Critical Design and Effective Tools for E–Learning in Higher Education:
Theory into Practice

Roisin Donnelly
Dublin Institute of Technology, Ireland

Jen Harvey
Dublin Institute of Technology, Ireland

Kevin O'Rourke
Dublin Institute of Technology, Ireland

INFORMATION SCIENCE REFERENCE

Hershey · New York

Director of Editorial Content:	Kristin Klinger
Director of Book Publications:	Julia Mosemann
Acquisitions Editor:	Lindsay Johnston
Development Editor:	Christine Bufton
Publishing Assistant:	Natalie Pronio, Sean Woznicki
Typesetter:	Keith Glazewski
Production Editor:	Jamie Snavely
Cover Design:	Lisa Tosheff
Printed at:	Yurchak Printing Inc.

Published in the United States of America by
Information Science Reference (an imprint of IGI Global)
701 E. Chocolate Avenue
Hershey PA 17033
Tel: 717-533-8845
Fax: 717-533-8661
E-mail: cust@igi-global.com
Web site: http://www.igi-global.com

Library of Congress Cataloging-in-Publication Data

Critical design and effective tools for e-learning in higher education : theory into practice / Roisin Donnelly, Jen Harvey, and Kevin O'Rourke, editors.
     p. cm.
  Includes bibliographical references and index.
 Summary: "The aim of this book is to bring together best practice in the development and use of E-Learning tools and technologies to support academic staff and faculty in universities, further education, and higher education institutes"--Provided by publisher.
   ISBN 978-1-61520-879-1 (hardcover) -- ISBN 978-1-61520-880-7 (ebook) 1. Education, Higher--Computer-assisted instruction. 2. Instructional systems-- Design. I. Donnelly, Roisin. II. Harvey, Jen, 1955- III. O'Rourke, K. C. (Kevin C.), 1964-
   LB2395.7.C75 2010
   378.1'734--dc22
                                              2009048637

British Cataloguing in Publication Data
A Cataloguing in Publication record for this book is available from the British Library.

All work contributed to this book is new, previously-unpublished material. The views expressed in this book are those of the authors, but not necessarily of the publisher.

Martin Ryan, *University of Manchester, UK*

Gearóid ŎSúilleabhain, *Cork Institute, of Technology, Ireland*

Julie-Ann Sime, *Lancaster University, UK*

Kay Mac Keogh, *DCU, Ireland*

Seamus Fox, *DCU, Ireland*

Francesca Lorenzi, *DCU, Ireland*

Yvonne Cleary, *University of Limerick, Ireland*

Eileen O'Donnell, *Dublin Institute of Technology, Ireland*

Barbara Geraghty, *Ireland*

Ann Marcus-Quinn, *Ireland*

C. Edward Watson, *Virgina Tech, USA*

Marc Zaldivar, *Virgina Tech, USA*

Teggin Summers, *Virgina Tech, USA*

Judith Kui, *University of Sunderland, UK*

Eugene O'Loughlin, *National College of Ireland, Ireland*

Frances Boylan, *Dublin Institute of Technology, Ireland*

Fionnghuala Kelly, *Dublin Institute of Technology, Ireland*

Helena Quinn, *Letterkenny Institute of Technology, Ireland*

Rachel Fitzgerald, *Northumbria University, UK*

Gerry Grogan, *Institute of Public Administration, Dublin, Ireland*

Muireann O'Keeffe, *Dublin Institute of Technology, Ireland*

Marian Fitzmaurice, *Dublin Institute of Technology, Ireland*

Brian Mulliga, *Institute of Technology Sligo, Ireland*

Sean Conlon, *Institute of Technology Sligo, Ireland*

Etain Kelly, *Institute of Technology Sligo, Ireland*

Diana Mitchell, *Dublin Institute of Technology, Ireland*

Claudia Igbrude, *Dublin Institute of Technology, Ireland*

Roisin Guilfoyle, *Dublin Institute of Technology, Ireland*

Vincent Farrell, *Dublin Institute of Technology, Ireland*

Table of Contents

Foreword xviii

Preface xxii

Section 1
Critical Design for E-Learning

Chapter 1
An Appreciation of Diverse Approaches to Learning Design in Higher Education 1
John Casey, Digitalinsite®, UK

Chapter 2
Designing Online Pedagogical Techniques for Student Learning Outcomes 22
Kay MacKeogh, Dublin City University, Ireland
Seamus Fox, Dublin City University, Ireland
Francesca Lorenzi, Dublin City University, Ireland
Elaine Walsh, Dublin City University, Ireland

Chapter 3
Online Identities in Virtual Worlds 39
Andrew Power, Dun Laoghaire Institute of Art, Design and Technology, Ireland
Gráinne Kirwan, Dun Laoghaire Institute of Art, Design and Technology, Ireland

Chapter 4
Do You See What I Mean? Computer-Mediated Discourse Analysis 55
Noel Fitzpatrick, Dublin Institute of Technology, Ireland
Roisin Donnelly, Dublin Institute of Technology, Ireland

Chapter 5
Educational Technology, Innovation and Habitus: What is the Connection? 72
Larry McNutt, Institute of Technology at Blanchardstown, Ireland

Section 2
Effective Tools: Web 2.0 and Beyond

Chapter 6
The Management and Creation of Knowledge: Do Wikis Help? 92
    Catherine Bruen, Trinity College Dublin, Ireland
    Noel Fitzpatrick, Dublin Institute of Technology, Ireland
    Paul Gormley, National University of Ireland at Galway, Ireland
    Jen Harvey, Dublin Institute of Technology, Ireland
    Claire McAvinia, National University of Ireland at Maynooth, Ireland

Chapter 7
Games for Learning and Learning Transfer 113
    Gearóid Ó Súilleabháin, Cork Institute of Technology, Ireland
    Julie-Ann Sime, Lancaster University, UK

Chapter 8
Anti-Plagiarism Software in an Irish University: Three Years Later 127
    Angelica Risquez, University of Limerick, Ireland

Chapter 9
iClassroom: Opportunities for Touch Screen Handheld Technologies
in Learning and Teaching 141
    Eugene F. M. O'Loughlin, National College of Ireland, Ireland

Chapter 10
ePortfolios for Learning, Assessment, and Professional Development 157
    C. Edward Watson, Virginia Tech, USA
    Marc Zaldivar, Virginia Tech, USA
    Teggin Summers, Virginia Tech, USA

Chapter 11
Learning to LOLIPOP: Developing an ePortfolio and Integrating
it into a First-Year Research and Study Skills Module 176
    Jennifer Bruen, Dublin City University, Ireland
    Juliette Péchenart, Dublin City University, Ireland
    Veronica Crosbie, Dublin City University, Ireland

Chapter 12
Constructing Disciplinary Inquiry Communities Using Web 2.0 Technologies 195
    Jamie Wood, University of Manchester, UK
    Martin J. Ryan, University of Manchester, UK

Section 3
Practitioner Insights

Chapter 13
Developing Educational Screencasts: A Practitioner's Perspective.. 213
Damian Raftery, Institute of Technology, Carlow, Ireland

Chapter 14
Applying E-Learning Technologies to Library Information Literacy Instruction 227
Jamie Ward, Dundalk Institute of Technology, Ireland

Chapter 15
E-Mentors: A Case Study in Effecting Cultural Change... 244
Barbara MacFarlan, Oaklands College, UK
Richard Everett, Oaklands College, UK

Chapter 16
The Student Perspective: Can the Use of Technologies Transform Learning?................................ 262
Eileen O'Donnell, Dublin Institute of Technology, Ireland

Chapter 17
Online Support for Students' Writing Skills Development in a Technical
Communication Introductory Module 280
Yvonne Cleary, University of Limerick, Ireland

Chapter 18
Design and Development of a Reusable Digital Learning Resource:
A Case Study Teaching Japanese Script 294
Ann Marcus-Quinn, University of Limerick, Ireland
Barbara Geraghty, University of Limerick, Ireland

Chapter 19
Web 2.0 to Pedagogy 2.0: A Social-Constructivist Approach to Learning
Enhanced by Technology 310
Judith A. Kuit, University of Sunderland, UK
Alan Fell, University of Sunderland, UK

Chapter 20
Sustainability through Staff Engagement: Applying a Community of Practice
Model to Web 2.0 Academic Development Programmes 326
Paul Gormley, National University of Ireland at Galway, Ireland
Catherine Bruen, Trinity College Dublin, Ireland
Fiona Concannon, National University of Ireland at Galway, Ireland

Chapter 21
Strategic Deployment of E-Learning 346
    Pat Gannon-Leary, Bede Research & Consultancy, UK
    James Carr, University of Edinburgh Business School, UK

Compilation of References 366

About the Contributors 408

Index 417

Detailed Table of Contents

Foreword xviii

Preface xxii

Section 1
Critical Design for E-Learning

Chapter 1

An Appreciation of Diverse Approaches to Learning Design in Higher Education 1
John Casey, Digitalinsite®, UK

This chapter makes the case for acknowledging and appreciating the diverse paths that lead to the generation of designs for e-learning in higher education. It identifies and critically examines some of the tensions between current design practices in the higher education sector and those assumed by interoperability standards such as IMS Learning Design and learning objects. The likely imperatives of a more design-intensive model of e-learning for the organisation and culture of the academic workplace are considered and some simple practical techniques to support the generation of designs are described. The chapter introduces a proposal for the combination of pedagogic and generic design knowledge as a means for improving practice by promoting a collaborative multidisciplinary approach to help reverse the current dominance of technology. Finally, the chapter briefly outlines suggestions for further areas of interdisciplinary enquiry and development.

Chapter 2

Designing Online Pedagogical Techniques for Student Learning Outcomes 22
Kay MacKeogh, Dublin City University, Ireland
Seamus Fox, Dublin City University, Ireland
Francesca Lorenzi, Dublin City University, Ireland
Elaine Walsh, Dublin City University, Ireland

The concept of identifying and measuring student learning outcomes has been embraced by a wide range of international policy makers and institutions across the globe, including the European Union through the Bologna Process, the USA, the OECD and other international organisations, while at national level many states have adopted, or are in the process of adopting a new national qualifications framework, based on student learning outcomes. The challenge for educators is to develop ways of enabling students to achieve, and to demonstrate their achievement, of these outcomes. The aim of this chapter is to explore ways in which online pedagogical techniques can be designed to provide solutions to the challenge of clearly demonstrating that students are achieving intended learning outcomes. While the techniques have been developed in the context of distance education programmes, the chapter includes an example of how these methods have been adapted for blended learning for on-campus students. A note of caution is sounded on the need to adopt effective techniques which do not impact unduly on lecturer workload.

Chapter 3
Online Identities in Virtual Worlds 39
    Andrew Power, Dun Laoghaire Institute of Art, Design and Technology, Ireland
    Gráinne Kirwan, Dun Laoghaire Institute of Art, Design and Technology, Ireland

Online identities need not reflect the true identity of the user. Relatively little is known about the use of online identities during e-learning and blended learning programmes, and if these reflect the students' true self. Online identities may impact on student achievement and satisfaction and as such are an important consideration for educators. Following an overview of the relevant literature regarding online identities, this paper describes findings from a survey of students currently engaged in a programme delivered using these techniques and where an awareness of online identities is to the fore. Several strengths and weaknesses of online identities in education are identified, and while students generally felt that they were portraying their own true identity online, many felt that others in the group were not. Implications for practice are described.

Chapter 4
Do You See What I Mean? Computer-Mediated Discourse Analysis 55
    Noel Fitzpatrick, Dublin Institute of Technology, Ireland
    Roisin Donnelly, Dublin Institute of Technology, Ireland

This chapter explores a sociolinguistic approach to computer-mediated communication (CMC), by examining how higher education teachers use digital media to manage interpersonal interaction in their online courses, form impressions, shape and maintain relationships with their students. Previous studies have often focused on the differences between online and offline interactions, though contemporary research is moving towards the view that CMC should be studied as an embedded linguistic form in everyday life. The study of language in these contexts is typically based on text-based forms of CMC, (often referred to as computer-mediated discourse analysis). Within this, focus in the chapter is on the devising and implementation of pragmatic linguistics of online interactions; at a high level this refers to meaning-making, shared belief systems and intercultural differences; at a specific level this includes issues such as turn-taking and the sequential analysis and organisation of virtual 'interlocution'.

Chapter 5
Educational Technology, Innovation and Habitus: What is the Connection? 72
    Larry McNutt, Institute of Technology at Blanchardstown, Ireland

Information and communications technology has radically transformed many aspects of modern life. However, this is in marked contrast to its impact on education. The purpose of this chapter is to explore why educational technology has done little to transform our higher education system. This is in spite of the emergence of the formal role of educational technologist, the improved ICT infrastructure and the evolving recognition of the importance of teaching and learning within the sector. Yet it is also apparent that within a given academic community there are many individually motivated innovators, i.e. those characterised by their willingness to experiment with new approaches and embrace change. Whilst there are also many who resist and avoid any possible alterations (or interference) in how they teach their subject matter.

Section 2
Effective Tools: Web 2.0 and Beyond

Chapter 6
The Management and Creation of Knowledge: Do Wikis Help? 92
    Catherine Bruen, Trinity College Dublin, Ireland
    Noel Fitzpatrick, Dublin Institute of Technology, Ireland
    Paul Gormley, National University of Ireland at Galway, Ireland
    Jen Harvey, Dublin Institute of Technology, Ireland
    Claire McAvinia, National University of Ireland at Maynooth, Ireland

Wikis are frequently cited in higher education research as appropriate and powerful web spaces which provide opportunities to capture, discuss, and review individual, group, project or organisational activities. These activities, in turn, offer possibilities for knowledge development by utilising wiki collaborative active spaces. The chapter uses selected case studies to illustrate the use of wikis to support online community based tasks, project development/processes, collaborative materials development and various student and peer supported activities. A key focus of the chapter is on evaluating the effectiveness (or otherwise) of wikis to create online communities to support knowledge management, development, retention and transfer. By way of contextualising the studies, a variety of examples of the use of wikis in higher education are reviewed. While there are relatively few studies of the use of Web 2.0 for the creation of knowledge, there are a number of reports which indicate the preference for the use of Web 2.0 technologies over the standard virtual learning environments. The chapter concludes with a review of the emergent themes arising and lessons learned from the case studies. This leads into a series of recommendations relating to the effective establishment, design, management and use of wikis to support knowledge creation and collaborative enterprise.

Chapter 7
Games for Learning and Learning Transfer... 113
    Gearóid Ó Súilleabháin, Cork Institute of Technology, Ireland
    Julie-Ann Sime, Lancaster University, UK

Research findings are at best mixed with regard to the effectiveness of computer and video games in promoting learning transfer or learning, but much of this research makes use of the same unsuccessful methods of classic transfer experiments which offered research subjects limited initial practice in the learning to be transferred. Learning transfer however, like expertise, may need to be based on extended practice, an idea supported by studies of habitual or expert game players and recent non-game related developments in transfer research. Practice however must be joined to a certain kind of game complexity and cognitive or experiential game fidelity before deep learning and instances of significant transfer can be facilitated. Implications of these transfer conditions for the design of games for transfer are discussed as well as the need for research with regard to the various learning processes underlying the game-play behaviour of expert and habitual gamers.

Chapter 8
Anti-Plagiarism Software in an Irish University: Three Years Later.. 127
    Angelica Risquez, University of Limerick, Ireland

A variety of anti-plagiarism software applications have appeared in recent years, but the pedagogical and institutional practices underpinning their use remains largely unexplored. It is essential to increase the amount of evidence-based literature that investigates the use of anti-plagiarism software in higher education. In the light of this, this chapter explores the integration of anti-plagiarism software in an Irish university since early 2006 and the progress made to date. We use data gathered from our own context to show how instructors are using this software to date, what trends emerge and what can be deduced about the adoption of the system to guide future research questions. Best practices are suggested for educators in order to help them to use anti-plagiarism software in proactive, positive, and pedagogically sound ways.

Chapter 9
iClassroom: Opportunities for Touch Screen Handheld Technologies
in Learning and Teaching.. 141
    Eugene F. M. O'Loughlin, National College of Ireland, Ireland

Hand-held technologies such as Apple's iPod/iTouch/iPhone devices are now capable of being used for educational purposes as well as for entertainment. The purpose of this chapter is to discuss the issues, content authoring, usage, workload, and pedagogical consequences of creating an iClassroom for mobile learning based on these devices. Use of podcasts and vodcasts by students, and their rate of success are varied as shown by studies reviewed from the literature and carried out by the author for this chapter. Several strategies for reducing workload at an individual and institutional level are proposed for adoption by educators. Key recommendations from this chapter are an increased emphasis on evaluation, usage of models for developing content, and an inclusion of iPod/iTouch/iPhone devices as part of an overall architecture for m-learning.

Chapter 10
ePortfolios for Learning, Assessment, and Professional Development 157
    C. Edward Watson, Virginia Tech, USA
    Marc Zaldivar, Virginia Tech, USA
    Teggin Summers, Virginia Tech, USA

ePortfolios are becoming increasingly popular as a means to address a variety of challenges in higher education, such as academic assessment requirements, specific teaching and learning goals, and emerging student professional development needs. This chapter explores these three applications of ePortfolios to provide administrators and faculty the information they need to make informed decisions regarding ePortfolios in academic settings. The relevant history of portfolios, assessment, and associated pedagogies sets a context for this discussion. Current trends in ePortfolios usage are outlined, including a survey of available technologies. This chapter concludes with a primer regarding the management of ePortfolios campus implementations as well as a brief examination of the key questions regarding the future of ePortfolios.

Chapter 11

Learning to LOLIPOP: Developing an ePortfolio and Integrating
it into a First-Year Research and Study Skills Module 176

Jennifer Bruen, Dublin City University, Ireland
Juliette Péchenart, Dublin City University, Ireland
Veronica Crosbie, Dublin City University, Ireland

The focus of this chapter is twofold: firstly, on the development of an electronic version of a European Language Portfolio, known as the LOLIPOP ELP,1 and, secondly, on its integration into a study and research skills module for first-year students on the BA in Applied Language and Intercultural Studies at Dublin City University. The chapter begins with an introduction to the concept of a European Language Portfolio (ELP) in the context of current trends in foreign language learning and teaching. It then describes the development and key features of the LOLIPOP ELP. It explains how it was integrated into a first-year, undergraduate research and study skills module focusing on elements of course design and assessment. Finally, the chapter concludes by analysing the output from the participants in this study which indicates that they appreciated the opportunity to engage with the LOLIPOP ELP and found it beneficial to their language learning although issues remain around its design and integration into an academic programme.

Chapter 12

Constructing Disciplinary Inquiry Communities Using Web 2.0 Technologies 195

Jamie Wood, University of Manchester, UK
Martin J. Ryan, University of Manchester, UK

This chapter explores the utility of Web 2.0 technologies for supporting independent inquiry-based learning, with a particular focus upon the use of blogs and social bookmarking tools. It begins by outlining the key issues confronting practitioners wishing to engage with such technologies before moving on to describe the approaches that were adopted in a range of first-year History seminar classes in two research-led universities in the UK. The chapter closes with an evaluation of the positive impact of the use of Web 2.0 on student learning and any drawbacks that were encountered. Web 2.0 is judged to have had a positive impact upon student engagement with course materials, encouraging student to conduct independent research outside of class and generating significant interactions between students and their peers as well as with tutors. Future avenues for research include investigations into how the use of such technologies can be scaled up for larger student groups and what impact summative assessment might have upon student engagement.

Section 3
Practitioner Insights

Chapter 13
Developing Educational Screencasts: A Practitioner's Perspective..213
 Damian Raftery, Institute of Technology, Carlow, Ireland

YouTube to iTunes, company to college websites, there is a seemingly exponential explosion in creating screencasts. A screencast is a digital recording of computer screen activity, often with an audio commentary. Short and engaging, screencasts have the potential to enable learning in new and exciting ways. They are becoming easier to create and, as a teacher in higher education, I have gradually increased my use of screencasts, learning with experience and from the generally positive feedback from students. Drawing on existing research and personal experience, this chapter will introduce screencasts and discuss their potential. The importance of integrating screencasts thoughtfully and carefully into the teaching and learning process will be examined, including pedagogical and instructional design issues. Next a four-step process for creating a screencast will be presented – prepare, capture, produce and publish. Prior to conclusions and final reflections, future research directions will be examined.

Chapter 14
Applying E-Learning Technologies to Library Information Literacy Instruction 227
 Jamie Ward, Dundalk Institute of Technology, Ireland

Academic libraries have adopted and adapted the e-learning technologies for delivery of their Information Literacy programmes. This chapter describes some of the ways in which academic librarians have been very inventive in using emerging technologies to enhance their instructional content. By using a case study of DkIT the chapter details how information literacy and the e-learning technologies emerged together. E-learning platforms like the virtual learning environments (VLE) are the natural place for libraries to use as portals for their IL instruction. This chapter argues that using the VLE (with the inherent instructional interaction made possible by this technology), and adopting some amalgam of the newer teaching styles like problem-based learning and blended learning techniques completes the IL circle for librarians. Librarians now have the tools at their disposal to finally fulfil the promises we undertook when we embarked on our information literacy programmes.

Chapter 15
E-Mentors: A Case Study in Effecting Cultural Change..244
 Barbara MacFarlan, Oaklands College, UK
 Richard Everett, Oaklands College, UK

The e-mentors scheme encapsulates the concept that the person in the home most likely to be able to programme the audio-visual equipment is the teenager. The scheme harnesses the digital generation's propensity for technology by using the students to teach their teachers how to make appropriate use of electronic resources in the classroom. We present a case study that focuses on both staff and student experiences of the e-mentoring system at a further education college in Hertfordshire, UK and outlines the strategy for ongoing staff development and support. The scheme has given lecturers the confidence to develop new technology-enhanced pedagogical practices and has given students the opportunity to play an active part in the development of their own learning environments and to influence policy on the use of technology. We believe that this model has been an effective element in a concerted approach to changing the prevailing attitudes to designing pedagogy for 21st century learners.

Chapter 16
The Student Perspective: Can the Use of Technologies Transform Learning?....................................262
    Eileen O'Donnell, Dublin Institute of Technology, Ireland

This chapter explores students' perspectives on the transformations that the use of technology has brought to higher education. The use of technologies in higher education facilitates flexible learning environments but the benefits to students who engage with these technologies will only be realised if the design is pedagogically sound. The pedagogic approach employed by lecturers when designing their e-learning platforms or learning management systems has the capability to transform learning. The author's discipline is Information Technology and Business Information Systems; from experience and case studies there is ample evidence to suggest that the use of technology does not always necessarily meet user requirements. Students are the end users of the technologies that educators use to enhance students' learning experiences. This chapter was undertaken to obtain students' perspectives (as the end users) on the uses of technologies in higher education to assist educators in improving the pedagogical design of their e-learning platforms. The responses received from students clearly indicate they are of the opinion that the use of technologies in higher education beneficially transforms learning but will never replace lecturers. In essence, the benefits that can be achieved through the use of technologies are totally dependent on the ways they are employed pedagogically by lecturers.

Chapter 17
Online Support for Students' Writing Skills Development in a Technical
Communication Introductory Module 280
    Yvonne Cleary, University of Limerick, Ireland

This chapter explores the development of online support for writing skills in one technical communication module taught at the University of Limerick. It demonstrates the need for writing support by exploring the many complexities of teaching and learning writing skills. Central to the discussion is the principle of process, rather than product, orientation. Students on the module have been surveyed over the past two years to determine their attitudes to, and perceptions of, their writing strengths and weaknesses. The chapter outlines and exemplifies the types of writing-problems students and instructors identify. Online support is posited as an intervention which facilitates autonomous learning. The chapter concludes by discussing how online resources, and especially the university virtual learning environment, Sakai (called Sulis at University of Limerick), can support students. It also suggests related research opportunities, especially in the area of using Web 2.0 technologies to foster autonomy.

Chapter 18
Design and Development of a Reusable Digital Learning Resource:
A Case Study Teaching Japanese Script 294
    Ann Marcus-Quinn, University of Limerick, Ireland
    Barbara Geraghty, University of Limerick, Ireland

This chapter describes the collaborative design and development process of a digital learning object in terms of roles, resources and user requirements. The example used to illustrate this process is a computer-assisted language learning (CALL) adaptation of a colour-based method of teaching one of the phonetic Japanese writing systems to zero beginners. This learning object combines as many of the positive features as possible of previous teaching methods with the advantages of mobile learning, facilitating autonomous learning on demand. It is time and cost effective and contains additional resources best supplied by a digital resource. The chapter also discusses the role and development of digital repositories in higher education.

Chapter 19
Web 2.0 to Pedagogy 2.0: A Social-Constructivist Approach to Learning
Enhanced by Technology 310

Judith A. Kuit, University of Sunderland, UK
Alan Fell, University of Sunderland, UK

Despite the extensive use of technology in teaching and supporting learning, teaching methods and approaches have for some academic staff remained largely unchanged. However, 21st century learners appear to have a different approach to learning and have different expectations regarding the use of technology in learning than their predecessors. For some academic staff this can be seen as a threatening scenario since they appear to believe that they have no role in future learning because it has been usurped by technology. Many suggest therefore, that the role of academic staff must change in the 21st century if they are to remain at the core of the learning process. The new learning paradigms of connectivism, navigationism, pedagogy 2.0 and heutagogy are described and discussed in the light of the role of academic staff. All of these paradigms have strong social constructivist learning theory underpinning their foundations and as such still have at their centre a fundamental role for academic staff. This is a role not in spite of the technology but rather one that is supported and enabled by the technology, particularly with respect to the Web 2.0 social networking tools.

Chapter 20
Sustainability through Staff Engagement: Applying a Community of Practice
Model to Web 2.0 Academic Development Programmes 326

Paul Gormley, National University of Ireland at Galway, Ireland
Catherine Bruen, Trinity College Dublin, Ireland
Fiona Concannon, National University of Ireland at Galway, Ireland

In many third-level institutions the innovative potential of technology has not been fully recognised or exploited at a strategic organisational level or embedded in mainstream educational work processes at a micro level. The sustainable integration of effective e-learning practices into higher education establishments remains a major challenge. This chapter discusses the challenges of designing staff development programmes which support the integration of e-learning into higher education by (1) leveraging the affordances presented by Web 2.0 technologies, coupled with (2) utilising a community of practice model to provide a sustainable peer-driven framework to share, support and embed technology-mediated teaching and learning practices. The chapter presents a practical example how a model of staff engagement was implemented within an Irish university, and concludes with suggestions on how others may benefit in considering a similar approach.

Chapter 21
Strategic Deployment of E-Learning..346
    Pat Gannon-Leary, Bede Research & Consultancy, UK
    James Carr, University of Edinburgh Business School, UK

Changes in higher education (HE) have continued in response to, or indeed in anticipation of, an increasingly competitive environment, technological advances and shifting demands of users. Introducing new technologies into a Higher Education Institute (HEI) requires management of complex change processes to deliver their full potential. Innovative ideas for technology and practice may be constrained, and compromised by people and cultural reactions thereby reducing their effectiveness and limiting their potential for improving teaching and learning. The management of change in organisational practices therefore involves attention to three aspects: processes, people, and culture. This paper presents a longitudinal study of one HEI through the lens of two active participants in a number of e-learning initiatives, and discusses process, people and cultural change challenges. It proposes that new evaluation frameworks are required to establish success in the implementation of new and emergent delivery modes mediated through the use of ICTs, and provides one example, the Learning Technology Practice Framework. The use of such frameworks may help with engaging academics in thinking about how to embed e-learning successfully within courses, and at a broader level within the organisation. The changes in the roles of lecturers/tutors and learners is particularly important in light of the disorientation faced by both of these user groups as a result of changing organisational culture and work practices. Lecturers and students have to adapt to their new roles and be allowed the opportunity, time, rewards and training to allow them to adapt the technology to meet their needs in their different and particular contexts of use. Overall it is found that the adoption and diffusion of e-learning in higher education is likely to develop more slowly than imagined by some educational visionaries owing to the complex nature of technology implementation that is common across all sectors, be it industry or education.

Compilation of References 366

About the Contributors 408

Index..417

Foreword

E-Learning – like e-anything – has made a dramatic entrance onto the world stage. While distance learning can be traced to the English instruction in shorthand by correspondence in the 1840s, e-learning – using the electronic computer and data communication networks – is a recent development. The electronic computer itself is only slightly more than 60 years old and as recently as 1977, some, like Digital Equipment Corporation founder and CEO Ken Olsen, told the World Future Society that "there is no reason for any individual to have a computer in his home."[1] Of course Apple Computer did introduce home computers at this time and personal computing became mainstream in 1982 with the introduction of the IBM PC. By 1983, there were about 2 million computers in the USA. By 1990, this number had grown to 54 million, and by 2000, 60 percent of all US households owned at least one of the 182 million personal computers in use at that time.[2] In 2008, the number of computers in the world passed 1 billion![3]

The history of networking is similarly spectacular. In 1969, the first four nodes of the ARPANET exchanged packets in the U.S. By 1973, University College London connected to the ARPANET via Norway's NORSAR, while Louis Pouzin led French networking efforts. By 1982, TCP/IP was adopted as the protocol for the ARPANET and the growth of networking exploded. By 1984, backbone networks had been initiated in England, continental Europe, Japan, and Canada, as well as in the USA. By 1987, the number of (computer) hosts connected to the US network backbone exceeded 10,000. The rest, as they say, is history. In 1991, Tim Berners-Lee and his colleagues at CERN had developed the World Wide Web and by 1998, the Canadians had created the first national optical network. Today, nearly one-quarter of all men, women and children – 1.4 billion people – are connected to the global Internet, using more than 1.5 billion networked devices.[4] Today, specialized computers in automobiles, appliances, and telephones comprise an increasingly diverse soup of smart devices regularly and persistently connected to the Internet. Not only has access to computing and the Internet become nearly ubiquitous, the capacity of the global Internet is continually growing. Breakthroughs in fiber optics and in optronics and wireless networking are facilitating a series of long-anticipated convergences that are literally putting multiple media in the hands – or pockets – of students, teachers, and others.

This history is central to the history of e-learning. Critical design for e-learning cannot likely predate the emergence of e-learning. E-learning, in turn, cannot predate the emergence of a standardized palette of hardware, software, and communications protocols that together constitute an *e-learning environment*. As important, critical design for e-learning cannot predate widespread ownership of the technologies that comprise the e-learning environment, or a widespread knowledge of how to place these technologies in the service of teaching and learning. Importantly, this dependency places burdens on both the learner and the teacher.

Amazingly, in many parts of the globe, preconditions have been met in less than three decades. The breathtaking and inexorable march of Moore's Law and related laws are ensuring that more and more computing, networking, storage capacity and human connections are available to teachers and learners at a constantly declining price. Having more and more people connected to the global Internet means that more software, more services, more information resources, and more expertise are available to all. The status of e-learning has moved – as a result – from the realm of the diabolical (see David Noble's early villlification of Educom and other early supporters of e-learning), to the quixotic (see Bob Zemsky's characterization of e-learning as a case of "thwarted innovation"), to the satisfactory (No Significant Difference), to the mainstream, to the exciting in less than 20 years.[5]

Two additional important developments facilitated the progress of computing in the service of education. Not only did computers become economically accessible features of the educational landscape, they became technically accessible. Early personal computers and their operating systems were anything but friendly, but by the early 1990s, even instruction manuals had gone the way of dip switches from the computer user's perspective. Hardware and software standards meant an increasingly standardized user interface, eliminating the need to spend hours figuring out how to navigate the software one would need to encounter in educational settings. Additionally, efforts in England, Canada, the USA, Norway and elsewhere – sporting mysterious and tantalizing names like Athena, Cyclops, Delta, and others – were developing an understanding of smart classroom environments and were creating environments designed to facilitate teachers in the management of educational courses for their students using computer hardware and software, which they called learning management systems or virtual learning environments. As with other technologies, these systems too became highly standardized across many parts of the world and across educational systems creating a common means and metaphor for delivering a great deal of educational content.

And so we conclude that, by this writing, most of the critical preconditions for the technology-mediated *improvement* of teaching and learning in the higher education sector have been met. A robust e-learning environment can now be put in place and made economically and technically accessible to a very wide variety of teachers and learners.

Pedagogy (that is, the principles and practices of instruction), like so many other social practices, has lagged the emergence of the e-learning environment. The popular and professional literature crackles with excitement (or anxiety) about the emergence of those NetGen learners who are storming our classrooms and the Internet with their skills as digital natives and their passion for all things digital. In too many cases, we digital immigrants are left in a state of hapless confusion. The literature that is informed by large-scale data tells other stories as well.[6] This literature describes the simultaneous emergence of (1) a digital *cognoscenti* among our students, (2) an equipped and connected student mainstream that can hardly be described as fluent with the academic uses of technology, and (3) a sizeable digital underclass that is equipped with hand-me-down tools, narrow band connections, untrained parents, and a generally unfriendly relationship with the new tools of the emergent e-learning environment. Not surprisingly, our instructional cadre arrays in much the same way. While a number of instructors have embraced the possibilities presented by e-learning, a great majority is using technology dominantly as a means to *administer* their courses (e.g. distribute syllabi and assignments, post grades, take attendance, etc.), and another large swathe is holed up in pre-technology bunkers, clinging to the course notes of another era. Importantly, some are eschewing the e-learning environment because they have well and truly mastered the conventional pedagogy. For one, I'd hate to insist that our finest stage sages abandon the lectern.

So here we have it. Another case of technology outrunning social and professional practice. The gap between emerging technological possibilities and pedagogical response in fact lies at the heart of the issues examined in this volume. If such gaps between technological innovation and the socialization or diffusion of new practices are commonplace, can't we conclude that time is on our side? In fact, I believe that we do not have time on our side, and the absence of time makes the reading of this book and the taking of recommended actions matters of grave urgency. I urge the instructor who reads this book to become an activist. Become a discriminating advocate for the integration of emerging technologies into the dominant pedagogies around you. Either commit to integrating new technologies into your classroom practice immediately, or if you already do this, commit to becoming an active agent in spreading the case for urgent action to your colleagues. Open your hearts and minds at the same time to securing the place of the magnificent lecture or teaching techniques where they make positive contributions to student learning and experience.

Why so urgent? Unlike many innovations that diffuse at rates that do not challenge core elements of the existing order, information technologies in general and e-learning technologies in particular are disruptive technologies. Disruptive technologies are new technologies that may be simpler and cheaper than the prevailing technologies but initially offer reduced performance. As these technologies improve, their simplicity and cost might allow them to supplant the prevailing technology. In the case of e-learning, the focus of modern pedagogy and of IT and e-learning technologies is student learning. In effect, e-learning, and in particular the remarkable tapestry of people, tools, and resources on the Internet are making it easier and easier for students to learn in ways that are remote from the classroom and ultimately, remote from the instructor. The results can in many cases be breathtaking for the learner and simultaneously devastating for the traditional instructor or the institution.

Earlier this decade, Oxford University considered requiring students to sign contracts that would obligate the to attend lectures and tutorials, complete written work and attend practical lessons. It seems that lecture halls and even tutors' apartments have been emptying of students, a problem by no means unique to Oxford University. So what has happened? Where are the students? Why are our lecture halls, seminar rooms, tutors' apartments empty? I suspect that we all know the answer to these and other questions. The answer is *not* that contemporary students have become lazy and irresponsible and simply prefer sleep or videogames to classroom instruction. What is far more likely is that our breathtaking global information system is being crafted – on an increasingly personal basis – by our students into the educational environment they need. While at this writing our institutions of higher learning, our faculties, our academic staff, remain secure as *certifiers of academic accomplishment and qualifications*, we are at risk of being replaced as the dominant suppliers of that which we certify. Students are coming to our institutions with substantial hardware and software, with lifetimes of network connections, with intact social networks, and in many cases with behaviors and norms for participating in network-situated learning. It is also clear that others – like publishers or Google – who control vast tracts of cyberspace and the rights to considerable intellectual property will also compete with traditional institutions for the learner's time, attention, and ultimately money.

The modern college or university and every modern academic then needs to understand that they are no longer the exclusive channel that our students must daily tune in to. And we must recognize that unless we develop active strategies to extend the relevancy and appeal of our pedagogical practice, that our lecture theaters may come to resemble our newspapers, television broadcasters, or others in the age of the Internet.

We are lucky to live and work in what Jim Duderstadt labeled the "knowledge-driven era." The challenge for those of us who toil in higher education's traditional fields is to secure the place of the modern college or university as a central force in a knowledge-driven world.[7] We will accomplish this only by thoughtfully situating our tradition-honoring and place-centric institutions clearly in the emerging e-learning environment, and by pressing hard to evaluate and adopt learning designs and tools that leverage this environment. While technology's uses will be conditioned and constrained by institutions out of respect for their spectacular historical successes, we must now work actively to balance our historical roles, standards, practices, and techniques, with emerging tools, practices, and pedagogies if our institutions and we are to remain relevant in the knowledge-driven era. The authors of this volume demonstrate how the respect for historical scholastic standards and methods can be carried forward and woven into the evolving e-learning environment. Their messages are at once relevant and exciting. They deserve our urgent attention.

Richard N. Katz
Boulder, Colorado

Richard N. Katz *has been Vice-President of EDUCAUSE since 1996 and in 2001, he founded the EDUCAUSE Center for Applied Research (ECAR). EDUCAUSE is a nonprofit association whose mission is to advance higher education by promoting the intelligent use of information technology. Before joining EDUCAUSE, Katz held a variety of management and executive positions spanning 14 years at the University of California (UC). At UC, Katz was awarded the Gurevich Prize, the Olsten Award, and was the 2nd recipient of that University's Award for Innovative Management and Leadership. Katz is the author, co-author or editor of seven books, four research studies, and more than 50 articles and monographs on a variety of management and technology topics. His book Dancing with the Devil was deemed one of the 10 most important education-related books of 1999 by Lingua Franca. He received his B.A. from the University of Pittsburgh, and his MBA from UCLA.*

ENDNOTES

[1]   See http://www.snopes.com/quotes/kenolsen.asp

[2]   See The Physics Factbook, http://hypertextbook.com/facts/2004/DianeEnnefils.shtml

[3]   See Science Portal, http://www.science-portal.org/in/71

[4]   IDC, IDC Finds More of the World's Population Connecting to the Internet in New Ways and Embracing Web 2.0 Activities, at http://www.idc.com/getdoc.jsp?containerId=prUS21303808

[5]   See David Noble, *Digital Diploma Mills*, October 1997, at http://www.handshake.ca/noble.html. See also Robert Zemsky, *Thwarted Innovation: What Happened to E-Learning and Why?*, West Chester, PA: The Learning Alliance for Higher Education at Http://www.irhe.upenn.edu/WeatherStation.html. See also See also Thomas L. Russell, *The No Significant Difference Phenomenon*, International Distance Education Certification Center, 2001, at http://www.nosignificantdifference.org/

[6]   See studies by the Pew Internet and American Life or the EDUCAUSE Center for Applied Research (ECAR).

[7]   James J. Duderstadt, "New Roles for the 21st Century University, in *Issues in Science and Technology Online*, Winter 1999, at http://www.issues.org/16.2/duderstadt.htm

Preface

Introducing change in higher education has never an easy nor a swift process. For almost two decades, information and communication technologies have been vaunted as the herald of a new age in learning, transforming both the traditional classroom and breaking down the barriers to education. The ubiquitous availability of information via the World Wide Web, facilitated by the rapid development of tools to harness, adapt and interact with this information, is welcomed by educators in theory. But in practice it has put many out of their comfort zone, especially those whose confidence in the online environment is not equal to that which they feel at the front of a classroom. For such people involved in higher education, technology was (and for some perhaps still is) regarded as a threat rather than an opportunity. And in many ways it is not difficult to see why: when the technology was merely a concern of the business processes of an institution, facilitating the registration and payroll functions, it did not impinge directly on the actual practices of teaching and learning. The subsequent advent in the 1990s of learning management systems (in Europe known as virtual learning environments) was often seen as an attempt to encroach on the traditional privacy of the classroom and lecture theatre. With this tool, the skills of the lecturer were of necessity going to have to expand to include design of materials for delivery on the web, the ability to facilitate online communications with ever-more demanding students, to change their presentation style in order to satisfy shortening attention spans and at the same time to ensure that learning is taking place to the standards required by an exacting quality assurance regime. Students, it seemed, were being put at an advantage: not only are they regarded as being more confident with new technologies, the technologies themselves were seen as empowering and emboldening students in a way that many of their lecturers were not. And in some cases the the position of lecturers themselves was seen to be at risk. The change was not always for the good.

However, such change must be seen as but a first (and indeed necessary) phase in the overall evolution that is happening within higher education. Alongside the fear of change there have been many good stories to tell. *Critical Design and Effective Tools for E-Learning in Higher Education: Theory into Practice* represents an attempt to gather some of those stories into a single handbook which can provide those who work in higher education with both a source of information and inspiration. Here, the thoughts of almost 40 professionals from across the English-speaking world share their theoretical and practical perspectives on the impact which technology is having, could have and should have on the learning experiences of our future graduates. Richard Katz's preface provides a good overview of many of the emergent themes, and the contributions are divided into three parts which, we believe, reflect the concerns of many of us at this phase of development.

In Section 1, entitled "Critical Design for e-Learning", we have gathered some of the contributions that offer a critical look at the bigger picture of e-learning, both from a theoretical and a practical perspective.

Thus with begin with an attempt to promote a more collaborative approach to learning. John Casey's appreciation of diverse approaches to design in higher education proposes a combination of pedagogic and generic design knowledge as a means to reverse the current dominance which technology tends to play in almost all discussions of e-learning. An e-learning specialist working in Scotland, he helpfully suggests further areas of interdisciplinary enquiry and development which the reader may find useful. Next, Kay MacKeogh, Seamus Fox and their colleagues at Dublin City University take a close look at the concept of identifying and measuring student learning outcomes, while maintaining a realistic eye on lecturer workload. Drawing from their experience in the field of distance education, they explore ways in which online pedagogical techniques can be designed to provide solutions to the challenge of clearly demonstrating that students are achieving the intended learning outcomes, both with a fully online and a blended environment. The non-personal world of the online environment is often a concern for lecturers, who may worry about issues such as appropriate online behaviour, etiquette, impersonation and so on. Just how the online environment impacts on student identity and behaviour is the subject addressed in the following two chapters. In "Online identities in virtual worlds" Andrew Power and Gráinne Kirwan from the Institute of Art and Design in Dun Laoghaire, Dublin, acknowledge that online identities do not necessarily reflect the true identity of the user. They identify strengths and weaknesses of online identities in education, and describe implications for practice. Noel Fitzpatrick and Roisin Donnelly next explore how higher education teachers use digital media to manage interpersonal interaction in online courses. At a theoretical level, issues of meaning-making, shared beliefs and intercultural differences come to the fore, while at a practical level they discuss issues such as turn-taking and the sequential analysis and organization of virtual communications. Section 1 concludes with a discussion of educational technology, innovation and habitus by Larry McNutt, a lecturer in information technology. This chapter involves a review of what we mean by educational technology itself, and takes a broad look at the characteristics of innovators in other domains before considering how applicable their experiences may be considered to education.

In the second section, we look at particular technologies and their implementation in the context of the web 2.0 phenomenon. The aim here is to offer insights into strengths and weaknesses of particular pedagogical approaches to the use of tools rather than providing a how-to guide to the actual tools themselves. To that end, the section opens with an exploration of the emergence of wikis in higher education. Catherine Bruen and her co-authors employ case studies to illustrate the use of wikis to support learning, focusing on evaluating the effectiveness (or otherwise) of wikis to create online communities to support knowledge management, development, retention and transfer. The chapter concludes with a review of the emergent themes and offers a series of recommendations relating to the effective establishment, design, management and use of wikis to support knowledge creation and collaborative enterprise. The effectiveness of digital games in the learning process is next explored: Gearóid Ó Súilleabháin and Julie-Ann Sime from Cork Institute of Technology hold a question mark over much of the research surrounding the effectiveness of computer and video games in promoting learning transfer. They discuss the design of games for learning, and advocate further research into the learning processes underlying the game-play behaviour of expert and habitual gamers. Such work suggests a new epistemological framework which will permit designers and educationalists to take the first steps in creating and adopting more effective games for learning.

While plagiarism is not a new phenomenon, the internet has certainly put it higher on the agenda within the higher education sector. Angelica Risquez from the University fo Limerick argues that the pedagogical and institutional practices underpinning the use of anti-plagiarism software applications remain largely unexplored. She suggests best practices for educators in order to help them to use such software in a proactive, positive, and pedagogically sound ways. Eugene F. M. O'Loughlin from the National College of Ireland examines the impact which hand-held technologies such as Apple's iPod/iTouch/iPhone might have on higher education. The iClassroom, he believes, will lead to at least a review of traditional pedagogical practices and may suggest new forms of pedagogy for the digital age. His recommendations include an increased emphasis on evaluation, usage of models for developing content, and an inclusion of such mobile devices as part of an overall architecture for any mLearning strategy within an institution. The increasing popularity of ePortfolios is addressed by Virginia Tech's C. Edward Watson, Marc Zaldivar and Teggin Summers, who outline the challenges which they bring to higher education, such as academic assessment requirements, specific teaching and learning goals, and emerging student professional development needs. These three applications of ePortfolios are used to provide administrators and lecturers with the information needed need to make informed decisions regarding the introduction of ePortfolios in academic settings. Taking a slightly different approach, Jennifer Bruen and her colleagues focus on the development of an electronic version of a European Language Portfolio, and its integration into a study and research skills module for first-year students at Dublin City University. Building on the success of their venture, they identify issues which remain around design and integration of ePortfolios into an academic programme. Section 2 concludes with Jamie Wood and Martin J. Ryan's exploration of the utility of Web 2.0 technologies for supporting independent inquiry-based learning, with a particular focus upon the use of blogs and social bookmarking tools. Drawing on case studies at two UK Universities, they evaluate the positive impact of the use of Web 2.0 on student learning (and the drawbacks encountered), which encouraged students to conduct independent research outside of class and generated significant interactions between students and their peers as well as with tutors.

In Section 3 we have gathered together a series of practitioner insights, from the perspectives of both learning and teaching. Damien Raftery describes his experiences of developing educational screencasts, holding that they have the *potential* to enable learning in new and exciting ways. He outlines a four-step process for creating pedagogically-sound screencasts and discusses future research directions. Librarian Jamie Ward employs a case study to demonstrate that student information literacy can be enhanced through the combined use of an institutional virtual learning environment, with some amalgam of problem-based and blended learning techniques. In their chapter entitled "eMentoring, a Case Study in Effecting Cultural Change" Barbara Macfarlan and Richard Everett describe a scheme whereby teenage students teach their teachers how to make appropriate use of electronic resources in the classroom. They believe that this model has been an effective element in a concerted approach to changing the prevailing attitudes to designing pedagogy for twenty-first century learners, and they outline a strategy for ongoing staff development and support. Eileen O'Donnell, a lecturer in Information Technology and Business Information Systems, examines learning from the student perspective by surveying student attitudes. The responses received clearly indicate that the use of technologies in higher education beneficially transforms learning, but will never replace lecturers. In essence, the benefits that can be achieved through the use of technologies are totally dependent on the ways they are employed pedagogically by lecturers. Next, Yvonne Cleary explores the development of online support for writing skills on a technical communication module taught at the University of Limerick. She outlines the types of writing problems most commonly identified by students and instructors, and posits online support as an intervention which facilitates autonomous learning. She further suggests related research opportunities, especially in the area of using Web 2.0 technologies to foster autonomy.

The design of a reusable digital learning resource for teaching Japanese forms the basis of the contribution by Ann Marcus-Quinn and Barbara Geraghty. Their chapter describes the collaborative design and development process in terms of roles, resources and user requirements. The positive features of more traditional teaching methods are combined with the advantages of mobile learning, facilitating autonomous learning on demand. The chapter also discusses the role and development of digital repositories in Higher Education. Judith A. Kuit and Alan Fell hold that, despite the extensive use of technology in teaching and supporting learning, teaching methods and approaches have remained largely unchanged. However, today's students appear to have a different approach to learning and certainly have different expectations regarding the use of technology in learning than their predecessors. The new learning paradigms of connectivism, navigationism, pedagogy 2.0 and heutagogy are described and discussed in the light of the role of academic staff. This is a role supported and enabled by the technology, particularly with respect to the Web 2.0 social networking tools. Applying a community of practice model to Web 2.0 academic development programmes is the basis of the contribution from Paul Gormley, Catherine Bruen, and Fiona Concannon. They argue that the sustainable integration of effective e-learning practices into higher-education establishments remains a major challenge both at organisational and local levels. Their chapter presents a practical example how a model of staff engagement was implemented within an Irish university, and concludes with suggestions on how others may benefit in considering a similar approach. Finally, Pat Gannon-Leary and James Carr discuss the strategic deployment of e-learning in higher education, holding that the introduction of new technologies requires management of complex change processes to deliver their full potential. The management of change in organisational practices, they argue, involves attention to processes, people, and culture, and as active participants in a number of e-learning initiatives they present a longitudinal study of one such institution. They suggest that new evaluation frameworks may help with engaging academics in thinking about how to embed e-learning successfully within courses, and at a broader level within the organisation. Overall they conclude that e-learning in higher education is likely to develop more slowly than we had imagined owing to the complex nature of technology implementation that is common to both industry and education alike.

Overall, the book aims to give a ground-level picture of e-learning as it is currently being practised in Ireland, the UK and the USA. It is not our intention that this book should be diligently read from cover to cover: rather, those who gain most from this book are likely to find different parts of it relevant at different times and in different situations. To that end, we have enjoyed the process of gathering these experiences to share with readers across the world, in the hope that they will offer you some guidance and insight into what has been happening over the past two decades. Above all we hope that this book will inspire readers to look with confidence towards the future of e-learning in higher education and, as Richard Katz urges in his preface, become an activist in the cause of integrating technologies into your teaching and learning practices. Together we can actively make a change for the better. But if we are ever going to change the world, each of us needs to start in our own classrooms.

KCO'Rourke
23 November 2009

Section 1
Critical Design for E-Learning

Chapter 1
An Appreciation of Diverse Approaches to Learning Design in Higher Education

John Casey
Digitalinsite®, UK

ABSTRACT

This chapter makes the case for acknowledging and appreciating the diverse paths that lead to the generation of designs for e-learning in higher education. It identifies and critically examines some of the tensions between current design practices in the higher education sector and those assumed by interoperability standards such as IMS Learning Design and learning objects. The likely imperatives of a more design-intensive model of e-learning for the organisation and culture of the academic workplace are considered and some simple practical techniques to support the generation of designs are described. The chapter introduces a proposal for the combination of pedagogic and generic design knowledge as a means for improving practice by promoting a collaborative multidisciplinary approach to help reverse the current dominance of technology. Finally, the chapter briefly outlines suggestions for further areas of interdisciplinary enquiry and development.

INTRODUCTION

This chapter describes the present, largely informal, approaches to developing designs for e-learning in higher education (HE) and examines how they relate to the emergence of interoperability standards, particularly that of IMS Learning Design (CETIS, 2009; IMS, 2009). This is con-

trasted to the situation in the distance learning, commercial and military training sectors where the abstraction, sharing and reuse of pedagogic designs and learning resources is comparatively well developed. In what might be described as 'mainstream' HE this kind of shared and formalised design-intensive activity is still relatively rare. This chapter aims to provide a critical commentary both on current learning design practice

DOI: 10.4018/978-1-61520-879-1.ch001

in HE and aspects of IMS Learning Design and describes the possible adoption of simple tools and methods to support improvement in practice. The chapter argues that a multidisciplinary approach is needed to overcome the current e-learning implementation problems that are frequently reported by practitioners from a variety of backgrounds.

The need to improve the quality of the design of the student learning experience in higher education is a longstanding issue and one that has been recognised by many influential educational authors including Biggs (2006), Ramsden (1992) and Laurillard (2002). For instance, the ambition for the 'Aligned Curriculum' in HE proposed by Biggs (2006) still remains a substantial challenge; where teaching aims, learning outcomes and assessment criteria are set in a coherent relationship with each other, supported by activities that facilitate the desired learning. So, questions relating to learning design also go straight to the heart of current major debates about quality and efficiency in higher education and learning. It is important to recognise that teaching in HE continues to be dominated by the traditional patterns of the campus-based face-to-face model, which can exert a tenacious hegemony over any attempts to change it (Agostinho, Harper, Oliver, Hedberg, & Wills, 2008). Yet, despite this, systems of HE teaching and education are also in a period of transition to meet the challenges posed by the need to supply quality flexible learning opportunities to a mass student population from increasingly diverse academic backgrounds.

This chapter is grounded in the practical experience of the author in helping subject matter experts to design online courses and learning resources over several years at the University of Stirling, Scotland, and participation in UK research projects that examined practitioners dealing with reuse and redesign of resources as learning objects. The chapter also draws on involvement in action research at the University of the Highlands and Islands Millennium Institute, Scotland that ex-

plored issues surrounding the extension of a more flexible curriculum in a federated geographically remote institution. From a wider perspective this chapter also includes inputs from the discussions and publications of the European UNFOLD project (UNFOLD, 2009) that brought together IMS Learning Design technical developers with teachers to discuss a wide range of issues involved in making usable software tools that teachers and institutions could use.

The chapter starts by reviewing some of the tensions between existing design practice in HE and the requirements of e-learning interoperability standards and identifies some important gaps in discussions about the creation of learning designs. The concept of a learning design continuum is then introduced, which can contain different types of representation and degrees of formalism. Next, some practical tried and tested approaches to generating learning designs are described. The discussion then goes on to combine some useful perspectives from the fields of pedagogic research and design studies. The chapter concludes with a discussion of how the topics covered may be integrated to provide a unified approach that is both broadly inclusive and supports diversity and creativity in e-learning design, and makes suggestions for further areas of work.

TENSIONS BETWEEN THE TECHNICAL DEVELOPER COMMUNITY AND MAINSTREAM EDUCATION

The IMS Learning Design specification aims to be able to supply a vocabulary, which teachers using any pedagogical method can use to express their designs for teaching. The core of this vocabulary assumes that the learning/teaching process can be expressed in terms of people in specified *groups* and *roles* engaging in *activities* in an *environment* that contains appropriate *resources* and *services*

– the terms in italics are part of the vocabulary. The aims for the specification are ambitious: to provide a common system of notation that can describe any pedagogic strategy in both human and machine-readable forms and originated from previous work carried out by the Open University of the Netherlands into educational modelling languages (Koper, 2005). The specification makes use of a theatrical metaphor with the stage play script providing a model for the notation system (Koper, 2005). The interest generated by this work in the educational and e-learning fields has been extensive and has also helped to encourage a wider reconsideration and exploration of how general learning design activities are conducted in mainstream education.

To date, educational institutions have proved remarkably resistant to change induced by e-learning technology and the hegemony of campus-based face-to-face teaching in many cases remains intact. This extract from the editorial of an e-learning research journal describes the situation:

Furthermore, most investments have been devoted to content authoring, and developing interoperability standards for content and virtual learning environments. Great economic investment have been made for Learning Objects (LOs) and for developing Learning Management Systems. The coupling between LO and LMS is a leitmotiv in every context of network learning, from schools to universities to the corporate sector.

This way of interpreting e-learning is running into a crisis: the promised economic effectiveness of content re-use is often hard to demonstrate or it is limited to specific contexts, while a general feeling of discontent is arising. (Fini, 2007, p. 5)

To understand this apparent impasse Friesen (2004) and Friesen and Cressman (2006) helpfully point out there is a set of important political and economic sub-texts connected to the proposed uses of technical standards and technologies in education that still need to be explored. This chapter takes the view that neglecting such 'soft' issues is a major cause of the problems cited above by Fini (2007). In this connection it is important to differentiate between the characteristics of mainstream HE and those areas that are already embracing the technologies involved in interoperability standards as exemplified by learning objects and IMS Learning Design, and the implications of this difference for future development. At the moment those most involved in these technologies are the distance learning sector, the research community, aviation and military training providers. It is questionable to assume that an effective approach to e-learning in the mainstream is one that replicates the use of technologies and methods imported from these sectors. The experience of such specialist 'early adopters' cannot simply be projected onto the mainstream educational institutions. Such institutions do not function in the same way, their structures and the cultures of those working in them are not the same and their actual missions and purpose are very different. Teaching and learning in the mainstream is a far more messy, less controlled and contingent enterprise than in the military, the distance learning sector and aviation, where an 'industrialised' Fordist style workplace is the norm with a much greater investment in up-front design activities. In contrast, much of the main mode of university teaching production is still pre-capitalist and dominated by the medieval communication tool of the lecture (Laurillard, 2002). Casey and Wilson (2006) suggest that understanding what might be termed the 'political economy' of e-learning lies at the heart of the success (or otherwise) of incorporating technology into mainstream HE. This presents some difficult questions, both for the reorganisation of the present academic workplace and the underlying philosophies of e-learning innovators.

IMPLICATIONS FOR INSTITUTIONAL AND PROFESSIONAL CHANGE IN RELATION TO E-LEARNING STANDARDS

To work at their best (in terms of quality and efficiency), many of the technologies related to e-learning effectively assume and require the re-design of the educational workplace. Pollock and Cornford (2000) make the insightful observation that these technologies carry strong implicit organisational and business models. Friesen (2004), gives a good description of these implicit models (including some of their military origins) in an often-referenced paper called 'Three objections to learning objects and e-learning standards' and calls for more research into this area, especially into an examination of their pedagogical, epistemological and ideological implications. Friesen and Cressman (2006) have also observed that the domains of education and learning can be best understood as being especially local, heterogeneous and contextual in ways that few other organised activities are. Similarly, Downes (2003) in an article entitled 'Design, standards and reusability' makes the same points about the contextually determined nature of education and limits to the ideas of reuse and economy than can be expected in this domain as opposed, for instance, to the military sector.

In contrast to the situation described by Fini (2007) above, those initiatives that are addressing the contextual aspects of implementing e-learning, what may be termed the tricky realities of implementing the political economy of e-learning, are tending to have more success than those that do not. Support for this analysis comes from the work of the National Centre for Academic Transformation (NCAT) in the USA, which administers large charitable grants to higher education institutions to improve the quality and efficiency of their educational provision with the use of information technology. The funding from the NCAT comes with tight conditions, such as a ban on creating new learning materials, and

concentrates on re-designing the curriculum and academic work practices using relatively lo-tech approaches with positive results (Twigg, 2005). Similar work in the UK has found that sharing and reuse of learning resources works best when combined with the organised re-engineering of a curriculum and associated working practises. Boyle (2003) outlines some guidelines for authoring learning objects from a pedagogic point of view and provides a description of a mass deployment of learning objects to support undergraduates (approx. 600) in computer science. In a later evaluation of the same initiative Bradley and Boyle (2004) report on encouraging results (fewer drop-outs and higher exam scores). Even more dramatic results are recorded by Trayner (2002), with a very large decline in drop-out rates, using the simple expedient of persuading lecturers to forego using their own notes and use a common set of learning materials in electrical engineering courses.

The heart of the challenge posed by the current status-quo in HE is that a considerable number of teaching staff generally do not share and reuse learning resources and learning designs, instead they concentrate on preparing 'their' content to deliver to 'their' students (Koper, 2003). The teaching activities are embedded in an institutional context (almost in the 'bricks and mortar' of the institution) and are therefore difficult to share and abstract. In this pedagogic environment lecturers find it difficult to conceptualise and abstract the design of learning activities for their students (Koper, 2003), and sharing these conceptions with colleagues is even rarer. As Allison Littlejohn (2003, p. 226) observes, 'Designing for reuse means designing with multiple users in mind and this is a new experience for most teachers in all sectors of education'. In this connection, Casey, Brosnan and Greller (2005) argue that one of the keys to understanding the emotional attachment of lecturers to their own materials is that in many cases they have created them in the process of learning how to understand and teach their discipline. As such, they are a crucial part of a lecturer's personal support system and contain their accumulated and embedded pedagogic and institutional knowledge, which in turn supplies a framework for their teaching and design activities. These patterns of academic work and administration need to be understood and factored in by those involved in the development and improvement of e-learning design activities in HE. The mission-critical nature of the design processes that are required to effectively implement e-learning make the acquisition of collaborative design skills a key area to address. In this connection there is much to learn from a consideration of other fields of professional activity where design is recognised as a fundamental component.

THE LEARNING DESIGN CONTINUUM

The developers working on the IMS Learning Design specification and associated tools have had, by necessity, to simplify their working problem domain space by assuming that the design process starts with the production of a formalised, structured and detailed design narrative. While convenient and necessary for technical developers this does not represent actual practice – a common tension in software projects. In fact, the requirement to produce a formalised and rather abstract design narrative (using a controlled vocabulary) was one that caused considerable difficulty to the mainstream educators involved with the European UNFOLD project that brought together teachers and the IMS Learning Design development community. Expecting teachers to be able to produce an abstracted narrative description (as required by IMS Learning Design) that uses a controlled vocabulary to choreograph and record the proposed interactions of learners, teachers, environments and resources over time and space currently represents a really serious challenge.

However, the useful thing about IMS Learning Design, from the point of view of this chapter, is its insistence on being able to produce a shareable and structured narrative that stands as a formal design document. The benefit of this is the ability to have a useful shared reference point for the production of design documentation. This can, in turn, support the critical activities for improving the design skills in HE that are required to implement e-learning effectively, which include:

- Development of more reflective practitioners and institutions
- Changing the teaching model from individual to team (important for flexible/ blended learning)
- Improving the quality of the design of learning experiences
- Providing a context for identifying organisational factors that impinge on design.

The difficulties teaching practitioners face with the use of a controlled vocabulary and other technical representations of design, such as Universal Modelling Language diagrams, was recognised during the discussions of the UNFOLD project. Out of these discussions came the acceptance of the need to recognise the less formal, rougher and more tentative conceptions of pedagogy that practitioners really use: 'primitives' and 'artefacts'– were the terms that emerged to describe these kind of conceptions (Griffiths & Blat, 2005). It was recognised that these may in turn become the building blocks of more elaborated and structured representations that may still be 'fuzzy', that lie midway between actual embedded practice and the more abstract and formalised narrative required to initiate an IMS Learning Design. This leads to the useful notion of a 'learning design continuum' as shown in Figure 1.

The *IMS Learning Design best practice and implementation guide* (IMS, 2009) describes the starting point of creating a design as an analysis phase that results in a structured narrative. As

Figure 1. The Learning Design Continuum

Primitives/Artefacts.....................Semi-Structured........................Formal

Griffiths and Blat (2005) point out, no structure or methodology is recommended to support this activity. This is an important gap in current understanding about learning design in mainstream education – what needs to occur before a formal learning design can be produced. This is also a problem that concerns many other creative design professions and education can profit from the experiences and insights from those involved in the field of design studies. Of course, one of the potential benefits of IMS Learning Design is that it provides part of the solution to this problem itself by providing a common reference point at the formal end of the continuum in the form of a shared and structured vocabulary to do just that. Having such design formalisms is something that is important to aid communication and development in many professional fields, architectural plans and engineering specifications being two examples. It is also worth noting that there are strong informal design traditions in these fields, especially in the visual forms of drawing and sketches.

The learning design language usage classification box in Figure 2 is inspired by Botturi, Derntl, Boot, and Figl (2006), and is a useful aid to help think about the purpose of a design and indicates that a design may well pass through all the four stages in this classification from (1) generative/reflective through to (4) finalist/communicative – i.e. from individual reflective use to a finalised and shared use. This is particularly useful in relation to categorising the types of communication needed to support the move from individual ways of working to a more collaborative team-based approach that a flexible e-learning curriculum requires. If this usage classification is superimposed onto the learning design continuum it results

in a useful combined conceptual tool, shown in Figure 3. This tool can be used to help understand, categorise and describe different types of learning designs, their uses and how they might support a move towards team working (indicated by the arrow). The formal end of the continuum being defined by the narrative required to produce an IMS Learning Design.

BRIDGING THE GAP: PRACTICAL APPROACHES TO GENERATING LEARNING DESIGNS

The gap referred to in this section title is that between the informal personal ideas of practitioners and the more finalised communicative designs that are needed to support a shared design effort. As Stubbs and Gibbons (2008) observe: 'Bridging this gap requires a process of externalising the designer's conceptual world. This externalisation

Figure 2. Learning Design Usage Classification Framework

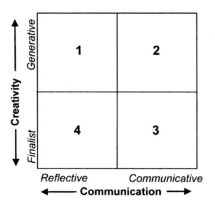

Figure 3. Learning Design Continuum Combined with Usage Classification

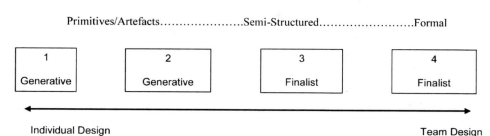

may be expressed verbally, visually, or physically – with words, drawings, or models' (p. 34).

The approaches in this section are based on experience of working with subject specialist teachers and helping them articulate and clarify their own, mostly internalised, pedagogic strategies in order to start representing them in a shareable way. Once they are externalised they can be reflected upon and when they are shareable, the teacher can discuss them with colleagues and develop them further.

Standard instructional and educational design wisdom is that after a period of analysis the aims, learning outcomes and assessment criteria are developed with some rigour and then content is added. This is fine if the teacher can work in this way and has the skills to do so. However, the reality is that many teachers feel most comfortable working outwards from what they already know and do (the content – especially 'their' content, their own notes, etc.). This perspective fits very well with taking a 'scaffolded' approach to developing design skills in mainstream teachers based on a cognitive apprenticeship model (Brown, Collins & Duguid, 1989). A good way of facilitating such an approach is to utilise communities of practice (Wenger, 1998), which is what two learning resources repository projects have done – the NDLR (National Digital Learning Repository) project in Ireland and the Merlot (Multimedia Educational Resources for Learning and Online Teaching) project in the USA have been pursuing this course with some success. In this scenario shared learning

objects and learning designs become social objects that help mediate meaning and understanding between different parts of the same community and across the borders of different communities – such as between subject matter experts and media developers (Wenger, 1998).

Some of the design approaches described below (especially related to content) may seem obvious or banal to existing experienced designers, but it needs to be borne in mind that these are aimed at teachers who may never have articulated or shared a learning design before. The division between content and activity is fluid and one will lead to the other and vice versa. It is worth noting that in the Instructional Systems Design tradition it is also generally recognised that activities like needs analysis and requirements gathering can include a fair amount of iteration and serendipity for experienced practitioners – even if the output is a relatively short and abstract design statement. There are some striking parallels in the methods described below to knowledge elicitation and representation in the field of artificial intelligence. In this connection, the two most important factors are (i) of finding suitable representations and elaborating them (Wenger, 1998), and (ii) the importance of a rapport between the 'knowledge engineer' (the designer/facilitator) and the subject specialists in a team setting (Irgon, Zolnowski, Murray, & Gersho, 1990).

For those readers less familiar with the Instructional Systems Design (ISD) tradition Reigeluth (1999) provides an authoritative introduction to the changing nature of the ISD community that is useful for those coming to that area for the first time and Clark (2004) provides a comprehensive and accessible online resource base covering the subject and its history

Working on Content

Hierarchical Lists, Concept Maps, Mind Maps

Many subject experts find it difficult to separate teaching activity (and hence design) from the actual content itself. Some are prone to producing long texts for their students (often unstructured), which are in effect internal narratives. A useful first step in this situation is to get them to produce a hierarchical list of the constituent topics of a subject, this begins to break down the subject area into the main components that are linked in order of precedence in the subject domain – this is surprisingly useful. Of course not all domains fall into a neat hierarchical list: this is where mind maps and concept maps come in useful in helping to define the type of structure inside the subject area. Boyle (1997) presents useful advice on how to go about the structuring (and restructuring) of content to support the process of curriculum design. Often the structure of the domain will suggest an initial order for teaching the material – this needs to be tested later in the design process. At this stage the first draft version of what is to be covered and taught is obtained. As a general observation it is worth noting that the use of graphical representations, particularly design drawings, is greatly underused in this area (Stubbs & Gibbons, 2008).

Structured Writing

It can be very useful to supply some guidelines and house styles to promote and support structured writing. This is simply writing and formatting materials in such a way that the inner structure of the material is obvious to the other members of the team (and of course the students). It is very similar to the techniques used in 'traditional' correspondence courses. In this approach the lo-tech concept of a contents list is used to make the document structure apparent, by dividing the material into hierarchical 'chunks'. For this it is essential that the relevant heading and sub-headings appear in the body text of the study material as well. Consistently formatted and well-named headings also act as useful 'prior organisers' for the reader. It is striking how such small factors can have a big impact – again this can help the teacher in conceptualising the structure of the course, this approach is recommended in a guide to designing for reuse produced in the UK (Casey & McAlpine, 2002).

Accessibility Issues

This is a common concern (and rightly so) although not always addressed coherently, the anxiety about this can be a useful lever in persuading teachers to organise their content in a clearer manner. The structured writing methods advocated above also produce more accessible web and text documents for screen readers (if standard heading styles are used). Developing content in layers as proposed below can also be a good basis for producing more accessible materials, as well as lightening the cognitive load on the authors by providing a useful incremental design framework.

Delivery Platforms, Bandwidth and Media Choices

Thinking about delivery platforms (both hardware and software) and bandwidth limits (the speed of a network connection) are good for helping to conceptualise students' situations and the choice of presentation modes available. It can be useful to develop content in layers (like an onion), with each layer adding more sophistication and presentational power (with possible implications for choice of platforms and bandwidth). This also provides an incremental way for subject matter experts and learning designers to engage with the extra cognitive load involved in translating their content and designs into different forms. A rough working rule of thumb that also represents the costs and skills of producing resources would be a hierarchy like that shown below:

Text > Diagrams (black and white schematic) > Colour Graphics/Photographs > Sound > Video > Animation > Interactive Multimedia

This layered approach to content design also makes it easier to identify and take account of important cultural factors, amongst both teachers and students, which may affect the design process. These cultural factors are mediated in face-to-face campus-based teaching in a relatively informal and rapid manner but can become much more explicit and problematical in online environments and this needs need to be factored into the design activities. For instance, in the textual form of the content the introduction of specialist terminology needs to be referenced to assumptions about prior learning. So do conceptions about what constitutes academic literacy – the assumed norms governing academic communication and interaction held by the teachers for that subject at that level. While in the visual media assumptions about visual literacy (such as in the use of diagrams) needs to be verified with the characteristics of the target student population and, where appropriate, additional explanatory resources provided.

Mode of Use

The intended context of use will affect the design of the content and related activities. Three useful modes to consider are:

- Face-to-face/classroom
- Distance/online learning
- Blended learning (a mix of the above two modes)

Often it is only possible to envisage activities by thinking about how the same content will be used in different modes: this is often enough to trigger a description of learning activities that can be associated with the content and, if needed, a redesign of the content.

Aims/Publicity

A useful exercise to go through is to examine the existing aims/purpose of the course with a view to clarifying them, especially when converting a campus-based course to flexible online delivery. Such statements are often drafted in a rush for a validation committee and can be difficult to understand – both for prospective students and other teachers – and are often remediated in a campus setting. But remediation in an online setting is much harder, so writing the aims/purpose with some rigour to be as clear as possible is one of the most important design tasks and should be done early on in the process. Good support tools to help in this process are the stock questions of journalistic enquiry such as: What is this about? Whom is this for? How will it benefit the student? When does it run? How is the teaching conducted? What is being taught? How is assessment carried out? What is special about this course, i.e. What is the selling point to students? Clarifying the answers to these questions can be a great help in preparing clear and meaningful learning outcomes – it is an iterative process. A useful side product of this is that it also produces good 'copy' for marketing the course. Another useful benefit of this approach is that it helps to make sure the public descriptions of the course do not 'drift' away from the internal validation documents and vice-versa.

Two Design 'Classics' for Educational Content Developers

It would be remiss not to mention in this section two design guides (that are still in print) relating to content development, one from the field of commercial publishing design and the other from the distance-learning sector. *The non-designer's design book: Design and typographic principles for the visual novice* by Robin Williams (1994) is an excellent and very readable introduction to the design of documents and use of typography. The principles described also have much to benefit the design of online documents and websites. As text documents in one form or another constitute the great bulk of academic communication and word-processing is within the skill set of most teachers, development in this area will provide a quick and high payback in terms of improvement in content design. Derek Rowntree, a professor of educational development at the Open University in the UK, has produced many books and guides about learning. In the context of this chapter his action-guide book *Preparing materials for open, distance and flexible learning* (Rowntree, 2002) is a guide that all e-learning designers should consult. He shows just how much can be achieved with a principled and lo-tech approach. It is interesting to note that both Rowntree (2002) and Williams (1994) advocate creating a design library or scrapbook in which to keep noteworthy designs for future reference and inspiration, a practice also used in many design and art disciplines.

Working on Activities

Organisational Issues: Encouraging a Systems Approach

Teachers are very influenced by their institutional context and it strongly affects their designs. When making the move to e-learning they need to take into account aspects of the organisational context that affect their design decisions. This requires relating to their own institutions in a more analytical manner. In a case study Postle et al. (2003) give a striking account of having to work around the limitations of the administrative systems in an Australian university when introducing e-learning. Issues such as delays in registration and hence access to an e-learning system are much more critical in an online scenario than a face-to-face one. Common workarounds are to have separate registration procedures, temporary log-on credentials and sending the first few weeks' worth of materials on CD-ROM or in print to ensure students can get started. This all connects to the closely related areas of 'customer relations and satisfaction' that more and more institutions and teachers are having to factor into their activities. The development of shared organisational models to facilitate a systems approach to identifying these kinds of contextual factors in e-learning design activities is likely to prove useful. Casey, Proven, and Dripps (2006) introduce an adaptable visual model intended for such applications.

Teaching Aims, Learning Outcomes and Assessment Criteria

Getting these factors right continues to represent a longstanding challenge in HE, as observed by Ramsden (1992) and Biggs (2006) and forms the basis of any good quality learning design. Although e-learning is relatively new in HE it involves elements of continuity as well as discontinuity with the past, this being a case in point. Jennifer Moon has written a useful practical guide to this difficult process, *The module and programme development handbook* (Moon, 2002). The outcomes-based approach to design still represents a difficult task for many teachers and organisations precisely because it calls for a fair degree of abstraction, precision and formalism in expression. Because of this, it represents an essential precursor to creating a formal learning design narrative and as such it occupies a pivotal position on the learning design continuum, as represented in Figure 4.

Figure 4. Aims, Outcomes, Assessment in the Learning Design Continuum

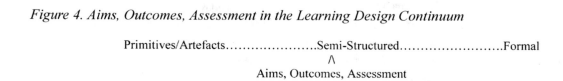

Primitives/Artefacts.....................Semi-Structured........................Formal

/\

Aims, Outcomes, Assessment

The module design and development model proposed by Moon (2002) stresses the iterative aspect of the design process and it is worth noting the primary input into this process is the creation of the Aims of the module, as described above. The outputs of this development cycle (learning outcomes, assessment criteria and methods and the teaching strategy) become an essential input to the learning design process and are an essential prerequisite to the creation of any formal learning design document.

Journalistic Enquiry Mapped to IMS Learning Design

The usefulness of adopting the questions of journalistic enquiry has already been referred to above in the context of writing the aims of the course.

The same questions can also be asked about the design of the course activities. A tool to support and record the outcomes of this process is shown in Figure 5. This kind of approach and tool can be useful for teachers to conceptualise what it is they think the student (or the teacher) might be doing at any point in the course. Larger cells will allow more detail and this can be accomplished by decreasing the number of rows in the grid. Another useful aspect of templates such as this is that they begin to introduce some of the abstractions needed to create a formal IMS Learning Design narrative. For instance the roles of teacher and student are represented, as are the learning outcomes, the resources needed, the type of environmental services used, the parts of the knowledge domain involved, and relations to assessment activities. This type of representation could also be used

Figure 5. Blended Learning Template

Module title:						
Module ref no.			Week no.			

	A Teacher/tutor activity	B Student activity	C Teaching and learning materials and resources	D Teaching topic, concept, knowledge, etc	E Learning outcomes (whole or partial) supported	F Formative or summative assessment	G VLE service – or classroom requirements: content delivery, discussion, chat, private mail, test, share files etc
1							
2							
3							

at different levels of granularity from an entire programme through to a module and down to an individual lesson, thus giving a common lo-tech 'vocabulary' and expressive framework to a team. This approach also fits well with the type of basic design visualisation tools advocated by Sloep, Hummel, and Manderveld (2005).

Online Tutoring and Student Activity Design

The highly successful guide books by Gilly Salmon, *E-moderating: The key to teaching and learning online* (2001)and *E-tivities: The key to online learning* (2006), are ideal for development in this area and show the demand from teachers for clear, accessible and well-written guidance to support their development. This also demonstrates that some of the experience and techniques from the distance-learning sector can be imported into the mainstream; Gilly Salmon previously worked at the Open University. Both Salmon (2001, 2006), and Rowntree (2002) adopt similar approaches to offering guidance to practitioners, especially in the use of case studies and practical exemplars that give a feeling of authenticity. Both writers also take it as a given (and advocate) that the design of the programme of instruction will have considerable time devoted to it beforehand and that this more design-intensive background provides the context for their advice about the design of content and activities. The success of these two writers' books also indicates that a number of important factors are particularly valued by practitioners in regards to sources of support:

- Compendium style training resource, i.e. a comprehensive but brief account of a subject
- Accessible conceptual models such as Salmon's 5 stage model
- Access to quick reference material for Just In Time Learning (JITL)

- Enduring appeal of paper-based resources
- Case-based 'stories' provide authenticity that teachers can relate to

Graphical Tools

These kinds of tools are relatively underused but increasing interest is being shown in the visual aspect of learning design and a useful handbook devoted to the subject was published in 2008 by Botturi and Stubbs. The ability of such visual tools, from pen and paper to more sophisticated software, to help practitioners visualise their designs is an important factor that is recognised in other design-intensive professions. However, it is not uncommon for some academic teachers to be uncomfortable with visual tools for learning design. There are strong cultural factors behind this as Stubbs and Gibbons (2008) identify:

We live in a world, especially in academia, over-shadowed by words. Lockard (1977) observed that, 'Our cultural heritage is dominated by a linear, verbal, and "rational" tradition which can inhibit the use of drawing in design.' The implication of this tradition is a belief that decisions are made rationally (meaning in the mind verbally), and drawing is merely an act of the hand printing the decisions out. (Stubbs & Gibbons, 2008, p.37)

In a techno-centric field, as is currently consti-tuted by much e-learning practice, it can be hard to make the case for lo-tech solutions such as the use of pen and paper. However, Hokanson (2008) provides powerful arguments for the important and central role that pen and paper techniques continue to play in the design process in hi-tech professions. It is the immediacy and control of the hand-drawn medium of paper that is unmatched by any other current technology and provides the least resistance to the externalisation of creative ideas both for individual reflection and for shar-ing. For these reasons it makes a great deal of sense to deliberately include graphical tools in the repertoire of learning design activities and to make a special point of using freehand drawing to release creativity and act as a communicative tool.

IMPROVING DESIGN SKILLS

Useful Lessons from Teaching Theory

Biggs (2006) and Ramsden (1992) both make the point that everyone has an implicit personal theory of teaching and learning and that the first step in the process of improving teaching is to start to externalise these internal conceptions in order to change them. In this section useful insights are introduced from research to serve as a foundation to build upon. In his influential book, *Learning to teach in Higher Education,* Ramsden (1992) outlines three theories of teaching in HE that co-exist and build upon each other in a hierarchical manner. They also nicely represent the stages a university teacher progresses through as their pedagogic expertise improves, as well as providing useful ways of analysing the proposed and actual uses of technology to support teaching. These three theories see teaching as concerned respectively with:

1. Delivering content
2. Organising and supervising student activity
3. Teaching as adapting to circumstances and context in order to make student learning possible

Theory 1: Teaching as Telling or Transmission

The 'teaching as telling' scenario is consistent with the 'subject specialist' model of teaching that has historically dominated HE. The experience of students in this kind of environment is often

unsatisfactory. Typically a student on a course will pass through the hands of different lecturers all teaching from their own notes, not working as a team from the same 'script'. This has the effect of fragmenting the learning experience and subject matter. It also places a higher load on the student than is necessary and presents obvious barriers to 'non-traditional' students who are not already familiar with this type of culture.

Theory 2: Teaching as Organising Student Activity

As Ramsden (1992) observes, the transmission model of teaching in HE (although still widespread) has in public discourse tended to be supplanted by concern about managing and directing student activity. Although this discourse sometimes acts as a 'cover' for the continuation of the transmission model it is a step in the right direction. Here the concentration is on what the student does, not on what the teacher does – or the content delivered.

Theory 3: Teaching as Making Learning Possible

At this third level teaching is an activity that includes delivering content and organising and supervising student activities; however, it is also fundamentally concerned with learning about teaching itself and applying the lessons learnt to new students and situations. In this view teaching is a constantly evolving, reflective, and reflexive process – in cognitive apprenticeship terms a sign of mastery of a discipline. To lay the foundation for working at the third level Ramsden (1992) is clear about the necessity for planning and incorporating the teachers' knowledge about common problem areas.

Note that this theory is very much concerned with the content of what students have to learn in relation to how it should be taught ... a teacher who uses this theory will recognise and focus especially on the key issues that seem to represent critical barriers to student learning. The content to be taught, and students' problems with learning it, direct the method he or she uses. (Ramsden, 1992, p. 114)

It is at this level (in a hybrid human-machine system) where the abilities of the human teacher can be used to best effect – the remediation of student knowledge. These three theories combined also corresponds closely to Laurillard's (2002) influential conversational model of HE teaching which also makes a number of useful recommendations for media choice and organisational restructuring.

Useful Lessons from the World of Design

The Nature of Design Knowledge

De Corte (1990) provides a description of the nature of the knowledge needed to underpin expertise in a domain that is also useful to frame a discussion about the nature of e-learning design skills and how to improve them:

a. The flexible application of a well-organised domain-specific knowledge base, involving concepts, rules, principles, formulae and algorithms, etc.
b. Heuristic methods
c. Metacognitive skills
d. Learning strategies that learners engage in to acquire the preceding types of skills.

This section looks towards how the field of design studies may help in developing the heuristic and metacognitive aspects of design expertise. Donald Norman (1999) has written a classic account about the profession of design in *The Design of Everyday Things*. There are some important ideas in this text in relation to

understanding the nature of the current design knowledge of teachers. Norman makes a strong and useful case for understanding the situated nature of such knowledge:

A major argument [in this book] is that much of our everyday knowledge resides in the world, not in the head. This is an interesting argument and, for cognitive psychologists, a difficult one. What could it possibly mean for knowledge to be situated in the world? Knowledge is interpreted, the stuff that can only be in minds. Information, yes, that could be in the world, but knowledge, never. Well, yeah, the distinction between knowledge and information is not clear. If we are sloppy with terms, then perhaps you can see the issues better. People certainly do rely upon the placement and location of objects, upon written texts, upon the information contained within other people, upon the artefacts of society, and upon the information transmitted within and by a culture. (Norman, 1999, p. xi)

It is precisely this situated, embedded, tacit and 'craft' nature of learning design in mainstream HE that needs to be comprehended in order to both understand and improve it.

Product Design

Those who design products experience many of the same problems as e-learning designers. They have to juggle with many conflicting elements in order to resolve the design problem, including purpose, resources, economics, the users, as well as more philosophical questions such as cultural values and aesthetics. It is useful to begin to explore what links there might be between the two professions. Achille Castiglioni was one of the most influential designers of the 20th century and taught Industrial Design at Milan Polytechnic. He is credited with many classic design creations and is cited in numerous design courses and handbooks. He is also famous for the many aphorisms and proverbs he used to describe his design methods. This particular use of language to express complex domain-specific concepts is typical of the existence of a community of practice – joint enterprises that create a shared repertoire (Wenger, 1998). With Castiglioni it is possible to get an insight into how a community makes special use of language (and drawings, etc.) to communicate internally; it allows practitioners to communicate to others at different levels of ability (including novices). In contrast, Beetham (2004) reports a relatively underdeveloped use of language and vocabulary in relation to descriptions of learning design in the mainstream HE educational community.

Looking at Castiglioni's statements it is clear he is operating at a meta-design level. What might be taken from this that may be of use in the field of learning design? For instance, he is credited with the viewpoint that if one is going to the trouble of designing something then the exercise must restructure an object's function, form and production process, and he applied this maxim to every work that he produced. Castiglioni described this process as 'Start from scratch. Stick to common sense. Know your goals and means' (Antonelli, 1997, p.1). How might this guidance be translated into the domain of learning design and objects? One useful interpretation might be (sentence for sentence):

- Start by identifying the learning needs as clearly as you can in terms of the problem, the learners and the context; don't try to reuse existing content and designs before doing this (a common problem), in fact: reuse last.
- Approach the design in terms of teaching aims and learning outcomes and take good time to develop the learning outcomes; from there develop the assessment criteria and methods in some detail.

- Return to check that the learning needs are correct, see if the design so far fits and adjust it according to the means and resources available.

Design Patterns

There is a need to find ways to mediate between the informal and situated designs of the mainstream and the more formalised design narratives needed to encourage wider sharing. One promising candidate is through the use of the concept of learning design 'patterns' (Bartoluci, Goodyear, & Retalis, 2004). For the purposes of this chapter a design pattern can be described as being a concise and accessible summary of a more complicated design instantiation. It is no coincidence that the use of patterns in this way emerged from the design-intensive profession of architecture (Alexander, 1979). The European E-LEN project (E-LEN, 2004) proposed a typical structure of a learning design pattern as follows:

- a name for the pattern
- a description of the problem/activity
- the context
- the forces and elements that play a role in coming to a solution
- the solution itself expressed succintly in terms of activities and resources, etc.

It would make sense for learning designs and learning objects to be filed in an online digital library together with their summary 'pattern' to help other teachers assess the design and the objects. The attraction of the pattern approach is that it provides an accessible shorthand summary that suggests a solution to the user who can then adapt or elaborate upon it in their own working context. The actual detailed designs and learning objects that the pattern is connected with may or may not be used in this process. The act of creating such simple structured patterns is also a good cognitive support tool to help designers to reflect upon their designs and externalise them in a shareable manner. McAndrew, Goodyear, and Dalziel (2006) provide a good explanation of both patterns and their possible applications to support learning design activities in the future.

CONCLUSION AND DIRECTIONS FOR FUTURE WORK

HE institutions are facing the challenges of delivering more flexible learning opportunities to greater numbers of students from more diverse academic backgrounds within limited budgets while maintaining and improving quality. In this situation, e-learning technologies and methods are increasingly being turned to in order to meet these challenges. To be effective, e-learning in HE will need to evolve into a more design-intensive process than it currently is, with accompanying changes in the academic workplace to be economically viable. One direction for change that many commentators and researchers foresee and recommend is a move towards a multidisciplinary team approach for the design and development of programmes of learning, a key component in this process being the increased sharing, reuse and adaptation of learning resources and designs. The type and degree of this change is likely be determined by factors such as disciplinary subject traditions, departmental structures, budgets, and institutional cultures.

The field of industrial product design is likely to be useful in helping to inform the development of effective e-learning designs and support tools and methods. This discipline often has to take a creative problem-solving approach to the redesign of products caused by changing markets and the introduction of new technologies and working methods. Higher education finds itself in just such a situation. Readers may be uncomfortable with the mass industrial production analogy, but

in many ways HE institutions have already drifted into becoming de-facto mass educational providers but without the benefit of a rational redesign of the workplace to make the best use of technology combined with educational research.

In this chapter the case has been made that it is not necessary to abstract and formalise the existing knowledge of teachers before it can be shareable or useful. Often it is precisely these informal 'craft' descriptions of knowledge, which are found valuable by others because they are accessible without being alienating. This is an important point to take on board for those involved in activities to support the development of learning design skills in mainstream HE. In this connection it is instructive to look to the design-intensive profession of architecture. There, it is recognised and understood that there is a parallel and longer tradition of what is called 'vernacular' design, which has developed to respond directly to the constraints of local conditions and to make best use of available resources as well as expressing cultural values. In their design activities architects often aim to have a 'dialogue' with this vernacular design tradition and in turn are influenced by it. Likewise, it is important to appreciate the veracity of teachers' conceptions about learning designs and their descriptions of them. An appreciation of this vernacular design tradition is particularly important for educational and technical researchers who, understandably, need to employ a more specialist and precise vocabulary with their peers but which is often found obscure and rebarbative by teachers. In this connection the work of researchers and authors like Salmon (2001, 2006), and Rowntree (2002) suggests that there is an important role for applied and action research to act as a nexus between the abstractions of 'high' research and teaching practice.

Effective solutions to the challenge of developing learning design skills in mainstream HE will need to recognise the diversity of ways people deal with their design tasks, often strongly influenced by contextual factors. This implies the need to work outwards from academic teachers' existing conceptual and skills bases. To support this, a cognitive apprenticeship model for their development is proposed. A natural adjunct to this is to develop communities of practice to situate such skills and knowledge within. A number of different tools, services and resources are likely to be required that reflect the diversity of contexts and working styles, as is the case in many other design-based disciplines. In this connection, it is likely to be best to think about how to create design environments (both online and lo-tech) that are 'convivial' to the production of effective learning designs (Illich, 1973). The development of such learning design support environments should be strongly linked to the wider study of creative design activities as well as research into the human-centred design of socio-technical systems that can effectively support those involved in such tasks.

REFERENCES

Agostinho, S., Harper, B., Oliver, R., Hedberg, J., & Wills, S. (2008). A Visual Learning Design Representation to facilitate dissemination and reuse of innovative pedagogical strategies in university teaching . In Botturi, L., & Stubbs, T. (Eds.), *Handbook of visual languages for instructional design: Theories and practices*. Hershey, PA: Information Science Reference.

Alexander, C. (1979). *The timeless way of building*. New York: Oxford University Press.

Antonelli, P. (1997). Curator's Essay. In *Achille Castiglioni: Design!* (A retrospective of the Italian architect and industrial designer), The Museum of Modern Art, New York. Retrieved July 27, 2009, from http://www.moma.org/exhibitions/1997/castiglioni/index.html

Bartoluci, S., Goodyear, P., & Retalis, S. (2004). E-LEN project: Working towards an e-learning design pattern language. *Learning Technology, 5*(4), 24–26. Retrieved July 27, 2009, from http://www.ieeetclt.org/issues/october2003/learn_tech_october2003.pdf

Beetham, H. (2004). Review: Developing e-learning models for the JISC Practitioner Communities. *JISC*. Retrieved July 27, 2009, from http://www.elearning.ac.uk/resources/modelsreview

Biggs, J. (2006). *Teaching for quality learning at university: What the student does*. Maidenhead, UK: Open University Press.

Botturi, L., Derntl, M., Boot, E., & Figl, K. (2006). A classification framework for educational modeling languages in instructional design. In *Proceedings of the Sixth International Conference on Advanced Learning Technologies* (ICALT2006) (pp. 1216-1220). Los Alamitos, CA: IEEE.

Botturi, L., & Stubbs, T. (Eds.). (2008). *Handbook of visual languages for instructional design: Theories and practices*. Hershey, PA: Information Science Reference.

Boyle, T. (1997). *Design for multimedia learning*. Hemel Hempstead: Prentice Hall Europe.

Boyle, T. (2003). Design principles for authoring dynamic, reusable learning objects. *Australian Journal of Educational Technology, 19*(1), 46-58. Retrieved July 27, 2009, from http://www.ascilite.org.au/ajet/ajet19/boyle.html

Bradley, C., & Boyle, T. (2004). Students' use of learning objects. *Interactive Multimedia Electronic Journal of Computer-Enhanced Learning, 6*(2). Retrieved July 27, 2009, from http://imej.wfu.edu/articles/2004/2/01/index.asp

Brown, J. S., Collins, A., & Duguid, P. (1889). Situated cognition and the culture of learning . *Educational Researcher, 18*(1), 32–34.

Casey, J., Greller, W., & Brosnan, K. (2005). *Prospects for using learning objects and learning design as staff development tools in Higher Education*. Paper presented at Cognition and Exploratory Learning in Digital Age, CELDA 2005, December, 14–16 2005, Porto, Portugal. Retrieved October 20, 2009, from http://trustdr.ulster.ac.uk/outputs/casey_brosnan_greller_final.pdf

Casey, J., & McAlpine, M. (2002). *Writing and using reusable educational materials: A beginners guide*. JISC Centre for Educational Technology Interoperability Standards. Retrieved July 27, 2009, from http://zope.cetis.ac.uk/groups/20010809144711/FR20020507112554

Casey, J., Proven, J., & Dripps, D. (2006). Modeling organisational frameworks for integrated e-learning: The experience of the TrustDR Project. In *Proceedings of the Sixth International Conference on Advanced Learning Technologies* (ICALT2006) (pp. 1216-1220). Los Alamitos, CA: IEEE.

Casey, J., & Wilson, P. (2006). *A practical guide to providing flexible learning in Further and Higher Education*. Gloucester: Quality Assurance Agency for Higher Education. Retrieved July 27, 2009, from http://www.enhancementthemes.ac.uk/themes/FlexibleDelivery/publications.asp

CETIS. (2009). *CETIS briefings on e-learning standards*. Retrieved July 27, 2009, from http://zope.cetis.ac.uk/static/briefings.html

Clark, D. R. (2004). *A brief history of instructional system design*. Retrieved July 27, 2009, from http://www.nwlink.com/~Donclark/history_isd/isdhistory.html de Corte, E. (1990). Learning with new information technologies in schools: Perspectives from the psychology of learning and instruction, *Journal of Computer Assisted Learning, 6*(2), 69-87.

Downes, S. (2003). *Design, standards and reusability*. Retrieved July 27, 2009, from http://www.downes.ca/post/54

E-LEN Project. (2004). *Design expertise for e-learning centres: design patterns and how to produce them. E-LEN project workpackage deliverable*. Retrieved July 27, 2009, from http://www2.tisip.no/E-LEN/documents/ELEN-Deliverables/booklet-e-len_design_experience.pdf

Fini, A. (2007). Editorial: Focus on e-learning 2.0. *Journal of e-Learning and Knowledge Society: The Italian e-Learning Association Journal, 3*(2).

Friesen, N. (2004). Three objections to learning objects and e-learning standards . In McGreal, R. (Ed.), *Online education using learning objects* (pp. 59–70). London: Routledge.

Friesen, N., & Cressman, D. (2006). The political economy of technical e-learning standards. In A. Koolhang, & K. Harman (Eds.), *Learning objects: Theory, praxis, issues, and trends* (pp. 507-526). Warsaw: Informing Science Press. Retrieved July 27, 2009, from http://learningspaces.org/n/papers/standards_ant.doc

Griffiths, D., & Blat, J. (2005). The role of teachers in editing and authoring units of learning using IMS Learning Design. *International Journal on Advanced Technology for Learning, Special Session on Designing Learning Activities: From Content-based to Context-based Learning Services, 2*(4). Retrieved July 27, 2009, from http://dspace.ou.nl/handle/1820/586

Hokanson, B. (2008). The virtue of paper: Drawing as a means to innovation in instructional design . In Botturi, L., & Stubbs, T. (Eds.), *Handbook of visual languages for instructional design: Theories and practices*. Hershey, PA: Information Science Reference.

Illich, I. (1973). *Tools for conviviality*. London: Harper & Row.

IMS. (2009). *IMS Learning Design best practice and implementation guide*. Retrieved July 27, 2009, from http://www.imsglobal.org/learning-design/ldv1p0/imsld_bestv1p0.html

Irgon, A., Zolnowski, J., Murray, K. J., & Gersho, M. (1990). Expert system development: A retrospective view of five systems. *IEEE Expert, 5*(3), 25–40. doi:10.1109/64.54671

Koper, R. (2003). Combining reusable learning resources and services with pedagogical purposeful units of learning. In Littlejohn, A. (Ed.), *Reusing on-line resources: A sustainable approach to e-learning*. London: Kogan Page.

Koper, R. (2005). An introduction to Learning Design. In Koper, R., & Tattersall, C. (Eds.), *Learning Design: A handbook on modelling and delivering networked education and training*. Berlin: Springer.

Laurillard, D. (2002). *Rethinking university teaching*. Abingdon: Routledge and Falmer.

Littlejohn, A. (2003). An incremental approach to staff development in the reuse of learning resources. In Littlejohn, A. (Ed.), *Reusing on-line resources: A sustainable approach to e-learning*. London: Kogan Page.

McAndrew, P., Goodyear, P., & Dalziel, J. (2006). Patterns, designs and activities: unifying descriptions of learning structures. *International Journal of Learning Technology, 2*(2/3), 216–242. doi:10.1504/IJLT.2006.010632

Moon, J. (2002). *The module and programme development handbook: A practical guide to linking levels, outcomes and assessment criteria*. London: Routledge.

Norman, D. (1999). *The design of everyday things*. Cambridge, MA: MIT Press.

Pollock, N., & Cornford, J. (2000). Theory and practice of the virtual university. *ARIADNE, 24*. Retrieved July 27, 2009, from http://www.ariadne.ac.uk/issue24/virtual-universities/

Postle, G., Sturman, A., Reuschele, S., McDonald, J., Mangubhai, F., Vickery, B., & Cronk, P. (2003). *On-line teaching and learning in Higher Education: A case study*. University of Southern Queensland. Retrieved July 27, 2009, from http://www.dest.gov.au/sectors/higher_education/publications_resources/profiles/online_teaching_and_learning_in_higher_education.htm

Ramsden, P. (1992). *Learning to teach in Higher Education*. Abingdon: Routledge and Falmer.

Reigeluth, C. (1999). What is Instructional-Design Theory and how is it changing? In Reigeluth, C. (Ed.), *Instructional-Design theories and models: A new paradigm of instructional theory* (*Vol. 2*). New Jersey: Lawrence Erlbaum Associates.

Rowntree, D. (2002). *Preparing materials for open, distance and flexible learning*. Abingdon: Routledge Farmer.

Salmon, G. (2001). *E-moderating: The key to teaching and learning online*. London: Kogan Page.

Salmon, G. (2006). *E-tivities: The key to active online learning*. Abingdon: Routledge Farmer.

Sloep, P., Hummel, H., & Manderveld, J. (2004). Basic design procedures for e-learning courses. In Koper, R., & Tattersall, C. (Eds.), *Learning design: A handbook on modelling and delivering networked education and training* (pp. 139–160). Berlin: Springer.

Stubbs, T., & Gibbons, S. (2008). Design drawing outside of ID . In Botturi, L., & Stubbs, T. (Eds.), *Handbook of visual languages for instructional design: Theories and practices.* Hershey, PA: Information Science Reference.

Trayner, T. (2002). *Practical approaches to electronic engineering – an SFEU funded teaching intervention.* Falkirk: Falkirk College of Further and Higher Education. Retrieved July 27, 2009, from http://www.sfeu.ac.uk/projects/falkirk_intervention_1

Twigg, C. (2005*). Keynote summary: Improving learning and reducing costs – New models for on-line learning.* Paper presented at the ALT-C 2005 Conference, Manchester. Retrieved July 27, 2009, from http://www.alt.ac.uk/altc2005/keynotes.html#carol

UNFOLD Project. (2009). *Welcome to Unfold.* Retrieved July 27, 2009, from http://www.unfold-project.net

Wenger, E. (1998). *Communities of Practice.* Cambridge: Cambridge University Press.

Williams, R. (1994). *The non-designer's design book: Design and typographic principles for the visual novice.* California: Pearson Education.

ADDITIONAL READING

Botturi, L., & Stubbs, T. (Eds.). (2008). *Handbook of visual languages for instructional design: Theories and practices.* Hershey, PA: Information Science Reference.

Boyle, T. (1997). *Design for multimedia learning.* Hemel Hempstead: Prentice Hall Europe.

Conole, G. (2008). Capturing practice: The role of mediating artefacts in learning design . In Lockyer, L., Bennett, S., Agostinho, S., & Harper, B. (Eds.), *Handbook of research on learning design and learning objects: Issues, applications and technologies.* Hershey, PA: Information Science Reference.

Goodyear, P. (2001). *Effective networked learning in higher education: Notes and guidelines.* Lancaster University: CSALT. Retrieved July 27, 2009, from http://csalt.lancs.ac.uk/jisc/guidelines.htm

Jochems, W., van Merriënboer, J., & Koper, R. (2004). *Integrated e-learning: Implications for pedagogy, technology and organisation.* Abingdon: Routledge and Falmer.

Lockyer, L., Bennett, S., Agostinho, S., & Harper, B. (Eds.). (2008). *Handbook of research on learning design and learning objects: Issues, applications and technologies.* Hershey, PA: Information Science Reference.

Mumford, E. (1995). *Effective Systems Design and Requirements Analysis: The ETHICS Approach.* Basingstoke: Macmillan.

Pavio, A. (1986). *Mental representations.* New York: Oxford University Press.

Sharples, M. (2006). Socio-cognitive engineering . In Ghaoui, C. (Ed.), *Encyclopedia of human computer interaction.* Hershey, PA: Information Science Reference.

Shuell, T. (1992). Designing instructional computing systems for meaningful learning . In Winne, P., & Jones, M. (Eds.), *Adaptive learning environments: Foundations and frontiers.* New York: Springer Verlag.

Sodhi, T., Miao, Y., Brouns, F., & Koper, R. (2007). *Bottom-up and top-down: An alternate classification of LD authoring approaches*. Paper presented at Open Workshop on Current Research on IMS Learning Design. June, 21-22, 2007, Barcelona, Spain. Retrieved July 27, 2009, from http://dspace.ou.nl/handle/1820/978?mode=full

Vosniadou, S., De Corte, E., Glaser, R., & Mandl, H. (Eds.). (1996). *International perspectives on the design of technology supported learning environments*. Mawah, NJ: Lawrence Erlbaum Associates.

Chapter 2
Designing Online Pedagogical Techniques for Student Learning Outcomes

Kay MacKeogh
Dublin City University, Ireland

Seamus Fox
Dublin City University, Ireland

Francesca Lorenzi
Dublin City University, Ireland

Elaine Walsh
Dublin City University, Ireland

ABSTRACT

The concept of identifying and measuring student learning outcomes has been embraced by a wide range of international policy makers and institutions across the globe, including the European Union through the Bologna Process, the USA, the OECD and other international organisations, while at national level many states have adopted, or are in the process of adopting a new national qualifications framework, based on student learning outcomes. The challenge for educators is to develop ways of enabling students to achieve, and to demonstrate their achievement, of these outcomes. The aim of this chapter is to explore ways in which online pedagogical techniques can be designed to provide solutions to the challenge of clearly demonstrating that students are achieving intended learning outcomes. While the techniques have been developed in the context of distance education programmes, the chapter includes an example of how these methods have been adapted for blended learning for on-campus students. A note of caution is sounded on the need to adopt effective techniques which do not impact unduly on lecturer workload.

DOI: 10.4018/978-1-61520-879-1.ch002

INTRODUCTION

The chapter will discuss the impact of the shift to the learning outcomes paradigm, which is leading to demands on higher education systems to move from traditional ways of designing learning towards more innovative forms of assessment and teaching: approaches which, it is argued, have been pioneered by e-learning and distance learning institutions (see for example the work of the Institute of Educational Technology http://oro.open.ac.uk/). The chapter starts by outlining some of the sources of pressure on systems to adopt a learning outcomes approach, before describing some generic learning outcomes schemas which have been proposed. This leads to a review of a number of pedagogical techniques which were initially designed to enable distance education students to achieve generic competences, such as ability to learn, ICT and information management skills, capacity to analyse and synthesise, research and project management competence, and interpersonal skills including team and group work. The objective of this chapter is to demonstrate the potential of online learning, not only to facilitate an outcomes focused curriculum design, but also clearly demonstrate that learning outcomes have been achieved. The type of tasks and structures which are designed into the curriculum to provide students with the opportunity to develop, perform and demonstrate their competence and achievement of specific learning outcomes will be explored through a series of examples and case studies of practice located mainly in a distance learning environment. However, as one of the case studies demonstrates, these techniques can be successfully adapted for delivery in a blended environment for on-campus students. The potential and challenge in 'blending' e-learning pedagogies with on-campus provision is discussed.

THE SHIFT TO LEARNING OUTCOMES: IMPLICATIONS FOR INSTRUCTIONAL DESIGN

Learning outcomes can be defined as 'statements of what a learner is expected to know, understand, and/or be able to do at the end of the learning process' (CEDEFOP, 2009, p. 17). While sometimes regarded as synonymous with objectives, the key difference is that objectives can also refer to inputs, and what is to be taught, while outcomes specifically refer to what the student can accomplish. Learning outcomes have acquired increasing importance at a political level and are seen as supporting diverse functions including: quality assurance; transparency of qualification systems; transnational mobility; tools to relate practical and theoretical learning; formulation of lifelong learning policies; and crucially, as a catalyst for reform or modernisation (CEC, 2006; Nusche, 2008; OECD, 2007).

Many countries have now adopted national qualifications frameworks, based on learning outcomes: for example, Ireland has adopted a National Framework of Qualifications (NFQ) which identifies ten award levels, with detailed descriptors for learning outcomes for each level (NQAI, 2003). All higher education institutions in Ireland are required by law (Government of Ireland Qualifications [Education and Training] Act 1999 Section 7a) to adapt their curricula and award structures to the new levels, and all programmes and modules are required to adopt learning outcomes (described as 'standards of knowledge, know-how and skill, and competence) which match the NQF guidelines (Maguire, Mernagh, & Murray, 2007).

Similar initiatives are taking place in other EU member states and those which have signed up to the Bologna Process (2009), albeit some countries and institutions are adopting at a slower pace than others (CHEPS, 2007). In a comprehensive survey carried out in 32 European countries, CEDEFOP, the European Union Agency for Vocational Education, claims that the 'shift to learning outcomes' is an 'integrated part of European and national lifelong learning strategies, addressing the need to create bridges between different parts of the education and training system' (CEDEFOP, 2009, p. 1). The survey found that, in some countries, learning outcomes were guiding changed assessment practices, and replacing traditional teacher and input focused methods based on tests of mastery of content, with more student and outcomes focused methods such as portfolios, projects, negotiated assignments, work and community based learning (CEDFOP, 2009, pp. 109–110).

In the USA, student learning has been identified as one of the six challenges confronting post-secondary education and higher education institutions have been urged by the Commission on the Future of Higher Education to adopt student learning outcome measures which would be comparable across institutions (Millett, Payne, Dwyer, Stickler, & Alexiou, 2008). The pressure for a learning outcomes approach is evidenced in many jurisdictions, for example Gallagher (2008) states that the accrediting agency for the California Community College system requires evidence of student learning as a measure of institutional effectiveness, and found that the colleges were in the process of designing strategies for developing and assessing student learning outcomes.

The European Qualifications Framework identifies three main types of learning outcomes: knowledge, skills, and competences (European Commission, 2005). The Tuning Project (http://www.tuning.unideusto.org/tuningeu/), which was influential in establishing the learning outcomes focus of the Bologna process, identified three categories of generic competences (Instrumental, Interpersonal and Systemic), with some 30 generic competences or transferable skills which were essential for preparing students for their future role as employees and as citizens. (See the section on Online Pedagogical Techniques for a more detailed list of these competences.)

The focus on learning outcomes has led to a questioning of fundamental aspects of the traditional educational paradigm including what is taught, how and where it is taught, and how it is assessed. Traditionally, many programmes were designed only to assess knowledge and skills, usually in a subject and discipline based context. The more generic skills and competences were often assumed to have been achieved, without being in any way assessed. Increasingly, however, it is recognised that not all learning outcomes, particularly those based on competences, can be achieved in the classroom or assessed by time delimited examinations (CEDEFOP, 2009, p. 101). According to Millett et al.:

The notions of transparency and accountability for student learning outcomes represents a paradigm shift for higher education. Although higher education has been evaluating student learning for centuries, the current societal pressure for data beyond course grades, degree granting rates, and similar 'production' measures represents a sea change of considerable magnitude. (2008, p. 3)

Thus, the shift to learning outcomes implies a shift of focus from the teacher and course content to a more flexible student-focused independent learning approach. This then has unavoidable consequences for instructional design and pedagogy. However, it is clear that merely writing a series of learning outcomes does not lead to change in the quality of education unless a radical and holistic approach is taken to instructional design, which will involve changes in teaching, learning and assessment strategies. There is evidence (CEDEFOP, 2009) that the attachment to traditional, summative assessment approaches remains strong despite the requirement inherent in the shift to learning outcomes for a fundamental change in the established forms of assessment.

It is now widely accepted that there is a need for 'constructive alignment' between outcomes, teaching/learning methods, and assessment. As

Ramsden (1992, p. 187) is often quoted: 'From our students' point of view, assessment always defines the actual curriculum. In the last analysis, that is where the content resides for them, not in lists of topics or objectives' (or indeed outcomes). According to Biggs there are two aspects to constructive alignment:

the 'constructive' aspect refers to the idea that students construct meaning through relevant learning activities. That is, meaning is not something imparted or transmitted from teacher to learner, but is something learners have to create for themselves. Teaching is simply a catalyst for learning. (2003, p. 2)

The main task of the teacher is to start by defining the intended learning outcomes, then to select teaching/learning activities designed to achieve these outcomes, then assess the learning outcomes to identify how they match what was intended. The final grade is then matched with the quality of the performance. Thus, the alignment of assessment strategies with outcomes is crucial. Biggs claims that the classroom provides very limited opportunities for attaining generic higher order skills and comments that resourcing pressures and the changing nature of higher education can be 'blessings in disguise' as many rich sources of learning are forced to take place outside of the classroom including 'interactive group work, peer teaching, independent learning and work-based learning' (2003, p. 3).

Distance and e-learning techniques and methodologies have the potential to deliver on learning outcomes which can be difficult to develop in the traditional time and place bound lecture format. Prensky (2001) argues that the achievement of different learning outcomes requires a mix of pedagogical approaches, and Anderson (2009) suggests that most outcomes can be achieved through e-learning, using a combination of online community and independent study activities and an 'appropriate mix of student, teacher and content

interaction [which] is uniquely designed for each learning outcome' (Anderson, 2009, p. 63). In a comparative review of developments in the USA under the Pew grant system and the eLearning Benchmarking programme in the UK, Mays and Morrison (2008) pointed out that both projects found the introduction of technology-enhanced learning led to improved learning outcomes as project participants 'redesigned their approach towards a more constructivist student-centred task-based form of learning and teaching, with technology playing an important role only to the extent that it facilitated the pedagogy' (p. 13).

The move to learning outcomes is also raising questions about the skills required to redesign teaching and assessment strategies and many institutions are now providing training for academic staff in instructional design and pedagogical strategies (e.g. Bowe & Fitzmaurice, 2006). Distance educators have much to offer traditional campus-based education in this context. They have long experience in instructional design and in developing innovative ways to support student learning outside of the classroom. Distance educators have used a wide range of media, including self-instructional texts, audiovisual media, and more recently e-learning involving the use of virtual learning environments (VLE), and there is considerable research on the efficacy of different pedagogical approaches. (See Moore & Anderson, 2004 in relation to the USA, and Bernath, Szucs, Tait, & Vidal, 2009 in relation to Europe.) The authors, as academics in Oscail, the National Distance Education Centre, based in Dublin City University, have developed and tested a number of innovative pedagogical methods designed to achieve a range of generic competences (see Fox & MacKeogh, 2003; Fox & Walsh 2007; Lorenzi, MacKeogh, & Fox, 2004; MacKeogh, 2006). In the following section we will synthesise some of the outcomes of the design research carried out, illustrated with examples of the alignment of generic competences with online pedagogical techniques in distance education undergraduate programmes in information technology and the humanities.

ALIGNING GENERIC OUTCOMES WITH ONLINE PEDAGOGICAL TECHNIQUES

Dublin City University, through Oscail, the National Distance Education Centre (http://www.oscail.ie), has been a major provider of distance learning in Ireland since 1982, providing graduate and postgraduate qualifications in information technology, humanities, social sciences, nursing, and management. Up to 2001, Oscail used mainly 'second generation' distance education technologies in delivering its courses, utilising a mix of correspondence texts, video and audio tapes, some computer-based learning and supported by face-to-face tutorials in a distributed network of study centres. Since its establishment, Oscail staff have evaluated and experimented with various forms of technologies, however, the introduction of VLEs, combined with online library full-text journal databases, together with increased student access to the internet, finally enabled the move of all programmes to online delivery between 2001 and 2005. With support from the EU Minerva programme, the PICTURE project (2000–2002) developed a number of online techniques which demonstrated the potential of developing higher order learning, as well as generic competences such as team work, which did not create excessive demands on tutor time (see Fox & MacKeogh 2003). The key to achieving this outcome is devolving responsibility on the student to engage in peer-learning and peer-support, with the tutor providing scaffolding support as the student constructs their own learning (Lorenzi et al., 2004). While the result is often perceived as increased workload for students, the efficacy of the approach in terms of deep learning is acknowledged by students (Fox & Walsh, 2007).

Since 2001 a number of online pedagogical techniques have been adopted to achieve specific generic competences, which have been subject to rigorous evaluation and continuing enhancement based on student feedback (MacKeogh & Lorenzi, 2007). Three of these approaches will be discussed here:

- **SPeL (the Student Passport to eLearning):** this approach is designed to enable first-year undergraduate students to develop the generic study skills required to succeed in specific disciplines, including planning and time management, IT skills, capacity for analysis and synthesis, as well as the ability to interact with other students and tutors.
- **TOOL (Task Oriented Online Learning):** this approach is designed to foster critical thinking, interpersonal, team working and group work and collaborative skills among students in their third year of an Information Technology undergraduate degree.
- **POURS (Peer and Group Online Undergraduate Research Supervision):** this approach is aimed at final-year undergraduates undertaking research dissertations, and fosters research skills, critical and analytical skills, project design and management, and ethical awareness.

While each of these methods focuses on students at different stages of undergraduate honours degrees, and prioritises specific sets of outcomes, each cluster of approaches has been used to achieve a far greater set of outcomes which will be discussed in further detail below.

SPeL: Student Passport to eLearning

The majority of students enrolling on Oscail undergraduate programmes are adults, ranging in age from 23 to over 80 years, with a widely varied background in terms of prior education and experience. Such students can find it difficult to adjust to the demands of studying at third level, as well as the need to adapt to new ways of learning using technology. The SPeL modules were introduced in 2003, initially as voluntary access type courses, and following review and evaluation, it was decided to embed the modules into the first-year (foundation) modules of the Bachelor of Arts programme. The learning outcomes specified for the modules incorporating the SPeL programme include the following.

- Students will demonstrate an understanding of the specific content, concerns, techniques, methods of enquiry and discourse typical of the subject.
- Students will develop the skills necessary for effective learning (e.g. researching, sourcing, recording, analysing and interpreting information, writing essays, reviews and reports) as well as the more generic skills of time management and reflective practice.
- Students will be able to access a wide range of printed and online resources comprising the body of scholarship in the subject.
- Students will develop their capacity for independent and self-directed learning through the use of information and communications technologies (ICTs).
- Students will apply their skills and knowledge of the subject through a portfolio of assessment tasks including:
  - Producing notes on course units
  - Writing reports and evaluations of subject-related weblinks and databases
  - Preparing bibliographies and reference lists derived from searching library online catalogues, and using the appropriate subject specific referencing and citation systems

  - Summarising and reviewing research-based journal articles accessed through online databases
  - Analysing and interpreting primary sources relevant to the subject (e.g., historical documents, literary or philosophical texts, psychological or sociological data)
  - Preparing essay structures and plans
  - Writing essays using the writing conventions of the subject
  - Engaging in subject related discussions online in Moodle.

Students take Foundation Modules (15 ECTS credits, 225 hours of learning over a period of 24 weeks) in their first year of study. The modules are designed over three 'blocks' comprising a series of tasks intended to allow students to develop generic competences in the context of the discipline which they are studying. (See Table 1.)

In Block 1 *'Exploring the subject'*, students set up study schedules (time management); they start reflective diaries; they discuss subject-related topics online (thus developing writing skills, analysis and debate, IT skills); they search online for sources for a bibliography related to an essay topic and learn how to use the referencing system related to the discipline (e.g., psychology students use the APA system, whereas history students use a system developed by the Irish Historical Association); they make notes on course units; and they download an article from the online databases and post a summary online.

In Block 2 *'Building knowledge of the subject'*, students build on the learning and IT skills developed in Block 1; they analyse primary sources (e.g., statistical data, historical documents, literary texts); they review a journal article; they prepare a mindmap and outline structure for an essay; and they continue to interact online, developing their writing and critical analysis skills.

In Block 3 *'Applying knowledge of the subject'* students apply their knowledge of the subject

Table 1. Assignment tasks: psychology foundation module

Block	Task and Contribution to Assessment
Block 1: Exploring the subject	• Post at least one contribution to the online weekly discussion topics on the Moodle discussion forum. One discussion topic per week, e.g., 'One could argue that language development begins at birth. Do you agree? Give reasons for your answer.' (25%)
	• Prepare a study schedule for the course, listing for each day the time you will make available for study. (formative)
	• Prepare a reflection at the end of each week of study under the following headings: learning process; course content; experience of learning with technology; Summary comments. (formative)
	• Make notes on Unit 4: Cognitive development. (formative)
	• Explore the range of web resources relevant to Psychology accessible through the DCU Library Psychology Portal. Evaluate and write a short review of two websites relevant to Psy1 Unit 4 and Unit 6. (25%)
	• Search the DCU online library catalogue for possible sources for an essay on bilingual language development. Prepare a bibliography using the approved referencing system of at least 15 items which are potentially relevant for the essay. (25%)
	• Download an article from DCU online resources: Flavell, John H. (1999). Cognitive development: Children's knowledge about the mind. *Annual Review of Psychology, 50,* 21–45. Prepare a 300-word draft summary of the article. (25%)
Block 2: Building knowledge of the subject	• Post at least one contribution to the discussion forum on Moodle per week. One topic per week, e.g., 'Can the psychometric approach capture the "humanness" of people? Can any scientific theory?' (12.5%)
	• Primary source analysis – Statistical analysis of data on self-esteem of participants on a personal development course. (50%)
	• Review (600 words) of article downloaded from bibliographic database: Furnham et al. (2002). Estimates of ten multiple intelligences: Sex and national differences in the perception of oneself and famous people. *European Psychologist, 7,* 245–255. (25%)
	• Using the information on brainstorming and patterned note-taking in the Study Skills text, formulate a spider diagram and outline structure for an essay on: Compare and contrast schema in adults and children in relation to either cognitive or social behaviour. (12.5%)
Block 3: Applying knowledge of the subject	• Post at least one contribution to the discussion forum on Moodle per week, e.g., 'Groupthink – does it exist in real life? Give examples where possible in your contribution. Do you agree with the examples posted by others and why/why not?' (12.5%)
	• Essay on topic for which bibliography and structure prepared in Block 2.
	• Examination question. (750–1000 words approx.) Formative

Source: Psy1. *Psychology Workbook* 2006/7 Oscail.

through writing an essay on the topic for which they have already planned in Block 2 and for which they will have received feedback from their tutor; they will prepare for examination assessment by completing an examination in self-regulated examination conditions, posting their answer online, and receiving peer and tutor feedback. The online discussion topics relate to the course content and require students to make a minimum number of contributions which all contribute to the overall assignment mark.

While the SPeL modules are evaluated and adaptations made on a regular basis, the main concern of these modules is to provide students with the skills to become effective learners in an online world. There is some concern that standalone study skills interventions tend to be unsuccessful as these skills need to be contextualised within specific disciplines (Lorenzi et al., 2009; Wingate, 2006). By using the affordances of online, asynchronous technologies, and appropriate pedagogical design strategies, it has been demonstrated that students can develop these competences, and become effective learners (Lorenzi et al., 2004, 2009). Table 1 above provides an example of the type of tasks students undertake in a Psychology Foundation module.

TOOL: Task Oriented Online Learning

The B.Sc. in Information Technology (comprising modules in Computing, Management Science, Communications Technology and Human Sciences) was converted to online delivery in 2002 leading to the development of a series of innovative online pedagogical techniques (Fox & Walsh, 2007). One of these techniques, TOOL – Task Oriented Online Learning, comprises an integrated series of tasks designed to generate interpersonal competences, in particular the ability to work in teams and groups, and to engage in collaborative projects, and peer learning. As the Human Sciences strand of the programme is primarily discursive in nature, the TOOL approach has been found to be particularly effective in achieving these outcomes. The TOOL approach is designed to improve student engagement and higher order learning through in-depth online discussion of the content of the module. Online engagement is an integral part of the summative assessment of the module. In addition, online support facilitates group work and collaboration, which had not been previously possible due to the logistical problems caused by dispersed student populations. The TOOL approach has been used extensively in the module: HSA Cultures of Technology. The intended student learning outcomes envisage that on completion of the module students should be able to:

- Demonstrate conceptual understanding of the main elements of the cultures of technology
- Analyse, evaluate and critique theories and constructs related to the course content
- Construct arguments and defend their views on a number of topics
- Apply research methods to the collection, analysis and reporting of empirical data
- Communicate effectively with diverse groups, including non-experts
- Demonstrate effective interpersonal skills

- Engage in collaborative work in groups, and understand and reflect on group processes.

As with the SPeL approach, the TOOL approach divides the academic year into three blocks which involve different assessment components:

Block 1. Online debates/resources: students engage in a series of debates on set topics related to the course content. Students are directed to a number of articles which can be accessed through the online databases. They are given two weeks to research the topic, following which they spend four weeks engaged in online debate on the topics with tutors and fellow students. Marks are allocated on the quality of the contributions.

Block 2. Peer tutoring: In the second phase, students are divided into groups of three and allocated a topic related to the second section of the course. The groups are given two weeks to research the topic, using internet sources and articles. They then agree a 200–300 word synopsis of the topic which is posted online. They post questions to other groups, and answer questions from students on the topic synopses. Finally, each group posts an amended synopsis which incorporates responses and reflections on the questions and discussion which has taken place during the 'peer tutoring' phase. The synopses are assessed on the basis of the quality of the contributions, and each member of the peer-tutoring group receives the same mark.

Block 3. Collaborative group project: In the final phase, students are engaged on a collaborative group project. Students work in groups of five or six and produce a report on a set topic relevant to the third section of the module text. The process of collaboration and group interaction is given equal emphasis with the production of a product – the final report. Students are given detailed guidelines on how to form groups, monitor progress, deal with conflict. Assessment is based on (1) the group report; (2) online progress reports; (3) personal evaluation of the collaborative learning process in which students are asked to evaluate their own contribution, i.e., a self-reflective piece and (4) a peer evaluation in which students assess the contribution of each of their group members both descriptively and numerically on a number of characteristics. The group decides which student names are listed on the group report. Where the group decides that an individual student has not contributed sufficiently, they may decide to omit that student from the assessment.

The three TOOL approaches have been found to be particularly effective in developing higher order learning and generic competences. The asynchronous nature of the online debates allows students time to reflect and consider their responses. The peer-tutoring assignment gives students experience of communicating difficult concepts to non-experts (their fellow students in this case). The collaborative group projects provide students with the experience of forming and maintaining a group, and engaging in a real collaborative enterprise. While student feedback indicates that the module is more time consuming than other more traditional modules, nevertheless, the quality and depth of learning is far superior. Some comments from students included:

- I feel that the online assessment during the year was probably a fairer way of assessing a person's knowledge on a subject than getting them to learn off-course material and spend three hours writing everything they know.
- I thought that the 'learning' experience was of a Higher Quality as the groupwork was in my opinion superior to the type of 'knowledge' required for an examination.
- The group work was rewarding … It was a good experience and challenge to build up trust and teamwork.

POURS: Peer and Group Online Undergraduate Research Supervision System

The development of research skills, project design and management, and ethical awareness are key generic graduate competences. In most undergraduate degree programmes, final-year students are expected to undertake a piece of independent research, yet increasing enrolments present challenges to effective supervision of the undergraduate dissertation, causing some institutions to dilute or abandon the traditional individual project. If it is accepted that students need to acquire research and enquiry-led approaches as a key component of their graduate outcomes, innovative ways of developing these skills must be adopted, within the context of diminishing resources. Supervising research and providing support to distance students present additional challenges. The challenges facing supervision at a distance include: part-time adjunct faculty; restricted time availability; student access to resources; students' research skills; ethics supervision; as well as authenticating the student's work. Another problem faced by students, not only in distance education, but also in on-campus education is that supervision is not 'on-tap' 24 hours a day, and access to supervision is normally limited to specific time slots, or by prior appointment only. These challenges have been addressed in the Oscail Humanities programme through the development of the Peer and Group Online Undergraduate Research Supervision System (POURS). With online interaction, students can post a query anytime, and will often receive advice and support from fellow students before the supervisor needs to intervene. Similarly students benefit from the knowledge gained from a more open discussion online of problems and solutions, and are exposed to a broader range of research topics and outcomes.

Students must be adequately equipped with the appropriate research and analytical skills to carry out their research. While students should have developed some skills in data collection and analysis in previous modules, often these skills need to be refreshed and oriented towards the more independent approach required for dissertation research. The POURS approach has been applied to research in psychology, sociology, history, and geography, with appropriate adaptations to allow for the unique research traditions in each subject. The main components of POURS are:

- Research exercises designed to refresh research skills, for example, statistical exercises, or analysis of historical documents
- Tasks related to research design, defining the research question, preparation of outlines, developing the literature review
- Online peer critiques of research outlines and proposals
- Supervisory online forums using threaded discussions, which are open to fellow students and supervisors
- Online presentations using PowerPoint
- Reflections on the research process.

The POURS approach was first developed in the context of a final-year psychology research module (see MacKeogh, 2006). This module includes a series of statistical exercises, using Statistical Package for Social Sciences (SPSS), which students carry out at home, while interacting online in Moodle in tutor-led discussions, with peer support. Students engage in peer support and supervision, by giving feedback on research topics, answering questions from other students on statistics, suggesting new approaches or references, offering to source participants for surveys or to distribute questionnaires, providing advice on technical issues with SPSS. The process of carrying out the research project is broken into distinct phases with milestones, followed by formative feedback from peers and supervisor. Students post research outlines on Moodle, review and critique outlines of other students, and prepare research proposals and literature reviews taking

into account both peer and supervisor feedback. A supervisory forum is set up with a discussion thread for each student. Students post questions to their supervisors in the discussion threads and either supervisors or other students post responses. Often, by the time the supervisor has checked in to the Moodle forum, other students have responded, or the student has worked out the answer for themselves. By discussing problems in an open forum, all students become aware of potential problems as well as solutions, thus reducing the need for one-to-one support from the supervisor.

Students prepare a draft report and a Power-Point presentation on their findings. The final report, the research dissertation, is the student's work and the supervisor provides no further direct support following the return of the draft report. Assessment of the module is on the basis of a portfolio which includes marks for practical exercises, online contributions, peer critiques, the literature review and research proposal, oral or PowerPoint presentation of results, and the final project report. Thus, students are assessed not only on the final product, but also on the process of becoming a researcher as evidenced by the outputs from the various set tasks. The POURS approach has led to a noticeable improvement in the quality of research reports, with some graduates being accepted as presenters in major disciplinary conferences. For example in 2006 five graduates of the Psychology module presented their research at the annual Psychological Society of Ireland conference.

In 2008/2009 the POURS approach was piloted with a group of 14 final-year Geography students studying full-time, on-campus in a traditional university, NUI Maynooth. In this format, a blended delivery approach was adopted, with face-to-face practical sessions in Semester 1 which included SPSS practicals and sessions on research design, literature reviews, and ethics. In parallel, students interacted on Moodle, posting weekly reports, posting their research proposal and outline, peer critiques of at least two other proposals, and

Table 2. Research module: Tasks

Semester	Task
Semester 1	Task A: Contributions to workshops and practicals, and online activities
	Task B: Research Proposal (300–500 words)
	Task C: Research Proposal Critiques (two critiques per student 300–500 words)
	Task D: Literature Review (1,500 words)
	Task E: Research Action Plan (500 words)
	Task F: Reflective Evaluation
	Task G: Ethics Approval Form
Semester 2	Task A: Contributions to online activities
	Task B: Weekly Progress Reports
	Task C: Project Report
	Task D: PowerPoint Presentation
	Task E: Reflective Evaluation

literature reviews. In Semester 2, all interaction was online on Moodle forums. Table 2 outlines the different tasks in the two semesters.

Student feedback indicates that the presence of online support from peers and the supervisor was a significant factor in stimulating confidence and removing feelings of isolation, as despite the fact that students were on-campus, the reality was that, given the large number of students in the programme, most students did not have regular contact with their peers in the supervisory group, especially in the second semester when no group activities are scheduled and students can call on supervisory support on a very limited basis.

In terms of the supervisor's workload, this format allows for more efficient use of time. Instead of allocating several hours per week to individual supervision, the supervisor spends in the region of two hours per week (on average 20 minutes per day) monitoring online interaction, answering queries and posting supportive reminders about deadlines. In addition, while the preparation of module handbooks and task descriptions takes up some time in the first presentation, the time is considerably reduced in later presentations as the handbook only requires minor editing and updating.

ONLINE PEDAGOGICAL TECHNIQUES: ISSUES AND OUTCOMES

As the case studies above have demonstrated, the SpeL, TOOL, and POURS tasks are designed to enable students to attain a wide range of key generic competences. Table 3 summarises the learning outcomes which the three approaches are designed to achieve in terms of the 30 Tuning competences referred to earlier. While the linguistic and intercultural competences have not been part of the outcomes for the disciplines described in this chapter, further application of the POURS approach to other disciplines in this area are planned for the 2009/2010 academic year.

These pedagogical techniques have evolved over a number of years, and have been guided by instructional design practices which focus on the application of constructivist, task-based approaches. The constructive alignment of learning outcomes with teaching and assessment methods is of key importance. Some scaffolding support is required in the form of detailed instructional schedules and clear assessment guidelines; while these can be time consuming to prepare for the

Table 3. Aligning generic competences with specific pedagogical techniques

Generic Competences	Description	SPeL	TOOL	POURS
Instrumental: • cognitive • methodological • technological • linguistic	Capacity for analysis and synthesis	√	√	√
	Capacity for applying knowledge in practice	√	√	√
	Planning and time management	√		√
	Basic general knowledge in the field of study	√	√	√
	Grounding in basic knowledge of the profession in practice	√	√	√
	Oral and written communication in native language	√	√	√
	Knowledge of second language	NA	NA	NA
	Elementary computing skills	√	√	√
	Research skills		√	√
	Capacity to learn	√	√	√
	Information management skills (ability to retrieve and analyse information from different sources)	√	√	√
	Critical and self-critical abilities	√	√	√
	Capacity to adapt to new situations	√	√	√
	Capacity for generating new ideas (creativity)	√	√	√
	Problem solving	√	√	√
	Decision-making	√	√	√
Interpersonal: • Social skills • Social interaction • Cooperation	Team work	√	√	√
	Interpersonal skills	√	√	√
	Leadership	√	√	√
	Ability to work in an interdisciplinary team	√	√	√
	Ability to communicate with non-experts in the field	√	√	√
	Appreciation of diversity and multiculturality	NA	NA	NA
	Ability to work in an international context	NA	NA	NA
	Understanding of the customs of other countries	NA	NA	NA
Systemic: • Understanding • Sensibility • Knowledge	Ability to work autonomously	√	√	√
	Project design and management	√	√	√
	Initiative and entrepreneurial spirit	√	√	√
	Ethical commitment	√	√	√
	Concern for quality	√	√	√
	Will to succeed	√	√	√

Source: Tuning Website http://www.tuning.unideusto.org/tuningeu/

first presentation, they can be relatively easily updated for subsequent presentations.

The instructional design cycle is a dynamic process involving the analysis of needs, design of learning outcomes, development of pedagogical interventions, implementation, and evaluation. Each year, modules are evaluated, based on 360 degree processes involving quantitative and qualitative measures, including student feedback and performance, extern examiners' reports, and monitoring of tutor teaching, assessment and student support quality. Evaluation reports are the basis on which modules are continuously improved and enhanced.

FUTURE DIRECTIONS

As we have indicated above, distance educators have developed a number of innovative pedagogical approaches which enable the achievement of learning outcomes which would be difficult to achieve in the conventional classroom. This has led to increasing interest from campus-based institutions for more blended solutions, where the advantages of face-to-face interaction can be enhanced by e-learning supported pedagogy (Garrison & Kanuka, 2004; Hughes, 2007; Kerres & de Witt, 2003). The authors are engaged in a process of 'mainstreaming' the approaches developed for their distance education programmes into the on-campus programmes currently offered in DCU. This follows an extensive consultative exercise which took place in 2008 aimed at introducing an overall e-learning strategy for the university (see MacKeogh & Fox, 2008). This process identified a number of drivers supporting adoption of e-learning, but also barriers in the form of academic attitudes and perceptions (Birch & Burnett, 2009; MacKeogh & Fox, 2009). The concern among academic staff with increased workload is a real challenge to wider adoption of new methods, particularly in large lecture-based classes. Traditionally, distance education courses have been designed and written by individual academics or course teams, with students supported and assessed in small tutorial groups by part-time tutors. However, in a traditional lecture-based module, assessed only by a terminal examination, the increased interaction and feedback required will inevitably increase the lecturer's workload unless consideration is given to employing teaching assistants to moderate online forums and provide formative and summative feedback to students. The challenge for academic managers, researchers and teachers is to find cost-effective ways of achieving learning outcomes without lecturer overload (Fox & MacKeogh, 2003). As has been indicated above, one key strategy is to involve students more actively in the process of knowledge construction through well-designed learning tasks involving peer interaction, self-directed and independent learning.

CONCLUSION

This chapter has discussed a number of trends that are changing the practice of higher education, in particular the shift to the learning outcomes paradigm which many expect will transform teaching and learning. The focus on outcomes, and what a student can actually do on completion of a course of study, is leading educators to explore a range of instructional design strategies and theories in order to ensure constructive alignment between course content, teaching, and assessment strategies. This in turn is leading to an awareness of the need for training and support for academics in pedagogical techniques to enable them to adapt their teaching practice for new types of students, new types of technologies, new types of societal demands. As we have seen, many of the new generic competences cannot be achieved within the confines of the traditional classroom, and cannot be assessed through closed book, time-limited examinations.

There is an opportunity here for convergence and synergies between conventional on-campus teaching, and the instructional design practices pioneered by distance educators and e-learning design researchers and practitioners. The advent of new educational technologies, especially virtual learning environments, has stimulated the development of a range of innovative online, task-based, constructivist, pedagogical techniques which can facilitate the achievement of a wide range of learning outcomes. This chapter has described a subset of such techniques which have been developed in a distance learning context. However, the competences and outcomes which these techniques are designed to address, such as, developing the capacity to learn, the ability to analyse, synthesise and critique, interpersonal, communication and group work skills, research design and data analysis, IT skills, are all outcomes which are equally relevant to on-campus students. This chapter has indicated that online pedagogical techniques which have proved successful for distance education students can, with refinement and adaptation, also provide powerful approaches to designing pedagogical strategies for achieving generic learning outcomes for traditional students in on-campus environments. It has also sounded a note of caution in relation to the potential impact on academic workloads and the need to design approaches which enhance learning without placing undue demands on the lecturer's workload.

REFERENCES

Anderson, T. (2009). Towards a theory of online learning. In T. Anderson, (Ed.), The theory and practice of online learning (2nd ed., pp. 45-74). Athabasca: Athabasca University Press.

Bernath, U., Szucs, A., Tait, A., & Vidal, M. (Eds.). (2009). *Distance and e-learning in transition. Learning innovations, technology and social challenges.* Hoboken, NJ: Wiley-ISTE.

Biggs, J. (2003). *Aligning teaching for constructing learning.* The Higher Education Academy. Retrieved October 20, 2009, from http://www. heacademy.ac.uk/assets/York/documents/resources/resourcedatabase/id477_aligning_teaching_for_constructing_learning.pdf

Birch, D., & Burnett, B. (2009). Bringing academics on board: Encouraging institution-wide diffusion of e-learning environments. *Australasian Journal of Educational Technology, 25*(1), 117-134. Retrieved October 20, 2009, from http:// www.ascilite.org.au/ajet/ajet25/birch.html

Bologna Process. (2009). Official Bologna Process Website 2009-2010. Retrieved October 20, 2009, from http://www.ond.vlaanderen.be/hogeronderwijs/bologna/

Bowe, B., & Fitzmaurice, M. (2006). *Guide to writing learning outcomes.* Dublin: Dublin Institute of Technology.

CEC Commission of the European Communities. (2006). *Communication from the Commission to the Council and the European Parliament: Delivering on the modernisation agenda for universities: education, research and innovation.* COM(2006) 208. Final. Brussels May 10, 2006. Retrieved October 20, 2009, from http:// eur-lex.europa.eu/LexUriServ/LexUriServ. do?uri=COM:2006:0208:FIN:EN:PDF

CEDEFOP. (2009). *The shift to learning outcomes: Policies and practice in Europe.* CEDEFOP Reference Series: 72 Luxembourg: Office for Official Publications of the European Communities. Retrieved October 20, 2009, from http://www. cedefop.europa.eu/etv/Upload/Information_resources/Bookshop/525/3054_en.pdf

CHEPS. (2007). The extent and impact of higher education curricular reform across Europe. Final report of the Directorate-General for Education and Culture of the European Commission. Part 1. Comparative Analysis and Executive Summary. Enschede: Center for Higher Education Policy Studies (CHEPS) Retrieved October 20, 2009, from http://ec.europa.eu/education/pdf/ doc244_en.pdf

European Commission. (2005). Towards a European qualifications framework for lifelong learning. Commission Staff Working Document. Brussels (SEC(2005)957). Retrieved October 20, 2009, from http://ec.europa.eu/education/policies/2010/doc/consultation_eqf_en.pdf

Fox, S., & MacKeogh, K. (2003). Can e-learning promote higher-order learning without tutor overload? *Open Learning, 18*(June), 121–134. doi:10.1080/02680510307410

Fox, S., & Walsh, E. (2007). Task Oriented Online Learning (TOOL)—Social interaction in an online environment. In G. O'Neill, G. et al. (Eds.), *Case Studies of Good Practice in Assessment of Student Learning in Higher Education* Dublin: AISHE/HEA. Retrieved October 20, 2009, from http://www.aishe.org/readings/2007-1/No-06.html

Gallagher, M. (2008). Improving institutional effectiveness: The relationship between assessing student learning outcomes and strategic planning in California Community Colleges. *Journal of Applied Research in the Community College, 15*(2), 101–108.

Garrison, D. R., & Kanuka, H. (2004). Blended learning: Uncovering its transformative potential in higher education. *The Internet and Higher Education, 7,* 95–105. doi:10.1016/j.iheduc.2004.02.001

Hughes, G. (2007). Using blended learning to increase learner support and improve retention. *Teaching in Higher Education, 12*(3), 349–363. doi:10.1080/13562510701278690

Kerres, M., & de Witt, C. (2003). A didactical framework for the design of blended learning arrangements. *Journal of Educational Media, 28*(203), 101–113. doi:10.1080/1358165032000165653

Lorenzi, F., MacKeogh, K., & Fox, S. (2004). Preparing students for learning in an online world: An evaluation of the Student Passport to eLearning (SPEL) model. *European Journal of Open Distance Learning (EURODL)* Jan–June 2004/1. Retrieved October 20, 2009, from http://www.eurodl.org/materials/contrib/2004/Lorenzi_MacKeogh_Fox.htm

Lorenzi, F., MacKeogh, K., & Fox, S. (2009). Preparing students for learning in an online world: The Student Passport to eLearning (SPeL) model. In Tait, A., Vidal, M., Bernath, U., & Szucs, A. (Eds.), *Distance and e-learning in transition? Learning innovation, technology and social challenges* (pp. 439–456). London: ISTE/Wiley.

MacKeogh, K. (2006). Supervising undergraduate research using online and peer supervision. In M. Huba (Ed.) *7th International Virtual University Conference, Bratislava 14–15 December 2006* (pp. 19–24). Technical University Bratislava: Bratislava. Retrieved October 20, 2009, from http://doras.dcu.ie/82/

MacKeogh, K., & Fox, S. (2008). *An eLearning Strategy for DCU.* Dublin: DCU. Retrieved October 20, 2009, from http://www.dcu.ie/~foxs/elearning

MacKeogh, K., & Fox, S. (2009). Academic staff in traditional universities: Motivators and demotivators in the adoption of elearning . In Bernath, U., Szucs, A., Tait, A., & Vidal, M. (Eds.), *Distance and E-learning in Transition: Learning innovation, technology and social challenges* (pp. 217–233). London: ISTE/Wiley.

MacKeogh, K., & Lorenzi, F. (2007). Learning from the past and looking at the future. Closing the evaluation-revision-implementation cycle in an elearning module. *European Association of Distance Teaching Universities Annual Conference,* Lisbon, November 8–10, 2007. Retrieved October 20, 2009, from http://www.eadtu.nl/conference-2007/files/SAA2.pdf

Maguire, B., Mernagh, E., & Murray, J. (2007). Aligning learning outcomes descriptors in national and meta-frameworks of qualifications: Learning from Irish experience. *European Journal of Vocational Training, 42*(3), 70–83.

Mays, J.T., & Morrison, D. (2008). You take the high road: National programmes for the development of elearning in higher education. *Reflecting Education*, 6-16.

Millett, C. M., Payne, D. G., Dwyer, C. A., Stickler, L. M., & Alexiou, J. J. (2008). *A culture of evidence: An evidence centred approach to accountability for student learning outcomes*. Washington, DC: Educational Testing Services.

Moore, M. G., & Anderson, W. G. (Eds.). (2003). *Handbook of distance education*. Mahwah, NJ: Lawrence Erlbaum Associates.

NQAI. (2003). *National Framework of Qualifications. A framework for the development, recognition and award of qualifications in Ireland*. Dublin: National Qualifications Authority of Ireland.

Nusche, D. (2008). Assessment of learning outcomes in Higher Education: A comparative review of selected practices. OECD Working Papers No 15. Paris: OECD.

OECD. (2007). Assessing Higher Education learning outcomes: Summary of a first meeting of experts. EDU (2007)8. Retrieved October 20, 2009, from http://www.oecd.org/dataoecd/15/5/39117243.pdf

Prensky, M. (2001). *Digital game based learning*. New York: McGraw Hill.

Ramsden, P. (1992). *Learning to teach in higher education*. London: Routledge. doi:10.4324/9780203413937

Wingate, U. (2006). Doing away with 'study skills'. *Teaching in Higher Education*, *11*(4), 457–469. doi:10.1080/13562510600874268

ADDITIONAL READING

Arbaugh, J. B., Godfrey, M. R., Johnson, M., Leisen Pollack, B., Niendorf, B., & Wresch, W. (2009). Research in online and blended learning in the business disciplines: Key findings and possible future directions. *The Internet and Higher Education, 12*, 71–87. doi:10.1016/j.iheduc.2009.06.006

Aworuwa, B., & Nkoge, B. (2007). The new taxonomy of educational objectives and implications for designing instruction for distance learning delivery. In T. Bastiaens, & S. Carliner (Eds.), *Proceedings of World Conference on E-Learning in Corporate, Government, Healthcare, and Higher Education* 2007 (pp. 1394-1398). Chesapeake, VA: AACE.

Brenton, S. (2009). An introduction to eLearning. In Fry, H., Ketteridge, S., & Marshall, S. (Eds.), *A handbook for teaching and learning in higher education: enhancing academic practice* (3rd ed., pp. 85–98). London: Routledge.

Conole, G., Dyke, M., Oliver, M., & Seale, J. (2004). Mapping pedagogy and tools for effective learning design. *Computers & Education, 43*, 17–33. doi:10.1016/j.compedu.2003.12.018

Dempsey, J., & Litchfield, R. (2007). The direct design and assessment of e-learning. In D. Remenyi, (Ed.), *Proceedings of the Second International Conference on E-learning. Columbia University New York 28–29 June 2007*. (pp. 131-138). Reading: Academic Conferences.

Garrison, D. R., & Kanuka, H. (2004). Blended learning: Uncovering its transformative potential in higher education. *The Internet and Higher Education, 7*, 95–105. doi:10.1016/j.iheduc.2004.02.001

Lorenzi, F., & MacKeogh, K. (2007). SPEL – Student Passport for eLearning: an integrated approach to assessment. In G. O'Neill, S. Huntley-Moore, & P. Race (Eds.), *Case studies of good practices in assessment of student learning in higher education* (pp.104–110). Dublin: AISHE. Retrieved October 20, 2009, from http://www.aishe.org/readings/2007–1

MacKeogh, K., & Lorenzi, F. (2005). Preparing students for online learning – the Oscail experience in A. Gaskell, & A. Tait (Eds.), *Reflective practice in open and distance learning: How do we improve? Proceedings of the 11th Cambridge International Conference in Open and Distance Learning.* (pp. 101–109). Milton Keynes: Open University. Retrieved October 20, 2009, from http://www2.open.ac.uk/r06/conference/papers2005.pdf

MacKeogh, K., & Lorenzi, F. (2006). An embedded approach to learning to learn online: Strategies to increase student retention through developing subject-based competence. *Proceedings of EAD-TU Annual Conference, Tallinn, 20–24 November 2006.* Retrieved October 20, 2009, from http://www.eadtu.nl/proceedings/2006/Master%20of%20the%20presentations%20overview.pdf

Mason, R., & Rennie, F. (2008). *Elearning and social networking handbook: Resources for higher education.* London: Routledge.

Rees, P., MacKay, L., Martin, D., & Durham, H. (Eds.). (2009). *E-learning for geographers: Online materials, resources and repositories.* London: IGI Global.

Sharpe, R., & Oliver, M. (2007). Designing courses for e-learners. In Beetham, H., & Sharpe, R. (Eds.), *Rethinking pedagogy for a digital age: Designing and delivering e-learning* (pp. 41–63). London: Routledge.

Vaughan, N. (2007). Perspectives on blended learning in Higher Education. *International Journal on E-Learning, 6*(1), 81–94.

Weller, M. (2007). The distance from isolation: Why communities are the logical conclusion in e-learning. *Computers & Education, 49,* 148–159. doi:10.1016/j.compedu.2005.04.015

Chapter 3
Online Identities in Virtual Worlds

Andrew Power
Dun Laoghaire Institute of Art, Design and Technology, Ireland

Gráinne Kirwan
Dun Laoghaire Institute of Art, Design and Technology, Ireland

ABSTRACT

Online identities need not reflect the true identity of the user. Relatively little is known about the use of online identities during e-learning and blended learning programmes, and if these reflect the students' true self. Online identities may impact on student achievement and satisfaction and as such are an important consideration for educators. Following an overview of the relevant literature regarding online identities, this paper describes findings from a survey of students currently engaged in a programme delivered using these techniques and where an awareness of online identities is to the fore. Several strengths and weaknesses of online identities in education are identified, and while students generally felt that they were portraying their own true identity online, many felt that others in the group were not. Implications for practice are described.

INTRODUCTION

Online teaching and learning offers both opportunity and danger. It can offer quality learning experiences in different modes and provide a democratisation of learning opportunities to students in a more flexible way. Online teaching encompasses the different and sometimes overlapping areas of e-learning, which may be a fully online distance learning approach or blended learning,

DOI: 10.4018/978-1-61520-879-1.ch003

which may combine elements of e-learning with more traditional classroom interaction. This paper will focus on the experience of the authors in using e-learning as part of an integrated or blended approach, and the issues of identity this has posed.

Identity is an important part of building an online community, such as an educational community. An awareness of others' identities informs our reactions to them and helps us to evaluate their behaviour. Over time members of an online community can become attuned to the nuances of each other's communication style as they develop an online 'voice'. These clues are not always reliable and a number of documented accounts of 'trolling' and impersonation within such communities are cited by Demiris (2005, p. 184).

This chapter aims to determine how online identities can impact on the student experience in e-learning in a blended learning environment, and how online identities can be best utilised in these programmes to improve the student experience. It will also attempt to determine if online identities reflect the students' true self. The chapter will accomplish these aims through reviewing and analysing the relevant literature in the fields of education and cyberpsychology, and also describing and analysing the experiences of students who have used online identities as part of a blended learning Masters in Cyberpsychology in Dun Laoghaire Institute of Art, Design and Technology, Ireland.

The chapter will address the question of what is an online identity, considering the types of identity that are often employed by individuals, and considering how these may be affected by the online environment. The impact of online identities in education will then be addressed, firstly by considering the types of online identity portrayed by students as part of an educational programme, and then considering how these may impact on student achievement and satisfaction. Finally, the potential benefits of online identities in education will be considered, along with an overview of how educators can make the most of online identities to improve the student experience.

BACKGROUND

Some work has been done on the impact of online teaching on the role and identity of educators (Wallace, 2002) which has shown that the identity of academics can be blurred as the educational process becomes 'productised'. This distancing of the teacher from the student has been an aspect of e-learning that has tried to be addressed in a

number of ways in the past. Email contact, video conferences, and individualised assignments, have all sought to bridge the gap left by the absence of face-to-face teaching. Using virtual environments appears to offer a solution to the one-to-many learning experience which can be offered to greater numbers at greater distances without the loss of a sense of personal contact.

Teachers are beginning to use social networks to hold distance education classes and report that the discussion can get livelier when students assume a digital persona (Foster, 2007, p. 24). Over one hundred and fifty colleges in the USA have some form of presence in Second Life, as do colleges from more than a dozen other countries. Foster (2007, p. 26) goes on to describe the different approaches of educators in the fields of architecture, ethnography, creative writing, literature, and technology in their use of virtual environments to promote better learning.

Studies of computer-mediated communication in the 1980s suggested that email removed many of the clues such as gender, age, race, social status and facial expression which we use to identify with each other. This reduced the inhibitions of participants (Williams, 2007, p. 7). Three-dimensional virtual environments, and the ability to represent oneself as an avatar, have provided opportunities not just to hide these clues but to create alternative ones. The visual representation of self, and the ability to alter it, has introduced a new dimension to communication within online communities.

In the early 1990s researchers were finding distinctions between the use of computers as standalone tools or as tools for communication. Turkle (1994, p. 159) found that individuals working alone in a gaming environment used the computer to work through issues of control and skill development. When the computer was used as a communications medium the control provided by the computer helped to develop skills for collaboration and even intimacy. The medium allowed for the exploration of self and social context. Exploring virtual worlds provides the opportunity to alter or control the exploration experience. The virtual environment provides opportunities to manufacture developmental experiences and allow users to explore in safety different elements of their personality. The cloak of an avatar can be used to encourage a cautious person to be more experimental (Junglas, Johnson, Steel, Abraham, & MacLoughlin, 2007). This process of a constantly evolving resolution of conflict between positive and negative developmental experiences is key to identity theory.

Community of practice refers to a process of social learning which occurs when people collaborate over a long period of time to share ideas, find solutions and build innovations, and the term was first coined by Lave and Wenger (1991). This collaboration can occur in the physical world, or via online communities (White, 2005). When becoming a member of an online community of practice, the user engages in a process of developing their online identity, both as an individual and as a member of the community (such as researcher, student, facilitator, and so on) and as a result of this, the community's identity also develops (Gray, 2004). Kreijns, Kirschner and Jochems (2003) indicate that online learning is most effective when social interaction is recognised as being just as important as development of the cognitive aspects for the development of an effective learning community. Rafaeli, Raban and Kalman (2005) suggest that online platforms that take social aspects of learning into account will fare better than those that ignore them.

As technology has become more prevalent, barriers to entry are falling. The baby boomers are now retiring and the students of the dot.com explosion are the parents and teachers of today. In their turn the children of the dot.com generation, are becoming the students of today. Prensky (2001) discusses the generation differences in the way we use and interact with technology. He suggests that students today think differently and process information differently from previ-

ous students because of their interaction with technology. These students that he calls digital natives, are increasingly living in a dual world of virtual reality via environments like Second Life, a social networking environment created by Linden Labs of San Francisco which allows users to create their own world communities with images, sound, and video from the 'real' world. Users can form communities for discussion, buy online property, and develop businesses and other organisations. Second Life, despite its rapid growth and its current population of more than 13 million users is still one of the smaller virtual worlds. It is dwarfed by the number of children using clubpenguin.com, webkinz.com, and barbiegirls.com amongst many others. This exposure suggests that these children will have none of the reluctance of their parents about online interaction. These children born after 1980, referred to as Millennial (Junglas et al., 2007) have grown up surrounded by digital media and are said to be sociable, collaborative, open-minded, confident, and achievement-oriented. They also are said to learn differently. Felder and Silverman (1988) provided a classification of learning styles in four dimensions; active/reflective, sensing/intuitive, visual/verbal, and sequential/global. Millennial students seem to be strong in the active, sensing, and global learning styles but their visual and auditory senses have been so stimulated from a young age that they seem capable of visual and verbal learning styles simultaneously. It makes sense in this context to provide an educational experience that suits the learning styles of this new generation of learners.

ONLINE IDENTITY

Online identities are not restricted by corporeal reality. They 'need not in any way correspond to a person's real life identity: people can make and remake themselves, choosing their gender and the details of their online presentation' (Mnookin,

1996). When a person is online, their identity does not need to reflect their offline identity. It is possible to change our gender, make ourselves younger, thinner and more attractive than we really are, or even change our species (for example, the various supernatural creatures that inhabit online games such as 'World of Warcraft'). Impression management is the process of controlling the impressions that other people form, and aspects of impression management normally outside our control in face-to-face interactions, can be controlled in online environments (Chester & Bretherton, 2007). In the online context, we can easily manage and alter how other people see us in ways that were never before possible.

Identity and the ability to change or disguise identity has been a subject much discussed in literature. Whether the story of Pygmalion is understood as the Greek myth of the sculptor who falls for his creation, or as Professor Higgins who tries to change Eliza into his image of the ideal, it is an idea that has captured the imagination. Cyrano could only romance Roxanne by presenting an 'avatar' in the form of a more handsome friend and it now seems we continue to enhance our sense of self in mediated virtual environments in much the same way. In a survey of Second Life avatars (Au, 2007) 45% said they tried to portray a 'better' body image, 37% chose to portray themselves as younger, and more than 20% altered their gender.

However, the most common forms of online impression management do not relate directly to physical appearance, but to changes in personality. Sometimes these changes are so subtle that even the individual themselves does not realise that they are altering their behaviour. When a person is online they can choose more easily what aspects of their personality they portray. In many cases this can result in the person emphasising the positive aspects of their personality (such as friendliness, extraversion, and helpfulness) and downplaying the more negative sides (such as shyness, frustration or jealousy). So even when our primary goal is not impression management, rarely will

we intentionally behave in ways that will create disadvantageous impressions (Leary, 1995).

The negative impact of this is the disinhibiting effect on a person's actions and the removal of a sense of responsibility for the actions of their avatar. The objectification of a 'character' in a game is also common and in some situations it can be unclear if a user is interacting with another 'real' player or with a software creation of the game. The potential to undermine an individual's inhibitions combined with the ability to act anonymously has the potential to lead to a breakdown in acceptable behaviour.

The possibility of several 'selves' is not new in psychology. Higgins (1987) argues there are three domains of the self: the *actual self* (attributes an individual possesses), the *ideal self* (attributes an individual would ideally possess), and the *ought self* (attributes an individual ought to possess). More recently, Bargh, McKenna, and Fitzsimons (2002) found that in comparison to face-to-face interactions, Internet interactions allowed individuals to better express aspects of their *true selves* – aspects of themselves that they wanted to express but felt unable to.

A further aspect of online identity involves the anonymity that online interactions can allow. Rather than discrete entities of identifiable versus anonymous, anonymity is more of a continuum. At one end, a person may be completely identifiable, disclosing their full name, date of birth, location, occupation, interests and hobbies – this is common for social networking websites such as Facebook. At the other end of the spectrum, the person may also choose to make their online identity completely untraceable, choosing a pseudonym and not disclosing any personal information (although even in this case, an individual is often more identifiable than they may wish due to the collection of information by Internet Service Providers or the website involved). However, in many cases online, individuals fall somewhere between these two extremes, providing some personal information but choosing what details to provide depending on the circumstances. This is common for online communities such as discussion boards, chat rooms and graphical virtual environments and was referred to by Joinson (2003) as 'visual anonymity' – those interacting online may not see each other, but still have access to some identifying information.

Various reasons have been suggested as to why we manage our impressions online. Early research such as Leary (1995) suggested that these may include goals such as social gains (for example, to get a date), material gains (such as to get a job), or less tangible goals such as the development of identity or the maintenance of self-esteem. Turkle (1995) suggested similar motives such as a desire to establish relationships and to express unexplored parts of identity that are normally inhibited in face-to-face interactions, but she also identified that some of those who engage in impression management gain a sense of power from deceiving others. Similarly, Wallace (1999, p. 48) suggested that the Internet was an 'identity laboratory, overflowing with props, audiences and players for our personal experiments'. As such, much of the early work concluded that many impressions were directly related to the users' hoped-for selves, allowing the opportunity to present highly desirable self-images and providing a chance for wish-fulfilment (Curtis, 1997; Reid, 1994; Romano, 1999).

However, more recent research suggests that impression management is not as common as it has previously been. It is possible that this change has occurred because people now think about cyberspace as an aspect of everyday life, rather than a different and separate world (Wellman & Haythornthwaite, 2002). This change is recent and generational. Johnson and Post (1996) argued that cyberspace constituted a new and different space where different rules must apply. Their argument was that in the offline world there is generally a correspondence between borders drawn in physical space, between nation states, and borders in legal space. The idea of cyberspace as a place an

individual can go to where new laws might apply is supported by the fact that the individual must make a decision to go there, normally by deciding to access a computer and enter a password. In this sense there is a boundary the individual crosses to get 'there'. Now to those millennials and digital natives the Internet has become just another part of life, rather than a place where different rules apply. For example, Chester (2004) found that online self-presentations were influenced more by participants' current perceptions of themselves than desirable future selves and those aspects of identity which the participants considered central to their identity were more likely to be presented online than those rated of lesser importance. Chester (2004) also found that the intention to present the 'real self' is quite strong, possibly due to participants' desires to connect with others online. With the current popularity of social networking websites, which are based on creating links between people who already know each other, there is no benefit in altering the online identity and people generally continue to express the 'actual self' to those whom he or she initially met in person, whether the interaction takes place online or not (McKenna & Seidman, 2005).

This research suggests that online impression construction is fundamentally similar to impression construction in offline contexts. It is possible that we now prefer others to recognise and validate us as we are than try to impress them with our hoped-for selves. However, Chester (2004) also indicated that while the identities presented online were not idealised, they were still self-promoting, and tended to focus on the positive aspects of personality. At the same time, it cannot be said that all Internet users only depict themselves in an accurate manner, and Boyd (2004) and Jung, Hyunsook and McClung (2007) describe the use of false information on social networking websites. Chester (2004) also noted that while some individuals did engage in identity management, these were more likely to be people who were relatively inexperienced online – those who spent more time in online environments were more likely to be truthful. Participants also noted that it was difficult to maintain a dishonest online identity. The accuracy of many online representations has also been supported by researchers such as Gosling, Gaddis and Vazire (2007) who compared impressions that people formed after regarding a Facebook profile with those who knew the profile owner from everyday life – the personality impressions showed some consensus for the two groups.

In some cases, it is possible that online identities are closer to 'true' identities than our offline depictions of ourselves. McKenna and Green (2002) indicate that some people feel that they are better able to express their true self on the Internet than offline, finding it easier to develop close online relationships which may later progress into real life. Similar to Rubin's (1975) 'strangers on a train' phenomenon, some individuals find it easier to communicate in online environments as they remain relatively anonymous. Other research, such as that of Hancock, Thom-Santelli and Ritchie (2004) has suggested that some forms of computer-mediated communication involve less deception than phone or face-to-face interactions as a record exists of e-mail or discussion forum correspondence, lying and misrepresentation may be actually reduced.

It should be noted that it is often important to have the 'right' kind of online identity, and this is not always within the control of the person involved. For example, the number of 'friends' in a person's social network seems to be important with people evaluating a person more positively if they are connected with many other people (Baumeister & Leary, 1995; Kleck, Reese, Ziegerer-Behnken, & Sundar, 2007). Walther, van der Heide, Kim, Westerman and Tong (2008) also noted that the comments left by friends on a person's profile also affect the evaluation of the profile owners, and comments which suggested negatively perceived behaviours, such as excessive drinking, decreased viewer's favourable ratings of the individual. Walther et al. also noted that even the physical attractiveness of the profile owner's friends affect the evaluation of the profile owner.

Having considered how online identities can be accurate or inaccurate portrayals of the individual concerned, the consequences for these online identities in blended and e-learning programmes will now be considered. This will commence with a discussion of why online identities need to be considered when providing these programmes, and the types of online identities that students portray in these programmes.

Online Identities in Virtual Learning Environments

In order to determine how online identities impact the student's learning experience a study was conducted of students in the Institute of Art Design and Technology in Dun Laoghaire, Ireland. The aim of this study was to determine how closely students' online identities reflected their offline selves, and how this influenced their interactions with other students and lecturers on the programme.

Participants and Methodology

Cluster sampling was employed, and the students selected were those enrolled on the M.Sc. in Cyberpsychology, run by the School of Creative Technologies. The M.Sc. in Cyberpsychology is a blended learning programme, which allowed the authors to probe if students identified differences between their classmates' online and offline identities. Students were also asked to hypothesise as to how their behaviour may have differed if the programme had been entirely conducted in online environments, with no real-life interactions with staff or other students.

The participants were mature students ranging in age from 26 to 48 and with an above average awareness of the issues of online technology. As part of the M.Sc. in Cyberpsychology students are required to engage in a variety of online communication methods, including blogging, microblogging (such as Twitter), online graphical virtual environments (such as Second Life), online gaming, instant messaging, discussion lists, and social networking, as well as using a Virtual Learning Environment (VLE). All students were currently registered on the programme and were attending classes one day each week. The M.Sc. in Cyberpsychology is a part-time programme so students were also informed by their professional backgrounds which include education, information technology, journalism, psychology and marketing. Twenty-eight students were invited to participate in the study via e-mail, of whom fifteen responded, providing a response rate of 53.6%. The survey was created and distributed using an online survey tool. It asked a variety of questions relating to the online identities students employed during their participation in the Masters, including how closely they felt their online identity matched their true identity, if they had ever used deception online, and how having an online identity may have impacted on their learning and satisfaction with the programme. The survey was primarily qualitative in nature, and the majority of questions were open-ended. All responses were anonymous, and confidentiality was ensured. Student participation in the study was entirely voluntary, and no incentives or rewards for participation were offered. The results of the study are compared with similar research completed in education.

Portrayed Self

Students were initially asked which self they portrayed during the programme. In the survey, all students indicated that their online identity closely matched their true identity, although they frequently felt that they could present different aspects of themselves or be slightly more adventurous or experimental than they could in real life.

'...the real self has many aspects whether online or offline. We present different sides of ourselves for different purposes.' (Participant 12)

'[I'm] a bit more likely to express my opinions due to [the] increased thinking time afforded.' (Participant 4)

'[I'm] a bit more experimental, but again it's a feature of online anonymity...' (Participant 5)

This finding corresponds with much of the more general research on online identities outlined above. Particularly in blended learning programmes, it is unlikely that a student will try to significantly alter their online identity. As they interact with other students in the classroom once a week, there is little purpose in trying to manage physical aspects of identity. This finding is consistent with those of Hemmi, Bayne and Land (2009) who suggested that even in pure e-learning environments, it is likely that students will maintain a high degree of overlap between their 'virtual' and 'real' identities. Interestingly, Hemmi et al. (2009) also noted cases of the online disinhibition effect amongst their participants, as some students felt more able to disclose personal information while blogging.

While all students felt that they represented themselves accurately online, interestingly, they did not always feel that other students represented themselves accurately in online environments. When asked about this a significant minority felt that their classmates behaved quite differently online.

'I was quite shocked by the behaviour of some people on the course in their online behaviour, I didn't expect people to be so different at times while communicating online, for example their use of language, avatar choices, "net names", behaviour and composure online.' (Participant 2)

'... people portray more of themselves or their more experimental selves online than offline – but its not that this side of them is not there in the first place. So taking all that into account, I DO think that people portrayed themselves accurately in their online activities – sometimes possibly more accurately than offline.' (Participant 5)

Portrayal of the Self in Entirely Online Programmes

For e-learning programmes, it is possible that students would have larger distinctions between their online and offline identities, as they would not have to meet with their classmates and lecturers. It was put to the students that they might have behaved differently online if they had never physically met the others on the course. Students were equally divided on this question with those who believed they would have behaved differently citing caution as the common reason.

'yes – would have been more cautious' (Participant 14)

'definitely. I like to know who I am talking to.' (Participant 12)

However when asked if classmates and lecturers would have a different perception of them if they had never met in real life, a clear majority (80%) felt that would be the case.

'I think body language and tone are important factors in communication and these are clues that are not visible with online communication. Even having the time to type a response to an email or online chat, allows time to think a question over and then reply when your response is clear, defined and precisely how you want it to be, this opportunity is not afforded in "real world" ... I think it's possible that when others who have not met me view my online communications they may have a very different view of me. This is a huge factor in why I try to create an online identity that resembles my "real" self.' (Participant 2)

'Meeting in real life is probably a fuller experience than just meeting online. However both online and offline is a very interesting mix and is possibly greater than either on its own.' (Participant 7)

Part of the reason for this difference in perception is due to the absence of the social context clues such as gender, age, race, social status, body posture and facial expression as discussed above. In addition to the absence of these clues students have the opportunity to create an alternative perception of themselves online. Students were asked if they used deception, alternate personae or masks during blended or e-learning programmes.

Some did:

'[It's] not appropriate to use [my] real name in Second Life ... [I] also choose not to reveal identity in other areas where information disclosed might impact on professional life.' (Participant 12)

'Sometimes I am concerned about future possibilities of being too visible on the web.' (Participant 2)

'... you would be probably less under stress, and you start interaction with other avatars from an advantageous situation [if] you have created a self as you would have liked it to be therefore, you are more confident, I think.' (Participant 9)

Others did not use deception during the programme:

'I'll use my real name where I'm happy for anyone to know my identity, this is usually in environments where to participate you need to have or appear to have a valid identity.' (Participant 4)

'I behave exactly as I am ... or at least I feel I do. I don't use the Internet to embellish or exaggerate my personality, possibly because my interactions are generally with friends who know what I am like.' (Participant 6)

'I like to have an online identity that reflects my real self as I think it is more professional, and gives an honest portrayal of who I am. I also find "net names" for example, hunnybunny@email.com or sexygal@email.com, extremely childish and kind of cringe worthy if you know the person with this "net name" in person ... is their "net name" how they view themselves?' (Participant 1)

'I use my real name online because I want to be positively associated with the information/ thoughts/opinions that I post.' (Participant 15)

Overall, these findings are in contrast to those of Bayne (2005) who suggested that online identity formation for the students was a quite negative experience, 'fraught with anxiety', as they feared loss of control of their real selves due to the development of their online identities. In some cases, these online identities included deceit or even separate personalities to those of the students involved. It is possible that the students who responded to the current survey did not experience this negative reaction to such an extent due to their increased familiarity with online personae and interactions because of the nature of their studies in cyberpsychology.

Other research in this field is quite rare, although Meskill and Sadykova (2007) examined student self-introductions in pure e-learning programmes using asynchronous computer-mediated communication. These students self-identified either via their academic status and/or as professionals. Some also included more personal information, such as family and home life. Meskill and Sadykova note that students may experience

a certain degree of tension between their 'global' and 'local' identities, and that they may be unsure as to what is appropriate to include in these self-introductions. They suggest that this may be resulting in a 'standard' style of self-introduction. Meskill and Sadykova's (2007) research suggests that students did not intentionally use any deception or online masks while introducing themselves, but were uncertain as to which aspects of the self to portray in online educational settings.

Online Identity and Student Achievement/Satisfaction

The students were asked to reflect on the impact, if any, of their online identities on their achievements and satisfaction with the programme. Some felt it had made a difference to their studies, having a mostly positive effect. Many indicated that online identities allowed them to draw upon the resources of others more effectively.

'Blogging and using twitter have brought resources to my attention that I wouldn't have necessarily found on my own. Blogging about topics I'm studying has also helped me to synthesis my learning.' (Participant 15)

'It enabled me to link in with other people and extend my learning experience.' (Participant 3)

'... they allow for collaboration, access to information and other online identities, for example lecturers, academics. Communicate with educators around the world.' (Participant 6)

Other students felt that the primary positive effect of online identities in education related to their perceived increase in anonymity.

'... anonymity facilitates exposure and trial, without fearing a negative feedback; the more you

try the more you learn; exploring your potential online.' (Participant 5)

'It can allow shy people to ask questions they might not in real life.' (Participant 4)

This positive aspect of the online disinhibition effect appears to be a very useful instrument for those students who under normal circumstances would be less inclined to participate in classroom discussions and activities.

However, not all students felt that having online identities provided any benefit, and a minority felt that they subtracted from the educational experience.

'In the context of a blended learning approach I don't really see any advantage.' (Participant 15)

'You lose some of the personal touch you get in face to face teaching.' (Participant 11)

Interestingly, some students felt that online identities added most to the educational experience when others used their true identities and did not engage in deception.

'I think there are benefits when people use their real names, less so when people are anonymous.' (Participant 6)

It was also clear that in a number of cases there were changes not just to the method of study but in the way students felt about themselves or the way they chose to interact with each other.

'Sometimes harder to communicate online.' (Participant 11)

'I don't consider my online identity is any different from my real life identity ... however I am some-

times apprehensive ... commenting or responding in group discussions online and notice that I am much more guarded or careful about what I write.' (Participant 15)

'Vulnerability. There were times when people would talk to you, their point may make no sense or be aggressive. It was difficult to figure out if I should talk back and in what tone.' (Participant 4)

Implications for Practitioners

The survey of students indicates that there are mixed consequences for the use of online identities in blended and e-learning programmes. While overall the students indicated many benefits, and few students seemed to experience any significant distress or difficulties due to their online identities, there seems to be a great deal of ambivalence regarding online identities in education. Again, it should be noted that these students have a higher than average awareness of online interactions due to the nature of their studies, and this may explain the somewhat more positive reaction than that noted by Bayne (2005). However, the survey does indicate the importance of online identities in blended and e-learning programmes, and provides direction for future research in the field.

The implications for practitioners of the theory and research considering online identities in higher education e-learning and blended learning programmes are numerous. When critically designing such a programme, the tutor or lecturer should consider the student identity in the design of learning engagements, the degree to which these identities may vary from reality, and ways in which this variation can be minimised. It should be recognised that students feel better able to engage in open discussion, and ask questions due to the anonymous nature of online identities. As such, it is useful for at least some group interactions to occur in wholly anonymous settings. The benefits for student work that were obtained from interacting with others online seemed to significantly improve student experience and satisfaction, and these activities should be actively encouraged.

Regardless, the harmful aspects of online identities cannot and should not be ignored, and it is advised that all students on e-learning or blended learning programmes be provided with some initial guidelines and instruction at the start of their programmes on the nature of online identities and their appropriate usage in educational environments. Students should be reminded that online interactions with staff or fellow students should be professional in nature, and that mutual respect is a requirement regardless of what types of interactions are taking place. It is suggested that all online student groups should be monitored closely. If necessary the practitioner should consider moderating all online discussions by students (preventing any negative comments from being published before they are approved by the tutor or lecturer). This will help to ensure that students are protected from any malicious comments that are made by others who are abusing their anonymous or remote status. This guidance may help to reduce the negative consequences of developing and maintaining an online identity as uncovered both in this study and by Bayne (2005). Students should be advised on an appropriate level of personal information which should be provided about themselves to others, and it may be useful to create a social network for students, which permits them to describe themselves in this way. Discussions about topics that may cause offence to any individual or group should be avoided wherever possible.

It is important that the guidance provided considers a variety of computer-mediated communication methods, including graphical online worlds, wikis, blogs, Voice over Internet Protocol (such as Skype), instant messaging, chat rooms, discussion boards, e-mail, virtual reality collaborative environments and software which may incorporate a variety of methods, such as learning

management systems. It is possible that virtual teams in the workplace may experience similar phenomena to the students, and so employers and managers should consider providing similar guidelines to them.

FUTURE RESEARCH AND CONCLUSION

In reviewing how online identities can be best utilised in e-learning and blended learning programmes to provide the best possible student experience a number of lessons are clear. Student success in online classrooms is especially dependent on the ability of the instructor to effectively organize content, provide clear assignments, and use assessment methods that provide timely feedback on student progress (Sujo de Montes, Oran, & Willis, 2002). Instructors in online settings are more likely to be facilitators than lecturers (Rogers, 2000), and it was noted by Bayne (2005) that instructors tended to have fewer problems with online identities than students did, as they primarily used them to assert authority.

It is evident that the research to date in this field is quite limited, and would greatly benefit from further studies. In particular, an extended survey with appropriate controls (including a greater number of participants, from a wider variety of disciplines and institutions) is required in order to make any decisive conclusions as to the benefits and difficulties of online identities in education. Objective research identifying potential relationships between online identities, student satisfaction and student achievement are also required in order to gain a more thorough understanding of the phenomenon. What is beyond doubt is that as more programmes employ blended learning and e-learning pedagogies the topic of online identities will become an increasingly important consideration for educators.

REFERENCES

Au, W. J. (2007, April 30). Surveying Second Life. *New World Notes*. Retrieved February 15, 2009, from http://nwn.blogs.com/nwn/2007/04/second_life_dem.html

Bargh, J. A., McKenna, K. Y. A., & Fitzsimons, G. M. (2002). Can you see the real me? Activation and expression of the 'true self' on the Internet. *The Journal of Social Issues, 58*(1), 33–48. doi:10.1111/1540-4560.00247

Baumeister, R. F., & Leary, M. R. (1995). The need to belong: Desire for interpersonal attachments as a fundamental human motivation. *Psychological Bulletin, 117,* 497–529. doi:10.1037/0033-2909.117.3.497

Bayne, S. (2005). Deceit, desire and control: The identities of learners and teachers in cyberspace . In Land, R., & Bayne, S. (Eds.), *Education in cyberspace*. London: RoutledgeFalmer.

Boyd, D. M. (2004, April). *Friendster and publicly articulated social networking*. Paper presented at the Conference on Human Factors in Computing Systems, Vienna, Austria.

Chester, A. (2004). *Presenting the self in cyberspace: Identity play online*. Unpublished doctoral dissertation, University of Melbourne.

Chester, A., & Bretherton, D. (2007). Impression management and identity online . In Joinson, A., McKenna, K., Postmes, T., & Reips, U. (Eds.), *The Oxford handbook of Internet psychology* (pp. 223–236). New York: Oxford University Press.

Curtis, P. (1997). Mudding: Social phenomena in text-based virtual reality . In Keisler, S. (Ed.), *Culture of the Internet* (pp. 121–142). Mahwah, NJ: Erlbaum.

Demiris, G. (2005). The diffusion of virtual communities in health care: Concepts and challenges. *Patient Education and Counseling, 62,* 178–188. doi:10.1016/j.pec.2005.10.003

Felder, R. M., & Silverman, L. K. (1988). Learning and teaching styles in engineering education. *English Education, 78*(7), 674–681.

Foster, A. L. (2007, September 21). Professor Avatar: In the digital universe of Second Life, classroom instruction also takes on a new personality. *Chronicle of Higher Education*. Retrieved February 12, 2009, from http://chronicle.com/weekly/v54/i04/04a02401.htm

Gosling, S. D., Gaddis, S., & Vazire, S. (2007, March). *Personality impressions based on Facebook profiles*. Paper presented at the International Conference on Weblogs and Social Media, Boulder, Colorado.

Gray, B. (2004). Informal learning in an online community of practice. *Journal of Distance Education, 19*(1), 20–35.

Hancock, J. T., Thom-Santelli, J., & Ritchie, T. (2004). Deception and design: The impact of communication technologies on lying behaviour. In E. Dykstra-Erickson and M. Tscheligi (Eds.), *Conference on computer human interaction* (pp. 29-134). New York: ACM Press.

Hemmi, A., Bayne, S., & Land, R. (2009). The appropriation and repurposing of social technologies in higher education. *Computer Assisted Learning, 25*(1), 19–30. doi:10.1111/j.1365-2729.2008.00306.x

Higgins, E. T. (1987). Self-discrepancy: A theory relating self and affect. *Psychological Review, 94*(3), 319–340. doi:10.1037/0033-295X.94.3.319

Johnson, D., & Post, D. (1996). Law and borders – The rise of law in cyberspace. *Stanford Law Review, 48*(5), 1367–1402. doi:10.2307/1229390

Joinson, A. (2003). *Understanding the psychology of Internet behaviour: Virtual worlds, real lives*. Basingstoke: Palgrave Macmillan.

Jung, T., Hyunsook, Y., & McClung, S. (2007). Motivations and self-presentation strategies on Korean-based 'cyworld' weblog format personal homepages. *Cyberpsychology & Behavior, 10*(1), 24–31. doi:10.1089/cpb.2006.9996

Junglas, I. A., Johnson, N. A., Steel, D. J., Abraham, D. C., & MacLoughlin, P. (2007). Identity formation, learning styles and trust in virtual worlds. *The Data Base for Advances in Information Systems, 38*(4), 90–96.

Kleck, C. A., Reese, C., Ziegerer-Behnken, D., & Sundar, S. (2007). *The company you keep and the image you project: Putting your best face forward in online social networks*. Paper presented at the annual meeting of the International Communication Association, San Francisco, California.

Kreijns, K., Kirschner, P. A., & Jochems, W. (2003). Identifying the pitfalls for social interaction in computer-supported collaborative learning environments: A review of the research. *Computers in Human Behavior, 19*(3), 335–353. doi:10.1016/S0747-5632(02)00057-2

Lave, J., & Wenger, E. (1991). *Situated learning: Legitimate peripheral participation*. Cambridge: Cambridge University Press.

Leary, M. R. (1995). *Self-presentation: Impression management and interpersonal behaviour*. Madison, WI: Brown and Benchmark.

McKenna, K., & Seidman, G. (2005). You, me, and we: Interpersonal processes in electronic groups. In Amichai-Hamburger, Y. (Ed.), *The social net: Human behaviour in cyberspace* (pp. 191–217). Oxford: Oxford University Press.

McKenna, K. Y. A., & Green, A. S. (2002). Virtual Group Dynamics. *Group Dynamics, 6*(1), 116–127. doi:10.1037/1089-2699.6.1.116

Meskill, C., & Sadykova, G. (2007). The presentation of self in everyday ether: A corpus analysis of student self-tellings in online graduate courses. *Journal of Asynchronous Learning Networks, 11*(3), 123–138.

Mnookin, J. L. (1996). Virtual(ly) law: The emergence of law in LambdaMOO. *Journal of Computer-Mediated Communication, 2*(1). Retrieved April 12, 2009, from http://jcmc.indiana.edu/vol2/issue1/lambda.html

Prensky, M. (2001). *Digital natives, digital immigrants*. Bradford: MCB University Press.

Rafaeli, S., Raban, D., & Kalman, Y. (2005). Social cognition online. In Amichai-Hamburger, Y. (Ed.), *The social net: Human behaviour in cyberspace*. New York: Oxford University Press.

Reid, E. (1994). *Cultural formations in text-based virtual realities*. Unpublished master's thesis, University of Melbourne, Australia.

Rogers, D. L. (2000). A paradigm shift: Technology integration for higher education in the new millennium. *Educational Technology Review, 13*, 19–27.

Romano, S. (1999). On becoming a woman: Pedagogies of the self. In Hawisher, G. E., & Selfe, C. (Eds.), *Passions, pedagogies and the 21st century technologies* (pp. 249–267). Logan, UT: Utah State University Press.

Rubin, Z. (1975). Disclosing oneself to a stranger: Reciprocity and its limits. *Journal of Experimental Social Psychology, 11*, 233–260. doi:10.1016/S0022-1031(75)80025-4

Sujo de Montes, L., Oran, S. M., & Willis, E. M. (2002). Power, language, and identity: Voices from an online course. *Computers and Composition, 19*, 251–271. doi:10.1016/S8755-4615(02)00127-5

Turkle, S. (1994). Constructions and reconstructions of self in virtual reality: Playing in the MUDs. *Mind, Culture, and Activity, 1*(3), 158–167.

Turkle, S. (1995). *Life on the screen: Identity in the age of the Internet.* New York: Simon & Schuster.

Wallace, M. (2002). Managing and developing online education: Issues of change and identity. *Journal of Workplace Learning, 14*(5), 198–208. doi:10.1108/13665620210433891

Wallace, P. (1999). *The psychology of the Internet.* Cambridge: Cambridge University Press.

Walther, J. B., van der Heide, B., Kim, S. Y., Westerman, D., & Tong, S. T. (2008). The role of friends' appearance and behaviour on evaluations of individuals on Facebook: Are we known by the company we keep? *Human Communication Research, 34,* 28–49.

Wellman, B., & Haythornthwaite, C. (2002). *The Internet in everyday life.* Oxford: Blackwell. doi:10.1002/9780470774298

White, M. (2005). Communities of practice: Sources of information. Retrieved on June 2, 2006, from http://www.intranetfocus.com

Williams, M. (2007). Avatar watching: participant observation in graphical online environments. *Qualitative Research, 7*(1), 5–24. doi:10.1177/1468794107071408

ADDITIONAL READING

Allan, B., & Lewis, D. (2006). Virtual learning communities as a vehicle for workforce development: A case study. *Journal of Workplace Learning, 18,* 367–383. doi:10.1108/13665620610682099

Amichai-Hamburger, Y. (2005). Internet minimal group paradigm. *Cyberpsychology & Behavior, 8,* 140–142. doi:10.1089/cpb.2005.8.140

Bailenson, J. (2008, April 4). Why digital avatars make the best teachers. *Chronicle of Higher Education.* Retrieved February 12, 2009, from http://chronicle.com/weekly/v54/i30/30b02701.htm

Barak, A., & Gluck-Ofri, O. (2007). Degree and reciprocity of self-disclosure in online forums. *Cyberpsychology & Behavior, 10,* 407–417. doi:10.1089/cpb.2006.9938

Brandon, D. P., & Hillingshead, A. B. (2007). Characterizing online groups. In Joinson, A., McKenna, K., Postmes, T., & Reips, U. (Eds.), *The Oxford handbook of internet psychology* (pp. 105–120). Oxford: Oxford University Press.

Brukman, A. (2006). Learning in online communities. In Sawyer, R. K. (Ed.), *The Cambridge handbook of the learning sciences* (pp. 461–472). Boston, MA: Cambridge University Press.

Chang, C. K., Chen, G. D., & Li, L. Y. (2008). Constructing a community of practice to improve coursework activity. *Computers & Education, 50,* 235–247. doi:10.1016/j.compedu.2006.05.003

Donath, J. S. (1999). Identity and deception in the virtual community. In Kollock, P., & Smith, A. S. (Eds.), *Communities in cyberspace* (pp. 29–59). London, UK: Routledge.

Fogel, J., & Nehmad, E. (2009). Internet social network communities: Risk taking, trust, and privacy concerns. *Computers in Human Behavior, 25,* 153–160. doi:10.1016/j.chb.2008.08.006

Guadagno, R., & Cialdini, R. (2005). Online persuasion and compliance: Social influence on the Internet and beyond. In Amichai-Hamburger, Y. (Ed.), *The social net: Human behaviour in cyberspace* (pp. 91–114). Oxford: Oxford University Press.

Haythornthwaite, C. (2007). Social networks and online community. In Joinson, A., McKenna, K., Postmes, T., & Reips, U. (Eds.), *The Oxford handbook of Internet psychology* (pp. 121–138). Oxford: Oxford University Press.

Haythornthwaite, C., & Nielsen, A. L. (2007). Revisiting computer-mediated communication for work, community, and learning . In Gackenbach, J. (Ed.), *Psychology and the Internet: Intrapersonal, interpersonal and transpersonal implications* (2nd ed., pp. 167–186). San Diego, CA: Elsevier Academic Press.

Hsu, J.-L., & Chou, H.-W. (2009). The effects of communicative genres on intra-group conflict in virtual student teams. *International Journal of Distance Education Technologies, 7,* 1–22.

Hughes, M., Ventura, S., & Dando, M. (2007). Assessing social presence in online discussion groups: A replication study. *Innovations in Education and Teaching International, 44,* 17–29. doi:10.1080/14703290601090366

Joe, S.-W., & Lin, C.-P. (2008). Learning online community citizenship behavior: A socio-cognitive model. *Cyberpsychology & Behavior, 11,* 367–370. doi:10.1089/cpb.2007.0109

Kreijns, K., Kirschner, P. A., Jochems, W., & Buuren, H. V. (2004). Determining sociability, social space, and social presence in (a)synchronous collaborative groups. *Cyberpsychology & Behavior, 7,* 155–206. doi:10.1089/109493104323024429

Lin, H. (2006). Understanding behavioral intention to participate in virtual communities. *Cyberpsychology & Behavior, 9,* 540–547. doi:10.1089/cpb.2006.9.540

Malamuth, N., Linz, D., & Yao, M. (2005). The Internet and aggression: Motivation, disinhibitory, and opportunity aspects . In Amichai-Hamburger, Y. (Ed.), *The social net: Human behaviour in cyberspace* (pp. 163–190). Oxford: Oxford University Press.

McKenna, K. Y. A. (2008). Influences on the nature and functioning of online groups . In Barak, A. (Ed.), *Psychological aspects of cyberspace: Theory, research, applications* (pp. 228–242). Cambridge, UK: Cambridge University Press.

Michinov, N., Michinov, E., & Toczek-Capelle, M. (2004). Social identity, group processes, and performance in synchronous computer-mediated communication. *Group Dynamics, 8,* 27–39. doi:10.1037/1089-2699.8.1.27

Postmes, T., Spears, R., & Lea, M. (2002). Intergroup differentiation in computer-mediated communication: Effects of depersonalization. *Group Dynamics, 6,* 3–16. doi:10.1037/1089-2699.6.1.3

Postmes, T., Spears, R., Sakhel, K., & De Groot, D. (2001). Social influence in computer-mediated communication: The effects of anonymity on group behavior. *Personality and Social Psychology Bulletin, 27,* 1243–1254. doi:10.1177/01461672012710001

Quan-Haase, A., Wellman, B., Witte, J. C., & Hamptom, K. N. (2002). Social contact, civic engagement, and sense of community . In Wellman, B., & Haythornthwaite, C. (Eds.), *The Internet in everyday life* (pp. 291–324). Malden, MA: Blackwell. doi:10.1002/9780470774298.ch10

Rafaeli, S., Raben, D., & Kalman, Y. (2005). Social Cognition Online . In Amichai-Hamburger, Y. (Ed.), *The social net: Human behaviour in cyberspace* (pp. 57–90). Oxford: Oxford University Press.

Schwartzman, R. (2006). Virtual group problem solving in the basic communication course: Lessons for online learning. *Journal of Instructional Psychology, 33,* 3–14.

Smith, G., & Kurthen, H. (2007). Front-stage and back-stage in hybrid e-learning face-to-face courses. *International Journal on E-Learning, 6*(3), 455–474.

Swan, K., & Shea, P. (2005). The development of virtual learning communities . In Hiltz, S. R., & Goldman, R. (Eds.), *Learning together online: Research on asynchronous learning networks* (pp. 239–260). Mahwah, NJ: Erlbaum.

Taylor, J., & MacDonald, J. (2002). The effects of asynchronous computer-mediated group interaction on group processes. *Social Science Computer Review, 20*, 260–274.

Weisband, S., & Atwater, L. (1999). Evaluating self and others in electronic and face-to-face groups. *The Journal of Applied Psychology, 84*, 632–639. doi:10.1037/0021-9010.84.4.632

Xu, Z. (2008). When hybrid learning meets blended teaching: Online computer-mediated communication (CMC) discourse and classroom face-to-face (FTF) discourse analysis. In Fong, J., Kwan, R., & Wang, F. L. (Eds.), *Hybrid learning and education* (pp. 157–167). New York: Springer. doi:10.1007/978-3-540-85170-7_14

Yee, N., Bailenson, J. N., Urbanek, M., Chang, F., & Merget, D. (2007). The unbearable likeness of being digital: The persistence of nonverbal social norms in online virtual environments. *Cyberpsychology & Behavior, 10*, 115–121. doi:10.1089/cpb.2006.9984

Yu, C.-P., & Young, M.-L. (2008). The virtual group identification process: A virtual educational community case. *Cyberpsychology & Behavior, 11*, 87–90. doi:10.1089/cpb.2007.9929

Chapter 4
Do You See What I Mean?
Computer–Mediated Discourse Analysis

Noel Fitzpatrick
Dublin Institute of Technology, Ireland

Roisin Donnelly
Dublin Institute of Technology, Ireland

ABSTRACT

This chapter explores a sociolinguistic approach to computer-mediated communication (CMC), by examining how higher education teachers use digital media to manage interpersonal interaction in their online courses, form impressions, shape and maintain relationships with their students. Previous studies have often focused on the differences between online and offline interactions, though contemporary research is moving towards the view that CMC should be studied as an embedded linguistic form in everyday life. The study of language in these contexts is typically based on text-based forms of CMC, (often referred to as computer-mediated discourse analysis). Within this, focus in the chapter is on the devising and implementation of pragmatic linguistics of online interactions; at a high level this refers to meaning-making, shared belief systems and intercultural differences; at a specific level this includes issues such as turn-taking and the sequential analysis and organisation of virtual 'interlocution'.

INTRODUCTION

This chapter provides a critical view of the present state of play in different strands in computer-mediated communication (CMC) research. By focusing on the literatures of social interaction, constructivism and linguistics, a critical discussion of key theories and resulting emergent arguments in the use of CMC in higher education (HE) is provided. Given the rapid development of technologies and their resulting literatures of usage in higher education today, it is argued that this chapter is very relevant to all whose practice is influenced by learning technologies – such as educational technologists, education policy makers and administrators, higher education teaching and research staff, advanced education students, designers of virtual education environments and similar teaching tools, psychologists of third-level education.

DOI: 10.4018/978-1-61520-897-1.ch004

Throughout the chapter we reflect openly on current difficulties in several areas. The chapter begins with consideration of the selective and nearly exclusive reliance on social constructivism as the 'philosophy' underpinning computer-mediated learning, while its legitimacy has not been validated by formal research with adequate control groups. A subsequent section explores the validity of assessing knowledge construction through merely quantitative, or even exclusively automatic, analysis of interactions, implying that there is nothing else to knowledge that is different from quantitative factors. Thereafter, a section looks at the attribution of the benefits of asynchronous CMC to the technology rather than to tutor intervention and the underplaying of the value of memorisation as opposed to 'real understanding'.

Specific problematics in the field are then highlighted including the excessive claims of the benefits of online collaboration as a method of creating learning, which is based in no more than anecdotal evidence and an inherent confusion between theory and practice with regard to the nature of knowledge. Alongside this, there is contemplation on the emphasis of constructing afresh online communities of practice which are essentially organic structures that should be encouraged to grow, live and die naturally.

Finally, the chapter explores the severe difficulties of automatic content analysis, which remains at an unsatisfactory impasse to this day. Impediments here centre on the observation that meaning-making has taken place or can take place outside the formal learning space provided and the continuing need for frequent, personal, direct, real-time interaction between tutor and student, to supply direct encouragement and feedback. Of utmost importance is the need to take into account physical and cultural context, which is currently unrealised in computer communication.

Terminology and History

As all of the terminology used in the chapter is well known to the target audience of the chapter, we do not define terms per se; however, we believe it will be useful to deconstruct 'social constructivism' in the context of the work. Constructivism is not a unitary theoretical position; rather, it is frequently described as a continuum. The assumptions that underlie this continuum vary along several dimensions and have resulted in the definition and support for multiple types of constructivism. Typically, this continuum is divided into three broad categories: cognitive, social and radical constructivism.

Computer-mediated communication first appeared in the 1960s in the USA as means of transferring computer programs and data between remote computers in the interest of national defense (Levy, 1984; Rheingold, 1993). The educational potential was soon explored through early experimental dialogue systems, based on a 'socratic dialogue' methodology (Feurzeig, Munter, Swets, & Breen, 1964). The first analysis of computer-mediated discourse appeared in 1985, where Dennis Murray gave a very detailed analysis of the types of discourses which were prevalent in CMC. Since the early 1990s there has been a rapid growth in research into computer-mediated communication and computer-mediated discourse, the complexity of communicative situations with humans interacting together through computers has turned out to be much more multifaceted than originally envisioned. In the extensive literature on asynchronous online discussions, within the realm of computer-mediated communication, there is widespread agreement that online discussion enables interaction which would otherwise be difficult to achieve in face-to-face situations. (Conole & Oliver, 2007). There is a widespread acceptance, for example, in second language acquisition, that the use of electronically mediated communication has definite benefits for learners (Thorne, 2006; Warschauer, 1996). The benefits which are cited range from the acquisition of metalinguistic structures such as grammar to pragmatic competence and intercultural competence. Language learning was one of the early adopters of CMC, and the benefits of usage to second language acquisition have been well documented in the field for over two decades (Belz & Kinginger, 2002; Thorne, 2006; Warschauer, 1996). From a general educational perspective Henri (1992) sees CMC as 'a goldmine of information concerning the psycho-social dynamics at work among students, the learning strategies adopted, and the acquisition of knowledge and skills' (p. 118). Computer-mediated communication is fast becoming an area of active research in a number of disparate fields: psychology, digitial media studies, e-learning educational research and linguistics, in particular computational linguistics and pragmatic linguistics. However, when one examines the typologies being used, in general there is a commitment to the two main forms of online interaction, between students themselves, and students and tutor, which is often associated with a social constructivist approach to learning and teaching (Angeli, Valanides, & Bonk, 2003; MacDonald & Twining, 2002). Indeed, computer-mediated communication is often cited as a prime example of social constructivism in action. Computer-mediated communication is seen to have wider educational and social implications including from an egalitarian perspective the democratic development of students. Yates's 'democratic theory' focuses on the emancipatory aspects of its use (Yates, 1996).

A review of the research literature shows that reports centre on relatively high rates of student participation with evidence of two fundamental facets of social constructivism: co-operative learning (Aviv, Erlich, Ravid, & Geva, 2003; Hawkey, 2003; Hiltz, Coppola, Rotter, & Turoff, 2000), and higher order thinking and knowledge building (Curtis & Lawson, 2001; McConnell, 2000; Thomas, 2002). However, analysis of participation rates and evidence of co-construction of

knowledge based on quantitative data from learning management systems have misconstrued the issue slightly. The evaluation of co-construction of knowledge based on quantitative analysis of discussion posting underestimates the complexity of the issue at hand. More fundamental questions about what these participation rates mean and what does it mean to co-construct knowledge are beginning to emerge. There is *discontent* with content analysis of online discussion fora because the methodologies being used are not yielding the expected results of evidenced construction of knowledge online (Guevarra Enriquez, 2009). The widespread use of CMC in higher education and the need to assess students' performance, the attaining of the learning outcomes, in measurable terms is leading to developments in the analysis of CMC data. There is an inherent relationship, therefore, between the search for evidence of learning and the types of technology that are being used to facilitate the learning.

Various aspects of CMC have received scrutiny across a number of disciplines. Yet the adoption of CMC in university courses has developed faster than the understanding of how it should best be used to promote higher-order thinking and learning (Garrison, Anderson, & Archer, 2001). There is much debate within linguistic circles about the influence electronically mediated communication is having on language usage; there have been rapid developments in linguistic expression, such as the use of abbreviations, emoticons and textspeak alongside the developments of technology. Perhaps it is still too early to fully encapsulate how communication has changed with the widespread adoption of internet technologies (Baron, 2008). Currently, within educational research and practice, diagnosing the online interactions specifically related to knowledge and expertise exchanges is challenging. Much research is concerning itself with the identification and exploration of frameworks for the understanding and measurement of high level thinking in computer conferences. The underpinning presumption is that through the online exchange there is a record of knowledge being constructed before our very eyes.

Traditional theories of learning treat learning as a concealed and inferred process something that 'takes place inside the learner and only inside the learner'. CSCL[1] research has the advantage of studying learning in settings in which learning is observable and accountably embedded in collaborative activity. Our concern, therefore, is with the unfolding process of meaning-making within these settings, not so-called 'learning outcomes'. (Koschmann, 2001: 19)

We are being afforded a unique opportunity to glimpse at the learning taking place, the unfolding of new meaning-making before our very eyes on the discussion boards. The traces of social constructivism should, therefore, be present within the online exchanges. However, as we shall see, this is very much an oversimplification of what computer-mediated discourse is and, at a more profound level, an oversimplification of what knowledge construction, communication and indeed what language are.

CMC is defined here as predominantly text-based human–human interaction mediated by networked computers or mobile telephony, which includes, email, asynchronous discussion boards, blogs and wikis. Whilst many tools available to education today may be used in CMC, such as social networking, bookmarking sites, and Twitter to name a few, the evaluation of the technology seems to be mixed.

Nonetheless, the very classification of what CMC is and how it should be classified is an object of debate in itself, at the moment there is no consensus as to how this should be done. Susan Herring has advanced a faceted classification scheme for computer-mediated discourse (Herring, 2007). This classification adapts the traditional typology of discourse analysis to the online environment, including modality, number of discourse participants, text type and discourse type, and genre or register. Her new typology includes facets of online communication in educational environments such as purpose, topic, tone and activity. Claimed benefits of the asynchronous and virtual worlds are opportunities for multiple connections, the easy storage and manipulation of the text, the opportunity to interact more thoughtfully, to more people, more often, in a way in which both teacher and student feel comfortable (Ham & Davey, 2005). Other HE-level studies report advantages such as extending classroom discussions, increasing time management ability, self-directive behaviour, self-confidence and self-discipline (Hammond & Wiriyapinit, 2005; McFerrin, 1999). Arguably, creating such effects is more a function of tutor intervention and planning than it is a built-in benefit of the technology itself.

BACKGROUND

It is interesting to point out that the widespread adoption of social constructivism in higher education has been coupled with the rush to put in place large virtual learning environments and learning management systems. The virtual learning environment Moodle, for example, explicitly expounds social constructivism as part of its learning and teaching philosophy. It appears that social constructivism has become the acceptable face of higher education (Fitzpatrick, Hayes, & O'Rourke, 2009). The social constructivist perspective of learning and teaching regards computer conferences as a virtual space where knowledge is codified, exchanged and constructed (Curtis & Lawson, 2001; Wilson & Stacey, 2004). It has been privileged in CMC research over other common philosophical theoretical constructs. While it covers a grouping of theories and should not be seen as an all-encompassing unified theory of learning, there are common traits which are presuppositions about the nature of language and knowledge; following on from Vygotsky (1978), language is seen to be socially constructed and knowledge is also taken as a social construct. Likewise, from our own research experiences and practices into CMC, the philosophical approach which appears to be most convincing is the paradigm of social constructivism. Perhaps not in practice, but certainly in the literature, other theoretical constructs tend to be devalued. Indeed, published views are surprisingly normative, almost ideological, in favour of a collaborative and dialogic practice that excludes other theoretical paradigms. Other learning theories such as, behaviourism, humanism, situated learning and activity theory are generally skipped through in the literature relating to technology enhanced learning and CMC. Although the significance of CMC, in relation to the social constructivist theory is well documented in research literature (Berge, 1995; Jonassen & Reeves, 1996; Resnyansky, 2002), the research relationship is often tentative. Indeed Hendricks and Maor (2004) argue that hard evidence linking CMC to social constructivism has not been fully supported by research, as the majority of studies were often anecdotal or descriptions centering on individual experiences. The main problem with this is the use of small samples of discourse data, and as a result, the studies often do not accurately describe the cognitive processes of the students nor illustrate how knowledge develops and grows across time and across topics. Not surprisingly, CMC researchers continue to urge further investigation into the quality of student learning through CMC. However, there is a movement towards other types of content analysis such as speech acts, genre, roles and goals of interlocutors which are beginning to show some interesting results (Guevarra Enriquez, 2009).

In its conceptual presuppositions and in the diverse applications derived from them, social constructivism has applications in the following aspects of learning strategies which are of great relevance to our own practice as educational developers in higher education:

- It is centred on the learner more than on the content. Such a personally targeted approach, means the learner can learn more than is possible from an abstracted approach where there is a common objective for all.
- It is focused on 'deep' rather than 'surface' learning and on 'productive' rather than 'reproductive' tasks.
- It encourages a real understanding of content rather than a mere memorisation; essentially this is the ability of the individual student to appropriate/assimilate content and to give it personal meaning rather than an ability to replicate information.
- It is interested in the transference of learning from the classroom to real-life situations/context.
- It facilitates the development of cognitive, metacognitive and social abilities, which are fundamental to continuous learning in today's so-called 'knowledge society'.

However, there is an appearance that collaboration follows a neat cycle of student-to-other dialogue with better learning as the presumed result. Within this neat cycle there are presuppositions made about the speaking subject, interlocution[2] and creation of meaning. Too much evidence for broad, sweeping claims about the efficacy of online collaboration is based on anecdote, lending the appearance, if not the reality, of an ideology rather than researched CMC practice. A further issue to compound this is that collaborative methods quite often represent a mix of pedagogies, difficult to sort out and test in empirical research, that remain unproven in terms of validity. This chapter addresses this by delving into CMC research practices, specifically on CMC discourse analysis. One of the presumptions behind the models currently being used to analyse discussion fora is that the construction or co-construction of knowledge will be present within the dialogues taking place.

However, when tested this presumption seems to lead to oversimplifications about the nature of online communication and the nature of new meaning-making. It might be more judicious to speak of the evidencing of knowledge construction which takes place on the educational discussion boards rather than the co-construction of knowledge itself. The underlying epistemological confusion in social constructivism comes to fore once research for co-construction of knowledge is examined in detail. There is an inherent confusion between theory and practice in much of what is reported under the social constructivism banner in regard to what knowledge construction is. Those of a more philosophical bent stand back in horror when the ultimate epistemological relativism of social constructivism is overlooked (Boghossian, 2006). There is, therefore a tension between how knowledge is viewed in social constructivism and the very hierarchical structure of most educational institutes.

The analysis of discussion boards needs to take into account the context of the language usage. It should never be far from our minds that we are dealing, in higher education, with education discourse where students are required to demonstrate that they have learnt. A more Foucauldian analysis would point to the inherent power structures which are in place and which make up that discourse:

discourse is not the majestically unfolding manifestations of a thinking, knowing, speaking subject, but, on the contrary, a totality, in which the dispersion of the subject and his discontinuity with himself may be determined. It is a space of exteriority in which a network of distinct sites deployed. (Foucault, 1966: 55)

The speaking subject and the manifestation of thinking are presuppositions in most analysis of what is taking place on CMCs in higher education. It is, therefore, worthwhile opening the space where a re-evaluation of the learning that is supposedly manifest could take place.

Once language and knowledge building are presumed to be socially determined and socially constitutive, the analysis of the 'community' becomes of paramount importance. The 'community' will be the bedrock of meaning-making, knowledge building and knowledge sharing. Based on extensive research in the field, McConnell (2006) has concluded that there have been many attempts to characterise Internet 'communities', and educational communities, but surprisingly little examination of actual, existing educational communities. Much is now known about the theory of establishing communities but very little about how these theories (such as social learning theory) work in practice. Little is known about what actually takes place in an e-learning community and what members of communities do in those settings. Wenger's model of communities of practice (1998) has been widely discussed and adopted and has been very influential in the area of online communities. It would seem, at first glance, slightly contradictory to construct communities of practice which are essentially organic structures which should be encouraged to grow, live and die naturally. The challenge is, perhaps therefore, to harness the organic benefits of online communities for sharing and learning within more formalised educational structures.

However, Holmes, Tangney, FitzGibbon, Savage, and Mehan (2001) have argued for an expanded definition of social constructivism that takes into account the synergy between the more recent advances in information technology, which are increasing our potential for communication and these ideas outlined above. With communal constructivism, students and teachers are not simply engaged in developing their own information but actively involved in creating knowledge that will benefit other students and teachers; the focus is on learning with and for others. Within the context of professional development courses in higher education, peer tutoring is an obvious outlet for a communal constructivist approach. A social and communal constructivist approach adopted in the design and delivery of such courses can emphasise active and student-centred learning. Developing lifelong learning skills is also important, alongside learning in context.

Content Analysis and the Co-Construction of Meaning

The ultimate aim of adopting a concerted approach to researching CMC in higher education is to understand how students interact online as well as factors affecting their interaction. This is to assist with the development of more effective instructional strategies and better use of the technology. There are several different methodologies that have been used to provide evidence of online meaning-making. Research into online discussions has drawn, not surprisingly, on similar sources of evidence: online questionnaire survey, interviews and message analysis. Some researchers have adopted more recognisably ethnographic perspectives (Taylor, 2001), while others have used experimental and comparative methods (Koory, 2003; Weller, 2000). Indeed, others have been inspired directly from areas of discourse analysis in general such as critical discourse analysis (Fairclough, 1993). Fairclough bases his methodology on the multifunctional linguistic theory of Halliday's functional-systematic linguistics (Halliday 1978, 1985). As we shall see later, the tension between language as socially determined and socially constitutive comes to the fore once analysis of computer-mediated communication tries to take into account language as language use, or the social context to language usage. Another approach, has been to adopt a more structured analysis of the chat, synchronous communication. Holmes (2008) proposes a discourse structure analysis (DSA) which provides both a quantitative and qualitative analysis of the online exchanges, he explores such issues as turn-taking and discourse coherence.

Many CMC researchers argue that one of the most powerful methods of investigation is content analysis of conference transcripts, and a range of seminal research studies over a decade exists as testament to this (Donnelly & Gardner (2009). Content analysis has provided these researchers with a direct means to understand the processes of learning and teaching, the quality of interactions, and the relationship between interaction and knowledge construction. Despite the perceived benefit of having large volumes of conference data readily available to researchers through the tracking mechanisms in virtual learning environments, recurring criticisms of this method are the lack of a reliable model of content analysis. A number of instruments of content analysis have been developed from a social constructivist perspective (Weinberger & Fischer 2006). Within these instruments for content analysis the unit has ranged from message, to thematic unit, to sentence and complete discussion. Moreover, the validity and theoretical foundation of the majority of instruments available for content analysis have been called into question (De Wever, Schellens, Valcke, & Van Keer, 2006). The discourse analysis of discussion boards in higher education has been closely associated with semantic analysis. The content, whether it be the sentence, the theme or the overall utterance (posting, or overall discussion) is closely related to the generation of new meanings. At a basic level, this would indicate that if students have adopted the semantics, the terminologies, then they have integrated the new concepts, and the learning has taken place. The analysis of large amounts of data available to tutors has led to the development of automatic language treatment software packages where the interaction of students can, for example, be represented visually (Holmes, 2008). Learning management systems have been given advanced tracking functionalities which include not only numbers of postings but also detailed data about pages visited and time spent. Early analysis of computer-mediated communication using asynchronous tools tended to focus on more quantitative analysis of the data, focusing primarily on word counts and numbers of postings. Nonetheless, this means of analysis gives an initial good overview of the interactions which are taking place online but does not take into account the content of what is posted on the discussion boards. The analysis of the content of the discussion boards, therefore, moved towards a more semantic labeling of content or propositions. For, example, Campos (1998) gives a detailed formal semantic means of analysis whereby each proposition is qualified in terms of specific typology of discourse, i.e. affirmation, negativity, response. This semantic labeling is based on formal semantics which breaks down content into 'if and then' clause structure. Once the semantic labeling of the content has been carried out the analysis knowledge construction can take place. The co-construction of knowledge is evidenced from the use of propositions and based on conditional reasoning. This methodology demonstrated that new meaning was being created through the advances in the 'if and then' structures present on the discussion boards. Ravenscoft (2000) focused on the use of argumentation structure of the discussion boards; this analysis enables a clear labeling of content in terms of new argument and counter argument. Another means of semantic labeling has been inspired by a cognitive approach to what learning is, the co-construction of knowledge is evidenced through the acquisition of certain meta-cognitive activities online. The levels of cognition are labeled in terms of semantic propositions, the propositions contain new concepts or new ideas which are expressed, and the new proposition can in turn be taken as evidence of learning.

Content analysis, therefore, is inherently linked to the analysis of new meaning-making. One of the most interesting issues in this field is online meaning-making, specifically where and how it happens. The design of online formal learning spaces should enable us to glimpse the learning which is taking place online. However, the meaning-making which is present in online discussion fora, through analysis, is quite different to what is expected. As far back as the late 1990s,

studies such as that by Gunawardena, Lowe, and Anderson (1997) attempted to find appropriate interaction analysis techniques that assist in the examination of the negotiation of meaning and co-construction of knowledge in CMC environments. The nature of the online dialogue between student/student or student/tutor raises some fundamental questions about the structure of asynchronous discussion for education. The meaning-making which is hoped for or evidenced tends to have taken place outside the formal learning space. For example, sometimes the discussion board is used to provide evidence for the tutor of the learning expected and students have subverted the formally designed online learning space and communicated with each other by other means outside the view of the learning management system through MSN or Skype or quite simply by SMS and telephone (Fitzpatrick et al., 2009).

There is, perhaps, an over-emphasis placed on the quantitative data extracted from the virtual learning environments which has a tendency to become a panopticon; an all-seeing, powerful, observing presence in the learning process (Land & Bayne, 2005). When examined in detail, the nature of the interlocution taking place online tends to have awareness of the educational panopticon's presence. Students, just as in face-to-face classroom situations, are aware that their performance is being scrutinised for evidence of learning. In the online environment the interaction becomes, in some cases, an evidencing of knowledge construction rather than knowledge construction itself. The *duologue* between the students could be compared to a dialogue on stage where the ever-present audience is the ultimate addressee rather the characters on stage. There is a triad of communication, student–student–tutor, the silent partner in this case being the tutor whose presence is constantly being acknowledged. Advances in pragmatic linguistics have led to a detailed analysis of this triad of communication, how the addressee and the duologue can be different in the exchange. In French pragmatic linguistics (la linguistique d'énonciation) interlocution is an area of research in itself and has been providing a very interesting analysis of dialogue, duologue, and triad in the theatre (Fitzpatrick, 2008). The analysis of the online interlocution should not be simply reduced to quantitative data about the number of postings, number of thematic units, number of sentences, nor the number of utterances in the exchanges on the virtual learning environment. Coupled with the intensity of time and labour required to organise the volume of data, identify an appropriate unit of analysis and code the transcripts into suitable categories, the whole process leaves this as out of favour for many practitioners. However, with advances in the field of computational linguistics there are a number of automatic methods available which enable content coding to be done. Nonetheless, even with these advances, the language analysis tends to be based on more formalised parsing structures which label content as specific units of meaning but do not take into account the wider communication context of the online interactions. There have been developments in the analysis of multimodal communication techniques which focus on behaviour and linguistic expression at the same time. The analysis needs to include aspects of the communication which are intimately linked to the medium of communication which is being used.

The Pragmatics of Online Communication

In terms of computer-mediated communication, advances within the field of pragmatic linguistics have important consequences. Pragmatic linguistics is considered as a part of sociolinguistics where the focus is on the social use of language. Pragmatics focuses on the use of language and hence upon the context of language usage. In the methods briefly mentioned above, there is no mention of the context of the utterances under analysis and yet in terms of human computer interaction, it is this context that is lacking. The paralinguistic

features of language or context, linguistics would argue, give meaning to the utterances. The analysis of the discussion needs to take into account the context, both in the sense of physical context but also in terms of educational context. In the area of research of CMC there has been a recent growth of interest in terms of methodologies which take into account the context of the discussion taking place. It has been shown that there is a higher frequency of pragmatic errors in CMC communication than there is elsewhere. The forms of presence online have a direct influence upon this; for example, if the addressee and addressor know each other, have spoken to each other previously then the grounding of the online communication can be more easily established. The lack of visual clues, tone of voice have all been analysed in earlier research which tended to focus on the comparisons between face-to-face communication and online communication. With recent developments in pragmatics, the areas of research have included grounding, theory of mind, multimodal analysis of exchanges. The context of the use of language is therefore of primal importance for a pragmatic linguistic analysis of the discussion boards. Indeed, even in terms of the co-construction of meaning, the establishment of context through the simple question about who is being addressed, or put more simply, who is talking to whom. The discussion does not take place without context – context here is meant in the wider sense of physical embodiment of language and educational context of the online communication. One of the fundamental principles of pragmatic linguistics is to investigate the wider context of the utterance, to juxtapose what is said with what is meant, or the said and the unsaid or not needed to be said. The establishment of means of analysing language in terms of wider contextual meaning-making is the main focus of this approach to linguistic analysis.

Susan Herring has developed a specific methodology for online discourse analysis which is called computer-mediated discourse analysis (CMDA) and from a linguistic perspective there is an extension of analysis beyond content to include key features of computer-mediated discourse such as the online community (see Herring, 2004a, 2004b). The methodology is on the surface very similar to traditional types of content analysis that have been mentioned above, however, although the methodology is language-focused it allows the inclusion of aspects of communication or context which are specifically related to computer-mediated communication. In this way it enables the analysis of language which is related to the specific medium of communication, related to the semiotics of online communication. For example, turn-taking in synchronous communication online can be influenced by specific features of the technology being used, i.e. the buffer or page renewal features. The lag in the conversation, which can be technical but also due to the physical speed of typing, can lead to over-talking and non-sequential turn-taking. In face-to-face communication, these would have specific inferred meanings. The pragmatics of the social use of language would indicate that we do not talk over each other as this would be considered as impolite or rude. However, in the online environment the turn could be considered as the overall thread of the discussion within which turn-taking rules would be adapted to the communicative context. Certain advances in technology have enabled these new pragmatic rules to be taken into account. For example in instant messaging, whether it be on MSN or on Facebook, when our interlocutor is typing their message we are given notice of the fact. This would be equivalent to signaling that it is going to be my turn to talk. For asynchronous communication the turn can be considered as each individual posting on the discussion board where more time is given for each turn to take place. Another feature of pragmatic analysis is sometimes referred to as grounding, of finding the common ground in the conversation, or being able to infer what is meant. Grounding in the widest sense includes complex notions of belief systems and theory of mind. The interlocutors need to understand the social context,

and grounding is used for reference resolution. If our interlocutors are in the same geo-political space and reference is made to 'our president' then the addressee can infer which president is being referred to. In online communication grounding or reference resolution can pose specific challenges. The nature of online communication can put speaking subjects in communicative situations who lack the certain grounding mechanisms to resolve simple references of the here and now. In online chat sequences the establishment of physical presence can at initial stages be very prevalent, where interlocutors refer to the time and distance present in the communication and refer to their own physical environment through references to the weather and such. In Herring's model of CMDA therefore we are given the possibility of including these specific features of online pragmatics into the analysis of the discussion boards.

Social Interaction, Collaborative Learning Tools

Interaction in education is a complex phenomenon. Online interaction as a means of communication is one of the most widely researched issues in higher education today. Donnelly (2008) argues that interaction has been and continues to be one of the most hotly debated constructs in the realms of distance and e-learning. The literature identifies several taxonomies that classify various types of online interactions. However, Moore's (1989) seems to be the most well-known taxonomy in the field of online education. He described three types of interaction: learner–content, learner–instructor, and learner–learner; these were later extended by Hillman, Willis, and Gunawardena (1994) to include learner–interface interaction. There is little doubt in the literature that social interaction is one of the most important components of the learning experience premised on social constructivist principles (Picciano, 2002). Interaction, using language as a tool of mediation among a community of learners, becomes a social mode of thinking where students learn by engaging in dialogue.

From a constructivist viewpoint, studies on web-based learning environments have shown that a critical component to interaction online is this interpersonal, social component; this occurs when learners receive feedback from the instructor or peers and colleagues in the form of personal encouragement and motivational assistance. Social interaction can contribute to learner satisfaction and frequency of interaction in an online learning environment. Indeed, Grabinger and Dunlap (2000) have reported that without the opportunity actively to interact and exchange ideas with each other and the instructor, learners' social as well as cognitive involvement in the learning environment is diminished.

For the purposes of this chapter, interactions are defined as reciprocal events that require at least two objects and two actions. Interactions occur when the objects and events mutually influence one another. A number of schools of thought have emerged in the last two decades that explore interaction in the context of technology-mediated learning. There are two commonly held beliefs. Firstly that the perceived quality of a learning experience is directly proportional to and positively correlated with the degree to which that experience is seen as interactive. Secondly, if technology-mediated learning designs are to have any significant impact on current and future pedagogical practices, then learning design decisions need to maximise the benefit of interaction.

Interaction has long been regarded as the vital ingredient upon which success depends in technology-related education. Research studies by Frankola (2001) and Charp (2002) on attrition rates in online courses have provided a rationale for the emphasis on promoting interaction and sound instructional strategies in online courses. More recently, Yun (2005) has concluded that there is evidence that instructional strategies which incorporate various types of interaction can be the key to teaching a high-quality online course

that engages students. Student perceptions also provide a reason why interactivity is important in e-learning. A number of studies have shown that students tend to judge a distance education course according to their perception of the instructor–student interaction (Abbey, 2000; Flottechmesch, 2000; Lynch, 2002).

According to Vygotsky's social development theory (1978), learning does not happen in isolation. A number of respected scholars including Ramsden (1988), Garrison (1990), and Wagner (1994) have reported that increased levels of interaction have been shown to increase motivation, positive attitudes toward learning, higher satisfaction with instruction, deeper, more meaningful learning and higher achievement. Owston, Garrison, and Cook (2006) believe that 'sustained interaction between and amongst tutor and students leading to knowledge construction and validation requires an opportunity to share and test ideas in a secure environment and with a manageable number of students' (p. 339). Information and communication technologies have both the capability of supporting and enhancing this engagement and the capacity to extend the learning experience to critically consider the technology itself and critically access and evaluate the wealth of information available in a virtual learning environment.

The explosion of internet communication tools over the last 10 years has enabled the creation of new forms of interaction such as virtual learning environments, learning management systems, and, more recently, blogs and wikis, all of which have changed the way interaction is taking place. Asynchronous forms of communication have advanced with the development of Web 2.0 tools; asynchronous communication now extends well beyond the use of discussion boards and includes a number of means of collaboration. Web 2.0 tools have changed the nature of the internet from *publication to participation* (Warschauer & Grimes, 2008) or from *linking pages to linking people* (Wesch, 2007). Warschauer and Grimes present a very interesting analysis of an emerging semiotics of these new means of online communication, which are at the same time tools of communication and tools of collaboration. Initially the internet was a static space, where webpages could be created by the few people who knew how to create and publish HTML pages. The second generation internet enables millions of people to create webpages together through blogs and wikis. In terms of the classification of CMC these new forms are challenging, they are both asynchronous and synchronous forms. The forms of CMC have become more fluid and mixed. Web 2.0 social networking sites (for example Facebook) enable members to be informed when they are online, the distinction is becoming more and more challenging to uphold. Wikis such as pbwiki have seen a massive increase in usage. The use of wikis is already having an impact in higher education, where participants can share the creation of online webpages and documents. Wikis, in particular, are lauded as exemplifying social constructivism, where, for example one study in *Nature* magazine purported that Wikipedia was as accurate as or slightly less accurate than the Encyclopedia Britannica (Giles, 2005). The collective knowledge construction which is taking place at a rapid pace online is challenging traditional notions of expert and expertise. The very notion of the university and traditional academe will ultimately be challenged by the egalitarian nature of Web 2.0 technologies. The post-structuralist collaboratively written, multi-authored text, raises questions about the role of the author and the role of the audience. The traditional boundaries between authorial intention and reader's receptive hermeneutics are becoming more and more blurred. At a more philosophical level, these new forms of interaction are calling into question the well-demarcated notions of authorship and reader. The technical advances of computer-mediated communication tools and collaboration tools are presenting challenges to what writing and reading are.

CONCLUSION

This chapter has been ambitious in trying to put forward new pointers for such a wide field of research. However, there is a need to re-evaluate research which is ongoing into computer-mediated communication and claims of co-construction of knowledge. Although large amounts of data and a growing number of methodologies are available to us, there is a need to take into account the semiotics and the social context of these online dialogues. The case can be made through a more interdisciplinary approach to the issues being raised. Current research, for example, in pragmatic linguistics around interlocution enables the inclusion of certain specific traits of the communicative context of CMC. Stahl (2003) argues that the form of communication that appears in computer-mediated interaction 'has special requirements and needs its own theory of communication'. The nature of the medium being used to communicate with, whilst it has afforded immense possibilities for communication amongst tutors and students, and students amongst themselves, has also brought with it specific needs for a theory of online communication. In this chapter we have limited ourselves to the most widespread usage of CMC in higher education in Ireland with asynchronous communication on learning management systems. Higher education has yet to come to terms with the consequences of adopting the use of this means of communication on its courses. It remains a significant challenge to socially construct knowledge through a new medium of communication, within an area which has been traditionally conservatively hierarchical and academically protective of that same knowledge.

REFERENCES

Abbey, B. (2000). *Instructional and cognitive impacts of web-based education*. Hershey, PA: Idea Group.

Angeli, C., Valanides, N., & Bonk, C. (2003). Communication in a web-based conferencing system: The quality of computer-mediated interactions. *British Journal of Educational Technology, 34*(1), 31–43. doi:10.1111/1467-8535.00302

Aviv, R., Erlich, Z., Ravid, G., & Geva, A. (2003). Network analysis of knowledge construction in asynchronous learning networks. *Journal of Asynchronous Learning Networks, 7*(3), 1–23.

Baron, N. S. (2008). *Always on: Language in an online and mobile world.* Oxford: Oxford University Press.

Belz, J.A., & Kinginger, C. (2002). The cross-linguistic development of address form use in telecollaborative language learning: Two case studies. *The Canadian Modern Language Review/ La revue canadienne des langue vivantes, 59*(2), 189-214.

Benveniste, E. (1971). *Problems in general linguistics (trans. Mary Elizabeth Meek), 2 vols.* Coral Gables, FL: University of Miami.

Berge, Z. L. (1995). Facilitating computer conferencing: Recommendations from the field. *Educational Technology, 35,* 22–30.

Boghossian, P. (2006). *Fear of knowledge: Against relativism and constructivism.* Oxford: Oxford University Press.

Campos, M. (1998). Conditional reasoning: A key to assessing computer-based knowledge-building communication processes . *Journal of Universal Computer Science, 4*(4), 404–428.

Charp, S. (2002). Wireless vs. hard-wired network use in education. *T.H.E. Journal, 29*(8), 8–10.

Conole, G., & Oliver, M. (Eds.). (2007). Contemporary perspectives in e-learning research: Themes, methods and impact on practice. Abingdon: Routledge.

Curtis, D., & Lawson, M. (2001). Exploring collaborative online learning. *Journal of Asynchronous Learning Networks, 5*(1), 21–34.

De Wever, B., Schellens, T., Valcke, M., & Van Keer, H. (2006). Content analysis schemes to analyze transcriptions of online asynchronous discussion groups: A review. *Computers & Education, 46*(1), 6–28. doi:10.1016/j.compedu.2005.04.005

Donnelly, R. (2008). Activity systems within blended problem-based learning in academic professional development. *International Journal of Applied Educational Studies, 3*(1), 38–59.

Donnelly, R., & Gardner, J. (2009). Content analysis of computer conferencing transcripts. *Journal of Interactive Learning Environments, 20*(4), 469–485.

Fairclough, N. (1993). *Critical discourse analysis: The critical study of language.* New York: Longman.

Feurzeig, W., Munter, P., Swets, J., & Breen, M. (1964). Computer-aided teaching in medical diagnosis. *Journal of Medical Education, 39*(8), 645–754.

Fitzpatrick, N. (2008). *Les Je(ux) de discours dans l'oeuvre de Brian Friel.* Lille: CNT.

Fitzpatrick, N., Hayes, N., & O'Rourke, K. C. (2009). Beyond constriction and control: Constructivism in online theory and practice . In Payne, C. (Ed.), *Information technology and constructivism in higher education: Progressive learning frameworks.* Hershey, PA: IGI Global.

Flottechmesch, K. (2000). Building effective interaction in distance education: A review of the literature. *Educational Technology, 40*(3), 46–51.

Foucault, M. (1966). *The order of things: An archaeology of the human sciences.* New York: Pantheon.

Frankola, K. (2001). Why online learners dropout. Retrieved August 30, 2005, from http://www.workforce.com/feature/00/07/29/

Garrison, D. R. (1990). An analysis and evaluation of audio teleconferencing to facilitate education at a distance. *American Journal of Distance Education, 4*(3), 13–24. doi:10.1080/08923649009526713

Garrison, D. R., Anderson, T., & Archer, W. (2001). Critical thinking, cognitive presence and computer conferencing in distance education. *American Journal of Distance Education, 15*(1), 7–23. doi:10.1080/08923640109527071

Giles, J. (2005). Internet encyclopaedias go head to head. *Nature, 438*, 900-901 (December 15).

Grabinger, R. S., & Dunlap, J. C. (2000). Rich environments for active learning: A definition. In Squires, D., Conole, G., & Jacobs, G. (Eds.), *The changing face of learning technology* (pp. 8–38). Cardiff: University of Wales Press.

Guevarra Enriquez, J. (2009). Discontent with content analysis of online transcripts. *Association for Learning Technology Journal, 17*(2), 101–113.

Gunawardena, C., Lowe, C., & Anderson, T. (1997). Analysis of a global online debate and the development of an interaction analysis model for examining social construction of knowledge in computer conferencing. *Journal of Educational Computing Research, 17*(4), 397–431.

Halliday, M. A. K. (1978). *Language as social semiotic*. London: Arnold.

Halliday, M. A. K. (1985). *An introduction to functional grammar*. London: E. Arnold.

Ham, V., & Davey, R. (2005). Our first time: Two higher education tutors reflect on becoming a 'virtual teacher'. *Innovations in Education and Teaching International, 42*(3), 257–264. doi:10.1080/01587910500168017

Hammond, M., & Wiriyapinit, M. (2005). Learning through online discussion: A case of triangulation in research. *Australasian Journal of Educational Technology, 21*(3), 283–302.

Hawkey, K. (2003). Asynchronous text-based discussion: A case study with trainee teachers. *Education and Information Technologies, 8*(2), 165–177. doi:10.1023/A:1024558414766

Hendricks, V., & Maor, D. (2004). Quality of students' communicative strategies delivered through computer-mediated communications. *Journal of Interactive Learning Research, 15*(1), 5–32.

Henri, F. (1992). Computer conferencing and content analysis. In Kaye, A. R. (Ed.), *Collaborative learning through computer conferencing: The Najaden Papers* (pp. 117–136). Berlin: Springer-Verlag.

Herring, S. C. (2004a). Computer-mediated discourse analysis: An approach to researching online behavior. In S.A. Barab, R. Kling, & J.H. Gray (Eds.), *Designing for virtual communities in the service of learning* (pp. 338-376). New York: Cambridge University Press. Preprint. Retrieved April 26, 2009, from http://ella.slis.indiana.edu/~herring/cmda.pdf

Herring, S. C. (2004b). Content analysis for new media: Rethinking the paradigm. In *New research for new media: Innovative research methodologies symposium working papers and readings* (pp. 47-66). Minneapolis, MN: University of Minnesota School of Journalism and Mass Communication. Retrieved April 26, 2009, from http://ella.slis.indiana.edu/~herring/newmedia.pdf

Herring, S. C. (2007). A faceted classification scheme for computer-mediated discourse. *Language@Internet*, 4, Article 1. Retrieved April 26, 2009, from http://www.languageatinternet.de/articles/2007/761

Hillman, D. C., Willis, D. J., & Gunawardena, C. N. (1994). Learner–interface interaction in distance education: An extension of contemporary models and strategies for practitioners. *American Journal of Distance Education*, *8*(2), 30–42. doi:10.1080/08923649409526853

Hiltz, S. R., Coppola, N., Rotter, N., & Turoff, M. (2000). Measuring the importance of collaborative learning for the effectiveness of ALN: A multi-measure, multi-method approach. *Journal of Asynchronous Learning Networks*, *4*(2), 103–125.

Holmes, B., Tangney, B., FitzGibbon, A., Savage, T., & Mehan, S. (2001). Communal constructivism: Students constructing learning for as well as with others. Retrieved December 5, 2006, from https://www.cs.tcd.ie/publications/tech-reports/reports.01/TCD-CS-2001–04.pdf

Holmes, T. (2008). Discourse structure analysis of chat communication. *Language@Internet*, *5*. Retrieved October 26, 2009, from http://www.languageatinternet.de/articles/2008/1633

Jonassen, D. H., & Reeves, T. C. (1996). Learning with technology: Using computers as cognitive tools . In Jonassen, D. H. (Ed.), *Handbook of research on educational communications and technology* (pp. 693–719). New York: Macmillan.

Koory, M. A. (2003). Differences in learning outcomes for the online and f2f version of 'an introduction to Shakespeare'. *Journal of Asynchronous Learning Networks*, *7*(2), 18–35.

Koschmann, T. (Ed.). (2001). *CSCL: Theory and practice of an emerging paradigm* (pp. 1–23). Mahwah, NJ: Lawrence Erlbaum.

Land, R., & Bayne, S. (Eds.). (2005). Education in cyberspace. London and New York: RoutledgeFalmer.

Levy, S. (1984). *Hackers: Heroes of the computer revolution*. New York: Dell.

Lynch, M. M. (2002). *The online educator: A guide to creating the virtual classroom*. New York: RoutledgeFalmer. doi:10.4324/9780203458556

Macdonald, J., & Twining, P. (2002). Assessing activity-based learning for a networked course. *British Journal of Educational Technology*, *33*(5), 603–618. doi:10.1111/1467-8535.00295

McConnell, D. (2000). *Implementing computer supported cooperative learning* (2nd ed.). London: Kogan Page.

McConnell, D. (2006). *E-learning groups and communities*. Maidenhead: Society for Research into Higher Education & Open University Press.

McFerrin, K. M. (1999). Incidental learning in a higher education asynchronous online distance course. In J.D. Price, J. Willis, M. Jost, & S. Boger-Mehall (Eds.), SITE 99: Proceedings of the Society for Information Technology & Teacher Education International Conference (pp. 1418-1423). San Antonio TX, 28 Feb. to 4 Mar. (Charlotteville, VA: Association for the Advancement of Computers in Education (AACE)).

Moore, M. (1989). Editorial: Three types of interaction. *American Journal of Distance Education*, *3*(2), 1–7. doi:10.1080/08923648909526659

Murray, D. (1985). Composition as conversation: The computer as a medium of communication . In Odell, L., & Goswami, D. (Eds.), *Writing in non-academic settings* (pp. 203–227). New York: The Guilford Press.

Owston, R., Garrison, D., & Cook, K. (2006). Blended learning at Canadian universities: Issues and practices . In Bonk, C. J., & Graham, C. R. (Eds.), *The handbook of blended learning. Global perspectives, local designs* (pp. 338–350). San Francisco: Pfeiffer.

Picciano, D. (2002). *Educational leadership and planning for technology* (4th ed.). Columbus, OH: Prentice Hall.

Ramsden, P. (1988). *Improving learning: New perspectives*. London: Kogan Page.

Ravenscoft, A. (2000). Designing argumentation for conceptual development . *Computers & Education, 34*, 241–255. doi:10.1016/S0360-1315(99)00048-2

Resnyansky, L. (2002). Computer-mediated communication in higher education: Educators' agency in relation to technology. *Journal of Educational Enquiry, 3*(1), 35–58.

Rheingold, H. (1993). *The virtual community: Homesteading on the electronic frontier*. Reading, MA: Addison-Wesley.

Stahl, G. (2003). *Communication and learning in online collaboration*. Paper presented at GROUP_03, Sannibel Island, Florida. Retrieved April 26, 2009, from http://www.cis.drexel.edu/faculty/gerry/publications/conferences/2003/group/group03.doc

Taylor, S. (Ed.). (2001). *Ethnographic research: A reader*. London: Sage.

Thomas, M. J. W. (2002). Learning within incoherent structures: The space of online discussion forums. *Journal of Computer Assisted Learning, 18*, 351–366. doi:10.1046/j.0266-4909.2002.03800.x

Thorne, S. L. (2006). Pedagogical and praxiological lessons from internet-mediated intercultural foreign language education research . In Belz, J. A., & Thorne, S. L. (Eds.), *Internet-mediated intercultural foreign language education* (pp. 2–30). Boston, MA: Heinle & Heinle.

Vygotsky, L. S. (1978). *Mind in society: The development of higher psychological processes* (Cole, M., John-Steiner, V., Scribner, S., & Souberman, E., Trans.). Cambridge, MA: Harvard University Press.

Wagner, E. D. (1994). In support of a functional definition of interaction. *American Journal of Distance Education, 8*(2), 6–29. doi:10.1080/08923649409526852

Warschauer, M. (1996). Computer assisted language learning: An introduction . In Fotos, S. (Ed.), *Multimedia language teaching* (pp. 3–20). Tokyo: Logos International.

Warschauer, M., & Grimes, D. (2008). Audience, authorship and artifact: The emergent semiotics of Web2.0. [from http://www.gse.uci.edu/person/warschauer_m/docs/aaa.pdf]. *Annual Review of Applied Linguistics, 27*, 1–23. Retrieved October 26, 2009.

Weinberger, A., & Fischer, F. (2006). A framework to analyze argumentative knowledge construction in computer-supported collaborative learning. *Computers & Education, 46*, 71–95. doi:10.1016/j.compedu.2005.04.003

Weller, M. (2000). The use of narrative to provide a cohesive structure for a web based computing course. *Journal of Interactive Media in Education*, 1. Retrieved, April 26, 2009, from http://www-jime.open.ac.uk/00/1/

Wenger, E. (1998). *Communities of practice: Learning, meaning and identity*. Cambridge: Cambridge University Press.

Wesch, M. (2007). Web2.0: The machine is us/using us [Video], Retrieved, April 26, 2009, from http://www.youtube.com/watch?v=6gmP4nk0EOE

Wilson, G., & Stacey, E. (2004). Online interaction impacts on learning: Teaching the teachers to teach online. *Australasian Journal of Educational Technology, 20*(1), 33–48.

Yates, S. J. (1996). Oral and written linguistic aspects of computer conferencing: A corpus-based study . In Herring, S. C. (Ed.), *Computer-mediated communication: Linguistic, social and cross-cultural perspectives*. Philadelphia: John Benjamins Publishing Co.

Yun, K. (2005). Collaboration in the semantic grid: A basis for e-learning. *Applied Artificial Intelligence, 19*(9 & 10), 881–904.

ADDITIONAL READING

Goertler, S. (2009). Using computer-mediated communication (CMC) in language teaching. *Unterrichtspraxis/Teaching German, 42*(1), 74-84.

Hull, D. M., & Saxon, T. F. (2009). Negotiation of meaning and co-construction of knowledge: An experimental analysis of asynchronous online instruction. *Computers & Education, 52*(3), 624–639. doi:10.1016/j.compedu.2008.11.005

Land, R. (2004). Embodiment and risk in cyberspace education. In R. Atkinson, C. McBeath, D. Jonas-Dwyer, & R. Phillips (Eds.), *Beyond the Comfort Zone: Proceedings of the 21st ASCILITE Conference*. Perth, Western Australia, 5–8 December: ASCILITE. Retrieved April 26, 2009, from http://www.ascilite.org.au/conferences/perth04/procs/contents.html

Mäkitalo, K., Weinberger, A., Häkkinen, P., Järvelä, S., & Fischer, F. (2005). Epistemic cooperation scripts in online learning environments: Fostering learning by reducing uncertainty in discourse? *Computers in Human Behavior, 21,* 603–622. doi:10.1016/j.chb.2004.10.033

Paulus, T. M. (2009). Online but off-topic: Negotiating common ground in small learning groups. *Instructional Science: An International Journal of the Learning Sciences, 37*(3), 227–245.

Scardamalia, M., & Bereiter, C. (1994). Computer support for knowledge-building communities. *Journal of the Learning Sciences, 3*(3), 265–283. doi:10.1207/s15327809jls0303_3

So, H. J. (2009). When groups decide to use asynchronous online discussions: Collaborative learning and social presence under a voluntary participation structure. *Journal of Computer Assisted Learning, 25*(2), 143–160. doi:10.1111/j.1365-2729.2008.00293.x

Zeng, G., & Shigenobu, T. (2009). Text-based peer-peer collaborative dialogue in a computer-mediated learning environment in the EFL context. *International Journal of Educational Technology and Applied Linguistics, 37*(3), 434–446.

ENDNOTES

[1] Computer Supported Collaborative Learning

[2] Interlocution refers to the social context of the use of language. The utterance is grounded in the context through the positions of interlocutors as addressee and adressor. The analysis of interlocution rather than dialogue allows the wider context of communication to be considered; see Benveniste (1971).

Chapter 5
Educational Technology, Innovation and Habitus:
What is the Connection?

Larry McNutt
Institute of Technology at Blanchardstown, Ireland

ABSTRACT

Information and communications technology has radically transformed many aspects of modern life. However, this is in marked contrast to its impact on education. The purpose of this chapter is to explore why educational technology has done little to transform our higher education system. This is in spite of the emergence of the formal role of educational technologist, the improved ICT infrastructure and the evolving recognition of the importance of teaching and learning within the sector. Yet it is also apparent that within a given academic community there are many individually motivated innovators, i.e. those characterised by their willingness to experiment with new approaches and embrace change. Whilst there are also many who resist and avoid any possible alterations (or interference) in how they teach their subject matter. This chapter will argue that Bourdieu's concepts of habitus and field could provide a suitable lens to investigate why this apparent dichotomy has developed. This will involve a review of what we mean by educational technology; a broad look at the characteristics of innovators in other domains and to consider how applicable their experiences are to education. Finally, I will propose that rather than identifying and classifying shared characteristics of innovators it would be more valuable to examine and capture the innovative educator's habitus.

INTRODUCTION

Is it possible that educational technologists contributed to the current crises facing our planet, i.e. global warming and the collapse of the world economy? Or perhaps I should rephrase that question and ask did the higher education sector contribute to these unfolding catastrophes? This may seem preposterous, however, I found myself pondering these questions recently, prompted by comments from two authors.

DOI: 10.4018/978-1-61520-897-1.ch005

The first was Anne Goodman who commented that:

I have previously examined education in the broad context of our culture, looking at our present situation as a crisis in which our civilisation and indeed life on earth is threatened. I suggest that the crisis exists because the taken-for-granted assumptions of our society are no longer appropriate and that our education system, which is based on the same assumptions, perpetuates the situation. (2003, p. 3)

This led me to question the role that technology was currently playing in our rapidly changing higher education sector, where education and other public services have been redefined as market commodities. In response colleges and universities have adopted many of the frameworks of successful corporations, e.g. quality assurance frameworks, performance management systems, unit costing and strategic plans. This encroachment of neo-liberalism and commercialism into higher education is the topic addressed by the second author Kathleen Lynch (2006) who writing on this issue says:

The neo-liberal position is fundamentally Hobbesian in character, focusing on creating privatised citizens who care primarily for themselves. The privatised, consumer-led citizenry of the neo-liberal model are reared on a culture of insecurity that induces anxiety, competition, and indifference to those more vulnerable than themselves. (p. 3)

It would appear that our education system reproduces the societal norms that currently prevail. A regime that is dominated by vested professional interests and limits class mobility. This year, in 2009, entrants to higher education will be largely drawn from the same higher socio-economic groups:

Years of research evidence on the patterns of class inequality in education have shown that not only has there been little class mobility in education over the last 50 years but there is little hope of social mobility through education for many even in prosperous countries like the USA. (Lynch, 2006, p. 2)

Yet we live in a society in which we are witnessing significant changes in our daily lives enabled by the same technology which allows us to bank, shop and book exotic holiday destinations from the comfort of our own sitting rooms. The world of technology is at our fingertips and it is having a profound effect on how we experience and view the world. This conundrum is the background to this chapter – to investigate why the transformative capability of technology when deployed in education contributes to the maintenance of the status quo rather than leveraging its capabilities to address these inherent inequalities that characterise the modern higher education sector.

Another trend in higher education in the past decade has been the establishment of Centres for Teaching and Learning and the creation of allied posts such as E-learning Coordinators. In many instances these centres are staffed by educators who have an interest in technology and how it relates to the current challenges in the teaching and learning domain. A key role is to encourage and support academic staff to adopt alternative delivery models that exploit the advantages of digital technology. Oliver (2002) comments on the emergence of the 'new professionals' and the importance of 'learning about how and why these varied groups work, in order to understand how their practices have developed to suit the current nature of institutions in the sector' (p. 251).

A secondary issue in this area is to also recognise that faced with this 'cauldron' of change many academics do not adopt new practices. The question that this scenario poses is described by Gunter (2000) as to 'why the individual researcher, lecturer, or professor does what he/she does and in the way that he/she does it' (p. 625). In the current climate where the dominant discourse of quality assurance prevails and performativity is the central tenet of measuring success it would be simplistic to dismiss such resistance as Luddite without exploring the underlying beliefs and values of these academics.

This perspective is shared by other commentators; Robertson (2003) contends that 'There is clearly a need for a different account of the attempts to transfer new information and communication technologies into school based education systems. Essentially rational explanation has proved inadequate' (p. 340). Within higher education, Kanuka and Kelland (2008) reflect that

the higher education literature on e-learning technology is replete with research that tinkers with, and then tests the effects of, instrumental practices. The ultimate aim is to determine, once and for all, what works and what does not – passing by the question of why. (p. 61)

This chapter will propose that Pierre Bourdieu's concept of habitus and field could provide a suitable lens to investigate the practices of educational technologists. The importance of habitus and field as 'thinking tools' to explore current practice is highlighted by Bourdieu who contends that 'to understand practices we need to understand both the evolving fields within which social agents are situated and the evolving habituses which those social agents bring to their social fields of practice' (Bourdieu, 1990, p.52).

Webb, Schirato and Danaher (2002) explain that:

Habitus can be understood as, on the one hand, the historical and cultural production of individual practices – since contexts, laws, rules and ideologies all speak through individuals, who are never entirely aware that this is happening – and, on the other hand, the individual production of

practices – since the individual always acts from self-interest. (p. 15)

For the purpose of this chapter the individual practices of educational technologists will encompass new specialists, including educational or technical developers, researchers and managers and academics who have a formal responsibility for learning technology (Oliver, 2002, p. 246).

This chapter will initially review existing research literature on the the characteristics of innovators in other domains and consider how applicable their experiences are to education. This will be followed by a review of the field of educational technology and an exploration of the relevance and suitability of Bourdieu's concepts as the rationale for an exploratory study designed to examine and capture the innovative educator's habitus.

FOSTERING INNOVATION – CHARACTERISTICS OF INNOVATORS?

There have been several papers investigating the characteristics of innovators over the past few decades. Innovation is not necessarily related to developments in technology. An early definition provided by Rogers (1963) suggests that innovators are the 'first members of a social system to adopt new ideas' (p. 252). Conversely, Uhl and Poulsen (1970) describe laggards as 'the last group or segment of persons to adopt' (p. 51), but importantly they do eventually adopt. So what do we know about the common characteristics of an innovator? Hannah (1995, p. 219) has described the following as key correlates of innovative people. (See Table 1).

As Table 1 illustrates there are a number of key differences between public and private sector innovators. For public sector employees the rewards are intrinsic compared to the often financial incen-

Table 1. Innovative People

Private and public sector innovators	Public sector innovators
See things from different angles	Often work alone
Have a broad perspective	Depend almost solely on intrinsic rewards
Are risk takers	Understand and work well with their political environment
Communicate effectively	Are very committed and very persistent
Know how to build support	
Are flexible but committed	
Are persistent	

tives offered by the private sector. Hannah (1995, p. 221) also adds that public sector innovators add an extra 'very' to committed and persistent and importantly can work well within their political system. This is an important characteristic for innovators in the education domain and is recognised as critical for the role of educational technologists who operate at the boundaries between academia and administration.

This tension was captured by Gosling (2008) in a study of Educational Development Units (EDU) in the UK where they state that 'EDUs have to work hard to ensure that they work alongside academic staff, and learning support staff, in a way that is based on conversation and dialogue, and not on the assumption that ED professionals are always right' (p. 43).

There is no doubt that in an education setting 'educational change is technically simple and socially complex' (Craft, 2000, p. 175). A review of some of the literature examining innovation in education would certainly support this point of view. Kirschner, Hendricks, Paas, & Wopereis, (2004) who investigated the success factors of large-scale educational innovation projects in Dutch higher education have noted that 'Innovating (or changing) the structure of an organization often comes up against a wall of resistance. Not surprisingly the human factor is often considered the most influential factor on the chance of success' (p. 362).

Crawford & Gannon-Cook (2002) also comment that the rewards systems are of primary importance to faculty. Davis (1979) offered a different approach by exploring the variables that influence changes in the instructional behaviour of faculty members. People are not just 'pushed' into action by drives; they are also 'pulled' by incentives. The performance of the faculty member is determined by motivation and learning acting together. A criticism of many faculty development programmes is that they emphasise one or other of these two variables but not both.

Craft (2000, p. 183) refers to the work of Hall and Oldroyd who have articulated the view that teachers will not commit themselves to innovations which:

- are not seen as beneficial
- cannot be clearly understood
- are at odds with their professional beliefs
- are inadequately resourced

In another study by Lee (2001) four categories of concerns were identified in relation to teacher's perceptions of technology, as shown in Table 2.

A common theme in both studies is the recognition of the importance of taking on board the concerns of teachers from the first instance the project is initiated and giving due regard to their professional beliefs.

This area received further elaboration by Surry, Jackson, Porter, and Ensminger (2006) who describe Ely's eight conditions for implementation of educational technologies: (1) to be motivated to accept change there must be dissatisfaction

Table 2.

Category 1	Concerns of individual incompatibility
Category 2	Concerns of unknown
Category 3	Concerns of organizational support
Category 4	Concerns of organizational incompatibility

with the status quo, (2) all involved in the implementation process must have adequate skills and knowledge, along with (3) sufficient resources and (4) time to train, practice, and apply the innovation, (5) rewards and incentives exist, (6) participation in the decision-making process (7) commitment from senior management and administrators, and (8) day-to-day leadership through support, encouragement and procurement of resources, by direct managers.

It is apparent from these studies that the profile of innovators has taxed the minds of researchers for some time. Rogers and Beal (1958) make reference to the importance of personal influence in an individual's decision-making process 'In most cases the people who interact have similar values, a common level of discourse and important referents to each other' (p. 329). This would suggest that access to formal and informal networks are considered a dominant factor in innovation.

Of particular note is a subsequent study by Rogers (1963) who describes innovators as 'venturesome individuals; they desire the hazardous, the rash, the avant-garde and the risky' (p. 253). In fact he describes innovators as *cosmopolite*: the cliques and formal organisations to which they belong are likely to include other innovators. He also comments that teachers who attend out-of-town meetings are more innovative. A similar observation described by Johnson (1984) 21 years later refers to a study by Evan's into the use of interactive television. The 'pro-ITV' faculty were characterised as more pragmatic and cosmopolitan. This could be accounted for by the fact that faculty with experience outside of academia have a more cosmopolitan perspective.

The online equivalent of the 'out of town meetings' is the membership of virtual learning communities. Allan and Lewis's (2006) recent study suggests that the impact of membership of a virtual learning community is significant on individual members. Two different personal development processes were identified: (1) some members used the experience to develop confidence and expertise to support their career progression through a process of incremental changes, and (2) members at early stages in their careers appeared to work through a transformational process that enabled them to change their identity by identifying and working towards new career opportunities. Are we now witnessing the virtual or online manifestations of the same characteristics of innovators identified in earlier research? Could these experiences sow the seeds of interest for future innovations?

Oliver (2002) comments that the practices of educational technologists emphasise learning by doing, the importance of context and involve learning with an expert. A process that can be adequately described in terms of communities of practice (p. 251).

It is interesting to note that although how we innovate may have changed many of the issues and indeed the characteristics of innovators have not. Of particular interest is the importance of taking into account the beliefs and values of individuals involved in any project designed to bring change to existing approaches and methods. The next section will take a closer look at innovations in the evolving field of educational technology in the context of the knowledge economy.

THE FIELD OF EDUCATIONAL TECHNOLOGY AND THE KNOWLEDGE ECONOMY

It is apparent that an innovative academic must be nurtured and supported by their organisational structure at all levels. However this may not be sufficient as commented by Hannah (1995) 'Innovative ideas and individuals however are not always enough. At some point, the idea must be adopted and institutionalized to have an impact' (p. 222).

The dilemma for many Higher Education Institutions today is justifying why they should engage or support these activities? In particular why invest significant capital investment in educational technology and its related support and training requirements without any apparent significant return? To explore this question it is necessary to chart briefly the history of educational technology.

The last decade in particular has seen a remarkable growth and subsequent decline in the educational technology marketplace. I use the word 'marketplace' deliberately – it was the recognition that education and training could be productised that proved to be major incentive for venture capitalists. Many Irish companies led the way – and still do. CBT Systems, Financial Courseware and Electric Paper carved out an international niche in the training market place.

The technology was also developing and evolving, offering the potential of greater functionality to eager learners. The BBC Micro heralded an era of colour; the Apple Mac an intuitive graphical interface with a pointing device (mouse); optical storage such as CD-ROM offered greater storage capacity with the accompanying dynamic media such as video and animation. Our vocabulary changed to suit the evolution of the technology: Computer Based Instruction (CBI) became Computer Based Learning (CBL) to Computer Aided Learning (CAL) to Computer Based Multimedia Learning (CBML) to interactive multimedia (IM).

A similar burst of activity was in the mid-1990s as the Internet heralded a new model: E-learning had arrived. A new age of computer-mediated communications offering additional functionality to the weary stand-alone multimedia CD-ROMs. Online courses, communities and activities: in fact E with everything!

An interesting comment made by Bruce and Levin (1997) is that the classification systems used for educational technology are treated as universally valid rather than 'as a statement about a particular set of values and beliefs about technology, teaching and learning' (p. 2). The important aspect of these classifications is that each of them expresses a view of the world that has 'significant ontological, epistemological and pedagogical implications' (Bruce & Levin, 1997, p. 3). This would suggest that a person's ontological, epistemological and pedagogical views are a critical factor in their adoption of technology in an educational setting. Furthermore the marked shift in emphasis over the past decade from technology centered to a learner centered taxonomy would suggest that this area is being influenced by a greater range of practitioners offering a wider spectrum of viewpoints. The significance of this point is related to the earlier contentions that innovators tend to interact with people with similar values and that teachers will not adopt new innovations that are at odds with their professional beliefs. Classification systems can also be used to normalise ways of thinking about educational technology which in turn can lead to the production of criteria for what is deemed 'best practice'. This in turn shapes the accepted possibilities for what educational technology can be deployed to address and just as importantly which cohort of students should benefit.

Technology and in particular educational technology has largely emerged from a positivist tradition; however the current nature and use of technology with the advent of what has been termed Web 2.0 and addressing the needs of the NET-generation, has witnessed a change in emphasis. Current usage patterns are predominately in the domain of communications (e.g. email/blogs/Skype), end user content design and development (YouTube) and online communities (e.g. MySpace, bebo). This is user-driven and would suggest that current educational technology innovators are also drawn from a different discourse. A discourse that is learner centered rather than technology led. However we are still debating the benefits of educational technology using a vocabulary that has limited impact and in arenas that are not debating the core challenges facing education and society today. A language that is often driven by a narrow economic rationale, at times disguised in the language of educational pragmatism.

There are two areas where the impact of this narrow economic rationale can be seen. Firstly, education and training are now recognised as an important factor in developing and sustaining economic growth. This is a cause for concern particularly as the rise of neo-liberal politics has redefined education as a market commodity and this trend has become a key tenet of international policy discourse (Grummell, Devine, & Lynch, 2009). This is also evident in the strategic imperatives underpinning some e-learning initiatives. Education is reduced to the production of a library of learning objects to be delivered in a cost-effective manner to a population of learners whose profile fits the 'digital native' characteristics. Secondly, lifelong learning appeared to be on the political agenda, Brine (2006) refers to the EU 1996 'Year of Lifelong Learning' and the subsequent White Paper (CEC, 1995). She notes that this paper made two shifts in the discourse on lifelong learning:

The concepts of exclusion and societal risk inherent in the threat of the 'dual society' were linked with differing degrees of knowledge and two types of learner: those that know (the high-knowledge skilled) HKS and those that do not know (the low knowledge-skilled) LKS. (p. 651)

However, currently Brine (2006) contends:

Despite, the very close association of the concept of lifelong learning with the knowledge economy, there is only one lifelong learner who is directly employed in it: the high knowledge-skilled graduate and postgraduate learner, a learner who, in contrast to the low knowledge-skilled learner below, is only ever referred to in terms of educational status, and whose particular learning needs are never identified. (p. 659)

The importance of this issue for educational technologists is to question who is driving the agenda for investment in technology in higher education. At an organisational level in Ireland third-level institutes have seen enormous change in relation to governance, funding, quality assurance, National Qualifications Frameworks and performance management systems. Metrics exist which will measure our success: throughput, retention, unit costs and funding. The integration of IT systems is already a hallmark of most Institutions: student registration, e-marketing, financial control and e-mail. E-learning fits neatly into this array of technology.

There is a danger that developments and support for e-learning will be viewed as another tool in a bureaucratic framework that will foster suspicion rather than innovation. According to the Observatory on Borderless Higher Education (OBHE) resistance by faculty members to e-learning can be explained 'by a lack of time or motivation to carry out what is basically an additional task, since e-learning mostly supplements rather than replaces classroom based teaching' (OECD, 2005, p. 5).

Another development that could inhibit innovation is the imposition of an 'audit culture':

Much of the literature on innovation in higher education is often written from the perspective of change advocates rather than from the point of view of the persons – usually faculty members

– who are expected to implement change. Consequently behavior that does not affirm a particular innovation may be labeled 'non-innovative' and regarded as the root of the problem, whereas the difficulties may actually lie either in the innovation itself or in other factors, such as characteristics of the academic organization. (Johnson, 1984, p. 496)

This is also echoed in the work of Grummell et al. (2009) who state that 'The highly individualised capitalist-inspired entrepreneurialism that is at the heart of the new academy has allowed old masculinities to remake themselves and maintain hegemonic male advantage' (p. 192). Academics must now show the relevance of their work in relation to new institutional mission statements, a feature that is 'generating a mixture of anomie and alienation' (Beck & Young, 2005, p. 184). This concern is also raised by Barcan (1996) who describes contemporary academics as situated within three different models of professional practise, i.e. scholarly, bureaucratic and managerial/corporate. However, the scholarly model sits uncomfortably with the service-provider model which promulgates the neo-liberal values of individualism and performativity. Beck and Young (2005) contend that probably those who have 'felt most traumatized and hostile to marketization' (p. 194) would have enjoyed high levels of autonomy earlier in their careers. The very ingredient needed to foster innovation in a public organisation.

It could be argued that innovation and innovators are being 'colonised' by the normative processes and discourses of quality and accountability. Barcan (1996) contends that the requirements of the evaluation system soon comprise the academic practices under scrutiny: 'practices change in order to meet the evaluation criteria' (p. 1). The ease of increasing the number of registered students on an online course may be the main criterion that dictates a continuation of funding and support by management rather than assessing its suitability as an optimal learning environment for a group of

adult learners. Similar commentary is offered by Fleming (2008) who refers to the 'inappropriate deployment of technology' and how e-learning offers another example of 'how system imperatives can invade pedagogical practice' (p. 8).

Clearly, the juxtaposition of educational technology, innovation and higher education provides a fertile ground for discussion and debate. The research agenda in relation to educational technology has largely been dominated by investigations into all aspects of the technology: educational technologists are often criticised for being too concerned by the next 'shiny new gadget'. This is also echoed by Seidensticker (2006) who comments in his book *Future Hype*: 'The result is that we don't see technology clearly; we don't soberly weigh today's new development against the technologies we already have. The value of today's technology is inflated, and some revaluation is needed to restore a balance' (p. 9).

Issroff and Scanlan (2002) refer to the work of Rowntree, one of the initial Open University innovators, describing educational technology as concerned with the design and evaluation of curricula and learning experiences and with the problems of implementing and renovating them. This is a very utilitarian view with no apparent scope for considering theory or indeed any underlying philosophy of education. However by the 1980s there was a noticeable shift. Issroff and Scanlan (2002) referring to the work of O'Shea and Self who suggested that educational technology was a branch of the behavioural sciences, which currently carries no commitment to any particular theory of learning.

Educational technologists would not therefore consider the computer as just another piece of equipment. If educational technology is concerned with thinking carefully about teaching and learning, then a computer has a contribution to make irrespective of its use as a means of implementation, for the design of computer based learning environments gives us a new perspective on the nature of teaching and learning and indeed on general educational objectives. (p. 3)

This redefined educational technology within the domain of teaching and learning, a domain that encourages self-reflection and the articulation of personal beliefs and theories with regard to pedagogy. Hammond (2003) also contends that 'Traditional ideas about pedagogy are already under question both through ICT use and through other demands on the HE system' (p. 12).

So how can we encourage educational technologists to give voice to their values, beliefs, and motivations within the context of a rapidly changing higher education sector? The next section will attempt to answer this question by proposing that the habitus of educational technologists could be the key to unlocking the answer to this question.

BOURDIEU, HABITUS AND EDUCATIONAL TECHNOLOGY

Habitus is a concept that mediates between relatively structured social relations and relatively 'objectified' forms of social agency or interest (Sterne, 2003). The term 'field' is used to describe 'groups of interrelated social actors, and 'capital' to describe the specific forms of agency and prestige within a given field'.

As argued above one of the challenges facing the field of educational technology is to capture the collective sense of assumptions and presuppositions which contribute to the motivations, values and beliefs of many of the innovators in higher education today. According to Webb, Schirato, and Danaher (2005):

Each field (medicine, philosophy, law, politics, economics) has its own set of discourses and styles of language, and that not only determines what is seen (for instance, philosophy tends to exclude the social, medicine tends to exclude abstractions),

but what things are valued, what questions can be asked, and what ideas can be thought. (p. 13)

Turning our gaze on the field of educational technology may allow us to answer these questions. To identify what things are valued by educational technologists; to identify the questions we are not asking and to ask what ideas can be thought.

According to Jenkins (2002):

a field in Bourdieu's sense, is a social arena within which struggles or manoeuvres take place over specific resources or stakes and access to them.... A field, therefore, is a structured system of social positions – occupied either by individuals or institutions – the nature of which defines the situation for their occupants. It is also a system of forces which exist between these positions; a field is structured internally in terms of power relations. Positions stand in relationships of domination, subordination or equivalence (homology) to each other by virtue of the access they afford to the goods or resources (capital) which are at stake in the field. (p. 84)

The field of educational technology is witnessing a number of developments that represent these 'struggles or manoeuvres'. Examples include attempts to define standards for learning objects and the associated accreditation of academic staff as teaching and learning 'experts'. The struggle could be viewed as exercising control over not just how learning is packaged – but who will be authorised to do the packaging and how. Bourdieu recognises that the game that occurs in social spaces or fields is competitive, with various social agents using differing strategies to maintain or improve their position (Thomson, 2008, p. 69). Within this struggle Bourdieu (1991, p. 229) has identified that 'These goods can be principally differentiated into four categories: economic capital, social capital (various kinds of valued relations with significant others), cultural capital (primarily legitimate knowledge of one kind or another) and symbolic capital (prestige and social honour)' (p. 229).

Within the educational technology field examples of social, symbolic and cultural capital are evident. For example social capital could comprise membership of various communities of practice and representative organisations in the related fields of education and technology; cultural capital is evident in the struggle to gain formal recognition of teaching and learning knowledge and associated learning technologies; whilst symbolic capital is the authentication of 'best practice' either through the awarding of credentials following the successful completion of accredited programmes of study or alternatively in judgements made at national competitions which acknowledge particular innovative accomplishments. However, this dynamic within a field is to be expected as Webb, Schirato, and Danaher (2005) have stated: 'Not only is the identity of a particular field always up for grabs to a certain extent but, as a corollary, so its relation to the social and political spheres of society'.

The concept of a field is further complicated by the recognition that people occupy more than one social field at a time (Thomson, 2008). Currently, the field of educational technology often appears as a collection of individuals without any shared values or beliefs brought together by a common interest in technology. On other occasions a common set of fundamental principles about education in general are apparent. However there is no doubt that the field has its own distinct 'logic of practice'. As Thomson explains, 'It is a human construction with its own set of beliefs (or theodicies), which rationalize the rules of field behavior: each field has its own distinctive 'logic of practice' (p.70).

Similarly, Jenkins (2002) has suggested that the existence of a field creates a belief on the part of participants in the legitimacy and value of the capital which is at stake in the field. The estab-lishment of Centres for 'Teaching and Learning' (there are various other titles in vogue) which often control and direct the activities of the field in many higher education institutes would suggest a form of 'legitimacy' in the apparent formal recognition by the 'field of power'. The 'field of power' is Bourdieu's term to represent the dominant or pre-eminent field in any society; it is the source of the hierarchical power relations which structure all other fields (Jenkins, 2002, p. 86).

The field of educational technology is clearly dependent on other subfields: e.g. quality assurance, finance, research, academic departments, teachers unions, government policy, demographics. As noted by Thomson (2008, p. 73) 'the fields that make up the field of power are not all on a level playing field: some are dominant and the game in subordinate fields is often dependent on activity in another'. One possible representation of the field of educational technology and its various relationships with other dominant and associated sub-fields is shown in Figure 1.

What is not captured in Figure 1 is the dynamic ever-changing characteristics of the field. These external factors include current government policies in relation to the creation of the knowledge society; the parallel requirements of needing to up-skill those in employment and now the even greater challenge of addressing the needs of the unemployed. Much of this agenda is predicated on a need for greater flexibility which could be met by deploying technology.

The field is the crucial mediating context wherein external factors–changing circumstances–are brought to bear upon individual practice and institutions. The logic, politics and structure of the field shape and channel the manner in which 'external determinations' affect what goes on within the field, making them appear a part of the ongoing history and operation of the field itself (Jenkins, 2002, p. 86).

This now leads to the important question of how we can use Bourdieu's concept of field to further explore the 'world' of educational technology. To

Figure 1. The Field of Educational Technology in Higher Education

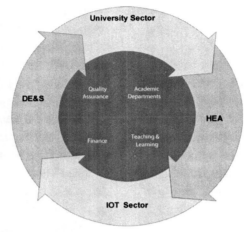

DE&S: **Department of Education and Science**
IOT : **Institutes of Technology**
HEA : **Higher Education Authority**

do this Bourdieu has suggested that his field must be understood as a scholastic device–an epistemological and methodological heuristic–which helps researchers to devise methods to make sense of the world. (Thomson, 2008, p. 74). He was also adamant that the notion of 'field' was not a system:

A field is a game devoid of inventor and much more fluid and complex than any game that one might ever design ... to see fully everything that separates the concepts of field and system one must put them to work and compare them via the empirical objects they produce. (Bourdieu & Wacquant, 1992, p. 104)

The concepts of habitus, field and capital constitute the most successful attempt to make sense of the relationship between objective social structures (institutions, discourses, fields and ideologies) and everyday practices, i.e. what people do and why they do it.

The next section will examine Bourdieu's concept of habitus as an additional lens with which to examine the identity of educational technologists.

THE HABITUS OF EDUCATIONAL TECHNOLOGISTS

Connolly (2004) contends that for Bourdieu 'our internalised modes of thought are not naturally given (i.e. essentialist) but are socially constructed: developed and generated (i.e. genetic) from our lived experiences'. This is further developed by Maton (2008) who describes how the

choices we choose to make, therefore depend on the range of options available at that moment (thanks to our current context), the range of options visible to us, and on our dispositions (habitus), the embodied experiences of our journey. Our choices will then in turn shape our future possibilities, for any choice involves foregoing alternatives and sets us on a particular path that further shapes our understanding of ourselves and of the world. (p. 92)

Bourdieu also wanted to use the concept of habitus to stress its formative qualities – in other words the way it moulds and shapes behaviour. A theme also reported in Barnett & Adkins (2004), referring to the work of Wacquant, that 'The relationship between an individual and a field or domain of interest is mediated by the habitus, a collective and individual disposition that is unconsciously formed over time and exhibited through both cognitive and physical actions (p. 4).

This is a very exciting observation. As pointed out by Sterne (2003) habitus is a powerful concept because it is historical, it changes over time: our habitus confronts us as a 'kind of second nature'. Habitus can be used as 'thinking tool' to understand the predispositions of the players in the field of educational technology. It raises the question of whether it is possible that innovators share similar 'second natures'?

Connolly's (2004) view is that:

habitus incorporates a more holistic understanding of the broader dispositions that individuals come to embody and which unconsciously shape and guide not only the way they think and behave but also the particular investments they have in certain forms of knowledge and ways of acting. (p. 87)

Many educational technologists have contributed to the development of the field: for some this has been based on their own technology-related backgrounds which recognised applications in the education domain. Others have been attracted to the field through their own positions within education and allied interests in pedagogical research. In addition individuals with skills sets from commercial multimedia or e-learning companies have found new opportunities within the academic field. This rich tapestry of backgrounds and expertise within a field was anticipated by Bourdieu:

Social agents do not arrive in a field fully armed with god-like knowledge of the state of play, the positions, beliefs and aptitudes of other social agents, or the full consequences of their actions. Rather they enjoy a particular point of view on proceedings based on their positions, and they learn the tempo, rhythms and unwritten rules of

the game through time and experience. (Maton, 2008, p. 54)

According to Morrison (2005), Bourdieu's habitus, operating as a theory of reproduction, provides an explanation as to why teachers perpetuate practices that seem anti-educational. The imposed or self-imposed control operates to reproduce the status quo. However he also argues that in situations where new, emergent practices present themselves these are not easily explained by theories of reproduction, structuration and habitus. The habitus 'both enables creativity and constrains actions and practices' (p. 314). Sterne (2003) contends that habitus is a generative principle; it does allows for creativity and improvisation. This would suggest that the real challenge is how to examine and capture the innovative educator's habitus, rather than identifying and classifying shared characteristics of innovators as outlined in Table 1 earlier? One approach is to examine the use of theory in educational technology research. An eclectic mix with some disciplines represented including psychology, computer science and cognitive science whilst others are not, e.g. sociology, business and education. The choice of theories (and also of research cited) in papers provides an insight into the habitus of educational technology researchers (Oliver, Conole, Cook, Ravenscroft, & Currier, 2002).

Bourdieu's concept of social power comprises not just economic capital (i.e. wealth) but also cultural and symbolic capital. The accumulation of capital within a field can encourage competition between social agents operating within the same field and also between different fields. In relation to individual academic departments or faculties, Pagnucci (1998) discovered that economic capital is represented by budget allocations, cultural capital by staff qualifications and symbolic capital as the 'right' to teach a particular discipline. This struggle to accumulate capital can prove to be an obstacle in the creation of cross-disciplinary courses: Who 'owns' the cultural capital? This is also an issue for the field of educational technology which often relies on cross-discipline collaboration and inter-departmental cooperation.

Connolly's (2004) work on *Boys and schooling in the early years* provides a good example of how Bourdieu's concept of habitus can be adopted as a research method. In order to gain a better understanding of how children learn and develop through internalising the sets of social relations in which they are engaged, he used Bourdieu's concept of habitus.

Reay's (1995) research work–looking at habitus in the primary classroom–concludes that habitus is a way of looking at data that renders the 'taken for granted' problematic. For example how well adapted is the individual in the context they find themselves in? How does personal history shape their responses to the contemporary settings? These questions are just as relevant in understanding the spectrum of responses from educators in relation to adopting educational technology.

There have been a number of other interesting examples using the concept of habitus as a vehicle to explore similar issues. The areas explored have been quite diverse from Hulme's (2004) study on technology use, Reay's (1998) work on individual preferences, Dumais (2002) on participation and Atkins (2000) on views of policy makers.

Could an innovative educator's habitus be the key that unlocks the creative desires and drives innovation? This is an important question in the current context where the main 'vehicle' for fostering innovation in third level has been formalised through the establishment of Centres for Teaching and Learning. Many Centres endeavor to capture the essence of 'best practice' in pedagogy and educational technology and offer staff development programmes designed to motivate educators to adopt, adapt and innovate within their current practice. However, it is now critical that we deepen our understanding of two key areas: (i) how the portfolio of best practice knowledge has been authenticated and (ii) what are the philosophical arguments underpinning the claims of superior pedagogic approaches.

We need to investigate the habitus of the teaching and learning staff in addition to that of educators who have engaged with these staff development programmes. The hope would be that this greater understanding would not only serve to enhance our understanding of the habitus of innovative educators but would also augment the integrity of evolving academic professional development courses. Such programmes developed and delivered by staff working in or associated with Centres for Teaching and Learning could be seen to represent the new 'game' in relation to acceptable pedagogy in higher education. Academic staff engagement will reflect each academic's 'feel for the game'. However, as stated by Cunningham (1993), the 'feel' will be measured in accordance with the expectations determined by the habitus of the teaching and learning authorities.

Can educational technology transform education? I believe that it can, however, as suggested by Mezirow (1996), 'The process of transforming our frames of reference begins with critical reflection. What I mean by critical reflection is the process of assessing one's assumptions and presuppositions' (p. 2). To achieve this there is a need to create and nurture a public sphere to discuss and debate these issues and to put forward the position of educational technologists either individually or as a collective.

Webb, Schirato and Danaher (2002) have outlined how Bourdieu has tried to explain the relationship between people's practices and the context in which these practices occur. Education is the mechanism through which the values and relations that make up the social space are passed on from one generation to the next. Bourdieu also points out that while academics are disposed to turn an inquiring gaze on others, they are reluctant to turn the gaze onto themselves. There needs to be a self-reflective understanding of the person's own position and resources within the field they are operating. We need a reflexive relationship with our own practice.

An interesting account by Kleiman (2004) reflecting on key themes in an article he wrote in 2000 accepts that in many places the myths persist and progress has been limited.

The investment in technology for schools resembles the investments being made in many 'dot-com' Internet companies. In both cases, the investments are based on the potential of new technologies, in the hope that this potential will be fulfilled in the coming years. And in both cases, the investments involve significant risks and may be a long way from yielding adequate returns. (p. 7)

Interestingly he also commented that one of the key determinants will not be the number of computers purchased or cables installed but rather 'how we define educational visions, prepare and support teachers, design curriculum, address issues of equity, and respond to the rapidly changing world' (Kleiman, 2000, p. 14).

It is critical that agents in the field of educational technology are encouraged to turn an enquiring gaze on themselves. The need for a reflexive practice has never been greater. Brockbank and McGill (2007) have posed the questions What prevents practitioners investigating the impact of the very process that is supposed to promote learning? Why is there a tendency to hold back from the exploration of process?' (p. 112). Apple (1979) would claim that this is to be expected.

There is nothing very odd about the fact that we usually do not focus on the basic set of assumptions which we use. First, they are normally known only tacitly, remain unspoken, and are very difficult to formulate explicitly. Second, these basic rules are so much a part of us that they do not have to be expressed. (p. 126)

The current unthinking commitment to the logic, values and capital of a field corresponds to what Bourdieu calls 'illusio' (Webb, Schirato & Danaher, 2005, p. 26).

The agent engaged in practice knows the world ... too well, without objectifying distance, takes it for granted, precisely because he is caught up in it, bound up with it; he inhabits it like a garment ... he feels at home in the world because the world is also in him, in the form of the habitus. (Bourdieu, 2000, pp. 142–143)

A reflexive practice that exceeds the bounds of a purely technocentric discourse would allow educational technologists an opportunity to voice their views and beliefs in relation to the challenges facing higher education. The need to assert a greater influence on current policies and practices in the wider domain is of paramount importance. Rather than educational technology being viewed as simply an economically more advantageous means of 'delivering' education – a commodity exchange model endorsed by current neo-liberal policies. However, it could also be argued that the emergence of Centres for Teaching and Learning signifies that it is too late. That these developments represent, as Brookfield quoting Foucault contends, the colonisation of educational technology: 'when members of the dominant group begin to recognize that specific practices could become economically advantageous and politically useful they become colonized' (2005, p. 127).

SUMMARY

Let me now try to pull these thoughts and deliberations into some form of summary and conclusions. This chapter represents a journey of enquiry for me as I pondered this seemingly paradoxical situation of rapid change in technology with a concomitant lack of real change in education. The educational technologist inhabits both worlds—we see both sides of the coin—and for me I am quite perplexed. My own decision to return to study at NUI Maynooth has afforded me a space to reflect on why this dichotomy still persists. Technologies that can transform the world of commerce can seemingly only contribute to the reproduction of our core education systems.

The purpose of this chapter is to explore the field of educational technology from one key perspective: that of the individuals who adopt the technology and seek to change their current approaches. Whilst, innovation in education and the characteristics of the innovators has been the subject of research studies over the past decade, many of the approaches adopted attempt to identify the key characteristics of these innovative individuals. Their personal beliefs, values and motivations are often absent from the public sphere at a time when they are needed to contribute to the debate on the future direction of education and the role that educational technology can play. The challenge is to establish how best to investigate the habitus of this group. The vista of educational technology failing to yield a rich harvest of tools and technologies and enthused educators intent on transforming education is sufficient motivation to encourage further investigation into this field of dreams.

The key points for consideration that arise from previous research and literature are:

- Our professional beliefs can inhibit innovation.
- Our education system as structured is perpetuating current inequities.
- We place too much emphasis on the 'next shiny gadget'.
- We fail to express our underlying motivations and values, and so need to reflect on our own personal beliefs and values.
- Centres for Teaching and Learning have emerged as the main vehicles for innovation.
- We need to debate and articulate the WHY and not always the HOW.
- We need to restore the balance and flow between education and technology.
- Educational technology has not had a transformative impact on education.

- The field of educational technology needs to encourage a critical reflective practice.

There is an opportunity for educational technology to become a radical force in the transformation of education. We must become advocates for change and not simply a cog in the wheels of reproduction. We need to put the 'I' back into educational technology – we need to articulate the rationale in human terms. We need to capture our own beliefs and views and give voice to them. Rather than to assume that the technology will speak for us.

REFERENCES

Allan, B., & Lewis, D. (2006). The impact of membership of a virtual learning community on individual learning careers and professional identity. *British Journal of Educational Technology*, 37(6), 841–852. doi:10.1111/j.1467-8535.2006.00661.x

Apple, M. W. (1979). *Ideology and curriculum*. London: Routledge & Kegan Paul. doi:10.4324/9780203241219

Atkins, C. (2000). Lifelong learning – attitudes to practice in the rural context: A study using Bourdieu's perspective of habitus. *International Journal of Lifelong Learning*, 19(3), 253–265.

Barcan, R. (1996). The Body of the (Humanities) Academic, or, 'What is an Academic'. *Australian Humanities Review, 1*(3) September/November. Retrieved October 20, 2009, from http://www.australianhumanitiesreview.org/archive/Issue-Sept-1996/barcan.html

Barnett, K., & Adkins, B. (2004). Engaging with the future: Older learners see the potential of computers for their lifestyle interests. Paper presented at *Social Change in the 21st Century Conference*. Queensland University of Technology: Centre for Social Change Research. Retrieved October 20, 2009, from http://eprints.qut.edu.au/643/1/barnett_adkins.pdf

Beck, J., & Young, M. (2005). The assault on the professions and the restructuring of academic and professional identities: A Bernsteinian analysis. *British Journal of Sociology of Education, 26*(2), 183–197. doi:10.1080/0142569042000294165

Bourdieu, P. (1990). The logic of practice (R. Nice, trans.). Cambridge: Polity Press. (Originally published 1980 as Le Sens pratique. Paris: Les Editions de Minuit.)

Bourdieu, P. (1991). *Language and symbolic power.* Cambridge: Polity Press.

Bourdieu, P. (2000). Pascalian meditations (R. Nice, trans.). Cambridge: Polity Press. (Originally published 1997 as Meditations pascaliennes. Paris: Seuil.)

Bourdieu, P., & Wacquant, L. (1992). An invitation to reflexive sociology. (L. Wacquant, trans.). Cambridge: Polity Press. (Originally published 1992 as Responses: Pour une anthropologie reflexive. Paris: Seuil.)

Brine, J. (2006, October). Lifelong learning and the knowledge economy: Those that know and those that do not – the discourse of the European Union. *British Journal of Educational Research, 32*(5), 649–665. .doi:10.1080/01411920600895676

Brockbank, A., & McGill, I. (2007). *Facilitating reflective learning in higher education* (2nd ed.). London: Open University Press, McGraw Hill Education.

Brookfield, S. D. (2005). *The power of critical theory for adult learning and teaching.* Berkshire, England: Open University Press.

Bruce, B. C., & Levin, J. A. (1997). Educational technology: Media for inquiry, communication, construction and expression. *Journal of Educational Computing Research, 17*(1), 79–102.

Connolly, P. (2004). *Boys and schooling in the early years. Abingdon.* Oxon, UK: Routledge-Falmer, Taylor and Francis Group.

Craft, A. (2000). *Continuing professional development: A practical guide for teachers and schools* (2nd ed.). New York: Routledge Falmer. doi:10.4324/9780203420041

Crawford, C. M., & Gannon-Cook, R. (2002). *Faculty attitudes towards distance education: Enhancing the support and rewards system for innovative integration of technology within coursework.* Paper presented at 13th International Conference of the Society for Information Technology & Teacher Education. Nashville, TN. Retrieved March 4, 2007, from http://www.eric.ed.gov/ERICDocs/data/ericdocs2sql/content_storage_01/0000019b/80/1a/99/d5.pdf

Cunningham, J. (1993). Habitus and misrecognition: An essay in response to Scahill. *Philosophy of Education.* University of Illinois Urbana-Champaign College of Education, Philosophy of Education Society 1996-2004. Retrieved September 8, 2007, from http://www.ed.uiuc.edu/EPS/PES-Yearbook/93_docs/CUNNINGH.HTM

Davis, R. H. (1979, March). A behavioral change model with implications for faculty development. *Higher Education, 8*(2), 123–140. .doi:10.1007/BF00138376

Dumais, S. A. (2002, January). Cultural capital, gender, and school success: The role of habitus. [from http://socofedcomps.wikispaces.com/file/view/cult+capital+and+habitus+quant+article.pdf]. *Sociology of Education, 75*(1), 44–68. Retrieved September 17, 2007. doi:10.2307/3090253

Fleming, T. (2008). We are condemned to learn: Towards higher education as a learning society. *DIT-Level3, 6*(1). Retrieved October 20, 2009, from http://level3.dit.ie/html/issue6/fleming/fleming_1.html

Goodman, A. (2003). *Now what? Developing our future: Understanding our place in the unfolding universe.* New York: Peter Lang Publishing.

Gosling, D. (2008, February). *Educational development in the UK*. Retrieved November 4, 2009, from Heads of Educational Development Group (HEDG) website http://www.hedg.ac.uk/documents/HEDG_Report_Final.pdf

Grummell, B., Devine, D., & Lynch, K. (2009). The care-less manager: Gender, care and new managerialism in higher education. *Gender and Education, 21*(2), 191–208. doi:10.1080/09540250802392273

Gunter, H. M. (2000, December). Thinking Theory: The field of education management in England and Wales. *British Journal of Sociology of Education, 21*(4), 623-635. Retrieved December 6, 2006, from JSTOR database http://www.jstor.org/pss/1393386

Hammond, N. (2003). Learning technology in higher education in the UK: Trends, drivers and strategies. In M. van der Wende and M. van der Ven (Eds.), *The use of ICT in higher education: A mirror of Europe* (pp. 109–122). Utrecht: Lemma Publishers. Retrieved October 20, 2009, from http://www.psychology.heacademy.ac.uk/Publications/HammondMirror2003.pdf

Hannah, S. B. (1995, December). The correlates of innovation: Lessons form best practice. *Public Productivity & Management Review, 19*(2), 216–228. doi:10.2307/3380499

Hulme, M. K. (2004). Examining inter-space: A working paper exploring Bourdieu's concepts of 'habitus' and 'field' in relations to mobility related empirical research. Centre for the Study of Media, Technology and Culture. Retrieved November 4, 2009, from http://www.lancs.ac.uk/fass/centres/cemore/pastevents/altmobs/hulme.doc

Issroff, K., & Scanlon, E. (2002). Educational technology: The influence of theory. *Journal of Interactive Media in Education,* 2002(6). Retrieved from www-jime.open.ac.uk/2002/6

Jenkins, R. (2002). *Pierre Bourdieu. Abingdon.* Oxon, UK: Routledge. (Original work published 1992)

Johnson, L. G. (1984). Faculty receptivity to an innovation: A study of attitudes toward external degree programs. *The Journal of Higher Education, 55*(4), 481–499. doi:10.2307/1981444

Kanuka, H., & Kelland, K. (2008). Has e-learning delivered on its promises? Expert opinion on the impact of e-learning in higher education. *Canadian Journal of Higher Education, 38*(1), 45–65.

Kirschner, P. A., Hendricks, M., Paas, F., Wopereis, I., & Cordewener, B. (2004, October). Determinants for failure and success of innovation projects: The road to sustainable educational innovation. Paper given at *27th Association for Educational Communications and Technology*. Retrieved March 4, 2007, from http://www.eric.ed.gov/ERICDocs/data/ericdocs2sql/content_storage_01/0000019b/80/1b/a7/36.pdf

Kleiman, G. M. (2000). Myths and realities about technology in K-12 Schools . In Gordon, D. T. (Ed.), *The digital classroom. How technology is changing the way we teach and learn.* Cambridge, MA: The Harvard Education Letter.

Kleiman, G. M. (2004). Myths and realities about technology in k-12 schools: Five years later. *Contemporary Issues in Technology and Teacher Education, 4*(2). Retrieved October 20, 2009, from http://www.citejournal.org/vol4/iss2/seminal/article2.cfm

Lee, H. (2001, November). Teachers' perceptions of technology: Four categories of concerns. Paper given at *24th National Convention of the Association for Educational Communications and Technology: Vols. 1–2. Annual Proceedings of Selected Research and Development [and] Practice Papers* (pp. 239-244). Atlanta GA. Retrieved March 4, 2007, from http://www.eric.ed.gov/ERICDocs/data/ericdocs2sql/content_storage_01/0000019b/80/1a/85/fc.pdf

Lynch, K. (2006). Neo-liberalism and marketisation: The implications for higher education. *European Educational Research Journal, 5*(1), 1–14. doi:10.2304/eerj.2006.5.1.1

Maton, K. (2008). Habitus. In Grenfell, M. (Ed.), *Pierre Bourdieu key concepts* (pp. 49–66). Stocksfield, UK: Acumen Publishing Ltd.

Mezirow, J. (1996). Adult education and empowerment for individual and community development. In Connolly, B., Fleming, T., McCormack, D., & Ryan, A. (Eds.), *Radical learning for liberation. Maynooth Adult and Community Education Occasional Series No. 1. Maynooth: MACE.*

Morrison, K. (2005, July). Structuration theory, habitus and complexity theory: Elective affinities or old wine in new bottles? *British Journal of Sociology of Education, 26*(3), 311–326. .doi:10.1080/01425690500128809

Murphy, M., & Fleming, T. (2006). The application of the ideas of Habermas to adult learning. In Sutherland, P., & Crowther, J. (Eds.), *Lifelong learning: Concepts and contexts* (pp. 48–57). London: Routledge.

OECD. (2005). *E-learning in tertiary education: Where do we stand?* Paris: Organisation for Economic Cooperation and Development.

Oliver, M. (2002). What do learning technologists do? *Innovations in Education and Teaching International, 39*(4), 245–252. doi:10.1080/13558000210161089

Oliver, M., Conole, G., Cook, J., Ravenscroft, A., & Currier, S. (2002). Multiple perspectives and theoretical dialogue in learning technology. In *ASCILITE 2002 Proceedings*. Retrieved April 2, 2007, from http://www.ascilite.org.au/conferences/auckland02/proceedings/papers/075.pdf

Pagnucci, G. S. (1998). Crossing borders and talking tech: Educational challenges. *Theory into Practice, 37*(1), 46-53. Retrieved March 4, 2007, from JSTOR database http://www.jstor.org/pss/1477512

Reay, D. (1995). 'They employ cleaners to do that': Habitus in the primary classroom. *British Journal of Sociology of Education, 16*(3), 353–371. doi:10.1080/0142569950160305

Reay, D. (1998). 'Always knowing' and 'never being sure': Familial and institutional habituses and higher education choice. *Journal of Education Policy, 13*(4), 519–529. .doi:10.1080/0268093980130405

Robertson, J. W. (2003). Stepping out of the box: Rethinking the failure of ICT to transform schools. *Journal of Educational Change, 4*, 323–344. doi:10.1023/B:JEDU.0000006047.67433.c5

Rogers, E. M. (1963). What are innovators like? *Theory into Practice, 2*(5), 252–256. doi:10.1080/00405846309541872

Rogers, E. M., & Beal, G. M. (1958). The importance of personal influence in the adoption of technological changes. *Social Forces, 36*(4), 329–335. doi:10.2307/2573971

Seidensticker, B. (2006). *Future hype: The myths of technology change.* San Francisco: Berrett-Koehler Publishers.

Sterne, J. (2003). Bourdieu, technique and technology. [from http://sterneworks.org/BourdieuTechandTech.pdf]. *Cultural Studies, 17*(3/4), 367–389. Retrieved April 2, 2007.

Surry, D. W., Jackson, M. K., Porter, B. E., & Ensminger, D. C. (2006). An analysis of the relative importance of Ely's Eight Implementation Conditions. [Online] Retrieved March 4, 2007, from http://www.eric.ed.gov/ERICDocs/data/ericdocs2sql/content_storage_01/0000019b/80/1b/cf/1f.pdf

Thomson, P. (2008). Field . In Grenfell, M. (Ed.), *Pierre Bourdieu key concepts* (pp. 67–84). Stocksfield, UK: Acumen Publishing Ltd.

Uhl, K., & Poulsen, L. (1970). How are laggards different? An empirical inquiry. *Journal of Marketing Research, 7*(1), 51-54. Retrieved March 4, 2007, from JSTOR database http://www.jstor.org/pss/3149506

Webb, J., Schirato, T., & Danaher, G. (2002). *Understanding Bourdieu.* London: Sage Publications.

ADDITIONAL READING

Bonal, X. (2003). The neoliberal educational agenda and the legitimation crisis: Old and new state strategies. *British Journal of Sociology of Education, 24*(2), 159–175. doi:10.1080/01425690301897

Fleming, T. (2000). Habermas, democracy and civil society: Unearthing the social in transformative learning. In Wiessner, C., Meyer, S., & Fuller, D. (Eds.), *Challenges of practice: Transformative learning in action* (pp. 303–308). New York: Columbia University.

Mezirow, J. (2006). An overview on transformative learning . In Sutherland, P., & Crowther, J. (Eds.), *Lifelong learning: Concepts and contexts* (pp. 24–39). London: Routledge.

Reay, D. (2005). Thinking class, making class. *British Journal of Sociology of Education, 26*(1), 139–143. .doi:10.1080/0142569042000305496

Section 2
Effective Tools:
Web 2.0 and Beyond

Chapter 6
The Management and Creation of Knowledge:
Do Wikis Help?

Catherine Bruen
Trinity College Dublin, Ireland

Noel Fitzpatrick
Dublin Institute of Technology, Ireland

Paul Gormley
National University of Ireland at Galway, Ireland

Jen Harvey
Dublin Institute of Technology, Ireland

Claire McAvinia
National University of Ireland at Maynooth, Ireland

ABSTRACT

Wikis are frequently cited in higher education research as appropriate and powerful web spaces which provide opportunities to capture, discuss, and review individual, group, project or organisational activities. These activities, in turn, offer possibilities for knowledge development by utilising wiki collaborative active spaces. The chapter uses selected case studies to illustrate the use of wikis to support online community based tasks, project development/processes, collaborative materials development and various student and peer supported activities. A key focus of the chapter is on evaluating the effectiveness (or otherwise) of wikis to create online communities to support knowledge management, development, retention and transfer. By way of contextualising the studies, a variety of examples of the use of wikis in higher education are reviewed. While there are relatively few studies of the use of Web 2.0 for the creation of knowledge, there are a number of reports which indicate the preference for the use of Web 2.0 technologies over the standard virtual learning environments. The chapter concludes with a review of the emergent themes arising and lessons learned from the case studies. This leads into a series of recommendations relating to the effective establishment, design, management and use of wikis to support knowledge creation and collaborative enterprise.

DOI: 10.4018/978-1-61520-879-1.ch006

INTRODUCTION

Second generation web technologies, including podcasting, blogs, and wikis, are increasingly being used in higher education (HE) both to support and capture processes employed across a range of different kinds of project-based collaborative activities. Lamb (2004) argues that these emergent technologies are starting to fill a gap in existing practice not filled by other institutional systems, while Dede (2008) suggests that Web 2.0 technologies are redefining how, what, and with whom, we learn. But is the full potential of these new technologies being fully realised within these institutional settings? Can and are these new online spaces affording users with the opportunity to create new knowledge easily as a collaborative enterprise, or are these technologies just being used as cost-efficient knowledge management systems?

CHAPTER OVERVIEW

This chapter focuses on how wikis might influence the creation and management of knowledge in HE. A wiki is defined as 'a freely expandable collection of interlinked web pages, a hypertext system for storing and modifying information–a database where each page is easily editable by any user with a forms-capable Web Browser client' (Leuf & Cunningham, 2001). Wikis' flexibility, adaptability and potential for increased functionality via Web 2.0 plug-and-play features, has led to their adoption across a wide range of social, educational and business contexts. Wikis are easy to create, use and deploy. Wiki support and functionality is available for mainstream virtual learning environments (VLEs) such as Blackboard, WebCT and Moodle, either integrated within the VLE or provided via third-party plug-ins. Many free providers, for example PBWorks (http://www.pbworks.com), offer free wikis with excellent usability and functionality, including content management functionality and storage space.

This chapter will present and describe selected case studies illustrating the use of wikis to support online community based tasks, project processes, collaborative materials development, and various student and peer supported activities. The intention within each of the case studies was to use a wiki to support the collaborative creation of new knowledge as an ongoing process. Structured and unstructured online activities were combined with face-to-face meetings. The level of experience of using Web 2.0 technologies varied: some of the wiki designers had limited or no experience of using wikis to support community development, but all had extensive experience of supporting online community development. Many of the users had never worked online as part of a group. A key question for the authors was to evaluate the effectiveness (or otherwise) of wikis to create online communities to support knowledge management (development, retention and transfer).

The chapter concludes with a review of the emergent themes arising and lessons learned from the case studies. These focus on the affordances of the technology, the collaborative nature of the tasks and how these facilitated engagement by users and explores whether these resulted in the co-construction of new knowledge. A series of recommendations relating to the effective establishment, design, management and use of wikis to support knowledge creation and collaborative enterprise concludes this chapter.

THEORETICAL UNDERPINNINGS

In pedagogical terms, a key attraction of using wikis is that their structure is shaped from within, rather than being imposed from above by proprietary institutional systems. Therefore, users do not have to adapt their practice to the 'dictates of a system', but can allow their practice to define the structure of that system instead (Lamb, 2004). It could be argued, therefore, that wikis provide a technology which is more akin to the development of a socio-constructivist pedagogical approach in HE than traditional virtual learning environments.

Wikis as a Way to Support Socio-Constructivist Pedagogical Approaches

The predominant philosophy of education, or psychological theory of learning, underpinning technology-enhanced learning is social constructivism. Constructivism, as a theory of learning is prevalent across higher education in its attempts to move away from traditional approaches to learning and teaching. The widespread adoption of technology-enhanced learning by higher education institutions is lauded as part of this paradigm shift towards a more student-centred approach to learning and teaching. However, constructivism should be seen as continuum encompassing radical constructivism, social constructivism and cognitivism (Jordan, Carlile, & Stack, 2008). The characteristics of social constructivism, which at first glance appear to align themselves with Web 2.0 technologies, are cooperative learning and knowledge building. The move towards more participative web technologies such as wikis has opened up a space for what is referred to as Learning 2.0 (Seeley Brown & Alder, 2008) where learning is characterised by content creation, critical thinking and collaboration.

The creation of content on the internet is no longer the remit of a few well-briefed HTML handlers but is available to anyone who can navigate through the web. By the very nature of wikis, participants can collaborate, create and reflect together in an online environment. This change in emphasis from Publication to Participation further reflects the paradigm shift towards student centred learning. The affordances of Web 2.0 technologies, it would appear, might enable such a move to take place. The responsibility is on the students/users to collaborate and create

together. Though the use of wikis in higher education is becoming more and more widespread and has become a particular area of interest for educationalists, their use is also highlighting certain fundamental paradoxes around the use of social constructivist learning in higher education. Epistemological questions about the nature of knowledge come to the fore when academia is required to revisit questions of ownership of 'content' and who is creating the 'content.'

The adaptive and 'constructivist' nature of wikis make them an interesting technology to investigate, particularly as research indicates that wikis may provide the potential to adapt and support a range of teaching, learning, research and organisational activities in HE. However, the use of Web 2.0 technologies within higher education does pose questions about the nature of knowledge within academia, and how such technologies support co-construction of knowledge. Dede (2008) cites a Web 2.0 definition of knowledge as being a 'collective agreement about a description that may combine facts with other dimensions of human experience, such as opinions, values, and spiritual beliefs' (p. 80); where traditionally new knowledge is seen as being created through 'formal, evidence-based argumentation, using elaborate methodologies to generate findings and interpretations' (p. 80).

Wikis and the Characteristics of Community Processes

Before presenting the case studies, and any consideration of how wikis can support community processes, it is important to highlight some of the indicators demonstrated in research as denoting 'community.' According to Wenger, the concept of community is demonstrated by positive interdependence, combination of individuals to generate group responses, mutual engagement, shared understanding of 'rules and tools' (Wenger, 1998). Preece (2000) emphasizes the importance of trust, collaboration, style of communication and different stages of online community development. Goodfellow (2005) cites a sense of belonging, expected learning and obligation. Specifically in relation to learning, Palloff and Pratt (2005) comment that '[a] community can provide the social interaction and relationships which are essential for learners to collaboratively construct social shared knowledge.'

Wikis can support community-based activities in a variety of ways (Choy & Ng, 2007; Doolan 2006; Grierson, Nicol, Littlejohn, & Wodehouse, 2004; Jones, 2007; Raman, Ryan, & Olfman 2005). Studies describe the need to create a healthy community (Shirky, 2008) and to be aware of the importance of building trust–buying into the wiki ideology is evident (Lamb, 2004). A wiki in the hands of a healthy community works. A wiki in the hands of an indifferent community fails. Elgort, Smith, and Toland (2008) also identify that student attitudes to group work, in general, are mixed, and that the use of wikis per se is not enough to improve these attitudes.

Staff and students have a range of perceptions about, and responses to wikis as part of their teaching and learning activities, particularly as part of assessed programmes. For example, lecturers have expressed concern about a lack of control over authoring: 'If anybody can edit my text, then anybody can ruin my text.' A lack of hard security and privacy are also commonly cited, as is a lack of a predefined structure and organisation as users become familiarised with what is perceived as a different way of working. While wiki systems are fully transparent, user issues regarding ownership and intellectual property rights can arise if clear policy guidelines or ways of working are not pre-defined. Logical context may be gleaned by checking the list of 'recent changes' on the wiki system, or by following links in and out, however, first-time users can experience an initial feeling of disorientation (Lamb, 2004). It is suggested that for effective use of a wiki to support learning (as in any learning design process) clear goals and learning outcomes need to be made explicit to learners in advance. Then, learning resources, supports and structured activities should be put in place and made easily accessible (Powazek, 2002).

Lamb (2004) comments that wikis function in a way that perhaps contrasts with traditional lecturer-controlled approaches to online group based activities, and for wikis to fulfil their promise, 'the participants need to be in control of the content–you have to give it over fully. This process involves not just adjusting the technical configuration and delivery, it involves challenging the social norms and practices of the course as well' (Lamb, 2004, p. 45).

Similar to the experience with other online systems in HE settings, a perception of less academic rigour is noted by some users. Meaningful learning, and the control underpinning learning processes, become the responsibility of the group rather than residing with the lecturer. Often, the full and optimal functionality of wikis is not used, perhaps as a result of a lack of familiarity with the technology or way of working. Wikis might only be used as a bulletin board rather than a collaborative enterprise, if this is the established way of working. Shirky (2008) observes that the software makes no attempt to add 'process' in order to keep people from doing stupid things.

WIKI CASE STUDY INTRODUCTION

Rationale for Case Study Selection and Analysis

A narrow sample of higher education implementations of wikis include: student individual ePortfolio development; student group case study analysis and reporting (e.g. in Medical studies for patient cases, and in Commerce studies for organisational marketing projects); as staff development training resources (e.g. as a 'Useful Resources' repository for trainers and participants, and as a collaborative space to develop participant case studies); and across virtual organisations for project management and information dissemination. The authors have each been involved in the development and implementation of wikis for teaching and learning, professional development, and project management. We have therefore selected five case studies which represent each of these areas of work. From these case studies, a number of factors influencing effective usage of wikis for higher education will be identified. We consider whether and how roles and responsibilities should be delegated. In line with other studies the importance of nature/authenticity of task, familiarity/use of technology and wiki functions, time and support provided for use, and the relevance of usage of the wiki will also be considered.

As will be seen from the case studies, not all community-based activities were supported through their wikis. Online activities were combined with face-to-face meetings. Our discussion will explore how these online communities and selected tasks have functioned. How was community evidenced? Patterns of wiki usage by the communities and the effect of various interventions will be explored—identifying features that have worked well. The case studies include commentaries relating to the way in which the communities were formed, when and how the wikis were used to support community-based processes and how these were supported. We examine how the wiki activities were tailored by the originator, and then altered as the community evolved. How have the different communities utilised/personalised the different wiki functionalities in order to further develop a sense of ownership over their online space?

Case Study Overview

The case studies that follow describe the creation of online communities to support student learning, professional development, and project management. All are concerned either with knowledge management or development. See Table 1.

The case studies are derived from different kinds of community:

1. A group of students learning in an interdisciplinary context
2. A group of staff and student representatives authoring a document collaboratively
3. A formally convened national network for learning in HE
4. A sub-group of partners from a national e-learning project
5. A national network of e-learning practitioners, formed separately from funded projects or initiatives, and independent of any HE institution

FIVE WIKI CASE STUDIES

Case Study 1. Operations Strategy: Third-Level Interdisciplinary Collaborative Student Learning

The increasing need for effective collaboration among third-level interdisciplinary groups suggests the necessity of developing teaching pedagogy that infuses teaching techniques with technologies. This case study analyses an undergraduate target module titled '0809-IE319: Operations Strategy' which has been developed by Dr Mary Dempsey at the National University of Ireland, Galway (NUIG). The course develops students' expertise in innovation. It also seeks to provide opportunities for students to meet with colleagues from other cultures. The Operations Strategy module combines approximately 40 third- and fourth-year Business and Engineering students from Ireland (58%), EU States (29%), the USA (10%) and the Far East (3%) comprising 55% female and 45% male students. A key element of the student learning environment centres on individual, small group and whole group activities aimed at developing problem-solving approaches

Table 1. Potential Factors contributing towards effective use of case study wikis

	Case Study 1	Case Study 2	Case Study 3	Case Study 4	Case Study 5
Clear purpose for using wiki	yes	yes	yes	yes	yes
User familarity	yes	mixed	mixed	mixed	yes
User designed	no	no	yes	no	yes
Motivation to collaborate	high	low	high	high	high
Private/group spaces	both	all group	all group	all group	all group
Defined Wiki roles	yes	no	yes	no	yes
Wiki supports f2f meetings	yes	yes	yes	yes	yes
Moderated tasks	yes	yes	yes	no	yes
Finite project	yes	yes	yes	yes	no
Motivation to use wiki	high	low	high	high	high

and strategies to resolve issues identified across a range of case-study scenarios. The face-to-face teaching and learning environment was supported by the NUIG Blackboard virtual learning platform which utilised the Learning Objects Teams LX building block to create group wikis.

The lecturer created inter-disciplinary and multi-cultural groups at the commencement of the module. Groups were then allocated a wiki which served as a communication and collaboration space to develop group response trigger questions. During class contact time, the lecturer distributed a common case study to each group for discussion and then presented a number of trigger questions for group consideration and group resolution. Groups were asked to upload their co-constructed response via their group wiki in real-time. The lecturer called on particular groups to present their responses to particular questions to trigger whole-group discussion. While wiki membership editing rights were restricted to the immediate group, all members of the module could view each other's wikis. This opened up the prospect of peer-review and evaluation exercises and allowed knowledge sharing amongst the wider cohort.

The principle wiki activities took place in the classroom setting. However, wiki access was available outside the class contact time for further edits, additions, comments and reflections. All group members had permission to export a .zip file copy of their wiki and this could be used to demonstrate team work and collaborative working practices to external stakeholders, such as potential employers.

Evaluation Methodology

This case study was evaluated using student questionnaires, group reflective exercises, individual student video interviews and lecturer video interviews.

Affordance of the Technology

While 84% of the students had not used a wiki prior to this module, the entire student cohort found the wiki software easy (58%) or very easy (42%) to use. It was easy to edit (95%) and add (87%) a new wiki page. There were some issues concerning the formatting of text that had been copied from MS Word into the wiki space. Students contributed reflective comments such as:

'I am not great at computers but it's really easy to use the wikis.' [Student 1]

'It's very very easy; very very simple.' [Student 2]

The students found that the technology was stable (90%) and were very pleased with the 24/7 access to their group wikis (96%).

Collaboration

The students explained how they used the group wikis:

'We use the group wikis to tie in the class theory with practical case studies. It gets you to think outside the box. You think "this is the real world".' [Student 3]

'We can edit together as a group in class, and then go afterwards and contribute online strategies amongst the team. We use the wikis to coordinate groups so that we can work together outside the classroom. It has transformed the learning from two hours in class to several hours outside the classroom.' [Student 4]

Co-Construction of Knowledge

The students appreciated the benefit of working in groups and clearly identified the 'real-world' relevance of replicating industry scenarios and problem-solving activities in their Operations Strategy module:

'It's about learning by doing; by interacting and getting ideas from other people. We have shared our details within the group. It's a challenge to work in a group but it's also fun. If there are conflicting issues, we can challenge them as a group and come to a consensus.' [Student 3]

'The wikis allow multiple ways to come up with a final answer and opens up new ideas. It's a great way to get group and class feedback. You learn a lot from that. It's a good challenge for future life and working in industry.' [Student 2]

While the international mix of students was clearly seen as an advantage to inform problem-solving approaches:

'We have a mix of Irish and international students. We have an American guy in our group and it's a really interesting mix. He provides a totally different view to us. It's great to learn from people with other backgrounds and perspectives to approach a problem.' [Student 7]

Engagement

Students liked working in groups and saw the relevance of using their wikis to aid their activities:

'You are helping your classmates. It helps to learn how to work in a group which is essential for project work. It's definitely a better way of learning because it's practical and more of a real working environment.' [Student 6]

The students identified opportunities to apply their learning to wider contexts:

'I did a placement with Boston Scientific and will be returning there in the summer. Wikis would be great to use with colleagues in the United States. I could see that this could work very well for collaborative projects between Galway and Boston and if you were dispersed throughout the company.'

Students commented that a motivating factor in their engagement with the environment was the opportunity to take a personal copy of their wiki to showcase their achievements to external audiences, such as potential employers.

The following comment indicates student use of the group wiki to aid personal reflection on learning and knowledge gained through the learning activities:

'Because we can access the wiki permanently, and take our own copy of the wiki, I can look back see what I wrote and how I wrote it. That's when I'll really recognise the learning.' [Student 4]

The Course Co-ordinator felt that the use of wikis has proven successful in facilitating knowledge construction and exchange:

'The Operations Module has really engaged the students. I have had a wonderful time observing the group dynamics and evolving problem solving approached demonstrated in the class. The wiki tool was seen as cool and novel, and very much supported the real-world element of the course. We aim to expand this module to incorporate a student cohort located in Germany for the 2009–10 academic cycle.'

Case Study 2. Three Month Review of a Policy Document within an HEI

The General Assessment Regulations (GAR) wiki was set up as a collaborative space between a group of nine members of a panel undertaking a review over a four month period of an institutional assessment policy document. After this time, the document was to be presented to the institutional academic council for approval. The panel comprised academic staff and student representatives. Members were initially asked to consult with colleagues, review the sections under discussion and attend a series of face-to-face sessions during which to agree edits to the document. Any changes would be captured by the administrator and circulated via email to the group, before finally being signed off at the next meeting.

A final review meeting of the full document was organised at the end of the collaborative period.

The use of a wiki was suggested during the first meeting of the group and there was agreement from all members that a wiki would provide a useful way for the group to collaborate. It was felt that it would be useful to have a live working document and all the associated materials and comments in one location, rather than collecting electronic documents via email. In addition, it was felt that individuals who were not able to attend meetings could also make comments that might then be included as part of the meeting. As the face-to-face meetings progressed, the panel also discussed memos, comments and feedback from members of academic council and the implications on any decisions.

The wiki was structured round the 15 sections and appendices of the policy document, with each section being allocated a separate wiki page. A copy of the existing regulations in their entirety alongside various other external, internal policy documents and relevant materials were also incorporated. An additional section that included questions pertinent to the document for example, the possible introduction of grade point average was also included. These questions had already been discussed within each faculty, but agreement regarding any changes in policy remained outstanding.

Before the wiki was created, there was a suggestion that some time subsequently be spent going through the site at the next (second) meeting to familiarise the group with the layout. However, partly due to the difficulties in booking a room with internet access, it was decided that there was no need to take time from the meeting to do this. The only people who expressed an interest in receiving training were the panel chair and administrator. This was provided. It was also at this time that these two individuals expressed some concern regarding the possibility of several people editing the document and the document being openly available, although access and editing rights were limited to within the reviewing group.

Evaluation Methodology

This case study was evaluated using a review of contributions on the wiki and a follow-up short questionnaire (5 out of the original group of 9 responded).

Affordance of the Technology

In the survey, all the panel members except one, the administrator, indicated that they had used a wiki before. Responses in the survey supported the original comments regarding the ease of using and navigating a Wiki.

'It was very straightforward and user-friendly.' *[Staff B]*

However, one member of staff did indicate that they felt that there was a lack of familiarity for some members of the panel:

'... it was a new tool for most members of the review panel. Group membership may have had mixed levels of IT competencies'. *[Staff D]*

The administrator was the only person to express some difficulty in making use of the wiki:

'the System in this building is very slow so it was very slow to load and took a lot of time to access each area.' *[Staff E]*

Having never formally introduced the wiki as part of working practice of the group, there was no agreement as to how the wiki should be used by the group.

'I feel that many of these issues may have been ameliorated by more extensive early discussions on how the wiki would help the group to achieve its objectives'. *[Staff D]*

As a result, initial contributions to the wiki related to the structure of the site and how the group should work collaboratively. Questions were directed at the person who had set up the site, rather than to the members. At an early stage it become evident that use of the wiki was becoming a separate activity, rather than one supporting the review process.

'There seemed to be to two parallel processes – one where you could make changes to the documents on wiki and another where changes where made to the documents at the meetings'. *[Staff A]*

A sense of ownership in determining the process was never really created:

'... there did not appear to be much "buy in" from the beginning'. *[Staff D]*

'Too many participants in the review weren't familiar with wiki. Again it worked out as a doubling up of work for me as even if I used wiki myself other participants weren't familiar with it so I still had to use my old format (Word).' *[Staff E]*

Interestingly, in week three, there were requests that other staff from two faculties that other staff might have access to the wiki in order to make comments. However, none of these staff ever contributed to the wiki and none of the students ever made comments.

Collaboration

The potential use of the wiki as a tool for a collaborative process was recognised by most of the members:

'This tool, or something like it, holds great potential for managing review processes in general. It allows the collaborative benefits of the meeting process to extend into the days/weeks between meetings. This I feel would help the group to maintain more consistency and focus in its work'. [Staff C]

But there was a need for the wiki to have an agreed but well-defined function within the group process.

'Yes, potentially [useful], but only if everyone was going to use it and it was the only way you could make changes to the document or leave comments for discussion.' [Staff A]

'I also feel that the wiki should have been used as the basis for the deliberations of the group at the various meetings, therefore requiring that all meetings be held in rooms with internet access.' [Staff D]

The roles of the various members within the group was also of concern to the administrator.

'... it wasn't my role to use the wiki. I had never heard of or worked with wiki as I think it is mostly academics [who] use it.' [Staff E]

Neither minutes nor document changes were ever formally captured in the site. Some disappointment was expressed by the members:

'If it had actually been used in the way it was intended, those who used the Wiki from the start might have continued to use it.' [Staff B]

'After using the Wiki initially, I found it was just as easy to make changes to the circulated [through email] documents and then suggest the changes

at the meeting. In this way, there was no need to go to the Wiki site.' [Staff A]

Co-Construction of Knowledge

Within the first week the process of making comments rather than edits appeared to become the established working practice of the group. With any final decisions being made on any changes on the policy at the face-to-face meetings, one individual expressed concern regarding making edits on the wiki

'... I was wary of using the "edit" function as I felt any change needed to be agreed before implementation.' [Staff D]

'It was pointless going to the wiki, if it was not being used to actually make the changes to the documents.' [Staff A]

'Interesting comments were made on the wiki but never discussed at the meetings, same material already commented upon on the wiki were then covered in the meetings.' [Staff A]

The administrator also commented

'From an administrative point of view it seemed working with wiki would be a doubling up of work that I already had to complete on Word etc.' [Staff E]

Engagement

Out of the 53 comments made on the Wiki, 18 posed questions in several cases indicating a desire for comments and feedback; for example, 'Is this a reference to ...?' 'Is this restriction necessary?'

There were only three instances where responses were given to comment, only four references to discussion to meetings or points that had been made.

One individual contributed consistently throughout the process, while five contributed initially but involvement gradually decreased.

'After the first few meetings I and a few others stopped making contributions because the Chair went through each chapter line by line at each meeting, irrespective of input from committee members via the wiki, so it seemed like a duplication of effort'. [Staff B]

'Lack of familiarity by some, which in turn reduced its effectiveness for others.' [Staff C]

'Though I was somewhat sceptical initially when the wiki was first suggested, I am very pleased with the experience that I have gained. I will certainly be adopting this tool as part of my own work in future.' [Staff D]

Case Study 3. Learning Innovation Network: Collaborative Online Curriculum Design

As part of the Learning Innovation Network (LIN) project goals, the establishment of shared academic development programmes required collaboration and sharing of a curriculum design process. As the LIN comprises the 13 Institutes of Technology and the DIT it became apparent that the development of shared academic programmes would require a design and development process which would have to be innovative. Initially the sub-group charged with Academic Programme Development[1] held a number of face-to-face meetings where the overall model for the academic programmes was discussed. A pilot programme was rolled out in a blended learning format in two of the institutes and a short course was developed and piloted in one institute. The model that was agreed by the sub-group was a 10 ECT (European Credit Transfer) Level 9 (Postgraduate) Special Purpose award which would include aspects of reflective practice and personal development planning. Once the model had been agreed, work had to begin on the design and development of the seven modules. While the face-to-face meetings worked well for brainstorming and creating an environment where the sharing of content and processes could start it became clear that these meetings required a considerable commitment of all those involved, both in terms of travel and time.

Affordance of the Technology

The philosophy behind the development was to be one of collaboration and sharing of the design and development. Each institute would in the future be able to integrate these programmes into their own staff development programmes. In October 2008 it was decided to use a PBWiki (now PBWorks) which was password protected to facilitate the design and development process; because of the nature of the collaboration the modules would be designed collectively online. The collaborative curriculum design process was based on a backward model adapted from Finks's model (2003). The wiki would enable partners to collaborate in defining their own philosophy of education, to critique and create course descriptors, and then to evaluate the courses. The wiki provided the creation of a space where the documents could be made available to the group before going through the standard quality assurance process in the developing institute. A wiki would allow documents in process to be shared, commented upon, amended together and then presented for the appropriate validation process for quality assurance. From the screenshot below, it can be noted that each module under development was given its own space where the individual module

Figure 1. LIN Front Page of Wiki

descriptor could be developed and commented upon. The lead institute, the institute being funded for the development and design, placed the module descriptor which they were presenting for validation in this space for comment and discussion.

There was a certain reticence about the curriculum design process and a lack of clarity was felt by certain members. After the process had begun, there was a need to have a look at the overall philosophy behind the development of the programmes and a need to refocus the development and design of the programmes. Collaborative curriculum design can be a challenging process and requires clear buy-in to the overall process. In December 2008, a face-to-face meeting was held and facilitated by Dr David Baume. This session allowed the group to decide on the underpinning values that the programme development would be based on. The values were made available on the front page of the wiki, as shown in Figure 1. The sub-group were following a process of online

collaborative design which needed to be more philosophically grounded. The value system was then published on the wiki and made available as the front page.

Collaboration and Engagement

The wiki also provided a valuable support from an administrative point of view. As the project has a limited span and will finish at year end 2009, there was a need to relay information in a centralised format to members developing and designing programmes. The structure of the wiki reflected the structure of the breakdown of the development: each folder contains the collaboratively agreed module outline and documents under discussion, while the pages were used for discussion about the document under review. It would be fair to say that the administrative perspective of the wiki proved to be invaluable; it enabled participants to see how the other partners were proceeding with the document creation and to be up to date with their progress.

Knowledge Creation

In this case study the creation of knowledge is represented by the final product of the process, a shared document which while written collectively is validated by Quality Assurance by one of the partners. The use of the wiki has varied radically amongst the members/participants. Some module descriptors were posted at the beginning of the process which allowed more time for amendments and comments while other members/participants used the wiki to present more 'fixed' documents where there was less room for discussion. The use of the wiki has enabled the positive inter-institutional collaboration, which has been one of the major hallmarks of the Learning Innovation Network, to be transferred into an accessible online environment. However, while the limited success of the wiki does pose questions, it might be in line with an emerging semiotics of Web 2.0 technologies (Warshauer & Grimes, 2007). The traditionally isolated writer is here placed at the centre of a collaborative writing activity where the final product is a representation of the success or failure of that collaboration. There is an inherent tension in the process which was undertaken on the LIN wiki, a tension between authorship, ownership and collaboration. A wiki enables open visible collaboration in the writing of documents—which edits and by whom are clearly visible. The demarcation between author and audience becomes blurred where the audience participates also in the authorship. The tension in our case arose between the open-ended nature of the collaboration afforded by the wiki and the ownership over curriculum design processes which tend to be institutionally led.

Case Study 4. NDLR Evaluation 2008

Background

The National Digital Learning Repository (NDLR) provides a shared online resource bank of teaching materials for HE institutions in the Republic of Ireland. It is currently in transition to becoming a full service, following a pilot phase, which was evaluated in 2008. Three phases of evaluation were undertaken: one focusing on users' responses, one on the technical aspects of the project, and one on the subject networks established under the auspices of the project.

The NDLR includes all Universities and Institutes of Technology, and therefore the three phases of work were carried out across all partner institutions by a team representative of all partner institutions. Working to tight deliverables and deadlines, the team needed close collaboration, but had limited capacity to meet face-to-face.

Affordance of the Technology

Email initially served adequately for the evaluation group in the drafting of evaluation plans. Face-to-face meetings of the NDLR Board also took place; these are a core function of the project's management and have been convened quarterly since its inception. However, outside these meetings the evaluators were working at disparate sites. Email became difficult in terms of version control for project documents. Partners who had joined the group but who had not previously been involved in the NDLR had limited or no access to legacy data-gathering instruments and draft materials from the early stages of the pilot. The team had no means of collectively editing text without repeated rounds of email correspondence.

To facilitate our work, we initially used a Google Groups space as a means to share documents. However, some members of the team reported difficulties accessing the Google Groups and/or non-receipt of email from the Groups area owing to the network settings for their work computers. More importantly, with increasing need to write together, a wiki appeared to afford much greater functionality to support the work of the group.

Collaboration and Engagement

We decided to use a wiki to support the evaluation project, and set up the 'Evaluation' wiki on PBWorks. This was a password-protected space which would be secure to the project team in the first instance.

The wiki was set up to reflect the three separate strands of evaluative work, and it provided a safe space to share data and documentation. Reports and 'fixed' documents (such as agreed plans and deadlines) could be stored for ongoing reference, with commentary pages describing their status, or updating on progress towards particular deliverables. Legacy documents were included to support newer members of the team, and to provide easy reference points for the current evaluation. Versions of different documents were visible within the wiki's content management structure. We could see clearly when changes and additions had been made, and the wiki included an alert feature which emailed partners to advise when changes had been made by someone in the team. Therefore, the wiki functioned in the first instance as a valuable administrative support to the evaluation work. As such, everyone had 'buy-in', as it became our principal workspace, and facilitated collaboration on both small and large tasks associated with the evaluation.

Co-Construction of Knowledge

The wiki came to play a more important role when we moved towards analysis of the data collectively across the three strands of work. What might otherwise have been an unwieldy and messy process was instead clear and simple. However, it is important to mention that a face-to-face meet-

ing instigated the work that we were then able to continue in the wiki. At the mid-point of the evaluation, with data from surveys, interviews and repository logs gathered, we met to begin our analysis. Paper and pen brainstorming identified some of the emerging outcomes. The wiki then allowed us to transfer the broad themes and findings to an online space, and to continue brainstorming for some weeks afterwards. We could also indicate where relevant data was coming from to support our findings, and even hyperlink to that data or relevant documentation if it was already stored in the wiki. Each member of the team could revise and refine the broad findings, and annotate them with information about where data would support each one. This process provided the backbone for our reporting, giving us a thematic structure which could be addressed in each of three reports for the project.

While we have not undertaken a separate analysis of our use of the wiki, it is reasonable to suggest that its successful use stemmed from a number of factors. We were highly motivated to use it in order to complete a range of detailed tasks within a tight timescale. We were a small team of people who already knew each other. We were all fairly confident users of the technology, even though we might not have used wikis extensively before. We needed a shared space to function as an archive for previous work and completed work, which was essential for reference, but which had been clogging email Inboxes. The wiki afforded a useful administrative support, but also a vital means of collaborative authoring as our analysis took shape. While the work could have been completed without the wiki, it would likely have taken longer, or our data analysis could potentially have suffered without adequate appropriate spaces to compare our findings.

Case Study 5. Irish Learning Technology Association: Project Management

Background

The Irish Learning Technology Association (ILTA) is a voluntary community of Irish professionals committed to the development and exchange of knowledge by sharing expertise and the promotion of best practice in technology-enhanced learning across all sectors in Ireland. In 2008/2009, a number of innovative activities were rolled out to mark the tenth anniversary of the association and to refine a new future strategic direction enabling a move towards a more formalised structure and formation of the association as a professional body. The association's steering committee grew from a core group of seven individuals to nine sub working groups consisting of approximately 44 individuals across 15 organisations. The central activities of the association, and the key annual milestone–the EdTech annual conference–were extended in scope and objectives. To facilitate the centralised progression of this project work at a pivotal milestone in the association's lifecycle, a wiki was set up as a collaborative space where the new extended steering committee could progress the central aims and deliverables of the association.

At the inaugural meeting of the new committee (in which the majority of members had vast experience in the use of Web 2.0 tools to moderate online communities), the decision was taken to replace the existing CMS and Google groups area with a single wiki [http://iltaworkinggroup.pbwiki.com]. The majority of committee members had used some form of wiki technology previously and all agreed that typical features of wiki functionality would best lend themselves to the project management needs of the working group. The most important of these were sharing and storage of ongoing private documentation; in-context commentary describing status and version; instant visibility of task status, schedule and key docu-

ments; virtual coordination and collaboration on tasks outside of regular face-to-face contact and meetings; reducing the number of emails and overlap of tasks between sub-groups; supporting any handover activities; and knowledge creation and exchange.

The wiki was structured to reflect the strands of work across the nine working groups (Education, Events, External links, Finance, Information, Publication, Research, Web development and Conference organisation). Each sub-group had its own folder and home page to enable them to plan and collaborate on their activities. See Figure 2.

Affordance of the Technology

The wiki technology was found to be easy to use and navigate. It provided a safe secure space to share data, survey feedback from the membership, and documentation from face-to-face meetings. Configuring the customised security settings did not require any IT supports but was authorised by the sub-group administrator. The project files were stored online, eliminating the need to send and store electronic versions to all stakeholders. This reduction in email traffic served as a significant productivity booster. The wiki software recorded a full audit of all changes, making it easy for all to see who had made modifications to shared resources. The wiki also integrated seamlessly with other platforms (e.g. existing forum, CMS and website) and necessitated little investment in hardware, software, installation or training.

Collaboration, Co-Construction of Knowledge and Engagement

The wiki structure made it possible to aggregate a wide range of organisational knowledge from the diverse group, enabling partners to work across tasks. Project-specific pages were set up for each group to disseminate focused and timely information so that priority tasks could be completed rapidly. The wiki allowed for increased transpar-

Figure 2. ILTA Front Page of Wiki

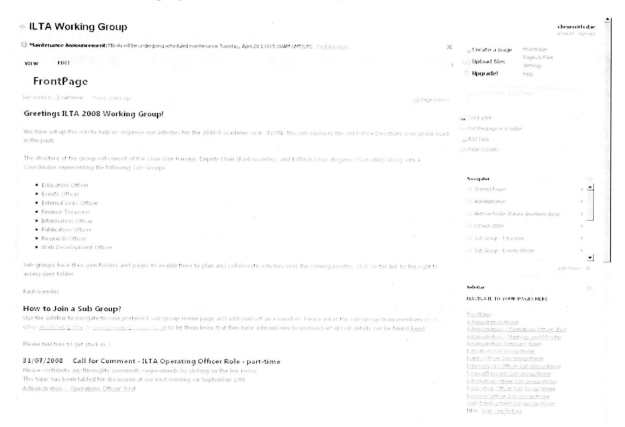

ency so individuals were able to work faster on their focused tasks while being able to engage with the full range of sub-groups involved. This meant that much of the editing, review and rewrite processes were reduced. The wiki also succeeded in creating its own momentum. Aided and abetted by the association chairs, the wiki became a dynamic knowledge base for the association. The wiki continued to expand to include minutes and agenda of meetings, contact details and roles for those working on the project as well as scheduling functionality for online and face-to-face meetings.

DISCUSSION

Our five case studies, drawn from the broad range of contexts in which people in HE are working,

show how these online communities functioned, and how they undertook their tasks. In this section we address common themes, but also points of difference, between each case.

Decisions to Use the Wikis

All case studies had selected to use a Wiki, rather than an institutional virtual learning environment or other facility, both as an easy to use, collaborative space and as an alternative to email correspondence. For students in CS1, the wiki offered a more authentic learning environment, and one that they would be likely to use again in the business world after graduation. In the other case studies, wikis offered the means to transcend institutional systems and boundaries, overcoming administrative issues (such as account creation and login distribution).

All case studies reflect a need to complete key tasks within deadlines, and used wikis to facilitate these tasks. Case studies 2–5 reflect the need for a disparate group to work together within constrained time periods. The wikis were used in different ways, often simultaneously supporting tasks at the administrative level, while also functioning as the medium through which tasks were undertaken.

Affordance of the Technology

All case studies reported that users found the wikis easy to use and navigate. Most users were already comfortable in using technology although not necessarily familiar with use of wikis. The structure was initially defined by an individual with prior experience of using a wiki. Most structures were defined by the principal reason for using the wiki. In CS4, the NDLR team had a pre-existing work package. In CS3, LIN had a remit to develop its various programmes. In CS2, the document sections determined the structure of the wiki, and in CS1, group case studies provided the framework for the online writing.

Wikis provided the flexibility to support a range of different structures. In CS4 and CS2, work arose from collaborative strands, and ongoing activities 'offline', in particular the creation and review of documents and reports. In CS3 and CS4, the wiki site structures evolved as the collaborative activities evolved, and enabled the editing of documents.

Most groups reported administrative value of a wiki. In CS4, the wiki alerted members to changes, which was important for their work. A shared space is useful not only for current work, but also for the storage and archiving of previous work. Managing large numbers of documents would have been unwieldy for a number of the projects discussed, had they not used the wiki for this purpose.

Engagement and Collaboration

The openness of the wiki could be problematic unless a clearly defined structure and managed way of working was established. CS2 highlights that the lack of an introduction to using the wiki may have influenced the ways in which it was used. CS3 discusses the tensions that can arise between ownership of curriculum design, and the open-ended nature of collaboration in the wiki. In CS1, individual or group management of tasks was felt to be important in determining the quality and relevance of group output.

There is need to have buy-in and commitment to make use of the wiki by the groups at an early stage. All of our case studies illustrate the need for perceived relevance and usefulness of wiki by all or a critical mass of its users. In all cases, the wiki was incorporated as part of the group's activities, and group processes were structured around the wiki. CS1 and CS3 in particular show a focus on group activities within different working spaces of the wiki. Where this didn't happen, there appeared to be a perceived lack of clarity related to the roles, editing rights and relevance of using the wiki (CS2, CS3).

Wikis were selected to support online activities between face-to-face meetings of the groups and worked most effectively when used in this way. In CS1, the student group incorporated use of the wiki as part of face-to-face meetings. But the cases demonstrate that it was important for the use of wiki to be integrated into the other activities of the groups. CS3 and CS4 show that the wiki allowed people to continue activities started in the face-to-face context or conclude them prior to meetings. In CS4, the wiki was also a vital means of collaborative authoring as the data analysis took shape.

Flexibility of wikis enabled groups to work together in different ways. Early working practice appeared to become established working practice for a number of groups (CS1, CS2). The students in CS1 worked together on structured face-to-

Table 2. Summary of case study outcomes under chapter themes

	Case Study 1	Case Study 2	Case Study 3	Case Study 4	Case Study 5
affordance	√	√	√	√	√
collaboration	√	√	√	√	√
co-construction	√	X	X	√	X
engagement	√	√	√	√	√

face case studies in groups and then contributed online, comparing and contrasting other student work. In CS2, the GAR group noted that the wiki was used more as a bulletin board rather than a collaborative space, although users posted comments posing open-ended questions, and seeking some kind of response.

Wikis also enabled changes in working practice as the communities evolved. In CS4, the evaluation authors revised and refined their broad findings, and annotated them with information about where data would support each one. They also 'inducted' newcomers to the team with the support of the wiki, uploading legacy information for these members to access. In CS3, module descriptors were posted at the beginning of the process which allowed more time for amendments and comments, while other participants used the wiki to present 'fixed' documents for which there was less room for discussion.

Co-Construction of Knowledge

The need for a shared safe space was felt to be important by all groups. Editing rights were of concern to all groups. GARS members in CS2 felt that editing decisions should be made face to face and then uploaded. Editing rights were limited to group members within the CS1 group spaces: groups were asked to upload their co-constructed responses via their group wiki in real-time. All groups could see other wikis but not edit the work. CS3 discusses the need for clear guidelines regarding editing rights in the wiki, and draws

out the tension between sharing authorship and 'owning' curriculum development.

Wikis as Reflections of Community

To what extent do these case studies present wikis as reflections of the communities using them? They appear to show the importance of interdependence, evidence of group responses to issues, joint efforts to address issues of concern to each group, and mutual engagement in the task at hand (Wenger, 1998). However, we suggest that understanding of the wiki as a 'tool', but also the potentially challenging 'rules' of that tool, is something still evolving (Wenger, 1998). A tension emerges in some cases between trust, and open authorship/editorship, and this may be linked to the stage of the community's development (Preece, 2000). Obligation and motivation were important factors in driving the communities, and the wikis provided engines for their work. However, our findings would appear to support those of Shirky (2008) and Lamb (2004), who suggest the need for a healthy community in order to make effective use of a wiki, and to get 'buy-in' to the wiki as a medium. See Table 2.

CONCLUSION

Do Wikis Afford Knowledge Creation? And if So, How?

'The basic idea of the Web is that it is an information space through which people can communicate, but communicate in a special way, by sharing their knowledge in a pool'. Berners-Lee (2000) foresaw the web as a place where ideas would be produced, as well as discovered.

Our findings suggest that wikis can function as both supports to, and engines of, community activity. The affordances of wikis support communities in their development, although that development is dependent in part on other factors. If well-functioning communities generate knowledge, then we can suggest that these case studies lend some evidence to the view that wikis afford knowledge creation. Moreover, wikis support knowledge management in complex collaborative projects, which are increasingly a feature of the Irish HE landscape. However, varying success in terms of knowledge creation has been reported by Choy and Ng (2007), Lamb (2004), Elgort et al. (2008), Raman et al. (2005). Researchers report that wikis are often used more to provide information, manage and update existing knowledge, but are of limited use to collaboratively create new knowledge.

FUTURE DIRECTIONS

The case studies and discussion presented in this chapter point the way to a number of areas for further research. We are interested in examining in more detail the relationship between well-formed 'offline' communities, and how quickly and effectively they begin to use wikis. The point at which the wiki stops being primarily a support for collaboration, and instead becomes the means for new knowledge to be produced, is a further question for more detailed investigation. Additionally, we ask whether institutions which seek to engage in collaborative projects to an increasing extent, can offer institutional systems to compete with those already 'out there'. If not, are there implications for the management and storage of sensitive information? Or implications for the creation of new knowledge which may have commercial or other advantage for a particular institution? New

ways of exploiting the affordances of wikis may also emerge, and we will continue to examine how these affordances interact with the communities of which we are members.

REFERENCES

Berners-Lee, T. (2000). The web's brainchild [Interview]. Retrieved October 20, 2009, from http://www.unesco.org/webworld/points_of_views/berners-lee.shtml

Choy, S. O., & Ng, K. C. (2007). Implementing wiki software for supplementing online learning. *Australasian Journal of Educational Technology, 23*(2), 209-226. Retrieved October 12, 2009, from http://www.ascilite.org.au/ajet/ajet23/choy.html

Dede, C. (2008). New Horizons: A seismic shift in epistemology. *EDUCAUSE Review, 43*(3), 80-81. Retrieved October 12, 2009, from http://net.educause.edu/ir/library/pdf/ERM0837.pdf

Doolan, M. A. (2006). Effective strategies for building a learning community online using a Wiki. *Proceedings 1st Annual Blended Learning Conference* (pp. 51-55). Retrieved October 12, 2009, from https://uhra.herts.ac.uk/dspace/bitstream/2299/1721/1/901867.pdf

Downes, S. (2005). *E-learning 2.0. eLearn Magazine.* October 16, 2005. Retrieved October 12, 2009, from http://www.elearnmag.org/subpage.cfm?section=articles&article=29–1

Elgort, I., Smith, A. G., & Toland, J. (2008). Is wiki an effective platform for group course work? *Australasian Journal of Educational Technology, 24*(2), 195–210.

Fink, L. D. (2003). *Creating significant learning experiences: An integrated approach to designing college courses.* San Francisco: Jossey-Bass.

Franklin, T., & van Harmelen, M. (2007). *Web 2.0 for Content for learning and teaching in Higher Education*. Bristol: JISC. Retrieved October 12, 2009, from http://ie-repository.jisc.ac.uk/148/1/web2-content-learning-and-teaching.pdf

Goodfellow, R. (2005). Virtuality and the shaping of Educational Communities. *Education Communication and Information, 5*(2), 113–129.

Grierson, H., Nicol, D., Littlejohn, A., & Wodehouse, A. (2004). Structuring and sharing information resources to support concept development and design learning. Paper presented at the *Network Learning Conference*, Exeter, UK (pp. 572-579), April 2004. Retrieved October 12, 2009, from http://www.networkedlearningconference.org.uk/past/nlc2004/proceedings/individual_papers/grierson_et_al.htm

Jones, P. (2007). When a wiki is the way: Exploring the use of a wiki in a constructively aligned learning design. In R.J. Atkinson, C. McBeath, S.K.A. Soong, & C. Cheers (Eds.), *ICT: Providing choices for learners and learning*. Proceedings ascilite Singapore 2007. Centre for Educational Development, Nanyang Technological University, Singapore, 2-5 December. Retrieved October 12, 2009, from http://www.ascilite.org.au/conferences/singapore07/procs/

Jordan, A., Carlile, O., & Stack, A. (2008). *Approaches to learning*. Maidenhead: Open University Press.

Lamb, B. (2004). Wide open spaces: Wikis ready or not. *Educause Review*, September/October, 36-48. Retrieved October 12, 2009, from http://net.educause.edu/ir/library/pdf/ERM0452.pdf

Palloff, R. M., & Pratt, K. (2005). *Collaborating online: Learning together in community*. San Francisco: Jossey-Bass.

PBWiki (now PBWorks) (2009). [Homepage] http://pbworks.com

Powazek, D. M. (2002). *Design for community. The art of connecting real people in virtual places*. Indianapolis, IN: New Riders.

Preece, J. (2000). *Online communities: Designing usability, supporting sociability*. Chichester, UK: John Wiley & Sons.

Raman, M., Ryan, T., & Olfman, L. (2005). Designing knowledge management systems for teaching and learning with wiki technology. *Journal of Information Systems Education, 16*(3), 311.

Seely Brown, J., & Alder, R. P. (2008). Minds on fire: Open education, the long tail, and learning 2.0, *EDUCAUSE Review, 43*(1). Retrieved October 12, 2009, from http://net.educause.edu/ir/library/pdf/ERM0811.pdf

Shirky, C. (2008). *Here comes everybody: The power of organizing without organizations*. New York: Penguin Press.

Warschauer, M., & Grimes, D. (2007). Audience, authorship, and artifact: The emergent semiotics of Web 2.0. *Annual Review of Applied Linguistics, 27*, 1–23. doi:10.1017/S0267190508070013

Wenger, E. (1998). *Communities of practice: Learning, meaning and identity*. Cambridge: Cambridge University Press.

ADDITIONAL READING

Barkley, E. F., Cross, K. P., & Major, C. H. (2005). *Collaborative learning techniques: A handbook for college faculty*. San Francisco: Jossey-Bass Publishers.

Campbell, L. M. (2003). Engaging with the learning object economy . In Littlejohn, A. (Ed.), *Reusing online resources: A sustainable approach to e-Learning*. London: Kogan Page.

Corporate Wikis. (2005). http://c2.com/cgi/wiki?CorporateWikis

Davies, J. G., Subrahmanian, E., Konda, S., Granger, H., Collins, M., & Westerberg, A. W. (2001). Creating shared information spaces to support collaborative design work. *Information Systems Frontiers*, *3*(3), 377–392. doi:10.1023/A:1011469727367

Ebersbach, A., Glaser, M., & Heigl, R. (2006). *Wiki: Web collaboration*. Berlin, Heidelberg: Springer-Verlag.

Hubert, C., Newhouse, B., & Vestal, W. (2001). *Building and sustaining communities of practice. Next-generation knowledge management: Enabling business processes*. Houston, TX: APQC.

Jonassen, D. H., & Carr, C. S. (2000). Mindtools: Affording multiple knowledge representations for learning . In Lajoie, S. P. (Ed.), *Computers as cognitive tools* (pp. 165–196). Mahwah, NJ: Lawrence Erlbaum Associates.

Nicol, D. J., & MacLeod, I. (2004). Using a shared workspace and wireless laptops to improve collaborative project learning in an engineering design course. *Computers & Education*, *44*(4), 459–475. doi:10.1016/j.compedu.2004.04.008

Prensky, M. (2001). Digital natives, digital immigrants. *On the Horizon, 9*(5). Retrieved October 20, 2009, from http://www.marcprensky.com/writing/Prensky%20-%20Digital%20Natives,%20Digital%20Immigrants%20-%20Part1.pdf

Rollett, H., Lux, M., Strohmaier, M., Dosinger, G., & Tochtermann, K. (2007). The Web 2.0 way of learning with technologies. *International Journal of Learning Technology*, *3*(1), 87–107. doi:10.1504/IJLT.2007.012368

Seely Brown, J., & Solomon Grey, S. (1995). The people are the company. *FastCompany Magazine*, 1. Retrieved October 20, 2009, from http://www.fastcompany.com/magazine/01/people.html

Wenger, E., McDermott, R., & Snyder, W. M. (2002). *Cultivating communities of practice*. Boston, MA: Harvard Business School Publishing.

Wenger, E., & Snyder, W. (2000). Communities of practice: The organizational frontier. *Harvard Business Review*, *78*(1), 139–145.

ENDNOTE

[1] The APD sub-group is made up of the following representatives, Dr Noel Fitzpatrick and Dr Jen Harvey (DIT), Dr Attracta Brennan (GMIT), Dr Etain Kiely (Silgo IT), Dr Liam Boyle (Limerick IT), Marion Palmer (IADT), Nuala Harding (Athlone IT), Hugh Mc Cabe (Blanchardstown IT), Anne Carpenter (Carlow IT), Dr Averil Meehan (LetterKenny IT), Dr John Wall and Sean Moran (Waterford IT).

Chapter 7
Games for Learning and Learning Transfer

Gearóid Ó Súilleabháin
Cork Institute of Technology, Co. Cork, Ireland

Julie-Ann Sime
Lancaster University, UK

ABSTRACT

Research findings are at best mixed with regard to the effectiveness of computer and video games in promoting learning transfer or learning, but much of this research makes use of the same unsuccessful methods of classic transfer experiments which offered research subjects limited initial practice in the learning to be transferred. Learning transfer however, like expertise, may need to be based on extended practice, an idea supported by studies of habitual or expert game players and recent non-game related developments in transfer research. Practice however must be joined to a certain kind of game complexity and cognitive or experiential game fidelity before deep learning and instances of significant transfer can be facilitated. Implications of these transfer conditions for the design of games for transfer are discussed as well as the need for research with regard to the various learning processes underlying the game-play behaviour of expert and habitual gamers.

INTRODUCTION

Research into learning transfer, broadly, relates to the influence of prior learning on new contexts of learning or performance. In its classic conceptualisation transfer involves the use of learning gained in one context, or setting, in a second subsequent context or setting. Ever since the formal introduction of the concept of learning transfer in 1901 in

DOI: 10.4018/978-1-61520-879-1.ch007

a series of papers by Edward E. Thorndike and Robert Sessions Woodworth, the concept has been controversial (1901a, 1901b, 1901c). Many studies and experiments have failed to facilitate transfer responses in subjects, even when, in many cases, the odds seemed to be very much stacked in favour of its occurrence (Detterman, 1996).

In this chapter the older tradition of transfer research is linked to more recent research into and development of games for learning. An argument is made that many of the concerns of researchers and other stakeholders in the emerging 'serious games' industry relate directly, if not explicitly, to the question of learning transfer. Games, it is argued towards the end of this piece, might also represent a useful environment within which to study some outstanding issues with regard to learning transfer. Games, for instance, offer affordances for empirical research simply not obtainable in more traditional learning environments–not least in the ability to use usability software and methods to closely monitor, capture and analyse a range of game-world and real-world actions and reactions.

Research findings, however, are at best mixed in their conclusions with regard to the pedagogical or transfer effectiveness of games, but, in another link between games for learning and learning transfer, many of these studies may be said to make use of the same unsuccessful methodologies of classic 'in vitro' transfer experiments in which research subjects, after only a limited exposure or practice, are prompted to demonstrate transfer into a new experimental setting. We suggest that one of the key reasons this approach has not tended to produce transfer is that transfer, like expertise, needs to be based on extended and perhaps considerable practice. Indeed, studies of habitual or expert computer and video game players do seem to provide encouraging results with regard to the 'transfer power' of games. Based on this and other evidence we propose three key necessary conditions for transfer: extended practice; game complexity; and cognitive or experiential fidelity. Together these key conditions provide the central structure and concerns of the chapter. First, however, some context is offered with regard to the history of research into transfer, its importance, and its relationship as both a phenomenon and concept to the use of computer and video games for learning.

BACKGROUND

Learning Transfer Research

In 1901, two well-known and influential academic psychologists Thorndike and Woodworth published a series of articles in *Psychological Review* entitled, 'The influence of improvement in one mental function upon the efficiency of other functions' (Thorndike & Woodworth, 1901a, 1901b, 1901c). In it they present the results of a series of experiments that suggest the influence of 'improvement' in one cognitive skill or 'function' does not necessarily imply an improvement in skills in what might be taken to be a closely related area, concluding, 'that spread of practice occurs only where identical elements are concerned in the influencing and influenced function' (Thorndike & Woodworth, 1901a, p. 250). But what are these 'identical elements'? Why is it so difficult to find evidence of this spread of practice, this *transfer of learning*? What are the factors which govern its occurrence? How can we, as it were, control and predict transfer?

Since the publication of Thorndike and Woodworth's articles these questions have been tackled by successive generations of researchers. Thorndike and his followers' initial focus on more or less physically identical elements in the original and target transfer contexts eventually gave way to what might be described as a more cognitivist interest in 'structural or conceptual similarities between contexts or tasks' (Carraher & Schliemann, 2002, p. 2) which was again replaced more recently by a more constructivist/situationalist approach, like that presented by Greeno, Smith, and Moore (1996) whereby transfer is seen as an active and constructive process.

Despite the efforts of these generations of researchers, examples of successful facilitation of transfer–beyond transfer of the largely reflexive kind between highly similar learning and target contexts–are a relative rarity in the research literature (see Bransford, Brown, & Cocking, 2003;

De Corte, 2003; Leberman, McDonald, & Doyle, 2006; Singley & Anderson, 1989).

As a result some commentators have gone so far as to venture we should now simply forget about the concept of transfer and find a more satisfactory way to analyse the interplay between prior learning and new learning challenges. For instance, Carraher and Schliemann (2002) argue that the underlying and irresolvable problem at the heart of the learning transfer concept is the central metaphor of knowledge or solutions being *transferred* unchanged and intact into a new situation. Arguing from a different perspective, Douglas K. Detterman proclaims 'significant transfer' is in general 'probably rare' and suggests that even those few studies which seem to indicate otherwise 'often tell subjects to transfer or use a "trick" to call the subject's attention to the similarity' of the original and target transfer contexts (Detterman, 1996, p. 21). Other researchers, for example Bransford and Schwartz (1999), try to save the concept of transfer but only by arguing for a rather radical reconceptualisation of transfer as 'preparation for future learning' where the focus is on metacognition and assessing transfer by the ability to learn in new, resource-rich contexts. This changes the emphasis from sequestered problem solving to problem solving in authentic contexts where collaboration and interaction with resources may affect performance in the transfer situation. In realistic working contexts people rarely work in isolation and are generally surrounded by numerous supports and opportunities to 'bump up' against the world.

The Importance of Learning Transfer

It is no exaggeration to say that the training and education systems of the world are predicated not merely on the existence of transfer but on the ability to manipulate and control it, to assure its continued occurrence. Across the world there is an assumption, rarely challenged, that learning facilitated in the classroom, lecture hall or laboratory will be of genuine and direct use in the world of work and in engagement with other future learning challenges (Bransford et al., 2003, p. 51). As has already been touched upon, however, 'Most research on transfer has been bad news for educators. It gives the impression that transfer usually doesn't happen' (Bereiter, 1995, p. 26).

In the developed world, perhaps more than anywhere else, the demand to, more deeply, understand the transfer phenomenon is ever more pressing. Haskell (2001) makes the point that 'in slow-changing traditional societies, there's much less need for transfer of learning' (p. 37). By contrast, in the developed world the rapid growth of information and communications technology has led to a sea change in the learning needs of the workforce and workplace. Traditional formal education, which was typically concentrated in the earlier stages of life, is no longer imagined to be sufficient to carry an individual through his or her working life in today's rapidly changing world. In addition to simply 'stopping over' every now and then for more formal or informal learning, today's working individual, to put it basically, needs 'information and thinking that will transfer' (Leberman et al., 2006, p. 3).

One symptom of this interest in transferable skills and knowledge is the growth of research and development of courses and programmes relating to, what are variously referred to as key skills, core skills, and generic skills. These primarily cognitive skills, subsumed by some policymakers under the lifelong learning agenda (e.g., OECD, 2007), are hard to define but may be said to be 'conceptualised as being skills applicable to different situations after initial teaching/learning and capable of slight adaptation to suit the varying needs of the new situation' (Cornford, 2005, p. 27). They are in other words generic skills with a high transfer potential and refusal to acknowledge as much here and elsewhere can only, as Cornford (2005) concludes, result in 'unrealistic and unachievable policy.' (p. 41).

Recent interest and debate in the USA with regard to so-called '21st century skills', which may be taken to include what is generally meant by 'generic skills' but also specifically to include a range of media and technology related skills would likewise appear to revolve, at least in part, around the issue of transfer and the conditions promoting it (e.g., Sawchuk, 2009).

Transfer and Games for Learning

The recent renewed interest in the use of computer and video games for learning brings with it a fresh perspective to the century-old transfer debate. Although it is not often remarked upon, many of the concerns of researchers and other stakeholders in the study and development of games for learning relate directly to transfer. Often, in point of fact, when it is asked 'Are games useful?' or, 'What do we learn from games?' what is being asked is if there is a specific piece of learning gained 'in there', as it were, in the game world, which can be of help 'out here' in the real one; or, in other words, a question is being asked about the learning transfer potential of games (Ó Súilleabháin, 2008).

The point can also be made that the vendors of many learning and conventional entertainment games make explicit or implicit claims about the ability of their products to promote transfer. One conspicuous case in point here is the highly popular *Brain Training* series for the Nintendo DS (Nintendo, 2007), a series of games clearly marketed to users wishing to develop transferable key cognitive and meta-cognitive skills. What are sometimes dubbed 'Exergames' (Bergeron, 2006, pp. 35–28) or more simply 'fitness games', that is, games which integrate exercise and game elements generally through the use of alternative input devices such as a dance mat or camera, also tend to make implicit or explicit promises with respect to the development of transferable physical skills. Certain game titles with strong simulation elements such as *SimCity* and *Civilization* are often supposed to facilitate transferable knowledge and

indeed have, with mixed results, been the subject of a number of empirical studies (Adams, 1998; Betz, 1996; Squire, 2004). In addition, what might be termed 'professional' or 'vocational' games have enjoyed a long history in both the health/medicine and the military/defence sectors, with many of these games–or versions of these games–'crossing over' as entertainment titles, for example, America's Army (US Army, 2009); Pet Pals: Animal Doctor (Legacy Games, 2009b) and 911 Paramedic (Legacy Games, 2009a)

Research into Games for Learning: Some Issues

Despite some promising links, drawn above, between the study of games for learning and learning transfer, it may be said that research, at best, returns mixed results when it comes to trying to decide on the learning or transfer capacity of games. Hays (2005), for instance, in his extensive review of the literature on the pedagogical effectiveness of games concludes that, 'In most cases, the research shows no instructional advantage of games over other instructional approaches' (p. 43). In their meta-analysis Randel, Morris, Wetzel, and Whitehill (1992) compared the pedagogical effectiveness of games with that of 'conventional classroom instruction' over the course of 67 reviewed research studies, and found 38 of these (56% of the total of reviewed studies) showed no difference between games and face-to-face teaching while 22 favoured games (32%), with a further 5 (7%) also favouring games but with controls that were considered 'questionable'. Just three studies (5%) favoured conventional teaching in this meta-analysis. Another meta-analysis (Vogel et al., 2006) initially, gives more support to the idea that games are more effective. In this analysis, incorporating 32 studies of computer games and interactive simulation, strong, positive effect sizes are found for interactive simulations and games by contrast to traditional teaching methods for both cognitive gains and attitude;

however, games taken by themselves, i.e. considered separately from interactive simulations, yield a much lower reliability.

Conditions for Transfer from Games

Some background has been offered, above, with regard to the history of research into transfer, the theoretical and practical importance of the concept and phenomenon of transfer and its relationship to the study and use of computer and video games for learning. It has been described moreover how, and in spite of some promising continuities between transfer and the games for learning, the research, at best, seems to return mixed results when it comes to trying to decide on the learning or transfer capacity of games. In the following section the general failures to find evidence for either transfer, or significant examples of learning from games, are compared to similar results in well-known studies of conventional learning transfer. Extended practice emerges from this discussion as the first of three proposed conditions of learning transfer from games. The section begins with a discursive account of the–appropriately– 'conservative' nature of transfer and the role of particular kinds of practice in facilitating it.

Transfer Condition 1. Game Transfer and Extended Practice

Many studies into learning and transfer from games are based on the kind of one-off 'in vitro' experimentation often associated with classic transfer studies, which often themselves end in failure. Such failures are often used, in fact, to suggest the concept of transfer should be abandoned entirely. Douglas Detterman (1996) is one such critic: at the end of his overview of the history of studies of what he terms 'general transfer' he comments that:

The amazing thing about all these studies is not that they don't produce transfer. The surprise is the extent of similarity it is possible to have between two problems without subjects realizing that the two situations are identical and require the same solution. (p. 13)

The studies Detterman refers to–which include well-known studies by Gick and Holyoak (1980) and Reed, Ernst and Banerji (1974) into what is more specifically termed 'analogical problem-solving'–are, without exception, studies in which participants were given only one-off chances to absorb and then later apply problem solutions.

Detterman (1996) is particularly critical of Gick and Holyoak (1980) who describe a series of experiments into analogous problem-solving, all based around a story which holds a solution to, structurally, highly similar problems. In the first, most basic, experiment Gick and Holyoak provide a participant group with a written account of a story, the group is told that this story could provide help in the solving of an analogous problem; the group are asked to summarise the story–presumably to ensure comprehension and a certain amount of retention–they are furthermore allowed to refer back to it at any point in the solving of the analogous problem. Despite having the odds somewhat stacked in favour of the 'right' solution being arrived at, just 57% of the group produce the looked-for result.

Should we be surprised at this result? Does transfer really work like this? The question may usefully be linked to work by Medin and Ross (1989, cited in Detterman, 1996, p 18) concerning the specific characteristics of abstract thought which suggests that induction/transfer is, in fact, necessarily and appropriately 'conservative', i.e. that transfer is rare and that this is due to an in-built and useful 'caution control' with regard to the use of prior learning in novel situations. Perhaps, notwithstanding all that has been said with regard to the importance of transfer, it is not the wisest or more practical course to try to make one's way in the world looking constantly to apply, wholesale, solutions from past learning experiences to entirely new settings. The conservative nature of transfer, according to Medin and Ross, effectively protects us from this kind of constant over-generalisation and interference.

Fisch, Kirkorian and Anderson (2005), in an article summarising their work on learning transfer from educational television, see various learning transfer solutions vying, as it were, for position in new learning contexts and offer an axiomatic formulation to predict those solutions most likely to emerge victorious: 'The probability with which the content acquired [in a prior learning context] will be applied is a function of the associative strength of that content relative to all of the other competing material that is stored in memory' (p. 383).

These points suggest that 'one-off' shots at producing transfer may be unlikely to succeed (Ó Súilleabháin, 2008). If we accept the idea that transfer is a conservative process and that there is competition between candidate transfer problem solutions then, despite all that has been done to encourage transfer–in Gick and Holyoak the group receiving a hint that the story might be of help in the problem coupled with the frankly striking similarities between the two scenarios– the experiment design still seems fated to failure from the start.

Similar methods and approaches to those of Gick and Holyoak can be found throughout the research on learning and learning transfer from computer and video games, including those studies surveyed by Hays (2005), Randel et al. (1992) and Vogel et al. (2006) indicated above. The, broadly, negative results for these 'one-exposure/ one-shot-at-transfer' studies may usefully be contrasted with those studies based on learning, or learning transfer, by habitual or expert computer and video game players. For instance a study by VanDeventer and White (2002) revealed expert behaviour–encompassing, for example, superior short-term and long-term memory and strong self-monitoring skills–in what the authors classified as 'outstanding video-game-playing children'.

Constance Steinkuehler's 'cognitive ethnography' of Massive Multiplayer Online Games (MMOGs) such as *Lineage* and *World of Warcraft* (WoW) belong very much to the same category of research. In a recent article, Steinkuehler (2008) presents evidence from her studies of these gaming communities of constant collaborative problem solving, digital media literacy practices, information scientific reasoning–here, she includes evidence from WoW online fora of specific forms of scientific literacy such as model-based reasoning, etc.–and 'computational literacy.'

Frequent practice, then, may well emerge as a key condition for learning and transfer in games. Quite how much practice is required, of course, cannot be stated here and the amount would, in any case, likely vary according to a number of complex factors (e.g. depth, breadth, and complexity of the learning, as well as individual differences) but, it could well be that it exceeds what is generally provided for within a typical research study or even a longer term research project. Researchers into the development of expertise, for instance, reckon its achievement in certain domains might take as many as 10 years' experience or 10,000 hours of 'deliberate practice' (see, e.g., Goleman, 1994). Boot, Kramer, Simons, Fabiani, and Gratton (2008) describe attempts to boost a range of cognitive abilities in non-gamers by exposing them to 20+ hours of game play which failed to bring them up to the levels recorded for expert players as part of the same study suggesting, again, that far more extensive game play experience is required to facilitate transfer than is often supposed. (*Note*: results may also be due to a self-selection effect in the participating video game players.)

Condition 2. Game Transfer and Game Complexity

Practice, then, may be one of the most important conditions for transfer. If so, there are some immediate implications for the use, development and study of games for transfer purposes. We can immediately say, for instance, that computer and video games which are not sufficiently compelling, which do not offer sufficient intrinsic motivation to make sure players are sufficiently inspired and rewarded to 'put in' the requisite amount of deliberate practice first day, may be unlikely to ever succeed in facilitating deep learning or significant learning transfer. Indeed, it may well be that this characteristic, this 'stickiness', in the language of web marketers, should be looked at first in developing what are sometimes termed 'serious games' (i.e. games intended for learning purposes) or in selecting entertainment titles for educational use. Stickiness, however, though it may be an important and necessary condition for transfer from games is hardly a sufficient one. Much of the scepticism that still surrounds the use of games for learning may, for example, be due in no small part to the association of games with early repetitive shoot 'em ups which, while utterly compelling, were unlikely to give rise to much in the way of sophisticated learning.

Marc Prensky, long time advocate for the use of games in education, makes a distinction, useful in this context, between these basic or trivial 'coin-op' games–alongside of which he also lists traditional board games and certain 'so-called' educational games–and what he wishes to call 'complex games' (Prensky 2005). The second, more pedagogically interesting group, he says, includes games which 'typically require tens of hours of concentrated attention to master' (p. 4) and include 'almost every [contemporary] game that comes in a box, whether for PC, or for console' (p. 10). The 'time to master', Prensky suggests, can be taken as a proxy for complexity, but it is more to the point to say that whereas trivial games offer only one kind of learning challenge or a variation on one kind of challenge, complex games offer 'a sophisticated mixture of difficult challenges that typically intertwine and support each other' (p. 5).

Johnson (2006) adds another complexity symptom to Prensky's list when he comments on what he calls the 'clearest measure of the cognitive challenges posed by modern games' (p. 28), i.e. the 'sheer size of the cottage industry devoted to publishing game guides' (p. 28). He could have added to this, of course, the range of active online communities players themselves have developed to share solutions and strategies for the games they play. This kind of support for the game player is a relatively new phenomenon, and Johnson again makes the point well when he says: 'you didn't need ten pages to explain the PacMan system, but two hundred pages barely does justice to an expanding universe like Ever-Quest or Ultima [the leading massive multiplayer games at Johnson's time of writing]. You need them because the complexity of these worlds can be overwhelming' (p. 30).

An excess of task complexity of course in terms, for example, of undue path-goal multiplicity (Terborg & Miller, 1978) or excessive conflict between interrelated completion/success criteria (Campbell, 1988) could easily threaten to overwhelm the learner in a conventional educational setting but contemporary and, in Prensky's sense, *complex* games are adaptive in the sense that they can, to a greater or lesser degree, adapt or manipulate difficulty levels dynamically, in keeping with player progress and performance. Many games also allow players to choose their own level of challenge and complexity, not merely in terms of simply choosing a level but in choosing which goals, or quests, or other objectives to pursue and when to do so. This kind of choice and adaptivity links to the kind of balance positive psychologist Mihaly Csikszentmihalyi (2002) has in mind when he speaks of the special zone where activities have for their actors neither too much challenge (provoking anxiety) nor too little challenge (provoking boredom). This special zone is where 'flow' takes place, Csikszentmihalyi's mental state characterised by, inter alia, 'merging of action and awareness' (p. 53), utter 'concentration on the task at hand' (p. 58), and 'loss of self-consciousness' (p. 61). In this way it can be said the requirement for games for transfer to be both complex and compelling meet and may be seen to be interdependent.

Transfer Condition 3. The Issue of Fidelity

The development of significant transferable learning with a high probability of occurrence may take time and may, it has been suggested above, be based, like the development of expertise, on a certain and perhaps considerable amount of deliberate practice. Games for learning, then, need to be sufficiently compelling, to make sure players are sufficiently inspired and rewarded to put in the requisite amount of deliberate practice, first day. 'Edutainment' titles which lack intrinsic motivation are to be criticised on this score (Egenfeldt-Nielsen, 2005, p. 84), as too, is the over-emphasis on what games are ostensibly 'about' over and above the complexity and sophistication of the games themselves. But does it matter at all what games are about or how they resemble or represent facts, objects, relationships, processes, and so on, related to the real world? In the older and, it can be argued, antecedent tradition of simulation-based training such questions are addressed under the heading of 'fidelity'.

The public perception of simulation-based training has traditionally revolved around efforts to replicate as much of the physical operating environment as possible. With regard to flight simulator design, for instance, this might be seen to involve what the pilot should see out of a cockpit window, the 'look and feel' of the controls and instruments, the physical sensations associated with flying, and so on. This form of verisimilitude is termed 'physical fidelity' by researchers and developers in the field and in the context of flight simulators 'equates the quality of a flight simulator device with the capability of the device to represent a physical replica of the aircraft cockpit environment' (Lee, 2005, p. 65). The inclination associated with the term to focus on physical realism is traced interestingly by Elliot, San Antonio, Dalrymple, Schiflett, and Miller (2004, p. 120) all the way back to Thorndike's identical element theory of transfer which was briefly described at the beginning of this chapter; this theory states that learning in one domain improves learning in another only 'in so far as and because [the new domain is] in part identical with it, because it contains elements common to [the original domain]' (Thorndike, 1906, p. 243).

Against this background one might expect that simulation-based learning systems with the greatest degree of physical fidelity, with the greatest number of physically 'identical elements,' should facilitate, or promote, the greatest amount of transfer to the target context. Research and reflection tells a different story, however. Even keeping the most ardent supporter of the (physically) identical element theory of transfer would be unlikely to disagree that:

if the pilot experiences a control feel that is indistinguishable from the actual control feel of the aircraft, then the simulation will be successful. This is true regardless of how closely the control loading system actually replicates control feel as measured by other means. (Lee, 2005, p. 65)

It is *perceived fidelity* then that counts not true physical fidelity. But there is more: to extend the concept of perceived physical fidelity to the facilitation of cognitive processes and activities we need to begin to talk about 'cognitive fidelity', i.e. the 'degree to which scenario content is similar in cognitive demand (i.e. difficulty)' (Elliott et al., 2004, p. 122) or, more simply, the extent to which the environment requires the exercise of a particular cognitive skill or set of skills.

Daniel Gopher, a well-known figure in the simulation-based learning tradition, views the pursuit of physical fidelity as less important than that of cognitive fidelity and with some justification too: a low-tech *Space Fortress* training game of his design with high cognitive fidelity succeeded in a

NASA-sponsored research project where a highly expensive flight simulator with high physical fidelity, it seems, could not (SharpBrains, 2006).

Against research findings that suggest performance in a game about moving a monkey inside a ball around a series of platforms collecting bananas appears to transfer to surgical skills (Rosser et al., 2007) or where skill in driving gorillas and Italian plumbers around in souped-up go karts (*Super Mario Kart*) may correlate with cognitive skills, such as superior short-term and long-term memory and strong self-monitoring skills (VanDeventer & White, 2002), maybe, we are well advised to concern ourselves less with the cosmetic detail of what a game appears to be about or the fictitious realm or world it is based in. Instead, perhaps—unless it is low-level comprehension and factual knowledge which is at issue—we should be very aware of the fidelity of games to real world cognitive requirements in terms both of those noted in the game-based learning research—for example, problem-solving, divided attention, means-ends analysis—and those skills and cognitive processes incorporated in frameworks and theories arising from, for example, the instructional design, cognitive development and productive thinking traditions.

Persuasive games, i.e. games with an agenda or games 'developed to deliberately alter or modify the values, wants, beliefs and/or actions of its players' (Lavender, 2008, p. 261) employ what Ian Bogost calls a 'procedural rhetoric' in the sense that they 'embody an idea or an argument that you explore by doing' (cited in, Mileham, 2008, p. 244) and may be said to aim for a kind of experiential or rhetorical fidelity. The fidelity requirements, here, are distinct certainly from those required for games more focused on the transfer of cognitive skills but bring related design requirements, if only insofar as it is, again, not so much the replication or modelling of a physical setting or physical phenomenon which is key for transfer but repeated practice or exposure to the salient characteristics of the lived experience or lived meaning of other human beings.

FUTURE RESEARCH DIRECTIONS

As indicated at the outset of this chapter, the ability to control and manipulate transfer has, perhaps, never been so keenly felt as it is today in our post-industrial, knowledge-based society. Reskilling, upskilling, lifelong and lifewide learning are not merely the rhetorical stock in trade for governments and policy makers, but genuine, hard-to-meet realities for us all, for living, for working and for generally engaging with the world around us. The, consequently important task of creating games for transfer may need to begin with the development and validation of a new epistemological framework with which, initially, to understand the learning engaged and evidenced in the playing of computer and video games. Such a framework will, likely, need to be drawn both from what is already known with regard to the acquisition, improvement and transfer of a range of cognitive and conative skills from digital game play—for example, problem-solving, divided attention, means-ends analysis—but also those skills and processes incorporated in older cognitive and epistemological frameworks and theories arising from the instructional design, cognitive development and productive thinking traditions.

As noted earlier, games offer opportunities for empirical research simply not achievable in more traditional learning environments. Desktop usability testing software, for example, that records and synchs user onscreen activity and user 'offscreen' verbal and non-verbal activity, can cheaply—in contrast to expensive traditional usability labs—be combined with tried and tested, if not quite unproblematic, qualitative data gathering methods such as talk-aloud and think-aloud protocol and/or post-hoc reflections to create rich data sets for analysis of the various learning processes underlying the real game-playing behaviour of expert and habitual game players. It is only after this kind of work, in validating a new epistemological framework with real data sets, that designers and educationalists can systematically and with confidence take the first steps in creating and adopting games for specific transfer purposes.

CONCLUSION

This chapter began with an overview of what might be termed the 'transfer debate' and proceeded to link transfer, as a concept and phenomenon, to the recent renewed interest in the use of computer and video games for learning. Some key research arising from this fresh interest was discussed and it was noted that a range of studies seeking to investigate the pedagogical effectiveness or 'transfer power' of games at best return mixed results. However, there may be a link between the frequency, or extent, of practice in the original game-based context and the occurrence probability of transfer, (i.e. extensive practice is a key condition for transfer). The complexity of the game environment and the tasks within it were identified as a second interrelated transfer condition. In the context of these two proposed transfer conditions we asked if it matters, much, what games are ostensibly about? Some answers were offered with reference to the antecedent tradition of simulation-based training from which the concept of 'cognitive fidelity' was borrowed to argue that it is the cognitive requirements of games–and also, perhaps in the case of persuasive games, their experiential or rhetorical fidelity–that we should direct our interests and research towards.

Prescriptions for the design of games for transfer arising from these suggestions are threefold:

- To encourage extensive practice, games for transfer should be compelling and intrinsically motivating.

- To ensure deep learning and significant transfer of any kind, games for transfer should be non-trivial but also adaptive.
- To ensure they articulate with the 'content' of our learning or transfer requirements, games for transfer should have an appropriate degree of cognitive and/or experiential fidelity.

These are not simple demands: entertainment game developers, for instance, have traditionally been sufficiently taxed by the need to create products to meet only the first two points, (i.e. to develop games that are 'fun' or compelling while being simultaneously sophisticated and, increasingly, adaptive) scanning the contents of any game review site or magazine reveals just how often they appear to get this wrong. The industry has only, in very rare cases, been required to attempt to join these characteristics to a systematic analysis of the learned or learning processes relating to the playing of their games. As was discussed earlier in this piece, however, this has not stopped a range of implicit and explicit claims–one thinks particularly of brain-training titles, here, but also a range of vocational and simulation games–being made about the ability of the products of the gaming industry essentially to assure the occurrence of what generations of educational researchers have often been at a loss to find or explain (i.e. learning transfer). Against this backdrop this chapter suggests how such claims, from a research and user perspective, could be framed and tested and how, from an industry perspective, these claims might possibly be made with more confidence and veracity.

This work has implications for more than just the traditional computer and video game industry: potentially revolutionising the somewhat staid SCORM/LMS-based product of the e-learning industry; offering something of a rallying call for the burgeoning serious games industry; bridging a gap to the antecedent, but still extant and vital, tradition of simulation-based learning and training;

and, in general, presenting a fresh perspective on a very, very, old problem.

REFERENCES

Adams, P. (1998). Teaching and learning with SimCity 2000. *The Journal of Geography*, *97*(2), 47–55. doi:10.1080/00221349808978827

Army, U. S. (2009). America's army offical website. Retrieved May 7, 2009, from http://www.americasarmy.com

Bereiter, C. (1995). A dispositional view of transfer . In McKeough, A., Lupart, J., & Marini, A. (Eds.), *Teaching for transfer: Fostering generalization in learning* (pp. 21–34). Mahwah, NJ: Lawrence Erlbaum.

Bergeron, B. P. (2006). *Developing serious games*. Hingham, MA: Charles River Media.

Betz, J. (1996). Computer games: Increase learning in an interactive multidisciplinary environment. *Journal of Educational Technology Systems*, *24*(2), 195–205.

Boot, W., Kramer, A., Simons, D., Fabiani, M., & Gratton, G. (2008). The effects of video game playing on attention, memory, and executive control. *Acta Psychologica*, *129*(3), 387–398.

Bransford, J., Brown, A., & Cocking, R. (2003). *How people learn: Brain, mind, experience, and school*. Washington, DC: National Academy Press.

Bransford, J. D., & Schwartz, D. L. (1999). Rethinking transfer: A simple proposal with multiple implications. *Review of Research in Education*, *24*, 61–100.

Campbell, D. (1988). Task complexity: A review and analysis. *Academy of Management Review*, *13*(1), 40–52. doi:10.2307/258353

Carraher, D., & Schliemann, A. (2002). The transfer dilemma. *Journal of the Learning Sciences*, *11*(1), 1–24. doi:10.1207/S15327809JLS1101_1

Cornford, I. (2005). Challenging current policies and policy makers' thinking on generic skills. *Journal of Vocational Education and Training*, *57*(1), 25–45. doi:10.1080/13636820500200273

Csikszentmihalyi, M. (2002). *Flow: The classic work on how to achieve happiness* (Rev. ed.). London: Rider.

De Corte, E. (2003). Transfer as the productive use of acquired knowledge, skills, and motivations. *Current Directions in Psychological Science*, *12*(4), 142–146. doi:10.1111/1467-8721.01250

Detterman, D. K. (1996). The case for the prosecution: Transfer as an epiphenomenon . In Detterman, D. K., & Sternberg, R. J. (Eds.), *Transfer on trial: Intelligence, cognition and instruction* (pp. 1–25). New York: Ablex.

Egenfeldt-Nielsen, S. (2005). *Beyond edutainment: Exploring the educational potential of computer games*. IT-University of Copenhagen.

Elliott, L., San Antonio, T., Dalrymple, M., Schiflett, S., & Miller, J. (2004). Scaling scenarios: Development and application to c4isr sustained operations research . In Schiflett, S. G. (Ed.), *Scaled worlds: Development, validation, and applications* (pp. 119–133). Aldershot: Ashgate.

Fisch, S., Kirkorian, H., & Anderson, D. (2005). Transfer of learning in informal education: The case of television . In Mestre, J. (Ed.), *Transfer of learning from a modern multidisciplinary perspective* (pp. 371–390). Greenwich: IAP.

Gick, M., & Holyoak, K. (1980). Analogical problem solving. *Cognitive Psychology*, *12*(3), 306–355. doi:10.1016/0010-0285(80)90013-4

Goleman, D. (1994, October 11). Peak performance: Why records fall. *The New York Times*.

Greeno, J., Smith, D., & Moore, J. (1996). Transfer of situated learning . In Detterman, D. K., & Sternberg, R. J. (Eds.), *Transfer on trial: Intelligence, cognition, and instruction* (pp. 99–167). New York: Ablex.

Haskell, R. E. (2001). *Transfer of learning: Cognition, instruction, and reasoning.* San Diego, CA: Academic Press.

Hays, R. (2005). *The effectiveness of instructional games: A literature review and discussion.* Orlando, FL: Naval Air Warfare Center Training Systems Division.

Johnson, S. (2006). *Everything bad is good for you: How popular culture is making us smarter.* London: Penguin.

Lavender, T. (2008). Homeless: It's no game – measuring the effectiveness of a persuasive videogame. In T. Conolly, & M. Stansfield (Eds.), *2nd European Conference on Games Based Learning* (pp. 261-266). Barcelona: Academic Publishing Limited.

Leberman, S., McDonald, L., & Doyle, S. (2006). *The transfer of learning: Participants' perspectives of adult education and training.* Aldershot: Gower.

Lee, A. T. (2005). *Flight simulation: Virtual environments in aviation.* Aldershot: Ashgate.

Legacy Games. (2009a). *911 paramedic.* Retrieved May 7, 2009 from http://www.legacygames.com/download_games/861/911_paramedic

Legacy Games. (2009b). *Pet pals: Animal doctor.* Retrieved May 7, 2009 from http://www.legacygames.com/download_games/154/pet_pals:_animal_doctor

Mileham, R. (2008). *Powering up: Are computer games changing our lives?* Chichester: Wiley/Dana Centre.

Nintendo. (2007). *Brain age.* Retrieved May 7, 2009 from http://www.brainage.com

OECD. (2007). Qualifications systems: Bridges to lifelong learning. Paris: Organisation for Economic Co-operation and Development.

Prensky, M. (2005). *Complexity matters.* Retrieved October 20, 2009, from http://marcprensky.com/writing/Prensky-Complexity_Matters.pdf

Randel, J., Morris, B., Wetzel, C., & Whitehill, B. (1992). The effectiveness of games for educational purposes: A review of recent research. *Simulation & Gaming, 23*(3), 261–276. doi:10.1177/1046878192233001

Reed, S., Ernst, G., & Banerji, R. (1974). The role of analogy in transfer between similar problem states. *Cognitive Psychology, 6*(3), 436–450. doi:10.1016/0010-0285(74)90020-6

Rosser, J. Jr, Lynch, P., Cuddihy, L., Gentile, D., Klonsky, J., & Merrell, R. (2007). The impact of video games on training surgeons in the 21st century. *Archives of Surgery, 142*(2), 181–186. doi:10.1001/archsurg.142.2.181

Sawchuk, S. (2009). Backers of '21st-century skills' take flak. *Education Week, 28*(23), 1–14.

SharpBrains. (2006). Cognitive training for basketball game-intelligence: Interview with Prof. Daniel. Gopher. Retrieved March 10, 2009, from http://www.sharpbrains.com/blog/2006/11/02/cognitivesimulations-for-basketball-game-intelligence-interview-with-prof-daniel-gopher/

Singley, M. K., & Anderson, J. R. (1989). *The transfer of cognitive skill.* Cambridge, MA: Harvard University Press.

Squire, K. (2004). *Replaying history: Learning world history through playing Civilization III.* Dissertation, Instructional Systems Technology Department, Indiana University.

Steinkuehler, C. (2008). Massively multiplayer online games as an educational technology: An outline for research. *Educational Technology Magazine: The Magazine for Managers of Change in Education, 48*(1), 10–21.

Súilleabháin, Ó. G. (2008). Player transfer: How learning transfer and serious games answer serious (and transferable) questions about one another. In T. Conolly & M. Stansfield (Eds.), *2nd European Conference on Games Based Learning* (pp. 349-357). Barcelona, Spain: Academic Publishing Limited.

Terborg, J., & Miller, H. (1978). Motivation, behavior, and performance: A closer examination of goal setting and monetary incentives. *The Journal of Applied Psychology, 63*(1), 29–39. doi:10.1037/0021-9010.63.1.29

Thorndike, E., & Woodworth, R. S. (1901c). The influence of improvement in one mental function upon the efficiency of other functions. (III). Functions involving attention, observation and discrimination. *Psychological Review, 8*(6), 553–564. doi:10.1037/h0071363

Thorndike, E. L. (1906). *The principles of teaching based on psychology.* New York: A.G. Seiler. doi:10.1037/11487-000

Thorndike, E. L., & Woodworth, R. S. (1901a). The influence of improvement in one mental function upon the efficiency of other functions. (I). *Psychological Review, 8*(3), 247–261. doi:10.1037/h0074898

Thorndike, E. L., & Woodworth, R. S. (1901b). The influence of improvement in one mental function upon the efficiency of other functions. (II). The estimation of magnitudes. *Psychological Review, 8*(4), 384–395. doi:10.1037/h0071280

VanDeventer, S., & White, J. (2002). Expert behavior in children's video game play. *Simulation & Gaming, 33*(1), 28–48. doi:10.1177/1046878102033001002

Vogel, J. F., Vogel, D. S., Cannon-Bowers, J., Bowers, C. A., Muse, K., & Wright, M. (2006). Computer gaming and interactive simulations for learning: A meta-analysis. *Journal of Educational Computing Research, 34*(3), 229–243. doi:10.2190/FLHV-K4WA-WPVQ-H0YM

ADDITIONAL READING

Alexander, P., & Murphy, P. (1999). Nurturing the seeds of transfer: A domain-specific perspective. *International Journal of Educational Research, 31*(7), 561–576. doi:10.1016/S0883-0355(99)00024-5

Baldwin, T., & Ford, J. (1994). Transfer of training: A review and directions for future research . In Schneier, C. E., Russell, C. J., Beatty, R. W., & Baird, L. S. (Eds.), *The training and development sourcebook* (pp. 180–205). Amherst, MA: Human Resource Development Press.

Barnett, S., & Ceci, S. (2002). When and where do we apply what we learn? A taxonomy for far transfer. *Psychological Bulletin, 128*(4), 612–637. doi:10.1037/0033-2909.128.4.612

Beach, K. (1999). Consequential transitions: A sociocultural expedition beyond transfer in education. *Review of Research in Education, 28*, 101–139.

Besnard, D., & Cacitti, L. (2005). Interface changes causing accidents. An empirical study of negative transfer. *International Journal of Human-Computer Studies, 62*(1), 105–125. doi:10.1016/j.ijhcs.2004.08.002

Burke, L., & Hutchins, H. (2007). Training transfer: An integrative literature review. *Human Resource Development Review, 6*(3), 263. doi:10.1177/1534484307303035

Cheng, E., & Hampson, I. (2008). Transfer of training: A review and new insights. *International Journal of Management Reviews, 10*(4), 327–341. doi:10.1111/j.1468-2370.2007.00230.x

Clark, R., & Voogel, A. (1985). Transfer of training principles for instructional design. *Educational Technology Research and Development, 33*(2), 113–123.

Cree, V. E., & Macaulay, C. (2000). *Transfer of learning in professional and vocational education*. London: Routledge.

Detterman, D., & Sternberg, R. (1996). *Transfer on trial: Intelligence, cognition and instruction*. New York: Ablex.

Ellis, H. C. (1965). *The transfer of learning*. New York: Macmillan.

Gopher, D., Weil, M., & Bareket, T. (1994). Transfer of skill from a computer game trainer to flight. *Human Factors, 36*(3), 387–405.

Helfenstein, S. (2005). Transfer: Review, reconstruction and resolution. [Dissertation] University of Jyväskylä.

Mayer, R., & Wittrock, M. (1996). Problem-solving transfer . In Berliner, D., & Calfree, R. (Eds.), *Handbook of educational psychology* (pp. 47–62). New York: Macmillian.

McKeachie, W. (1987). Cognitive skills and their transfer [Discussion]. *International Journal of Educational Research, 11*(6), 707–712. doi:10.1016/0883-0355(87)90010-3

McKeough, A., Lupart, J., & Marini, A. (1995). *Teaching for transfer: Fostering generalization in learning*. Mahwah, NJ: Lawrence Erlbaum.

Mestre, J. P. (2005). *Transfer of learning from a modern multidisciplinary perspective*. Greenwich, CT: Information Age.

Postman, L., & Stark, K. (1971). Encoding variability and transfer. *The American Journal of Psychology, 84*(4), 461–471. doi:10.2307/1421162

Reed, S. (1996). A schema-based theory of transfer . In Detterman, D. (Ed.), *Transfer on trial: Intelligence, cognition and instruction* (pp. 39–67). New York: Ablex.

Royer, J. (1979). Theories of the transfer of learning. *Educational Psychologist, 14*(1), 53–69. doi:10.1080/00461527909529207

Salomon, G., & Perkins, D. (1989). Rocky roads to transfer: Rethinking mechanism of a neglected phenomenon. *Educational Psychologist, 24*(2), 113–142. doi:10.1207/s15326985ep2402_1

Thorndike, E. L. (1923). The influence of first year Latin upon the ability to read English. *School Sociology, 17*, 165–168.

Thorndike, E. L. (1924). Mental discipline in high school studies. *Journal of Educational Psychology, (15)*: 1–22. doi:10.1037/h0075386

Tuomi-Gröhn, T., & Engeström, Y. (2003). *Between school and work: New perspectives on transfer and boundary-crossing* (1st ed.). Amsterdam, London: Pergamon.

Vogel, J. F., Vogel, D. S., Cannon-Bowers, J., Bowers, C. A., Muse, K., & Wright, M. (2006). Computer gaming and interactive simulations for learning: A meta-analysis. *Journal of Educational Computing Research, 34*(3), 229–243. doi:10.2190/FLHV-K4WA-WPVQ-H0YM

Chapter 8
Anti–Plagiarism Software in an Irish University:
Three Years Later

Angelica Risquez
University of Limerick, Ireland

ABSTRACT

A variety of anti-plagiarism software applications have appeared in recent years, but the pedagogical and institutional practices underpinning their use remains largely unexplored. It is essential to increase the amount of evidence-based literature that investigates the use of anti-plagiarism software in higher education. In the light of this, this chapter explores the integration of anti-plagiarism software in an Irish university since early 2006 and the progress made to date. We use data gathered from our own context to show how instructors are using this software to date, what trends emerge and what can be deduced about the adoption of the system to guide future research questions. Best practices are suggested for educators in order to help them to use anti-plagiarism software in proactive, positive, and pedagogically sound ways.

INTRODUCTION

Academic dishonesty is far from a new phenomenon, yet claims that it is on the rise are widespread and often associated to the use of the Internet (Chaky & Diekhoff, 2002; Scanlon & Neumann, 2002). Several plagiarism scandals, the proliferation of 'paper mills' and websites offering assignments 'à la carte', and the widespread use of the Internet for learning purposes have also amplified

awareness of it. The concern of higher education institutions is manifested in their websites, where students are advised on correct referencing and plagiarism avoidance, and educators are given tools and guidance to detect cheaters. A variety of free and commercial software designed to detect plagiarism from Internet sources has also appeared and has been made available to teachers as a means to deter plagiarism and detect it when happening (Turnitin, My Drop Box, Eve, WcopyFind are some of these). The plethora of educational institutions that have adopted the use

DOI: 10.4018/978-1-61520-879-1.ch008

of plagiarism prevention software indicates that its popularity is thriving.

Both practical and ethical issues can be argued for and against the use of technological solutions for the investigation of the originality of students' work. While distributors like Turnitin assert that their plagiarism prevention module can enhance teaching by 'deterring plagiarism before it happens' (from www.turnitin.com), detractors regard the service pedagogically inappropriate, untrustworthy and even unethical. For example, Carbone (2001) denounces that 'the service is not about teaching, it's about catching, it's a pedagogic placebo'. Similarly, Sutherland-Smith and Carr (2005) express their concerns that teachers could view Turnitin as a purely punitive tool. The authors report that some members of staff participating in their study felt that that 'where students were caught for plagiarism and punished, that would be the educative value of the anti-plagiarism software, as students would be unlikely to re-offend'. This approach implies a reactive attitude to the behavioural manifestations of academic dishonesty, which neglects the reasons that underpin it and the actions that may prevent it from happening. On the other hand, it is arguable that the effectiveness of plagiarism-prevention services has been assumed rather than confirmed, and only a few studies have addressed their actual impact on the student population (Baker, Thornton, & Adams, 2008; Draaijer & van Boxel, 2006; Goddard & Rudzki, 2005; Rees & Emerson, 2009). In the light of this discussion, we believe it is essential to increase the amount of evidence-based literature that investigates the use of anti-plagiarism software in higher education.

BACKGROUND

Turnitin (www.turnitin.com) is a widely used online tool which addresses academic honesty in students' work (plagiarism prevention); formative and summative feedback (online marking); and student-centred assessment (peer review). The tool has also an important level of acceptance in Ireland, as the last conference of the Irish Educational Technology Users' Conference saw the first meeting of the Turnitin user group, with around 20 attendees from Institutions across Ireland.[1] The University of Limerick adopted the use of the software in 2005 and it has been used since 2006, with training and support provided by the Centre for Teaching and Learning. As it is the case with many other educational technologies offered by the institution, the use of the system has remained the prerogative of each lecturer, and voluntary training sessions have been organised on demand, with one-to-one support being offered on an ongoing basis. All seminars and support are underpinned by a positive, proactive attitude towards plagiarism prevention that puts student learning in the centre of the process. During this period, around 150 teachers' faculty have attended training, and one-to-one support has been provided for many more. Appendix B shows a piece of documentation distributed across the institution which gives basic information about Turnitin, warns of its limitations, gives an example case scenario and provides further resources.

Almost three years after the initial introduction of the software at the institution, the statistics collected along six semesters of use offer some insights into the patters of use of the system. In this chapter we use data gathered from our own context to show how instructors are using this software to date, what trends emerge and what can be deduced about the adoption of the system to guide future research questions.

OUR EXPERIENCE SO FAR

According to cumulative statistics collected in April 2009, 210 instructor accounts[2] had been created in the system since 2006, there were 7,802 student accounts,[3] 11,970 submissions had been completed, 10,144 originality reports produced,

Figure 1. Number of New Student Accounts Each Semester

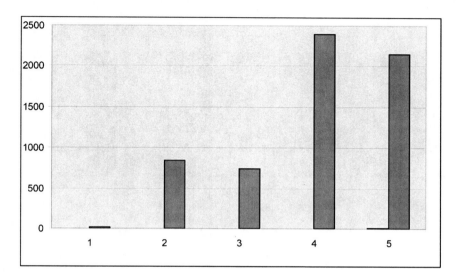

1,783 peer reviews[4] had been performed and 226 papers had been marked online. Therefore, although the online marking and peer review features of the system have been used by a minority, most faculty members approaching the system have used the plagiarism prevention tools. The statistics presented next correspond to the first five semesters of use of the system (from early 2006 to mid 2008), when 140 instructor accounts were active in the system.

Number of Accounts

There are indications from the rate of creation of new student accounts in the system that the teachers who adopted the use of Turnitin after its introduction did not do so with whole classes. Figure 1 shows the creation of student accounts largely increased in the last part of the second year of implementation (semester 4), indicating a progressive standardisation of the use of Turnitin with full classes. We can reasonably assume that if the system had been integrated with the institutional learning management system the early rate of adoption could have been higher and the use across full cohorts would be likely to become the norm.

The representation of student registrations across colleges was however very uneven: while the College of Engineering and Humanities was largely represented by the student accounts in the system, the use by the College of Education, Informatics and Electronics and Science was minimal. We have no reasons that justify this distribution and this could possibly be an area for further exploration, although this trend mirrors the adoption of other proposed educational technology at the institution, which suggests there are different motivators towards technology enhanced teaching innovation across departments and colleges. See Figure 2.

The number of total reports by college reflects the number of student accounts created in the system, with Humanities and the Kemmy Business School leading (with approximately 2,300 and 1,700 originality reports produced respectively), followed by Engineering with roughly 1,450 reports.

Figure 2. Representation of Student Accounts in Turnitin (relative to student registration records in academic year 2007/08)

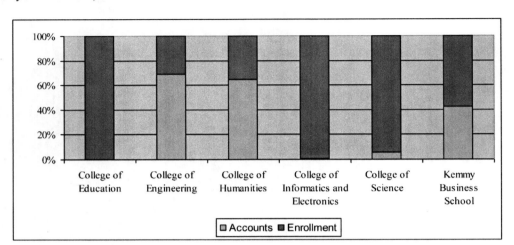

Originality Reports

It is also interesting to explore the results of the originality reports produced by Turnitin (the system provides an originality report with a 'similarity index' per submission, corresponding to the percentage of text in the student's work which matches text in publicly available online sources and every single document submitted to Turnitin in the past). During the first five semesters that the system was used, over 11,200 were generated, including both all the submissions made by students and by faculty. While just over 40% of the reports were found to have an overall similarity index of 24% or less with publicly available sources in the Internet or the Turnitin database, almost 27% of the originality reports produced rendered a similarity index of 75% matching text or higher. These results are inclusive of bibliographies, as the feature that allows the lecturer to exclude them from the originality report was only included later on. It must be noted too that the university does not adhere to a particular percentage as an acceptable level of plagiarism, and it is left to the lecturer to judge, according to personal teaching experience, when the 'matching text' identified constitutes actual plagiarism.

When looking at the evolution of the results of the originality reports semester by semester, we can observe that the number of reports where less than 24% text was matched to online sources has progressively increased, from around 45% in the first semester to approximately 75% in the fifth semester of use. In contrast, the number of originality reports containing more than 75% of text matching other sources has decreased overall, representing less than 5% of all documentation submitted into the system in the same semester (from around 20% in the first semester of use of the system). This could indicate an increasing trend to use Turnitin with whole classes, as opposed to each lecturer submitting student material which is deemed to be suspected of plagiarism.

Emerging Practices

These results pose questions on how the instructors used Turnitin with their classes, in order to further understand the high number of reports (which amount to over 1,100 potential plagiarism cases) in which a high level of matching text was found. The 140 faculty accounts created in the system at that stage represented 31% of their population. When examining the online records closely, we discovered that 73 of them (52% of the total) did not create student accounts so their students could submit their work into Turnitin; instead they submitted all assignments into the system themselves. 48 of them (34.3%) have at least one student account created, which allows students to submit their own work, although we cannot guarantee from the records this was always the case. Finally, 19 of them have created instructor accounts in the system, but have not submitted any documents. See Figure 3.

We were particularly interested to learn who had submitted the documentation into the system, so we proceeded to examine further the group of lecturers who created student accounts. From the 48 lecturers that created student accounts or facilitated their students doing so, 22 had classes with more than eight students (the size of a small tutorial class) and at least eight submissions, the other 26 seem to have created a few student accounts to cater for special cases. That is, out of 121 instructors with submissions in the system, only 18% had organised student submissions with their classes.

It is also noticeable that the trend of results of the originality reports changes with the method of submission used. When the faculty created student accounts with group sizes of 8 students or more,

the results of the reports tend to cluster around the low similarity index of 0–24% of matching text. See Figure 4.

These results indicate that anti-plagiarism software is best used integrated in an assessment strategy for the whole class that addresses the issue of academic honesty, aided by Turnitin as a learning tool. Some of the informal interactions with our faculty give us indications the system may be best used with proactive practices which emphasise writing skills and specific training in referencing practices, as the excerpt from one email received in Appendix C shows.

DISCUSSION AND FURTHER RESEARCH DIRECTIONS

The results rendered by the plagiarism-prevention system throughout five semesters of use at the institution have shown that the majority of submissions fall below the level of 25% matched text. However, a significant percentage has been found to contain over 50% of verbatim text from websites and other submissions to the system, which is largely due to the lecturer's submitting into the system only those assignments that are deemed suspicious of plagiarism. When instructors

Figure 3. How Teaching Staff Used the System

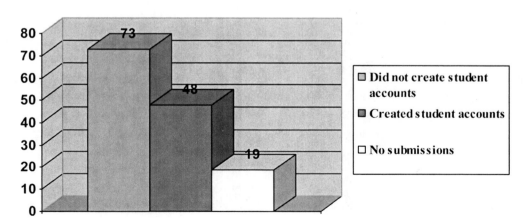

Figure 4. Results from Originality Reports Per Mode of Submission

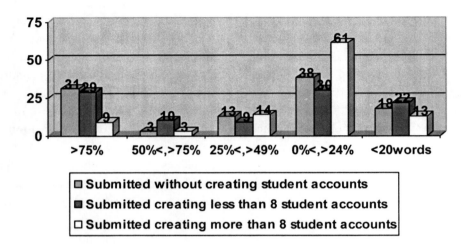

facilitate their students submitting their own work the picture shown by the originality reports is quite different compared to when it is the faculty member who submits the work. The results in our context suggest therefore that the statistics offered by Turnitin cannot be used to make inferences about the incidence of plagiarism in any given institution, as the system can be used in very different ways. This in turn relates to underpinning assumptions on the role of students and instructors, trust, and collective responsibility at the institution.

We have also seen that only a small minority of faculty members have had all their students submitting work into the system. However the escalating rate of creation of student accounts and the progressively increasing number of submissions with low similarity indexes seems to indicate the system is starting to be used with full classes in a standardised fashion.

From the results presented, two distinctive practices emerge. On one hand are those lecturers who are proactive, encouraging students to submit their assignments and take responsibility in the process. On the other hand are those who themselves use the system to submit documents written by students that are likely to have been plagiarised. It remains to be seen how these different practices are intertwined with a comprehensive approach to plagiarism prevention, how they affect academic performance, student learning, and development of attitudes towards academic honesty. We could hypothesise that the fact that the majority of faculty members are using the system without creating students accounts, submitting assignments when they are flagged as 'suspicious', constitutes an ad-hoc approach which may alienate students from the use of the system and can provoke reactions of resistance, fear, etc. We could also conjecture that the use of the software may actually provide more added value if students are encouraged to submit their work through the semester, are allowed to see their own originality reports, and have an available tutor (or peer support) to learn the conventions of referencing and academic honesty.

Of course there is a need to find out more from lecturers on how and why they are using the system. (See proposed survey questions in Appendix 1) Also, questions can be asked about the reasons why around 70% of the teaching population at this particular institution do not use the system at all, and whether they are they addressing the issue of academic honesty and how. It may well be that, despite managerial support for the use of Turnitin, many remain sceptic about the effectiveness of technology-enhanced, plagiarism-prevention methods or oppose its use for pedagogical reasons. However, it has also been well established in the literature that the issue of plagiarism is likely being neglected, as faculty often avoid the issue (Vandehey, Diekhoff, & LaBeff, 2007). There is also interest in gathering students' views on the use of the system, complementing the picture drawn by some other emerging research (Dahl, 2007; Ledwith & Risquez, 2008; Savage, 2004; Sheridan, Alany, & Brake, 2005; Smith, Evans, Jastram, & Leader, 2008).

CONCLUSION

In a context where academic honesty is actively promoted and rewarded, it would be expected that values of integrity and honour would be internalised, based on the principles of individual freedom and mutual responsibility. On the other hand, it is also possible that educational contexts based on student competitiveness and control result in 'self-fulfilling prophecies' of deceit and fraud. In this sense, I believe the use of anti-plagiarism software can play a role as a learning tool within comprehensive approaches to plagiarism prevention, in which students have an available tutor (or peer support) and learn the conventions of referencing and academic honesty. The knowledge creation and informal learning that happens through collaborative work in wikis, blogs and other social networking Web 2.0 tools based on the principles of sharing and repurposing poses new challenges but also offers new exciting learning opportunities as students are immersed in knowledge creation and informal learning which challenges traditional notions of authorship. Learning tasks should be underpinned by the principles of authentic assessment, as the dangers of plagiarism are greatly reduced when students are set authentic work assignments where 'learners should demonstrate, rather than tell

about, what they know and can do' (Cole, Ryan, & Kick, 1995). Positive and creative, rather than punitive ways, of introducing anti-plagiarism software in the class are recommended (for example, peer assessment exercises, allowing students to see their own originality reports, giving feedback on writing skills, and so on) in order to 'practice what we preach.'

REFERENCES

Baker, R. K., Thornton, B., & Adams, M. (2008). An evaluation of the effectiveness of turnitin. com as a tool for reducing plagiarism in graduate student term papers [Electronic Version]. *College Teaching Methods & Styles Journal, 4.* Retrieved October 19, 2009 from http://www. cluteinstitute-onlinejournals.com/archives/abstract.cfm?ArticleID=2096

Carbone, N. (2001). Turnitin.com, a pedagogic placebo for plagiarism [Electronic Version]. *Technical Notes.* Retrieved October 10, 2007 from http://bedfordstmartins.com/technotes/techtiparchive/ttip060501.htm

Chaky, M., & Diekhoff, M. (2002). A comparison of traditional and internet cheaters. *Journal of College Student Development, 43*(6), 906–911.

Cole, D. J., Ryan, C. W., & Kick, F. (1995). *Portfolios across the curriculum and beyond.* California: Corwin Press.

Dahl, S. (2007). Turnitin. The student perspective on using plagiarism detection software . *Active Learning in Higher Education, 8*(2), 173–191. doi:10.1177/1469787407074110

Draaijer, S., & van Boxel, P. (2006). *Summative peer assessment using 'Turnitin' and a large cohort of students: A case study.* Paper presented at the Computer-Assisted Assessment (CAA) Conference. Retrieved October 20, 2009, from http://hdl.handle.net/2134/4559

Goddard, R., & Rudzki, R. (2005). Using an electronic text-matching tool (Turnitin) to detect plagiarism in a New Zealand university. *Journal of University Teaching & Learning Practice, 2.*

Ledwith, A., & Risquez, A. (2008). Using anti-plagiarism software to promote academic honesty in the context of peer reviewed assignments. *Studies in Higher Education, 33*(4), 371–384. doi:10.1080/03075070802211562

Rees, M., & Emerson, L. (2009). The impact that Turnitin has had on text-based assessment practice. *International Journal for Educational Integrity, 5*(1), 20–29.

Savage, S. (2004). *Staff and student responses to a trial of Turnitin plagiarism detection software.* Paper presented at the Australian Universities Quality Forum 2004, Australia.

Scanlon, P., & Neumann, D. R. (2002). Internet plagiarism among college students. *Journal of College Student Development, 43*(3), 374–385.

Sheridan, J., Alany, R., & Brake, D.-J. (2005). Pharmacy students' views and experiences of Turnitin®—an online tool for detecting academic dishonesty. *Pharmacy Education, 5*(3/4), 241–250. doi:10.1080/15602210500288977

Smith, G., Evans, J., Jastram, C., & Leader, W. G. (2008). *Enhancing plagiarism awareness and understanding among students through didactic review and TurnItIn.* Paper presented at the annual meeting of the American Association of Colleges of Pharmacy, July 19, 2008.

Sutherland-Smith, W., & Carr, D. (2005). Turnitin.com: Teachers' perspectives of anti-plagiarism software in raising issues of educational integrity. *Journal of University Teaching and Learning Practice, 3*(1b), 94–101.

Vandehey, M., Diekhoff, G., & LaBeff, E. (2007). College cheating: A twenty-year follow-up and the addition of an honor code. *Journal of College Student Development, 48*(4), 468–480. doi:10.1353/csd.2007.0043

ADDITIONAL READING

Devlin, M. (2006). Policy, preparation, and prevention: proactive minimization of student plagiarism. *Journal of Higher Education Policy and Management, 28*(1), 45–58. doi:10.1080/13600800500283791

Jenson, J., & De Castell, S. (2004). 'Turn it in': Technological challenges to academic ethics. *Education Communication and Information, 4*(2-3), 311–330. doi:10.1080/1463631041233130473 5

Macdonald, J. C. (2006). Plagiarism—a complex issue requiring a holistic institutional approach. *Assessment & Evaluation in Higher Education, 31*(2), 233–245. doi:10.1080/02602930500262536

Marsh, B. (2004). Turnitin.com and the scriptural enterprise of plagiarism detection. *Computers and Composition, 21*(4), 427–438. doi:10.1016/S8755-4615(04)00039-8

Martin, D. (2005). Plagiarism and technology: A tool for coping with plagiarism. *Journal of Education for Business, 80*(3), 149–152. doi:10.3200/JOEB.80.3.149-152

McKeever, L. (2006). Online plagiarism detection services—saviour or scourge? *Assessment & Evaluation in Higher Education, 31*(2), 155–165. doi:10.1080/02602930500262460

Underwood, J., & Szabo, A. (2003). Academic offences and e-learning: Individual propensities in cheating. *British Journal of Educational Technology, 34*(4), 467–477. doi:10.1111/1467-8535.00343

Walden, K., & Peacock, A. (2006). The i-Map: A process-centered response to plagiarism. *Assessment & Evaluation in Higher Education*, *31*(2), 201–214. doi:10.1080/02602930500262510

ENDNOTES

[1] For more information see http://www.tcd.ie/CAPSL/academic_practice/index.php?page=turnitin

[3] Student accounts are created by lecturers administering a class or can be created by the student when provided with a username and passwords. Student accounts are unique and non transferable. Students submit their work through their student account and can receive feedback from the lecturer or tutor, and by default cannot see other peers' submissions.

[4] There is a peer review feature in Turnitin which allows lecturers to set up a peer review assignment for students to evaluate each others' work. Once students have completed their own submission, they are randomly assigned one or more assignments for anonymous peer review.

[5] Adapted from the cases available in the webpage of the Instruction Technology Services of Diego State University, http://its.sdsu.edu/resources/turnitin/index.html

APPENDIX A.

Table 1. Proposed questions for faculty study

Survey Questions
1. Do you use Turnitin? yes/no
    (if 'no', respondents are taken automatically to question 'Why did you choose not to use it?')
2. Please select what feature(s) in Turnitin you use (tick as many as apply):
    ☐ Plagiarism prevention
    ☐ Peer review
    ☐ Online grading
3. What type of classes do you use Turnitin with?
    ☐ Small (1–49 students)
    ☐ Medium (50–99 students)
    ☐ Large (over 100 students)
4. When do you use Turnitin? (tick as many as apply):
    ☐ At the beginning of the semester
    ☐ During the semester
    ☐ At the end of the semester
5. Please describe in a few lines your main purpose for using Turnitin:
    ....
    ....
6. What of the following do you do? (tick as many as apply)
    ☐ I personally submit students' work into Turnitin
    ☐ I get students to submit their work into Turnitin themselves
    ☐ Other (please explain):
    ....
    ....
7. Which of the following you do? (tick as many as apply)
    ☐ I only submit/get my students to submit work into Turnitin thst is deemed suspicious of plagiarism to get an originality report for those students only
    ☐ I submit/get my students to submit into Turnitin all students' work to get an originality report for all students
    ☐ Other (please explain):
    ....
    ....
8. How are your students introduced to Turnitin? (tick as many as apply)
    ☐ They are not introduced to it
    ☐ It is mentioned in the syllabus for the module
    ☐ They get a handout with instructions for Turnitin
    ☐ They get a demo on a main screen in class/tutorial
    ☐ They get a hands-on demo in a pc lab
    ☐ They are requested to submit a test document into the system
    ☐ They get to see their originality report
    ☐ Other (please explain):..
    ....
9. What do you use the originality report for?
    ....
    ....
10. Do you allow students to see their originality reports? Yes/no
    Please explain why:..
    ....
11. Do you give your students any feedback on the result of their originality reports? Yes/no
    Please explain why
    ....
    ....

12. Do you use Grade Mark? Yes/no
Which of these features of Grade Mark do you use?
□ the Highlighter Tool
□ the Comment List
□ the Rubrics Library
□ the Quick Mark Sets
□ the Clipboard Library
□ Statistics Tool
□ Student Mode
□ the Edit feature
13. Finally, please explain how using Turnitin has aided your teaching and your students' learning?
....
....
14. Why did you choose not to use it?
....
....

This survey is anonymous and confidential. However in order to understand better our findings we would greatly appreciate you giving us some demographic information. All details will be strictly used for research purposes only.
Department (drop down menu of all departments here)
Role:
□ Lecturer
□ Teaching Assistant
□ Researcher
□ Working status
□ Full time
□ Part time
Number of years teaching at UL:
Number of years teaching in total (UL and elsewhere):
Number of modules taught by semester:
Size of module(s):
□ Small (1–49 students)
□ Medium (50–99 students)
□ Large (over 100 students)

APPENDIX B.

RECOMMENDATIONS FOR FACULTY USING TURNITIN.COM

What is Turnitin?

Turnitin (www.Turnitin.com) is an online resource for educators and students, which offers varied diverse web-based class management solutions. This document deals with the Plagiarism Prevention module only.

What Does the Plagiarism Prevention Module Involve?

Submitted papers are compared to millions of pages of content located on the Internet and Turnitin.com proprietary databases. The results of those comparisons are compiled, one for each paper submitted, in custom 'Originality Reports' (Figure 5). These reports are sent to the lecturer.

Some Important Points about the Plagiarism Prevention Module

- It can identify matching text even when a student has added, deleted or substituted significant amounts of text

Figure 5. Originality report

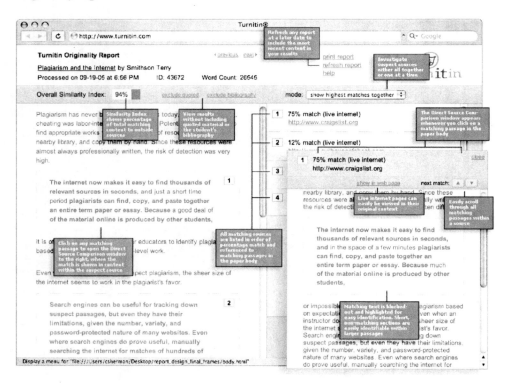

- It is faster and more effective than investigating for the original sources through conventional search engines (i.e. Goggle), allowing for citation verification and providing documentation of any alleged plagiarism
- Turnitin stores in its database every new submitted piece of work, but your work can not be released without the permission of the instructor who submits and/or is responsible for the class
- **All the software does is matching text, not examining citation correctness**, in other words, it is perfectly possible that a document full of quotations properly referenced returns an originality report with a high percentage of similarity with other source. Therefore, instructors must judge, according to personal teaching experience, when the 'matching text' identified constitutes actual plagiarism.

Possible Case Scenario[5]

An originality report has shown a match for the following passage:

According to the authors of the Report for the Policy Center on the First Year of College at Brevard College numerous studies use Tinto's model as a springboard from which to explore further the dynamics of departure; in doing so, the authors often draw attention to several features of first-year student persistence that the model fails to fully address.

Upon clicking on the comparison link, your lecturer finds that the text is found in an on-line report, entitled 'Designing an Assessment of the First College Year: Results from the 1999–2000 YFCY Pilot Study. Report for the Policy Center on the First Year of College at Brevard College'. This may be interpreted as an instance of poor citation instead of plagiarism. While the student makes an effort to attribute the proper source, the citation itself is incorrectly done, and your lecturer may decide to drop some marks for this.

UL Resources to Avoid Plagiarism

```
http://www.ul.ie/ctl/plagiarismhttp://www.ul.ie/~library/referenc-
inghttp://www.desktop.ul.ie/lskills/TLTP3/IS/plagiarism.htmlhttp://
www.ul.ie/studentacademicadmin/files/student_handbook_2005-2006.pdf
```

(Appendix 5: Plagiarism at College)

```
http://www.ul.ie/%7Elibrary/tutorials.html
```
   (Library online tutorials on Harvard referencing style, Refworks, researching with the internet, etc.)

APPENDIX C. A LECTURER'S VIEWS ON THE USE OF TURNITIN

… it seems that I am the only one that requested that students submit all of their texts to Turnitin. I have found them reluctant to do so, but I'm not sure why. At this point, only a few have been exposed for documentation violation through Turnitin.

In fact, Turnitin doesn't pick up everything. For instance, paraphrased and summarized information is not picked up by the software. During the editing and proofing process, tutors have to inform students when it is appropriate to document information. Electronically, I edit using Microsoft Track Changes. I think that next time, I will try to use the program available on Turnitin to make commentary and flag errors, but I just wasn't ready to do it this time. I would only have to convert my code list into rubrics on the website, but it just seemed like a time-consuming task that I just wasn't up for. Anyway, to indicate that a passage needs to be documented, I use the code 'Cit.', for 'citation necessary here'. I'm finding that these first year students are, understandably, uncertain about what kind of information needs to be cited. As a result, many of the errors detected by Turnitin were related to the fact that the students are altogether uninformed and uncertain about how to reference. We should expect more of these students in second year.

As to the lack of submissions, there was a simultaneous lack of tutorial attendance. There's speculation that a number of the students have jobs, but I don't buy it. They just don't seem that industrious. Who knows. For the few students who did attend tutorials and submit regularly, I think the combination of essay writing tutorials, feedback and originality verification was a boon of a benefit. We'll see.

Chapter 9
iClassroom:
Opportunities for Touch Screen Handheld Technologies in Learning and Teaching

Eugene F. M. O'Loughlin
National College of Ireland, Ireland

ABSTRACT

Hand-held technologies such as Apple's iPod/iTouch/iPhone devices are now capable of being used for educational purposes as well as for entertainment. The purpose of this chapter is to discuss the issues, content authoring, usage, workload, and pedagogical consequences of creating an iClassroom for mobile learning based on these devices. Use of podcasts and vodcasts by students, and their rate of success are varied as shown by studies reviewed from the literature and carried out by the author for this chapter. Several strategies for reducing workload at an individual and institutional level are proposed for adoption by educators. Key recommendations from this chapter are an increased emphasis on evaluation, usage of models for developing content, and an inclusion of iPod/iTouch/iPhone devices as part of an overall architecture for m-learning.

INTRODUCTION

Recent advances in hand-held, touch-screen devices open up many opportunities for learning and teaching. Already, many third-level institutions world-wide have introduced such devices in many different ways to both engage learners and teachers, as well as to provide administration support. While there are many such devices now available, this chapter will concentrate on the

use of Apple technology with video capabilities: specifically the iPod/iTouch/iPhone devices, as these are the devices that the author has most experience with. The power of these devices lies in their portability, connectivity, and flexibility. They can be used for a wide variety of education types such as the delivery of HIV/AIDs educational material to a college population (Shim, Crider, Kim, & Raffin, 2008), the provision of College services to students (Sacco, 2008), and the use of podcasts by students for reflective learning (Ng'ambi, 2008).

DOI: 10.4018/978-1-61520-879-1.ch009

This chapter reviews:

- the existing literature on the use of iPod/iTouch/iPhone devices in the classroom
- the pedagogical challenges in the use of iPod/iTouch/iPhone devices in the classroom for e-learning content
- existing uses of such technologies in third-level institutions
- examination of both student and teacher perceptions on the use of iPod/iTouch/iPhone devices in the classroom
- workload implications for educational technologists
- an exploration of m-learning and the use of iPod/iTouch/iPhone devices

BACKGROUND

Since the introduction of the original iPod from Apple on the October 23, 2001, advances in hand-held technology have opened up many opportunities for educational use of iPod/iTouch/iPhone devices. Early Apple devices were used mainly for entertainment purposes only: they were capable of little more than playing music. With the introduction of iPods with colour display in 2005, and video capability in 2006, educators started to get interested in looking at ways to use these devices to enhance the educational experience for students. Innovative teachers and lecturers started to use podcasts–sometimes recording entire classes–which were then made available to students. In the meantime, the storage capacity of hand-held devices soared: by 2007 the capacity of the iPod had reached up to 160GB. Suddenly file size was no longer a major technological issue: recordings (podcasts) that needed many megabytes of storage capacity could easily fit on an iPod. Videos (vodcasts) were now also available for the iPod.

In January 2007, Apple announced the introduction of the iPhone that 'completely redefines what users can do on their mobile phones' (Apple Press Release, 2007a). While the storage capacity of the initial iPhone was smaller than the then available iPods, it was instead a feature rich device that had touch-screen capabilities. By September 2007, Apple had also introduced the iTouch: essentially the same as an iPhone, but without mobile phone capabilities. By the end of 2007, Apple had a suite of products with Internet access and media rich audio and video capabilities: the iPod, iTouch, and iPhone. The iPhone 3G has recently become the top-selling mobile phone in the USA (NDP Group, 2008). In February 2009, the iPhone accounted for a 'staggering 66.61 percent of mobile traffic', though just '0.48 percent of the web' traffic (Malley, 2009).

Initially teachers had to distribute their podcasts and vodcasts through their own websites. In May 2007, Apple launched iTunes U which is a dedicated area within the iTunes Store that provides 'free content such as course lectures, language lessons, lab demonstrations, sports highlights and campus tours' (Apple Press Release, 2007b). To date there are over 200 universities and colleges such as Oxford, Cambridge, Yale, Trinity College Dublin, and The Open University UK, with a presence on iTunes U. iTunes U makes content available for download onto iPod/iTouch/iPhone devices. Currently there are over 100,000 educational audio and video files available ranging in content from lectures on quantum mechanics at Stanford University, to Creative Writing at the Open University, and to Genetics at the Université Paris Descartes.

In July 2008, Apple launched the App Store–a resource for third-party developers to create their own applications for the iTouch and iPhone and making them available online through iTunes, many of which are free. At the time of writing there are over 15,000 applications available with over 500 million downloaded so far (Burrows, 2009). Of these, over 3,000 are education related applications. These range from applications that teach a variety of subjects such as: languages, mathematics, history, geography, science, web development, and law. There are also other educational tools such as dictionaries, thesauri, calculators, quizzes, brain teasers, e-books, phrase books, and study aids available–some of them free of charge. As the App Store continues to be a successful platform for developers, there are many opportunities to provide many more educational tools at an affordable price.

Today, Apple and many other companies have provided an environment with rich possibilities for educators as well as learners in higher education. According to the website of Abilene Christian University (ACU), a third-level institution in Texas, ACU has developed online tools and resources, called 'ACU Mobi', specifically optimized for iPod/iTouch/iPhone technology. With this technology, ACU students can do many things such as:

- check calendar and webmail
- contact classmates and university staff
- get news and directions around campus
- check when assignments are due
- gather information about classes
- check balances for college accounts such as printing and meals
- view files stored on the college network
- view guides to student and local services
- answer in-class polls and quizzes

All of the above features can now be added to the existing functionality that iPod/iTouch/iPhone devices already provide, such as:

- full web browsing
- checking email
- listening to podcasts
- viewing vodcasts
- reading eBooks
- communicating through text messaging and voice (iPhone only)

This means that with a hand-held device, students have all the ingredients for the 'iClassroom,'

or what Bell (2008) refers to as 'The university in your pocket' (p. 178). For the purposes of this chapter, the iClassroom can be described as a virtual classroom that provides access to all types of online content, as well as to student services as in ACU, and media-rich podcasts and vodcasts. Some institutions such as ACU (Murph, 2008), provide incoming first-year students with a choice of an iTouch or an iPhone, but most still do not provide these devices. Students may have to rely on providing these devices themselves; however, ownership is increasing at a rapid rate. Salmon and Nie (2008) report that there is a 'renaissance for audio in learning' (p. 2), based on British Market Research Bureau (BMRB) (2006) figures such as that 69% of the 16–24 age group owned an MP3 player. For its fiscal 2009 third quarter ended June 27, 2009, Apple reported sales of iPods (which includes the iTouch) at 10.2 million and iPhone sales of '5.2 million, representing 626 percent unit growth over the year-ago quarter' (Apple Press Release, 2009). As these devices become more ubiquitous, the opportunity to build the iClassroom becomes greater.

TOUCH-SCREEN HAND-HELD TECHNOLOGIES IN LEARNING AND TEACHING

To get a deeper understanding of the issues involved in using iPod/iTouch/iPhone devices in the iClassroom, we need to look at the pedagogy of this form of mobile learning, the costs involved, technical problems that may arise, usage statistics for podcasts and vodcasts, content development, and the workload implications of this technology for educators.

Pedagogy

Pedagogy in the 21st century faces challenges in a new environment where technology is reaching into all levels of education. Prensky (2009) suggests that society in the 21st century will reach a level of 'digital wisdom' as all will eventually have grown up in the 21st century and will have become comfortable with technology. Beetham and Sharpe (2007) conclude that we should reconsider the 'pedagogical practices that underpin education' (p. 1) in the digital age. Students are connected to data and information in ways never seen before. Siemens (2005) proposes a new learning theory for the digital age: 'Connectivism'. This theory presents a 'model of learning that acknowledges the tectonic shifts in society where learning is no longer an internal, individualistic activity'–and recognises the role of technology, networks, and knowledge in the way people learn. It takes into account modern trends in learning and proposes that learning theories such as behaviorism, cognitivism, and constructivism are limited in an environment where learners are now connected to vast amounts of information in the digital age. Therefore, in all levels of education, faculty and teachers will need to focus on 21st century skills, re-think the profession of teaching and the nature of learning, and keep up with far-reaching and ongoing changes in technologies such as iPod/iTouch/iPhone devices. Edirisingha, Salmon, and Nie (2008) have recognised that there is now a need for guidelines for developing both audio and video podcasts in higher education and propose a detailed 10-factor design model as a guide for development. The model when applied to new technologies provides a new perspective on using tools such as audio and video podcasts in higher education. Each step in the model can have several options and is especially recommended to be followed step-by-step by academics new to podcasting. The model covers all aspects of podcasting from deciding the pedagogical rationale, through media used, content, style and structure, to reusability and deployment.

However, new more sophisticated models may be needed to face the challenge of educational development for the iClassroom. Unless specialised software is used to develop content,

podcasts and vodcasts are largely non-interactive and will not include desirable instructional design features such as questions and exercises. The delivery format offered by the iClassroom on iPod/iTouch/iPhone devices will require new research into the way that these devices are used for learning and teaching. It would be a mistake for both educators and students to look on the iClassroom as a complete substitute for attending lectures and tutorials. These traditional methods of learning and teaching may not transfer easily to hand-held devices–as this chapter will show, it is not certain where the iClassroom can be positioned in an educational framework. Adopting the iClassroom will almost certainly lead to at least a review of our traditional pedagogical practices, and perhaps even new pedagogies for the digital age we live in. Instructional designers will have to rethink the best way in which content is developed in order to maximise educational value so that the delivery method, whether in a traditional classroom setting or on an iPhone, is not a barrier to learning and teaching. Developing content for two or more methods of delivery is time consuming, and as you will see later in this chapter, it is possible to develop content using traditional tools like PowerPoint that can be delivered in classroom as well as on iPod/iTouch/iPhone devices.

Cost

The major issue for most students is the cost of hand-held devices. iPods currently range in price from over €100 for the iPod Nano to over €200 for the iTouch (price quoted at Apple Store online on April 15, 2009). However, the cheapest option currently available for a pre-pay 8GB iPhone 3G is over €400 and can go up to over €700 for a pay-monthly version (prices quoted at O_2 Shop online on April 15, 2009). For many students this is a prohibitive price–in the case of ACU, many students opt to keep their own mobile phones and opt for the iTouch for College purposes. Disadvantaged students from poorer backgrounds may not be able to afford even the cheapest iPod or equivalent. However, recent evidence suggests that this may be about to change: in the 'All about iPhone', Wu (2008) reported that for the first time the iPhone has become a lower cost alternative to expensive multiple digital devices and services, transforming it from an expensive luxury item to a practical communication and entertainment device. According to the report, growth rates of iPhone penetration are three times higher in lower income groups when compared to high income groups. Cost barriers are being reduced all the time. Providing access to content online such as textbooks and course notes will save students on printing costs as well as reducing the need for purchasing sometimes expensive print versions of textbooks. In addition, almost all colleges provide free WiFi access to students, reducing the cost of potentially expensive data download charges.

Technical Problems

The launch of iPhone/iTouch devices for incoming first-year students in ACU was relatively successful with huge support from Apple and from ACU's IT staff. However, it was not a complete success at first with the college's WiFi system being overloaded (Sacco, 2008). Similar problems were encountered at Duke University (Cheng, 2007), where it was also reported (Baker, 2007) that a single iPhone could cause the freezing of the college's wireless network system. Third-level institutions must prepare for increased levels of wireless traffic. In the case of ACU, 243 additional wireless access points were installed to address coverage issues. These costs will place extra demands on already budget-conscious colleges. College authorities should plan carefully for the introduction of services for iPhone/iTouch/iPod devices as there will be inevitable IT support issues such as security, bandwidth, and access that will arise as with the introduction of any new service. The increased inter-dependency between

education and IT infrastructure may be one of the biggest road-blocks on the path to the iClassroom.

Usage

A major issue for educators is that they wonder whether students use their hand-held devices such as the iPhone/iTouch/iPod for viewing and listening to lecture notes, and question the need for the iClassroom in modern education. Many educators feel that digitally recorded lectures in any form will encourage students to skip classes—as they can download the recordings later. When iPods were first used at Duke University in the USA, Armstrong Moore (2005) reported that 'about 75 percent of freshmen surveyed said they used the iPods for their academic work'. At the University of Nottingham in the United Kingdom, where students were required as part of their course work to watch podcasts at least once, only 10% of them actually downloaded podcasts to devices such as iPods—most (79%) preferring to watch the podcasts through the university's virtual learning environment (Mount & Chambers, 2009). Lee and Chan (2007) reported in a survey of distance learning students at Charles Sturt University in Australia that '83% of the respondents reported that they had listened to seven or more of the nine available podcasts from start to finish, and a majority reported that they had listened to at least three of the episodes multiple times' (p. 94). Elsasser, Hoie, Destache, and Monaghan (2009) in a study at Creighton University in the USA on the use of digitally recorded lectures made available for students to download found that 91% of students 'reported using the audio files as a replacement for attending lectures' (p. 20). There was also an effect on attendance with all faculty reporting 'a decrease in student attendance by at least 25%' (p. 20) when compared to classes the previous year which did not have recordings. However, there is evidence that students perform better when viewing recorded lectures rather than

Figure 1. Percentage of Students Accessing Course Resources

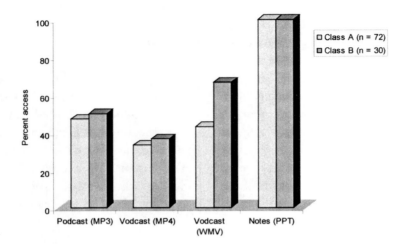

attending class. In a study at State University of New York Fredonia, McKinney, Dyck, and Luber (2009) found that students who watched vodcasts of lectures from iTunes U instead of attending the corresponding classroom lectures scored an average of 9% higher in tests. When students also took notes as well as watching the vodcasts, the gap rose to 15%. This study reports that it is clear that the ability to pause and rewind a vodcast was a major factor in improving student grades.

At the National College of Ireland, this author conducted a survey for this chapter of two classes where podcast and vodcasts were made available to students through the Moodle Learning Content Management System (LCMS). Class A (n=72) were business studies students, while Class B (n=30) were technology studies students. The same module was delivered to both classes in different semesters during 2008. Each week, the author recorded short (15–20 minutes) summaries of each lecture in three formats: MP3 audio-only podcast, Windows Media Video (WMV) vodcast, and MP4 vodcast. The MP3 versions were recorded using Audacity software (see http://audacity. sourceforge.net). The WMV version was created in Windows Movie Maker by combining the MP3 podcast with PowerPoint slides into one video.

The WMV video was then converted to MP4 format for delivery on iPhone/iTouch/iPod devices. Figure 1 summarises the findings of this survey.

Figure 1 shows the percentage of students accessing each type of podcast and vodcast at least once, plus the percentage of students accessing PowerPoint only lecture notes. In both classes, all students accessed the basic lecture notes in PowerPoint (PPT) format. For Class A this represents 72 students accessing the lecture notes 1,510 times. For Class B this represents 30 students accessing the lecture notes 876 times. Access to the podcasts and vodcasts was at a much lower rate. In Class A, there were a total of 436 accesses by 45 out of 72 students, with MP3 format being the most popular format (47%). For Class B there were 283 accesses by 24 out of 30 students with WMV format being the most popular format (67%). Figures for both groups were almost the same for each group except in the preference for WMV format with Class B students who have a higher rate (67%) of access compared to Class A (43%). These figures reveal that while availability of traditional PowerPoint lecture notes online remains popular, podcasts and vodcasts are less popular. Overall this study showed that despite the availability of podcasts and vodcasts in a variety of formats, that there is still a preference for traditional lecture notes in both classes surveyed.

Developing Content for the iClassroom

Developing content for the iPhone/iTouch/iPod devices is a critical process for educators. But how should content developers consider the overall goal of delivering educational material via mobile devices? Not all types of media and educational materials lend themselves to mobile delivery. However, with careful planning, content developers can create and deliver a wide variety of content to help those students who are on-the-go to learn. Content development for this type of media is in its early stages. Best practices for developing content for traditional desktop delivery may not translate well to these hand-held devices. As these devices gain more attention, new strategies and best practices will arise as content developers follow the changing trends in mobile technology.

Much existing commercial e-learning content depends on having an Adobe Flash plug-in which is not yet supported by these devices. Commercial authoring tools are now available for creating content for delivery on iPhone/iTouch/iPod devices. SumTotal Systems have released ToolBook 9.5 which features full support for the iPhone and iTouch (SumTotal Press Release, 2008). Authoring tools such as ToolBook can make it easy to create content for many types of online learning formats—interactive content, assessments, and simulations. They can provide 'the most innovative and comprehensive delivery options to ensure that our customers can engage employees across geographies, time zones and devices'. Not only is learning now more mobile than ever, it is very flexible in both its content development and delivery.

Some LCMS companies are now developing tools for iPhone support. Blackboard for example has introduced 'Blackboard Learn for Apple iPhone' (Blackboard Press Release, 2009). This is a product that allows students to access information such as 'updates and alerts on grades, assignments, tests and other information from courses as well as groups and organizations of which they are part on their iPhone or iPod touch'. In addition to providing the ToolBook 9.5 authoring tool, SumTotal also provides full support for content developed in ToolBook on its content deployment systems (SumTotal Press Release, 2008).

However, there are other options available to content authors. Most educators at third level will use presentation slides, such as PowerPoint, in some format for providing lecture notes to students. LCMSs are the most common method of making these notes available to students. However, getting this content onto iPhone/iTouch/iPod devices is not easy to do. Consideration should also be given to the need for this content to be compatible with other devices such as non-Apple MP3 players. The iPhone/iTouch/iPod devices do not provide native support for PowerPoint, though you can view presentations if sent as an attachment to an email. There are several simple ways to convert PowerPoint slides for viewing on iPhone/iTouch/iPod devices. For example, students could save each slide as a graphic in PowerPoint, add the graphics to their photographs library, and synchronize the device—each slide can then be viewed as a photograph. A PowerPoint presentation can also be saved in HTML format which, if uploaded onto a website or LCMS can be viewed like any other web page. However, these processes for making content available online can make it awkward for both teachers and students to get access to the content if they lack the necessary skills to create the content. Leaving it up to students to convert presentations themselves into a format for viewing on their iPhone/iTouch/iPod device is placing an unnecessary step for them to have to take, and may even prove to be a barrier for many students.

The iClassroom should remove obstacles on the path to accessible content, and make content available in formats such as podcasts and vodcasts.

Creating podcasts is now easier than ever as most desktop computers now feature multimedia tools such as microphones, speakers, and the software necessary to record audio. With only a few easily learned steps a teacher or lecturer can easily record an audio-only podcast using a tool such as Audacity. Whether the recording is of a whole lecture or a summary of a lecture, it can be saved as an MP3 file that will work on most mobile devices. As an MP3 file it can be uploaded to an LCMS like any other file–such as a PowerPoint presentation–therefore no special skill is required by educators to make it available to students. Equally, it is easy for students to download the file to their mobile device. Combined with printouts of lecture notes, students can listen to the podcast as if they were attending a lecture, with the added benefit of being able to pause and rewind whenever they want to.

For vodcasts, more skill is required than for creating an audio-only podcast. While some third-level institutions can provide video cameras to record entire lectures and make them available online through services such as iTunes U, the cost in money, time, and resources of doing this may be prohibitive for many other institutions. At its simplest, a vodcast can be created by running a PowerPoint presentation and recording the voice-over at the same time, i.e. exactly what a lecturer will do in class. This can be done using PowerPoint's own Record Narration tool–no specialist extra skills are required to get this far. To convert the resulting presentation into a vodcast can be done in several ways–one simple way is to import the presentation slides (as graphics) and audio files into Windows Movie Maker and create a Windows Media Video (WMV). WMV files will not work on iPhone/iTouch/iPod devices and need to be converted to MP4 format. Using Apple's own QuickTime Pro, or free tools such as the Jodix Free iPod Video Converter (see http://www.jodix.com), WMV files can easily be converted to MP4 format, which can then be synchronised with any iPhone/iTouch/iPod device.

Screen capture software such as CamStudio (see http://camstudio.org) also makes it much easier for educators to create vodcasts without using cameras or the people needed to operate them. This type of software creates industry standard AVI videos or more bandwidth-friendly Flash videos (SWF) and eliminates many of the steps needed to make conversions. In order to get videos of this type to work on an iPhone/iTouch/iPod device, they will still have to be converted to MP4 format. The big advantage of tools such as CamStudio is that they take the need for specialist skills out of the process of creating vodcasts so that almost any educator can create content for the iClassroom. Recent evidence suggests that use of videos created with screen capture software can enhance the learning experience greatly. Franciszkowicz (2008) reports in a survey of 1,074 students on video usage that there was 'overwhelming use of the resource for both pre-class preparation and pre-test review with nearly 80% utilizing at least 50% of the videos available' (p. 5), and that the videos 'improved their conceptual understanding and their problem solving skills' (p. 5).

Workload

An over-riding concern for many educators at third-level is that they are regarded as 'digital immigrants' while 21st century students are regarded as 'digital natives' (Prensky, 2001). Even though Prensky (2009) has since written that 'the distinction between digital natives and digital immigrants will become less relevant' as we move further into the 21st century–we are still mired in the fact that anyone over 30 years of age (most third-level educators today) did not grow up in the modern ubiquitous digital environment that we now live in. According to Heppell (2006) universities having just 'spent the 20th century trying to escape from their 19th century structures they seem to have greeted the 21st century by finally embracing 20th century instead'. Educators will need to adapt to new environments and rapidly changing technologies to remain relevant in order to adopt the iClassroom. For the sake of future generations educators must embrace new technologies–they are now preparing for the next generation of educators. This means that the iClassroom challenges the traditional role of the educator as well as the entire process of learning and teaching, including the spaces and structures of learning in higher education.

Embracing the iClassroom demands an increased workload for educators, in particular for pre- and post-class preparation of course content. Most educators have already embraced the convenience of using tools like PowerPoint and LCMSs for the presentation and deployment of lecture notes to students. LCMS tools make the task of providing presentations online an easy one for even the most technologically shy 'digital immigrant'. However, moving to the next step will increase significantly the amount of work that even a technologically aware educator must do in order to commit to the iClassroom. Recording the most basic of podcasts and developing simple vodcasts takes time and effort, and requires skill with using new tools and technologies. As Bell (2008) points out, this could lead to a new digital divide with 'm-friendly and tech-savvy on one side, and those assumed to be has-beens and Luddites on the other' (p. 186).

Workload is a factor to consider at the individual educator's level and also at the whole faculty level. Moving from a situation where a few tech-savvy educators create content for the iClassroom, to everyone in a school, department, or college doing so, has huge workload implications. While podcasts and vodcasts are gaining in popularity with students, preparation of these resources will have to be planned and scheduled at a faculty level. Even at college level, considerable effort is needed to implement a college-wide policy of providing podcasts to students. This is illustrated in a project by Kansas State University in late 2006 when the university announced that it planned to 'convert an unprecedented 6,000

recorded classes to enhanced podcasts' (Tegrity Press Release, 2006). While there is a perception among many faculty members that using technology for preparing online resources takes a lot of time, Zhen, Garthwait, and Pratt (2008) found that time was not a factor in a faculty member's decision to use technology in teaching. Instead, motivational factors such as self-efficacy and philosophy had a strong impact on the likelihood of using technology.

In general, producing high-quality audio and video will take the most time and effort. Consequently, producing lower quality material for the iClassroom will reduce workload dramatically. At its simplest, wearing a microphone to record audio during a standard lecture, is the easiest way to create a podcast. Without any editing, all a lecturer has to do is save the podcast and upload it to an LCMS–this is a quick-and-dirty approach that is an easy add-on to a standard class where the lecturer is already doing what comes naturally: teaching. To move up to the next level where some editing is required will increase the need for a new skill-set based on iClassroom technologies–hence workload will also increase.

There is also the need to consider reusability of podcasts and vodcasts. Many lecturers will reuse the same lecture notes when delivering the same class to students on different courses, or for the same course the following year. This suits classes where the content will not change that much over time–for example history, algebra, and some science subjects. For other content in rapidly changing subjects such as politics, economics, and bio-informatics–even lecture notes will have to be updated for almost every class. This has consequences for the iClassroom. A podcast on Pythagoras' Theorem for a mathematics class can be reused for years, therefore saving the lecturer considerable workload. However, a podcast on the variability of financial markets in an economics class may have reduced value within weeks of recording and will almost certainly have to be updated the next time the class is delivered.

Third-level educators must adopt strategies for reducing workload so that development of podcasts and vodcasts for the iClassroom becomes part of their teaching resource rather than an extra load on their time and effort. Some suggested strategies for reducing workload, based on author's experience, are as follows:

- Where possible, use tools and technology that you are already familiar with in developing iClassroom content
- If available, get training on any technology you use
- Use a model for development such as that proposed for podcasts by Edirisingha et al. (2008)
- Form a group of experienced and well-trained educators to aid innovation, collaboration, and shared experiences
- When planning and developing traditional content such as a PowerPoint presentation, keep in mind that you may use the same presentation in a vodcast at a later stage. Therefore you should avoid having to re-work your presentation by creating it in the most vodcast-friendly way in the first place
- Be sure to have a vision of what your podcast will sound like, and how your vodcast will look like on an iPod/iTouch/iPhone device
- Check that all your media equipment are working properly–especially in advance of recording live classes
- Test your podcasts and vodcasts on iPod/iTouch/iPhone devices
- Encourage your students to provide feedback on your use of iClassroom resources
- Share your experiences with faculty colleagues to help reduce their workload
- Consider using your content in future classes
- Improve your time management skills to better manage production

Whatever strategies are adopted, planning is crucial to the success of any iClassroom initiative. Many third-level educators take it upon themselves to create their own iClassroom for their own students, therefore resulting in some lecturers providing content for iPod/iTouch/iPhone devices while others do not. This can be particularly frustrating for students, especially those who learn best from podcasts and/or vodcasts, who may have recordings of some classes available but not of others. Third-level institutions should make it part of their strategic planning process to ensure that the iClassroom is available to all students and consequently that plans are implemented to ensure that faculty are in the best possible position to develop iClassroom resources. Some suggested strategies for reducing workload at institutional level are as follows:

- Institutions should ensure that their philosophy for the use of iClassroom technology is embedded into the institution's vision and mission statements.
- Course Committees should ensure that iClassroom technology is incorporated into courses in the most appropriate way to provide an enhanced learning experience for students.
- Promote the benefits of the iClassroom throughout the institution to both faculty and students.
- Provide appropriate hardware to faculty–this may be as simple as ensuring that headsets for recording are available.
- Ensure that necessary software tools are installed on each computer–careful planning is necessary here in the case of institutions where locked down desktops are the norm.
- Choose standard file formats for all content delivery, e.g. MP3 for all podcasts, and MP4 for all vodcasts.
- Even in budget-conscious times, consider providing some training on the use of hard-

ware and software necessary to develop content for the iClassroom.

- Ensure that the institution's information technology infrastructure can cope with the increased demands projected for the iClassroom.
- Ensure that there are no Intellectual Property (IP) issues arising in the iClassroom and that all content authors are aware of the institution's regulations in this area.

MOBILE LEARNING

Mobile learning (m-learning) is often defined as e-learning through mobile computational devices (Trifonova & Ronchetti, 2004). iPod/iTouch/iPhone devices can bring m-learning to the iClassroom by providing the connectivity and flexibility needed for learning on the move. These devices are now powerful enough to allow students to connect directly to content online: even live classes and seminars, or to uploaded content for viewing at a later time. With these devices it is almost impossible not to be connected to the Internet. While the endless possibilities provided by the iClassroom to deliver anywhere anytime education, there is some evidence that students do not take advantage of the mobility of podcasts and vodcasts for learning. McKinney et al. (2009) in their study at the State University of New York Fredonia found that only about 20% of students watched the podcast lecture on a mobile device, while 80% watched the iTunes download on a laptop. Clearly, while students continue to have access to both laptops and mobile devices such as the iPod/iTouch/iPhone, they will still opt for viewing content on larger screen laptops. This 20% figure will no doubt increase as students move towards a single media platform for mobility such as the iClassroom devices.

Whatever mobile devices are used for m-learning, it is advisable to implement an appropriate architecture for mobile learning. In addition to the obvious needs for an IT infrastructure to meet m-learning needs and for content suitable for a mobile device to be available, m-learning must be part of a learning architecture and not a separate entity. Trifonova and Ronchetti (2004) suggest that in order to 'to support the experimentation of any tool or technique of m-learning a rather complex information system is necessary' (p. 33). They propose a general architecture for m-learning where m-learning should first be an extension of an existing system such as an LCMS, secondly be general in providing all the necessary m-learning services, and thirdly be generic so that it is extensible for different mobile devices. This architecture can provide an m-learning environment where the system should 'automatically detect the devices' capabilities and limitations (software and hardware) and on that basis to select and propose the services proper for the device and adapt them the best way' (Trifonova & Ronchetti, 2004, p. 33). Using devices such as the iPod/iTouch/iPhone and tools like iTunes to synchronise content, bring the iClassroom closer to reality where it can be used to implement the Trifonova and Ronchetti general architecture.

FUTURE PERSPECTIVES

Embracing the iClassroom can only be effective if institutions, faculty, and students understand what it can as well as what it cannot do. As Elsasser et al. (2009) point out the 'importance of developing social skills, professionalism, self discipline, and mentoring facilitated through class attendance should not be minimized' (p. 22) when considering the introduction of iClassroom type technology. In an article entitled 'Technology Euphoria?', Rosenberg (2008) declares that in the corporate sector 'irrational exuberance around learning technology drove an unsustainable level of investment built on unrealistic expectations of what it could do' (pp. 24–25), and places an increasing importance on evaluation and success criteria for technology initiatives. Before we rush headlong into creating the iClassroom we need to establish what the expectation levels of success are. This means that first, the question 'What is the purpose and benefit of the iClassroom?' must be asked. While the purpose–to provide accessible educational content to students–might be relatively straight-forward to answer, the benefits will be more difficult to identify without evaluation. Rosenberg (2009) concludes that the best strategies are 'the ones that generate the most support, place a high value on evaluation' (p. 27). Using Kirkpatrick's (1959) model for the evaluation of training it is already clear that many initiatives using podcasts and vodcasts are popular with students (Level I–Reaction). What is less certain is that learning is taking place (Level II–Learning) and that behaviour is changing (Level III–Behaviour). While there is some evidence (McKinney et al. 2009) that students get better results with iClassroom technology, more evaluation needs to be done to determine the real effectiveness of iClassroom initiatives over the long term (Level IV–Results).

Since the 1980s, learning technology has been available in many different formats, but day after day in almost every college world-wide, students enter into lecture theatres to hear a lecturer speak and to take notes–much as their parents and grandparents did in the pre-learning technology days. In the last 20 years, researchers have been trying to find the best ways to deliver education with technology in an environment where the technology itself is changing faster than educators can keep up. After all, the iPod was introduced in 2001 as a device for playing music and nothing more: today less than eight years later, it is an invaluable learning and teaching tool if used appropriately. Researchers need to continue to investigate how effective the iClassroom will be, and what is the best formula for creating and delivering content using devices like the iPod, iTouch, and iPhone. More in-depth studies that evaluate the effectiveness and learnings are needed to understand truly where is the best place for iPod/iTouch/iPhone

devices in the iClassroom. This will not be determined easily: many long-term studies are needed to fill the research void in learning technology. As Bell (2008) states, 'This is a huge research agenda. But it is a vital one' (p. 184).

Third-level institutions will need to find the right balance between traditional classrooms and the iClassroom. They will also have to deal with the different needs of different Schools and Departments within the institution, as well as the financial constraints that difficult economic times will enforce. Overall, they will need to combine iClassroom strategies with the institutional vision and strategy in a way that makes the technology invisible, while learning and teaching remain visible. As most third-level institutions are part-funded by Government, there is also the need for a national strategy to align government educational responsibilities with the practices in third-level institutions. Government sponsored research funding should continue to provide learning technology researchers with the means to find the best strategies to provide engaging education for learners as well as value-for-money teaching methods. The challenge for all is to explore further the unique opportunities that iPod/iTouch/iPhone devices can provide.

CONCLUSION

The iClassroom provides for many learning and teaching opportunities in third-level education. There are several varied and widespread uses of iPod/iTouch/iPhone already in place. As these devices become more powerful and ubiquitous, they will provide many (if not most) of the services necessary for the iClassroom. From a pedagogical point of view, a model for use of podcasts and vodcasts is recommended to help overcome the issues of costs, technical problems, and content development. Evidence for successful usage levels is still inconsistent and requires more research to investigate how iClassroom technologies are best used in learning and teaching–it is not yet certain where the iClassroom fits in third-level education. Educators must adopt strategies for managing the extra workload implications that result from creating content for the iClassroom in addition to normal classroom content development–this must be done not only at an individual level, but also at an institutional level. In order to succeed, the iClassroom must be part of each third-level institution's m-learning architecture to remove difficulties and roadblocks in the way of both teacher and student engagement with this system.

While the iClassroom is here to stay, it has struggled to find its place for educators. More research needs to be done to establish the true value of iClassroom technologies and the appropriate pedagogies that may still have to be developed for this type of education. The possibility of third-level faculty lecturers recording lectures in an empty classroom that are later uploaded onto an LCMS for students to download at a time of their choosing is a real one. Students will naturally ask what the difference is between attending a lecture on the one hand, and watching a good quality vodcast on the other. The purpose of third-level institutions is not only to educate students in their chosen subjects, but also to prepare them for careers in the real world. The iClassroom will place huge challenges on the roles of educators at all levels, not just to lecturers in third-level institutions. The opportunities presented by touch-screen hand-held technologies in learning and teaching open up a vast array of possibilities for third-level education in the 21st century. There are unique affordances provided by iPod/iTouch/iPhone devices based on their mobility, ease of use, rapid development of support tools, huge variety of applications already in place, reduced barriers such as cost, and their ubiquity. Learning and teaching at all levels of education is moving towards an exciting horizon of educational possibilities that these technologies can now provide.

REFERENCES

Apple Press Release. (2007a). *Apple reinvents the phone with iPhone.* Retrieved April 15, 2009, from http://www.apple.com/pr/library/2007/01/09iphone.html

Apple Press Release. (2007b). *Apple announces iTunes U on the iTunes store.* Retrieved April 15, 2009, from http://www.apple.com/pr/library/2007/05/30itunesu.html

Apple Press Release. (2009). *Apple reports third quarter results.* Retrieved August 26, 2009, from http://www.apple.com/pr/library/2009/07/21results.html

Armstrong Moore, E. (2005). When iPod goes collegiate. *The Christian Science Monitor.* Retrieved April 15, 2009, from http://www.csmonitor.com/2005/0419/p11s01-legn.html

Baker, M. (2007). iPhone may be freezing college network. Retrieved April 15, 2009, from http://www.msnbc.msn.com/id/19836992

Beetham, H., & Sharpe, R. (2007). An introduction to rethinking pedagogy in the digital age . In Beetham, H., & Sharpe, R. (Eds.), *Rethinking pedagogy for a digital age: Designing and delivering e-learning* (pp. 1–10). London: Routledge.

Bell, D. (2008). The university in your pocket. In G. Salmon, & P. Edirisingha (Eds.), Podcasting for learning in universities (pp. 178-187). Open University Press: Society for Research into Higher Education.

Blackboard Press Release. (2009). New Blackboard Learn(TM) for Apple(R) iPhone(TM) application lets users take learning on the go. Retrieved August 26, 2009, from http://www.blackboard.com/Company/Media-Center/Press-Releases.aspx?releaseid=1270202

British Market Research Bureau (BMRB). (2006). A quarter of all adult internet users will listen to a 'Podcast' in the next 6 months. *British Market Research Bureau.* Retrieved April 15, 2009, from http://www.bmrb.co.uk/news/article/a-quarter-of-all-adult-internet-users-will-listen-to-a-podcast-in-the-next-Burrows, P. (2009). App Store hits 500 million downloads. *BusinessWeek.* Retrieved April 15, 2009, from http://www.businessweek.com/technology/ByteOfTheApple/blog/archives/2009/01/the_app_store_s.html

Cheng, J. (2007) Duke solves iPhone network problem. *Ars Technica.* Retrieved April 15, 2009, from http://arstechnica.com/apple/news/2007/07/duke-solves-iphone-network-problem.ars

Edirisingha, P., Salmon, G., & Nie, M. (2008). Developing pedagogical podcasts. In G. Salmon, & P. Edirisingha (Eds.), Podcasting for learning in universities (pp. 153-168). Open University Press: Society for Research into Higher Education.

Elsasser, G. N., Hoie, E. B., Destache, C. J., & Monaghan, M. S. (2009). Availability of Internet download lecture audio files on class attendance and examination performance. *International Journal of Instructional Technology and Distance Learning, 6*(2), 19-24. Retrieved April 15, 2009, from http://www.itdl.org/Journal/Feb_09/article03.htm

Franciszkowicz, M. (2008). Video-based additional instruction. *The Journal of the Research Center for Educational Technology, 4*(2), 5–14.

Group, N. D. P. (2008). The NPD Group: iPhone 3G leads U.S. consumer mobile phone purchases in the third quarter of 2008. Retrieved April 15, 2009, from http://www.npd.com/press/releases/press_081110.html

Heppell, S. (2006). Play to learn, learn to play. Retrieved April 15, 2009, from http://www.heppell.net/weblog/stephen/otherwriting/2006/10/20/Playtolearnlearntoplay.html

Kirkpatrick, D. L. (1959). Techniques for evaluating training programs . *Journal of American Society for Training and Development, 13*(11-12).

Lee, M. J. W., & Chan, A. (2007). Reducing the effects of isolation and promoting inclusivity for distance learners through podcasting, *Turkish Online Journal of Distance Education, 8*(1), 85-104. Retrieved October 26, 2009, from http://tojde.anadolu.edu.tr/tojde25/pdf/article_7.pdf

Malley, A. (2009). Apple iPhone controls over 66% of all mobile web use. *AppleInsider.* Retrieved April 15, 2009, from http://www.appleinsider.com/articles/09/03/01/apple_iphone_controls_over_66_of_all_mobile_web_use.html

McKinney, D., Dyck, J., & Luber, E. (2009). iTunes University and the classroom: Can podcasts replace professors? *Computers & Education, 52*(3), 617–623. doi:10.1016/j.compedu.2008.11.004

Mount, N., & Chambers, C. (2008). Podcasts and practicals. In G. Salmon, & P. Edirisingha (Eds.), Podcasting for learning in universities (pp. 1-11). Open University Press: Society for Research into Higher Education.

Murph, D. (2008). ACU dishing out iPhone/iPod touch to all incoming freshmen. *Endgadget.* Retrieved April 15, 2009, from http://www.engadget.com/2008/02/26/acu-dishing-out-iphone-ipod-touch-to-all-incoming-freshmen

Ng'ambi, D. (2008). Podcasts for reflective learning. In G. Salmon, & P. Edirisingha (Eds.), Podcasting for learning in universities (pp. 132-145). Open University Press: Society for Research into Higher Education.

Prensky, M. (2001). Digital natives, digital immigrants. *On the Horizon, 9*(5). Retrieved October 20, 2009, from http://www.marcprensky.com/writing/Prensky%20-%20Digital%20Natives,%20Digital%20Immigrants%20-%20Part1.pdf

Prensky, M. (2009). H. Sapiens Digital: From digital immigrants and digital natives to digital wisdom. *Journal of Online Education. 5*(3). Retrieved April 15, 2009, from http://www.innovateonline.info/index.php?view=article&id=705

Rosenberg, M. J. (2008). Taming the irrational expectations of high-tech learning. *T+D Training and Development.* Retrieved April 15, 2009, from http://www.marcrosenberg.com/images/ASTD_Technology_Euphoria_TD_0608.pdf

Sacco, A. (2008). iPhone University: At ACU, students navigate college life via Apple iPhone. *CIO.* Retrieved March 7, 2009, from http://www.cio.com/article/452714/iPhone_University_At_ACU_Students_Navigate_College_Life_via_Apple_iPhone?page=1&taxonomyId=1436

Salmon, G., & Nie, M. (2008). Doubling the life of iPods. In G. Salmon, & P. Edirisingha (Eds.), Podcasting for learning in universities (pp. 1-11). Open University Press: Society for Research into Higher Education.

Shim, A., Crider, D., Kim, P., & Raffin, J. (2008). Can the use of video iPods promote cognitive residue in college health and wellness students? In G. Richards (Ed.), *Proceedings of World Conference on E-Learning in Corporate, Government, Healthcare, and Higher Education* 2008 (pp. 3197-3200). Chesapeake, VA: Association for the Advancement of Computing in Education (AACE).

Siemens, G. (2005). Connectivism: A learning theory for the digital age. *International Journal of Instructional Technology and Distance Learning, 2*(1). Retrieved August 26, 2009, from http://www.itdl.org/Journal/Jan_05/article01.htm

SumTotal Press Release. (2008). SumTotal introduces ToolBook 9.5 for faster learning content creation and access anytime, anywhere. Retrieved April 15, 2008, from http://www.sumtotalsystems.com/press/index.html/2008/09/09/1

Tegrity Press Release. (2006). Kansas State University launches world's largest course podcasting initiative. Retrieved April 15, 2009, from http://www.tegrity.com/learn-more/press-releases/56-kansas-state-university-launches-worlds-largest-course-podcasting-initiative.html

Trifonova, A., & Ronchetti, M. (2004). A general architecture for M-Learning. *International Journal of Digital Contents, 2*(1), Special issue on 'Digital Learning-Teaching Environments and Contents'. In A. Méndez-Vilas, & J.A. Mesa González (Eds.), *Proceedings of the II International Conference on Multimedia and Information and Communication Technologies in Education (mICTE2003)*, Badajoz (Spain), December 3-6, 2003, pp. 31-36.

Wu, J. (2008). All about iPhone. *comScore Report.* Retrieved April 15, 2009, from http://www.comscore.com/press/release.asp?press=2545

Zhen, Y., Garthwait, A., & Pratt, P. (2008). Factors affecting faculty members' decision to teach or not to teach online in Higher Education. *Online Journal of Distance Learning Administration, XI*(III). Retrieved April 15, 2009, from http://www.westga.edu/~distance/ojdla/fall113/zhen113.html

ADDITIONAL READING

Beetham, H., & Sharpe, R. (Eds.). (2007). *Rethinking pedagogy for a digital age: designing and delivering e-learning.* New York: Routledge.

Biersdorfer, J. D., & Pogue, D. (2009). iPod: The missing manual. 8th ed. Sebastopol, CA: O'Reilly Media, Inc.

Bounds, J., Buechler, J., & DeHaan, J. (2003). *Windows Movie Maker 2 Zero to Hero.* New York: Friends of ED.

Guy, R. (2009). *The evolution of mobile teaching and learning.* Santa Rosa, CA: Informing Science Press.

Hart-Davis, G. (2009). *How to do everything iPod, iPhone & iTunes* (5th ed.). San Francisco, CA: McGraw-Hill Osborne.

Holtz, S., & Hobson, N. (2007). *How to do everything with podcasting.* San Francisco, CA: McGraw-Hill.

Kelby, S., & White, T. (2008). *The iPhone Book: How to do the most important, useful & fun stuff with your iPhone* (3rd ed.). Berkeley, CA: Pearson Education/Peachpit Press.

Kelby, S., & White, T. (2008). *The iPod Book: Doing cool stuff with the iPod and the iTunes Store* (5th ed.). Berkeley, CA: Pearson Education/ Peachpit Press.

King, K. P., & Gura, M. (2007). *Podcasting for teachers: Using a new technology to revolutionize teaching and learning (emerging technologies for evolving learners)* (2nd ed.). Charlotte, NC: Information Age Publishing.

Laurillard, D. (2008). *Rethinking university teaching: A conversational framework for the effective use of learning technologies* (3rd ed.). New York: Routledge.

Mason, R., & Rennie, F. (2008). *E-learning and social networking handbook: Resources for Higher Education.* New York: Routledge.

Metcalf, D. (2006). *MLearning: Mobile learning and performance in the palm of your hand.* Amherst, MA. HRD Press Inc. Microsoft, Windows How-To Movie Maker Centre. *Get started with Windows Movie Maker.* Retrieved September 27, 2009, from http://www.microsoft.com/windowsxp/using/moviemaker/getstarted/default.mspx

Richardson, W. (2008). *Blogs, Wikis, Podcasts, and other powerful web tools for classrooms* (2nd ed.). Thousand Oaks, CA: Corwin Press.

Roblyer, M. D., & Doering, A. H. (2009). *Integrating educational technology into teaching* (5th ed.). Berkeley, CA: Pearson Education/Allyn & Bacon.

Rosenberg, M. J. (2006). *Beyond e-learning: Approaches and technologies to enhance organizational knowledge, learning and performance.* Hoboken, NJ: Wiley/Jossey Bass.

Salmon, G., & Edirisingha, P. (Eds.). (2008). *Podcasting for learning in universities.* London: Open University Press, Society for Research into Higher Education.

Salmon, G., Edirisingha, P., Mobbs, M., Mobbs, R., & Dennett, C. (2008). *How to create podcasts for education.* London: Open University Press, Society for Research into Higher Education.

Siemens, G. (2006). Knowing knowledge. Raleigh, NC: Lulu.com.

Solomon, G., & Schrum, L. (2007). *Web 2.0: New tools, new schools.* Washington, DC: International Society for Technology in Education.

Chapter 10
ePortfolios for Learning, Assessment, and Professional Development

C. Edward Watson
Virginia Tech, USA

Marc Zaldivar
Virginia Tech, USA

Teggin Summers
Virginia Tech, USA

ABSTRACT

ePortfolios are becoming increasingly popular as a means to address a variety of challenges in higher education, such as academic assessment requirements, specific teaching and learning goals, and emerging student professional development needs. This chapter explores these three applications of ePortfolios to provide administrators and faculty the information they need to make informed decisions regarding ePortfolios in academic settings. The relevant history of portfolios, assessment, and associated pedagogies sets a context for this discussion. Current trends in ePortfolio usage are outlined, including a survey of available technologies. This chapter concludes with a primer regarding the management of ePortfolio campus implementations as well as a brief examination of the key questions regarding the future of ePortfolios.

INTRODUCTION

Drawing on literature from the areas of pedagogy, assessment, and portfolio practice, this chapter provides a comprehensive narrative regarding best practices of ePortfolios application in higher education. This chapter provides an overview of

ePortfolio applications and usage to help faculty, staff, and administrators make informed decisions regarding the adoption and implementation of these technologies to meet specific learning, assessment, and professional development goals.

While there exist as many definitions of electronic portfolios as there do uses, an ePortfolio can generally be described as an electronic means for students to collect artifacts and examples of their

DOI: 10.4018/978-1-61520-879-1.ch010

academic, co-curricular, and professional accomplishments, to reflect upon their work over time, to select materials highlighting specific strengths and interests, and to share these sub-collections with others via the web or other interactive forms of media. Because portfolios often employ processes of reflection, electronic portfolios have much in common with their print-based counterparts: for example, both incorporate reflection into the collection, selection, and demonstration of student experiences and achievements.

Portfolios bring together visibility, process, and reflection as students chart and interpret their own learning. Students are responsible ... for explaining what they did and did not learn, for assessing their own strengths and weaknesses as learners, for evaluating their products and performances, for showing how that learning connects with other kinds of learning (in the classroom and without), and for using the review of the past to think about paths for future learning. (Yancey, 2001, p. 19)

Further, portfolios encourage the inclusion of a variety of learning materials that help students, teachers and reviewers alike see patterns in learning that might otherwise go unnoticed. This inclusion of various materials also contributes to richer forms of formative and summative assessment. When ePortfolios are approached from a perspective that values student responsibility, reflection, and growth over time, they hold much of the value intrinsic to traditional portfolios. Additionally, they can potentially offer much more to their various constituents. As Yancey (2001) suggests, the main difference between print-based and electronic portfolios is 'the interactivity both of the digital medium and of social interaction' (p. 20), and it is from this perspective that this chapter is grounded.

ePortfolios also provide a unique means for addressing several student learning needs, including course-level challenges regarding the facilitation of learning, the transfer of knowledge from one learning event to the next, and the synthesis of content over time. Due to easily accessible online storage, ePortfolios provide a streamlined method for students and faculty to keep past assignments and projects active, potentially beyond graduation. Pedagogies that require students to reconsider past work and reflect upon its place in the current project foster meaning-making and help students synthesise their educational experience as a whole. This chapter describes these pedagogies, including how to structure capstone ePortfolio experiences to foster student learning and the mastery of programmatic learning goals.

While student-learning goals help to support an interest in ePortfolios, often the most powerful drivers in institutional adoption are assessment and accreditation pressures. These processes are currently evolving, but the overarching trend is toward continuous data-driven improvement and accountability. Colleges and universities are no longer simply being asked to describe what students learn in their programmes. They must now provide evidence, and the holistic and customisable nature of ePortfolios makes them more attractive than other assessment options, such as standardised tests. This chapter provides an overview of the assessment, accreditation, and accountability pressures facing institutions and includes case studies from higher education where ePortfolios are being implemented to provide evidence of student learning. These cases offer models that can be implemented at various types of institutions.

In addition to these student learning and institutional assessment needs, ePortfolios are also being used to assist students as they make the transition from undergraduate to graduate school and from higher education to career positions. Students can easily share their best work and greatest accomplishments with any audience, including admissions specialists and potential employers. Descriptive statistics and case studies from academic departments and career services units

provide evidence and exemplars for those engaged in promoting student professional development.

While the core focus of this chapter is on student learning, academic assessment, and professional development, also discussed are the evaluation of ePortfolios and the creation of rubrics to assist that process. A range of current ePortfolio technologies is reviewed, and the merits and drawbacks of each technology are provided.

This chapter also includes information on the diffusion of innovations within the context of higher education. Specifically, direction is given for those attempting to launch an ePortfolio initiative on their campus. Examples are provided that offer models for successfully fostering institutional buy-in. This chapter concludes by reviewing emerging questions and what they suggest for the future of ePortfolios in higher education.

BACKGROUND

While portfolios have existed in one form or another for many hundreds of years (Johnson, Mims-Cox, & Doyle-Nichols, 2006; Taylor, Thomas, & Sage, 1999), it is in the last three decades that they have gained attention in the field of higher education. Much of the early work in portfolios began as responses from faculty unsatisfied with the ways in which assessment of student learning was being conducted at the end of the 20th century (Challis, 1999; Elbow & Belanoff, 1986). While portfolios were in use prior to this time, they received increased attention in the mid-1980s when teachers of college composition, such as Elbow and Belanoff (1986), lauded them as viable alternatives to standardised tests and proficiency exams.

Concurrently, in the mid-to-late 1980s, in the UK, learning portfolios were becoming more prominent, partly through the Enterprise in Higher Education initiative (EHE) (Stefani, Mason, & Pegler, 2007) and the National Vocational Qualifications, which emphasised competence-based

assessment (Challis, 1999). The EHE initiative focused on personal development planning by emphasising transference of skills, connections between academic curriculum and professional work, adaptability to a changing world, active learning, and understanding and promotion of the skills related to lifelong learning. Portfolio development grew when the UK Open University gained funding to teach 'A Portfolio Approach to Personal and Career Development'. The Open University project was seen as 'possibly one of the first initiatives in the UK to emphasise, value, and credit 'the learning process'–through a portfolio of learning evidence' (Stefani et al., 2007, p. 23). Additionally, Challis (1999) has noted the use of portfolios within higher education as early as the late 1980s and the introduction of a professional portfolio in the field of nursing by the English National Board in 1991.

As a useful tool for documenting authentic learning and showcasing achievement in a variety of situations, portfolios have been used by artists, architects, students, and teachers for a multitude of purposes. As such, the term 'portfolio' has become increasingly harder to define; however, there are some fundamental qualities about which most can agree. An aggregation of several scholars' analyses of portfolios shows that all portfolios have at least some of these five qualities in common:

- They are purposeful and context-driven.
- They incorporate reflection and self-assessment into their creation process.
- They incorporate student responsibility, engagement, and ownership into their creation process.
- They demonstrate growth over time and enable students to project goals for the future.
- They are derived from a collaborative process, such as peer review, example portfolios, and teacher feedback. (Paulson, Paulson, & Meyer, 1991; Taylor et al., 1999; Yancey, 2001)

The great degree of disciplines using portfolios illustrates their capability of serving a variety of purposes; however, there are some broad categories into which many portfolios can be grouped, such as portfolios for learning, assessment, and professional development.

Learning portfolios, which often involve sets of classroom or course portfolios, can take many different forms and vary by elements such as type and level of course, objective of the portfolio, audience for the portfolio, and criteria for evaluation (Yancey, 2001). While they do vary widely, course portfolios typically all have one quality in common: student responsibility for including and contextualising pieces that exhibit learning of the course objectives. This process of interpretation of these learning objectives by the student helps to make learning more visible.

Portfolios for assessment often operate at the programme level and work to capture efforts of visible learning, usually in an attempt to review programme levels of effectiveness. Students show how effectively they have learned material, and programmes ascertain how effectively they are teaching (Knight & Gallaro, 1994). Students often complete programme portfolios to show that they have mastered a prerequisite for a major, to demonstrate senior capstone experiences, or to show that they have mastered areas for a degree and are qualified to join a professional community of practice. Johnson et al. (2006) emphasise two qualities typically inherent within all portfolios, reflection and facilitation of authentic assessment, that 'provide program developers with vital information about how well learners have integrated their values, knowledge, and meaning from their instruction and mentoring' (p. 9).

The act of reflection is a key feature of portfolio creation, and most 'portfolio advocates choose portfolios because of their understanding that reflection enhances learning' (Yancey, 2001, p. 17). Yancey (1998) defines reflection:

To reflect, as to learn (since reflection is a kind of learning), we set a problem for ourselves, we try to conceptualize that problem from diverse perspectives – the scientific and spontaneous – for it is in seeing something from divergent perspectives that we see it fully. Along the way, we check and confirm, as we seek to reach goals that we have set for ourselves. Reflection becomes a habit, one that transforms. (pp. 11–12)

The initial portfolio paradigm is described as one where students first collect all of their work, then select samples of work to share, and finally reflect on why they chose those samples, why the samples exhibit certain skills, or how their portfolio might help them plan for the future (Yancey, 2001). The act of reflection can occur throughout this entire process. Diez (1994) outlines three ways in which the portfolio encourages reflection. First, it supplies a structure which makes work visible to the student; second, by asking students to examine a collection of their work it provides the opportunity for self-assessment and peer assessment; and third, through self-assessment students can set goals for future growth and professional development. In many ways, portfolios remind us of the literal roots of 'reflection': 'The process of looking at one's development through a portfolio process functions like a literal mirror–when one sees one's own image or performance–the *literal* reflection sparks *internal* reflection' (Diez, 1994, p. 10).

Partly because of this reflection, richer forms of authentic assessment are often attributed to portfolios. During the last two decades there has been an increasing dissatisfaction with standardised testing along with an increasing demand for accountability among educational institutions (Shaklee, Barbour, Ambrose, & Hansford, 1997). As critique against standardised testing grows, there is a pressing need for forms of authentic assessment, which Johnson and Rose (1997) describe as 'performance-based, realistic, and instructionally appropriate' (p. 5). When assessing programme portfolios, candidates' reflections can provide a breadth of rich qualitative data for programme improvement regarding programme strengths, weaknesses, and types of implementation. These reflections can also help serve as a map to help students see both where they have been, in regards to their learning, and where they would like to go (Diez, 1994). Self-assessment builds the portfolio as a map:

Using explicit criteria, the student develops the ability to look at her own work and determine strengths and weaknesses evident in a particular performance or across a set of performances. She begins to set goals to address the areas she needs to develop and to deepen her areas of strength. (Diez, 1994, p. 12)

When viewed through the lens of the map, we can see portfolio assessment as a way to chart student learning, as well as programmatic and institutional curricular development by providing the means to more authentic forms of assessment.

Diez (1994) warns us not to view the portfolio as something that can *do* our assessment work for us: 'The portfolio may provide a form, but the agency remains with the teacher's and student's *use* of the form' (p. 6). The analogy of the sonnet can be used to describe the form provided by the portfolio: the sonnet form provides a structure, which the poet employs for expressive purposes (Diez, 1994). The type of portfolio best described by the sonnet metaphor is one in which the creator chooses a set of 'best' pieces to show a range of performance and skills achieved. This type of portfolio is usually projected toward a specific audience, with a specific objective in mind. It may be guided by a set of required elements, but it is the student's choice of materials to match those elements coupled with the student's voiced reflection about those materials that make the portfolio an individual expression of the student's learning. Teachers can then use this expression and self-assessment as a moment of significant learning,

about the student and about the curriculum, but the portfolio does not do that assessment without the student's and teacher's close involvement with the learning processes.

A portfolio that showcases best practices can certainly be used as a learning portfolio or one for assessment, and it can also contribute to professional development. Because the creator chooses pieces that best showcase her or his skills and achievements, the portfolio for professional development requires discipline. Diez (1994) asserts, 'In the work world, a similar discipline is required for communicating about one's qualifications to a potential employer' (p. 7). The types of self-assessment and reflection that go into building professional portfolios draw connections between lessons learned in school and the skills and criteria that make them professionally qualified.

Portfolios, then, can be seen as tools for the facilitation and assessment of students' reflections on learning and professional development. Portfolios also engender a certain type of thinking – what has been called 'folio thinking' (Chen & Mazlow, 2002). 'Folio thinking' values reflection and its role throughout the process of learning, and it views students as collaborators who are actively engaged in constructing and taking ownership in their educations (Garis, 2007; Roberts et al., 2005). When all of the processes of the portfolio are taken together–map, mirror, and sonnet–they can serve creatively and constructively to enhance student learning and promote forms of authentic assessment (Diez, 1994). However, as Johnson and Rose (1997) remind us, 'When we only focus on portfolios as a product, we've missed their potential power, which comes from the process of creating them' (p. 8). The process of creating portfolios is one on which we focus as we turn our attention to their popular, new electronic forms of development and presentation. Citing John Keats's poem, 'On the Sonnet,' Diez (1994) encourages us all to take as much liberty as needed to make the form serve our own purposes, helping our students make their portfolios '"interwoven and complete", weighing "the stress of every chord"' (p. 8). Electronic portfolios are the next step in 'stressing every chord' of student learning.

ePORTFOLIOS IN HIGHER EDUCATION: LEARNING, ASSESSMENT AND PROFESSIONAL DEVELOPMENT

From Folio to eFolio Thinking

Though portfolios have been used in academic settings for decades, the shift to students who are often digital natives creating portfolios has wide-ranging implications on the pedagogy, design, and deployment of portfolios in higher education. With the possibility of combining digital learning objects–video, audio, or animation to name just a few–with technologically mediated social interaction offers both new challenges and new potentials (Yancey, 2001).

Paper-based portfolios were and are good methods of bringing process-based pedagogies to classroom instruction. 'Folio thinking' has proven to be a useful way to encourage students to 'document and track their learning, develop an integrated, coherent picture of their learning experiences, and enhance their self-understanding' (Stanford Center for Innovations in Learning, 2002). However, paper-based portfolios have limitations that most research recognises. Non-electronic portfolios can be difficult to compile and distribute, depending upon the medium of distribution. All elements have to be conveyed on paper, or be able to be converted to some form of paper-based representation. Students and faculty alike find them to be exceptionally time-consuming to create and to assess, often requiring excessive incentive to motivate students to value their creation and to encourage faculty to take the instructional time necessary to encourage good portfolio practice. And everyone can relate to the frequent difficulty in finding all of the necessary

and required components of portfolios, as students lose drafts and input from peers. Finally, the accumulation of hundreds of portfolios over time can make the physical storage a pressing issue.

Electronic media provide affordances that make ePortfolios useful for overcoming the limitations of paper-based portfolios. This is a clear shift from 'Folio thinking' (Stanford Center for Innovations in Learning, 2002) to what might be called 'eFolio thinking.' It might serve best to organise these around a familiar organisational scheme, that of the portfolio process itself: collection, selection, reflection, connection, and evaluation.

In terms of collection, ePortfolio development and 'eFolio thinking' encourage the creation of digital formats for student work. These digital formats will be usable and re-usable for the longevity that some assessment efforts require. Digital formats encourage instructors to involve new forms of digital, participatory submissions to student portfolios, such as blogs, video, and audio podcasts.

Locating these resources online, typically in Internet-accessible environments, centralising the collection of portfolio elements so they are accessible to students, classroom instructors, and assessment administrators, eases selection processes. In past portfolio creation, multiple paper copies would have to be created for each individual viewing of the portfolio, requiring quite a few costly resources. In digital formats, each view of the portfolio can access the same digital artifact without creating permanent physical copies.

Reflective processes are most aided on two levels. Through the use of highly detailed, varied modes of prompting, instructors are able to scaffold deep reflective activities by their students. In addition, online environments allow easier integration of the artifacts and reflections. For example, clips of audio or video can be brought in alongside commentary from the learner, the learner's peers, and the classroom instructor, all within one page of an ePortfolio. The ability to create templates of reflective prompts in many portfolio systems also has important ramifications for the assessment capabilities of ePortfolios. Form-based collection of reflection prompts turns student thinking into meaningful, qualitative (or quantitative) data regarding the student's actual learning during course activities.

The growing social technologies on the Internet have changed the collaborative nature of ePortfolio projects. Now, rather than costly resources being devoted to reproduction and sharing of paper-based portfolios, Internet-based production allows for easy access by many parties. Often the student can control and limit access or choose to publish a portfolio to a wider, public audience for purposes of professional development or community participation. The work at Penn State University using blogging software as a base for their student learning portfolios is a good example of such a system (Education Technology Services, 2009). Indeed, as students in our classes are more comfortable working in digital environments, it becomes important to incorporate the types of media they are comfortable producing as artifacts of their own learning. Blogs and podcasts, video and animation, all become legitimate media for displaying evidence of student creativity, knowledge, and learning.

Finally, in terms of evaluation or assessment of portfolio work, again the centralising of data within institutional learning management systems greatly aids the ability for faculty and administrators to organise systematically the types of artifacts that they require to assess student learning, whether on a course, programme, or institutional level. While it was possible to organise this vast amount of information with paper-based portfolios, the effort was often very costly and time-consuming, particularly at the programmatic and institutional levels. With the advent of digital distribution and easy, centralised access to student learning portfolios, assessment teams have access to complex datasets, often alongside sophisticated assessment tools, managed through an online interface. eP-

ortfolio tools allow for a balanced approach to student learning and assessment (Barrett, 2009).

The shift to electronic environments poses a great opportunity for folio thinking to develop into a new mode of pedagogy, eFolio thinking. In this mode, students and faculty alike can find new ways to collaborate on the steps of student learning. This emerging pedagogy is at the heart of the most current trends regarding ePortfolio usage.

Current ePortfolio Trends

The interactive and social nature of ePortfolios speaks to current trends in higher education. Because ePortfolios allow for documentation of and central storage for various materials that can be accessed from multiple avenues, they can help contribute to two ongoing demands in all levels of education: accountability and authentic assessment (Reese & Levy, 2009). While these calls for accountability and authentic assessment are not new in the field of education, with the advent of the Spellings Report in the USA, there is increasing pressure on higher education to provide substantive evidence of student learning. Susan Kahn (2001) addresses electronic portfolios' authentic accountability: 'Web-based institutional portfolios are not only public and highly accessible to stakeholders; they are also especially useful tools for communicating evidence-based information demanded by higher education stakeholders' (p. 137). ePortfolios offer ways to answer these calls for assessment from a student-centered perspective. Since most ePortfolios involve deriving and describing a set of outcomes or objectives, and since they can be connected across courses, programmes, and institutions, they have the potential to facilitate dialogues that make competencies and outcomes central to curricular discussions. Moreover, since ePortfolios commonly make student involvement and responsibility a high priority (Yancey, 2001), assessment through portfolios is often student-centered.

The social element of electronic portfolios addresses a third trend in higher education: students' increased use of multimedia in their daily lives. Reese and Levy (2009) state that today's undergraduates share their experiences through such web-based multimedia outlets as Facebook, Flickr, and YouTube and are capable of utilising various media to communicate their ideas. When surveying the different trends in portfolio usage, it becomes clear that portfolios have been in use for a long time and are currently being used for a vast variety of purposes. Johnson et al. (2006) identify nine areas that show the multiple uses for portfolios; Cambridge, Kahn, Tompkins, and Yancey (2001) emphasise three main types of electronic portfolios; and, Abrami and Barrett (2005) describe three types of portfolios. Our discussion focuses on ePortfolios for learning, assessment, and professional development, with the understanding that many of the disparate uses of ePortfolios fall into one or more of these categories.

Zubizarreta (2004) describes a portfolio for learning, electronic or otherwise, as a 'flexible, evidence-based tool that engages students in a process of continuous reflection and collaborative analysis of learning' (p. 16). When portfolios established at the programme level include an emphasis on student learning, they can 'lead students to deeper reflection on programmatic goals and objectives that are promulgated to wider audiences' (Reese & Levy, 2009, p. 4). Ultimately, learning portfolios work to engage students in processes of inquiry, help to establish reflective learning environments that challenge students to evaluate and synthesise their learning in addition to stating and analyzing preexisting information, and ask students to reflect on what they have already learned and then project goals and improvements for future learning (Yancey, 2001; Zubizarreta, 2009). ePortfolios focused on learning facilitate processes of collaboration and mentoring between the student and teacher and can even provide 'an interactive, web-based set of goals, directions, advice, and models developed as a virtual mentor or guide to portfolio development' (Zubizarreta, 2009, p. 38). Learning-focused portfolios allow students to select and organise their content, which engages them in the assessment and evaluation process (Abrami & Barrett, 2005). This can lead to students being more engaged in their learning process, and it can contribute to more authentic forms of assessment (Abrami & Barrett, 2005). ePortfolios for learning provide authentic ways to gauge students' understandings of course and programme curriculum.

These models for learning overlap with the forms of assessment deployed throughout universities to improve student learning: 'A portfolio allows the student the opportunity to reflect and record learning process while offering teachers an authentic integrative approach of evaluating student growth and achievements as well as acting as a feedback mechanism for their teaching practices' (Abrami & Barrett, 2005, p. 8). Because electronic portfolios provide central spaces for storage, access, and presentation of student learning materials, they can provide the means for internal and external departmental review, as well as other forms of institutional accreditation and assessment (Reese & Levy, 2009). The task of integrating ePortfolios within an educational institution can renew critical interest in curricular development at the programme level, and ePortfolios can promote authentic assessment throughout every level of higher education accountability. ePortfolios are often associated with authentic assessment because they accommodate virtual exhibitions of competencies. Because of this, they can be useful for ascertaining prior learning, experiential learning, and non-credit forms of learning, which can be especially useful in the assessment of 'immigrants, minorities, and mature learners where life experiences, rather than credentials, are especially relevant to judge' (Abrami & Barrett, 2005, p. 4).

Because of their authentic nature, ePortfolios can contribute to forms of professional development and life-long learning. Ward and Moser (2008) recently conducted a survey of 5,310 employers, finding that 56% of all respondents planned to use ePortfolios as part of their applicant review process; the authors recommended faculty and career services encourage student use of ePortfolios. Turner (2007) claims that a well-designed work portfolio can provide students with a great advantage over other qualified candidates for competitive professional positions, noting that 'a good work portfolio can provide visual evidence to back up your verbal and written claims of competency' (Turner, 2007, p. 19). In regard to promoting professional development, ePortfolios can be used for academic advising and career planning (Reese & Levy, 2009). The ePortfolio can provide a useful tool for an academic advisor to review a student's degree progress and it 'illuminates a structured workflow toward academic and professional goals, making it easy to review past activities' (Reese & Levy, 2009, p. 4). In addition to the type of advising that reviews academic achievement and charts progress toward professional expertise, ePortfolios also offer students a comprehensive overview of their academic, extracurricular, and co-curricular achievements, and they provide a medium for students to present those activities, along with self-reflection and supporting evidence, to prospective employers. Ring and Foti (2006) note the relationship between portfolio creation and student connections between theory and practice, asserting, 'The ability to make these links contributes to the professional development of our students. A student's ability to make informed decisions about what best represents him/her as an educator reflects a high level of professional knowledge' (p. 344). Ultimately, the interactivity, reflective processes, and authentic forms of evidence that are so often associated with ePortfolios can contribute to more reflective professionals graduating from our institutions of learning.

The three types of portfolios we distinguish overlap in many ways and only represent one form of categorisation. There are in fact many uses for these tools, and they are being utilised in K-12, secondary, and post-secondary educational institutions the world over. ePortfolio tools, however, are just that: a set of tools. They can facilitate learning and provide alternatives to traditional forms of assessment, but they must be employed with those values in mind. Much like their namesake, ePortfolio initiatives often develop through iterative processes of reflection that value student engagement, curricular reform and refinement, and forms of experiential, authentic assessment. When viewed from this vantage point, ePortfolio initiatives within institutions promote notions of life-long learning. Taylor et al. (1999) cite a statement on life-long learning from the National Record of Achievement Review:

Many people are increasingly likely to live so-called 'portfolio lives', constantly needing to update their skills and knowledge in order to take advantage of opportunities as they arise. Their skills need to be transferable. ... This changing world will thus place much greater emphasis on individuals taking responsibility for reflecting on what they have already experienced, setting future learning goals and preparing plans for how these will be achieved. (as cited in Taylor et al. 1999, p. 147)

Institutions of higher education should promote life-long learning, and ePortfolios provide a meaningful way to assist this process.

Assessment Strategies with ePortfolios

As suggested above, growing institutional assessment needs are facilitating interest in ePortfolios in higher education. For many institutions, this is often the central driver of ePortfolio adoption (Bass & Eynon, 2009; Schneider, 2009). Even if the assessment is done on an individual, student-centered basis, one of the features that mark an ePortfolio as different from personal websites, social networking sites, or blogs, is that an ePortfolio should be guided by a sense of goal, purpose, or direction.

Take for instance, the often-cited definition of portfolios generated in a conference of the Northwest Evaluation Association in August, 1990:

A portfolio is a purposeful collection of student work that exhibits the student's efforts, progress and achievements in one or more areas. The collection must include student participation in selecting contents, the criteria for selection, the criteria for judging merit, and evidence of student self-reflection. (cited in Paulson et al., 1991, p. 60)

Nested within this definition is student self-assessment of progress. From this student-centered effort, much research has shown how students can learn to reflect on their own learning and professional development (Angelo & Cross, 1993; Davis, Ponnamperuma, & Ker, 2009; Johnson, et al., 2006; Murphy, 1997; Riedinger, 2006; Taylor, et al., 1999). Classroom instructors should be able to assess personal instructional practices and activities by looking over a class-sized sample of student work, not to mention having a richer method of assessing an individual student's progress in a course. Sliding up the scale, by sampling from potentially hundreds of student-created portfolios, entire programmes, departments, colleges and universities could have a more representative sampling of the work the students in the university are producing, which can be used for broad measures of assessment and to plan long-term programmes of development.

This section reviews the learning and assessment theories that ground work in electronic portfolios, and then turns to an exploration of the potential uses of ePortfolios within higher educational assessment settings, from an individual to an institutional framework.

Walvoord (2004) defines academic assessment in clear language: 'Assessment of student learning is the systematic gathering of information about student learning, using the time, resources, and expertise available, in order to improve the learning' (p. 2). ePortfolios offer an opportunity to enhance that systematic gathering of student learning, including non-traditional, but direct, evidence, such as videos of oral presentations and group work, blog posts, and a wide array of multimedia. This potential has gained recent attention from organisations such as the Association of American Colleges and Universities (Schneider, 2009). Assessment requires a 'systematic gathering of information about student learning,' (Walvoord, 2004). Portfolio assessment seems to stand in opposition to traditional modes of assessment, but, as the president of the AAC&U, Carol Geary Schneider (2009) recently put it, 'after nearly a century of experimentation with standardized testing in college admissions, we know that students' scores tell us much more about the test-takers' resource base–or lack of it–than about their potential or their capacity to learn' (p. 2).

Electronic portfolios offer an opportunity for unique forms of assessment on several levels: for the individual student, for the classroom instructor, and for programmes or even institutions. For the individual learner, an electronic portfolio can be an opportunity to reveal desirable, personal learning outcomes, and to chart progress towards those outcomes. In addition, typical uses of electronic portfolios as 'electronic résumés' offer an opportunity for student learners, typically novices in communities of professional practice, to demonstrate that they have skills desirable of that community. This goes beyond typical modes of 'résumé' sharing that merely list skills with no capability to demonstrate teamwork, communication, or design skills effectively, for example. Assessment, in this sense, allows individual learners to improve and to target their learning on a set of self-directed, but communally significant, skills.

For the classroom instructor, there are two levels of assessment that can benefit from ePortfolio use. The first is perhaps the most obvious: having students create electronic portfolios provides a method for assessing elements of student learning that are not captured through multiple-choice tests or even essays. As only one example, one faculty member in a secondary English education programme has her student teachers use vlogs, or video-based blogs, to capture their experiences with instruction. After they videotape themselves teaching a lesson, they are asked to record a 3–5 minute reflection on that lesson. Then, as part of the programme's final portfolio, the student-teachers are asked to compile a narrative using 10–15 second clips from the array of collected reflections, focused on the question of their developing skills as classroom instructors, informed by the standards of practice of the National Council of Teachers of English. This provides a powerful tool for the instructor to assess her students' individual progress, not only on content knowledge in English or in theoretical classroom practice, but in observable classroom presence and activity.

The second level at which electronic portfolios provide a good mechanism for classroom instructors begins when the instructor participates as well, collecting not only student portfolios, but creating a portfolio of his or her own alongside the students'. There is a long-standing, and growing, tradition in education of course portfolios. A quick search will find institutions such as Indiana University, the University of Wisconsin, the University of Nebraska, Georgetown University, Xavier University and others with organised efforts at supporting instructors in creating reflective course-development portfolios. Course portfolios can be especially beneficial if there are more than one faculty teaching a shared set of learning outcomes. They give the opportunity for the instructor to take the elements of a course–syllabus, assignments, lectures and course materials–and to create a reflection space around those elements. In an electronic environment, this is particularly easy, and using blogging software, for example, an individual instructor or a team of instructors could provide examples of student response,

analysis of effectiveness, and recommendations for revision. At the end of the semester, a good electronic course portfolio would provide a tool for more effectively assessing the activities of the course and the effectiveness of the learning environment. In addition, the electronic environment can provide a unique opportunity to collect forms of student-produced 'data' that might not typically be easy to organise or process (Bass, 1997).

Extending that work, a third level that benefits from electronic portfolios is the programme or institution (Kahn, 2001). This arena has garnered much international attention on assessment. In America, the Association of American Colleges and Universities' VALUE project seeks 'to contribute to the national dialogue on assessment of college student learning. It builds on a philosophy of learning assessment that privileges multiple expert judgments of the quality of student work over reliance on standardized tests administered to samples of students outside of their required courses' (Association of American Colleges and Universities, 2007). ePortfolios play a central role in this new form of assessment that the VALUE project supports:

Educators around the country are pointing to an accountability strategy that can provide, simultaneously, a framework for raising student achievement, evidence of progress over time, and transparency about the extent to which students are achieving. ... The strategy—well attuned to the technologies of our time—uses e-portfolios ... ePortfolios enable us to see what a student is working on over time, to discern an emerging sense of purpose and direction, and to review samples of writing, research projects, and creative work as well as progress in integrating learning across multiple levels of schooling and multiple areas of study and experience. An e-portfolio also opens windows into a student's field-based assignments by creating opportunities to present supervisor evaluations or even videos showing real-world performance. (Schneider, 2009)

For academic programmes and departments, and indeed entire institutions, electronic student portfolios provide a set of unique learning and programme assessment data (Blair & Takayoshi, 1997). Rather than course grades, graduation numbers, or retention rates, instead data from student responses to course assignments across the programme, as well as work samples representing specific programme outcomes are readily accessible to assessors.

In order to increase the effectiveness of portfolio collection schema, experts from the different communities of practice can be drawn into the portfolio assessment process (Dubinsky, 2003; McNair, Paretti, Knott, & Wolfe, 2006). For example, criteria for portfolio artifacts and reflection prompts for learners can be derived from asking experts in the field what types of artifacts are most often produced and are necessary for practitioners to master. In addition, alumni boards provide excellent candidates for assessment teams: practitioners in the field provide a valid, external source of expertise that can assess the effectiveness of the student's representation of learning in an electronic portfolio.

By taking advantage of contemporary learning theories, electronic portfolios provide a new approach to assessing learning in higher education. Walvoord (2004) reminds us that assessment should use 'the time, resources, and expertise available, in order to improve the learning' (p. 2). Rather than focusing on data that simply provides accountability for a programme or institution, assessment of student learning centered on ePortfolios can begin to focus on data that provides real evidence of student learning.

Rollout and Adoption Strategies

With interest in ePortfolios being driven by student, curricular, and institutional pressures, administrators and technology directors are in need of guidance that will enable them to implement their initiatives successfully. There are a number of general strategies useful to that end. Additionally, strategies from the field of diffusion theory specific to higher education provide valuable rollout direction.

Whether considering a small pilot or an enterprise-level launch, it is important that those in charge of these projects develop strategies to ensure the sustainability of their endeavour. A key strategy to reach this objective is to align the ePortfolio initiative to departmental, college, and/or institutional stated goals and missions strategically. For instance, finding language in a university's mission statement or strategic plan consistent with the goals of an ePortfolio initiative provides a skeletal framework onto which arguments for funding can be placed in the future. As Virginia Tech's Learning Technologies group launched its enterprise-level ePortfolio initiative, they paired discussions and presentations of capabilities with language taken directly from their institution's strategic plan. 'A culture of continuous improvement' and 'integrating learning technologies to enhance the teaching and learning process' were among the phrases used to generally describe ePortfolio's logical role and place within the university's future (Fowler, Watson, & Zaldivar, 2009).

In addition to this rhetorical strategy, Learning Technologies also developed and nurtured key partnerships with stakeholders who had parallel or similar missions across campus. The Vice Provost for Academic Affairs and the Director of Academic Assessment were among these collaborators and were dealing with institutional challenges associated with accreditation. By offering a viable alternative to less attractive assessment methods, such as standardised tests, that still aligned with institutional goals, advocates at the administrative level emerged (Fowler, et al., 2009). Other key partnerships include faculty development groups, teaching and learning centres, institutional research, campus technology support groups/units, career services, student affairs, and alumni relations. All the while, senior leadership should be kept aware of progress and status, as they will be able to advocate for the project as opportunities arise.

Prior to or in concert with partnership building, it is advisable, if possible, to run lengthy pilots. This will enable a project team to understand the capabilities of the system deeply, as well as learn its limitations. Being able to respond to critiques and criticisms with a thorough understanding of the issues will foster a sense of trust in those leading the project. These opportunities for relationship building are essential. Additionally, as pilots are being planned, it is wise to select carefully the faculty that will participate, as well as the projects that will ultimately serve as exemplars to the next round of adopters. Faculty who have a high tolerance for technical issues are ideal for early pilots. As the project continues, it is then essential to engage and include those that have a high degree of opinion leadership. Rogers (2003) defines opinion leadership as 'the degree to which an individual is able to influence other individuals' attitudes or overt behavior in a desired way with a relatively high frequency' (p. 388). Within the faculty ranks, department heads/chairs, full professors, and award winning faculty are likely to possess a high degree of influence while still being perceived a peer to other faculty. As adoption grows and resources are requested, these faculty will serve as key, influential advocates in support of your project.

Faculty development also serves as a key component to ePortfolio adoption; however, given the complexity of the concept and the commitment required by faculty to integrate ePortfolios into their course or curriculum, a sustained, ongoing commitment to engage faculty is required. Diffusion of innovations theorists agree that adoption is a process rather than an event, and ongoing contact with adopters is required to ensure adoption occurs (Ellsworth, 2000; Hall, 1979; Rogers, 2003). The Concerns-Based Adoption Model (CBAM) embraces this understanding and was developed

to provide strategies to those managing adoption processes (Hall, 1979).

This model provides direction for the types of messages that should be provided to different audiences at different stages. For instance, given that the typical response from adopters in the first stage (awareness) is concerns about the self and what the adoption might mean in terms of time investment, learning curve, etc., messages to those faculty should be appropriately tailored to include clear messages about benefits to the individual. As faculty progress in their consideration of ePortfolio, the messages should shift to address the concerns that are present in the audience/individual. This logic holds true as adoption campaigns turn their attention to students as well.

Institutional climate and context also play a role in the successful rollout of any initiative, and Ely (1990) has identified and validated eight conditions that facilitate change efforts and diminish resistance associated specifically with instructional technology in higher education. A practical way to apply these conditions is to phrase each one as a question (Ely, 1990). For instance, 'Are most in the university pleased with current academic assessment methodologies?' 'Is it clear to faculty who is sponsoring our ePortfolio project on campus?' While project managers may have limited ability to change some of the answers, awareness of these answers will enable leaders to understand the reasons for slow adoption or outright resistance. This information should then influence the structure, timeframe, and communication plans associated with rollout activities.

Challenges to ePortfolio Adoption

While electronic portfolios have the potential to be transformative at the course, programme, and institutional level, possible limitations and obstacles to adoption should be addressed when considering the launch of any ePortfolio initiative.

Whenever any new technology is considered in the field of education, the question of access needs to be addressed. While the concern for the 'digital divide' might be less prevalent today, it should be noted that as of 2000, 'seven percent of lower income households have a computer, compared with 32 percent in the $30,000–50,000 income bracket, 53 percent in households making more than $50,000 annually, and more than 70 percent in those with incomes higher than $75,000 annually' (as cited in Cambridge et al., 2001, p. 10). In many instances, educational institutions may provide computers for student and faculty use; however, additional resources should be supplied to prepare and support student and faculty use of these technologies. The issue of access to technology, while important, is not the only potential challenge to ePortfolio adoption. Electronic portfolio scholars have shown a wide range of ePortfolio tools that span the spectrum of accessibility and cost (Barrett, 2008; Cambridge et al., 2001). For this reason, it is possible to build an ePortfolio using easily accessible tools for minimal, if any, cost.

Perhaps more significant than access, student and faculty attitudes toward ePortfolios can greatly influence prospective adoption. From a faculty perspective, even armed with the best intentions, there are several obstacles that faculty have to overcome in order to successfully adopt an ePortfolio project. Some of the impediments to ePortfolio adoption may be related to the necessity of implementation; adoption may be directly related to whether or not the use of ePortfolios is mandated from the university. Required ePortfolio use may provide a catalyst for adoption, but it may not ensure that faculty see and utilise the benefits of ePortfolios and eFolio thinking. Conversely, optional ePortfolio use removes pressure from faculty but may not result in institution-wide ePortfolio adoption.

Additional challenges to ePortfolio adoption include time, pedagogical planning, and ease of technology. Faculty are often committed to multiple institutional and scholarly duties and may not have the time required to embark on a transformative ePortfolio initiative. Moreover, incorporation of ePortfolio into current curriculum may require time to revisit and revise curricula at the course, programme, and institutional levels. These concerns can be magnified depending on the ease of available technology.

On all of these fronts, it is best to view ePortfolio adoption from a long-term perspective. As described above, consider starting with small pilot projects and plan for growth and expansion over several years. Electronic portfolio projects do not need to begin with sweeping change; it is usually best to target one main priority, such as assessment of two or three goals or objectives or a particular common learning activity. Approaching portfolios from the perspective of learning, assessment, and professional development, it might also be suggested that one start an ePortfolio project by focusing on one of these three areas and work to incorporate the remaining two over time. Finally, additional conditions for ePortfolio success, gathered from multiple resources and cited in Knight, Hakel, and Gromko (2008) include thoughtfully incorporating ePortfolio into the curriculum; faculty promotion of the value of ePortfolio; multiple opportunities for and inclusion of feedback on ePortfolios; time allotted for development; inclusion of engagement and personalisation within ePortfolios; provision of multiple examples of ePortfolio; and provision of technical support (pp. 11–12).

While the challenges to ePortfolio adoption are not limited to those listed, and while the potential obstacles are significant, the school culture, or institutional attitude, towards learning, assessment, and technology may play the most important role in ePortfolio adoption and utilisation (Cambridge et al., 2001, p. 11). As Cambridge et al. (2001) suggest, 'As more technology becomes more and more universally available, institutions that have developed a culture of practice around student learning and a culture of assessment around improvement will be ready for the rich possibilities of electronic portfolios' (p. 11).

FUTURE RESEARCH DIRECTIONS

It is expected that ePortfolio usage on college and university campuses will increase as accountability continues as a growing practice in higher education. Regional and disciplinary accrediting bodies' requirements continue to evolve and become more rigorous, and the probability is high that holistic assessment methods, such as those that utilise ePortfolio, will continue to grow in popularity.

As a result of this powerful facilitator, questions associated with pedagogy, assessment, and professional development will certainly become more complex and intertwined. For example, how can a single ePortfolio initiative or system meet course-level pedagogical needs while still serving the assessment needs of the institution? Given the variety of ePortfolio systems on the market, is it possible to provide some sense of standardisation that would enable portability for students who might bring ePortfolios to campus and then wish to take them to graduate school and beyond? What are the long-term fiscal implications and liabilities for an institution that purchases a vendor-based solution for its ongoing assessment and data warehousing needs? What new capabilities are needed, given the breadth and power of numerous Web 2.0 applications, to ensure key data is captured to enable meaningful assessment? These are among the broad emerging questions.

Thinking specifically about teaching and learning, researchers are beginning to verify the value of ePortfolios. A recent pilot study at Bowling Green State University found that 'students with e-portfolio artifacts had both significantly greater cumulative grade-point averages and credit hours earned than undergraduates without e-portfolio artifacts' (Knight, Hakel, & Gromko, 2008). While correlation is not causation, this study does suggest an exciting line of inquiry as well as a desire to quantify the value of ePortfolios within the curriculum outside of the realm of academic assessment.

CONCLUSION

In many ways, the trajectory of ePortfolios resembles that of e-learning in the late 1990s. The concept is receiving a great deal of press, praise and promise are currently high, a variety of disciplines are engaging with the technology, and a broad spectrum of colleges and universities are exploring its efficacy. While the concept of web-based portfolios has existed almost as long as the World Wide Web, a unique triangulation of complimentary needs (assessment, pedagogy, and professional development) has brought ePortfolios to the forefront of e-learning discussions. Given its current historical placement and the variety of institutional pressures that continue to facilitate interest, this chapter was authored *in medias res*; however, the pedagogies and practices described above provide an overview of the foundations of ePortfolio usage in higher education now and for the foreseeable future.

REFERENCES

Abrami, P. C., & Barrett, H. (2005). Directions for research and development on electronic portfolio. *Canadian Journal of Learning and Technology 31*(3), 1-15. Retrieved April 12, 2009, from http://www.cjlt.ca/index.php/cjlt/rt/printerFriendly/92/86

Angelo, T. A., & Cross, K. P. (1993). *Classroom assessment techniques: A handbook for college teachers* (2nd ed.). San Francisco, CA: Jossey-Bass.

Association of American Colleges and Universities. (2007). *VALUE: Valid assessment of learning in undergraduate education.* Retrieved March 20, 2009, from http://www.aacu.org/value/index.cfm

Barrett, H. (2008, September 30). *Categories of ePortfolio tools.* Retrieved April 1, 2009, from http://electronicportfolios.org/categories.html

Barrett, H. (2009). *Balancing the two faces of ePortfolios.* Retrieved April 1, 2009, from http://electronicportfolios.org/balance

Bass, R. (1997). *Course portfolio page.* Retrieved March 19, 2009, from http://www9.georgetown.edu/faculty/bassr/portfolio.html

Bass, R., & Eynon, B. (2009, March 18). Electronic portfolios: A path to the future of learning. *Wired Campus.* Retrieved April 1, 2009, from http://chronicle.com/blogPost/Electronic-Portfolios-a-Pa/4582

Blair, K. L., & Takayoshi, P. (1997). Reflections in reading and evaluating electronic portfolios. In K.B. Yancey, & I. Weiser (Eds.), Situating portfolios: Four perspectives. Logan, UT: Utah State University Press. Cambridge, B., Kahn, S., Tompkins, D.P., & Yancey, K.B. (Eds.) (2001). Electronic portfolios: Emerging practices in student, faculty, and institutional learning. Sterling, VA: Stylus.

Challis, M. (1999). AMEE medical education guide no. 11 (revised): Portfolio-based learning and assessment in medical education. *Medical Teacher, 21*(4), 370–386. doi:10.1080/01421599979310

Chen, H. L., & Mazlow, C. (2002). Electronic learning portfolios and student affairs. *Net Results.* Retrieved April 6, 2009, from http://www.naspa.org/netresults/PrinterFriendly.cfm?ID=825

Davis, M. H., Ponnamperuma, G. G., & Ker, J. S. (2009). Student perceptions of a portfolio assessment process. *Medical Education, 43*(1), 89–98. doi:10.1111/j.1365-2923.2008.03250.x

Diez, M. (1994). *The portfolio: Sonnet, mirror, and map.* Paper presented at the conference on Linking Liberal Arts and Teacher Education: Encouraging Reflection through Portfolios, San Diego, CA.

Dubinsky, J. (2003). Creating new views on learning: ePortfolios. *Business Communication Quarterly, 66*, 96–102. doi:10.1177/108056990306600410

Education Technology Services. (2009). *e-Portfolios at Penn State.* Retrieved March 23, 2009, from http://portfolio.psu.edu

Elbow, P., & Belanoff, P. (1986). Portfolios as a substitute for proficiency examinations. *College Composition and Communication, 37*(3), 336–340. doi:10.2307/358050

Ellsworth, J. B. (2000). *Surviving change: A survey of educational change models.* Syracuse: Eric Clearinghouse on Information & Technology.

Ely, D. P. (1990). Conditions that facilitate the implementation of educational technology innovations. *Journal of Research on Computing in Education, 23*(2), 298–305.

Fowler, S., Watson, C. E., & Zaldivar, M. (2009, January). *Institutionalizing the ePortfolio: Addressing assessment, pedagogy, and professional development issues for widespread adoption.* Paper presented at the annual meeting of the Educause Learning Initiative, Orlando, Florida.

Garis, J. W. (2007). e-Portfolios: Concepts, designs, and integration with student affairs. *New Directions for Student Services, 119*(Fall), 3–15. doi:10.1002/ss.245

Hall, G. E. (1979). The concerns-based approach to facilitating change. *Educational Horizons, 57*(4), 202–208.

Johnson, N. J., & Rose, L. M. (1997). *Portfolios: Clarifying, constructing, and enhancing.* Lancaster, PA: Technomic Publishing Company.

Johnson, R. S., Mims-Cox, J. S., & Doyle-Nichols, A. (2006). *Developing portfolios in education: A guide to reflection, inquiry, and assessment.* Thousand Oaks, CA: SAGE Publications.

Kahn, S. (2001). Linking learning, improvement, and accountability: An introduction to electronic institutional portfolios . In Cambridge, B. (Ed.), *Electronic portfolios: Emerging practices in student, faculty, and institutional learning* (pp. 135–158). Sterling, VA: Stylus.

Knight, M. E., & Gallaro, D. (Eds.). (1994). *Portfolio assessment: Applications of portfolio analysis.* Lanham, MD: University Press of America.

Knight, W. E., Hakel, M. D., & Gromko, M. (2008). The relationship between electronic portfolio participation and student success. *Association for Institutional Research Professional File, 107*, 1–16.

McNair, L., Paretti, M., Knott, M., & Wolfe, M. L. (2006). *Using e-portfolio to define, teach, and assess ABET professional skills.* Paper presented at the annual meeting of the ASEE/IEEE Frontiers in Education.

Murphy, S. (1997). Teachers and students: Reclaiming assessment via portfolios . In Yancey, K. B., & Weiser, I. (Eds.), *Situating portfolios: Four perspectives* (pp. 72–88). Logan, UT: Utah State University Press.

Paulson, F. L., Paulson, P. R., & Meyer, C. A. (1991). What makes a portfolio a portfolio? *Educational Leadership*, 60–63.

Reese, M., & Levy, R. (2009). Assessing the future: e-portfolio trends, uses, and options in higher education. *ECAR Bulletin, 4*. Retrieved October 20, 2009, from http://portfolio.project.mnscu.edu/vertical/Sites/%7B0D936A3C-B3B2-48B8-838C-F5A3B3E0AF6C%7D/uploads/%7B2231316D-EFA9-4A6D-B382-734A350E4510%7D.pdf

Riedinger, B. (2006). Mining for meaning: Teaching students how to reflect . In Jafari, A., & Kaufman, C. (Eds.), *Handbook of research on ePortfolios* (pp. 90–101). Hershey, PA: Idea Group Reference.

Ring, G., & Foti, S. (2006). Using ePortfolios to facilitate professional development among pre-service teachers . In Jafari, A., & Kaufman, C. (Eds.), *Handbook of research on ePortfolios* (pp. 340–358). Hershey, PA: Idea Group Reference.

Roberts, G., Aalderink, W., Cook, J., Feijen, M., Harvey, J., Lee, S., et al. (2005). *Reflective learning, future thinking: digital repositories, e-portfolios, informal learning and ubiquitous computing.* Paper presented at the ALT/SURF/ILTA1 Spring Conference Research Seminar, Trinity College, Dublin.

Rogers, E. (2003). *Diffusion of innovations* (5th ed.). New York: Free Press.

Schneider, C. G. (2009). The proof is in the portfolio. *Liberal Education, 95*(1), 1–2.

Shaklee, B. D., Barbour, N. E., Ambrose, R., & Hansford, S. J. (1997). *Designing and using portfolios.* Boston, MA: Allyn and Bacon.

Stanford Center for Innovations in Learning. (2002). *Folio thinking: Personal learning portfolios.* Retrieved March 23, 2009, from http://scil.stanford.edu/research/projects/folio.html

Stefani, L., Mason, R., & Pegler, C. (2007). *The educational potential of e-Portfolios: Supporting personal development and reflective learning.* London, UK: Routledge.

Taylor, I., Thomas, J., & Sage, H. (1999). Portfolios for learning and assessment: Laying the foundations for continuing professional development. *Social Work Education, 18*(2), 147–160. doi:10.1080/02615479911220151

Turner, J. (2007). Creating a work portfolio: Interview tips for engineers and computer scientists. *Graduating Engineers + Computer Careers.* Retrieved April 1, 2009, from http://www.graduatingengineer.com/articles/20071023/Creating-a-Work-Portfolio

Walvoord, B. E. (2004). *Assessment clear and simple*. San Francisco, CA: Jossey-Bass.

Ward, C., & Moser, C. (2008). E-portfolios as a hiring tool: Do employers really care? *EDUCAUSE Quarterly, 4*, 13–15.

Yancey, K. B. (1998). *Reflection in the writing classroom*. Logan, UT: Utah State University Press.

Yancey, K. B. (2001). Digitized student portfolios . In Cambridge, B. (Ed.), *Electronic portfolios: Emerging practices in student, faculty, and institutional learning* (pp. 15–30). Sterling, VA: Stylus.

Zubizarreta, J. (2004). *The learning portfolio: Reflective practice for improving student learning*. San Francisco, CA: Anker Publishing Company.

ADDITIONAL READING

Acker, S. R., & Halasek, K. (2008). Preparing high school students for college-level writing: Using ePortfolio to support a successful transition. *The Journal of General Education, 57*(1), 1–14. doi:10.1353/jge.0.0012

Batson, T. (2002). *The electronic portfolio boom: What it's all about*. Retrieved April 10, 2009, from http://www.tc.columbia.edu/cis/newsletter/ospi-miniconf/The%20Electronic%20Portfolio%20Boom.pdf

Blomqvist, U., Handberg, L., & Naeve, A. (n.d.). *New methods for focusing on students' learning process and reflection in higher education*. Retrieved April 10, 2009, from http://kmr.nada.kth.se/papers/ConceptualModeling/IUT_New_methods.pdf

Brown, G., Peterson, N., Chida, M., & Desrosier, T. (2009, February 4). ePortfolios, the harvesting gradebook, accountability, and community. *Campus Technology*. Retrieved April 14, 2009, from http://campustechnology.com/articles/2009/02/04/eportfolios-and-communities-of-practice.aspx

Cambridge, D., Cambridge, B., & Yancey, K. B. (Eds.). (2009). *Electronic portfolios 2.0: Emergent research on implementation and impact*. Sterling, VA: Stylus.

Cambridge, D., Fernandez, L., Kirkpatrick, J., Kahn, S., & Smith, J. (2008). The impact of the open source portfolio on learning and assessment. *The Journal of Online Learning and Teaching, 4*(4), 490–502.

Desmet, C., Miller, D. C., Griffin, J., Balthazor, R., & Cummings, R. E. (2008). Reflection, revision, and assessment in first-year composition ePortfolios. *The Journal of General Education, 57*(1), 15–30.

Greenberg, G. (2004). The digital convergence: Extending the portfolio model . *EDUCAUSE Review, 39*(4), 28–36.

Hamp-Lyons, L., & Condon, W. (2000). *Assessing the portfolio: Principles for practice, theory, and research*. Cresskill, NJ: Hampton Press.

Hickerson, C., & Preston, M. (2006). Transition to ePortfolios: A case study of student attitudes . In Jafari, A., & Kaufman, C. (Eds.), *Handbook of Research on ePortfolios* (pp. 460–473). Hershey, PA: Idea Group Reference.

Lorenzo, G., & Ittelson, J. (2005). *Demonstrating and assessing student learning with e-portfolios*. Retrieved April 14, 2009, from http://net.educause.edu/ir/library/pdf/ELI3003.pdf

Rickards, W. H., Diez, M. E., Ehley, L., Guilbault, L. F., Loacker, G., & Hart, J. R. (2008). Learning, reflection, and electronic portfolios: Stepping toward an assessment practice. *The Journal of General Education*, *57*(1), 31–50. doi:10.1353/jge.0.0008

Roth, J., Loacker, G., Deutsch, B., Gardner, S., & Nevers, B. (2004). The offspring of doing: Framing experience at Alverno College. In Michelson, E., & Mandell, A. (Eds.), *Portfolio development and the assessment of prior learning*. Sterling, VA: Stylus.

Treuer, P., & Jenson, J. D. (2003). Electronic portfolios need standards to thrive: The proliferation of e-portfolio applications requires compatible software and design standards to support lifelong learning. *EDUCAUSE Quarterly*, *26*(2), 34–42.

Yancey, K. B., Cambridge, B., & Cambridge, D. (2009). *Making common cause: Electronic portfolios, learning, and the power of community*. Retrieved April 14, 2009, from http://www.academiccommons.org/commons/essay/making-common-cause-electronic-portfolios

Chapter 11
Learning to LOLIPOP:
Developing an ePortfolio and Integrating it into a First-Year Research and Study Skills Module

Jennifer Bruen
Dublin City University, Ireland

Juliette Péchenart
Dublin City University, Ireland

Veronica Crosbie
Dublin City University, Ireland

ABSTRACT

The focus of this chapter is twofold: firstly, on the development of an electronic version of a European Language Portfolio, known as the LOLIPOP ELP,[1] and, secondly, on its integration into a study and research skills module for first-year students on the BA in Applied Language and Intercultural Studies at Dublin City University. The chapter begins with an introduction to the concept of a European Language Portfolio (ELP) in the context of current trends in foreign language learning and teaching. It then describes the development and key features of the LOLIPOP ELP. It explains how it was integrated into a first-year, undergraduate research and study skills module focusing on elements of course design and assessment. Finally, the chapter concludes by analysing the output from the participants in this study which indicates that they appreciated the opportunity to engage with the LOLIPOP ELP and found it beneficial to their language learning although issues remain around its design and integration into an academic programme.

INTRODUCTION

Today's language undergraduates find themselves in a very different position to their counterparts 20 or even ten years ago. This difference is the result of several related factors. These include increased access to high quality internet connections and other information and communication technologies (Bruen & Sherry, 2007) as well as the development and implementation in the classroom of pedagogical frameworks which support

DOI: 10.4018/978-1-61520-879-1.ch011

the concepts of self-regulated and intercultural language learning.

For example, with regard to self-regulation, since the 1970s, a significant amount of research in second or foreign language learning has been devoted to studying the L2 learning strategies employed by language learners. The primary goal of much of this research has been the exploration of ways of empowering language learners to become more self-directed and effective in their language learning (Tseng, Dörnyei, & Schmitt, 2006). A related area of activity exists around the teaching of language learning strategies to L2 learners (Cohen, 1998; Zhengdong, Humphries & Hamp-Lyons, 2004). It appears that such training is most successful and likely to facilitate self-directed or self-regulated learning when the strategies, for example goal-setting, are explicitly taught and when strategy training is associated with language tasks that the learners are normally expected to accomplish (Hsiao & Oxford, 2002).

Furthermore, there have been calls in recent times for an increased integration of such research in the field of language learning strategies into the area of self-regulation in research on strategic language learning (Dörnyei, 2003; Gao, 2006; Tseng et al., 2006). Self-regulation is closely allied with the concepts of metacognition (Wenden, 1998, 2002), strategic competence (Bachman & Palmer, 1996) and learner autonomy. There is greater emphasis placed, particularly in the areas of self-regulation and metacognition on an underlying understanding of their learning process on the part of the learner. Learner autonomy, on the other hand, requires the learner to take conscious responsibility for and control of their language learning.

In parallel, there has been a growing recognition of the fact that language learning necessarily equates with intercultural education, as speaking a foreign language implies entering a foreign culture (Sercu, 2002). Byram and Zarate (1997) further define an interculturally competent language learner as one who can cross borders and mediate between cultures. Such a learner is dissatisfied with a mere view from the outside with a focus on difference and 'the exotic'. Instead he or she is determined to gain an inside view of the other culture and to function effectively and appropriately within that culture.

Against this backdrop, the Council of Europe (http://www.coe.int/) issued a recommendation to member states in 1998 that a document to be known as the European Language Portfolio (ELP) be introduced to learners in all educational sectors. In particular, the European Language Portfolio seeks to promote the following:

- The development of learner responsibility and learner autonomy;
- The deepening of mutual understanding and respect among citizens in Europe;
- The protection and promotion of linguistic and cultural diversity;
- The promotion of life-long language and intercultural learning;
- The clear and transparent description of competences and qualifications to facilitate mobility and personal growth.

The document itself has three components: a Passport, a Biography and a Dossier. The Passport contains an identity profile of its bearer relating to their experiences and abilities in the different languages in which they have some level of competence as well as to their experience of different intercultural contexts. In the Passport, the language learner records their formal qualifications as well as a self-assessment of their linguistic skills. Self-assessment is defined in terms of proficiency levels set out by the 'Common European Framework of Reference for Languages' (CEFR).

The CEFR is the result of lengthy consultation and widespread collaboration among applied linguists in Europe. One of its central tenets is a global scale containing descriptors for each of six levels of competence which range from A1 (complete beginner) to C2 (highly proficient).

In addition, the CEFR contains a series of five individual scales also ranging from A1 to C2 for the following skills: listening, reading, writing, spoken production and spoken interaction. The CEFR is becoming increasingly used and accepted, for example, in the definition of syllabi in Europe (Ruane & Gauthier, 2006).

The Biography section of the portfolio is an updateable record of how, why and where a learner has learned each language that he/she knows. It is intended to foster learner autonomy by assisting the learner in setting, monitoring and evaluating relevant language learning aims and objectives, and by encouraging them to reflect on their language learning and intercultural experiences. For example, the learner can progress through a checklist of performative statements such as 'I can describe myself, my family and other people' in a spoken context, or 'I can write about events and real or fictional experiences in a detailed and easily readable way', or perhaps 'I can understand fairly long demanding texts and summarise them orally'. The learner then indicates whether they can do these tasks and also asks themselves whether such a task is relevant to their needs. This enables the learner to focus on their language learning priorities in a more concrete manner and to select discrete areas/skills on which to concentrate. The learner is also encouraged to describe the most significant intercultural experiences that have influenced them, experiences which may have led them to a deeper appreciation of another way of life.

Thirdly, in the Dossier, the language learner is encouraged to showcase samples of work as evidence of competence in the target language. The Dossier helps the learner to reflect on their progress and can also be used to demonstrate capabilities to others, such as prospective employers or directors of academic courses. Sample work might include examples of good written language, audio or video recordings involving the learner, or descriptions and results of project work.

To begin with, the majority of ELPs developed were paper based and took the form of ring binders or folders to which pages could be added or from which pages could be removed. However, such a format can be cumbersome and, in some cases, awkward to use and transport (Dalziel, 2007; Wright, 2006). Furthermore, as well as being easier to use and transport, many researchers and practitioners in this field felt that online ELPs or e-ELPs would enjoy several additional advantages when compared with their hard copy counterparts. For example, online ELPs could potentially exploit the new opportunities offered by ICT in the field of language learning (Bruen & Péchenart, 2007) which, as indicated at the beginning of this section, define to an ever greater extent the learning environment in which today's undergraduates operate. Therefore, it was decided to consider the possibility of developing an online version of the ELP. The development and key features of this e-ELP are described in the following section.

THE LOLIPOP ELP

Aims and Objectives

The primary aim of the LOLIPOP project was the creation of a sophisticated and innovative tool in the form of an online, interactive ELP in a wide variety of languages ranging from French and German to Norwegian, Latvian and Polish. In line with the current trends in language teaching referred to in the introduction, the intention was also that the LOLIPOP ELP should display an enhanced intercultural dimension and be designed to assist learner autonomy, self-assessment and reflection on language and intercultural learning in the context of higher education. Once the online ELP described above had been developed, the objective was to use it to encourage and support particular pedagogical principles and didactic approaches, the most important of these being:

- learner autonomy, with its aims to foster independence of thought and action, thus fostering a set of values for European citizenship;
- reflective practice through methodological approaches, which include self-evaluation, goal-setting, monitoring of progress, and an active engagement with the learning process;
- student-centred and task-based learning;
- collaborative learning;
- active use of computer-mediated communication to enhance learning potential and reach a wider audience in a more accessible way;
- commitment to lifelong learning;
- support for the making of the many transferable skills developed through language learning such as goal-setting, critical thinking, time management, planning and

presentation skills more transparent for student and employer alike.

The LOLIPOP project itself represented a pan-European partnership of 12 higher education institutions from eight countries and was funded by the Socrates (Lingua 2) programme (2004–2007). The LOLIPOP ELP is currently available as freeware at http://www.lolipop-portfolio.eu in English, French, German, Latvian, Norwegian, Polish and Spanish. There is also a facility by which additional languages may be added. Some key features of the LOLIPOP ELP include increased connectivity, improved visuals and animation, increased ease of navigation and portability.

In particular, in the case of the LOLIPOP ELP, increasing its connectivity involved placing the Biography section of the ELP with its dual functions of reporting and planning at the heart

Figure 1. Biography Homepage

of the new online layout or structure of the ELP together with self-assessment. For example, when the user first enters the LOLIPOP ELP, they are directed to the Biography homepage where they are provided with the opportunity to *self-assess*, *report* and *plan*. See Figure 1.

Self-Assessment

With regard to self-assessment, the increased connectivity of the LOLIPOP ELP simplifies what can be a daunting process for the learner. For example, if the learner clicks on *self-assess*, a *Profile of Language Skills* appears for the selected target language. This takes the form of an interactive table indicating the skills down one side and the CEFR levels across the top (Figure 2). The process of self-assessment is then aided by the provision of a function whereby clicking on the relevant CEFR levels causes the related descriptors and

can-do statements to appear. Examples are also provided for all of the *can-do* statements with the exception of those relating to spoken interaction and production, and written production (Figure 2). For a *can-do* statement, the learner clicks on the relevant radio button, i.e. green column (can already do something), orange column (it is still an objective) or grey column to reset the function. If they are unsure whether or not they can do something, the examples provided can help them in their decision. The *can-do* statements and examples therefore assist in the self-assessment process in that if all or the majority of the *can-do* statements represent objectives for the learner, it is likely that their level is in reality a lower one and vice versa.

Once the learner has selected their level for each of the languages in which they have a degree of competence and have saved this information, it is automatically exported to the Passport and used to

Figure 2. Profile of Language Skills with Statements and Examples

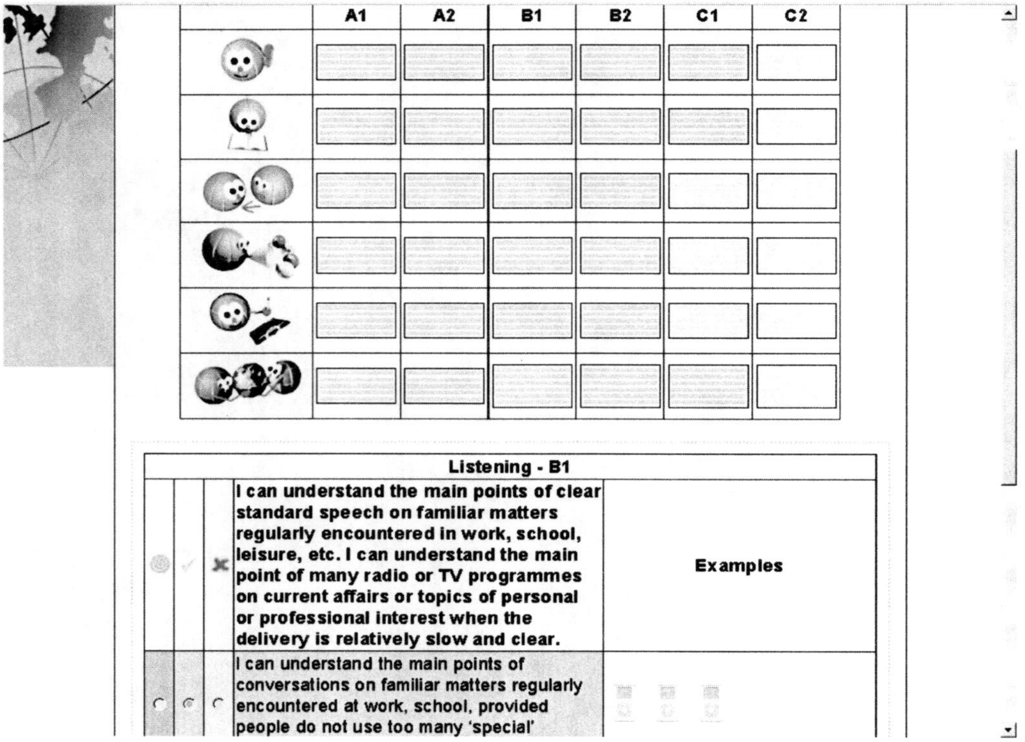

generate the *Profile of Language Skills* within the Passport. For example, a native English speaker who selects a B2 level knowledge of written and spoken German (interaction and production) and a C1 in reading and listening skills together with a C1 in intercultural competence would, on saving the self-assessment section of the Biography, generate the following table in their Passport. See Figure 3.

In addition, links are provided in the LOLIPOP ELP to suitable online language learning resources which can be accessed via the online, updateable resources section.

Reporting

As shown in Figure 4 other key pages within the LOLIPOP ELP include the reflections on learning (reporting) in which the learner is prompted to describe and then analyse an experience associated with their language learning. One criticism of this page in ELPs in general concerns a lack of guidance on how exactly learners should approach such reflection (e.g. Little & Simpson, 2003). Therefore, in designing the LOLIPOP ELP, specific questions in relation to both language and intercultural learning were included. As a result, the page facilitates the learner in identifying the type of intercultural experience currently being reflected upon, for example, meeting someone from another culture or watching a film or reading a book in their target language. They are encouraged to describe the experience and if they click on an icon to the left are given instructions on how to reflect using a three-step process. According to this process, they describe, analyse and then reflect on what they have gained from a particular experience. Finally, the yes/no questions assist

Figure 3. The Passport: Profile of Language Skills

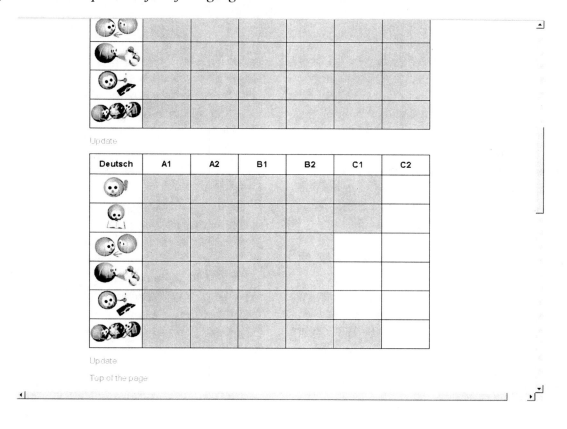

Figure 4. Reflections on Learning

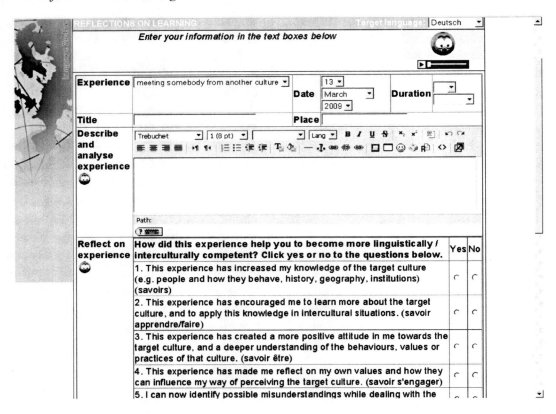

them in analysing the experience further. Such an exercise by students can provide a useful starting point for classroom discussion, for example.

A Transferable Skills page also encourages the learner to record skills which they have developed as part of their language learning which could be transferred to another context. This information is exported automatically to the Passport and could for example usefully be shown to an employer as part of a job application. See Figure 5.

Innovations within the LOLIPOP ELP

Within the portfolio itself there are many examples of creative use of visuals, animation, audio help-files, etc. In addition, the LOLIPOP ELP currently operates as a plug-in to the virtual learning environment, Moodle. This means that learners are able to access the tool in the 12 partner

institutions via the same server thereby increasing the potential for tandem learning. In addition, the possibility exists to download the LOLIPOP ELP to an individual institution's own server (with instructions available on the project website).

A further key example of innovation in the LOLIPOP ELP is the enhanced intercultural dimension. As is clear from Figure 1, an additional sixth scale designed to measure intercultural competence has been added. This encompasses intercultural descriptors developed for levels A1 to C2 which mirror the linguistic scales contained in the CEFR. Byram and Zarate's (1994) model of knowledge, skills and attitudes (described in the CEFR in terms of four *savoirs* and later developed by Byram (1997) as five *savoirs*), and to a lesser extent, the Bennett (1998) scale of intercultural sensitivity were used as conceptual models for the development of this component. In addition,

Figure 5. Transferable Skills

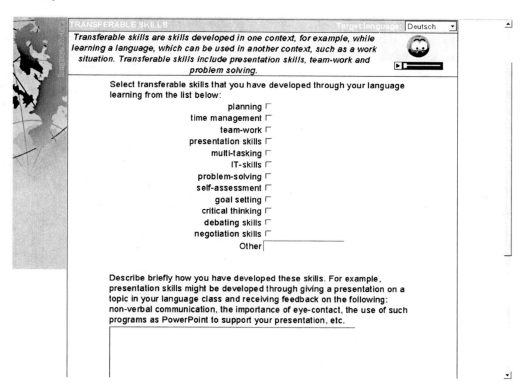

intercultural *can-do* statements were developed which display a progression from the acquisition of facts and figures to the quite sophisticated intercultural speaker or mediator, who can operate at a high and often complex level of intercultural interaction. As in the case of the linguistic scales, learners are assisted in the self-assessment of their intercultural competence by concrete examples for each of the statements and a glossary of specialist intercultural terminology.

Once an initial version of the LOLIPOP ELP had been developed, the next step in the process involved piloting it in classroom settings, a process which began informally before the completion of the LOLIPOP ELP in several of the institutions involved in its development. Furthermore, a key pedagogical aim underlying the development of this ELP is that all students studying a language should be introduced to the online ELP in their first semester.

The pilot studies referred to in the previous paragraph in addition to studies by other researchers investigating the use of ELPs at third level have stressed the importance of the embedding of the portfolio both in terms of curriculum and formal assessment (see e.g. Little, 2008; Wright, 2006). Additional studies (Ruane & Gauthier, 2006) also underline that using an ELP as a component of a language module also requires the learner to be introduced to the notion of self-assessment and goal-setting regarding what they would like to achieve in terms of their language proficiency and intercultural development at each stage of their college career.

Therefore, it was decided to pilot the LOLIPOP ELP as a key component of a core first-year module in research and study skills during the first semester of the academic year 2008/2009 on the BA in Applied Language and Intercultural Studies and BA in Languages for International

Communication (English Studies) at Dublin City University. It was envisaged that at least some of these students would then go on to engage with a target language version of the LOLIPOP ELP as part of their language modules in subsequent semesters. Issues around the design and implementation of this pilot project are discussed in the following section.

INTEGRATING THE LOLIPOP ELP INTO A FIRST-YEAR RESEARCH AND STUDY SKILLS MODULE: THE PILOT PROJECT

Approach

The 43 students selected for participation in this pilot project study one or two languages as part of their undergraduate degree programme and spend their third year studying and possibly working in the country of one of their target languages.

The research and study skills module, LC100, selected for this study is compulsory for all first-year undergraduate students on the BA in Applied Language and Intercultural Studies and on the BA in Languages for International Communication (English Studies). According to the current module descriptor, the learning outcomes for the course are as follows:

On completion of this module, students will be able to display greater awareness of their learning styles and become familiar with the conventions of academic writing and presentations. The module will contribute to facilitating the transition into a third level learning environment. (LC100 Module Descriptor 2008–2009)

On this module, the students have one weekly two-hour session on the following topics: language learning, library services, the LOLIPOP ELP, transferable skills, academic writing, searching journals and databases and evaluating sources,

citing referencing and plagiarism, and finally time-management. A session on the module assessment is given in the 12th and final week of the semester.

The two sessions on the LOLIPOP ELP were structured as follows. In the first week, all of the students involved attended a one-hour lecture. This began by looking at more general notions around language learning, learner autonomy, goal-setting, language learning strategies, intercultural competence and so on. The students were then introduced to the concept of an ELP and then to the objectives, structure and various elements of the LOLIPOP ELP in particular.

The next stage involved dividing the students into three smaller groups and devoting the second hour of the first session and the two hours in the subsequent week to hands-on training with the LOLIPOP ELP in a dedicated language learning room with wireless internet access and a laptop for each participant. During these sessions, the participants were encouraged to access the LOLIPOP ELP and engage with and complete the *Profile of Language Skills*. They were then encouraged to explore the rest of the portfolio at their leisure with the guidance of the researchers who were present to provide assistance or respond to queries. The researchers were also available for consultation over the remainder of the semester.

With regard to the formal assessment process for this module, the students were required to submit a Curriculum Vitae which included as a compulsory element a completed LOLIPOP ELP Passport in partial fulfillment (10%) of the requirements of the module, together with a 1,500 word essay (70%) on the following topic:

What is a good language learner? Is there evidence to suggest that they have a particular type of personality or approach the study of language in a particular way? In the light of your answer, to what extent and in what ways was the LOLIPOP ELP a useful aid in your approach to studying a foreign language?

The criteria by which the essay was graded were given to the students in advance and include evidence of self-reflection on the language learning process. The essay itself served the dual purposes of a summative assessment for the students and a source of research data for the lecturers involved in this course. All of the students involved were asked to indicate whether they were happy for their essay to be used for the purposes of research and were assured of confidentiality and that this aspect of their assessment did not influence their grade for this course in any way. No participant requested that their work not be used to inform this study.

Findings

The experience of the lecturers involved in delivering this module was that the students demonstrated an interest in and engagement with the LOLIPOP ELP. The level of attendance at both the lecture and the seminars was high. Analysis by the researchers of the students' Passports indicated a good understanding of the mechanics of this online ELP in that, for example, almost all students successfully completed the self-assessment section of the ELP, thus automatically generating a *Profile of Language Skills* in their Passport. Similarly, the section on Transferable Skills was completed by most of the students in the Biography, again generating the related graphic in the Passport. However, it was the essays, in particular, that yielded the most fruitful information regarding the students' attitudes and views concerning the value and quality of the LOLIPOP ELP as well as the purpose and effectiveness of its integration into this research and study skills module.

For example, a content analysis of the data generated by the participants in this study in response to the essay question posed above indicates that they recognise the position of self-assessment and goal-setting as being at the heart of European Language Portfolios in general and the LOLIPOP ELP in particular.

Some 89% or 37 of the 44 participants referred in their essays to the value of engagement in the process of self-assessment using the *Profile of Language Skills*. Specifically, they described identifying their proficiency levels for the different sub-skills in their different languages using the *can-do* statements and examples as motivating in that it showed them '...*how far they had come*' [19][2] as well as helping them to identify their weaknesses, what they still needed to achieve and how they might go about achieving it. For example, in the words of three participants:

It helped me drawing a clear picture of where I stand in each one of the three languages I acquire. It made me set short-term and long-term goals. It clearly showed me where I should concentrate more. [1]

I am considerably more aware of what areas I need to focus on and dedicate more time to. For example, my spoken production is at a considerably lower level than my writing (a fact that I had been somewhat aware of) but with the affirmation of this and the function of being able to set myself objective dates by which to achieve certain goals, I find my motivation to progress has certainly increased. [24]

[...] I have now set more challenging and exciting goals for myself and look forward to seeing them through. [34]

As well as:

It also made me assess where I was with my level of language proficiency in my target languages and also made me think about what level I wanted to obtain and what the best way to obtain it was. [6]

Indeed, the value of the links to potentially useful resources was stressed by several participants. These were perceived as being helpful in the achievement of the objectives mentioned above. For example:

This [resources] is the area of the portfolio I use most extensively as it allows me to practice, reflect on and to further my language and intercultural skills. [14]

Not all of the participants, however, valued the possibility of using the LOLIPOP ELP as a way of identifying areas in need of improvement. In the opinion of one, this feature was demoralising with regard to their ab initio language as it merely showed them that they had to learn '*everything*' [19]. A second disagrees with this comment in their claim that '[...] *realising what you cannot do is sometimes the only way one can start to succeed*' [35]. A third was of the opinion that there was insufficient emphasis within the LOLIPOP ELP on ways to eliminate weaknesses once they had been identified in their comment that:

It [the LOLIPOP ELP] does not put a great deal of emphasis on showing the student ways to improve the areas they are not so strong in. [10]

Another [21] felt that the classification of long-term and short-term objectives as expressed in the LOLIPOP ELP was inaccurate with many of the short-term objectives really being more long-term in nature such as, for example, '*I want to be able to understand discussions in standard language likely to be encountered in social, professional or academic life and identify the speakers' viewpoints and attitudes*'. The student continues by quoting Rebecca Oxford's (1990, p. 157) definition of a short-term objective as one which aims for achievement in the very near future, for tasks such as learning a list of vocabulary or trying to understand a radio programme in the target language.

However, these comments did not reflect the general view and the majority of the participants expressed their appreciation of the fact that en-

gagement with the LOLIPOP ELP allowed them to assess their level, identify their strengths and weaknesses and set goals accordingly, and finally provided them with links to resources which could support them in achieving these goals. The difficulty, however, of accurately assessing one's own level did not go unnoticed by the students concerned, one of whom commented that:

[...] during this technological self-analysis, I am at times unsure as to whether or not I am accurate in such an evaluation. [32]

The student goes on to refer to studies which report a discrepancy between self-assessment scores and scores in official examinations in order to emphasise this point. Surprisingly, though, the majority of those involved did not report on any significant difficulties associated with the self-assessment process. One issue, however, which was noted as a potential source of confusion by several participants was the fact that the CEFR scales go in the opposite direction to the grades awarded under the Irish Leaving Certificate where an A1 is the highest possible grade which can be achieved. A second student [18] described the CEFR scale as '*arbitrary and unhelpful*' and regretted the fact that links had not already been created and made explicit in the LOLIPOP ELP between the CEFR scale and Leaving Certificate grades. Finally, a native speaker of French also complained that the CEFR classifications were unfamiliar to her.

A second major theme which emerged from the data related to the relationship between engagement with the LOLIPOP ELP and learner autonomy. Conflicting views as to the direction of the relationship between autonomy and use of the LOLIPOP ELP emerged. For example, one student [3] commented that only language learners with a particular personality would benefit from using the LOLIPOP ELP. Such a learner, according to the student, is self-motivated and independent to begin with. They are also open-minded and flexible with regard to approaches to language learning as they '*will have had little or no previous experience of learning via such a medium*' [3]. Others, indeed the majority, expressed the belief that the relationship between autonomy in language learning and the LOLIPOP ELP to be the other way around with the LOLIPOP ELP assisting in the development of this quality in the learner in that it allowed '*[her] to be responsible for what and when [she] was learning as opposed to a lecturer or teacher*' [10].

As mentioned above, one of the key features of the LOLIPOP ELP was the enhanced intercultural dimension which included, in particular, an additional scale in the CEFR with related can-do statements and examples as well as additional exercises in the Biography. It appears that increased attention to the intercultural dimension found favour among several students (approximately 6 of the 44 participants) although it did appear to go unnoticed by the majority in the sense that they did not refer to it in their essay. Those who did make reference to the enhanced intercultural dimension noted that it encouraged and assisted the learner in reflecting on intercultural aspects of language learning, something that they might not otherwise have engaged in.

In addition, a number of participants' comments indicate that engagement with the LOLIPOP ELP made explicit to them the fact that language learning can continue to occur in parallel with and subsequent to formal classroom learning. This is indicated by, for example, the following comment:

I feel this LOLIPOP tool will be invaluable to me during the Summer months and then when I have successfully finished my studies at DCU, I can continue using this form of learning for my language development. [40]

An additional positive outcome from engagement with the LOLIPOP ELP was an increased awareness of the transferable skills associated with language learning such as presentation skills,

negotiation skills, goal-setting, etc. This point was, however, noted by only two of the participants.

There was also a considerable degree of discussion around the design, interactive and online nature of the LOLIPOP ELP. Unsurprisingly, this computer literate generation of students appreciated the fact that they were engaging with an e-ELP which did not require transportation and which could be accessed at any time, night or day. They also expressed positive attitudes towards the interactive nature of the tool and the fact that completion of, for example, the *Profile of Language Skills* in the Biography automatically generated pages in the Passport. As mentioned above, the links to suitable language learning resources were also deemed useful. However, several students referred to navigational difficulties in their use of the LOLIPOP ELP and complained of finding the tool difficult to use, user unfriendly and confusing. Comments of this nature were made by five of the 44 participants in this study. One student in particular [42] felt that the LOLIPOP ELP was time consuming to get used to and [...] *once this was done [they] felt that [they] had lost interest.* They posed the question as to whether their time would not be better spent learning the language rather than '*just reflecting*' on the process.

In terms of the integration of the LOLIPOP ELP into the first-year research and study skills module, analysis of participants' responses indicated that it helped them to make a link between the theory behind what makes an effective language learner and the practice of good language learning. They identified some of the qualities that make a good language learner such as high levels of motivation and autonomy and an ability to monitor progress and argued that the LOLIPOP ELP '*caters to*' these qualities [5]. For example, in relation to feedback one student [6] stressed the fact that Cotteral (1999) found in her research that feedback is particularly important for good language learning. They continued:

Before I undertook this module the only feedback I ever got was from the teacher, but now, after using LOLIPOP, I realised that by answering the questions, I could gauge for myself how well I am doing, for example, in Japanese.

However, some tensions in the integration of this e-ELP into this module also emerged. Several participants felt that the fact that the LOLIPOP ELP formed part of the assessment for the module, with students required to submit a completed Passport, *'something that should be fun was being turned into somewhat of a chore'* [5]. Others felt that the LOLIPOP ELP was not sufficiently integrated into the module and that it did *'not relate to the course work being done in the class at the time'* [10].

In general, though, responses to the LOLIPOP ELP were positive. In the words of the students themselves, it provided them with a *'different perspective'* on language learning and helped them realise *'the amount of effort involved'* [7]. Several commented that they have *'definitely had more success in [their] second language since beginning to use the programme'* [13], and the majority recognise it as being potentially a *'useful supplementary tool'* for [their] foreign language studies.

DISCUSSION

According to Ruane and Gauthier (2006, p. 64), the ELP is an 'accessible real-world tool intended to be integrated into day to day situations'. The pilot study described above represents an attempt to do just that with a particular online version of the ELP, the LOLIPOP ELP.

In terms of integration, it appears from student feedback that they appreciated the value of their engagement with the LOLIPOP ELP. In particular, they found it motivating as it helped them to monitor their progress. It was also described repeatedly as facilitating them in identifying their strengths and weaknesses, setting targets, linking to suitable resources to assist them in achieving these targets and, in general, helping them to become more independent learners, or in the words of Little (2005, p. 1) 'gradually developing metacognitive mastery of the learning process'.

The argument was also put forward that learners who are already self-motivated and independent would derive greater benefit from the LOLIPOP ELP although most appeared to agree with the findings of other, similar studies (e.g. Wright, 2006) that engagement with the LOLIPOP ELP could help to develop these qualities in the learner. Similarly, according to Little (2005), autonomous learners are already motivated learners. This is indicated by their generally proactive approach and their commitment to self-management. Little also notes, however, that success in learning strengthens intrinsic motivation. This in turn increases autonomy. In other words, the realisation on the part of the students that autonomy, motivation and performance are interrelated is one that is supported by the relevant literature.

Several of the participants, however, although admittedly fewer than anticipated given the reported difficulties by researchers and practitioners in this field (González, 2008) regarding learner self-assessment, described the self-assessment process as difficult. They reported being unsure whether their own assessment of their levels was a reliable one. However, the majority of participants found the experience of self-assessment to be a useful and motivating one, mirroring the comments of Chamot and O'Malley (1994) that 'self-rating requires the student to exercise a variety of learning strategies and higher order thinking skills that not only provide feedback to the students but also provide direction for future learning' (p. 119).

Several students did, however, express concern with the CEFR framework itself indicating a need for guidance from the lecturer in this area in particular given its importance within ELPs in general (see also Little & Perclová, 2001). One of the difficulties, for example, for both learner and teacher concerns matching the levels and related objectives to existing curriculum and classroom goals (*A teacher's guide to the Common European Framework*).

Finally, a third group felt that once they had engaged in the self-assessment process, they felt demoralised as it merely indicated to them how much they still had to do. It is possible, of course, that with hindsight, they will come to the belief that such a realisation in the first semester of their studies may actually act as a driving force for their future learning. It may also be desirable to provide additional links within the LOLIPOP ELP to online assessment tools such as the online assessment tool, Dialang (http://www.dialang. org), as they could provide further assistance to students in their assessment of their level.

A second key finding was that participants in this study liked the online, accessible nature of the ELP and the different ways in which (and times at which) they could interact with it directly. This is not surprising given that this generation of learners, as discussed in the introduction to this paper, enjoy an increased familiarity with ICT when compared with previous generations (Bruen & Sherry, 2007). In addition, as reported in the previous section, participants also expressed appreciation of the fact that they would be able to continue to access the LOLIPOP ELP independently of the particular research and study skills module in which it was used and, indeed, independently of their current course of study in the context of lifelong learning.

However, several students did report difficulties in using the LOLIPOP ELP. This was despite the fact that every effort was made in designing the tool to keep it as user-friendly as possible. For example, the same navigational menu was consistently placed in the same place at the bottom of each page and location-based feedback was provided using breadcrumbs. A site-map was also provided. However, the responses by the participants in this study indicate that scope for further improvements in software usability remain.

These are primarily concerned with navigation which continues to confuse some users requiring their attention to determine how it works and thus detracting from the actual task at hand. It is possible that the LOLIPOP ELP contains too many pages. The literature suggests that each time users are taken to a new page, there is a risk that they may become disoriented. Thus, fewer pages with more functionality might offer a possible solution as, in the words of Kreitzberg and Little (2008), 'Putting more functionality on a page can improve usability a lot, provided you're careful with the screen design so that the user is not confused or overwhelmed'. It is worth noting at this point that a possible follow-up project, which would have as one of its aims the simplification in navigational terms of the LOLIPOP ELP, is currently being considered.

It should also be noted that it is widely accepted that it takes time to become accustomed to working with an ELP with its various elements and components. This was the first time these students had been introduced to the concept of an ELP and while they were, in general, open and receptive to the approach it represented, two weeks of classroom exposure is unlikely to be sufficient if learners are to achieve a high degree of familiarity with and a level of comfort in using the LOLIPOP ELP.

This point could perhaps be linked to the view expressed by some of the participants that the LOLIPOP ELP could have been integrated to a greater extent into their module on research and study skills. With hindsight, it would perhaps have been useful to have revisited the LOLIPOP ELP in weeks five, eight and nine of the semester. This could also have perhaps prevented the intercultural dimension being somewhat overlooked by the students as a greater focus could have been placed on it at this stage. The same applies to the section on Transferable Skills. Clearly, the use of an ELP, and in this case an online version, constitutes a new element to language learning for many first-year undergraduates and one which, it appears, should be foregrounded as much as possible during class contact hours when being introduced for the first time. As a learner progresses through their degree, the degree of support required should diminish.

An alternative, or indeed complementary, solution in the case of this pilot would be to have commenced work with the LOLIPOP ELP through the target language during the language modules within a couple of weeks of introducing it in the study skills module. This might have helped to increase the students' familiarity with the tool and also have helped those who failed to see its direct relevance to what they were doing.

Thus, in summary, it appears that students derived benefit from their engagement with the LOLIPOP ELP primarily with regard to increasing their awareness of the centrality of self-assessment in becoming an autonomous language learner. However, they found the tool at times difficult and confusing and would like it to be integrated into their course to an even greater extent.

These findings echo, to a large extent, those of other small-scale pilots conducted by members of the LOLIPOP project in their home institutions and presented at a symposium entitled *Learning to LOLIPOP: Learners and teachers reflect* which took place in Dublin City University on 12 June 2009 [http://www.lolipop-portfolio.eu/symposium/index.html]. The presenters from various institutions of higher education in France, Germany, Poland and Ireland all spoke of the need for training and familiarisation of students and lecturers with the CEFR and the process of self-assessment in particular (Sudhershan, 2009).

Others spoke of a strong belief among students in France, in particular, that the role of the teacher was to assess and the role of the student to be assessed. It is also seen as ironic by some in France that the use of a tool, such as an ELP, which is intended for autonomous, reflexive learning and should remain the property of the learner, should be imposed (Gourvès-Hayward, Simpson, & Morace, 2009). In the words of Frath (2006), Tu seras un démocrate polyglotte, sinon

gare à toi! (You will be a multilingual democrat, or else!). Gourvès-Hayward et al. (2009) described an enthusiastic take-up of the LOLIPOP ELP on the part of their Chinese and Spanish students, but some reluctance on the part of the French. These findings echo previous studies at Dublin City University and Poznan Technical University which also indicated that culture, gender and discipline are contributing factors to attitudes towards the use of the LOLIPOP ELP (Bruen, Péchenart & Crosbie, 2007; Gourvès-Hayward, Kennedy & Sudershan, 2007; Gourvès-Hayward, Péchenart & Simpson, 2008).

CONCLUSION AND RECOMMENDATIONS

As mentioned at the beginning of this chapter, today's language learner has very different needs and expectations and operates in a very different learning environment from those who attended university 20 or even ten years ago. In addition to being more accustomed to interacting with different elements of ICT, many have part-time jobs and may not attend large numbers of language classes every week even if it is possible, in the current economic climate, for third-level institutions to continue to provide this form of intensive language teaching. Therefore, tools which facilitate the learner in becoming more autonomous, for example with regard to the dual processes of goal-setting and self-assessment, the centrality of which is increasingly accepted in the field of language pedagogy, and which permit them to work in their own time outside of formal contact hours are becoming increasingly important. This means that the ELP in particular in its online guise has the potential to play a key role in the education of tomorrow's language graduate.

The primary purpose of this study was to describe the development and initial piloting of an online version of the ELP, known as the LOLIPOP ELP, in a core first-year undergraduate module on research and study skills. The findings indicate that the participants in this study appreciated the opportunity to engage with this tool and found it beneficial to their language learning. In particular, they describe the opportunity to self-assess and set goals for themselves as informative and motivating.

However, the experience was not without its challenges for the learner. For example, one of the key lessons learned from this pilot was the need to prepare students for the process of self-assessment. According to Cram (1995) such preparation would ideally take place in a supportive environment and would not assume prior knowledge of self-assessment. Instead it would 'provide a series of experiences and opportunities for reflection so that learners could "operationalise" self-assessment concepts' (Cram, 1995, p. 296). In this context, learners also need to become familiar with the CEFR, in particular, the global scales, before engaging with an ELP. In addition, the CEFR encourages an autonomous approach by learners, generally with a focus on learning strategies. Consequently many teachers may need to adapt some of their existing approaches and materials to take account of and facilitate this heightened degree of student autonomy as well as engaging in the training of learner strategies.

The study also highlighted a need for simplification and refinement of the LOLIPOP ELP in order to make it more user friendly. In particular, there is a need for improved navigation: possible reduction in the number of pages in the learning tool and an increase in the functionality on each page.

Furthermore, in terms of integration into an academic programme, this process needs to be a more intensive one, requiring, ideally, more contact hours, increased guidance from the lecturers concerned and the parallel piloting of the LOLIPOP ELP in both a non language-specific module in an area relating to learning in general and in modules directly related to the acquisition of the target language(s). Research (e.g. Afoullouss, 2009; Little, 2008) also suggests that effective

integration of an ELP into such language-specific modules may require syllabus and assessment changes involving the expression of learning outcomes in the action-oriented terms favoured by the CEFR. Attempts by Higher Education Institutions throughout the European Higher Education Area to review learning outcomes in line with the Bologna Process may actually facilitate such changes (Moon, 2004). Finally, further case-study and action research in different institutional and cultural contexts is required in order to determine the validity of the above proposals.

REFERENCES

A teacher's guide to the Common European Framework. New York: Pearson/Longman. Retrieved June 23, 2009, from http://www.pearsonlongman.com/ae/cef/cefguide.pdf

Afoullouss, H. (2009, June). *Integrating LOLIPOP ELP in a language course: A pilot project*. Paper presented at the symposium Learning to LOLIPOP: Learners and Teachers Reflect. Dublin City University, Dublin. Retrieved June 23, 2009, from http://www.lolipop-portfolio.eu/symposium/index.html

Bachman, L., & Palmer, A. (1996). *Language testing in practice*. Oxford: Oxford University Press.

Bennett, M. J. (1998). *Basic concepts of intercultural communication: Selected readings*. Yarmouth, MA: Intercultural Press.

Bruen, J., & Péchenart, J. (2007, May). *Vorsprung durch Technik: Developing an online version of the European Language Portfolio*. Paper presented at EDTech 2007: Eighth Annual Irish Technology Users' Conference, Dublin Institute of Technology, Dublin. Retrieved March 2, 2009, from http://www.ilta.net/edtech2008/index_edtech2008.html

Bruen, J., Péchenart, J., & Crosbie, V. (2007). Have portfolio, will travel: The intercultural dimension of the European Language Portfolio . In Pearson-Evans, A., & Leahy, A. (Eds.), *Intercultural spaces: Language, culture, identity* (pp. 115–125). New York: Peter Lang.

Bruen, J., & Sherry, R. (2007). New perspectives in language learning: Transferable skills and the Language On-line Portfolio Project . In Conacher, J., & Kelly-Holmes, H. (Eds.), *New learning environments for language learning: Moving beyond the classroom* (pp. 111–122). Frankfurt am Main: Peter Lang.

Byram, M. (1997). *Teaching and assessing intercultural communicative competence.* Clevedon: Multilingual Matters Limited.

Byram, M., & Zarate, G. (1994). *Definitions, objectives and assessment of sociocultural competence.* Strasbourg: Council of Europe.

Byram, M., & Zarate, G. (1997). Defining and assessing intercultural communicative competence: Some principles and proposals for the European context. *Language Teaching, 29,* 239–243. doi:10.1017/S0261444800008557

Chamot, A., & O'Malley, J. (1994). *The CALLA handbook: Implementing the cognitive language learning approach.* Reading, MA: Addison Wesley.

Cohen, A. (1998). *Strategies in learning and using a second language.* New York: Addison Wesley Longman.

Common European Framework of Reference for Languages. (2001). *Learning, teaching, assessment.* Cambridge: Cambridge University Press.

Cotteral, S. (1999). Key variables in language learning: What do learners believe about them? *System, 27,* 593–613. doi:10.1016/S0346-251X(99)00047-0

Council of Europe [Website] Retrieved October 15, 2008, from http://culture2.coe.int/portfolio

Cram, B. (1995). Self-assessment: from theory to practice. Developing a workshop guide for teachers. In G. Brindley (Ed.), *Language Assessment in Action.* Sydney: NCELTR. Dialang [Website] Retrieved March 24, 2009, from http://www.dialang.org

Dalziel, F. (2007, June). *The European Language Portfolio: Its role and potential in university language teaching.* Paper presented at a Cercles Seminar, University College Dublin, Dublin. Retrieved February 24, 2007, from http://www.cercles.org/en/elp/seminar/presentations/Dalziel/ELP_Higher_Education.ppt

Dörnyei, Z. (2003). Attitudes, orientations and motivations in language learning: Advances in theory, research and applications. *Language Learning, 53*(1), 3–32. doi:10.1111/1467-9922.53222

Frath, P. (2006). Le Portfolio européen des langues et le Cadre européen commun de référence: entre normalisation institutionnelle et responsabilité individuelle . In Sachot, M., & Schneider-Mizony, M. (Eds.), *Education et normativité.* Caen: Presses Universitaires de Caen.

Gao, X. (2006). Has language learning strategy research come to an end? A response to Tseng et al. *Applied Linguistics, 28*(4), 615–620. doi:10.1093/applin/amm034

González, J. (2008). Promoting student autonomy through the use of the European Language Portfolio, *English Language Teaching (ELT) Journal, 10*(November), 1-10. Retrieved March 6, 2009, from http://eltj.oxfordjournals.org/cgi/reprint/ccn059v1.

Gourvès-Hayward, A., Kennedy, F., & Sudhershan, A. (2007, April). *The intercultural dimension in LOLIPOP. How interculturally competent are you?* Paper presented at the SIETAR EUROPA Annual Conference, East, West, North & South: Culture's Impact on Economy, Religion, Ecology, Politics. Sofia, Bulgaria.

Gourvès-Hayward, A., Péchenart, J., & Simpson, V. (2008, May). LOLIPOP, vers une plus grande autonomie dans l'apprentissage des langues. *Actes du 36ème Congres de l'UPLEGESS (Union des Professeurs de Langues des Grandes Ecoles)* (pp. 43-55). Paris, France.

Gourvès-Hayward, A., Simpson, V., & Morace, C. (2009, June). Using LOLIPOP for intercultural communication and management. Paper presented at the symposium *Learning to LOLIPOP: learners and teachers reflect*. Dublin City University, Dublin. Retrieved June 23, 2009, from http://www.lolipop-portfolio.eu/symposium/index.html

Hsiao, T., & Oxford, R. (2002). Comparing theories of language learning strategies: A confirmatory factor analysis. *Modern Language Journal*, *86*(iii), 368–383. doi:10.1111/1540-4781.00155

Kreitzberg, C., & Little, A. (2008). Usability in practice: Strategies for designing application navigation. *MSDN Magazine* (March). Retrieved June 23, 2009, from http://msdn.microsoft.com/en-us/magazine/dd458810.aspx

Language On-line Portfolio Project (LOLIPOP). Retrieved October 15, 2008, from http://lolipop-portfolio.eu

Little, D. (2005). *Learner autonomy: Drawing together the threads of self-assessment, goal-setting and reflection*. Graz: European Council for Modern Languages. Retrieved June 19, 2009, from http://www.ecml.at/mtp2/Elp_tt/Results/DM_layout/00_10/06/06%20Supplementary%20text.pdf

Little, D. (2008, August). David Little talks about the European Language Portfolio (ELP). *ELT News*. Retrieved February 24, 2009, from http://www.prosper.ro/EuroIntegrELP/materiale%20pentru%20site%20EuroIntegrELP.../EN_ELT%

Little, D., & Perclová, R. (2001). *The European Language Portfolio: A guide for teachers and teacher trainers*. Strasbourg: Council of Europe. Retrieved March 2, 2009, from http://www.coe.int/T/DG4/Portfolio/documents/ELPguide_teacherstrainers.pdf

Little, D., & Simpson, B. (2003). *European Language Portfolio: The intercultural component and learning how to learn*. Strasbourg: Council of Europe.

Moon, J. (2004, July). *Linking levels, learning outcomes and assessment criteria*. Paper presented at a conference Using Learning Outcomes, Edinburgh. Retrieved June 23, 2009, from http://www.bologna-bergen2005.no/EN/Bol_sem/Seminars/040701-02Edinburgh.HTM

Oxford, R. (1990). *Language learning strategies*. New York: Newbury House.

Ruane, M., & Gauthier, V. (2006). Implementing the European Language Portfolio in an institution-wide language programme . In Gallagher, A., & O'Laoire, M. (Eds.), *Language education in Ireland: Current practice and future developments*. Dublin: Irish Association for Applied Linguistics.

Sercu, L. (2002). Autonomous learning and the acquisition of intercultural communicative competence. *Language, Culture and Curriculum*, *15*(1), 61–74. doi:10.1080/07908310208666633

Sudhershan, A. (2009, June). *Savoir auto-évaluer: Exploring learners' experience of LOLIPOP self-assessment*. Paper presented at the symposium Learning to LOLIPOP: Learners and Teachers Reflect, Dublin City University, Dublin. Retrieved June 23, 2009, from http://www.lolipop-portfolio.eu/symposium/index.html

Tseng, W., Dörnyei, Z., & Schmitt, N. (2006). A new approach to assessing strategic learning: The case of self-regulation in vocabulary acquisition. *Applied Linguistics*, *27*(1), 78–102. doi:10.1093/applin/ami046

Wenden, A. (1998). Metacognitive knowledge and language learning. *Applied Linguistics, 19,* 515–537. doi:10.1093/applin/19.4.515

Wenden, A. (2002). Learner development in language learning. *Applied Linguistics, 23,* 32–55. doi:10.1093/applin/23.1.32

Wright, V. (2006). *Promoting and evaluating the use of the European Language Portfolio.* United Kingdom Higher Education Academy: Subject Centre for Languages, Linguistics and Area Studies. Retrieved March 2, 2009, from http://www.llas.ac.uk/projects/2570

Zhengdong, G., Humphries, G., & Hamp-Lyons, L. (2004). Understanding successful and unsuccessful EFL students in Chinese universities . *Modern Language Journal, 88*(ii), 229–244. doi:10.1111/j.0026-7902.2004.00227.x

ADDITIONAL READING

Bruen, J. (2005). 'How good am I really at German and how good would I like to be?' Some initial attempts to integrate self-assessment and goal-setting skills into a German language module using the European Language Portfolio: Developing students' transferable skills in the language classroom. *Report of the Transferable Skills Project* (pp. 7-21). Dublin: Transferable Skills Project. Retrieved March 2, 2009, from http://www.skillsproject.ie

Centre for Language and Communication Studies Portal, Trinity College Dublin, Dublin. Retrieved March 2, 2009, from http://www.tcd.ie/slscs/clcs/research/featuredresearch_european_language_portfolio.php

CILT The National Centre for Languages. *European Language Portfolio for adult and vocational language learners.* Retrieved March 2, 2009, from http://www.cilt.org.uk/further_and_adult_education/teaching_and_learning/resources/adult_elp.aspx

Confédération Européenne des Centres de Langues de l'Enseignement Supérieur (European Confederation of Language Centres in Higher Education). Retrieved March 2, 2009, from http://www.cercles.org

Cook, V. (2002). *Portraits of the L2 user,* Clevedon: Multilingual Matters Limited. Council of Europe: European Language Portfolio, Language Policy Division. Retrieved March 2, 2009, from http://www.coe.int/t/dg4/portfolio/default.asp?l=e&m=/main_pages/welcome.html

European Language Council European Language Portfolio for Higher Education. Retrieved March 2, 2009, from http://web.fu-berlin.de/elc/portfolio/index.html

Fleming, M. (2006). *Evaluation and assessment.* Strasbourg: Council of Europe, Language Policy Division.

Little, D. (Ed.). (2002). *The European Language Portfolio in use: Nine examples. Language Policy Division.* Strasbourg: Council of Europe.

Sherry, R., & Curry, P. (2005). *Developing students' transferable skills in the language classroom – A report on the pilot programme of the Transferable Skills in Third Level Modern Languages Curricula Project.* Dublin: Transferable Skills Project.

ENDNOTES

[1] The Language Online Portfolio Project

[2] Numbers were assigned at random to the participants in this study and appear in square brackets after their comments.

Chapter 12
Constructing Disciplinary Inquiry Communities Using Web 2.0 Technologies

Jamie Wood
University of Manchester, UK

Martin J. Ryan
University of Manchester, UK

ABSTRACT

This chapter explores the utility of Web 2.0 technologies for supporting independent inquiry-based learning, with a particular focus upon the use of blogs and social bookmarking tools. It begins by outlining the key issues confronting practitioners wishing to engage with such technologies before moving on to describe the approaches that were adopted in a range of first-year History seminar classes in two research-led universities in the UK. The chapter closes with an evaluation of the positive impact of the use of Web 2.0 on student learning and any drawbacks that were encountered. Web 2.0 is judged to have had a positive impact upon student engagement with course materials, encouraging student to conduct independent research outside of class and generating significant interactions between students and their peers as well as with tutors. Future avenues for research include investigations into how the use of such technologies can be scaled up for larger student groups and what impact summative assessment might have upon student engagement.

INTRODUCTION

Inquiry-based learning (IBL) is a form of active learning that seeks to engage students, either individually or in groups, in a process of self-directed and reflexive inquiry and research. Unlike the closely related problem-based learning (PBL) where learners are typically presented with a problem at the outset and tasked with defining and sourcing their own research questions, methods, and data (Barrett, 2005), IBL embraces a range of pedagogic frameworks and learning outcomes, linked only by their emphasis upon active student engagement and inquiry (Hutchings, 2006; Kahn & O'Rourke, 2005). Both IBL and PBL have strong links to constructivist epistemologies, which place emphasis not only on the active and experiential construction of knowledge by the subject but also

DOI: 10.4018/978-1-61520-879-1.ch012

on the essentially social nature of this process (Dewey, 1938; von Glaserfeld, 1989).

Web 2.0 is a term used to designate a range of internet-based technologies–blogs, social networking sites, social bookmarking sites, wikis–that facilitate active user engagement and collaboration (O'Reilly, 2005). As such, IBL should be strongly aligned to such technologies (Armstrong & Franklin, 2008; Cotterill, White, & Currant, 2007). Likewise, the social nature of Web 2.0 and the fact that IBL is often imagined as a collaborative venture, particularly at undergraduate levels, means that a priori we should expect a significant level of convergence, synergy even, between the technology and the pedagogy. Additionally, given existing student familiarity and engagement with social networking sites and other such technologies outside of formal learning situations (Thelwall, 2008), the use of Web 2.0 may minimise the uncertainties and anxieties that often mark students' first experience of IBL (Brew, 2007).

This chapter, therefore, will explore the various methods that the authors have employed to develop online inquiry communities through the use of Web 2.0 applications, specifically blogs and social bookmarking services, in History teaching at undergraduate level. This chapter will focus on the use of IBL-based pedagogies to facilitate and support these processes and the benefits and challenges the authors, students, and other teaching staff experienced. We will also reflect upon the reciprocal nature of this relationship: the extent to which inquiry and research-based learning is supported by Web 2.0. This will be accomplished through a series of case studies drawing upon the personal reflections of the authors, and evaluative feedback from students and fellow staff members. We will situate this discussion against the backdrop of the well-established literature on IBL and the emergent scholarship of Web 2.0 pedagogies, two areas which have, as yet, been insufficiently related on both the theoretical and practical levels (e.g. Armstrong & Franklin, 2008; Selwyn et al., 2008).

Indeed, because the Web 2.0 field as a whole is in its infancy, little research has been conducted into its pedagogic potential and impact.

BACKGROUND AND ISSUES: INQUIRY-BASED LEARNING AND WEB 2.0

We set out below the issues that interest us in particular in the use of Web 2.0 technologies to develop inquiry communities, ending each section with the key question that is to be explored.

1. Student Engagement

Despite the frequent perception that History is effectively applied common sense (Lloyd, 1996) and the avowal of some scholars that there is little specific historical methodology beyond the traditional *Hilfswissenschaften* (i.e. the 'Auxiliary Sciences' of palaeography, codicology, diplomatic, numismatics, etc.) (Elton, 1967), much work over the past few decades has emphasised the unnaturalness of historical inquiry and the concomitant need to encourage active student engagement with and reflection on historical methodologies as well as historical data (Warren, 2007). Promoting this active engagement, this inquiry, presents particular problems at first-year undergraduate level. History teaching at 'A' level may often have a relatively narrow, exam-driven focus (Lang, 2000) and the somewhat restricted syllabus, the so-called 'Hitlerisation' of History (Booth & Nicholls, 2005), means that first-year students may be encountering ancient or medieval history for the first time, at least in a formal educational setting. Whilst inquiry-based pedagogies, such as formal IBL or PBL projects, offer an obvious mechanism for promoting critical engagement and reflection, such open-ended learning can often be daunting or intimidating to students making the transition from 'A' level to university (Brew, 2007) and require a level of background knowledge that many students may lack (Crabtree, 2003). The incorporation of Web 2.0 technologies at a relatively informal level in first-year courses may present one method of encouraging critical inquiry, reflection, and questioning outside of a formal IBL setting.

• Can Web 2.0 technologies encourage students to engage with both the material being studied and the methods and techniques of historical inquiry?

2. Integration of Seminars and Lectures

The large modules commonly taught at level one on History degrees frequently mean that seminar teaching is often undertaken by teaching assistants, rather than module lecturers and/or course conveners. This can create difficulties for both lecturers and students. First, lectures permit only a limited level of interaction between lecturer and student. Although lecturers will encourage the asking of questions during the lecture, the formal setting of the theatre, the number of students, and the attendant fear of being perceived as less able tends to inhibit this. Web 2.0 technologies may offer the opportunity for students to pose questions and request clarifications or further information in an informal, non-threatening and, depending on the technology employed, an anonymous way. Secondly, lecturers and course conveners may have little sense of students' experiences and perspectives of the seminars. Again, Web 2.0 technologies may offer a way for lecturers and course conveners to gain insight not simply into what students are doing in seminars but their thoughts and ideas about their seminar learning and, most importantly, their particular interests and strengths. Such knowledge should allow for lectures and seminars to be more closely integrated and each to support the learning aims of the other.

• Can Web 2.0 technologies help to integrate seminars and lectures?

3. Freedom vs. Control; Process vs. Content

It has been suggested that inquiry-based pedagogies can be empowering for students because they have the potential to give students greater levels of control over two fundamental aspects of the learning process: setting inquiry questions or tasks, and determining the process by which those inquiries will be pursued (Brew, 2006; Kahn & O'Rourke, 2004). This raises several issues for educators wishing to utilise IBL in their teaching, depending upon their aims and objectives, the discipline, and the level of the students concerned. If, for example, the aim is to teach students about a specific area of disciplinary content knowledge, there are likely to be significant concerns about allowing students to conduct their inquiries independently of the tutor in case they come up with the 'wrong answer' or inquire into the incorrect area or knowledge. In such a case it is deemed safer to teach them the specified content via lectures, for example. If, however, the intention is to teach the students skills relating to the process of learning, then there may be more willingness to allow the students to engage independently in the inquiry process.

• What impact do Web 2.0 technologies have upon students' knowledge of subject content and their understanding of learning processes?

4. Cost

Resistance to the adoption of alternative teaching and learning approaches, including the introduction of new technologies, often focuses on the perceived cost to the adopter (Walters, Burhans, Kershner, & Alphonce, 2000). The investment in terms of resourcing, time and expertise is deemed too expensive compared to the uncertain benefits and the risk involved in making a change to tried and tested methods. Similarly, the pace of change in technologies, especially in the Web 2.0 context, is likely to be off-putting for some members of staff. Investment becomes more risky in such an uncertain environment. The potential mismatch between the expertise of staff and students in favour of the students, the majority of whom are now considered to be 'digital natives', is another factor mitigating against engagement. The training and support that are offered at the level of the institution to facilitate use of institutional virtual learning environments further encourages staff to make use of such learning spaces. In some cases this may be accompanied by policies and procedures that prevent staff and students from accessing certain Web 2.0 services from campus.

- Given the various motivational, resourcing and institutional barriers to engagement with Web 2.0 can we reasonably expect more colleagues to make use of such technologies?

5. Web 2.0 and Inquiry Communities

It has been argued that there is the potential for a strong degree of alignment between Web 2.0 technologies and IBL pedagogies due to the social constructivist roots of the latter and the fact that the former requires active engagement, often of a collaborative nature (Franklin & van Harmelen, 2007; Laru & Järvelä, 2008). Web 2.0 technologies may therefore offer adopters the chance to engage students in research and inquiry activities inside and outside of class, even facilitating the insertion of IBL into courses where there is no existing IBL component. Likewise, the fact that most Web 2.0 services allow users to interact with other users, including the production of work that can be viewed by the wider web, and the frequently collaborative nature of IBL activities means that

it has significant potential for supporting collaboration among participants and thus for creating communities of inquiry (Garrison, 2007; Zhang & Wang, 2008), although as yet these affordances are under-investigated (van Joolingen, de Jong, & Dimitrakopoulou, 2007). However, owing to the relative novelty of many of the technologies, few concrete evaluations have been conducted of their utility for supporting any kind of learning, let alone specific inquiry pedagogies.

- To what extent do these Web 2.0 technologies support the development of inquiry communities among participating students?

CASE STUDIES

The case studies in the following part of the chapter are intended to help to answer the questions raised by the preceding sections.

University of Sheffield

Context

These case studies are based on two second semester seminar classes for a first-year core course in the History Department at the University of Sheffield in 2008 and 2009. The students had to do two assessed presentations each (5–10 minutes, one presentation is in response to a question and the other is a source commentary) over the course of 11 seminars. In addition, students' oral contributions to seminar classes are assessed. Overall, the two presentations and general oral contributions account for 17% of the module assessment. The resources that the students built up in the course of these seminars were shared across two seminar groups.

Case Study 1: Blogging for Questioning

In 2008 the seminar leader set up a course blog (http://wordpress.com) for the seminar groups. Students posted a weekly question to the blog. This was based on the reading that they had done in preparation for the seminars. The rationale for this was threefold:

1. to motivate the students and encourage engagement with the seminar by giving them the opportunity to input into the selection of class topics and questions;
2. to give the tutor an impression of what the students had found particularly interesting about their homework, thus allowing the seminar to be tailored accordingly to meet the students' learning needs;
3. to develop the students' questioning skills in a supported, non-threatening environment.

The tutor read the student blog posts in advance of each class and then fed them into class activities. Different approaches were deployed, including:

*   selecting one question and using it as basis for class discussion;
*   working through a series of questions in turn as a class;
*   assigning questions to separate groups within the class;
*   giving students a choice of which questions to address.

Case Study 2: Social Bookmarking and Independent Learning

In 2008 the seminar leader set up a course account with the social bookmarking service delicious. com to encourage students to record their readings and to generate a dynamic list of online resources for the course. This approach was adopted as a response to the need to improve students' digital information literacy (Armstrong & Franklin, 2008;

Eshet, 2004). While students' uncritical use of sources derived from the internet is a problem, students themselves often fail to recognise that there is a gap in their skills in this area (Patrick, 2008) and attempts to modify their behaviours pedagogically have not developed very far, with some notable exceptions (Armstrong & Franklin, 2008; Morley, n.d.). Because students were recording their weekly research on the internet, the tutor was able to gain a perspective on the kind of resources that they were consulting and was thus able to develop activities that facilitated the development of more sophisticated approaches to the use of digital resources. In addition, by encouraging the students to record and share their journeys around the internet, the resource list meant that their efforts were not totally lost: they could return to resources which they had found whenever they wanted, as could their fellow students. Finally, because the bookmarks in delicious were visible to the course tutor, he was able to make the seminars more relevant to the students' interests and independent work.

For their weekly homework students were asked to log into the course account at delicious. com and bookmark three websites relating to the weekly topic. Having chosen these sites, the students were instructed to provide a short description of each site and 'tag' the site with a number of descriptive keywords. In preparation for each seminar the tutor read the course delicious site, using it as a basis for preparations for the coming seminar; for example, in determining the activities in which students were to be asked to engage and/or the sources/topics that were to be addressed in class.

Case Study 3: Integrating Social Bookmarking and Questioning

Building upon the student feedback and personal reflection on the 2008 iteration of the seminars, the course tutor decided to adopt a modified approach in 2009. The same objectives as described in the earlier iteration underpinned the 2009 version, but it was felt that two changes would improve student engagement: to provide the students with more direction regarding the activities that they were expected to do outside of class; and to improve integration between the different technologies that were being utilised. With this in mind, the social bookmarking site diigo.com was utilised to host both the course resource list and the questioning area. There were other specific motivations for using diigo, including:

- its wider functionality compared to delicious, meaning that students could be engaged in more kinds of activities inside and outside class;
- the recent development of a 'diigo for educators' account that enabled the tutor to register all of their students with separate accounts for the course and 'close' the account from the rest of the web (overcoming the problem of needing to have a class login for everyone in delicious and needing to keep the bookmarks and student names public).

It seemed, therefore, that diigo had the potential to offer a more structured, safer and more flexible environment for students to engage in activities. Other objectives for this iteration included:

- to integrate student activities in the social bookmarking site (outside class, mainly) with student tasks inside class;
- to provide the students with a broader range of activities to engage in outside class (instead of getting them to complete essentially the same task each week).

University of Manchester

Context

The case studies are based on two first-year courses, *St Augustine and the Last Days of Rome* and *The Origins of England c. 400–750* in the School of Arts, Histories, and Cultures at the University of Manchester in 2008–2009. Both courses were taught via a combination of lectures and seminars, *St Augustine* was assessed by means of written coursework and examination and *Origins* assessed by means of written coursework, group presentations, and examination. Seminars were constructed around the reading of specific texts (the *Confessions* of Saint Augustine of Hippo and a range of works from early medieval Britain respectively).

Case Study 4: Blogging for Interaction and Feedback

For *St Augustine*, the course convener, who was delivering the lectures but not seminars, set up a blog with Blogger for the entire course. Rather than sign up every student on the course as a blog author, a generic student author was set up and students were given details of how to post using this profile. The intention was for students to post questions about and reactions to the weekly lectures, both in terms of content and delivery, as well as to comment and reflect on their reading for seminars. The intention was for the course tutor to read student blog posts in advance of each lecture and to use them to shape the lectures and determine the particular supporting and supplementary material employed (handouts, PowerPoint presentations, etc.). Where necessary, clarification of previous lectures and further information could be fed into subsequent lectures or added directly to blog.

Case Study 5: Blogging for Questioning and Communication

For *Origins*, the course convener set up four blogs with Blogger, one for his own seminar group and the others for the three additional seminar tutors delivering the course. Each student was signed up as a blog author at the beginning of the course. As well as seeking questions and reactions about the twice-weekly lectures, the blogs were intended to be a means of communication between tutors and students (providing details of reading for the next seminar, links to useful web-sites, etc.) and a means for the students to reflect critically on the reading that they were undertaking for each of the five weekly seminars. Rather than seeking specific questions about the reading, tutors encouraged students to post more general reflections on the issues raised by each text and the problems they presented to the historian.

Case Study 6: Blogging for Group Communication and Research

As part of the assessment of *Origins*, seminars were divided into smaller groups who undertook projects culminating in an assessed 20-minute group presentation. These projects took up five weeks of seminars, with three devoted to research and two to group presentations. The course convener set up blogs with Blogger for each of the groups in his seminar, with each student signed-up as an author. Students were encouraged to use the blogs to communicate with other group members, to share research findings, and arrange additional meetings outside of seminars. They were also encouraged to post links to useful sites to the blog and to use the blog to make available supplementary material to their presentations.

FINDINGS

Overall, the approaches adopted for the Sheffield case studies proved successful in 2008. Although the activity was not compulsory, at least 75% of the students posted to the blog and the delicious resource list outside of class time (the number of anonymous posts suggests that the actual percentage was higher for both services). In total, over 150 bookmarks were added to the delicious resource list and 54 entries were made on the questioning blog. However, the actual number of questions posed was much higher than this as some posts contained 'chains' of questions, for example:

'Why would Romans want to be Christians? Why in a very tolerant and accepting society would people actively decide to join a new exclusive religion which was against some of the core values Rome stood for? A religion which they would also be persecuted for belonging to, so why did Christianity become as popular as it was?'

All the students had to engage with the resource to some degree in class even if they did not actively post to them outside of class as certain activities required that they consult the resource list.

In 2009, increased levels of engagement were observed in the course at Sheffield. Owing to the fact that the diigo site allowed the tutor to register students individually, he was able to monitor the number of postings made by individual students to the resource list and the forum. As at week 8 of the course every single student had posted at least two entries to the forum and two bookmarks to the resource list, with the top contributors having posted twelve bookmarks and eight forum postings respectively. Overall there were 122 postings to the discussion forum and 277 bookmarks on the resource list. Although it should be noted that this includes postings made by the course tutor and a significant number of bookmarks that were transferred over from the previous year's delicious resource list, there was a significant improvement in terms of engagement with the resource across the entire class.

The results of the Manchester case studies were more mixed, although, as will be explored below, this may provide some insight into more effective ways to employ Web 2.0 technologies. For Case Study 4 relating to *St Augustine* after a few comments in response the opening post by the course convener, there was only one further student post and was this made at the explicit suggestion of one of the seminar tutors. For Case Study 5, the first of the *Origins* case studies, levels of participation varied considerably between the different seminar groups, with one tutor opting not to make use of the blog. The blog for the course convener's group saw posts and comments made by 9 students, from a group size of 14, and attracted a total of 26 posts and comments, for the first of the seminar tutors the figures were 12 posts and comments and for the second, 16 posts and comments. For Case Study 6, the second of the *Origins* case studies, of the three groups one did not make use of the blog, one group made a total of 12 posts, and the other five posts. The two groups used the blogs very differently; the first used it primarily as a means of communicating and arranging meetings outside of the seminars, the other used it primarily to exchange information and bibliographical references. The second group also customised the blog, adding a number of gadgets to the sidebar.

LESSONS LEARNED AND RECOMMENDATIONS

1. Student Engagement

The levels of posting and bookmarking in the case studies suggest that Web 2.0 technologies have considerable potential for promoting active student engagement with both historical data and historical methodologies. The blog posts ranged from specific factual enquiries–'I don't understand whether or not Nennius is calling Arthur the cause of the Anglo-Saxons arriving in England'–to more complex questions, ranging across the categories of encyclopaedic, meaning-orientated, relational, value and solution-orientated questions identified by Abrandt Dahlgren and Öberg (2001) as being necessary for meaningful learning: 'How could Julian ever have expected to unite the Empire under such a fragmented and varied religion as paganism? All the different gods, approaches and personal preferences on rituals/practices stacked the odds heavily against him. So why did he attempt it? Was he aware of the challenges?'

The posts also showed that students engaged with methodological and source critical issues and showed an awareness of the relationships and potentials of different disciplines and source types. This is exemplified by the following quotation:

'My initial impression [...] was that piecing together the transition from a Roman to an Anglo-Saxon society would require a considerable degree of detective work in which snippets of information provided by each [source] would need to be brought together to generate a more coherent story. This might be a credible approach if the sources were truly independent of each other ... but they are clearly not. To the extent that the "Truth" can be found, I suspect that the answers do lie with modern archaeological practice, landscape history and genetics.'

One unexpected effect of blog posting–though this is necessarily impressionistic–was that in class discussions students tended to defend more strongly their own views when challenged by other students and also seem to have anticipated the kinds of critiques their positions would attract. It seems probable that composing a post may necessitate a more detailed reflection and consideration of the position being adopted, as well as generating a sense of 'ownership' of a particular idea or position. Similarly, in a number of cases, those students whose questions had been selected for discussion in class commented upon that fact in class and consequently were more motivated in the sessions.

The notable failure–the *Augustine* blog–might be explained by a number of factors. The very anonymity of the blog is likely to have discouraged contributions as in many ways it severs the direct link between a student's posting and their learning experience. Secondly, the large pool of potential authors and readers may have inhibited students from posting–diffusion of responsibility–and in general discouraged a sense of ownership of the blog. Thirdly, the precise functions of the blog may have been ill-defined from the outset–posts were invited about aspects of the lectures, the reading for the seminars, and the course overall–making students unsure as to what was expected from them or what role the blog played in their learning. It is also important to note that student engagement with all of the Web 2.0 technologies was variable, irrespective of the approach adopted by the tutor. Some students engaged very consistently, others used the technology quite frequently, while a minority used it infrequently and some not at all. This may have been related to the decision not to assess the work that students were doing on the blogs and bookmarking sites.

The successes and failures of the case studies suggest that while Web 2.0 technologies can promote active student engagement, it is necessary to ensure that:

- The aims and objectives of the exercise are made clear and are relatively concise and compact.
- Students understand precisely what is expected of them in terms of posting, commenting, and bookmarking.
- A clear link is made between students' use of Web 2.0 technologies and their learning, that is, it is integrated as fully as possible into both seminars and lectures.

2. Integration of Seminars and Lectures

Except for Case Study 4, the integration of seminars and lectures was not an explicit objective of the interventions. The blogs had considerable success in terms of generating interactions between students and integrating different aspects of their learning. A number of student postings/questions explicitly responded to previously posted questions and comments; it seems that the process of interacting with their peers had the effect of prompting further thoughts from students. In addition, a relatively large number of entries explicitly mentioned the contents of lectures, the revision of lecture notes or the reading of articles (often with links to such articles, if available electronically). This suggests that the blogs had an integrative effect by tying together the different activities which students had been engaged in across the entire course. For the Manchester case studies, where questions or comments about the lectures were raised, the course convener was able to respond directly to specific queries and, where necessary, alter or tailor lectures accordingly. Posting such questions or comments to a blog rather than asking them directly in a lecture allowed for continued dialogue and for additional comments and opinions from tutors and other students. In this way, the students gained a range of different ideas and alternative perspectives on the information presented in lectures, emphasising the essentially dialogic nature of historical inquiry.

The blogs also allowed seminar tutors to gain a sense of the particular strengths and abilities of their students and to tailor work or assessment accordingly. Thus one student posted a comment to a blog in Latin, leading to the exchange:

Tutor: *With your Latin, when writing essays or in the exam please do yourself a big favour and comment on the problems of translating the sources or the errors made by the editors! I can provide*

Latin versions of Bede, Nennius and Gildas if you would like.

Student*: Really? That would be great!*

The findings from the case studies suggest, then, that Web 2.0 technologies have considerable potential for furthering the integration of lectures, seminars, and other learning activities. Indeed, given that students tended to comment and reflect on the whole range of activities undertaken, even without explicit instructions to do so, the very nature of Web 2.0 technologies would seem to actively encourage such integration. This may be a product of the way in which the internet itself is navigated, with hyperlinking facilitating and encouraging the following of a long chain of information that can often move beyond the original object of inquiry. Information and ideas turned up in this way may not be immediately applicable to the specific task in hand but posting the details to a blog or social bookmarking site can preserve the information for later use.

3. Freedom vs. Control; Process vs. Content

The approaches that have been recounted in the preceding case studies demonstrate, to varying degrees, that Web 2.0 services can engage students productively in learning both about the process and the content of the subject. Virtual learning environments offer the possibility of monitoring which areas of the site the students have been accessing: where they have been *inside* the environment. Web 2.0 retains this functionality, but with the significant added benefit of allowing the tutor to see what the students have actually done on the site to which they have been directed, including their journeys *outside* of a closed environment into the rest of the internet. These technologies therefore represent a powerful way of using the internet constructively: encouraging the students

to go beyond Google and Wikipedia to explore the wealth of research and researchable material that is to be found there. Staff are therefore able to increase the relevance of the activities and resources they are asking the students to engage with because they can be confident about what work students have done outside of class and gain a perspective on what the students are actually interested in, a powerful motor for learning (Memory, Yoder, Bolinger, & Warren-Wilson, 2004; Plowright & Watkins, 2004). Students also learn about the research process, for example in being given the opportunity to practise their questioning skills. The research process can be supported by the technologies, through facilitating communication between members of a research team and aiding the collation and sharing of research materials they have collected separately. Subject specific skills and knowledge are developed in the process of finding, summarising and sharing material on the social bookmarking sites. Finally, the generic skills that students develop through engagement with Web 2.0 in the course of IBL (collaboration, communication and technical abilities) should not be underestimated.

From the viewpoints of the tutor there are additional benefits:

- The fact that tutors are able to see specific aspects of the students' work (readings, comments on readings, questions, comments on the blog) allows the tutor to tailor the content of seminars to meet student interests, to correct misapprehensions through the checking of content knowledge.

- Web 2.0 technologies are inherently open-ended and thus suited to engaging students in activities that allow them to research (perhaps on the web, but not exclusively), construct their own knowledge and interact with their peers.

- Likewise, Web 2.0 potentially makes visible to the tutor the process as well as the product of research, which may be important in terms of assessment or monitoring student behaviour.

- In Level 1 teaching staff often have a greater degree of freedom in deciding what and how to teach students than at later levels. Likewise, students may be more open at this level to engaging in different kinds of activities because assessment is less likely to count towards their final degree.

4. Cost

The experiences reported in this paper of how Web 2.0 technologies are used in teaching and learning indicate that the adoption of these technologies does not necessarily incur significant costs on the part of adopters. Indeed, the DIY nature of the technology means that staff members are free to tailor Web 2.0 services to meet their particular needs and respond to their own situations. The freedom of choice offered by the services and the rapid pace of change should actually be seen as a benefit: different Web 2.0 services were adopted between various iterations of the same module as the tutors realised that the new service was better suited to meeting his aims and objectives. Interchange between social bookmarking sites means that data from one site can be transferred between the services, so investment need not necessarily be lost. Indeed, the learning that takes place from using one service is perhaps the most valuable pay-off as it can be transferred to a range of different contexts, including into the use of the virtual learning environment, for example. It is also possible to see how meaningful activities could easily be constructed to involve students in interacting with different Web 2.0 services.

In terms of expertise, the Web 2.0 services which have been used in the curricular innovations reported here do not incur heavy costs. Both the Sheffield and Manchester tutors are of the opinion that the Web 2.0 technologies are more intuitive and far easier to use than virtual learning environments, also offering more rapid connection speeds on the majority of occasions. Web 2.0 services are thus relatively easy to set up and to use, while students are quite likely to be familiar with the services (or at least their 'look and feel'). In terms of commitment to engaging with the Web 2.0 sites, the tutor does not necessarily have to 'post' anything, although in some cases it may be preferable to model for students the specific activities in which they are to engage and it is clearly important that the tutor reads what the students have added to the site when preparing for classes. In addition, the unassessed nature of the tasks and the DIY nature of the technology mean that it is possible, preferable indeed, to start small and then build up as the course progresses or in subsequent iterations.

Experiences of using virtual learning environments can feed productively into the adoption of Web 2.0, and vice versa: the two should not be seen as opposing, but as potentially complementary technologies. Indeed, central university services are increasingly offering support for the use of Web 2.0 technologies to accompany their investment in the institutional virtual learning environment, while efforts to integrate Web 2.0 with the virtual learning environment are also moving forward (Hall, 2006). Web 2.0 service providers are also becoming increasingly aware of the potential educational uses of their technologies (e.g. pbwiki.com has an educational account feature; while diigo.com had recently launched a 'diigo for educators' service).

5. IBL and Community

Inquiry pedagogies at Level 1 often focus upon improving students' awareness of disciplinary research processes and developing basic research skills. This helps to prepare them for more in-depth inquiry experiences at higher levels (Levy & Petrulis, 2007). Evaluation of the approaches presented here demonstrates that the Web 2.0 technologies with which we have experimented effectively support collaborative student activity and encourage students to engage in IBL in their first undergraduate year. Blogging for interaction and questioning allows students to reflect upon their learning process and their subject knowledge, as well as developing specific research skills, such as the ability to ask questions based on their independent research and reading. Several of the activities discussed in the case studies mirror the early stages of inquiry process very closely. For example, in the case of the exercises in diigo, the students

- identify reading(s) of their own choice, based on the seminar topic;
- do that reading;
- briefly summarise the reading;
- and devise a question based on the research that they have conducted (sometimes they also explicitly connect it to lecture/seminar materials).

In other instances, for example in the use of blogs, the students are able to present their research findings or questions to the rest of the group and the tutor for discussion; these can easily be fed into the seminar to help structure further research. A number of these tasks could easily be scaled up to support larger scale IBL, for example in tying the blog explicitly to the assessed presentations that students have to do in some of the courses, perhaps by making the blog a compulsory activity in order to facilitate assessment of the collaborative learning process. In virtually all cases described above, the cognitive activity that is involved in processing and writing up the material that students have consulted outside of class is highly valuable: the thinking that goes on helps students to organise their thoughts on the topic more effectively.

FUTURE RESEARCH DIRECTIONS

The themes which we have explored in this chapter–inquiry/research-based teaching and learning, the first-year experience, and the use of Web 2.0 technologies in teaching and learning–are all rapidly changing fields of practice and of study, which are frequently high on national and institutional agendas. As such, they are ripe for future innovation and research. Based on our experiences and the research which we have undertaken, three issues strike us as particularly worthy of further attention:

- In none of the case studies above was engagement with the technologies a formal, compulsory component of the course. Students are not assessed on their contributions and although they are encouraged to engage with the Web 2.0 services, they have the freedom to choose not to do so. The idea was to encourage the students to actively engage with the subject matter, using Web 2.0 as a *forum* where this could occur. It would be interesting to observe the impact that assessing student engagement with the tasks and the technologies might have upon the quality of student work and the effort involved on the part of the tutor. In addition, if students were to be assessed on work produced and stored inside Web 2.0 services and therefore stored on servers that were external to the institution, account must be made of the security and longevity of the data across the life of the assessment. There is the potential to lose students' assessed work. Although this risk is unlikely to be great, it must be borne in mind and appropriate measures taken.
- It is important that we do not over-estimate the technological expertise of students. Just because a majority of students are familiar with some Web 2.0 technologies, does not mean that all students will be capable of

engaging with the technology that the tutor chooses (Krause, 2007). Effort must therefore be expended in determining which technologies are best suited to enhancing student learning and in supporting students through the process of engagement.

- The implementations of Web 2.0 discussed here are based on relatively small-scale interventions. The extent to which the technology scales up to meet larger student numbers is therefore, as yet, unknown. It is likely, however, that it would have some resourcing implications and this is certainly something that we intend to investigate further over the coming years. A comparison of the affordances offered by Web 2.0 with those of institutional virtual learning environments would also be worthwhile in this respect.

CONCLUSION

This chapter has explored, via a number of small-scale case studies, the ways in which Web 2.0 technologies–blogging and social bookmarking–could enhance student learning experiences and, in particular, foster an inquiry-based approach to this learning. The specific technologies used were relatively simple and in many ways represent the minimum engagement with the collaborative and interactive possibilities of Web 2.0. It is clear, however, that even at this level such technologies have considerable potential for encouraging active student engagement with the learning process, for tailoring teaching and supervision to the specific skills, needs, and interests of students, and for facilitating the acquisition of key technological and communicative skills. The process of blogging and social bookmarking promoted student inquiry and reflection, often at levels of some sophistication, and allowed this inquiry to be integrated into seminars and, to a lesser degree, lectures outside of a formal IBL setting. Web 2.0

technologies also allowed tutors to follow the processes of student learning, rather than simply the result, and to understand how students used the wider internet. Although the virtual learning environments used by some universities offer many facilities that mirror those provided by Web 2.0 services, at present the open-ended nature of such services as well as the non-institutional aspects of these technologies may allow them to promote student-centred, inquiry-driven learning more effectively than traditional VLEs. Likewise, the relative ease of set-up, low costs, and existing student familiarity allows such technologies to be integrated into existing courses with little difficulty and the customisable and modular nature of many of the services permits differing levels of tutor involvement in their creation and design.

REFERENCES

Abrandt Dahlgren, M., & Öberg, G. (2001). Questioning to learn and learning to question: Structure and function of problem-based learning scenarios in environmental science education. *Higher Education, 41*, 263–282. doi:10.1023/A:1004138810465

Armstrong, J., & Franklin, T. (2008). A review of current and developing international practice in the use of social networking (Web 2.0) in higher education. Retrieved December 29, 2008, from http://www.franklin-consulting.co.uk/Linked-Documents/the%20use%20of%20social%20networking%20in%20HE.pdf

Barrett, T. (2005). Understanding problem-based learning. In T. Barrett, I. Mac Labhrainn, & H. Fallon (Eds.), Handbook of enquiry and problem-based learning. Irish case studies and international perspectives (pp. 13-25). Dublin: All Ireland Society for Higher Education (AISHE).

Booth, A., & Nicholls, D. (2005). History teaching in Higher Education: Breaking down the barriers to progression and dialogue. Retrieved March 23, 2009, from http://www.history.ac.uk/education/conference/nichollsbooth.html

Brew, A. (2006). *Research and teaching: Beyond the divide*. Basingstoke: Palgrave Macmillan.

Brew, A. (2007). Research and teaching from the students' perspective. Retrieved March 23, 2009, from http://portal-live.solent.ac.uk/university/rtconference/2007/resources/angela_brew.pdf

Cotterill, S. J., White, A., & Currant, B. (2007). Using Web 2.0 to support PDP. *PDP-UK, 12,* 7–8.

Crabtree, H. (2003). Improving student learning using an enquiry based approach. Retrieved March 23, 2009, from http://www.ece.salford.ac.uk/proceedings/theme2.php?id=2

Dewey, J. (1938). *Logic: The theory of inquiry*. New York: Holt.

Elton, G. R. (1967). *The practice of history*. London: Fontana.

Eshet, Y. (2004). Digital literacy: A conceptual framework for survival skills in the digital era. *Journal of Educational Multimedia and Hypermedia, 13*(1), 93–106.

Franklin, T., & van Harmelen, M. (2007). Web 2.0 for content for learning and teaching in Higher Education. Retrieved March 30, 2009, from http://ie-repository.jisc.ac.uk/148/1/web2-content-learning-and-teaching.pdf

Garrison, D. R. (2007). Online community of inquiry review: Social, cognitive, and teaching presence issues. *Journal of Asynchronous Learning Networks, 11*(1), 61–72.

Hall, R. (2006). Battery farming or free ranging: Towards citizen participation in e-learning environments. *E-learning, 3*(4), 505–518. doi:10.2304/elea.2006.3.4.505

Hutchings, B. (2006). Principles of enquiry-based learning. Retrieved March 23, 2009, from http://www.campus.manchester.ac.uk/ceebl/resources/papers/ceeblgr002.pdf

Kahn, P., & O'Rourke, K. (2004). Guide to curriculum design: Enquiry-based learning. Retrieved March 27, 2009, from http://www.campus.manchester.ac.uk/ceebl/resources/guides/kahn_2004.pdf

Kahn, P., & O'Rourke, K. (2005). Understanding enquiry-based learning. In T. Barrett, I. Mac Labhrainn, & H. Fallon (Eds.), Handbook of enquiry and problem-based learning: Irish case studies and international perspectives (pp. 1-12). Dublin: All Ireland Society for Higher Education (AISHE).

Krause, K.-L. (2007). The Teaching-Research-Technology nexus: Implications for engaging the Net Generation. Retrieved March 30, 2009, from http://www.linkaffiliates.net.au/idea2007/files/IdeaConfKrauseFINAL.pdf

Lang, S. (2000). A-level history: Changes and methodology. *History Today, 50*(2), 16.

Laru, J., & Järvelä, S. (2008). Using Web 2.0 software and mobile devices for creating shared understanding among Virtual Learning Communities. Retrieved March 30, 2009, from http://ieeexplore.ieee.org/stamp/stamp.jsp?tp=&arnumber=4489827&isnumber=4489772

Levy, P., & Petrulis, R. (2007). Towards transformation? First year students, inquiry-based learning and the research/teaching nexus. Retrieved March 30, 2009, from http://www.srhe.ac.uk/conference2007

Lloyd, C. (1996). For realism and against the inadequacies of common sense: A response to Arthur Marwick. *Journal of Contemporary History, 31,* 192–207. doi:10.1177/002200949603100108

Memory, D. M., Yoder, C. Y., Bolinger, K. B., & Warren-Wilson, J. (2004). Creating thinking and inquiry tasks that reflect the concerns and interests of adolescents. *Social Studies*, *95*(4), 147–154. doi:10.3200/TSSS.95.4.147-154

Morley, N. (n.d.). Making Wikipedia work for you ... Making use of Wikipedia to promote learning, not just warning students against it. Retrieved March 23, 2009, from http://www.heacademy. ac.uk/hca/resources/detail/assessment_making_ wikipedia_work_for_you

O'Reilly, T. (2005). What is Web 2.0? Design patterns and business models for the next generation of software. Retrieved April 4, 2009, from http://www.oreillynet.com/pub/a/oreilly/tim/ news/2005/09/30/what-is-web-20.html

Patrick, M. (2008). Fostering effective and appropriate use of online resources: (Or: How do we stop students copying their essays from Wikipedia?). *Discourse (Berkeley, Calif.)*, *8*(1), 99–111.

Plowright, D., & Watkins, M. (2004). There are no problems to be solved, only inquiries to be made, in social work education. *Innovations in Education and Teaching International*, *41*(2), 185–206. doi:10.1080/1470329042000208701

Selwyn, N., Crook, C., Carr, D., Carmichael, P., Noss, R., & Laurillard, D. (2008). Education 2.0? Designing the web for teaching and learning: A Commentary by the Technology Enhanced Learning phase of the Teaching and Learning Research Programme. Retrieved December 29, 2008, from http://www.tlrp.org/tel/publications/ files/2008/11/tel_comm_final.pdf

Thelwall, M. (2008, January 15). MySpace, Facebook, Bebo: Social networking students. *ALT Newsletter*. Retrieved March 23, 2009, from http:// newsletter.alt.ac.uk/e_article000993849.cfm von Glaserfeld, E. (1989). Cognition, construction of knowledge, and teaching. *Synthese, 80*, 121-140.

van Joolingen, W. R., de Jong, T., & Dimitrako-poulou, A. (2007). Issues in computer-supported inquiry learning in science. *Journal of Computer Assisted Learning*, *23*, 111–119. doi:10.1111/ j.1365-2729.2006.00216.x

Walters, D., Burhans, D., Kershner, H., & Al-phonce, C. (2000). Early followers versus early adopters: The use of technology as a change lever leads to increased learning and decreased costs in a computer fluency course. Retrieved March 30, 2009, from http://connect.educause.edu/Library/ Abstract/EarlyFollowersversusEarly/37714

Warren, W. J. (2007). Closing the distance between authentic history pedagogy and everyday classroom practice. *The History Teacher*, *40*(2), 249–256. doi:10.2307/30036991

Zhang, X., & Wang, Z. (2008). The design and implement of knowledge building classroom based on Web 2.0. In *Proceedings of the 7th international conference on Advances in Web Based Learning* (LNCS 5145, pp. 405-412). Berlin: Springer.

ADDITIONAL READING

We have divided this section into four parts, each dealing with one of the main themes of our article.

1. INQUIRY-BASED LEARNING

Boyer Commission on Educating Undergraduates in the Research University. (1998). *Reinventing undergraduate education: A blueprint for America's research universities*. New York: Stony Brook. Retrieved April 7, 2009, from http://naples. cc.sunysb.edu/Pres/boyer.nsf

Brew, A. (2003). Teaching and research: New relationships and their implications for inquiry-based teaching and learning in Higher Education. *Higher Education Research & Development, 22*(1), 3–18. doi:10.1080/0729436032000056571

Hutchings, W. (2007). Enquiry-based learning: Definitions and rationale. Retrieved April 7, 2009, from http://www.campus.manchester.ac.uk/ceebl/resources/papers/hutchings2007_definingebl.pdf

Jenkins, A., & Healey, M. (2005). Institutional strategies to link teaching and research. Retrieved April 7, 2009, from http://www.heacademy.ac.uk/assets/York/documents/ourwork/research/Institutional_strategies.pdf

Justice, C., Rice, J., Warry, W., Inglis, S., Miller, S., & Sammon, S. (2007). Inquiry in Higher Education: Reflections and directions on course design and teaching methods. *Innovative Higher Education, 31*(4), 201–214. doi:10.1007/s10755-006-9021-9

Kinkead, J. (2003). Learning through inquiry: An overview of undergraduate research. *New Directions for Teaching and Learning, 93*(Spring), 5–18. doi:10.1002/tl.85

Kreber, C. (Ed.). (2006). *Exploring research-based teaching: New directions in teaching and learning.* San Francisco: Jossey Bass/Wiley.

Lee, V. S. (2004). *Teaching and learning through inquiry: A guidebook for institutions and instructors.* Sterling, VA: Stylus.

Rowland, S. (2006). *The enquiring university.* Maidenhead: McGraw-Hill/Open University Press.

Sharpe, R., & Savin-Baden, M. (2007). Learning to learn through Supported Enquiry: A literature review conducted for the L2L through supported enquiry FDTL5 project. Retrieved April 7, 2009, from http://www.som.surrey.ac.uk/learningtolearn/Resources.asp

2. WEB 2.0 IN TEACHING AND LEARNING

Alexander, B. (2006). Web 2.0: a New wave of innovation for teaching and learning? *EDUCAUSE Review, 41*(2), 32–44.

Blackwell, C., & Martin, T. R. (2009). Technology, collaboration, and undergraduate research. *Digital Humanities Quarterly. Changing the Center of Gravity: Transforming Classical Studies Through Cyberinfrastructure,* 3(1). Retrieved April 7, 2009, from http://www.digitalhumanities.org/dhq/vol/003/1/000024.html

Davis, B. G. (2009). *Tools for teaching.* San Francisco: Jossey Bass/Wiley.

Lew, A. A. (n.d.). *Web 2.0 teaching tools.* Blog at http://web20teach.blogspot.com

Solomon, G., & Schrum, L. (2007). *Web 2.0: New tools, new schools.* Washington, DC: International Society for Technology in Education.

Tapscott, D., & Williams, A. D. (2008). *Wikinomics: How mass collaboration changes everything.* New York: Portfolio.

3. INQUIRY PEDAGOGIES FOR HISTORY TEACHING

Hanlon, C. (2005). History on the cheap: Using the online archive to make historicists out of undergrads. *Pedagogy, 5*(1), 97–101.

Hicks, D., & Doolittle, P. E. (2008). Fostering analysis in historical inquiry through multimedia embedded scaffolding. *Theory and Research in Social Education, 36*(3), 206–232.

Sitch, B., Sutherland, E. L., Tatlock, J., & McTavish, K. (2007). Enquiry based learning in classics at Manchester. Retrieved April 7, 2009, from http://www.aishe.org/events/2006–2007/conf2007/proceedings/paper-03.doc

Slatta, R. W. (2004). Enhancing inquiry-guided learning with technology in history courses . In Lee, V. S. (Ed.), *Teaching and learning through inquiry. A Guidebook for institutions and instructors* (pp. 93–102). Sterling, Virginia: Stylus.

Slatta, R. W., & Atkinson, M. P. (2007). Using primary sources online: An inquiry-guided learning approach to teaching Western history. *Journal of the West, 46*(2), 14–21.

Stephens, R., & Thumma, J. (2005). Faculty–Undergraduate collaboration in digital history at a public research university. *History Teacher, 38*(4). Retrieved April 7, 2009, from http://www.historycooperative.org/journals/ht/38.4/stephens.html

4. TEACHING FIRST-YEAR UNDERGRADUATES

Greene, D., Odom, J., & Malinowski, A. (2004). Inquiry, critical thinking and first year programs . In Lee, V. S. (Ed.), *Teaching and learning through inquiry: A guidebook for institutions and instructors* (pp. 207–217). Sterling, VA: Stylus.

Oliver, R. (2007). Exploring an inquiry-based learning approach with first-year students in a large undergraduate class. *Innovations in Education and Teaching International, 44*(1), 3–15. doi:10.1080/14703290601090317

Oliver, R. (2008). Engaging first year students using a Web-supported inquiry-based learning setting. *Higher Education, 55*(3), 285–301. doi:10.1007/s10734-007-9055-7

Schnell, C. A., Louis, K. S., & Doetkott, C. (2003). The first-year seminar as a means of improving college graduation rates. *Journal of the First Year and Students in Transition, 15*(1), 53–76.

Starke, M. C., Harth, M., & Sirianni, F. (2001). Retention, bonding, and academic achievement: Success of a first-year seminar. *Journal of the First-Year Experience & Students in Transition, 13*(2), 7–35.

Section 3
Practitioner Insights

Chapter 13
Developing Educational Screencasts:
A Practitioner's Perspective

Damien Raftery
Institute of Technology, Carlow, Ireland

ABSTRACT

YouTube to iTunes, company to college websites, there is a seemingly exponential explosion in creating screencasts. A screencast is a digital recording of computer screen activity, often with an audio commentary. Short and engaging, screencasts have the potential to enable learning in new and exciting ways. They are becoming easier to create and, as a teacher in higher education, I have gradually increased my use of screencasts, learning with experience and from the generally positive feedback from students. Drawing on existing research and personal experience, this chapter will introduce screencasts and discuss their potential. The importance of integrating screencasts thoughtfully and carefully into the teaching and learning process will be examined, including pedagogical and instructional design issues. Next a four-step process for creating a screencast will be presented: prepare, capture, produce and publish. Prior to conclusions and final reflections, future research directions will be examined.

INTRODUCTION

The other day I wanted to embed a YouTube video into a PowerPoint presentation: to link and view directly a video on YouTube, rather than hyperlink out to an internet browser or embed the downloaded video file. I didn't know how to do this, so I searched YouTube and *hey presto*

a series of videos appeared. Selecting the first video, I watched a screencast showing how to do the task I wanted to do myself. I was able to watch it, pausing at places and switching to my presentation to embed the video I wanted. As well as the basic process, the screencast gave a number of tips. Less than ten minutes later I had completed my task.

A screencast is often used to capture *how-to-do-something*, for example how to use particular

DOI: 10.4018/978-1-61520-879-1.ch013

software. In the vignette above, I learnt and practiced a new skill: I had an immediate need, I found help in a form that was immediate, understandable and engaging, and I used that help to complete my task.

Increasingly educators are blending more online elements with traditional face-to-face teaching, often by simply using a virtual learning environment (VLE) to provide notes and other documentation as well as to communicate with students. As part of a multimedia approach (combinations of video, animations, images, text and sound) to blended learning, screencasts offer a multimedia-rich option to support student learning in particular contexts (such as learning a new skill as above). Thus a screencast can be a standalone multimedia learning object or can be part of a series that together comprise a fuller learning resource, or indeed be part of a learning object that integrates a screencast(s) with other hypermedia elements. Screencasts are becoming easier to create: a computer, some software and a microphone is enough. At the simplest, it could be adding a voiceover to a presentation, perhaps by using the narration feature within Microsoft PowerPoint. A little more complicated is recording on-screen activity with explanatory labels or a voiceover. With more effort, a screencast can integrate some interactivity, including clickable zones and quizzes. The time, resources and expertise required increases with the complexity of the screencast.

So what exactly is a screencast? How does one go about creating a screencast? What are the pedagogical and instructional design, technical and practical issues involved? And, of course, why do it? What are the benefits for learners? The rest of the chapter will explore these questions, starting with examining in more detail what a screencast is and sharing some personal experiences of using screencasts with students.

EDUCATIONAL SCREENCASTS

A screencast is a digital recording of computer screen activity, often containing audio narration. It is sometimes referred to as a video podcast or simply a video, and also as a *scrast* (verbally shortening the word screencast to one syllable).[1] A screencast gives a *look over my shoulder effect* similar to one-on-one instruction and can be accessed whenever and wherever it is convenient (Educause, 2006). Students particularly value this, flexibly using screencasts to support their learning and thereby allowing for greater learner independence. A screencast usually has control buttons, enabling it to be paused and particular sections to be replayed: this level of learner control over pace is important (Oud, 2009, p. 169). The combination of video and audio appeals to different learning styles (as an alternative to predominantly text-based learning materials) and, as it is produced locally, it may be more approachable than glitzy packaged instructional videos (Kanter, 2008).

Short, sharply focused screencasts can be very useful in supporting students, working at their own pace, to achieve learning outcomes. Screencasts are particularly useful for teaching software applications and showing how to use online tools such as websites and library catalogues, having the following benefits over reading step-by-step instructions, as identified by Mount and Chambers (2008): 'improving student cognition through improved information integration, reduced information redundancy and an improved representation of the dynamics of software operation' (p. 49). They can provide engaging revision materials and, like other learning materials, are particularly valued by students if focused on preparing for assessments. Screencasts can be used to give short presentations (mini-lectures of voiceovers over images or PowerPoint slides). These short teaching episodes are best used for topic overviews, difficult concepts and guidelines for the module, projects and assessments as well as for just-in-time support for project- or problem-based approaches.

Other potential uses include explaining model solutions, correcting and giving feedback, answering frequently asked questions (FAQs) and website testing. Using a tablet and wireless pen together with software for writing on the screen, *mathcasts* (screencasts where the solution to a maths problem is hand-written to an accompanying voiceover explanation (see Budgett, Cumming, & Miller, 2007; Bonnington, Oates, Parnell, Paterson, & Stratton, 2007; Fahlberg, Fahlberg-Stojanovska, & MacNeil, 2007) and other screencasts incorporating writing, drawings and highlighting can be created.

Personal Experiences

A number of years ago, as part of a quantitative techniques module, I introduced first-year students to spreadsheets and then looked at their applications to financial mathematics and statistics. In a computer lab, students first worked through some generic introductory exercises focused on basic skills and then progressed to applying these skills and learning new ones by tackling subject-specific exercises. I would often explain new spreadsheet features using a digital projector, requiring the entire class to stop and watch, irrespective of their progress. The disadvantage of these *helpful* interruptions was that the timing did not suit all the students and thus some would fail to get the full benefit of these explanations.

Changing to an alternative approach, I created a series of short screencasts (using the four-step process explained later in this chapter) that introduced the basic features of spreadsheets as needed by the introductory exercises (each exercise listed the relevant screencasts). Students were now free to work through the exercises, watching the relevant screencast(s) as required. This allowed a student to watch the screencast exactly when needed, as often as they wanted with full control to pause and replay particular sections. Thus students could spend more time on task, as well as freeing more time for me to assist individual

students. Together with a number of screencasts showing how to do a sample assessment, this series of screencasts formed a reference bank that students could draw upon as and when needed, including when revising.

Screencasts showing a suggested approach to completing the tasks of a sample assessment are, like everything explicitly linked to assessment, very popular with students. Useful also are screencasts of solutions to assessments, especially if released prior to results: they provide valuable feedback (and also can be used in future iterations of the module as further sample assessments). Moreover, a reference bank of screencasts introducing a topic, such as the 'introduction to spreadsheets' screencasts as described in the vignette above, can subsequently be used in more advanced courses as a quick revision for students to go through prior to classes; this has the benefit of encouraging students to engage prior to the first class as well as establishing a minimum starting level. Groups of screencasts can also be used as a first point of reference for former students who make contact asking for help on using software applications, which usually enables them to resolve their difficulties by themselves.

Initial feedback from students has been very positive (similar to Bush, 2008; Peterson, 2007; Winterbottom, 2007). Consistently for the past five years, in end-of-module evaluations for computer lab-based subjects, most students indicate that the available screencasts have been very useful and, that for future iterations of the module, more should be produced. Accessed through the college's virtual learning environment, the screencasts provide students with rich, multimedia online content to complement face-to-face classes. The VLE also provides a platform for the integration of screencasts into the module, so that they naturally support other activities and materials.

Recently, one week prior to a test, I uploaded to the VLE a series of four mathcasts (two to three minutes each) showing the handwritten development of the solution to a number of mathematics problems. The screencasts were presented with the questions, so that prior to viewing the screencast the student could read and indeed was encouraged to attempt the question. In the week prior to the test, over half the students in the class accessed the resource and nearly a quarter on two or three different days. A small number of students watched the screencasts over the weekend, with the heaviest use in the day before and the morning of the exam. The screencasts were viewed both during the day and into the late evening. Feedback from students a week after the exam (via a short anonymous in-class survey) showed a positive and enthusiastic attitude, indicating that almost all students would like to see more of this type of support and that using it helps to get a higher grade, with about three quarters of students thinking that this type of online solution is very useful for them personally. Students used the online solutions in a variety of ways, from just quickly watching them, through thinking carefully about the question before watching, to trying the question and then watching the solution (or fast-forwarding to the end to check their answer). Some students study together in groups, only resorting to the mathcasts if the group cannot solve the problem. A reservation that surfaced among a substantial minority, particularly from those who did not use the mathcasts, was the inability to print the solutions.

This vignette illustrates the potential of screencasts: students engaging with revision materials prior to an assessment. They did not all use the online solution, and those that did used the mathcasts in a variety of ways, a way that suited them. It raises the importance of being aware of individual differences and preferences for different ways of engaging with the materials. How screencasts are presented to students is important. Screencasts need to be integrated into the teaching and learning process, with attention to their design and use so as to avoid passivity and encourage engagement: students doing tasks, thinking and solving problems.

The profusion of screencasts on the internet, on YouTube and on specific websites such as www.teachertrainingvideos.com (a collection of screencasts for teachers to help them to incorporate technology into their teaching) and www.demogirl.com (a blog with short screencasts explaining new internet applications and services), links to a dilemma that faces a teacher considering using screencasts: should you just link to useful screencasts you find on the internet, or create your own? Creating screencasts involves time, pedagogy and technology, with an important trade-off between final screencast quality and sophistication, and the time taken to develop it. Getting the balance right can be difficult, but may be answered by keeping the benefits to students clearly in mind: sometimes it's better to link to a screencast produced elsewhere, other times preferable to create your own. Prior to presenting a four-step process for creating a screencast, the next section will consider some pedagogical and instructional design issues.

Integrating Screencasts into the Teaching and Learning Process

All teaching starts with a learner's need. Screencasts are created by teachers to assist the learning process of students, to help students achieve learning outcomes. As the goal is to support student learning, it should always first be asked whether a screencast approach is the most appropriate and effective way to accomplish this. Only after reflecting on this should screencasts be created. Thus screencasts should be *pedagogically led* rather than *technology led*: in short, when creating a screencast, think about the learner. It is advisable, like with other teaching innovations, to start small and build on initial successes, learning what works best for your students.

Create bite-sized screencasts: it is better for students to choose from a series of short, clearly focused screencasts than to have to navigate a smaller number of longer ones: two to four minutes, definitely less than ten minutes (see Cann, 2007). Shorter screencasts are more flexible for reusing with other learners and can be updated more easily. Each screencast should have a specific, clear purpose (ideally focused on one learning outcome), such as

- introducing a module
- providing guidelines or giving an overview
- reviewing a difficult concept
- previewing a forthcoming lecture, reviewing or summarising a previous lecture
- illustrating the steps to solve a problem
- explaining a technical diagram or picture
- demonstrating a software or website feature (particularly useful for software that students have limited access to)
- supporting an activity or project
- revising for a test
- answering frequently asked questions
- correcting or giving feedback

Combined together, a series of screencasts can form a reference bank (as discussed earlier) that can be used as a comprehensive resource for independent study and revision, a support for project work and a starting point for more advanced modules. Note that for students viewing on campus, particularly in computer labs, consideration of whether to use audio is required: Will all students have headsets or should an alternative no-audio screencast with captions also be produced? Veronikas and Maushak (2005) concluded, from a small research study, that students learning software applications prefer audio and text, rather than text only despite no statistically significant evidence that audio improves test scores (p. 204).

Careful preparation is crucial to the creation of high quality educational screencasts of high value to students. When creating a screencast, balance the time and effort involved against the potential benefits for learners. Also consider whether the screencast is to be of limited use, by

a small number of students for a short period of time? Or should you expend more time and effort to create a screencast of higher quality that can be productively used by a variety of learners over a longer time-span across different modules and contexts? This extra effort may be rewarded if screencasts can be shared, either internally within a college or externally via YouTube or a national repository of learning objects.

A potential and real criticism of screencasts is that they can have a teacher focus rather than student focus and can lack interactivity (Educause, 2006), and thus may encourage passivity in learners, an attitude of *just sit back and watch*. To counteract this, think carefully how students can be encouraged to be active when using screencasts (a criticism and response that was also considered by Franciszkowicz (2008) when using screencasts to teach problem-solving skills and conceptual understanding in a general chemistry module). If possible, add some interactions. These could be some quiz elements, such as answering multiple-choice questions or dragging and dropping. It could be the addition of clickable zones, for example where a student must click on the correct button to get a software demonstration to continue. At the most basic, it could simply be a requirement to click a button to continue, paired with an instruction or exhortation to think or do something before continuing. For example, if illustrating how to solve a question, such as an accounting or engineering problem, the screencast could display the question and then pause, instructing the student to read it carefully and consider how to proceed. The student could then click to view how to approach the question, with an audio explanation linked to underlining or highlighting on screen the key terms and numbers. Then the student might be requested to attempt the question, only viewing when having completed their solution as best they can. As the learner can forward and rewind, they can focus on specific areas of difficulty, watching these sections a number of times. The solution could be partitioned into stages, with pauses at each transition.

There is an element of 'watch what I do' in a screencast: this can be useful, enabling the student to watch an expert at work, thereby offering a scaffold for undertaking the activity herself/himself. Some interactivity giving feedback may be incorporated into the screencast itself, as discussed above. This increases the complexity of the screencast, requiring greater time and expertise to create it; indeed many screen capture softwares may not support this, or it may be easier to create a simple screencast and build the other elements separately. This latter approach is where screencasts may bring audio-visually rich media to an online learning activity, a form of reusable learning object (RLO). Alternatively, it may be better to create simple screencasts and then carefully consider how these can support learning in conjunction with activities designed for students to undertake.

Oud (2009) presents a useful summary of the implications stemming from the limited capacity of short-term or working memory and how this limits learners' capacities for information processing. When too much information is presented, learners' 'working memory is overloaded and they cannot process anything well, which leads to poor understanding, retention and learning' (p. 166). Thus when creating a screencast, it is important to minimise the cognitive load. This leads to practical recommendations (see below in the Capture section). Of particular importance is chunking, the splitting of longer or more complex content into small sections (p. 167).

Instructional design approaches are valuable for informing the screencast development process. An instructional design approach to the development of educational multimedia, specifically screencasts, is based upon the application of appropriate research, such as the psychology research on cognitive load theory summarised above. Instructional design is the use of systematic design procedures, thereby making, according to

Gustafson and Branch (2002), 'instruction more effective, efficient and relevant than less rigorous approaches to planning instruction' (p. 18). Fundamental to all systematic design approaches are the following elements: analysis, design, development, implementation and evaluation (often referred to by their acronym ADDIE). (Readers interested in instructional design are directed to the References and Additional Reading sections.) In the next section, the four-step model proposed for creating a screencast broadly corresponds to the middle three elements of the ADDIE model.

Creating a Screencast

The motivation for creating a screencast is to support learning. The process builds naturally on existing teaching expertise, often using low threshold applications (i.e. technology with a relatively short learning curve, Gilbert 2002). As shown in Figure 1 the process to create a screencast can be envisioned in four steps:

The process starts with preparation, careful consideration of a teaching activity and learning opportunity. With a computer, screen capture software and a microphone, educational screencasts can quickly be created that are of immediate use and value. Voiceovers can be captured when recording the screencast or added later during the production process. The production process can be elaborate, including the addition of captions and other visual cues, additional voiceovers and interactive elements such as quiz questions. Alternatively, given usual time pressures, this pre-deployment step can be minimised to simply publishing the screencast in the required technical format (Costello, 2008). Then the screencast can be deployed via a virtual learning environment, a blog, an intranet or the Internet. Although Figure 1 presents the four steps as a linear process, the boundaries are fuzzy and, similar to the ADDIE model, there may be jumps back and forth and reiterations.

Figure 1. Four-step Screen Capture Process (with a summary of each step)

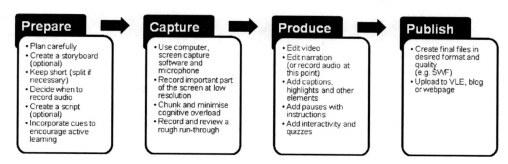

For capturing a screencast, there are both hardware and software requirements. The computer needs to be sufficiently powerful to run the capture software plus any target applications that you are recording. The same general issues apply to sound quality as when producing a podcast and an inexpensive microphone headset usually suffices. For capturing handwriting on the screen, such as for mathcasts, a tablet laptop is likely to result in much clearer handwriting than an external USB tablet and it is easier to use for annotations as you are writing on the actual screen. Software that is useful here includes Microsoft OneNote, PDF Annotator and Microsoft PowerPoint, as well as drawing tools such as Microsoft Paint.

There are many capture software options available, from sophisticated packages with powerful capture and editing features such as Adobe Captivate and Camtasia to simple, free options that simply publish what you capture without any editing such as Jing and Screenr.com.[2] These four software options all include screencasts showing how to use the particular software to create screencasts (see links in Additional Reading). Your choice of software should be dictated by the extent to which you wish to edit your screencasts, as well as the importance of particular features, such as being able to add quiz elements, modify menu options, accessibility features and publishing format options.

In the following four sections, each of the four steps will be discussed in terms of instructions and tips for creating educational screencasts.

Prepare

Plan your recording carefully. Know what you want to show, to do and what you want to say. Be aware of what your students already know. It may be useful to create a storyboard, a 'visual representation which illustrates the content, navigation and structure of the learning materials' (Clarke, 2001, p. 173). Use the storyboard to help the chunking of complex sections into simpler pieces. For short, simple screencasts, the storyboard can be an overview of the major elements. For longer screencasts, the storyboard may be more elaborate, detailing each major element or screen display. If the storyboard indicates a long screencast, consider whether it is possible to break it into a series of two or more shorter screencasts. Remember at this stage to think carefully how students are likely to use the screencast and what cues you can incorporate to encourage them to be active when using the screencast.

Decide when to record the audio. For short simple screencasts you may decide to record narration as you capture the screen activity. For longer screencasts, it may be easier to record the audio separately after capturing the screen activity. For example, if demonstrating how to use a website, it may be better to first edit out any time waiting for pages to load and any glitches before adding the voiceover. Also recording the audio afterwards allows you when screen capturing to focus on doing clear screen actions. Consider using a script: the trade-off is between spontaneity and naturalness versus a professional, confident narration mostly free of ums and ahs. An added benefit of a script is that it can be used as a transcript or for closed captions.

To summarise, a teacher creates screencasts to help learning happen. Creating good screencasts depends on 'planning a session with an eye toward its being recorded and on thoughtful editing afterwards' (Educause, 2006). Careful planning and thoughtful reflection can assist in translating teaching activities into useful screencasts: indeed this preparation is key to the *capture* stage in the creation of educational screencasts.

Capture

After your planning, you should know exactly what you are going to record. If recording audio, use a quiet room with telephones turned off. Ensure that any other applications will not interfere with the recording, for example an email application beeping or otherwise alerting that a new email has arrived. Indeed you should close any unneeded applications. A tip when recording is to record only the application window or a defined area, and to consider recording at low screen resolution (such as 800x600). It is important to be aware of any quirks of your screen capture software that may result in glitches in your recording. For software demonstrations, make clear mouse movements at a pace that is suitable for learners to follow.

Be conscious of instructional design principles. In particular use strategies to minimise cognitive load such as the following guidelines suggested by Oud (2009, pp. 176–177): start with an outline and end with a summary; split content into small segments/chunks; sequence content logically; use words (text or audio, not both) with graphics; pro-

vide clear interface, navigation and instructions; remove unnecessary graphics, text and audio; and, focus attention on important areas with visual or verbal cues.

A pragmatic approach is to record a rough run-through, review it and then record the main version. For a short screencast, if you make a mistake you could just restart recording rather than having to edit. For longer screencasts, errors can be edited out during the *produce* stage.

Produce

The *produce* stage may be extensive, short or omitted entirely (especially in the case of screencasts that are not to be used extensively). Start with editing the video, removing glitches and unneeded elements such as video showing the loading of webpages. Edit the audio, removing ums and ahs (or record the narration at this point). Make the modifications decided upon in the *prepare* stage: add captions as appropriate (or edit captions that have been automatically created by your screen capture software), whilst remembering not to overburden the viewer with too many simultaneous elements; use text animation, highlighting and zoom effects to focus attention and reinforce important points; and, add interactivity such as clickable zones and buttons, quiz elements or simply pauses with exhortations to think.

If your screen software capture allows, modify the default menu (player) options to your desired configuration, ensuring to allow learners substantial control. Now the screencast should be ready to *publish*.

Publish

The *publish* stage of the screencast creation process involves creating the final screencast file(s) in a technical format suitable for use by learners. Depending on the software used to capture and process the screencast, there may be a variety of options, such as Macromedia Flash (swf), Windows Media Video (wmv), Audio Video Interleave (AVI) or executable (exe). Screencasts can be delivered on a variety of platforms, primarily streamed via the internet for watching via a browser with suitable media player, but also downloadable for later viewing on a computer or portable device capable of playing video (although note that the small display size of some portable devices may be insufficient to display certain screencasts in sufficient detail). For example, Adobe Captivate creates Flash files to be viewed via a browser, also creating the HTML code for launching the screencast.[3] It can also create Windows executable files (not requiring any other software) and AVI (which can be further processed for uploading to YouTube).

It is straightforward to upload these files to a VLE, a blog, an intranet or the Internet. Decide whether to only allow the screencasts to be viewed online, or to permit downloading for offline viewing. Some issues may arise regarding file size and server space if uploading a large number of screencasts (particularly within a VLE where each file must be uploaded separately to different courses). A solution is to host separately and to post links to the VLE. For students viewing screencasts from home, large file sizes necessitate having broadband. A separate issue is how students should be notified of new screencasts. Within a VLE, they may be uploaded to the relevant section, possibly accompanied by an announcement or email notification.

FUTURE RESEARCH DIRECTIONS

Screencasts are very popular with students and many teachers in higher education are exploring their use. Although most practitioner-reported experience views screencasts positively, there may be questions as to the effectiveness of screencasts in improving learning for students; for example Lee, Pradhan, and Dalgarno, (2008) report on a research project in which screencasts were used to support the teaching of programming, finding 'no significant effect of the provision of screencasts during learning' (p. 75). The level of complexity of the task or subject matter for the screencast is important, with Bhowmick, Khasawnehb, Bowling, Gramopadhyea, and Melloya (2007) finding that for complex procedural tasks 'a combination of audio, video and synchronized text yields the best results both in terms of learning performance and process efficiency' (p. 615). Given the development of national repositories for reusable learning objects (RLOs) such as the National Digital Learning Repository Project (NDLR) in Ireland, Jorum in the United Kingdom and MERLOT in the USA, it is appropriate to consider the development of quality screencasts that are reusable by students on a variety of programmes, in different ways and contexts.

A potential criticism of the four-step screen capture process presented above is that, unlike the ADDIE model, it does not explicitly include an evaluation stage. There is a need for the evaluation of the use and effectiveness of screencasts in a variety of intents and contexts. These evaluations and related research should inform the development of evidence-based recommendations for good practice in the creation and use of educational screencasts.

It is incumbent on teachers who develop screencasts to become proficient with the technology. However those who create screencasts also need to become familiar and draw upon research in areas such as instructional design, pedagogy, educational psychology and accessibility. This should be viewed within the context of major change in higher education underpinned by technology and the attending change in the role of the academic (see Davidson-Shivers, 2002).

CONCLUSION AND REFLECTIONS

Simple, short screencasts are quick and easy to produce, popular with students and can help learning happen. The combination of text, audio and video is engaging. Screencasts can be used for many purposes, for instance to introduce a module, give an overview or review a difficult concept, illustrate how to solve a problem, explain a technical diagram or picture, show how to use software or a website, and give feedback. Students can flexibly use short, sharply focused screencasts how, when and where they want.

To create a screencast, you need a computer, some software and a microphone. There are many software choices, with more powerful options having a steeper learning curve. Time is often the major issue, whether to capture a simple screencast and publish with little editing or to expend greater effort in creating a screencast together with interactive elements that is of use by a greater number of students in a wider context.

When introducing screencasts into a module, there are some personal considerations. Screencasts, like full digital recordings of lectures, are a more public form of teaching. This combined with the possibility of the digital recording of mistakes (Do *you* want to appear on YouTube? See Young, 2009) may enable possible misuse by students and criticism of presentation style by colleagues (see Budgett et al., 2007). This openness is broadly positive, but requires a certain level of confidence. Another issue may arise: if recording mini-lectures, software demonstrations and explanations for model solutions of questions, will students stop coming to class? No, I would tentatively suggest; it is likely that screencast use and class attendance are positively correlated, consistent with the findings of Grabe and Christopherson (2007) who found that the use of online lecture resources, lecture attendance and examination performance were positively related. Screencasts do need to be thoughtfully integrated and their introduction may provide an opportunity to rethink the use of classroom time, to create space for implementing more active learning strategies.

Screencasts indeed have the *potential* to enable learning in new and exciting ways. Screencasts can be used to support greater learner independence and may allow for a change in how lectures, tutorials and lab sessions are used, with less time spent presenting and more time spent on students doing things. It is important to reflect on the strengths and weaknesses of screencasts to be able to harness their potential, as well as to draw upon pedagogical and instructional design principles in their development. In particular, it is essential to carefully integrate screencasts into the teaching and learning process to support students' active engagement with their learning.

REFERENCES

Bhowmicka, A., Khasawnehb, M. T., Bowling, S. R., Gramopadhyea, A. K., & Melloya, B. J. (2007). Evaluation of alternate multimedia for web-based asynchronous learning. *International Journal of Industrial Ergonomics*, *37*, 615–629. doi:10.1016/j.ergon.2007.04.004

Bonnington, C. P., Oates, G., Parnell, S., Paterson, J., & Stratton, W. (2007). A report on the use of tablet technology and screen recording software in tertiary mathematics courses. In A. D'Arcy-Warmington, V. Martinez Luaces, G. Oates, & C. Varsavsky (Eds.), *Vision and change for a new century, Proceedings of Calafate Delta'07: 6th Southern Hemisphere Conference on Mathematics and Statistics Teaching and Learning* (pp. 19-32). Retrieved April 1, 2009, from http://www.bonnington.org/publications/TabletLectureRecording.pdf

Budgett, S., Cumming, J., & Miller, C. (2007). *The role of Screencasting in statistics courses*. Paper presented at the International Statistical Institute conference, Lisbon.

Bush, M. (2008). Screencasting as a vehicle for learning & teaching. *Project application,* London: South Bank University. Retrieved April 1, 2009, from http://www.lsbu.ac.uk/lteu/documents/ltip0809/LTiPInd0809MBush.pdf

Cann, A. J. (2007). Podcasting is dead. Long live video! *Bioscience Education ejournal,* 10. Retrieved April 1, 2009, from http://www.bioscience.heacademy.ac.uk/journal/vol10/beej-10-C1.pdf

Clarke, A. (2001). *Designing computer-based learning materials.* Aldershot: Gower.

Costello, E. (2008). *Developing educational resources using Camtasia Studio.* National Digital Learning Repository Project (NDLR) workshop presentation. Retrieved March 20, 2008, from http://www.ndlr.ie/mshe

Davidson-Shivers, G. V. (2002). Instructional technology in higher education . In Reiser, R. A., & Dempsey, J. V. (Eds.), *Trends and issues in instructional design and technology* (pp. 256–268). New Jersey: Merrill Prentice Hall.

Educause (2006). 7 things you should know about ... Screencasting. *EDUCAUSE Learning Initiative Brief.* Retrieved April 1, 2009, from http://net.educause.edu/ir/library/pdf/ELI7003.pdf

Educause (2007). 7 things you should know about ... RSS. *EDUCAUSE Learning Initiative Brief.* Retrieved April 1, 2009, from http://net.educause.edu/ir/library/pdf/ELI7024.pdf

Fahlberg, T., Fahlberg-Stojanovska, L., & MacNeil, G. (2007). Whiteboard math movies. *Teaching Mathematics and Its Applications, 26*(1), 17–22. doi:10.1093/teamat/hrl012

Franciszkowicz, M. (2008). Video-based additional instruction. *Journal of the Research Center for Educational Technology, 4*(2), 5-14. Retrieved April 1, 2009, from http://www.rcetj.org/?type=art&id=90059& Gilbert, S. (2002). Low threshold applications. *Webpage.* Retrieved July 5, 2002, from http://www.tltgroup.org/resources/rltas.html

Grabe, M., & Christopherson, K. (2007). Optional student use of online lecture resources: Resource preferences, performance and lecture attendance. *Journal of Computer Assisted Learning, 24*(1), 1–10.

Gustafson, K. L., & Branch, R. M. (2002). What is instructional design? In Reiser, R. A., & Dempsey, J. V. (Eds.), *Trends and issues in instructional design and technology* (pp. 16–25). New Jersey: Merrill Prentice Hall.

Kanter, B. (2008). Screencasting primer. *Webpage.* Retrieved April 1, 2009, from http://screencastingprimer.wikispaces.com/primer

Lee, M. J. W., Pradhan, S., & Dalgarno, B. (2008). The effectiveness of screencasts and cognitive tools as scaffolding for novice object-oriented programmers. *Journal of Information Technology Education, 7,* 61–80.

Mount, N., & Chambers, C. (2008). Podcasting and practicals. In G. Salmon, & P. Edirisingha (Eds.), Podcasting for learning in universities (pp. 43-56). Berkshire: Open University Press.

Oud, J. (2009). Guidelines for effective online instruction using multimedia screencasts. *Reference Services Review, 37*(2), 164-177. Retrieved June 19, 2009, from http://www.ingentaconnect.com/content/mcb/240/2009/00000037/00000002/art00004

Peterson, E. (2007). Incorporating screencasts in online teaching. *The International Review of Research in Open and Distance Learning, 8*(3). Retrieved April 1, 2009, from http://www.irrodl.org/index.php/irrodl/article/viewArticle/495/935

Veronikas, S. W., & Maushak, N. (2005). Effectiveness of audio on screen captures in software application instruction. [from http://www.proquest.com.eresources.shef.ac.uk]. *Journal of Educational Multimedia and Hypermedia, 14*(2), 199–205. Retrieved July 20, 2009.

Winterbottom, S. (2007). Virtual lecturing: Delivering lectures using screencasting and podcasting technology. *Planet, 8.* Retrieved April 1, 2009, from http://www.gees.ac.uk/planet/p18/sw.pdf

Young, J. R. (2009). Caught (unfortunately) on tape. *The Chronicle of Higher Education, 55*(28), A17. Retrieved April 1, 2009, from http://chronicle.com/free/v55/i28/28a01701.htm

ADDITIONAL READING

a website of a professional screencast creation company, including examples, a blog and a short screencast overview of the company approach to creating screencasts (http://scraster.com/82/scraster-professional-screencasting-a-3-minute-introduction-2)http://scraster.com

http://screenr.com: a website that allows you to create screencasts directly from your browser with no software to install. For free, you can create your screencast, preview it (no editing) and then upload for hosting on screenr.com, download as MP4 or upload to YouTube. It integrates with

http://www.screencast.com: a website that allows you to upload and share screencasts, presentations, documents and images. Integrates with Jing and Camtasia.

Branch, R. M. (2009). Instructional design: The ADDIE approach. London: Springer. A general instructional design primer focused on fundamental ADDIE principles.

Oud, J. (2009). Guidelines for effective online instruction using multimedia screencasts. *Reference Services Review, 37*(2). Written from an academic library instruction perspective, this journal article presents a summary of research in cognitive psychology, education and librarianship from which useful guidelines for designing educational screencasts are derived.

http://www.teachertrainingvideos.com: Russell Stannard's website is a collection of screencasts to help teachers incorporate technology into their teaching. It demonstrates the usefulness of screencasts, and has a series of screencasts on using Camtasia.

Salmon, G., & Edirisingha, P. (Eds.). (2008). Podcasting for Learning in Universities. Berkshire: Open University Press. Comprehensive book on podcasting, including a useful chapter by Mount and Chambers on their research on screencasting for software practicals.

http://www.mathcasts.org: Tim Fahlberg's website is a useful starting point for those interested in creating mathcasts (or simply recording writing and drawing on a screen). He also showcases *pencasts*, created using the Pulse SmartPen which digitally records writing and your voice as you write on paper.

Twitter. http://demogirl.com: a blog with short screencasts explaining new internet applications and services, useful to see some good screencasts and Molly McDonald explains how she makes a screencast (http://demogirl.com/2008/01/14/want-to-see-how-i-make-a-screencast)

http://www.adobe.com: website for Adobe Captivate, where you can download a fully functioning trial, get help and tips from the Developer Center, watch example screencasts and visit the blog.

http://www.techsmith.com: website for Camtasia, where you can download a fully functioning trial, go on a product tour, watch tutorials and visit a section on using Camtasia in education.

http://www.jingproject.com: website for Jing, where you can download Jing or upgrade to Jing Pro, read about Jing's features, watch screencasts demonstrating how to use Jing and visit the Help Center.

http://www.lynda.com: website of provider of educational materials on using technology. Many of their courses comprise of a series of screencasts and the site provides an opportunity to review some high quality screencasts.

http://www.rlo-cetl.ac.uk: website of the Centre for Excellence in the design, development and use of learning objects. They define an RLO as 'a web-based interactive chunk of e-learning designed to explain a stand-alone learning objective'. RLOs can contain screencasts and this website has many good examples.

ENDNOTES

[1] Note Educause's (2006) definition of a screencast as 'a screen capture of the actions on a user's computer screen, typically with accompanying audio, distributed through RSS' (p.1); thus a student will have subscribed to the teacher's RSS feed which will automatically highlight any new screencasts that have been added since the student last logged in (Educause, 2007).

[2] I have used a variety of software, starting with Viewletbuilder (www.qarbon.com), then switching to Adobe Captivate (www.adobe.com) and most recently testing Jing (www.jingproject.com). Another very popular screen capture software, particularly in higher education, is Camtasia (www.techsmith.com). Note that there are many software options to choose from. The choice of software is a balance between sophistication of features, ease of use and financial cost. If you want to create a professional screencast, usable over time by many students and reusable by others, using a professional tool such as Captivate or Camtasia is advisable. Captivate, which I am more familiar with, has many features enabling full editing of your screencast (editing of recording and sound, adding captions, clickable zones and buttons, highlighting and much more) as well as the development of e-learning objects with quizzes and branching scenarios. It is part of a suite of e-learning tools. Captivate incorporates a good text-to-speech converter and supports accessibility features like closed captioning. Like Camtasia, it has a presentation feature seamlessly enabling the narration of a PowerPoint presentation. The power of Captivate does come with a learning curve, especially for those less technically literate. Both Captivate and Camtasia have fully functioning trial versions that can be used for 30 days, with integrated screencasts demonstrating how to use the main features. A simpler option that can be used to quickly produce screencasts, especially throwaway (one-use) or limited-use ones, is Jing. Jing makes the capture very straightforward. The free version allows screen captures of up to five minutes to be recorded, with audio if desired. Jing, in conjunction with Screencast.com (www.screencast.com), makes it easy to upload your screencast to the internet, in the process generating a unique URL to link to and the HTML code to embed it within your VLE, blog or other webpages (similar to the options for linking to a YouTube video). Disadvantages however include, as well as the five minute limit, not being able to add captions, indeed not to edit the screencast at all nor to add audio after screen capture, as well as the commercial branding of Jing at the end of screencasts produced. These can be partly overcome by moving to the professional version (which allows removal of commercial branding as well as an easy upload to YouTube) or by bringing the SWF file generated by Jing into Camtasia for editing. At this early stage of my experience of working with Jing, it seems a promising option for colleagues who wish to produce the occasional screencast for use by their

own students and I can see myself increasingly using it for limited-use screencasts (or alternatively Screenr.com, a new web-based option offering similar features). However the editing power of Captivate means it likely that I will continue to use it or similarly powerful screen-capture software for producing screencasts that will be used more widely.

3   It is sometimes useful to create a simple webpage with links to a series of screencasts that students can open as full screen in a separate browser window. These files can be put into one zipped file and uploaded as a package file (for example, when uploading content in Blackboard choose 'Unpackage this file' to allow the online display of the zipped material, pointing to the index page from which the screencasts will be launched).

Chapter 14
Applying E-Learning Technologies to Library Information Literacy Instruction

Jamie Ward
Dundalk Institute of Technology, Ireland

ABSTRACT

Academic libraries have adopted and adapted the e-learning technologies for delivery of their Information Literacy programmes. This chapter describes some of the ways in which academic librarians have been very inventive in using emerging technologies to enhance their instructional content. By using a case study of DkIT the chapter details how information literacy and the e-learning technologies emerged together. E-learning platforms like the virtual learning environments (VLE) are the natural place for libraries to use as portals for their IL instruction. This chapter argues that using the VLE (with the inherent instructional interaction made possible by this technology), and adopting some amalgam of the newer teaching styles like problem-based learning and blended learning techniques completes the IL circle for librarians. Librarians now have the tools at their disposal to finally fulfil the promises we undertook when we embarked on our information literacy programmes.

INTRODUCTION

We live in interesting times for librarians. The amount of information and means of access to this information has dramatically increased in volume and complexity. Methods of accessing this information and how people engage with the different information media are also in constant flux. This preponderance of networked information that has become available to library users has necessitated the expansion of librarians' instructional role to help equip our users in the skills required to access information effectively. The librarian's remit has been broadened and this has compelled us to explore the possibilities of e-learning technologies to assist us in this extended remit. The demand for library instruction has also required librarians to really engage with the science of teaching and how we employ different methods of instruction. We as a profession now accept that the increas-

DOI: 10.4018/978-1-61520-879-1.ch014

ing volume of information is only of value to an academic community when it is employed in a meaningful way within the process of learning.

This chapter is an attempt to examine the convergence of the factors that led to the new outlook for information provision and will look at the possibilities for library instruction using the new e-learning technologies. I will be detailing our own case study in Dundalk Institute of Technology in an attempt to draw all the elements together and endeavour to show that no single element can be taken in isolation from the other. By detailing our own evolutionary experience with information literacy and e-learning, I hope to demonstrate that an academic library has the instructional imperative and the skills to design the necessary e-learning instruments for user support and training. I will also show that whilst librarians working within the academic environment have tried to address and fulfil our duty to our community, we have found that a new collaborative model of engagement with academics will be the best template for designing future library instruction.

The case history is also an attempt to show how different technologies were employed for all our digitally facilitated instruction and engagement with library users and how this culminated in a 'blended learning' approach to helping students become information literate. Blended learning is using a variety of learning methods, teaching resources and techniques and applying them in an interactive way for students. The case history is also an attempt to highlight that libraries' sometimes uneven implementation of information literacy and their idiosyncratic adoption of different technologies, as vehicles for library instruction, have created a new fresh dynamic for academic libraries. This dynamic has had the effect of placing libraries as central, once again, within the learning processes for students in academic institutions. Finally, I will be examining some ideas on what more libraries can do to support the community we serve. The future trends section is based on our own experiences to date and is informed by an

examination of some of the developments that may emerge from the current trends within teaching practice and how these can help shape librarians' use of available e-learning technologies. Utilising networked information to enhance knowledge is a complex human as well as technical process that requires some background explanation of what librarians are dealing with.

BACKGROUND

The term 'Information Literacy' (IL) is widely used by the library profession to describe what we believe is an essential attainment for students and staff to be effective scholars. For librarians the main aims of IL is to participate in developing students who can 'recognise what information is needed and have the ability to locate, evaluate and use effectively the information needed' (American Library Association, 1989). One of the main avenues being used to achieve the standards set by IL is e-learning. E-learning is defined as 'learning facilitated and supported through the use of information technologies' (Melling, 2006, p. XII). To date libraries have been exemplars in adopting and adapting the e-learning technologies available in the furtherance of the goals of information literacy.

Yet there hasn't been, nor can there be, a consistent approach within the academic libraries of Ireland to the delivery of IL modules and therefore no correspondingly consistent approach to using the technologies available in the delivery of their IL training. Even with librarians having approximately the same definition of IL, a common set of standards on how to work towards IL and the same set of available e-learning resources, each library has come up with a different set of learning support mechanisms for its particular institute. So why do people trained in the librarian profession produce such a wide range of different instructional products and material? This may be a result of all academic libraries being unique and existing to serve the particular individual needs of their local scholarly community. Different institutions have different subject-based priorities, and subject or liaison librarians whose skills are largely acquired through experience have been the main drivers in IL and take their different, subject-specific, experiences to IL development. The use of different e-learning resources may also be a result of the different ICT skills amongst library staff. Any library will have a wide variety of skills within its staff members and ICT skills are only one of the many skills sets needed for a library to function. Another factor is that the age range of library staff is such that some staff have witnessed many developments and false dawns in learning technologies;

The development of learning technologies over the past 20 years can be roughly divided into three overlapping phases: the multimedia phase, the internet phase and the virtual learning environment (VLE) phase, which includes the development of managed learning environments (MLEs). (Liber cited in Melling, 2006, p. 31)

Some librarians have experienced the emergence of all of these learning technologies and the grand claims that attended their inception. Experience has made us innately cautious in approaching certain of the newer technologies. Some of our more experienced and valued librarians are also not necessarily content to embrace a new social networking 'folksonomy' or accept the Google page ranking algorithm as the best method of searching for information on the web: and rightly so.

A lot of the development of IL within libraries and the technological mechanisms used to deliver IL instruction could have been characterised as champion-based: in the sense that a few converts within any given institution drove IL and were at the forefront of investigating and adopting the suitable technologies for its delivery. Across the academic libraries now, one gets the distinct

impression that each is keeping a watching brief on other libraries, both here and abroad, and approximating other IL curricula into their own library IL programmes, and that something similar is occurring with the technologies being adopted. The danger in this localism approach is that some smaller libraries with fewer staff will get left behind. Although the new generation e-learning technologies, with their ease of use and development, provide great opportunities for libraries to promote their IL strategies, they also pose a challenge for resource stretched librarians who have to master these technologies before they can utilise them as platforms for IL delivery. There is also a fear that without any firm pedagogical reason for using certain technologies, some of the larger libraries may end up using the latest web offering because it is viewed as an advance.

It may be surprising to some that libraries in the academic sector in Ireland have no common strategy on information literacy and therefore no collective strategy on the best practice on using future technologies in the delivery of IL modules. This shouldn't be surprising though when we consider that the IL project is such a large topic for such a diverse profession that a singular, collective approach would seem to be almost impossible to achieve. What is beginning to emerge is that some libraries and partnership of libraries have sought funding to produce IL modules and online courses that would have some common IL approach for at least some aspect of the subjects covered by the institutions. Another method of advancing a common approach is to look at the IL digital content as reusable learning objects and allow libraries to share their e-learning content with each other. Recently the Higher Education Authority in Ireland funded the National Digital Learning Repository (NDLR) to provide a repository of reusable learning objects, and IL (or Information Skills) has now its own community of practice within the NDLR. The IL reusable learning objects do not constitute a full prescriptive curriculum, however, and can be viewed as a list of the ingredients towards making an IL curriculum. The search for a common generic IL curriculum and method of delivery has largely remained elusive and this goal could become the white whale to the Ahabs of librarianship.

The difference of application of e-learning technologies isn't just a phenomenon within libraries, as most third-level institutions and indeed most departments within these institutions operate almost autonomously from other institutes and departments. What is produced in the e-learning environment (because it is usually viewed as a non-core element of teaching and learning within academic institutions) has the hallmarks of departmental innovation trophies that show the department in a better light as it was produced unsolicited by the developers. However innovation, whatever the motivation, cannot be knocked. Innovation leads to advancement, however incremental this may be. This laissez-faire attitude to e-learning may be changing though, as department by department and institution by institution each attempt to devise their own guidelines and policies on e-learning and this groundswell of e-learning content will make the adoption of a common policy and set of objectives an imperative. The situation nationally remains that we have no comparable body to the UK's Joint Information Systems Committee (JISC) that exists to coordinate 'activities support education and research by promoting innovation in new technologies and by the central support of ICT' (JISC, 2009)

Another very real consideration is that the various Irish academic institutions have differing local governance structures within their institutes. Different stakeholders are charged with responsibility and ownership of the e-learning content and delivery. Most institutes have a legacy of rigid departmental structures that can act as a deterrent to development of e-learning because the skills that are needed to develop these resources are spread across so many different departments. The sound pedagogy may be found in the academic departments, the ability to find and access the in-formation with the library and the technical skills needed to develop and integrate the technology into the institution's infrastructure lies within the computer service departments. If not handled correctly the tensions that can exist between different departments with separate missions can be a very great impediment to developing a shared e-learning strategy. The level of collaboration to bring the different skill sets together may not be institutionalised and policy driven at the highest level. Often it comes down to how different departments within the institute interact with each other or even to how particular academics view the role of libraries and support departments, or indeed how these support departments actually view their own role. With all this in mind I will now describe our own experience with creating an e-learning environment for IL.

A Case Study of Information Literacy and E-Learning Development

The Dundalk Institute of Technology library's IL programme began with a growing need to organise and formalise a coherent structure for library instruction because of the increasing demand for instruction on the ever growing digital resources of the library. In 2005 we adopted the term Information Literacy more as a library ensign to march under rather than for any great love of the rather clumsy term. As we were coming quite late to the formulation and practice of IL we had many examples of structured IL implementations in other academic libraries to call on. Also the literature and research on IL was quite mature, particularly from the USA, and we, like a lot of other smaller institutions, assimilated ready-made definitions and standards that we felt most suited our needs. Looking back at the documents we produced about IL at this time it is clear that the adoption of standards and structuring the actual IL output was one of our main concerns.

The American Library Association definition of Information Literacy quoted above was adopted by us to serve as our IL definition and the SCO-NUL (Society of College and University Libraries) seven pillars model of information literacy was used to define what exactly we meant by IL in terms of quantifiable skills. The seven headline skills are identified as

1. The ability to recognise a need for information
2. The ability to distinguish ways in which the information 'gap' may be addressed
3. The ability to construct strategies for locating information
4. The ability to locate and access information
5. The ability to compare and evaluate information obtained from different sources
6. The ability to organise, apply and communicate information to others in ways appropriate
7. The ability to synthesise and build upon existing information, contributing to the creation of new knowledge. (SCONUL, 2003)

These became the basis for a practical working model. Learning from other libraries' IL syllabus we decided to divide the IL competency levels into three 'streams' that ranged from beginners in Stream One through to more advanced classes for postgraduate students in Stream Three. Within these three streams we constructed a series of modules with their own learning outcomes and lesson plans. These modules were primarily tool descriptors or instructional modules on the different resources the library could offer. At the time we decided to put our IL presentations on PowerPoint slides to deliver to students. There was a lot of good instructional material that we had already produced for instructional leaflets, web content, etc., and it was quite natural to adapt this to slide format. We did not examine any other alternatives to slide presentation at this stage, because frankly when producing a full IL suite of classes in a few summer months, the merits or otherwise of particular technological methods of delivery

seemed rather low down on the list of priorities.

The emphasis was on collecting our existing instructional material, creating new material to fill any gaps and structuring it around the IL philosophy. We may have used IL arguments to convince ourselves and academics of the need for IL but I'm not sure we had the material to meet all the standards set by IL. We were content to rely on creating the instructional content as a signifier of our intention to honour the lofty ambitions of IL. Not being trained instructors we perhaps overlooked what the students' experience of the IL instruction would be, and the final two pillars dealing with communicating and synthesising information were maybe a bit beyond our expertise at that time. We had no real conception of how to create interactive or challenging learning processes. How students actually learned was a sort of magical process that we had only a basic knowledge about.

The classes were devised as a list of hour-long instructions on searching the library catalogue, using the different databases we subscribed to, searching e-journals and websites, and using referencing and citation methods. Other more theoretic modules were devised on accessing the quality of information and devising search strategies. With these modules we were in many respects still within the traditional librarian comfort zone of familiarity. Library working groups were assigned to develop each module. There were intensive efforts made at compiling what we as an academic library collectively knew. The fact that staff were also upgrading their own skills was an unforeseen, but welcome, consequence of this process. Indeed the exercise served to enlighten some of us on the full capabilities of the databases, catalogue features, referencing procedures, etc. The IL development process became one of those all-inclusive efforts that served to make us re-evaluate most of what we were doing as an organisation.

An Information Desk was added as a visible sign of what could be characterised as our transition from information storage and provision to also being focused on user support and training. The IL modules were launched, amid much fanfare, upon the wider academic community. The modules were to be offered to lecturers in the new academic year as a service for academic staff to book for their classes. Lecturer buy-in was left purely to their own discretion. In the launch release statement at the time was the exhortation: 'Although we advise that the streaming system is followed as it brings new users progressively to information fluency we are flexible enough to allow academics to tailor their own information skills needs, by choosing the modules they wish their classes to take.'

So the modules were generic in origin and not prescriptive in any sense. Not having the temerity at this early stage to insist on students moving through our programme towards becoming information literate, and mindful also of the restrictions of time that academic staff had for delivering their own courses, we allowed this *à la carte* approach for academic staff to select what they felt was most relevant for their students. We understood IL as a process of students moving towards a set of competencies, however, what we were offering was in fact a list of individual instructional sessions on library resources that could be chosen in any fashion by lecturers.

There was also the thorny issue of librarians moving into what was seen as traditional teaching roles, and this was an obstacle for some librarians and academics. Were we now offering a course of IL and should this not be accredited or placed on a more formal recognition within the institute? This issue was somewhat diluted by the generic and optional element to our modules. There was a strong sense of IL being a library 'gift' for our users which sits happily with much of the ethos of librarianship. It was described almost apologetically as a natural extension of our previous working habits of user instruction. But the sheer amount of extra classes we were doing and the concept of IL that we were now espousing made the idea of it being just another development seem

quite hollow. In many respects we weren't giving the importance of IL its due respect. Nevertheless even with some design faults, misconceptions and political naivety, we at least had a start made from which to build.

The technology employed for the classes was slideshow presentation format stored on memory discs and delivered within a standard classroom environment, accompanied by paper handouts of the resources we were instructing. As we had no dedicated learning space designed within the library, a conference room facility was adapted for IL delivery, with all the attendant problems for network connectivity, and lack of hands-on PCs for students to do any searching themselves. We also systematically collected the opinions of students about what we were trying to achieve as a means to inform improvements of our content and processes. Storage and harvesting of this content was becoming an issue and quite elaborate spreadsheets with dates and numbers of students were devised. A lot of the initial feedback was quite positive, both from the students and the teaching staff, which gave us encouragement in the initial tentative stages. Our early phase was deemed a general success. We had over 2,300 students completing at least one of these modules within the first couple of months. Rarely had the library been in such demand and the increased use of our services and facilities was seen as a vindication of all the hard work the staff put in. But as the bedding-in process progressed it was becoming clear that we had a lot to learn about our new role.

Issues Encountered

Notwithstanding the first flush of success, a number of issues were becoming apparent. The first and most obvious one was that the sheer number of sessions booked placed a great deal of pressure on library resources, both in terms of personnel and facilities. We hadn't sought new staff or resources for this extended instructional function. This wasn't an oversight on our part but more an acknowledgement of the reality that no further resources would be forthcoming, and was also indicative of the 'gift' nature of the library's endeavour. Another issue highlighted was that because of the elective nature of many of the institute's courses, different lecturers had inadvertently double-booked some students into the same class. Clearly our booking system needed some modification. We were on a steep learning curve adjusting practices as we went along.

The academic staffs were initially enthused by the idea that we in the library would take students through the information resources that were available to them. The academics were engaging with the IL project as a mix-and-match list of resources to be booked rather than understanding the theories of the IL programme that was designed as a graduated process of training students on how to learn. This was, in fact, how the modules were structured and offered to lecturers and perhaps our timidity was undermining the important issue of guiding students on an IL project. From a library staff point of view, there was no distinction made between library staff that were subject liaisons and had better experience to present instruction on information resources and those who were not as well equipped to speak confidently about resource discovery. Having a small number of staff we may have created the mistake of placing some staff in stressful situations. The motivation for the staff in taking this extra workload on-board was not uniform. Some did it more as a duty than with conviction. These teething problems would create an unnecessary hostility towards IL in the future. Although we understood that the workload would be front-loaded, I don't think anyone was quite prepared for the disruption to their normal working day in the initial phases. Printing off attendance sheets, feedback forms, guides for particular classes and preparing for the class became a time-consuming part of our working day.

The lack of suitable technology was becoming an issue too. As the college didn't have a content management system, we resorted to storing all our new IL content on the shared drive of the institute server, which had its limitation because of access rights, etc. Having the class content available to students and staff became an issue also. Putting slideshows on the web without explanatory notes leaves a lot to be desired from an instructional point of view. What was becoming very evident was that the range of technologies and the facilities that had been adequate for previous library functions were beginning to creak under the stresses of being used for purposes for which they weren't initially designed. Indeed, it's a testament to the adaptability and patience of the librarians that the introduction of IL went so well. To continue with the broad base of classes we would have to examine new technologies.

Some of the feedback from students was less favourable, and from some of the bored expressions of students who had to sit through 45 minutes of screenshots of our library catalogue being explained to them and from some of the written feedback expressing annoyance at the method of our delivery, we became aware of the need for modification. The experience of sitting in a crowded library room improvised to seat 30 students looking at a projector attached to a laptop was perhaps more of a learning experience for the librarians than for the actual students.

A Work in Progress

The librarian/tutors began to ask: 'Could we be doing this any better?' Our experiences with classes had the effect of making some librarians think like teachers and learning technologists. The involvement of librarians in the process of IL delivery compelled us to search for new technologies and in particular the possibilities of using available e-learning technologies. What had become apparent also was that we needed to take a fuller, more holistic approach to IL looking at the interdependence of its parts. So in tandem with our prescribed IL instruction, we were beginning to look at the possibility of using newer e-learning resources in a 'blended learning' approach. As the IL project progressed, the discipline of IL began to infuse more of our services with the ethos of providing support and training to our users. The users' needs and our own efforts to bridge the gap in their ability to access information was almost imperceptibly brought centre-stage for us. Our concentration was focused on what we were offering students not only by way of instruction in the face-to-face sessions but also of what library instruction the students could get on the library's web pages and other available platforms. The determination was made that students should be able to access IL instruction from our online resources. We also needed to have the information available to them online, 24 hours a day and seven days a week. We were beginning to ask how and when students needed our services, and the web resources provided a cost effective method of providing these services. The public face of the library became important to portray a more user-friendly and user-focused library service. Posters, promotions, library events, and our on-line content all were judged in relation to how we could improve our dialogue and the instruction content for our users.

Perhaps the interaction between staff and students through the IL sessions encouraged us to look deeper at the issue of communicating to all our users. As we looked at how students were communicating and interacting with each other and correlatively how they were learning, we saw that the web was facilitating an immediacy of communication and simple connectivity solutions for students that could be adapted to our instructional output. These 'social software' solutions required little training on behalf of the users and were, to a large extent, free to use. Both of these factors were real positives for us.

One such example is a blog or weblog. The library developed its own blog around this time, primarily as an online notice board for library news and events. We felt that there was need to circumvent the cumbersome process of placing notification of library-related activities on the web pages hosted on our institutional web server. The immediacy of our blog entries and the feedback potential from students, with the ability of users to leave comments on the interactive and mediated comments board were viewed as important features in our drive for improved communication with students. There had been asynchronous solutions in our communication methods before, like simple email or an 'Ask a Librarian' facility, but these Web 2.0 technologies seemed more in tune with what present-day students were using. Web-based solutions proved inexpensive and were under our total control in the sense that we could easily learn to design and use the interfaces. A shift away from the rigidity of solutions like static web pages was a consequence of our efforts to connect with the users. IL had become the catalyst for change making us look to virtual technologies to support and train our users.

In keeping with the idea of directly interacting with our user to supply information assistance, we recently set up a web chat service, MSN Messenger, that we hope will be a synchronous virtual equivalent to our information desk and an adjunct function of the work done by staff at the information desk. The idea is that students can chat to librarians about queries they may have and receive live feedback to those queries. This service is only in its infancy with us, but its potential value has been verified in other academic libraries that use it. As with a lot of these new technologies, it is relatively easy to set up but requires some thought on the policies and procedures needed to use it, for instance, what sort of information we should respond with, how to deal with nuisance correspondence, how we log communications, etc.

Another simple but effective web-based technology is 'social bookmarking' software that can be used by subject librarians to disseminate their qualified recommendations of websites for specific subject areas. Social bookmarking allows you to create a list of links in one of the social bookmarking sites such as del.icio.us, Connotea, Citulike, etc. These can then simply be hosted as the link on your subject-specific webpage. The bookmarking sites have the advantage of being able to organise and tag sites into groups, so librarians can make searching the websites simpler for their students. Social bookmarking is also a good way for subject librarians to keep an eye on other good subject guides on library sites and keep up-to-date on what's new within the particular 'tags' they are interested in.

By including subject-relevant RSS (Really Simple Syndication) feeds into your web pages, blog or social networking site you can automatically keep your pages dynamic and fresh for users. In many ways these so-called Web 2.0 technologies are helping librarians to bridge the gap towards a semantic web that assists in the interaction between how humans express their information needs and what is understandable by computers. With Web 2.0 technologies like blogs, social bookmarking, and wikis the emphasis is on student interaction. Students should be able to add content, comments, or look for assistance as they deem necessary. The versatility of these software solutions encourages librarians to experiment and modify the uses of them for their own purposes. Most importantly for librarians, we do not have to undergo software training to be able to develop them. Another software tool that we now use to augment our online content is Camtasia software. Using this software we were able to produce a series of short instructional videos that can be broadcast over the Internet. We can record demonstration searches using screen capture and audio instruction and even insert flash animation to enliven the content. The files can be produced to allow students to download them as podcast or view them as embedded streaming media files within any browser. We use these primarily as a means of having instruction for students available on the web at any time. These were developed as a direct response to the inadequacies of uploaded traditional slideshows. Another driving motivation for developing webcasts was the idea that students were learning differently and that downloadable instructional webcasts would give them an option to find out about library resources whenever and wherever they chose.

An interesting development in the webcast project was the collaboration with the International Office to translate and dictate a webcast for our foreign students who spoke Cantonese. This came about because of the problem of giving library tours and basic instruction to new Chinese students, with the need for a translator being present. The idea was simply to script a webcast with all the basic information needed for these foreign language students and this would be available for them on the web to view as and when they wished to do so. The script was given to a translator from the International Office to translate and a recording was made of it and synced up to suitable screen captures and flash animation. The whole lot was then compiled and produced as a five to six minute webcast that was be put on the web for download.

The webcast project required a more labour-intensive approach and required a team of developers who had to quickly come to terms with many new and interesting skills such as script writing and voice delivery. Having a team member who knew how to develop and add Flash animation to the webcasts greatly enhanced the look and feel of these online instructional videos. The Camtasia software also allows you to create interactive instruction with navigation aides and pop quizzes at the end of instructional sections. Some libraries have developed very clever and innovative ways to demo their resources with these interactive audio tutorials. We are hoping to develop our webcasts along similar lines in the near future. It is also important to note that, as with much web-based content we do not have to re-invent the wheel and a lot of good information is freely available to access on the web, developed by database vendors, web search engines, etc. A trawl through the web and You Tube may produce some valuable material or at least a good indication of where you should start.

With our face-to-face IL sessions we were finding that some library staff began to become more comfortable in the classroom environment and were starting to improvise and experiment with the traditional class process. Some of our librarian/tutors were beginning to intuitively interact with their classes and were going off-script from the slideshow presentations. Librarian/tutors felt it more natural to ask the students questions and to do more 'live' searches on databases and web searches of student queries in order to engage the classes in the process of information retrieval. So network points for access to the web became a hardware requirement for the IL classes. Other basic interactive web-based tools were discovered to engage students in answering questions in class. Simple questions were put to the class looking for answers, which would then be answered on the browser screen via a java applet. The simple act of asking students for a response was engaging students' cognitive faculties and hopefully awakening their intellectual curiosity. This was an important development as it meant that we as instructors were now becoming more interested in eliciting responses from our students and more concerned that the instruction was being delivered in an effective manner. We were beginning to feel the pride of teaching well. We did look at how other libraries were dealing with conducting classes and options were examined such as the 'clicker' technique, but this was dismissed as being too expensive and time consuming to set up.

Another e-learning solution is an online learning tutorial that allows students to go through the tutorial at their own pace. Once again there is no need to develop your own software for this as ready-made packages exist for libraries to adapt and customise for their own needs. Some libraries went to great lengths to develop their own online tutorials but many different academic libraries have adapted their own version of these freely available tutorials. We went down the adopt-and-adapt route in order to have an online tutorial ready to roll out for the beginning of the academic year.

The range of resources and different links to completely separate sites managing your library content and services may begin to resemble a patchwork quilt and it is imperative that a well-structured library website is developed to capture all these different resources into a coherent easily navigable structure for users. As with so much else a proactive computer services department or cooperative institution web developer is a real bonus in managing the first portal that users go to. Our website was completely overhauled recently and the results are very satisfactory. The pages on library web interface are some of the most widely used pages on the whole institution site.

One question you need to ask yourself when developing any e-learning product is how effective it will it be and whether it warrants the time developing it for its perceived reward? There is a school of thought that suggests that purely online unmediated courses can leave the students cold and that the level of attainment of learning cannot go above proficiency with pure web-based instruction. Dreyfus (2009, p. 128) argues that 'acquiring skills requires involvement and risk', but that using e-learning technologies in conjunction with face-to-face teaching 'helps students stay informed as to what is going on in the course.' So we should temper our enthusiasm for stand-alone online courses, and always encourage users to engage with our IL sessions where possible.

At the same time as IL sessions were becoming integral to our working day, other developments elsewhere within the institute were taking shape. An institutional virtual learning environment was developed and some of our academics had begun using it. This was an Open Source product, Moodle, and was developed locally by interested champions. Moodle is a software e-learning platform, designed to help educators create online courses with opportunities for rich interaction with the students. Many of the academics have now progressed from using it as a type of document management system where they stored class materials to actually utilising its more interactive capabilities. It would be fair to say that at its inception the library hadn't fully appreciated the importance that this e-learning tool would have for our IL delivery. Initially the library only expressed an interest in having 'a presence' on the new VLE, to advertise our service on it and perhaps to investigate the possibilities of hosting our presentations and documents on it, as a sort of makeshift content management system. We did have some training in using the VLE but at that time we saw it primarily as a vehicle for the academics.

Embedded IL

Recently one of the more interesting developments in IL instruction occurred when a lecturer asked for a series of IL classes as part of the Research and Writing course for a first-year Business Studies group. The lecturer had decided to opt for the whole suite of Stream One IL instruction modules that were available. With this level of involvement the subject librarian was usually assigned the role of instructor. As I was the business studies liaison, I decided to ask the lecturer to arrange a lab in the Business Studies department for these classes. Learning from past experience, I wanted to incorporate some element of student activity within the class. The simple premise at the time was to give the IL presentations, and then give a sheet of questions to the students to answer on what had been presented using the PCs in the labs. The lecturer was happy to oblige with arranging lab bookings and I set about devising relevant questions for these classes. Given the level of involvement of students in the IL classes, the lecturer decided that the students should be awarded marks as part of their continuous assessment for the Research and Writing course. This accreditation was an important element in 'embedding' IL modules into a first-year course. This was an

opportunity to test the theory of best practice within IL of embedding IL into actual courses.

In its first year the course relied heavily on the presentations and printed material for instruction. The structure of the course was divided into the IL learning modules that were already on offer, such as searching the library catalogue, searching databases, searching the web, referencing and evaluation of information resources. The time in the class would be divided into tutor presentation time and time spent by the students using what they had learned to find information on the PCs. Different sets of questions were devised for the students to answer at the end of each presentation that related to the students demonstrating that they could access and find material on the particular resources that had been taught to them. The examination at the end of the course was answered on paper but required the students to use computers.

We began to really see the importance of students applying what was being taught in a lab situation. Having students apply their knowledge within the class was easier and more effective than talking at them for an hour. The exams were conducted and all students passed without exception, which wasn't really a surprise as the content of the examined material was well flagged in advance and not on the difficult side. There was a pretty steep learning curve for these sessions as you had to organise the classes like a teacher and make sure the technological hardware was working properly before-hand. It was also surprising to me how involved one became as a tutor and anxious that the students learn as much as possible when there were actual marks awarded for the course.

When it came to reviewing the project with the lecturer at the end of the first term, the lecturer expressed satisfaction with the experience and said that the students benefited greatly from the IL course. Unfortunately though, she revealed that she had witnessed no discernible improvement in the bibliographies and, evidently, the depth of research from these students in their other first-year assignments. No 'inductive transfer' or 'learning transfer' was taking place between what was being taught in the IL sessions and their other research. This was quite a surprising observation as a good deal of emphasis of the instruction was focused on broadening their resource discovery skills. The conclusion we made at the time was that students had the ability to compartmentalise the different strands of their first-year courses. This was after all what they were used to doing in secondary level education. They viewed the library part of their course in isolation from the rest of their studies. It was just another module to be passed and they hadn't made the connection that the library IL skills was a universal set of skills that should be transferred to the other aspects of their courses. This compartmentalising of IL into just another class to be passed was disappointing and defeated one of the main tenets of IL: that it gives students transferable skills they can utilise in other courses. The students demonstrated reluctance to use more in-depth search strategies which meant that they were falling back on their prior knowledge and had not learned how to learn differently. They were falling short of the goal we set ourselves of moving them towards being independent learners. It was becoming clear that the structure of the IL sessions and our methodology were at fault. A solution we thought would be to take some of the students' other course assignments and incorporate the information needs of these assignments into the IL part of the course. We needed to make the study skills and advanced research methodology a seamless part of what they did for third-level learning.

The following year we ran the same classes again, this time incorporating the assignments into the modules. If we were doing a class on database discovery I would have prior knowledge of student assignments and incorporate the assignment keyword searches into the class and require that the students use the PCs to find information on their assignments. Then we would spend some time evaluating the results. This was quite successful and the students were glad to have a library

facilitator there to help them get the information for upcoming assignments. Again the students did well with the formal examinations but this time from both the academics involved and from a librarian and an IL perspective it was felt that students took more away from the sessions than the previous year. By pure coincidence I had happened upon the teaching theory and methodology and was beginning to see the benefits of using a system that involved students more in their own learning process. Elements of problem-based learning and constructivist psychological theory of knowledge and teaching methods were creeping into these IL instruction sessions. In particular the idea that students should work in collaborative groups within a lab situation to discover for themselves what information resources were of value for their course work, and that these labs could be facilitated by information professionals such as librarians represents a new and more effective way to deliver IL

Using the Virtual Learning Environment

One of the key developments from these embedded sessions was the request by some of the students to have the material that was delivered in class accessible in electronic format. This made us examine how we could use the VLE to put presentations and other material onto it for students to access. In the process of doing this it became clear that using the VLE simply as a content management system was not using its full potential and we were simply placing all our existing documents into the VLE, without much care for adapting the content to the new platform; 'Shovelware' is a disparaging term to describe this practice. There were resources and activities that could assist in a more involved method of teaching the students that both the lecturers and librarians wished for. Not only could you lay out the structure of your weekly courses and upload the resources you wanted students to access from the class, but you could develop and add web pages and list web links suitable for each week's course. There were also facilities to add quizzes for each class, forums to allow students to post their queries and informational needs. Chat rooms, wikis and a facility to create blogs were also features that provided interesting avenues of interaction for instructor and student and from student to student. We could also interact with the students using the survey facility of the VLE. Another useful function within the VLE allows students to upload word documents, for instance, which means that tutors can set assignments for students and students can then upload these assignments for correction when they are finished. Also there was a facility to manage online quizzes or assignments that could be graded by the administrator and made available immediately to students. For the administrators and teachers there were question banks that were effectively repositories of questions that other librarians could use. We needed to quickly learn about SCORM, (Sharable Content Object Reference Model), standards compliant questions format that allowed us to create interactive questions for the VLE.

The potential for augmenting our IL classes in a blended manner using the VLE is so great, that a whole re-think of our content and what we can do in the classroom situation has opened up before us. We can truly incorporate collaborative content into the classroom environment using the VLE. The VLE is a clear instance where the technology has facilitated the development and future direction of what we intend to offer in IL over the coming years. In the future content will be structured into five different classes. The class time will be divided into the PAR model of teaching: Present, Apply and Review. There will be a presentation for 15 minutes, followed by structured application by the students of what they have learned using the lab PCs for a further half hour, followed by a class discussion and reviewing process of the quality of the information that they harvested at the end of the class. There is an online forum where students

are asked to post their questions either on their first-year assignments or on broader queries about information retrieval. These will be answered in the next class or as soon as possible. This approach has some aspects of computer-supported collaborative learning (CSCL) in the sense that the VLE provides the virtual scaffold for students to communicate and share the solutions to their information needs of a shared assignment. The lecturer also expressed an appreciation with the forum because the lecturer has been assigned the co-teaching role within the VLE module and can see what the class is discussing and what questions they are asking, which gives an insight into how they are progressing and whether they are asking the right questions.

The classes are now structured so that the IL sessions provide targeted intervention for first-year students at the beginning of their studies and just after they have been given their first assignments. This is in the hope that students feel that these sessions are actually addressing their real curricular needs. Contextualisation of what they are doing in the IL sessions, and relating their work to other parts of their curriculum, makes the work in the sessions more urgent and relevant for the students (and useful to the lecturer!). The fact that they are developing good IL practices about information seeking, retrieval and evaluation and that they are learning how to learn in a real environment is the IL bonus for the library.

FUTURE DEVELOPMENTS

One of the most interesting developments has been the collaboration between academic and librarian to achieve real progress in the provision of IL to embedded students, and how the VLE supplied some of the pressing issues we had with IL delivery. The constructivist psychological theory and the problem-based learning models that some academics are themselves adopting and developing, I believe, complement many of the

239

standards we set ourselves in IL and re-enforce what has been our experience of IL delivery. The roles of subject or liaison librarians are vital to fostering the collaborative partnership in this new dynamic between academics and library. It also requires trust to be built up between academics and librarians, to share their curriculum and proposed learning outcomes and a willingness to modify their classes to incorporate the IL principles. Meetings between lecturer and librarian must be timely and frank for a common structure and mutual trust to be developed.

There are two basic platforms for e-learning for librarians to consider in their delivery of IL. Firstly there is the stand-alone, web-based and unmediated platform where instructional content can be hosted. Websites with subject-based portals or resource guides, web-based tutorials, webcasts, audio recordings, virtual tours, synchronous and asynchronous methods of relaying information to students. These are some of the technologies employed through this platform. Secondly, there is the blended learning platform with a tutor/facilitator teaching an IL course and utilising a variety of technologies to enhance the classroom experience. These classes are particularly effective in instructing students how to use information resource locators like e-journal databases, or how to search the web with various search engines, or how to reference correctly. A further development of these classes is the embedded IL instruction that requires more design cooperation between librarian and academic. These embedded IL courses created in collaboration with academics and tailored to be subject-specific are delivered in an interactive and meaningful way to students that will augment their chosen course of study. Having IL and the course syllabus unite in the common purpose of creating independently minded and information-aware students seems to be a very promising development for academic librarians, academics and students alike. This is as far as we have come on our IL and e-learning journey, so far.

Looking to the future, the idea of student group work within the classroom or lab is an avenue that we intend to explore. Giving students problems to find information related to their course work and the librarian acting as a facilitator and guide within this learning environment seems like a very constructive approach, but one that needs to be developed in collaboration with lecturers: 'Instructors and librarians contribute to the session by collaborating on objectives and learning goals, creating research questions, recommending lists of resources, and questioning' (Snavely, 2004, p. 529).

As always we are looking to improve IL delivery for our users, and it may be that what is needed now is a systemic approach to creating a set of classes that would be obligatory as part of a first-year orientation course. This would need to be part of an institution-wide effort to develop instructional models that would seek to develop students as independent thinkers. Each school or faculty within the institution would need to be involved with the relevant support services to bring this about. The institutional VLE is an ideal e-learning environment to host such a suite of subject-based IL modules. The librarian's input would be needed in developing learning outcomes and instructional content to help students locate and evaluate resources. These agreed learning outcomes and instructions could be incorporated into problem-based learning classes that were based on the actual student's chosen course of study and something that the academics could perhaps instruct themselves upon. (As long as IL is devised and delivered correctly, there is no reason why librarians should be the sole instructors.) Such an approach may help address the phenomenon of web savvy-students 'getting by' with poor research and IL skills. It would also address some of the issues of librarians being over-stretched with their instructional duties and serve to firmly embed IL concepts into the teaching discourse. A systematic acceptance of IL would take a lot of management commitment and organisational coalescing that is beyond the remit of the library to affect. However, the overlap in philosophy and goals between IL and problem-based learning may allow librarians, working in collaboration with problem-based learning inclined lecturers, to further IL instruction. Of course there would be departmental considerations and timetabling issues to address, but just because it is difficult to achieve should not make it impossible, especially if we who work within the academic world are serious about creating an information society.

CONCLUSION

At present the variety and scope of the e-learning technologies available to librarians offer us diverse ways to present IL to the community we serve. I believe we must tailor our IL content for that community in a way that best suits our resources. The convergence of increasing volume of information, a need for librarians to instruct users how to access this information, new practices in the broader teaching world and emerging e-learning technologies has opened up a very real possibility of repositioning the academic library as central to the education process. It is tempting to say that technology and the discovery of e-learning tools revolutionised our IL output and therefore the way we as librarians work. But I think that this would be an over-simplification of the whole process of IL introduction that I have detailed. IL re-orientated our attention to a more student-focused agenda and informed many other practices we do within the library. The convergence of information literacy and e-learning technology, aligned with new teaching practices certainly makes it possible to create this new dynamic. Each of these forces, though, should not be taken in isolation, as it would distort our main aim to instruct library users in the skills needed to navigate the complex information world.

REFERENCES

American Library Association. (1989). *Presidential Committee on Information Literacy: Final Report.* Retrieved March 23, 2009, from http://www.ala.org/ala/mgrps/divs/acrl/publications/whitepapers/presidential.cfm

Dreyfus, H. L. (2009). *On the Internet* (2nd ed.). New York: Routledge.

Joint Information Systems Committee. (2009). *About us.* Retrieved March 24, 2009, from http://www.jisc.ac.uk/aboutus.aspx

Melling, M. E. (Ed.). (2006). *Supporting e-learning: A guide for library and information managers.* London: Facet Publishing.

Snavely, L. (2004). Making problem-based learning work: Institutional challenges. *Portal-Libraries and the Academy, 4*(4), 521–531. doi:10.1353/pla.2004.0071

Society of College, National and University Libraries. (2003). *Information skills in higher education: A SCONUL position paper.* Retrieved April 2, 2009, from http://www.sconul.ac.uk/groups/information_literacy/papers/Seven_pillars.html

ADDITIONAL READING

Blake, L. (2009). On Campus or out of town: How publishing online tutorials can help your patrons. *Computers in Libraries, 29*(4), 11–13.

Blummer, B. (2007). Utilizing webquests for information literacy instruction in distance education. *College & Undergraduate Libraries, 14*(3), 45–62. doi:10.1300/J106v14n03_03

Blummer, B. (2008). Applying Perkins's facets of a learning environment for information literacy instruction. *Community & Junior College Libraries, 14*(3), 179–189. doi:10.1080/02763910802035108

Buchanan, L. E., Luck, D. L., & Jones, T. C. (2002). Integrating information literacy into the virtual university: A course model. *Library Trends*, *51*(2), 144.

Burton, V. T., & Chadwick, S. A. (2000). Investigating the practices of student researchers: Patterns of use and criteria for use of Internet and library sources. *Computers and Composition*, *17*(3), 309–328. doi:10.1016/S8755-4615(00)00037-2

Callison, D. (2009). Instructional trends from AASL journals: 1972-2007. Part 3: From access-measured to evaluation-measured. *School Library Media Activities Monthly*, *25*(10), 25–28.

Corcos, E., & Monty, V. (2008). Interactivity in library presentations using a personal response system. *EDUCAUSE Quarterly*, *31*(2), 53–60.

Dreyfus, H. L. (2002). Anonymity versus commitment: The dangers of education on the Internet. *Educational Philosophy and Theory*, *34*(4), 369–378. doi:10.1111/j.1469-5812.2002.tb00510.x

Fosmire, M., & Macklin, A. (2002). Riding the active learning wave: Problem-based learning as a catalyst for creating faculty-librarian instructional partnerships. *Issues in Science & Technology Librarianship*. Retrieved October 26, 2009, from http://www.istl.org/02-spring/article2.html

Grafstein, A. (2007). Information literacy and technology: An examination of some issues. *Portal: Libraries & the Academy*, *7*(1), 51–64. doi:10.1353/pla.2007.0006

Griffin, D. K., Mitchell, D., & Thompson, S. J. (2009). Podcasting by synchronising PowerPoint and voice: What are the pedagogical benefits? *Computers & Education*, *53*(2), 532–539. doi:10.1016/j.compedu.2009.03.011

Johnson, D., & Eisenberg, M. (1996). Computer literacy and information literacy: A natural combination. *Emergency Librarian*, *23*(5), 12.

Kenedy, R., & Monty, V. (2008). Dynamic purposeful learning in information literacy . In Watts, M. M. (Ed.), *Information Literacy: One Key to Education. New Directions for Teaching and Learning, 114*. San Francisco: Jossey-Bass.

Lincoln, M. (2009). Information literacy: An online course for student library assistants. *School Library Media Activities Monthly*, *25*(10), 29–30.

Macklin, A. S. (2001). Integrating information literacy using problem-based learning. *RSR. Reference Services Review*, *29*(4), 306–314. doi:10.1108/EUM0000000006493

Orme, W. A. (2008). Information literacy and first-year students. *New Directions for Teaching and Learning*, *114*, 63–70. doi:10.1002/tl.317

Pope, A., & Walton, G. (2006). *Information literacy: Recognising the need*. Oxford: Chandos Publishing.

Rogerson-Revell, P. (2007). Directions in e-learning tools and technologies and their relevance to online distance language education. *Open Learning*, *22*(1), 57–74. doi:10.1080/02680510601100168

Slaouti, D. (2002). The World Wide Web for academic purposes: Old study skills for new? *English for Specific Purposes*, *21*(2), 105–124. doi:10.1016/S0889-4906(00)00035-1

Spence, L. (2004). The usual doesn't work: Why we need problem-based learning. *Libraries and the Academy*, *4*(4), 485-493. Retrieved October 20, 2000, from http://muse.jhu.edu/login?uri=/journals/portal_libraries_and_the_academy/v004/4.4spence.html. doi:10.1353/pla.2004.0072.

Stephen, M., Trywell, K., Kgomotso, M., & Justus, W. (2006). Design and implementation of an online information literacy module: Experience of the Department of Library and Information Studies, University of Botswana. *Online Information Review*, *30*(2), 168–187. doi:10.1108/14684520610659193

Sundin, O. (2008). Negotiations on information-seeking expertise: A study on web-based tutorials for information literacy. *The Journal of Documentation, 64*(1), 24–44. Retrieved from http://www.emeraldinsight.com/Insight/ViewContentServl et?contentType=Article&Filename=Published/EmeraldFullTextArticle/Articles/2780640102. html. doi:10.1108/00220410810844141. doi:10.1108/00220410810844141

Viggiano, R. G. (2006). When faculty behave like students: Teaching faculty about online library resources. *Journal of Library Administration, 45*(3/4), 563–563. doi:10.1300/J111v45n03_22

Williams, J., & Chinn, S. J. (2009). Using Web 2.0 to support the active learning experience. *Journal of Information Systems Education, 20*(2), 165–174.

Chapter 15

E–Mentors:
A Case Study in Effecting Cultural Change

Barbara Macfarlan
Oaklands College, UK

Richard Everett
Oaklands College, UK

ABSTRACT

The eMentors scheme encapsulates the concept that the person in the home most likely to be able to programme the audio-visual equipment is the teenager. The scheme harnesses the digital generation's propensity for technology by using the students to teach their teachers how to make appropriate use of electronic resources in the classroom. We present a case study that focuses on both staff and student experiences of the eMentoring system at a further education college in Hertfordshire, UK and outlines the strategy for ongoing staff development and support. The scheme has given lecturers the confidence to develop new technology-enhanced pedagogical practices and has given students the opportunity to play an active part in the development of their own learning environments and to influence policy on the use of technology. We believe that this model has been an effective element in a concerted approach to changing the prevailing attitudes to designing pedagogy for 21st century learners.

INTRODUCTION

Learning technology is spreading rapidly within further education (FE) and teachers are expected to incorporate Information and Communication Technologies (ICT) into their pedagogy. This necessitates huge investment most significantly in staff development and support. It is imperative that we recognise the ubiquitous incursion of technology into every aspect of our lives which necessitates a response from educational institutions whose role it is to prepare students for further study and employment. According to Abowd and Mynatt (2000) 'The proliferation of computing into the physical world promises more than the ubiquitous availability of computing infrastructure; it suggests new paradigms of interaction inspired by constant access to information and computational capabilities' (p. 29)

DOI: 10.4018/978-1-61520-879-1.ch015

At first it seems that teaching staff are resistant to the incursion of technology into the learning environment, however it is teachers' pedagogical beliefs that mediate their integration. (Ertmer, 2005; Donnelly & O'Rourke, 2007) 'few academics or teachers have all the necessary skills, or either the time or the desire to acquire them' (Salmon, 2002, p. 5). Any programme that sets out to addresses teachers' use of learning technologies needs to address the pedagogic issues, inspire and enthuse and give teachers the skills to implement these technologies into their methodology. To address this situation the college has developed a range of responses and we report, on one of those support systems: the eMentors programme. This system uses the students to teach the teachers how to use technology appropriately and aims to exploit the situation that students can take on the role of technical support at the point of need.

Oaklands College is a Further Education College in the UK. It delivers education to approximately 11,000 students supported by about 600 staff; just over half of the student population is in the 15 to 18 age group. The learners are enrolled on a range of courses including vocational and work-based; Adult and Community Learning; and academic to degree level professional courses. The college also caters for pupils drawn from local schools on vocational courses, and learners following modern apprenticeships.

This predominantly vocational curriculum requires the education of students to take place in classrooms and workshops within the college and real life settings outside. The college accepts students from a wide variety of social contexts and its mission is to provide 'outstanding learning opportunities and training solutions within a vibrant, inclusive College experience, leading to recognised qualifications and outcomes that contribute to personal development, and the economic growth and social well-being of our community' (Oaklands, 2009).

The college vision separates technology from e-learning: an important distinction that is reflected in the senior management hierarchy with a Director of Estates being responsible for Information Technology operation and support and a Director of E-learning, a post that is part of the curriculum structure, responsible for the use of that technology in the classroom, workshop and beyond.

The e-learning and technology vision (Everett 2008, p. 3) documents an entitlement to students that they will get a 'better technology experience than at home' aiming to deliver ' bleeding edge learning' utilising 'leading edge technology'. It should be noted that it also emphasises the concept of 'education requirements driving technology' and e-learning 'enhancing the learning experience', both aspects underpinning the rationale behind the whole eMentors concept.

The eMentors programme plays an integral part in a concerted programme of staff development and support designed to implement culture change. FE teachers often have large workloads, and this often impacts upon the adoption of, or even resistance to, new technology and attendance at professional development sessions. Students on the other hand, have strong intrinsic motivation to use new technology and have experience in its use.

BACKGROUND

For the effective use of learning technologies, it is generally recognised that educators have to integrate those technologies into a new personal pedagogical practice (Donnelly & O'Rourke, 2007; Jackson & Anagnostopoulou, 2001). However, this endeavour is unlikely to make progress if educators have a fear or lack sufficient knowledge of, the basic underlying technologies. Most institutions provide some form of initial training or staff development on the introduction of new technology (Laurillard, 1993). But this is rarely sufficient to overcome all staff anxieties. Most lecturers require more IT support than their institutions provide (Mason & Rennie, 2006). This is not surprising; education is largely a real-time activity and ideally requires real-time and situated support.

Our main theoretical influence is *situated learning* (Lave & Wenger, 1991; see also Brown, Collins, & Duguid, 1989; Wenger, 1998) and the related concept of *communities of practice*. Lave and Wenger's view of situated learning is that 'learners inevitably participate in communities of practitioners and that the mastery of knowledge and skill requires newcomers to move toward full participation in the sociocultural practices of a community' (p. 29). They describe the process by which newcomers become part of a community of practice as legitimate peripheral participation (LPP). They suggest that a 'person's intentions to learn are engaged and the meaning of learning is configured through the process of becoming a full participant in a sociocultural practice. This social process includes, indeed it subsumes, the learning of knowledgeable skills' (p. 29). It should be noted that Lave and Wenger do not intend LPP to be an educational form or a pedagogical strategy: 'it is an analytical viewpoint on learning, a way of understanding learning' (p. 40). They argue that learning through LPP takes place whatever the educational setting or even if there is no explicit educational setting at all. All learning and all activity is situated. Most theories based on social models of learning are influenced to some extent by the socio-cognitive theories of Vygotsky (1978). Vygotsky's attempt to create a Marxist psychology led to a rather fortuitous application of a *socio-historical* perspective to many issues in psychology that had previously been considered as largely individual processes.

Lave and Wenger's description of situated learning through LPP in communities of practice represents an ideal; a successful and efficient process of learning when all the conditions are right. Unfortunately communities of practice can also be dysfunctional. For example, Lave and Wenger themselves describe how newcomers can be prevented from fully participating in communities and Wenger, McDermott, & Snyder (2002) describe how the practice at the heart of a community can become stagnant. Within organisations communities often create their own informal support structures (Eales, 2003). However, formal interventions in communities of practice have become a standard approach to staff development in educational institutions. The recognition and support of e-learning champions, or advocates, has been a common approach to educational cultural change (Lucas, 2006; Sharpe, Benfield, & Francis, 2006). A more focused method of supporting cultural change is through personal mentoring (Kent, 2002). In addition to traditional face-to-face mentoring, technology can now support human online mentoring (Harris, 2008) and even computer-based virtual mentoring (Zhang, 2004).

The Need for Change

In late 2003 the college was inspected by the national Office for Standards in Education (Ofsted). Its report criticised the leadership and management of the organisation and the college was put into 'special measures' and a Post-Inspection Action Plan was put into operation to address the major issues. One of the key criticisms in the report was that Information and Learning Technologies (ILT) were not in evidence and the arrival and widespread integration of digital technology in education seemed to have been over-looked in the planning and delivery of courses. A severe underinvestment in technology and the infrastructure, processes and development of skills to utilise it was evident: certainly a radical change was required in the College.

The College embarked on the development of a vision that clearly set out where it wanted to be and a strategy that gave everyone a role in bringing about the cultural change that was needed. This addressed the learner experience through an ambitious plan to create an exciting, innovative and flexible environment for the 21st century that is safe and secure and provides the facilities needed for learning in modern accommodation. It aimed to facilitate multi-layered, innovative approaches to learning and teaching that would inspire and motivate students, optimise the use of resources, and improve access for all. The learner experience was becoming central to the strategy and the inspectors' report had made it clear that students of the 21st century needed to develop a modern range of skills. Prensky (2001) describes today's students as the first generation to grow up with technology all around them. He points out that these 'digital natives' have never known a time without computers, video games, mobile phones and all the other gadgets of the digital age and 'that as a result of this ubiquitous environment and the sheer volume of their inter-action with it, today's students think and process information fundamentally differently from their predecessors' (p. 1).

A new Principal brought energy and enthusi-asm to the achievement of these ambitious aims and a strategic approach was adopted and fully supported by the senior management team. A culture of change and innovation was fostered with opportunities provided for all to be part of the process. However, such a major shift relies on staff members recognising this need for change and to support and participate in the process along the way. As Brighouse (2005) puts it: 'leading in exceptionally difficult circumstances is the need to understand the way in which the forces of internally generated change can be structured and harnessed rather than, as so often happens, external suggestions imposed or accepted' (p. 113).

Everett (2006) harnessed student feedback which was very clear in its unanimous message that these digital natives had a preference for us-ing IT in their learning environment and that the College needed to provide a better IT experience than the students had at home. 'The research has clearly shown that there is a need in the college to move into the transitional stage, to embed e-learning into the organisation' (Everett, 2006, p. 46). This transitional stage refers to a stage of the

MIT90 model for benchmarking e-learning (Scott Morton, 1991).

The use of digital technologies in a learning environment is considered essential by students; they expect that the resources that they employ in their everyday lives will be incorporated into their learning. But as well as considering student perceptions, 'academic staff must balance the impact of e-learning activity development and its application with their workload and capability with educational technology' (Sheey, Marcus, Costa, & Taylor, 2006, p. 757). A coherent strategy for e-learning was developed by the Director of E-learning, that included provision for the support and resources that staff needed to scaffold them through the start-up phase and place e-learning in a pedagogic context that can be sustained and developed in the long term.

Creating and Supporting a Culture of Change

Leading teaching staff in anything that involves change is notoriously difficult and often feels next to impossible on occasions.

Leading in a culture of change means creating a culture: (not just a structure) of change. It does not mean adopting innovations, one after another; it does mean producing the capacity to seek, criti-cally assess, and selectively incorporate new ideas and practices – all the time. (Fullan, 2001, p. 7)

Without well thought through strategies, achieving the gains of competent e-learning usage can result in confusion for staff due to a lack of vision at the top of the organisation; anxiety for managers unable to get staff to take on the skills required for using the technology; extremely slow change due to a lack of incentives to encourage success; much frustration for those trying to sup-port an e-learning strategy because of a lack of resources being brought to bear; and many 'false

Figure 1. Table Adapted by the Authors from the Knoster, Villa, and Thousand (2000) Model for Successful Change

Vision	Skills	Incentives	Resources	Action Plans	Collaboration	Result
	✓	✓	✓	✓	✓	Confusion
✓		✓	✓	✓	✓	Anxiety
✓	✓		✓	✓	✓	Gradual Change
✓	✓	✓		✓	✓	Frustration
✓	✓	✓	✓		✓	False Starts
✓	✓	✓	✓	✓		Isolation
✓	✓	✓	✓	✓	✓	Change

starts' giving the feeling that things were going to change – but not the reality (Knoster, Villa, & Thousand, 2000). Their model for successful change identifies that it can only be implemented if all the elements of vision, skills, incentives, resources, and action plans are present. To this list we have added a sixth term of *collaboration* or alternatively helping users help each other (Eales, 2003) an element we feel is inherent and an important skill in today's workplace. We have drawn up a table (see Figure 1) which recognises the essential elements identified by Knoster, Villa, and Thousand, and includes our element collaboration. These are all needed to achieve successful change and we identify the results where any element was omitted. Thus the table in Figure 1 shows that without vision confusion results, with no resources frustration ensues, and so on; isolation is identified as the predominant outcome where collaboration is not achieved.

Management of cultural change requires a holistic approach that works from the top down and the bottom up simultaneously. Fullan (1999) describes the processes of human and organisational change as having an organic and evolutionary nature. He points out that 'each situation is complex and to a certain degree unique. And, living things grow, adapt and evolve' (p. 14).

We argue that in addition to a simultaneous top-down and bottom-up approach this has to be supplemented by support from the sides to be fully effective. In the case study it can be seen that the eMentors form an essential element of that approach.

1.   There is strong leadership from the top in the college made obvious, for example, by the Principal and his team investing in a coherent e-learning vision and strategy including the creation of the post of Director of E-learning at senior management level.

2.   An approach from the sides utilising staff support systems; and the building of team of educators into e-learning and Technology Support (eLTS), whose role it is to work with lecturers in group sessions and one-to-one, training them in the use of the new 'tools of the trade' and to guide them towards the development of a pedagogy that incorporates digital resources. In addition, each curriculum team is invited to nominate an eChampion, someone within a teaching team with an interest and enthusiasm for e-learning rather than expert knowledge. The object of the eChampion initiative is to encourage the cascading of e-learning skills and resources by fostering the enthusiasm of individuals within these teams.

3.   From the bottom up with students demanding a more technologically-rich learning experience (Everett, 2006) and leading the way by mentoring the lecturers in IT skills.

In addition enthusiastic staff or early adopters (Rogers, 1964) pushed the boundaries of pedagogy inventing new technology uses to create authentic and innovative learning experiences.

By its re-inspection the investment in infrastructure was beginning to show, however, the necessary cultural change from an e-learning perspective had not yet taken place and the inspectors' report observed that while the equipment was in evidence it was not being used sufficiently. Fullan (2001) describes this stalling when the initial excitement cannot be sustained as an 'implementation dip' when people are struggling with two issues 'The social-psychological fear of change, and the lack of technical know how or skills to make the change work' (p. 6). The College received a *Satisfactory* rating with a *Good* capacity to improve; the eMentors programme being mentioned as one of the support systems in place that was effective.

The eMentors Programme

The teacher-student nexus is also under threat; ... the notion of teacher as 'expert' and student as 'receiver' makes little sense. (Conole, 2008, p. 8)

A mentor is an experienced and trusted adviser or an experienced person in an organisation who trains and counsels new employees or students. Some institutions have mentoring programmes in which newcomers are paired with more experienced people to help them to adapt quickly to the organisational culture (Hargreaves & Fullan, 2000), and schools sometimes have mentoring programmes where an older student is paired with a new student.

The term eMentor in our case study refers to the student as a 'native speaker' (Prensky, 2001) of the digital language of computers, video games and the Internet. The lecturers confer and collaborate with their eMentors to help them communicate their 'still-valuable knowledge and wisdom in the world's new digital language' (p. 13). Other projects, notably New Zealand's Tech Angels (Bolstad & Gilbert, 2006) harness the valuable resource they have in their students, recognising that the student has digital experience and the lecturer is the one who needs support; they use the term 'reverse mentoring'. The 'e' element in our term refers to the mentoring being in the realm of electronic resources and technology, as the eMentors are guiding and supporting the lecturers while they adapt to the changing teaching and learning environment. The scheme works on the premise that digital-savvy 21st century students are more technically adept and are better placed to help 'digital immigrant' (Prensky, 2001) lecturers overcome their insecurities towards ICT while at the same time empowering and engaging students.

Recent research on students' experience of using technologies shows that many are comfortable in this technology-enriched environment. They are sophisticated users who appropriate the technologies to their own needs. The implications for educational Institutions both in terms of the technological infrastructure we provide and the way in which we support learners are profound. (Conole, et al, 2007, p. 1)

The programme was devised and initiated by Richard Everett in 2006 as a result of work on an MA in Educational Leadership and Management at the Institute of Education. It is managed on a day-to-day basis by the four members of the eLTS team.

The rationale of the eMentors programme was to support lecturers in the classroom or workshop in a more informal manner taking a 'just in time' approach. By situating the learning in this context staff had the support they needed and learners gained from this in developing mentoring skills they would not normally learn. The challenge being to bring together 'the cultures of youth and experience' (Hargreaves & Fullan, 2000, p. 54) in a collaborative manner.

Learner input encouraged staff to explore a range of multimedia and Web 2.0 resources previously not considered or known about. Add to that the considerable backup with the eLTS team being brought to bear and electronic resources became deployable in places hitherto unexplored. The ICT equipment was kept running because eMentors were reporting faults accurately and technology was getting fixed when inoperable.

Initially, lecturers from all courses who had shown an interest in using technology in their teaching were invited by members of the eLTS team to participate and nominate a student eMentor. This was chiefly because these lecturers had demonstrated an interest in trialling something new and had the confidence to allow a student to help them with managing the ICT demands of the new e-learning strategy. The lecturer/student pairs were then briefed together about the programme and its expectations and a Memorandum of Understanding was signed by each of them. This mutual understanding of shared meaning does not suggest that the participants carry equal responsibility for the management of the learning but rather that 'mutuality of [our] participation' (Wenger, 1998, p. 56) has the potential to transform each of them. This new relationship of lecturer and eMentor joins each pair in a wider community of tutors and eMentors who share an understanding that using ICT will lead to the provision of a curriculum that will better cater for a diverse range of learners. Participation shaped the classroom experience of both lecturers and students, who in turn, had the potential to shape the practice of their own communities which they rejoined for training and other activities. The lecturers continued to attend the staff development sessions, while the students, although invited, chose to attend training organised by the eLTS team specifically for the eMentors as well as attending eMentors meetings once a term.

While the main advantages for the student of being an eMentor would be the opportunity to work more closely with the tutors and take a more active role in the management of learning, there are other incentives and rewards to encourage taking on this role. These include USB data sticks, music vouchers for attending meetings once a term, and a reference for any future employers or educational institutions. In addition, training is provided for the eMentors with members of the eLTS team helping them develop their technical skills. Perhaps more importantly, they were supported in the development of their communication and mentoring skills. Comments gathered from eMentors reveal that the main benefit that they get from being involved is gaining soft skills that they would not normally have learned.

For the lecturer, the advantage of having an eMentor would be to have assistance at the point of need, providing situated support for the electronic resources that are being integrated into the learning environment. The programme creates a mentoring relationship that exploits the fearless attitude of the digital native students to guide the lecturers through a maze of technical uncertainty to a more confident integration of e-learning resources.

Such a shift in the dynamics of the classroom requires lecturers to challenge their own pedagogical beliefs and make changes in classroom teaching practices. By joining the programme, they participate in a community of practice that discusses 'new materials, methods and strategies, and that supports the risk taking and struggle involved in transforming practice' (Ertmer, 2005, p. 34). In the first year, there were 42 eMentors and the next year there were 75 all drawn from across a wide range of areas, courses and levels. Generally, when a student had several classes with the same lecturer then that relationship continued through all classes, but when the eMentor also had classes with a different lecturer the eMentoring was not established unless the tutor was willing to get involved. The lecturers in the eMentor programme were gradually influencing the wider community of lecturers by their membership in both groups; and the eMentors were identified by other students as belonging to a group to which they wanted to belong. So lecturers who were initially reluctant to take part were influenced by their peers to see the eMentor scheme as being valuable and they were also encouraged by their students who wanted to be an eMentor and become actively involved in incorporating ICT into their learning environment. To quote from one tutor in the programme: '*Yes I think it is an excellent idea as you have extra support if things go wrong. You can also learn from your eMentor.*'

However, the programme did not always go to plan. Some eMentors became less active and stopped coming to the meetings or posting on the eMentors' forum and did not respond to efforts to contact them. This attrition accounts for about 20% of the initial eMentors in the programme and we continue to try to ascertain why this is so. While we cannot point to particular factors as to why students stop participating, feedback from students indicates that those who remain in the programme do so because they were enjoying the experience of being involved in their own community and active participants in their learning.

Recruiting for the eMentors programme has now become part of the induction process and students receive information in their orientation package and posters appear around the student areas. Lecturers are reminded of the programme through notices in the staff bulletin and members of the eLTS team also visit classes to talk about the eMentor role and encourage students to become part of the programme. Often a class will choose an eMentor when electing other roles of responsibility, such as class representative and in some cases these roles will be undertaken by one and the same person.

The eMentors programme has played an integral part in a concerted programme of support designed to implement a much-needed culture change. The lecturers were subjected to a programme of change in order to raise the public perception of the college being competitive in the education sector and the introduction of ICT into every aspect of the operation, but particularly learning and teaching, was central to this vision of excellence.

Initially it seemed that the eMentors programme had no incentives for staff to participate and that they would be very reluctant to allow students to help them. However, this was shown not to be the case very quickly as the eMentors proved their worth and other lecturers joined the programme seeing its widespread benefits for all. Our studies have shown that in the first year of operation, classes which had an eMentor showed an increased success (retention x achievement) rate of 6%.

One of the eMentors, James Belmont, had his role expanded into that of eMentor liaison officer and he began to organise the regular eMentor meetings; feedback the comments and criticisms from the eMentors to relevant people; and co-ordinate the eMentor training with the e-learning team. He became a member of the student council, a student representative and was invited to become a student ambassador. The scheme has impacted in unexpected ways as eMentors now contribute to the development of policy by highlighting procedures that could be managed in a more digitally efficient way.

Evaluation

To evaluate effectiveness we focused on interviews with key members of the scheme. After reading the results of the staff (48 responded) and student (37 completed) questionnaires we selected five interviewees who represented different viewpoints ranging from the corporate view of the vision and necessary change, to the views from the lecturers who must integrate this change into their beliefs and understandings of learning and teaching. All the interviewees agreed to be identified.

We had collated questionnaire responses gathered from eMentor James Belmont's project report distributed to all staff and students via the virtual learning environment (VLE). We felt that in order to tease out some of the attitudes and feelings from the participants we needed to conduct one-to-one interviews. These interviews, lasting between 60 and 90 minutes, were recorded on video and later transcribed into text. Informants were interviewed and in some cases interviews were followed up at a later date by additional clarifying questions. The questions were based on a semi-structured and generally open-ended format. There was a fixed initial list of questions, with changes made to fit the general conversation or questions added to clarify answers or develop points. The questions centred on issues of changing work practices in education and how they impact on teaching and learning both in terms of what managers expect and what learners demand in the way of technological expertise; and the contribution of the eMentoring programme. The lecturers were asked about their attitude to adapting their teaching practices to incorporate learning technologies; and the eMentors were asked about their role as an eMentor and what that entailed. We have summarised the main points of the interview and direct quotations are shown in italics.

Interviews

Mark Dawe, Principal of Oaklands College

This huge investment in technology, new building, staff development, e-learning and all the rest, is ultimately an investment in learning.

Through his work with other colleges Mark Dawe had developed the view that technology was important in teaching and learning, especially to the learners, and he recognised that there was a lot of work to do in order to develop a fully integrated learning experience. While Mark observed pockets of good practice he also saw that there was no consistency and no policy guiding the integration of IT into teaching and learning. It was clear that technology resources were limited and that the staff had little or no enthusiasm for change. Once the problem was identified then the implementation of the process of change and development could begin because it was clear that if the college did not replicate the changes that were taking place in the wider society then it was not meeting the needs of the market, the employers, learners, and staff. Mark comments:

Jobs are changing; workplace requirements are very different now and we are trying to prepare learners who can grow and develop as new employment opportunities open up; learners who can be flexible and adapt to accommodate new workplace roles and responsibilities that haven't yet been imagined.

Oaklands College was committed to training and educating people to make them employable, now and in the future. An investment in the infrastructure and training was made. The first priority was the network which had to be upgraded and a significant investment went into the development and installation of a college-wide wireless network; laptops were provided to staff members for access to the college's resources via the wireless network; and a comprehensive system of training and support as well as one-to-one training and advice from the eLTS team was put in place.

Mark realised that the College had a fantastic resource in its student cohort many of whom had the knowledge and understanding of what technology can do and what they want in a learning environment. This eMentor programme is successful because of widespread support from the tutors who allowed their eMentor to share the responsibility of managing the IT and contributing to the e-learning for the class. This approach to learning has widespread benefits as the tutors and learners are involved in a more collaborative construction of the learning which fosters a deeper understanding of the work as topics are discussed and explored by students who are active participants in their learning. The Principal notes:

It is fantastic that the students involved in this eMentoring scheme are not only helping us immensely to ensure that new technology is used smoothly in the classroom, but they are also gaining valuable work experience, which will benefit them greatly when looking for work once they have finished their studies.

The learners coming through the system now expect a high level of interaction; they are always connected with their friends and the world through their high-powered 3G phones: they do not turn off, they are always online and our learning environment must cater for that. *Our investment in this vision of the future is firmly grounded in our understanding that it is the demands of our learners and their changing needs from a learning environment that drives this e-agenda.*

James Belmont, eMentor

Being an eMentor gave me the opportunity to get to know the tutors better who gave me more personal feedback on my work.

The role of eMentor was taken up by James when he began studying for a Foundation Degree in ICT and Multimedia and he saw the scheme as a chance to develop new skills and gain work experience. He enjoyed helping others who were less comfortable with technology and appreciated the opportunity to work more closely with his tutors. The sort of problems he was often called to assist on were helping connecting and calibrating the interactive board; offering a few tips about its use; and helping logging on to the network. He was proactive in his development of electronic resources and set up a peer-to-peer site for the sharing of files between tutors and students. This site was used by his peers to build a repository of useful resources and links for the duration of the course. This sharing helped develop a stronger sense of ownership of the learning for the students and created a valuable reference for tutors to use on other courses.

James's final research project was a study of the effectiveness of the eMentor scheme. He designed questionnaires which were placed on the College's VLE and collated the responses. He discovered a wide range of reactions to the scheme from the lecturers who actively involved their eMentor when developing online resources, creating podcasts of the class for revision, or integrating the social and collaborative facilities of Web 2.0 technologies; to the lecturers at the other end of the spectrum, who did not integrate ICT into the learning and teaching. The following are some of the lecturers' anonymous comments from James's questionnaire:

I have eMentors in all my groups and find them very useful.

Using the student expertise to assist myself and other students with computer technology has been very helpful.

Yes, having an eMentor in the classroom has saved time during a class and also enhanced the teaching and learning experience by being able to be more experimental in teaching methods and utilisation of on-line resources.

James recognises that being a part of this scheme has given him the opportunity to develop a wide range of skills.

Being an eMentor has given me lots of experience that I wouldn't have had otherwise. Presenting at meetings has improved my communication skills and I have learned to adapt my technical explanations to suit the audience. Although presenting at conferences still makes me nervous.

Matthew Reid, eMentor

I really enjoy this role. It has given me the chance to meet lots of people and learn new things and I feel as if I am part of the bigger picture at College.

Matthew is enrolled in the BTEC National Diploma in Animal Management. When he graduates, Matthew has several options which include continuing his study at University, pursuing a work option in a variety of areas in the animal sector, or going into business for himself. Matthew volunteered to be the eMentor in his class because he saw it as an opportunity to get valuable training in IT and to develop mentoring and communication skills. Matthew likes his role as he enjoys helping others and brings enthusiasm to the task of finding solutions when there is a technical breakdown. For example, the Animal Management area does not have good wireless connectivity and Matthew has at times had to help the tutor connect the computer to the projector via cables. They are still talking about the time he set off the projector alarm when using a broom handle to turn it on … the sheds in which they work have very high ceilings. But mostly Matthew finds that things run smoothly and the tutor is more relaxed knowing that he is there to help with technological glitches.

One of the ways that Matthew helps is in organising the student presentations. He gathers all the presentations for a session onto one memory stick so that there is no delay waiting for students to load and unload individual pen drives. It seems obvious, but it adds to the smooth running of a once complicated session in the classroom. Matthew has also been given editing rights in the VLE to the online course managed by his tutor. He uses

this to upload items related to their course of study and he also edits the Land-Based Studies page on the student intranet which is used to inform learners of current events.

The regular eMentor meetings are very helpful for Matthew who enjoys the developing sense of community in the group. They use them to say how they have helped the lecturers; to discuss ideas for further incorporating ICT; to share expertise or demonstration of new software; comment on systems and procedures; to review and recommend new resources. Matthew attends these meetings as often as he can to gain new perspectives on the role and maintain contact with other eMentors.

Antoinette Abunaw-Akinola, lecturer

Having an eMentor to help me in the class makes it possible to create a more open and relaxed environment where the learners can actively participate in their learning and share the responsibility of finding resources and presenting these to the rest of the class.

Antoinette teaches a variety of subjects and levels in the Health and Social Care curriculum area. Most of her learners are between the ages of 16 and 19. She has been at the College for two and a half years and has noticed a different institutional culture that encourages everyone to develop their IT skills and use technology more widely.

Antoinette is very conscious of her learners, all of whom have computers at home and are highly proficient in their use of multimedia and Web 2.0 technologies and as a consequence, they have high expectations of their learning environment. The pressure is on to provide a learning experience for these students that seamlessly blends available online and electronic resources with an interactive, stimulating experience that facilitates learning on every level. The students are regularly directed to their online learning space to get feedback on their work, revise using an online game that the tutor or her eMentor has developed or to get information about what to read or research before the next class so that it can be discussed in more detail and add more depth to the understanding of the topic.

The eMentor chosen for this class was very quiet and shy, struggled a bit with his written work but was intuitive with technology and had very good verbal skills; being an eMentor gave him an opportunity to shine in a different area. He was good at acting so he was able to use these skills to interact with the class and he became a completely different person when he was helping others; the eMentor went from being very shy and reserved to being able to stand in front of the class to give a demonstration. His enthusiasm encouraged Antoinette who developed a blended learning pedagogy (Garrison & Kanuka 2004) which allowed the students greater flexibility in managing their studies. She sourced materials suitable for online delivery and with the help of her eMentor, developed interactive learning activities and incorporated a range of communication channels, forums and wikis, largely managed by the eMentor. Being the eMentor gave him confidence and he used this confidence to encourage others to participate as well.

The lecturer's collaborative approach to learning means that the students have the opportunity to grow and develop as learners, building skills that they will need for the rest of their lives. Students are encouraged to check information from different sources during the class and report possible anomalies, thus developing essential critical thinking skills and over-riding the tendency to accept information on the internet at face value.

Clearly, the widespread use of IT at the College has really suited Antoinette. She is now at the stage where she will use IT automatically and naturally as part of her regular working practice: '*I don't even think about it anymore.*' She enjoys learning new things and is always looking for ways to be more efficient. '*I think I have managed the transition and I am always looking for new opportunities to learn something that will help me work better.*'

Sue Nicholls, lecturer

It is frustrating and unnerving for me when my skills don't match the technology introduced, it seems that I have just learned something and then it changes to something more complex. I need help with the technology when things go wrong, not later when I can get to the phone.

Sue Nicholls has worked at the college since 1993 and has taught Maths and Numeracy across many levels and classes ranging from adult numeracy for beginners to senior high school level as well as working closely with curriculum areas to embed key skills into their courses. She is lucky enough to have some of her classes in rooms with computers and she regularly directs learners to online resources for practice and revision. In the classroom, Sue likes having resources online which gives her more flexibility for managing the learning as she can divide her class according to individual needs with some students working independently online and others working one-to-one with her. Learners who are at different concept stages will need different teaching and learning activities and using a variety of IT resources makes this management easier for her.

Sue declined to be part of the formal eMentor scheme but the role of coping with the technology is shared by those in the class. She will occasionally try new resources in her classroom and often calls on the students to help with the set-up. So connecting to the projector or playing a CD becomes a collaborative effort and the responsibility is shared by the class. However, she has found that the adult classes are better at coping with trial and error and they have expertise and ideas to develop the resource. Sue does not use this tactic with the

14–19 year olds because she feels that they are not as patient and so she says she '*won't risk the innovation*' with the very group that needs it most.

Sue's expectations of herself as a teacher are very high and she is committed to providing a personalised learning classroom environment to a diverse range of students. She comments that '*the skills required of lecturers now have changed and it's assumed that everyone has IT skills*'. Sue feels that it does not allow for the fact that within a group of tutors there is a vast array of different skills and that her set of skills, which she is trying to update, is not appreciated. She feels isolated by the increasing pressure to develop a blended learning pedagogy which she does not feel she needs to do. She is happy using online resources when her students have access to computers, but she does not consider that the range of online and communicative technologies that are available have anything to do with her, or her teaching. However, in the classroom whenever Sue calls on the skills of her adult students she feels more relaxed about using IT and is encouraged to make use of the range of online resources available for her students.

DISCUSSION

The college's journey to enhance the learners' experience is not an isolated phenomenon. It is placed in a wider political context where various stakeholders all influence what is essentially, an education agenda. James and Biesta (2007) describe this as 'a complex interaction between many factors, dimensions and influences that shape the learning opportunities for students' (p. 4). Our approach is to take what is a national, or even a global phenomenon of change sweeping through the education sector, and make it personal. We recognise that 'changing culture is difficult because it is people who make cultures' (James & Biesta, 2007, p. 4). The dynamic relationship between members of a learning culture, their

differing life experiences and attitudes to learning, and their relative status in that group create a culture that is far from static. Each classroom, workshop, study group, workplace and so on creates a group of participants who share an understanding that learning is facilitated through the process of becoming a full participant in the sociocultural practice of the community. Students who expect to find technology as ubiquitous in their learning environment as it is in every other aspect of their lives exert pressure to include it. The lecturer, as a member of the community who is trying to engage the learners, needs to consider ways in which technology can facilitate progress towards a shared goal.

Sociocultural practice can also be one of the inhibiting factors in effecting wider cultural change. Although the college was committed to providing a learning experience for its students who expected a technology-rich environment it relies on a shift in teachers' pedagogical beliefs about learning and technology to fundamentally affect teaching practices (Ertmer, 2005; Sharp et al., 2006). Teachers were found to be more likely to change their beliefs about incorporating learning technologies into their practice when they 'were socialized by their peers to think differently about technology use' (Ertmer, 2005, p. 35). This shows the strong influence of the teachers' community of practice facilitating the exploration of new technologies and pedagogies and supporting each other in the transformation of classroom practice. Whilst in the classroom the teacher is encouraged by the community of learners who appreciate the pedagogic shift towards using technology, and supports this in the form of an eMentor who can offer technical assistance.

The Tech Angels project (Bolstad & Gilbert, 2006) describes a student mentoring programme that is similar in that it sets up a 'reverse mentoring' situation where the teacher is mentored by a student in using technology. The secondary school students were given training in applications and software and paired with a teacher to work together outside the classroom to develop the teacher's IT skills. It was hoped that the students would reinforce their own learning through their helping others to learn; and develop a better understanding of learning in general and their own learning in particular. For the tutors it gave them an opportunity to learn much-needed IT skills, although many resisted learning something if they did not think that it fitted into their pedagogy. All the teachers reported that they became involved for the benefit of the students so that those students could 'experience "the power of leadership" by becoming teachers' (p. 22). The role reversal was clearly unsettling for some. As for changing the culture, the authors note that 'Most did not recognise the project's possibilities for producing pedagogical change. Those who did were not convinced that this was a good thing' (Bolstad & Gilbert, 2006, p. 23).

So if the eMentors programme is so successful and the lecturers who have eMentors are so happy, why is it not adopted by everyone? The lecturers who were the first to take part in the eMentors scheme were those who were already very flexible in their approach to learning and teaching and who often tried new ideas and approaches to enhance the learning experience. They were confident enough to allow a student to step in and show them how to manage a technical element; their classrooms were organised on a shared understanding of respect and trust; and the growth and development of students' knowledge and understanding is just one of the outcomes. It could also be the case that many lecturers are already involving their students in the learning process and that there is an environment of participation and engagement, and they feel part of the process without formally joining the eMentor scheme. Sue Nicholls is an example of this. She is certainly not a signed-up member of the corporate eMentors scheme but she calls on her students to help with the management of the technology that she finds difficult. She demonstrably resents the increased emphasis that the college places on e-learning, and although she does have many online resources for her learners she resists the corporate insistence of change at every turn. She uses technology in the classroom to diversify the activities for the learners but hers is essentially a teacher-centred methodology and her students are not using technology to develop higher-order constructivist thinking and interpreting skills. Sue feels isolated by the increasing pressure to adopt a blended learning pedagogy and she is unwilling to change her fundamental beliefs. Her isolation is clearly mapped on the table (Figure 1) of the model described by Knoster, Villa and Thousand (2000) as she does not buy into the vision or participate in any of the activities or processes designed to ease the pain of change. On the other hand, Antoinette has clearly demonstrated an openness and willingness to adapt to the changing environment and review her learning and teaching strategies. She uses technology in every aspect of her course and collaborates with her eMentor to further develop its use. She encourages her students to take a critical approach to information they gather, checking sources and cross-referencing for consistency. Her student-centred, constructivist pedagogy develops high level critical thinking skills that students will use across all contexts.

Just because conditions seem right for change does not mean that change will take place. Change by its very nature stimulates resistance and people need time to adjust. The Tech Angels project and the eMentors scheme highlight common understandings about key principles that need to be in place to foster culture change. There needs to be strong leadership and a culture that supports an innovative approach to learning and teaching and supports the staff through relevant, inspiring staff development programmes; opportunities for staff to evaluate critically the purposes and practices of curriculum and pedagogy; an understanding that learning is socially constructed and that everyone in that community contributes; commitment to preparing the learners to the high demands of the 21st century community. (Bolstad & Gilbert, 2006)

The college's vision document recognises the ubiquitous incursion of technology into every aspect of our lives and it has a commitment to preparing its graduates, as the Principal put it in his interview: '*as learners who can be flexible and adapt to accommodate new workplace roles and responsibilities that haven't yet been imagined*'. This includes the learners who are on courses that are traditionally hands-on such as plumbing, trowel trades, beauty therapy, animal management. These lecturers come from an apprenticeship tradition which involves practical demonstration by the 'master' and then practice by the 'apprentice' as the skills required for the discipline are developed and honed. This traditional approach is an effective methodology when fostering skills and professional understandings in those entering a community of practice. The lecturers in these courses must now also incorporate skills required in new working practices that their 'apprentices' will face when they leave the college; skills that include competence with digital technology if an independent business person is to be visible in the competitive market. What we have observed is that these initially resistant lecturers, are leading the way in the production of video podcasts of a process or skill, demonstrated by the lecturer and filmed by a student which they then upload onto the VLE for later review. The eMentors and other students are also adding their own resources (from, for example, YouTube, Videojug) to develop a range of online demonstrations of something that was previously only seen in the workshop, salon or out in the field.

The role of eMentor is a formal recognition that all participants have a role in the learning and teaching environment. It recognises the collaborative, social nature of learning and develops the notion that roles can change according to the dictates of the situation. For example, one moment the lecturer is outlining the requirements of an assignment or class activity and in the next moment, the eMentor is demonstrating how to access these materials on the college's VLE. One of the unexpected, and in many ways immeasurable, consequences was the shift of the lecturers from 'pedagogic authoritarians viewing [students] as novices who *should*

be instructed' (Lave & Wenger, 1991, p. 76) to active participants in the learning and teaching environment. Lecturers felt that it was acceptable to admit to not knowing how to operate IT equipment that was unfamiliar; they were able to accept the assistance of a student which freed them from the anxiety of trying something new.

CONCLUSION

The eMentors scheme recognises that everyone has something to contribute to the group to which they belong. In the classroom context, the lecturer is the subject expert whose role is to guide the students towards their goal of achieving competency in a field of study or vocational programme; and the students also have expertise that can contribute to this learning. Many lecturers lack the skills and understanding to use the technology provided by the new ICT initiative and are unsure of introducing an element into the classroom that they cannot control. Although staff development is provided in regular scheduled sessions on a variety of topics and the staff have the opportunity for one-to-one help from the eLTS team, they are often unable to transfer what they learn from these sessions into the classroom environment. By situating the support in the classroom at the very time that it is needed, the lecturer has the opportunity to learn by doing at the very time that the instruction is required. This approach is more effective and gives the tutor the confidence to try something new knowing that there is assistance on-hand. For the student, this opportunity to share expertise helps to develop a strong sense of participation and fosters a sense of ownership. These improved relationships where expertise in different disciplines is recognised and respected can profoundly affect a student's perception of himself/herself as an active member of his/her learning community.

The evidence from case studies of the programme clearly shows that a much more collaborative and interactive teaching style ensued from the experience. Staff identified that relationships between eMentors and the staff they supported improved markedly and subsequently this created a better relationship between all students in the class and their lecturers. This more collaborative and active approach can be argued to have resulted in the significant gains in retention and achievement that resulted. When the lecturers were given a trusted eMentor in the classroom/workshop it broke down the resistance to using technology by making it easy to access help when needed and removing the stress often associated with implementing unfamiliar systems.

REFERENCES

Abowd, G. D., & Mynatt, E. D. (2000). Charting past, present, and future research in ubiquitous computing. [TOCHI]. *ACM Transactions on Computer-Human Interaction*, *7*(1), 29–58. doi:10.1145/344949.344988

Bolstad, R., & Gilbert, J. (2006). Creating digital age learners through school ICT projects: What can the Tech Angels project teach us? New Zealand Ccouncil for Educational Research. [Online] Retrieved November 3, 2009 from http://www.educationcounts.edcentre.govt.nz/__data/assets/pdf_file/0017/6614/ict-tech-angels.pdf

Brighouse, T. (2005). 'Remote' leadership and cultural change . In Coleman, M., & Earley, P. (Eds.), *Leadership and management in education* (pp. 102–114). Oxford: Oxford University Press.

Brown, J. S., Collins, A., & Duguid, P. (1989). Situated cognition and the culture of learning. *Educational Researcher*, *18*(1), 32–42.

Conole, G. (2008). Stepping over the edge: The implications of new technologies for education. In M. Lee,& C. McLoughlin (Eds.), *Web 2.0-based e-learning: Applying social informatics for tertiary teaching*. [Online] Retrieved July 28, 2009, from http://www.online-conference.net/jisc/content2008/conole/Conole_in_lee_mcloughlin.doc

Conole, G., Thorpe, M., Weller, M., Wilson, P., Nixon, S., & Grace, P. (2007). *Capturing practice and scaffolding learning design*. Paper presented at the Eden Conference. Milton Keynes, The Open University. [Online] Retrieved July 28, 2009, from http://labspace.open.ac.uk/file.php/1/kmap/1176712833/references/eden_conole_et_al_learning%20design%20final.doc

Donnelly, R., & O'Rourke, K. (2007). What now? Evaluating e-learning CPD Practice in Irish Third-Level Education. *Journal of Further and Higher Education*, *31*(1), 31–40. doi:10.1080/03098770601167864

Eales, R. T. J. (2003). Supporting informal communities of practice within organizations . In Ackerman, M., Pipek, V., & Wulf, V. (Eds.), *Beyond knowledge management: Sharing expertise*. Cambridge, MA: MIT Press.

Ertmer, P. (2005). Teacher pedagogical beliefs: The final frontier in our quest for technology integration? *ETR&D*, *53*(4), 25–39. doi:10.1007/BF02504683

Everett, R. (2006). *Addressing 'E': A pedagogic rationale for embedding e-learning in a large Further Education College*. Unpublished MA thesis, University of London: Institute of Education.

Everett, R. (2008). *Oaklands College Vision*. St Albans. [Online] Retrieved July 21, 2009, from http://info.rsc-eastern.ac.uk/file_security/get_file.aspx?id=1525

Fullan, M. (1999). *Change forces the sequel*. London, Philadelphia: Open University Press.

Fullan, M. (2001). *Leading in a culture of change*. San Francisco: Jossey-Bass.

Garrison, D., & Kanuka, H. (2004). Blended learning: Uncovering its transformative potential in Higher Education. *The Internet and Higher Education*, *7*(2), 95–105. doi:10.1016/j.iheduc.2004.02.001

Hargreaves, A., & Fullan, M. (2000). Mentoring in the new millennium. *Theory into Practice, 9*(1), 51–56.

Harris, J. (2008). eMentoring: The Future of online learner support. *Scientific Commons.* [Online] Retrieved April 10, 2009, from http://en.scientificcommons.org/40674734

Jackson, B., & Anagnostopoulou, K. (2001). Making the right connections: Improving quality in online learning . In Stephenson, J. (Ed.), *Teaching and learning online: Pedagogies for new technologies.* London: Kogan Page.

James, D., & Biesta, G. (Eds.). (2007). *Improving learning cultures in further education.* Oxon: Routledge.

Kent, T. (2002). Supporting staff using WebCT at the University of Birmingham. *Proceedings of the European Conference on E-Learning* (pp. 157-168). Brunel University, Uxbridge, UK.

Knoster, T., Villa, R., & Thousand, J. (2000). A framework for thinking about systems change . In Villa, R., & Thousand, J. (Eds.), *Restructuring for caring and effective education: Piecing the puzzle together* (pp. 93–128). Baltimore, MD: Paul H. Brookes Publishing Co.

Laurillard, D. (1993). *Rethinking University Teaching: A framework for the effective use of educational technology.* London: Routledge.

Lave, J., & Wenger, E. (1991). *Situated learning: Legitimate peripheral participation.* Cambridge: Cambridge University Press.

Lucas, B. (2006). Bringing e-learning home: An experiment in embedding e-learning using e-learning departmental advocates. In L. Markauskaite, P. Goodyear, & P. Reimann (Eds.), *Proceedings of the 23rd Annual Conference of the Australasian Society for Computers in Learning in Tertiary Education: Who's Learning? Whose Technology?* (pp. 479–482). Sydney: Sydney University Press.

Mason, R., & Rennie, F. (2006). *Elearning: The key concepts.* Oxon: Routledge.

Oaklands (2009). *Oaklands 2011–Vision to Reality.* St Albans. [Online] Retrieved July 21, 2009, from http://www.oaklands.ac.uk/about/strategy.aspx

Prensky, M. (2001). Digital natives, digital immigrants *On the Horizon, 9*(5). [Online] Retrieved October 20, 2009, from http://www.marcprensky.com/writing/Prensky%20-%20Digital%20Natives,%20Digital%20Immigrants%20-%20Part1.pdf

Rogers, E. M. (1964). *Diffusion of innovations.* Glencoe: Free Press.

Salmon, G. (2002). *E-tivities: The key to active online learning.* Oxon: Routledge.

Scott Morton, M. S. (Ed.). (1991). *The Corporation of the 1990s: Information technology and organizational transformation.* Oxford: Oxford University Press.

Sharpe, R., Benfield, G., & Francis, R. (2006). Implementing a university e-learning strategy: Levers for change within academic schools. *ALT-J. Research in Learning Technology, 14*(2), 135–151.

Sheey, M., Marcus, G., Costa, F., & Taylor, R. (2006). Implementing e-learning across a faculty: Factors that encourage uptake. *Proceedings of the 23rd Annual Conference of the Australasian Society for Computers in Learning in Tertiary Education: Who's Learning? Whose Technology?* [Online] Retrieved July 21, 2009, from http://www.ascilite.org.au/conferences/sydney06/proceeding/pdf_papers/p120.pdf

Vygotsky, L. S. (1978). *Mind in society: The development of higher psychological processes.* Cambridge, MA: Harvard University Press.

Wenger, E. (1998). *Communities of practice: Learning, meaning and identity.* Cambridge: Cambridge University Press.

Wenger, E., McDermott, R., & Snyder, W. M. (2002). *Cultivating Communities of Practice.* Boston, MA: Harvard Business School Press.

Zhang, D. (2004). Virtual mentor and the LBA System: Towards building an interactive, personalized, and intelligent e-learning environment. *Journal of Computer Information Systems, 44*(3), 35–43.

ADDITIONAL READING

Ackerman, M., Volkmar, P., & Volker, W. (2003). *Sharing expertise: Beyond knowledge management.* London: The MIT Press.

Bruner, J. (1996). *The culture of education.* London: Harvard University Press.

Ford, P., Goodyear, P., Heseltine, R., Lewis, R., Darby, J., & Graves, J. (1996). *Managing change in Higher Education.* Buckingham: Society for Research into Higher Education.

Gallacher, J., Crossan, E., Mayes, T., Cleary, P., Smith, L., & Watson, D. (2006). *Expanding our understanding of the learning cultures in community based further education.* Paper presented at the British Educational Research Association Conference, Warwick, 2006.

Hannan, A., & Silver, H. (2000). *Innovating in Higher Education.* Buckingham: Society for Research into Higher Education.

Hargreaves, A., & Fink, D. (2000). The three dimensions of reform. *Educational Leadership, 57*(7), 30–33.

Hodkinson, P., Anderson, G., Colley, H., Davies, J., Diment, K., & Scaife, T. (2007). Learning cultures in Further Education. *Educational Review, 59*(4), 399–413. doi:10.1080/00131910701619290

Hodkinson, P., & James, D. (2003). Transforming elearning cultures in Further Education. *Journal of Vocational Education and Training, 55*(4), 389–406. doi:10.1080/13636820300200236

James, D., & Bloomer, M. (2001). *Cultures and learning in Further Education.* Paper presented at British Educational Research Association Annual Conference, University of Leeds, September 13-15, 2001.

Kleiman, G. M. (2004). Myths and realities about technology in K-12 schools: Five years later. *Contemporary Issues in Technology and Technology and Teacher Education, 4*(2), 248–253.

O'Connell, B. (2005). *Creating an outstanding college.* Cheltenham: Nelson Thomas Ltd.

Chapter 16

The Student Perspective:
Can the Use of Technologies Transform Learning?

Eileen O'Donnell
Dublin Institute of Technology, Ireland

ABSTRACT

This chapter explores students' perspectives on the transformations that the use of technology has brought to higher education. The use of technologies in higher education facilitates flexible learning environments but the benefits to students who engage with these technologies will only be realised if the design is pedagogically sound. The pedagogic approach employed by lecturers when designing their e-learning platforms or learning management systems has the capability to transform learning. The author's discipline is Information Technology and Business Information Systems; from experience and case studies there is ample evidence to suggest that the use of technology does not always necessarily meet user requirements. Students are the end users of the technologies that educators use to enhance students' learning experiences. This chapter was undertaken to obtain students' perspectives (as the end users) on the uses of technologies in higher education to assist educators in improving the pedagogical design of their e-learning platforms. The responses received from students clearly indicate they are of the opinion that the use of technologies in higher education beneficially transforms learning but will never replace lecturers. In essence, the benefits that can be achieved through the use of technologies are totally dependent on the ways they are employed pedagogically by lecturers.

INTRODUCTION

Increasingly technology is pervading all areas of education. As part of the Dublin Institute of Technology's Strategic Plan, a Learning Tech-

nology Team was established in 2003 to roll out the institutional virtual learning environment. Students are the end users of the information systems that educators use to enhance students' learning experiences. This chapter was undertaken to obtain students' perspectives (as the end users) on the uses of technologies in higher education

DOI: 10.4018/978-1-61520-879-1.ch016

to assist educators in improving the pedagogical design of e-learning platforms alternatively known as learning management systems.

The use of technology has modified the ways that some lecturers distribute course materials to students, i.e., no longer do all students transcribe notes from blackboards/whiteboards. Course materials are disseminated online through files of course notes, PowerPoint presentations, podcasts, video casts and web links. The use of technology has also brought alterations to students' ability to communicate with lecturers and fellow students, through the use of e-mail, discussion boards, online chat rooms and wikis. In addition, technology has changed the ease with which students can access further information to read outside of the course material and conduct research through the use of online journals and databases.

Academics are very often encouraged to create an online presence without ever having studied online themselves or even considered the pedagogical impact that technology can have on the students' learning experience. Salmon (2000) stated that the use of the World Wide Web for learning and teaching was set to dramatically increase, and the onus was on all lecturers using technology to ensure that they familiarised themselves with the pedagogical skills necessary to ensure that the technologies used effectively enhanced the learning experience of students.

An important point to note is that technologies are simply tools at the disposal of educators. The beneficial transformations in learning that can be achieved through the use of technologies depend on the skill levels and commitment of the educators, similar to all professionals' effective use of tools. When employing the use of technologies to transform learning a number of issues need to be considered, amongst them student perspectives, the learning experience, teacher–student and student–student relationships, learning outcomes, and so on, to ensure that the lecturers' pedagogical skills are utilised to best effect. Should any educators believe that their pedagogical approach does not require enhancement from the use of technologies that is their prerogative.

Broad, Matthews, and McDonald (2004) proposed that despite students' prolific use of new technology, there is no need for academics to presume that students are disposed towards academic use of the Internet in the higher education sector, and they question whether the use of technology in education is supported by sound educational rationales and that 'this strategy has not yet been pedagogically proven' (p. 135). All the effort that lecturers, who employ the use of technologies with their students, put into creating suitable content is wasted unless students actively engage with and gain some benefits from using the material provided. As a result of a study conducted by Löfström and Nevgi (2007) at the University of Helsinki, Finland, the authors suggest that 'Experiences of relevance and meaningfulness are central facilitators of learning. In this context, meaningful learning entails learner activity and intentionality, application of constructivist principles, collaboration, dialogue, reflection, connection to context and transferability of knowledge' (p. 315). Educators should keep this in mind when designing material for use with technological devices.

McLoughlin's (2000) experiences from working in the Teaching and Learning Centre at the University of New England in Australia, lead her to suggest that despite the prolific availability of online teaching tools there is no established approach on how to develop quality learning programmes that make the best use of these tools, which can only be achieved by educators forming a deeper understanding of how technology can affirm and extend the principles of good teaching. Slevin (2008) from Roskilde University in Denmark, states that concentration upon practical problems associated with the opportunities afforded by modern technology draws attention away from the theoretical concerns posed by e-learning. Apart from reading books and articles on the use of technologies in higher education, educators who attend e-learning and teaching

Summer schools, conferences and seminars, afford themselves the opportunity to form a deeper understanding of how technology can affirm and extend the principles of good teaching through shared experiences.

BACKGROUND

On commencing an introductory course to using an electronic learning (e-learning) platform, the extent of the task can seem quite daunting, even to educators who are literate in Information and Communications Technologies. 'Developing an e-learning course demands a range of contributions: subject, technical, design and resource expertise' (Connolly, Jones, & Jones, 2007, p. 164). It takes time for lecturers to familiarise themselves with the use of an electronic learning platform, to compile learning material in a suitable format to use technologically with students and to realise the pedagogical benefits that can be achieved by using technologies in different ways. Trial and error and discussions with colleagues on their experiences of using technologies with their students is possibly the best way forward for lecturers embarking on using technologies with their students. However, in order to make e-learning courses successful student perspectives and feedback on the use of technologies in higher education must be heeded and taken into consideration.

The use of technologies in higher education has increased the modes of delivery of information to students by making information more readily available and ubiquitous. The association between classrooms and lecture halls as primary places of learning has ceased to exist (Slevin, 2008). Learning is now perceived as ubiquitous, occurring any time regardless of location, which makes further education more accessible to people who previously would not have had the opportunity, for example, people who work shifts and are unable to attend structured classes on a regular basis; alternatively students who fall ill or pregnant during the course of their study can still continue to keep up with the class even though their presence in the classroom is no longer feasible. James, Bexley, Devlin, and Marginson (2007) conducted a national survey of Australian university student finances and found that '22.7% of full-time undergraduate students and 37.4% of part-time undergraduate students regularly missed classes because they needed to attend employment for survival and to purchase study materials, as did around one quarter of all postgraduate students' (p. 2). The learning materials designed by academics to use with technological tools increase the opportunity for students who are unable to attend all lectures provided to attain higher educational qualifications.

Some educators have expressed concerns that students lack the skills to critically evaluate the information they find on the Internet and that use of the Internet can lead to information overload. Hence, lecturers should provide guidance to students to assist them in focusing their ability to identify reliable and peer-reviewed sources of information and supply students with links to websites that provide suitable learning activities. Students can also learn from online learning activities in ways not previously envisioned by the lecturers 'Many researchers and theorists have observed that much learning occurs online, even if it seems to be off-task from a well-identified learning activity' (Shank, 2008, p. 255). The use of technology in education has altered the ways in which lecturers and students can interact and has expanded the volume of information that students can access in order to develop a broader knowledge of the subject under consideration. This chapter explores some examples of where the use of technologies can transform student learning, and provides some students' perspectives on academic use of technologies in higher education.

The objectives of this chapter are to establish students' perspectives on a number of issues related to the use of technologies that educators employ to augment and possibly enhance their teaching methods in higher education and to obtain students' views on whether it is possible for the effective use of technological tools to transform learning. In the context of this study, the term transform learning implies all the changes, alterations, modifications, improvements, developments, and so on, that the functionality, made possible through the use of technology, can make to the students' learning experience. The functionality provided by e-learning platforms enabled by the use of technology includes ubiquitous access to course documentation, PowerPoint presentations, podcasts, video casts, e-mail, discussion boards, chat facilities, and so forth. The competence of the lecturers' skills when designing course content is paramount to the learning achieved by students who engage with e-learning platforms.

Communications technology enables students to connect to the World Wide Web in order to access e-learning platforms, learning management systems, electronic journals and the wealth of information that is available through this medium. In addition, technology facilitates communication with lecturers and other students through the use of e-mail, discussion boards, chat facilities, wikis, blogs, and so on.

Methodology

This study was conducted in the Faculty of Business, Dublin Institute of Technology. An evaluation of current literature was performed to identify key attributes to be explored; from these attributes statements were devised to seek student perspectives regarding the issues identified. A survey was compiled to ascertain students' perspectives on the use of technology in transforming learning.

The survey was designed with three sections:

(i) A list of 27 statements was created, for students to evaluate using a five point Likert scale, (i.e. strongly agree, agree, neutral, disagree, strongly disagree).

(ii) Very basic personal information was sought such as gender, level of study and current year of study.

(iii) The third section provided students with the opportunity to share any other perspectives that they had on the questions 'Can the use of technologies transform learning?' and 'What use of technology has the most beneficial impact on student learning?'

A sample of full-time business students were approached in April 2009, and requested to complete a paper-based survey to establish their perspectives on 'Can the use of technologies transform learning?' The questionnaires were collected soon after distribution. A controlled group was not selected to avoid the opportunity of the students being biased by what they perceived expectations to be, which would inadvertently influence responses and skew statistical analysis derived from this data.

The students surveyed were advised in writing before completion of the survey that their perspectives were sought to enable the author to write a chapter for a book. Permission was sought and granted from the Dublin Institute of Technology's Research Ethics Committee (2009) to conduct this study in the Dublin Institute of Technology. The survey was reviewed by several academic colleagues and their comments taken on board before distribution to students for completion.

Results and Discussion

From the initial survey completed by 164 students, 4 surveys were not included in the analysis because of missing data. 74 respondents were male, 66 were female and 20 chose not to identify their gender. Further research could be conducted to establish if there are dominant preferences for particular uses of technological tools attributed to gender. Statistics were compiled on students' perspectives regarding the use of technology in higher education from data collected and a comparison of the findings of this study with the findings of other peer reviewed studies follows.

Student Perspectives

Overall, students' perspectives on the use of technology in higher education are quite positive. However, their perspectives clearly show that they still appreciate the benefits of having face-to-face tutorials with lecturers and face-to-face interaction with peers.

In this study 91% of business students agreed that the use of technologies in higher education makes a positive difference to studying. Similar to this study, Rogers (2004) sought students' opinions on the use of online learning and how it had impacted on their learning; his findings on students' perceptions of online learning are also positive with 79% responding that 'online learning made a positive difference to studying history' (p. 244).

Rogers (2004) found that 72% of students responded that online learning had developed their ability to work as a team members. In contrast to Rogers' (2004) findings this study found that 39% of business students agreed that online learning develops students' ability to work as team members, 39% were neutral in this instance and 21% disagreed. The high number of students that were neutral in this instance could be related to the fact that they lacked personal experience of working online in teams; this area possibly needs to be explored in more detail. However, 68% of business students agreed that technology facilitates a student-centred environment that was not possible before. It is important to remember that it is the design skills and implementation methods employed by lecturers that influence the online environment that students engage with and subsequently the learning outcomes achieved by students from using online learning environments.

Podcasts and video casts are used by teachers to provide alternative ways of delivering course material to the student population. This technology can also be used to record student activity from which they can also learn, for example, students participating in a civil discourse, public-speaking class at a private comprehensive university in the Pacific Northwest, North America, through the use of technology, for instance recording their presentation on video tapes, were able to judge previous presentations that they had made in order to reflect upon their changing stance on various controversial topics under discussion (Gayle, 2004). This example showed how students involved in a debating class were able to use technology to record and review their debating techniques, which enabled them to compare changes in their attitudes after exposure to multiple perspectives on a controversial topic. In this instance it has been shown that the use of technology can transform learning. As students reflected on their presentations they got the chance to identify shortcomings and confront their own assumptions, which enabled them to improve their delivery and more importantly forced them to open their minds to the thoughts and opinions of others.

As part of this survey, business students were asked for their agreement or disagreement on the ability of discussion boards to force students to open their minds to the thoughts and opinions of others. Discussion boards provide students with the opportunity to review their own submissions and reflect upon their previous submissions and how their views might have changed as a result of alternative viewpoints presented by fellow students (peers). This study of business students found that 55% agreed that online discussion boards force students to open their minds to the thoughts and opinions of others, 30% had no opinion on this statement. The high number of students who contributed no opinion on this statement could be attributed to the fact that they had no personal experience of using discussion boards. In a previous study conducted on business students in the DIT, only 20% of students had used an e-learning platform to participate in discussion boards (O'Donnell, 2008).

The Learning Experience

Churchill (2005), an Educational Developer in the United Kingdom, recommends that in order for the use of technologies to effectively enhance the students' learning experience, minimum requirements should be clearly outlined for the students by the lecturers, thus informing students of the lecturers' expectations of their participation with e-learning; for example 'The absolute minimum requirement to be able to continue on the course is logging on twice a week' (p. 50). Students should be given clear guidance on how the lecturer expects them to use technologies to enhance their learning. Blended learning is where a suitable combination of traditional teaching and e-learning are combined to enhance students' level of attainment from a particular course of study.

In this research 68% of business students agreed that the quality of students' learning is enhanced by using technology to augment lectures: this would be in the form of blended learning. This level of agreement implies that students believe that online learning or distance learning on its own does not achieve the same level of student attainment as blending e-learning with traditional teaching methods. Condie and Livingston (2007), while conducting a study of one particular online programme designed for students in the post-compulsory years of secondary schooling in Scotland, also found that while online learning did appear to have a positive influence on attainment, the evidence suggested that attainment might have been greater had the teachers modified their methods by combining online learning with more traditional methods (blended learning). Gilbert, Morton, and Rowley (2007) conducted a study of 19 students across the globe participating in an online course of study leading to M.Sc. Information Technologies and Management (e-Learning) to obtain an insight into the students' perspective on the experience and concluded that more in-depth studies would enhance understanding of how e-learning can contribute to enhancing the quality of learning.

This study found that 54% of business students agreed that podcasts and video casts of lectures would facilitate student learning more so than handouts. McKinney, Dyck, and Luber (2009) on examining student attitudes about using podcasts found that 'students believed that pod-casts helped them revise notes more effectively than textbooks' (p. 618). In this study 59% of business students agreed that using podcasts or video casts for revision purposes improves recall more so than revising course notes, 26% were neutral, 15% disagreed and one student commented that 'Yes, it makes things quicker, more entertaining and easier to revise'.

Web teaching can effectively enhance the learning experience of students through the use of bulletin boards, resources and databases, online quizzes, student portal pages, e-journals, assignment submission, sharing of files, graphics, and so on, to augment course material (McLoughlin, 2000). Results from the student survey showed that 82% of students agreed that using technology in higher education effectively enhances the learning experience of students. O'Donnell (2008) came to the same conclusion in a study for a master's thesis; 77% of students and 61% of lecturers agreed that using an e-learning platform as a form of blended learning improves the learning experience of students more than using traditional teaching methods. In addition 68% of students and 59% of lecturers agreed that using an e-learning platform as a form of blended learning is better for preparing students for work than traditional teaching methods (O'Donnell, 2008).

Several times over the last few years at various seminars and courses, lecturers have expressed concerns that using e-learning platforms will effectively lead to the demise of the teaching profession and ultimately their redundancy. Donnelly and O'Rourke (2007) also noted that some academic staff in Irish higher education institutions believed that the introduction of an online learning environment could lead to their own redundancy.

In this study, 66% of business students disagreed that the use of technology in higher education will make lecturers disposable. Two thirds of students disagreeing that the use of technology in higher education will make lecturers disposable should be reassuring to lecturers who believe that the use of technology in education is a threat to their employment. One of the students commented that 'Yes, technology can transform learning, but only as an aid, not as a replacement'. The third section of the survey afforded students the opportunity to share any other perspectives on the question 'Can the use of technology transform learning?' Over 50% of the 32 students that completed this section commented that technology could never replace lectures/lecturers/class discussions/debates and interaction. O'Neill, Singh, and O'Donoghue (2004) came to the same conclusion that technology can be used to enhance the learning experience of students, but not replace the lecturer. In addition to this argument, 58% of business students disagreed with the statement that the use of technology in education could successfully replace the learning achieved through interaction with lecturers.

The third section of the survey gave students the opportunity to share their opinions regarding 'What use of technology has the most beneficial impact on student learning?' Seventy-six of the students responded to this question, responses were analysed as per Table 1. Some students referred to more than one beneficial use of technology.

Attendance at Lectures

Professors/lecturers will not be replaced any time soon according to Wilson and Christopher (2008), two educators based in Colorado, United States of America, who also suggest that e-learning depends on lecturers in order for the whole system to run effectively, from planning and design to management and delivery, as well as being role models and providing guidance for students (p.65). The overall findings of the research conducted in the Faculty of Business concur with the above opinions as 72% of the students surveyed disagreed with the statement that there is no longer any need to attend lectures because course notes available online are a good substitution. This may be the case, but still 52% of business students agreed that having course notes available online makes them more likely to skip the occasional lecture. Yet again, 80% of students agreed that attending formal lectures facilitates a deeper understanding of course content than online access. One student

Table 1. Students' Opinions on What Use of Technology Has the Most Beneficial Impact on Student Learning?

What use of technology has the most beneficial impact on student learning?	Number of students who mentioned this use
Online lecture notes/podcasts/video casts/e-learning	40
Ability to access a large selection of information	20
Access to academic journals/databases/books/library	13
Internet access	12
No time constraints, access anytime, day or night	5
Contact e-mail	3
Ubiquitous – accessible from anywhere in the world	2
Home office packages	2
Multiple choice testing	1

commented that 'Yes, I think technologies can transform learning but also that lectures and class interaction increase further learning'. So even though half of the student population that completed this survey agreed that having course notes available online makes them more likely to skip the occasional lecture, they still appreciate the fact that attending formal lectures facilitates a deeper understanding of course content.

This study found that 52% disagreed that watching a video cast of a lecture would be as educationally beneficial as attending the lecture in person. Similar to the findings of this study McKinney et al. (2009) found that although 60% of undergraduate general psychology students felt that computer-based lectures were appealing, they still preferred the traditional lecture.

Teacher–Student and Student–Student Relationships

Computer-mediated communication is increasingly being used in higher education, along with other technological enabling opportunities to supplement face-to-face interaction with lecturers and fellow students. Lecturers need to shift the level of control from that of the lecturer to that of the student to enable students to become self-regulated, reflective learners who have developed independent study habits (Jelfs & Colbourn, 2002). Light, Nesbitt, Light, and Burns (2000) recognise that the atmosphere between students within the computer-mediated communication area must be supportive, rather than hostile or competitive in order for successful learning to be achieved. When designing online interactive communication tools for students it is paramount for the success of the learning activity that educators advise their students that the rules of netiquette should be observed when working online. This is possibly significantly more important than the way that etiquette should be observed during discourse with lecturers and fellow students in a classroom situation. Body language, a nudge and a wink can

convey a joke is intended in a real life situation, but in an online environment, the written word or recorded electronic data can have a more lasting effect on an individual, than a quick, murmured comment. Because of the nature of stored electronic data, the data can be revisited again by the victim and the hurt occasioned repeatedly, also, more people may be privy to the exchange, which can increase the hurt felt by the victim.

In this survey, 31% of business students agreed that computer-mediated communications achieve a more in-depth insight than classroom discussions, 33% were neutral, and 36% disagreed with the statement. The findings on this statement are inconclusive possibly due to students' lack of experience using computer-mediated communication or students' insufficient knowledge of what learning can be achieved through effective use of computer-mediated communication. This is a very interesting area, and further investigation is needed to establish whether or not beneficial learning can take place as a result of students using computer-mediated communication. An interesting comment on this issue made by one student was:

Yes, technology can transform learning, it enables people to work to their own pace, e.g. if they are a night time student. However, attending lectures allows students to engage in debates and discussions which are fundamental to social skills because online discussions mean people don't have to think on their feet.

This students' perspective is very intuitive, because in life there is a need to know when to respond immediately and when to pause and think before making a contribution, and of course, students need the ability to do both.

Students' satisfaction can be influenced by quality instruction, instruction that accommodates various learner/student characteristics/learning orientations (Overbaugh & ShinYi, 2006). When designing content suitable for electronic delivery, the designer must consider contemporary student characteristics and identify the tools most appropriate for each learning orientation and create a range of course activities that will encompass as many of the preferred learning orientations as possible. 'The Felder & Silverman theory categorizes an individual's preferred learning style by a sliding scale of four dimensions: sensing-intuitive, visual-verbal, active-reflective and sequential-global' (Park, 2005, p. 2). Course material that has been purposely developed to suit the learning abilities and learning styles of a wide range of students should be instrumental in keeping the attention of a broader range of students. Mainemelis, Boyatzis and Kolb (2002) conducted research on student learning preferences and suggested that web-based learning as a pedagogical approach poses an interesting research question.

One of the dilemmas for lecturers in trying to accommodate various learning preferences is whether to give out all course material at the start of the academic year or to enable student access to each topic prior to or subsequent to each individual lecture. This research found that 80% of business students agreed that if course material was available online at the commencement of term it would markedly change students' ability to learn at their own pace. 'These electronic opportunities theoretically allow students to organize their own learning to suit their lifestyle' (Light, Nesbitt, Light, & Burns, 2000, p. 85).

Once the material provided by lecturers is sufficiently absorbing, students should be suitably engaged to ensure satisfaction with the course, therefore, improving student attrition rates. This research found that 80% of business students agreed that the use of technology in higher education increased their satisfaction with their course of study. Obviously other factors such as personal circumstances, change of course preference, and so on, will also influence student attrition rates and satisfaction with courses in all disciplines.

In this study 47% of students agreed that the use of video casts would be superior to podcasts for enhancing students' understanding of course material. Video casts enable students to observe the body language of the lecturer which is an important factor of communication and, in addition, to see any supporting blackboard/whiteboard or PowerPoint (2009) presentations displayed, or even any demonstrations that are taking place, while also benefiting from responses to any questions posed by students attending the class.

Access to Information

Some 55% of students disagreed with the statement that they prefer accessing journal articles from hardcopies in the library to accessing journals online. Online journals make access to peer-reviewed work much more easily obtainable and less time-consuming than visiting libraries and trawling through hardbound copies of journals, which subsequently have to be photocopied. Numerous files and articles from electronic journals can be magnetically stored by academics and students conducting research on a technological device called a memory key. Memory keys or USB (Universal Serial Bus) keys are small portable electronic storage devices which are compatible with most desktops and laptops. Printing from the electronic version is more user friendly than photocopying page by page. The time that is saved by using technology when conducting research can be better spent critically evaluating the relevance of the identified work.

Another 63% of students disagreed with the statement that when they come across an acronym or new concept with which they are unfamiliar, they seek clarification in the library first and then online. Hardbound encyclopaedias are no longer a first call of reference to seek information on any subject; the Internet offers an abundance of information on all topics. It is generally accepted in today's society that people expect immediate gratification. Students' satisfaction with their course of study is enhanced by the use of the Internet to aid them in understanding any new terms or concepts introduced with which they are unfamiliar. This speed of access to information was not previously achievable. 'Four out of five students believe that Internet use has had a positive impact on their academic experience, and three out of four say they use the Internet for research more than they do the library' (Hartman, Moskal, & Dziuban, 2005, p. 6.3).

A wiki is a web-based document which enables a group of users to add and edit content using only their web browser (Bayne, 2008). In this study 40% of business students agreed that using wiki interfaces increases the value of the students' learning experience, 42% were neutral and 18% disagreed with this statement. The fact that 42% of students were neutral in their opinions on the use of wiki interfaces increasing the value of students' learning experience could be through lack of experience of using wiki interfaces in the higher education learning environment. This could be an interesting area to explore in future research. The objective when getting students to work collaboratively online through the use of wikis using Web 2.0 is to ensure that the pedagogical requirements of the learning experience are met and that the students are involved in content generation and social networking. Jelfs and Colbourn (2002) concluded that there were positive correlations between how comfortable students felt while taking part in virtual seminars and the value of the learning experience undertaken.

Gilbert et al. (2007) conducted a student evaluation of an e-learning module on an M.Sc. in Information Technology and Management, and found that the use of discussion boards and support from other students (peers) were the most frequently cited aspects of the learning process and in general, students felt that they learnt from their peers. In this study 55% of business students disagreed that the use of technology in education could successfully replace the learning achieved through face-to-face interaction with fellow students (peers), 24% were neutral and 21% agreed with the statement. Lea (2001) suggested that

computer conferencing can enable students to reflect upon subject-based knowledge in ways that were not possible in more traditional teaching environments and emphasised the importance of students learning from each other in a collaborative learning environment.

Learning Outcomes and Skills Development

Learning outcomes must be realised, developed and fine tuned over time, and interventions made based on the findings. Broad et al. (2004) tentatively concluded that the use of an Integrated Virtual Learning Environment (IVLE) can facilitate student learning, however, their measurements of improved student performance were less conclusive. Assessment of critical thinking is one of the most difficult to quantity as per the experience of Peach, Mukherjee, and Hornyak (2007). 'Increased scrutiny about student learning outcomes seems ubiquitous at a time when higher education and accreditation agencies are still grappling with identifying the best measures of these outcomes' (Sullivan & Thomas, 2007, pp. 321–322). This may be so, but it is paramount to the success of the educational system to establish a recognised process to identify the best ways to improve students' critical thinking skills and how to measure student learning outcomes. Rogers (2004) researched the ability to measure improvement in critical thinking skills in history students and how this ability would be influenced by students' pre-conceived ideas and the nature of the assessments used, and referred to the fact that it would be audacious to claim that his study had found solutions to the difficult questions encountered. When the question regarding critical thinking skills was put to the student participants in the Faculty of Business 54% of them agreed that the use of technology in higher education improves students' critical thinking skills.

In this study 45% of business students agreed that the learning experience of students would be altered for the better if lecturers discussed topics in class prior to making the notes available online. This statement could well depend on the maturity of the students. Some students, for instance, prefer to study the topic to be discussed prior to the lecture to enable them to put questions to the lecturer to facilitate their understanding of the topic. A comparison of undergraduate and postgraduate student perspectives on this topic would be an interesting study for future research.

'In traditional lecture formats, students are note-takers, listeners, and observers' (Trees & Jackson, 2007, p. 23). This research found that 49% of business students agreed that they would be forced to learn more in lectures if they had to make their own notes (as opposed to having the notes available online). 'Personally taking notes (as opposed to being given full notes of a lecture) was more important to higher educational outcomes. Higher scores were obtained by students that created their own notes' (McKinney et al., 2009, p. 618). These findings are interesting and perhaps may lead lecturers towards enabling students' access to lecture notes subsequent to the lecture taking place, to encourage students to make their own set of notes during the lecture. Due to a basic fact of life that lecturers can speak faster than students can write, students have to summarise what lecturers say in order to keep up with the class. This process of summarising content forces students to consciously think about what the lecturer is saying in order to select the most salient points to note. The mere process of writing engages brain activity which will also improve retention. Although, one student's perspective was that 'Being able to add your own notes to the notes available online ... learning is decreased if you're concentrating on taking lots of notes instead of listening to the lecturer'. Here different viewpoints have come to light on note-taking; this could be attributed to the acknowledged existence of different learning preferences and styles.

Ambrose (2001), an e-learning officer based in Brisbane, concluded from personal experience as an online learner that in order for lecturers to be successful in their delivery of e-learning they must possess organisational, intellectual and social facilitation skills in order to provoke intelligent responses from students and create group harmony. The fact that 81% of business students agreed that the use of technology in higher education improves student engagement with course material indicates that the lecturers that do use technologies as part of their pedagogical approach with students are obviously using the right approach and gaining student recognition for their efforts.

Treleaven and Cecez (2001) from the University of Western Sydney, New South Wales, found that approaching assessment and submission dates had the effect of rapidly increasing the number of postings students made to the bulletin board. Lecturers can monitor students' engagement and participation in online discussion boards, quizzes and multiple choice attempts, in order to identify the students who are actively getting involved with the course material and fellow students, and those who are not. This research found that 50% of business students agreed that collaborative online research affords the lecturer the opportunity to identify the students that are making the most worthwhile contributions.

FUTURE RESEARCH DIRECTIONS

One future research direction which is of particular interest to the author is the appropriateness of the employment of adaptive e-learning, to personalise the online learning experience of the individual student. This approach to online learning would facilitate students' individual learning styles and preferences.

The findings of this research have identified several areas requiring further investigation, which may provide a more valuable insight, including:

- To establish whether or not beneficial learning can take place as a result of students using computer-mediated communication.

- Can the use of wiki interfaces increase the value of students' learning?
- To conduct a comparison of undergraduate and postgraduate students' perspectives on whether studying class notes prior to a lecture facilitates deeper understanding.
- To establish if there are dominant preferences for particular uses of technological tools attributed to gender.

An interesting comment made by a student was 'It should be noted that even with the increase in technology within academic learning situations, both lectures and lecturers will never become redundant. As the degrees of computer literacy in Ireland to-date varies too much.' Not only is computer literacy an issue, broadband access and speeds can also have a big influence on students' ability to engage with technology. In addition, with the current economic climate, people are not investing in the latest computer technology, as in desktops and laptops, although iPod sales are performing better than expected. This trend could also impact on students' ability to effectively work with technology on an equal footing, as some students will have access to higher performance desktops and laptops than others. Another area that could be explored is whether the current economic climate will impact on the volume of households subscribing to broadband access? This could be considered as a luxury, not a necessity to some, and could impact on students' ability to engage with learning technologies from their homes or rented accommodations.

CONCLUSION

The statistics outlined in this chapter indicate that even though students expect technologies to be used in higher education, they realise that lecturers form the backbone of third-level education, and while technologies can effectively be used to enhance students' learning experience, the use of technologies in higher education will never replace the lecturers.

There is no indication at all to suggest that students wish to see academic staff removed from their educational experience. Students realise the benefits to be achieved from face-to-face interaction with lecturers and peers. Even though students have identified some beneficial uses of technologies in their learning experience, the human aspect is missing, as one student commented 'Technology's major fault is that you cannot easily ask a question. Lecturers will be able to answer immediately, while searching through computer data may lead the answer seeker astray.' Hence, the use of technologies can enhance the learning experience of students, but lecturers are required for guidance and support.

The use of technology in higher education has certainly made information more readily available to students than before, but providing adequate guidance and instruction, basically educating students on how to effectively turn this information into knowledge, is still the responsibility of lecturers. One student commented that 'Lecturers will always be needed. Technology cannot always be trusted.'

In order for e-learning to be a success, university management and staff must take ownership of e-learning and satisfy themselves that pedagogy can be maintained, even though the medium of delivery is changing. The use of technological devices as enabling tools in higher education appears to bring some advantages, however, to quote one student 'It helps definitely, but I do not think it can, or ever will, replace lecturers, interaction in class is how I feel I learn best.' I think this comment nicely sums up the findings of this study.

ACKNOWLEDGMENT

I would like to acknowledge the co-operation that I received from students of the Faculty of Business, Dublin Institute of Technology, who gave their time so graciously to complete surveys. Their involvement in this study was paramount and I am deeply indebted. In addition, I would like to thank Liam O'Donnell for all the technical support he so willingly provided.

REFERENCES

Ambrose, L. (2001). *Learning online facilitation online*. Brisbane: Intellectual Property Unit, Southbank Institute of TAFE.

Bayne, S. (2008). Higher education as a visual practice: Seeing through the virtual learning environment. *Teaching in Higher Education, 13*(4), 395–410. doi:10.1080/13562510802169665

Broad, M., Matthews, M., & McDonald, A. (2004). Accounting education through an online-supported virtual learning environment. *Active Learning in Higher Education, 5*(2), 135–151. doi:10.1177/1469787404043810

Churchill, T. (2005). E-reflections: A comparative exploration of the role of e-learning in training higher education lecturers. *Turkish Online Journal of Distance Education, 6*(3), 48–57.

Condie, R., & Livingston, K. (2007). Blending online learning with traditional approaches: Changing practices. *British Journal of Educational Technology, 38*(2), 337–348. doi:10.1111/j.1467-8535.2006.00630.x

Connolly, M., Jones, C., & Jones, N. (2007). Managing collaboration across further and higher education: a cause in practice. *Journal of Further and Higher Education, 31*(2), 159–169. doi:10.1080/03098770701267630

DIT. (2009). Dublin Institute of Technology's Research Ethics Committee. Retrieved March 31, 2009, from http://www.dit.ie/researchandenterprise/research/researchsupportoffice/ethics/guidelines

Donnelly, R., & O'Rourke, K. (2007). What now? Evaluating eLearning CPD practice in Irish third-level education. *Journal of Further and Higher Education, 31*(1), 31–40. doi:10.1080/03098770601167864

Gayle, B. M. (2004). Transformations in a civil discourse public speaking class: Speakers' and listeners' attitude change. *Communication Education, 53*(2), 174–184. doi:10.1080/0363452041 0001682438

Gilbert, J., Morton, S., & Rowley, J. (2007). e-Learning: The student experience. *British Journal of Educational Technology, 38*(4), 560–573. doi:10.1111/j.1467-8535.2007.00723.x

Hartman, J., Moskal, P., & Dziuban, C. (2005). Preparing the academy of today for the learner of tomorrow. In D.G. Oblinger, & J.L. Oblinger (Eds.), *Educating the Net Generation*. Retrieved October 20, 2009, from http://www.educause.edu/Resources/EducatingtheNetGeneration/PreparingtheAcademyofTodayfort/6062.

James, R., Bexley, E., Devlin, M., & Marginson, S. (2007). Australian university student finances 2006: A summary of findings from a national survey of students in public universities. Canberra: Australian Vice-Chancellors' Committee.

Jelfs, A., & Colbourn, C. (2002). Do students' approaches to learning affect their perceptions of using computing and information technology? *Journal of Educational Media, 27*(1-2), 41–53. doi:10.1080/0305498032000045449

Lea, M. (2001). Computer conferencing and assessment: New ways of writing in higher education. *Studies in Higher Education, 26*(2), 163–181. doi:10.1080/03075070120052099

Light, V., Nesbitt, E., Light, P., & Burns, J. R. (2000). 'Let's you and me have a little discussion': Computer mediated communication in support of campus-based university courses. *Studies in Higher Education, 25*(1), 85–96. doi:10.1080/030750700116037

Löfström, E., & Nevgi, A. (2007). From strategic planning to meaningful learning: Diverse perspectives on the development of web-based teaching and learning in higher education. *British Journal of Educational Technology, 38*(2), 312–324. doi:10.1111/j.1467-8535.2006.00625.x

Mainemelis, C., Boyatzis, R. E., & Kolb, D. A. (2002). Learning styles and adaptive flexibility: Testing experiential learning theory. *Management Learning, 33*(5), 5–33. doi:10.1177/1350507602331001

McKinney, D., Dyck, J. L., & Luber, E. S. (2009). iTunes University and the classroom: Can podcasts replace Professors? *Computers & Education, 52*(3), 617–623. doi:10.1016/j.compedu.2008.11.004

McLoughlin, C. (2000). Creating partnerships for generative learning and systemic change: Redefining academic roles and relationships in support of learning. *The International Journal for Academic Development, 5*(2), 116–128. doi:10.1080/13601440050200725

O'Donnell, E. (2008). *Can the use of e-learning improve the learning experience to better prepare students for work in industry?* Unpublished master's dissertation. Dublin City University.

O'Neill, K., Singh, G., & O'Donoghue, J. (2004). Implementing e-learning programmes for higher education: A review of the literature. *Journal of Information Technology Education, 3*, 314–320.

Overbaugh, R.C., & ShinYi, L. (2006). Student characteristics, sense of community, and cognitive achievement in web-based and lab-based learning environments. *Journal of Research on Technology in Education, 39*(2), 205–223.

Park, H. (2005). Design and development of a mobile learning management system adaptive to learning style of students. Retrieved June 19, 2009, from http://ieeexplore.ieee.org/stamp/stamp.jsp?arnumber=01579236

Peach, B. E., Mukherjee, A., & Hornyak, M. (2007). Assessing critical thinking: A college's journey and lessons learned. *Journal of Education for Business, 82*(6), 313–320. doi:10.3200/JOEB.82.6.313-320

PowerPoint. (2009). Microsoft. Retrieved April 24, 2009, from http://office.microsoft.com/en-gb/powerpoint/default.aspx

Rogers, G. (2004). History, learning technology and student achievement: Making the difference? *The Institute of Learning and Teaching in Higher Education and SAGE Publications, 5*(2), 232–247.

Salmon, G. (2000). Computer mediated conferencing for management learning at the Open University. *Management Learning, 31*(4), 491–502. doi:10.1177/1350507600314005

Shank, P. (2008). Web 2.0 and beyond: The changing needs of learners, new tools, and new ways to learn . In Carliner, S., & Shank, P. (Eds.), *The E-Learning Handbook: Past Promises, Present Challenges* (pp. 241–278). San Francisco: Pfeiffer.

Slevin, J. (2008). E-Learning and the transformation of social interaction in higher education. *Learning, Media and Technology, 33*(2), 115–126. doi:10.1080/17439880802097659

Sullivan, B. F., & Thomas, S. L. (2007). Documenting student learning outcomes through a research-intensive senior capstone experience: Bringing the data together to demonstrate progress. *North American Journal of Psychology, 9*(3), 321–329.

Trees, A. R., & Jackson, M. H. (2007). The learning environment in clicker classrooms: Student processes of learning and involvement in large university-level courses using student response systems. *Learning, Media and Technology, 32*(1), 21–40. doi:10.1080/17439880601141179

Treleaven, L., & Cecez, K. (2001). Collaborative learning in a web-mediated environment: A study of communicative practices. *Studies in Continuing Education*, *23*(2), 169–183. doi:10.1080/01580370120101948

Wilson, B. G., & Christopher, L. (2008). Hype versus reality on campus: Why e-learning isn't likely to replace a professor any time soon . In Carline, S., & Shank, P. (Eds.), *The E-Learning Handbook: Past Promises, Present Challenges* (pp. 55–76). San Francisco: Pfeiffer, An Imprint of Wiley.

ADDITIONAL READING

Abouchedid, K., & Eid, G. (2004). E-learning challenges in the Arab world: Revelations from a case study profile. *Quality Assurance in Education*, *12*(1), 15–27. doi:10.1108/09684880410517405

Ajjan, H., & Hartshorne, R. (2008). Investigating faculty decisions to adopt Web 2.0 technologies: Theory and empirical tests. *The Internet and Higher Education*, *11*, 71–80. doi:10.1016/j.iheduc.2008.05.002

Arbaugh, J. B. (2000). How classroom environment and student engagement affect learning in internet-based MBA Courses. *Business Communication Quarterly*, *63*(4), 9–26. doi:10.1177/108056990006300402

Auerbach, P. R. (2007). U.S. decline in the context of formal education and in situ learning. *Journal of Economic Issues*, *41*(3), 715–728.

Beastall, L., & Walker, R. (2006). Effecting institutional change through e-learning: An implementation model for VLE deployment at the University of York. *Journal of Organisational Transformation & Social Change*, *3*(3), 285–299. doi:10.1386/jots.3.3.285_1

Becta. (2007). *Summary report—Harnessing technology review 2007: Progress and impact of technology in education*. Retrieved April 29, 2009, from http://publications.becta.org.uk/display.cfm?resID=33980&page=1835

Bell, M., & Martin, G. (2004). Engaging in the future of e-learning: A scenarios-based approach. *Education + Training, 46*(6/7), 296-307.

Bruner, J. (2006). *In search of pedagogy* (1st ed., Vol. II). London: Routledge Taylor & Francis Group.

Charp, S. (2002). Changes to traditional teaching. (Cover story). *T.H.E. Journal*, *29*(10), 10.

Cheng, K.-W. (2006). A research study on students' level of acceptance in applying e-learning for business courses. A case study on a Technical College in Taiwan. *The Journal of American Academy of Business, Cambridge*, *8*(2), 265–270.

Chu, P.-Y. (2007). How students react to the power and responsibility of being decision makers in their own learning. *Language Teaching Research*, *11*(2), 225–241. doi:10.1177/136216880607074613

Clegg, S., Konrad, J., & Tan, T. (2000). Preparing academic staff to use ICTs in support of student learning [Electronic Version]. *The International Journal for Academic Development*, 138-148. Retrieved January 22, 2009 from http://www.tandf.co.uk/journals

Cloud, J. (2007). Failing our geniuses. (Cover story). *Time*, *170*(9), 40–47.

Cooper, K. C. (2007). 12 unavoidable truths about e-learning. *Chief Learning Officer*, *6*(1), 42–45.

Cunningham, T., McDonnell, C., McIntyre, B., & McKenna, T. (2008). A reflection on teachers' experience as e-learners . In Donnelly, R., & McSweeney, F. (Eds.), *Applied e-learning and e-teaching in higher education* (pp. 56–83). Hershey: Information Science Reference.

De Jong, W. (2007). From 'doing' to 'knowing what you are doing': Kolb's learning theory in teaching documentary practice. *Journal of Media Practice*, 7(2), 151–158. doi:10.1386/jmpr.7.2.151_3

Dublin, L. (2006). E-learning success: Engaging organisations, motivating learners. *Chief Learning Officer*, 5(11), 24–56.

Flatow, S. (2007). Making the case for e-learning. *Associations Now*, 3(11), 63–69.

Fresen, J. W., & Boyd, L. G. (2005). Caught in the web of quality. *International Journal of Educational Development*, 25(3), 317–331. doi:10.1016/j.ijedudev.2004.12.002

Garvin, D. A. (2007). Teaching executives and teaching MBAs: Reflections on the Case Method. *Academy of Management Learning & Education*, 6(3), 364–374.

Gibbs, G. (1995). Training lecturers to value teaching. *People Management*, 1(7), 34–38.

Gordon, J., & Berhow, S. (2009). University websites and dialogic features for building relationships with potential students. *Public Relations Review*, 35, 150–152. doi:10.1016/j.pubrev.2008.11.003

Grant, D., Malloy, A., & Murphy, C. (2009). A comparison of student perceptions of their computer skills to their actual abilities. *Journal of Information Technology Education*, 8, 141–160.

Gros, B. (2007). Digital games in education: The design of games-based learning environments. *Journal of Research on Technology in Education*, 40(1), 23–38.

Hadsell, L., & Burke, G. T. (2007). Computers, learning outcomes, and the choices facing students. *Eastern Economic Journal*, 33(1), 111–124. doi:10.1057/eej.2007.7

Harris, R., Hall, J., Muirhead, A., McAteer, E., Schmoller, S., & Thorpe, G. (2004). *Impact of e-learning on learner participation, attainment, retention, and progression in Further Education: Report of a scoping study*. Glasgow: Scottish Centre for Research into On-Line Learning & Assessment, University of Glasgow.

Harrison, R., & Leitch, C. (2007). Developing paradigmatic awareness in university business schools: The challenge for executive education. *Academy of Management Learning & Education*, 6(3), 332–343.

Holsapple, C. W., & Lee-Post, A. (2006). Defining, assessing, and promoting e-learning success: An information systems perspective. *Decision Sciences Journal of Innovative Education*, 4(1), 67–85.

Kallkvist, M., Gomez, S., Andersson, H., & Lush, D. (2009). Personalised virtual learning spaces to support undergraduates in producing research reports: Two case studies. *The Internet and Higher Education*, 12, 33–44. doi:10.1016/j.iheduc.2008.10.004

Labrie, R., & Haveriner, B. (2007). Longview fibre protects knowledge, improves decision with e-learning. *Pulp & Paper*, 81(2), 33–35.

Levin, T., & Wadmany, R. (2006). Teachers' beliefs and practices in technology-based classrooms: A developmental view. *Journal of Research on Technology in Education*, 39(2), 157–181.

Li-Fen Lilly, L., & Jeng, I. (2006). Knowledge construction in inservice teacher online discourse: Impacts of instructor roles and facilitative strategies. *Journal of Research on Technology in Education*, 39(2), 183–202.

Lim, D. H., & Morris, M. L. (2006). Combined effect of instructional and learner variables on course outcomes within an online learning environment. *Journal of Interactive Online Learning*, 5(3), 255–269.

Livingston, K., & Condie, R. (2006). The impact of an online learning program on teaching and learning strategies. *Theory into Practice, 45*(2), 150–158. doi:10.1207/s15430421tip4502_7

McClelland, B. (2001). Digital learning and teaching: Evaluation of developments for students in higher education. *European Journal of Engineering Education, 26*(2), 107–115. doi:10.1080/03043790110033583

McFarland, D., & Hamilton, D. (2005). Factors affecting student performance and satisfaction: Online versus traditional course delivery. *Journal of Computer Information Systems, 46*(2), 25–32.

Pan, C. C., & Sullivan, M. (2005). Promoting synchronous interaction in an e-learning environment. *T.H.E. Journal, 33*(2), 27–30.

Reiners, T., & Dreher, H. (2009). Culturally based adaptive learning and concept analytics to guide educational website content integration. *Journal of Information Technology Education, 8*, 125–139.

Reynolds, J. R. (2003). E-learning effectiveness. *Association Management, 55*(10), 37.

Rieck, S., & Crouch, L. (2007). Connectiveness and civility in online learning. *Nurse Education in Practice, 7*, 425–432. doi:10.1016/j.nepr.2007.06.006

Roffe, I. (2002). E-learning: engagement, enhancement and execution. *Quality Assurance in Education, 10*(1), 40–50. doi:10.1108/09684880210416102

Sabry, K., & Baldwin, L. (2003). Web-based learning interaction and learning styles. *British Journal of Educational Technology, 34*(4), 443–454. doi:10.1111/1467-8535.00341

Segrave, S., Holt, D., & Farmer, J. (2005). The power of the 6[three] model for enhancing academic teacher's capabilities for effective online teaching and learning: Benefits, initiatives and future directions. *Australasian Journal of Educational Technology, 21*(1), 118–135.

Shen, D., Laffey, J., Lin, Y., & Huang, X. (2006). Social influence for perceived usefulness and ease-of-use of course delivery systems. *Journal of Interactive Online Learning, 5*(3), 270–282.

Shroff, R. H., Vogel, D., Coombes, J., & Lee, F. (2007). Student e-learning intrinsic motivation: A qualitative analysis. *Communications of the Association for Information Systems, 19*(1), 241–260.

Shroff, R. H., & Vogel, D. R. (2009). Assessing the factors deemed to support individual student intrinsic motivation in technology supported online and face-to-face discussions. *Journal of Information Technology Education, 8*, 59–85.

Stoyanov, S., & Kirschner, P. (2007). Effect of problem solving support and cognitive styles on idea generation: Implications for technology-enhanced learning. *Journal of Research on Technology in Education, 40*(1), 49–63.

Subramanian, R. (2006). Blended eLearning: Integrating knowledge, performance support, and online learning. *Academy of Management Learning & Education, 5*(2), 248–249.

Vonderwell, S., Xin, L., & Alderman, K. (2007). Asynchronous discussions and assessment in online learning. *Journal of Research on Technology in Education, 39*(3), 309–328.

Zhu, F. X., & McFarland, D. (2005). Towards assurance of learning in business programs: Components and measurements. *Journal of American Academy of Business, Cambridge, 7*(2), 69–72.

KEY TERMS AND DEFINITIONS

E-Learning: The skill of acquiring information through the use of technological devices which is subsequently turned into knowledge.

E-Teaching: The skill of augmenting teaching practice using technological tools.

Higher Education: Educational establishments which students may attend at some period in their life, predominantly after leaving secondary/post primary education in order to engage with further education.

Learning: The skill of acquiring information that is subsequently turned into knowledge.

Podcasting: Subject matter in audio format that can be downloaded to technological devices and played for the recipient to listen to at their leisure.

Student Perspective: The opinion, view, perception or regard, that student hold with respect to something.

Technologies: The use of any electronic device, for example, computer, laptop, iPod, mobile phone, for accessing information and for communication purposes.

Video Casting: Subject matter in multi-media format that can be downloaded to technological devices for viewing at a convenient time.

Chapter 17

Online Support for Students' Writing Skills Development in a Technical Communication Introductory Module

Yvonne Cleary
University of Limerick, Ireland

ABSTRACT

This chapter explores the development of online support for writing skills in one technical communication module taught at the University of Limerick. It demonstrates the need for writing support by exploring the many complexities of teaching and learning writing skills. Central to the discussion is the principle of process, rather than product, orientation. Students on the module have been surveyed over the past two years to determine their attitudes to, and perceptions of, their writing strengths and weaknesses. The chapter outlines and exemplifies the types of writing-problems students and instructors identify. Online support is posited as an intervention which facilitates autonomous learning. The chapter concludes by discussing how online resources, and especially the university virtual learning environment, Sakai (called Sulis at University of Limerick), can support students. It also suggests related research opportunities, especially in the area of using Web 2.0 technologies to foster autonomy.

INTRODUCTION

The University of Limerick (UL) is unique in Ireland in offering programmes and modules in Technical Communication. Writing style is an important aspect of all Technical Communication modules, but is a central focus of one introductory module, *Principles of Professional and Technical Communication and Information Design*. Un-

DOI: 10.4018/978-1-61520-879-1.ch017

dergraduate, postgraduate and distance-learning students take this module. Quite strong differences in their performances are evident, however. Many undergraduate students, especially, and for several reasons, have underdeveloped writing skills and lack a basic understanding of writing-related concepts. It is clear writing skills need to be an essential component of their curricula, however, since written communication skills consistently feature high in lists of transferable skills valued by employers (see for example Curry, Sherry,

& Tunney, 2003). Our own surveys and needs analyses of students on the module, conducted over the past two years, demonstrate that students are aware of their writing problems, but are often at a loss as to how to fix, or even describe, these problems. In part response to these challenges, we have in recent years used the University of Limerick virtual learning environment (VLE), Sulis (the UL name for Sakai[1]), together with other tools, to support writing skills development on this module.

The mission of this chapter is to explore the development of online support for writing skills, and to demonstrate the application of ICT support to the initiatives on this introductory module. The first section of the chapter demonstrates the need for writing support, and posits online support as an intervention which facilitates autonomous and creative learning. The second section describes the module, and outlines and exemplifies the types of writing problems students and instructors identify. The chapter goes on to discuss use of online resources, and especially the university VLE, to support students and address some of the problems highlighted in previous sections. Finally, conclusions and directions for future research are posed.

BACKGROUND: SUPPORT FOR WRITING SKILLS

This section explores the complexities of writing instruction and examines strategies that may address the challenges.

Why is Writing Instruction Problematic?

Most research on teaching professional writing emanates from the United States of America, where writing instruction has been an area of curricular and research interest for the past century. Much of the literature on the subject of writing instruction identifies problems with how students learn to write and practise professional writing.

Several traditional models of writing instruction have complicated students' ability to articulate their writing concerns, and undermined teachers' efforts to help students produce better work. Writing instruction has historically focused on mechanical and grammatical error correction (Elbow, 1999), often to the detriment of strengthening or evaluating fluency or value of content (Santa, 2008). The ambiguous and often esoteric definition of error in grammar and punctuation causes confusion about, and resentment of, error correction among students. The objectives of a piece of writing may be ignored at the expense of technical correctness. These objectives might include, for example, clear, coherent, cohesive expression, or the development of a persuasive argument. Elbow (1999) describes the frequent tension between meeting these objectives and writing 'correctly'.

During secondary school, we begin the process of learning to write discursively. The school system privileges articulate style, often over invention, sometimes even over content. We make the inductive leap as apprentice writers, therefore, that we are rewarded for how we say something, rather than what we say. In a provocative article on the subject, Edmund Weiss (1995) argues that many of us learn at an early age to use words to create an impression of, rather than demonstrate, understanding. He suggests that much writing that is valued (by educators and/or employers) is often the most mendacious, because the writer has managed to create a false, or at least exaggerated, impression of understanding, knowledge, or expertise.

Many teachers charged with teaching and assessing student writing focus almost exclusively on the product, rather than the writing process. Hairston (1982) suggests that we often assume that 'competent writers know what they are going to say before they begin to write; thus their most important task when they are preparing to write is finding a form into which to organize their content' (p. 78). This attitude ignores the reality of the writing process for most writers, where through writing we learn to articulate thoughts often we had only partially developed before we began (Elbow, 1973; Sharples, 1996).

A further problem for teachers of writing at third level is that some students arrive at university defeated by their belief that writing is a native skill, that cannot be learned and that they will therefore never master. Pajares and Valiante (2006) call students' perceptions of their writing competence 'writing self-efficacy beliefs' and note that self efficacy is affected by gender, and determines motivation, and often success, levels. (Peterson (2006) also explores studies that show the influence of gender on writing development.) Although efficacy at writing tasks increases as students practise, Pajares and Valiante note that confidence levels tend to decrease. In other words, we become less confident as we become more effective.

The converse is the 'good writer', who has learned well how to offer up carefully chosen words, often as a substitute for meaning. Such students may feel they have nothing left to learn about writing well. In both cases, the problem is the belief that good writing is a) a product, and b) not learnable. Bell and Motion (2001, p. xi) encounter the same phenomenon in attitudes to creative writing: 'There remains in circulation a myth that writing can't be taught. That despite the proliferation of writing courses, creative writing is something esoteric, unpindownable, something inspired by muses and shaped by genius.'

This problem is exacerbated, perhaps even partly caused, by the lack of explicit focus on English-language grammar, punctuation, or writing style, at primary- or second-level for native speakers. Many third-level students, even of Humanities disciplines such as languages, literature, and communications, do not have a basic vocabulary of grammar, syntax, or writing style. Without such a basic understanding of writ-

ing tools, a more developed academic literacy is impossible to foster.

The current Irish Leaving Certificate syllabus for English notes that 'students' knowledge and level of control of the more formal aspects of language, e.g. register, paragraphs, syntax, punctuation and spelling, should be given particular attention in the new syllabus' (Department of Education and Science). However, the practice is understandably to spend most class time focused on preparing students for examinations, which assess neither style nor grammar explicitly.

A further influence on the teaching and learning of writing are sociocultural factors. In one conservative college in the USA, Warschauer (1998) describes a writing class for English as a Foreign Language students where the focus was almost entirely on learning rules rather than expressing meaning. While rules are important because their implementation gives students access to a discourse community, Warschauer argues that developing autonomy and agency is more important. Sociocultural factors are important for native English speakers too. Elbow (1999) notes that Standard Written English is a largely white, middle-class phenomenon, which excludes other native speakers.

Online Support as a Potential Solution to Some Writing Problems

In the USA, over the past three decades, academic writing assessment has moved away from the punitive and mechanical model, and towards a more empowering one of autonomous, supportive, and process-oriented development of student writing (Flower and Hayes, 1981; Hairston, 1982; Perl, 1977; Santa, 2008). The objective of this approach is to enable students to reflect on *how* they write, what they say, and why they choose the words and style they do. In tandem with this approach has been the development of ICTs and the consequent range of tools available to support writing activities. Writing instruction supported by electronic tools and resources can enable students to improve their writing practice, and can empower students as authors (Lee, 2005). Furthermore, through online exposition, students negotiate meaning and construct knowledge socially (Jonassen, 2003).

Much early research on computer support for writing focused on the tools available to improve the superficial aspects of text production: grammar and spell checkers, speech recognition, track change features, and so on. Another focus was the area of computer-supported collaborative writing (see Sharples, 1993). More recently, research is concerned with building support networks online for students. This approach has emerged from the writing centres and Writing Across the Curriculum (WAC) initiatives of American universities (see, for example, McGrath, 2002; Palmquist, 2003), and from the communities of practice model (Wenger, 1998). Writing centres are a very common feature of US universities, offering a range of support services to student writers, and focusing on peer support and reflection, rather than a remedial or quick-fix response to writing. Writing centres have also become a phenomenon in the UK and Ireland over the past decade. There are now writing centres in London Metropolitan University, Liverpool Hope University, Nottingham Trent University, and the University of East London, for example. The University of Limerick is part of a consortium which runs a regional writing centre for third-level education institutions in the west of Ireland. Most writing centres are now also supported by online writing labs, where students can consult online grammars, take tests, submit writing queries online to tutors, and get referencing information. One of the best known such labs is the Purdue Online Writing Lab.[2]

VLEs, now commonly used in third-level institutions, can also support writing skills development in a number of ways. Although the VLE offers little that could not in some way be offered in a traditional classroom, it has the potential to support a more constructivist and creative learning environment (Jonassen, 2003). At a basic level, it can house useful resources for students, and help to organise materials. A further advantage is that it holds a record of participation, collaboration, and discussion which may be useful for students and teachers (Curtis and Lawson, 2001). Perhaps most importantly, the VLE enables collaboration among all students. They can read and comment on each others' discussion topics and share resources. The sense of engagement (cognitive presence) and collaboration (social presence) that the VLE can foster are central to the development of a community of enquiry (Garrison, Anderson, & Archer, 2000).

Because so many technologies are available and competing for users' attention, it is tempting to focus only on the technology. However, any technology used must support the achievement of learning outcomes. Savenye, Olina, & Niemczyk (2001) list several factors determining the success or failure of a course partly or wholly delivered online. These include using instructional design principles to design the content, analysing the learners and goals, determining whether the material is suitable for online delivery, developing strategies for delivery, and determining the technologies available. They also note that both students and teachers must be supported in their use of technologies.

Increasingly, there is also recognition that online and face-to-face teaching are not mutually exclusive, and that a blended solution may best support student needs. For example, Whithaus and Neff (2006) conclude that exclusively asynchronous communication reduces spontaneity and 'moments of liveliness' in the classroom. Synchronous, as well as asynchronous, communication helps to give a sense of 'social presence', which may be difficult to evoke in an online environment.

THE MODULE: PRINCIPLES OF PROFESSIONAL AND TECHNICAL COMMUNICATION AND INFORMATION DESIGN

Programmes in technical and professional communication are commonly taught in universities in the USA, though the discipline is less well known in Europe. Each year, approximately 100 students take the module *Principles of Professional and Technical Communication and Information Design*. This module was originally designed for postgraduate students as an introduction to the discipline of Technical and Professional Communication. Since 2004, it is also offered on several undergraduate programmes as part of a New Media stream of their degree programmes, and on two distance-learning postgraduate programmes.

Module Description

The objectives of this module highlight the emphasis on helping students to improve their professional writing skills. At the end of the module, students are expected to be able to:

- Choose appropriate writing styles for a range of technical and professional communication genres and diverse audiences.
- Critique graphics and text.
- Create different types of documentation: summaries, manuals, brochures.
- Design documents using principles of information design.
- Write clear, concise, correct English appropriate for technical and professional communication.
- Use software tools to design effective documents.

Through a range of writing assignments which are aligned with module objectives, students have several opportunities for writing practice on this module. The assignments are designed to replicate the kinds of texts technical and professional writers produce in the workplace. There is no final exam. The range of assignments includes:

- Writing a summary of a text: most writers have to produce summaries for reports, theses, training courses and so on. Some technical writers begin their careers as abstract writers.
- Rewriting a poorly written text: much of the focus of the module is on helping students to see the value of a clear, direct writing style. In this assignment, students rewrite a text which, although grammatically correct, has several stylistic problems which obscure its meaning.
- Critiquing graphics, brochures, instructions. The word count for each critique is limited to reduce repetition and unnecessary verbiage. Writing a critique is a valuable professional writing skill, and also enables students to explore the requirements and best practice for a variety of writing genres.
- Redesigning graphics, brochures, and instructions. Students are expected to match their redesigns to the rhetorical context, genre, and audience of the document.

Delivery of the Module

Since both full-time on-campus undergraduates, and distance-education postgraduates take this module, we use several strategies to deliver the content. Lectures, for full-time students, concentrate on summarising, and pointing students towards resources on writing style and information design for technical and professional communication. We also use lectures to examine exemplars of good and poor practice. We use bespoke examples and materials to facilitate distance-learning students in accessing and engaging with the lecture content. Tutorials concentrate on writing practice, with emphasis on genre writing, error correction, reflection on the writing process, and peer review. For full-time students, tutorials are classroom based, while distance students use the Sulis VLE to practise writing and to collaborate. Laboratory work covers advanced topics in word processing, graphic design, and an introduction to desk-top publishing. Distance students come on campus for Saturday workshops to learn the software tools.

Although full-time students attend face-to-face classes, they also use the VLE, and it has become an important delivery medium for the module. Firstly, the VLE functions as a repository for resources. In this way, it brings coherence to the content: because the content is organised thematically, students can see the materials (lecture notes, readings, exercises, discussions, and assignments) associated with each topic. This explicit rendering of the module organisation also helps to increase students' understanding of the range of topics covered. A second use of the VLE is to enable students to engage with course material. They can post their own resources and comments about a particular topic, which should increase their sense of involvement. We also organise frequent discussions which help to foster engagement with the content. For example, one popular topic I ask students to comment on early in the semester is the use of 'fashionable' words. They discuss words, phrases or clichés in common usage that irritate them. This discussion topic tends to be a good ice-breaker, and creates a sense of engagement both with the module, and with the other students, since posts frequently disagree with, or supplement, a previous post. It also begins the process of meaning negotiation and collaborative knowledge creation that subsequent tasks build on.

Writing Concerns

One of my objectives has been to use the VLE, and other online tools, to empower students to engage with the concept of writing, the writing process, and writing skills more generally. All groups that take the module should, ostensibly, have a strong interest in writing: postgraduates are following programmes in either e-learning design and development or technical communication, and undergraduates are studying new media and/or languages. However, there is considerable disparity in experience levels, age ranges, and academic backgrounds of students. Moreover, the objectives are varied and require students to be open to learning about writing, design, and relevant software applications.

We have noted extreme differences in performance levels across the group. Although the module is taught at introductory level, the experience gap often results in a performance gap. Typically, the postgraduate students perform significantly better than the undergraduates, who, for several reasons, have underdeveloped writing skills and have difficulty grasping writing-related concepts. In short, we face the challenge of maintaining standards despite increasing enrolments, a diverse cohort of learners, and a general deterioration in the standard of written English among the students.

The writing issues we encounter broadly fit into these categories:

- *Grammar and punctuation*: the most common problems are comma splices, general lack of punctuation in sentences, misuse of the apostrophe, non-parallel constructions, lack of subject-verb agreement, and incomplete sentences.
- *Writing style*: more fundamental than grammar and punctuation errors, frequently, are stylistic patterns. Overuse of passive constructions, colloquial language, clichéd expressions, meaningless words, misuse of terms, and excessive verbiage all help to mask the meaning behind a text. In some cases, these tactics are indicative of a more worrying lack of engagement with an assignment. It is a truism that many students throw words at assignments in an attempt to hide their lack of knowledge, understanding, or ideas.

Here are two brief samples of student writing which typify writing work at the low end of the class, and exemplify the kinds of issues we see. Both are from (different) critiques of information graphics.

'The areas for underground mapping are highlighted on the map in bold, although it stands out from the other features on the map I feel it would more so if it was done in colour. Positions on the map are explained through numbered text, these numbers alike the highlighted area is not obvious enough.'

'For students in primary school, studying a table such as this, one would expect a map to accompany this table to locate these 38 islands around the country but there was not ... It may not be able to be seen properly on the photocopied page but there are boundary lines going on as well as the two legends which have quite a few symbols in each. On top of that, there's actually a bit of text as it names each of the symbols locations.'

Our Solutions: Soliciting Student Feedback and Providing Online Support

The teacher's instinct, when faced with such a product from a student of writing, is to mark up the text, highlighting each example of concern. It quickly became apparent when using this approach to mark assignments, however, that the weaker students do not learn from such feedback on their errors. Only those students who have a very strong interest in improving as writers seem to be able to apply such feedback for subsequent assignments. The vast majority, on the other hand, become disillusioned and dismayed, begin to identify themselves as weak writers, or decide that the module just does not suit them. Moreover, this

method of presenting feedback is product- rather than process-oriented.

Surveying Students about Their Own Writing

Faced with concerns about how to support students and help them work autonomously on their writing skills, in the autumn semesters of 2007 and 2008, I surveyed students of the module on their attitudes to writing, their perceptions of themselves as writers, and their interest in developing their writing skills.

My reasons for surveying students were manifold. I wished to learn more about the problems students perceive with their own writing, and to solicit suggestions that might inform delivery of the module. For example, I wanted to learn about writing topics students felt most needed to be covered, the usefulness of feedback, and I also wanted to assemble suggestions about how the module could help them improve their writing.

Furthermore, the survey would highlight that this module places a strong emphasis on writing well. Many students, particularly undergraduates, do not know that 'technical writing' is much more about writing than it is about technology. They often imagine that this module's content relates to IT or some aspect of computing. That misunderstanding leads them to privilege learning the software tools over learning writing strategies. Surveying them at the start of the semester would, I hoped, increase their awareness of the module's focus. Through answers to the survey, I hoped to learn more about aspects of writing students needed help with. I hoped moreover to learn how we might facilitate them in identifying their own writing strategies. The introduction explained what the survey should achieve, and highlighted the importance of completing the survey:

'A major focus of this module is improving your writing skills. By completing this survey, you can

help ensure that the module addresses common writing problems and is pitched at the correct level for you. Therefore, it is very important that you answer the survey questions truthfully. Your responses will not have any bearing on your grade in the module. Rather, information from the survey will be used, as much as possible, to align module content to student needs.'

I posted the questionnaire on Sulis as a Word document. The survey was completed by 40 students in 2007 and 39 in 2008, in both cases approximately 40% of the group. This section briefly summarises the survey findings. Since the quantitative findings were largely similar in both years, findings for both years are presented together. Of the 79 respondents, 78 claim to enjoy writing, 70 consider themselves to be good writers, 67 claim to receive good grades for writing assignments, and 70 claim to edit their work before submitting. Although those who responded are probably among the better students in the class, these figures do not match our experiences of either the standard of writing or editing among the groups.

One hundred per cent of respondents in both years claim to read feedback on assignments, and the same percentage find feedback useful. While I

would like also to believe this statistic, our experience again does not tally with it. Since the same errors recur from one assignment to the next for many students, I have little reason to suspect that all students read and apply feedback.

Much more useful and credible data emerges through responses to our questions about aspects of writing the students would like to work on. Question 10, for example, asks the respondent to rank module topics in order of perceived importance, from a list. Table 1 shows the ranking of topics. Again, data from both surveys are presented.

The responses in the table appear to demonstrate that expression and writing development are more important to students than content on the 'nuts and bolts' of grammar, punctuation, editing, mechanics and so on. This information tallies with my own instinct about how students use the feedback they receive. Editing is of surprisingly little interest to them. While these responses have not altered the types of content delivered, they have made us more cognisant of how to package that content, and the need to emphasise the essential connection between, for example, drafting, writing practice, and clear expression. They have also underscored the importance of providing a space for students to practise and discuss writing. To this end, in addition to tutorial work, Sulis is

Table 1. Aspects of writing students would like to learn about

Topic	Ranked first or second by respondents
Expressing your ideas clearly	24
Developing your ideas through writing	16
Organising information	11
Grammar and punctuation	9
Writing consistently	9
The writing process	9
Writing coherent sentences	6
Error correction	5
Register/level of formality/tone	5
Editing	4

used for discussions of writing issues. This usage is discussed further in the section *Using Online Resources on the Module.*

The questionnaire included open-ended questions seeking information on aspects of writing students had concerns about, aspects that had been singled out for attention in feedback, ways that module feedback, and ways that the module more generally, could help them to improve their writing skills. Some responses to these questions are outlined and discussed below:

To the question, 'In assignment feedback, what areas of your writing have been suggested for improvement?', responses were thoughtful, honest, and informative in most cases. Most indicated that they had received feedback about stylistic, grammatical, and structural problems in their work. Here is a selection of the comments students made:

'... inclination to digress or go off on a tangent. I've been caught out trying to pad something I really didn't know before too.'

'Punctuation has been corrected on some occasions. I have a tendency to write long sentences which some teachers have advised me to avoid. Trying to keep paragraphs to one consistent length has also been advised to me in the past.'

'... sentence construction. It was said that I sometimes constructed overlong sentences and as a result their meaning became vague. On a personal level I feel I sometimes have a problem with slipping in between tenses, sometimes mid sentence.'

The above responses show that students internalise the feedback they receive and remember in considerable detail the types of comments, even if they continue to make the same errors. Such comments demonstrate that this is certainly not the only module where problematic writing is an issue, and many students are already aware of problems with their writing. Therefore, it is apposite to find a solution to these problems, rather than to highlight them yet again. One response to this question indicated a more worrying problem: teachers may mark-up items that are not incorrect, when grading.

*'Grammar as in my recent submission "It became clear that when the data **were** being collected for eventual analysis that the many and varied themes were emerging to enable a review of the categories." My supervisor referenced "data" and suggested replacing "were" with "<u>was</u>" commenting that **countable or uncountable noun??**'* [original emphases]

Here, the student is illustrating that the instructor who marked the use of a plural verb with 'data' as incorrect, had no more idea than the student of the perceived writing problem. In fact, the student's usage of the plural verb was technically correct.

Although our survey respondents report the converse, my instinct is that students do not use the feedback they receive. The entreaty, 'If you have suggestions for improving the quality of feedback on your writing, please list them here', was an attempt to discover if students might heed feedback presented in a particular fashion or using a specific technique. Here are some of the more useful suggestions:

'Just to be clear and not vague if writing recommendations or corrections, perhaps to circle the problem area or give an example.'

'List concrete steps that I could take to make the necessary improvements. What helped other people who were in a similar situation like me, had similar problems?'

Finally, I asked students to list ways the module could help them to improve their writing. This question was probably difficult to respond to, since they had only attended the first couple of weeks of classes when they completed the survey. Most listed items that had occurred earlier in the questionnaire, such as helping them to express themselves more clearly, increasing their awareness of grammatical infelicities, and improving their punctuation. There was a worrying tendency in these responses to suggest that the onus was on the teachers to deliver improved performances, underscored by comments such as:

'... ensure my grammar is correct, teach me how to edit properly, show me how to use computer programs to edit my writing.'

'... improving my punctuation, teaching me about editing, learning how to write clearly and concisely.'

'Make me write more coherently. Improve my punctuation. Improve my sentence structure.'

However, there were also many useful suggestions: several responses noted the importance of writing practice, and several also understood that improvements in writing would require significant effort on the part of the learner:

'I hope it will help me pinpoint areas I need to work on to improve. My ego tells me I'm a fantastic writer but in reality I know there are lots of areas I can improve.'

'I hope to be able to gain my own insight into different formulae writers [use]; get me researching about editing, which will help me develop a coherent framework for reviewing my own work;

help give me a framework for understanding what I already do well and should continue to do.'

Using Online Resources on the Module

The findings of the survey have informed delivery of the module, in as much as it has been possible to align module content to student responses. Particularly, they have validated my attempts to harness the potential for Sulis to facilitate autonomy and reflection on the writing process. Since UL adopted Sulis as the university virtual learning environment, we have used this system to support all students on the module. Following is a short discussion of the ways we have used tools to address pedagogical issues.

- **Resources:** Sulis acts as a repository for writing-related materials and exercises that students can access at any time: lecture notes, writing resources, tests and quizzes, articles, relevant multimedia files (YouTube clips, web resources, and so on.). We also post examples of previous assignments in the Resources area. Analysis of usage statistics of the VLE show that this is the most visited section of the site. Our main aim in using the Resources repository is to enable students to access writing-related materials at times and in locations that are convenient to them. This strategy facilitates autonomy, creates an additional learning space, and enables students with different learning styles to use materials that best suit their learning styles.
- **Assignments:** Two of the module's five assignments must be submitted online. Students submit and receive evaluations of much of their work through Sulis. We grade as much as possible online, using Track Changes and Comments features of Word™, for example, to provide feedback.

To ensure students understand our feedback and the reasons for their grades, we post grading schemes following our evaluations. For all assignments, we post results on Sulis. The VLE includes a Gradebook tool, which keeps a record of the marks students receive for each assignment. This tool enables them to evaluate their own progress. Our overall objective in using the Assignments space, therefore, is to enable students to reflect on the feedback they receive and to use it for future assignments. A further advantage of using Sulis to manage assignments is that the external examiner can be added as a guest user to view feedback given to students. Sulis also includes some automated testing tools. The potential of these tools is an area for module development and research, since feedback is automatic and grading is less onerous for large groups.

- **Discussions:** We use Sulis to run several discussions on topics related to writing, hoping that such discussions can foster a deeper awareness of, and reflection on, personal writing processes. For example, we have initiated and facilitated discussions on genre, word usage, writing likes and dislikes, the writing process, and so on.

Communicating online is fraught with problems. Many people communicate too informally, because the online medium is more immediate than traditional written communication, while the seemingly anonymous nature of the medium can also occasionally lead to rudeness. There is also far greater potential for misunderstandings because of the 'lean' character of communication. Yet, the potential benefits of discussion forums far outweigh the disadvantages, so to mitigate against miscommunication, we give guidelines for discussions, requesting students not to post trivial responses, to use language carefully, and

to take issue only with ideas, not with people.

The discussion forum has been significantly more effective with distance-learning students: most full-time students participate in such discussions more actively if there is a grade reward for participation. However, our analysis of usage statistics demonstrates that while students may not participate actively, they read all submissions and visit this section of the site frequently. Even those who never post responses to discussions 'lurk' to read discussion postings. We also insist that students post module-related queries to Sulis, rather than emailing teachers. This strategy eliminates unnecessary questions sent by email from students who have not attended class. It also ensures that all students have the benefit of answers to questions.

Sakai also includes blog and wiki tools, but our students have found these difficult to use, and different in format and organisation to the blogs and wikis they are familiar with. These tools may be more user-friendly in version 3.0 of Sakai.

FUTURE RESEARCH DIRECTIONS

We plan to continue developing the online support tools on this module. My intention is also to continue surveying students, but in future years I will conduct pre-and post-module surveys to determine whether student attitudes have changed on completion of the module, in respect of how they write, and in respect of the features of writing they consider important.

The problem of student engagement appears to have worsened in recent years, and may be a result of the experience gap, noted earlier, or a broader sociological phenomenon. It is possible that undergraduate students, intimidated by the level of experience of more mature postgraduates, become de-motivated and disengaged. It is certain that the varying abilities within the group make the module more difficult to teach, and may disadvantage both the strong and weaker students. This issue is also worth exploring in much greater detail than this chapter allows.

Related to the problem of student engagement is the issue of plagiarism. Using online technologies may lead to increased incidences of plagiarism, and anti-plagiarism software is not always a solution (Hinman, 2002). Plagiarism may increase in online collaborative environments. This related area requires further research.

CONCLUSION

Some responses in our surveys validate current practice, and underline the point that student awareness of resources available, and willingness to use resources, is central to their learning. For example, most respondents agree that writing practice is essential to improving technique. Many students have noted that writing samples could be a useful tool for helping them to learn good practice. We post sample assignments on Sulis and also work on each assignment in tutorials and labs, and through online discussions.

Many students clearly recognise that they will not improve without considerable personal commitment. However, we are grappling with an unprecedented level of disengagement among the undergraduate cohort, many of whom do not benefit from the module because they choose not to attend classes or participate in online activities. Many students are unaware of the amount of support available online for this module. Increasing the profile of the online component of the module is therefore critical.

The current Web 2.0 phenomenon and the expansion of the social web have further exciting potential for reflecting on students' and teachers' attitudes to writing. Students who use social networks such as Facebook and Bebo are continually creating texts, and experimenting with words. Tools such as wikis and blogs also facilitate

creativity and self-expression. How, indeed if, these phenomena affect both the writing process, and writing products are areas ripe for further research. Recent studies (see, for example, Witte, 2007) suggest that students view online writing activities as separate from writing assignments. Social networking tools such as blogs and wikis are already featured in Sakai, and these tools will become central to Sakai 3.0, due for release in 2010.

As a teacher, I have learned from these surveys, and from the changes made to the module as a result, that students are interested in improving their writing, that they recognise their own writing problems, and that they are open to using social networking tools to improve their writing skills. It seems important to continue the work we have started on this module: using the technologies available to enable students to negotiate meaning (Jonassen, 2003) and develop their writing self-efficacy (Pajares & Valiante, 2006) collaboratively.

REFERENCES

Bell, J., & Motion, A. (2001). *The creative writing coursebook*. London: Macmillan.

Curry, P., Sherry, R., & Tunney, O. (2003). *What transferable skills do employers look for in third-level graduates?* Dublin: Transferable Skills Project.

Curtis, D. D., & Lawson, M. J. (2001). Exploring collaborative online learning. *Journal of Asynchronous Learning Networks*, *5*(1), 21–34.

Department of Education and Science. Ireland *Leaving Certificate English Syllabus*. Retrieved October 26, 2009, from http://www.education.ie/servlet/blobservlet/lc_english_sy.pdf?language=EN

Elbow, P. (1973). *Writing without teachers*. London: Oxford University Press.

Elbow, P. (1999). Inviting the mother tongue: beyond 'mistakes', 'bad English', and 'wrong language'. *Journal of Advanced Composition, 19*(2), 359–388.

Flower, L., & Hayes, J. (1981). A cognitive process theory of writing. *College Composition and Communication, 32*(4), 365–387. doi:10.2307/356600

Garisson, D. R., Anderson, T., & Archer, W. (2000). Critical inquiry in a text-based environment: computer conferencing in higher education. *The Internet and Higher Education, 2*(2/3), 87–105.

Hairston, M. (1982). The winds of change: Thomas Kuhn and the revolution in the teaching of writing. *College Composition and Communication, 33*(1), 76–88. doi:10.2307/357846

Hinman, L. M. (2002). The impact of the Internet on our moral lives in academia. *Ethics and Information Technology, 4*(1), 31–35. doi:10.1023/A:1015231824812

Jonassen, D. H. (2003). *Learning to solve problems with technology: A constructivist perspective.* Upper Saddle River, NJ: Merrill.

Lee, S. (2005). Electronic spaces as an alternative to traditional classroom discussion and writing in secondary English classrooms. *Journal of Asynchronous Learning Networks, 9*(3), 25–46.

McGrath, O. (2002). *Building an instructional portal: Channeling the writing lab.* Paper presented at the 30th Annual ACM SIGUCCS Conference on User Services, New York.

Pajares, F., & Valiante, G. (2006). Self-efficacy beliefs and motivation in writing development . In MacArthur, C. A., & Graham, S. (Eds.), *Handbook of writing research.* New York: Guilford Press.

Palmquist, M. (2003). A brief history of computer support for writing centers and writing-across-the-curriculum programs. *Computers and Composition, 20*(4), 395–413. doi:10.1016/j.compcom.2003.08.013

Perl, S. (1977). The composing processes of unskilled college writers. *College Composition and Communication, 28*(8), 12–28.

Peterson, S. (2006). Influence of gender on writing development . In MacArthur, C. A., & Graham, S. (Eds.), *Handbook of writing research.* New York: Guilford Press.

Sakai (2009). Sakai 3 proposal: A proposal for a next-generation Sakai. Retrieved October 26, 2009, from http://confluence.sakaiproject.org/download/attachments/26444008/Sakai+3+Proposal+v08.pdf?version=1

Santa, T. (2008). *Dead letters: Error in composition 1873-2004.* Creskill, NJ: Hampton Press.

Savenye, W., Olina, Z., & Niemczyk, M. (2001). So you are going to be an online writing instructor: Issues in designing, developing, and delivering an online course. *Computers and Composition, 18*(4), 371–385. doi:10.1016/S8755-4615(01)00069-X

Sharples, M. (Ed.). (1993). *Computer supported collaborative writing.* London: Springer Verlag.

Sharples, M. (1996). An account of writing as creative design . In Levy, C. M., & Ransdell, S. (Eds.), *The science of writing: Theories, methods, individual differences, and applications.* New Jersey: Erlbaum.

Warschauer, M. (1998). Online learning in socio-cultural context. *Anthropology & Education Quarterly, 29*(1), 68–88. doi:10.1525/aeq.1998.29.1.68

Weiss, E. (1995). 'Professional communication' and the 'odor of mendacity': The persistent suspicion that skilful writing is successful lying. *IEEE Transactions on Professional Communication, 38*(3), 169–175. doi:10.1109/47.406731

Wenger, E. (1998). *Communities of practice.* Cambridge: Cambridge University Press.

Whithaus, C., & Neff, J. M. (2006). Contact and interactivity: Social constructionist pedagogy in a video-based, management writing course. *Technical Communication Quarterly, 15*(4), 431–456. doi:10.1207/s15427625tcq1504_2

Witte, S. (2007). That's online writing, not boring school writing: writing with blogs and the Talkback project. *Journal of Adolescent & Adult Literacy, 51*(2), 92–96. doi:10.1598/JAAL.51.2.1

Littlejohn, A., & Pegler, C. (2007). *Preparing for blended e-learning: Understanding blended and online learning*. New York: Routledge.

MacArthur, C. A., & Graham, S. (Eds.). (2006). *Handbook of writing research*. New York: Guilford Press.

Salmon, G. (2003). *E-moderating: The key to teaching and learning online*. New York: Routledge.

ADDITIONAL READING

Blythe, S. (2001). Designing online courses: User-centered practices. *Computers and Composition, 18*(4), 329–346. doi:10.1016/S8755-4615(01)00066-4

Danchak, M. M., & Huguet, M. (2004). Designing for the changing role of the instructor in blended learning. *IEEE Transactions on Professional Communication, 47*(3), 200–210. doi:10.1109/TPC.2004.833684

ENDNOTES

[1] Sakai an open-source VLE, which includes typical VLE course and collaboration tools. More information on Sakai is available at http://www.sakaiproject/org/portal

[2] Purdue University's Online Writing Lab (OWL) can be accessed at http://owl.english.purdue.edu

Chapter 18
Design and Development of a Reusable Digital Learning Resource:
A Case Study Teaching Japanese Script

Ann Marcus-Quinn
University of Limerick, Ireland

Barbara Geraghty
University of Limerick, Ireland

ABSTRACT

This chapter describes the collaborative design and development process of a digital learning object in terms of roles, resources and user requirements. The example used to illustrate this process is a computer-assisted language learning (CALL) adaptation of a colour-based method of teaching one of the phonetic Japanese writing systems to zero beginners. This learning object combines as many of the positive features as possible of previous teaching methods with the advantages of mobile learning, facilitating autonomous learning on demand. It is time and cost effective and contains additional resources best supplied by a digital resource. The chapter also discusses the role and development of digital repositories in higher education.

BACKGROUND

There are many definitions of digital learning objects. An early definition by Wiley (2000) states that digital learning objects are 'small (relative to the size of an entire course) instructional components that can be reused a number of times in different learning contexts'. In a later paper, Caws, Friesen and Beaudoin (2006) cite Harman and Koohang's definition for learning objects used in education: 'learning objects are digital resources of any kind that can be similarly combined, shared and repurposed in different educational contexts'. While Wiley favours the Internet as the mode of delivery for digital learning objects, this is rather

DOI: 10.4018/978-1-61520-879-1.ch018

restrictive. For the purpose of this chapter, we define digital learning objects as any object which enhances learning (a photo, an MP3, a map, etc.), that can be shared in digital form and delivered in various ways (virtual learning environment (VLE), online repository, CD, mobile phone, MP3 player).

Of course, the concept of reusable learning objects is as old as education itself: in particular, teachers have been using multimedia – various kinds of authentic materials – in the classroom for as long as they have been available. These materials, however, could not be shared and could only be accessed in the classroom, greatly reducing the possibility of autonomous use by learners. In addition, every teacher who wanted to use such materials had to build their own portfolio of resources.

In recent years, there has been a large increase in the number of third-level courses delivered online. Courses are either delivered completely online or using a blended approach whereby students may receive some coursework online but they may have to attend a limited number of workshops or lectures on campus. This change in delivery has necessitated a change in the type of course materials that learners are given. Many lecturers facing the challenge of developing materials for online delivery have had to evaluate their own teaching materials and in some cases have either had to redesign or develop teaching resources that match this new cohort's learning expectations and needs. Digital resources are being developed increasingly to meet these needs (Mohan, Greer, & McCalla, 2003).

Won and Shih (2004) are also among the many practitioners at third level who believe that one of the greatest challenges for distance learning is the creation of high quality course materials (lecture notes, references, tests, etc.). They stress the importance of sharing and reusing well-developed learning objects to 'reduce the load on instructors, and to make them available across a wide variety of platforms'. International best practice indicates that the successful development of high-quality

learning objects is collaborative, that there are sufficient resources available in terms of expertise and money and that the objects can be easily shared.

In October 2002 the Massachusetts Institute of Technology (MIT) began an initiative to make available online without any subscription fee all of the educational materials from its undergraduate and postgraduate courses. These materials, including learning objects, but also lecture content of all lectures, are available to anyone. The project is jointly funded by the William and Flora Hewlett Foundation, the Andrew W. Mellon Foundation, and MIT. In terms of its sheer size, comprehensiveness, level of coordination as well as its free global access, this project is now taken as an example of best practice for the development and sharing of high quality learning objects.

James Taylor from the University of Southern Queensland Australia, located in an area with a long history of distance education and consequently an international leader in off-campus education, asserts that the growth in the field of instructional design and technology has led to a marked increase in collaboration. He advocates 'a multi-disciplinary team approach, wherein a wide range of specialist expertise is applied to the generation of training programs' (Taylor, 1998, p. 9). Taylor states that the necessary level of expertise for the development of technical teaching and learning systems is usually beyond the skill set of individual teachers and appears to demand the deployment of an expert teaching team, with a wide range of specialist skills. These include specialists in instructional design, systems design, electronic information systems, database design, graphic design, student administration, electronic publishing and project management working alongside subject matter experts. Taylor continues to advocate this structured collaborative method of design and development of content in preference to what he terms 'random acts of innovation'. These random acts of innovation are the result of many individual lecturers spending time and money developing similar learning objects. If they shared their resources, perhaps in a repository, they could see where gaps needed to be filled rather than constantly reinventing the wheel.

Closer to home, the 81 Centres for Excellence in Teaching and Learning in the UK and Northern Ireland were funded from 2005 by the Higher Education Funding Council for England (HEFCE) and the Department for Employment and Learning (DEL) in Northern Ireland. These centres develop high quality learning objects and make them available online to the wider teaching community. Similarly, the Joint Information Systems Committee (JISC) is 'funded by the UK HE and FE funding bodies to provide world-class leadership in the innovative use of ICT to support education and research.' Both of these initiatives have access to enviable levels of expertise and money resulting in rapidly produced high quality learning objects. JISC also funds JORUM, the UK's digital learning repository which was launched officially in 2006. A national digital learning repository like this is both more economical and more efficient than the alternative which is each institution funding, hosting and populating its own repository.

Ireland's National Digital Learning Repository (NDLR) is a Higher Education Authority-funded initiative, in which the seven Irish universities and 14 Institutes of Technology are involved. Despite having a much lower level of funding than in the UK, the NDLR has proven successful in terms of cross-institutional collaboration and the development of learning objects. This may be because the HE community in Ireland is small enough to make collaboration easier. In addition to storing the learning resources, the project also provides infrastructure to support subject or discipline-based communities of practice in higher education. The development of these communities of practice is unique to the NDLR. The spirit of collaboration generated by many of these communities of practice facilitates the development of learning objects with very limited resources.

DESIGN AND DEVELOPMENT OF LEARNING OBJECTS

For higher education professionals wishing to develop digital learning objects, however, issues remain. One fundamental and long-running controversy is the doubt whether technology used in education results in a significant statistical difference in learning outcomes or not. This is neatly summarised in Conger (2005). She also makes the point that many media comparison studies (MCS) that examine the question of significant difference are methodologically flawed and lack a theoretical basis. Conger concludes citing Sener (2004): 'Rather than continuing to perform MCS, then, we should move towards developing teaching pedagogies that make best use of current technologies'. Oblinger and Hawkins (2006, p. 14) go so far as to query the usefulness of the question itself. 'We need to ask: "Difference in what?"'. They then go on to summarise their vision of learning as follows: 'Learning occurs as a result of motivation, opportunities, an active process, interaction with others, and the ability to transfer learning to a real-world situation'. The remainder of their article demonstrates that technology has a positive role in education when it is used to bring about beneficial change as a means to a clear pedagogical end and that use of technology is social: 'Being with others is now multimodal involving face-to-face *and* online communication, often simultaneously (Oblinger & Hawkins, 2006, p. 15). They conclude that it is crucial to exploit to the full the range of opportunities afforded by technology in education.

To make optimum use of digital learning objects, therefore, they need to have clear, achievable learning outcomes that are relevant to the skill they are trying to learn. While learning objects produced using word processing or presentation software have their place, their sustained use to produce learning objects does not exploit to their fullest extent the possibilities offered by technology in education.

While much of the literature encourages the development of digital learning objects, a number of issues remain which impede instructors from deciding to develop them. These include the following: concern about cost, lack of time, access to expertise and anxiety about the perceived quality of shared learning objects. Concerns about copyright also hamper sharing.

Instructional designers have a range of design and development models to choose from. There are hundreds of models to design and develop training materials, but nearly all are variants of the basic ADDIE model (Kruse, 2009). The five phases of this model are:

- Analysis
- Design
- Development
- Implementation
- Evaluation

The ADDIE model provides a simple but systematic approach to the design and development process. There are alternative systematic models in circulation outlining the most successful plan for the design and development process of a learning object. However, as Kruse (2009) comments, a systematic approach with distinct steps allows for more efficient use of time and resources. The stages recommended by the London Metropolitan University (Cook & Light, 2006) are as follows:

1. Concept
2. Specification
3. Peer Review 1
4. Development
5. Peer Review 2
6. Student Peer Review
7. Revision
8. Delivery
9. Packaging and Metadata
10. Deposited

Having limited resources can lead to more focused planning; resulting in a more successful learning object. Learning outcomes must be clarified at the very beginning of the process, ensuring that the object leads to the intended outcomes. While possibly time-consuming, this step is crucial. Another way of reducing costs is to identify existing resources that can easily be accessed, in-house recording and design facilities, at no additional cost, for instance.

Developing effective digital learning objects takes time. However, establishing a clear idea of the learning outcomes will save time in the long run, and successful reusable objects reduce teaching time far into the future. Collaboration also saves time because not everyone in the group will need to develop the same level of technical skill.

Another vital step is quality assurance through usability testing. This may seem superfluous, but it is the only method of ensuring that the object both meets the needs of learners and achieves its original purpose. Nielsen (2009), in his Usability 101, advocates that 10% of the overall budget be allocated to usability. This results in a more successful online object.

One of the advantages of repositories and communities of practice is the opportunity for collaboration. The following account describes a successful collaboration between two disciplines – Technical Communication and Japanese – at the University of Limerick leading to the development of an effective digital learning object for language teaching. The development process, which is an adaptation of the ADDIE model, was as shown in Figure 1.

SUCCESSFUL COLLABORATIVE LEARNING OBJECT DEVELOPMENT

The process begins with an existing learning activity. The instructor decides to explore the option of digital delivery. He or she meets the instruc-

Figure 1. Model of design and development process for HiraganaLearning Object

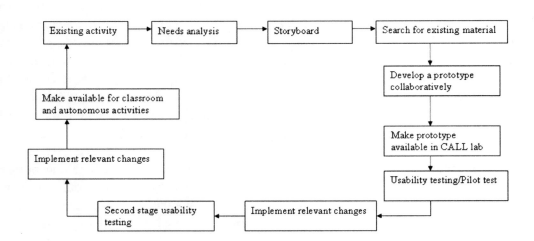

tional designer who has technical expertise. They conduct a needs analysis together. The instructor clarifies the learning outcomes required. Next, they make a rough draft of a storyboard (this can be as simple as a basic diagram of what is intended). After that, they both search for existing material that might meet these needs. If this material already exists, no further work may be needed. If there is no usable material in existence already, they develop a couple of possible prototypes together and the instructor selects the most appropriate one. These prototypes are not complete learning objects: they give an idea of what the eventual learning object will look like. Once the most appropriate prototype has been selected, it is developed as a full learning object. The team next carries out initial usability testing. On the basis of the findings from this testing, they implement required changes. They then carry out usability testing again with a different group, implement any additional changes and finally make the learning object available for use by learners.

The specific development model chosen is not as important as having a design and development process in place. Awareness of the stages in the process applicable to your project is essential. However, our experience shows that storyboard-ing and usability are the two areas that should not be omitted.

Existing Activity

The writing system is one of the great challenges in learning and teaching Japanese. Japanese has three writing systems: two phonetic syllabaries, hiragana and katakana, and the logographic system imported from China, *kanji*. In general, the rounder hiragana are used to write inflections as well as words that cannot be written in kanji, while the squarer katakana are used to write loan words and at times, scientific terms.

Given the challenges of learning the three character sets, some materials' writers have avoided Japanese character sets altogether and opted to use Roman characters to teach Japanese. In an attempt to avoid using Roman characters in introducing the pronunciation of hiragana, and also to make use of a greater variety of learning styles among learners, teachers of Japanese at the University of Limerick developed a method of teaching the hiragana inspired by the Silent Way's use of colour (Gattegno, 1978). [1] Silent Way pedagogy was not important: the association of colour combinations to teach the pronunciation of various characters was. The Silent Way uses charts or fidels as well as other learning aids. However, thinking that the use of cards rather than fidels would allow for a greater range of learner-centred activities in class as well as activating a greater number of learning styles, the method used at the University of Limerick used A4 sized cards with colour on one side and the hiragana on the other. This allowed for the introduction of the shapes and sounds of the hiragana and the order of the hiragana chart (important for making sense of grammatical inflections later as well as for dictionary use) to zero beginners at the start of their study of Japanese.

The cards were A4 sized, with colour on one side and the character written in black on the other (see Figure 2). The side with the character also had the colour or colours on the back of the card repeated in miniature at the top left-hand corner. The cards for vowel sounds in the first line of the table -- あ(a), い(i), う (u), え (e), お (o) – had single colours on the back: blue, white, green, yellow and red in that order. The first character in the second line, か(ka), had orange to represent the 'k' sound of the syllabet and blue to represent the 'a' sound. The card for the next syllabet in the table, け(ke), was coloured orange and white, and so on.

Needs Analysis

After some years using the card-based activity, the technology and expertise were available to develop a digital version of the cards. Because of four years' experience using paper-based materials, a focused learning outcome was in place from the beginning: that learners would be trained to recognise pronunciation and associate that sound with the correct character.

Storyboarding

Given the well-defined learning outcome, it was possible to sketch a rough plan of how the learning object would look. The initial idea was to replicate digitally the way the cards were used in class. It seemed that animation software would allow learners to 'turn over' the cards on screen as they did with the A4 sized cards. However, it soon became clear that this would not make optimal use of the technology; that learners needed to be only one click away from relevant information when they clicked on the character. Waiting for a card to be turned over on screen would take too long to no pedagogical purpose.

Accordingly, learners clicking on a character on the hiragana chart on screen were brought to a screen showing the colour coding associated with the character and a speaker which they could click to hear the pronunciation. As well as providing sound files, the software also had the capacity to animate the writing of the characters using the correct stroke order. The learning object was initially made available on CD. This was mobile,

Figure 2. Coloured cards showing first row front and back

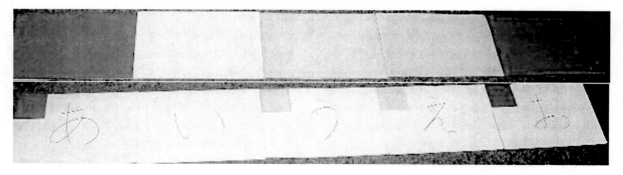

cost effective and allowed each learner to have a portable copy of the learning object.

Search for Existing Material

Before further development could take place, an internet search was necessary to indentify existing materials. At the time there was nothing available which provided simultaneous sound and of the hiragana system. Surprisingly little is available even now, and romanisation to give pronunciation (which this learning object avoided) is still common. Many of the online objects, while they showed the character being faded in, had the pronunciation playing in a separate window which often took a long time to load. Currently, a considerable amount of home video level material is available on You Tube. It is certainly a cheap way of producing learning material but it is not interactive, the information is not on demand (one click away), there is no assessment and it does not give pronunciation and writing simultaneously.

When the hiragana object was initially developed, there were sound reasons for choosing Flash as the authoring tool. However, more recently a number of more intuitive authoring tools have become available. It is worth examining the various options before choosing the authoring tool. If the object is to be distributed using a virtual learning environment, the authoring tool as well as the VLE should be SCORM compliant (SCORM stands for Shareable Content Object Reference Model). SCORM is a technical standard and allows communication and tracking between an interactive learning object and the learning management system. It is a set of rules governing the creation of 'shareable content objects' or 'SCOs' that can be reused in different systems and contexts (SCORM, 2009). It is not a standard but a model based on existing industry standards. SCORM can facilitate more interactive online assessment for objects developed using Flash and other authoring tools.

Prototypes

The developer created three very basic prototypes. It was at this stage that it became clear that the original specification of the cards being virtually 'turned', exactly replicating the classroom activity, was neither necessary nor making the best use of the potential offered by the technology: a simple click on the character gave the desired result. It is therefore important to maintain a flexible attitude in the development process as well as to maintain regular communication between instructor and developer.

Choosing the Prototype

At this stage it was obvious which of the three prototypes was the most suitable. The chosen prototype had the following features: a clean template, the minimum of English directions (this was to satisfy the pedagogical aim of teaching through the Target Language) and colours adapted from the existing cards to cater for the possibility of colour blindness among users (Figure 3). This version used a pattern in the areas which had previously been red, green and white as these colours are the most problematic for those with colour blindness (University of Illinois, 2007). A native speaker then recorded the pronunciation of the characters and wrote them using a pen mouse. This meant that the written examples were authentic giving a hand-written example for learners to copy and, coincidentally, avoiding copyright issues.

Delivery

We made the first prototype available on the PC desktops in the university's CALL Lab. This had the advantage of being cost-neutral as well as allowing access to the whole university population. This provided initial usability feedback and raised awareness of the existence of the new learning object within the institution.

Figure 3. Table with one character adapted for colour blindness

あ	い	う	え	お
か	き	く	け	こ
さ	し	す	せ	そ
た	ち	つ	て	と
な	に	ぬ	ね	の
は	ひ	ふ	へ	ほ
ま	み	む	め	も
や		ゆ		よ
ら	り	る	れ	ろ
わ				を
ん				

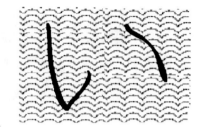

Usability Testing

Usability testing followed a task-based approach. This type of usability testing focuses on how typical users perform key tasks. The first group was given the CD and they were asked to perform a key task: to familiarise themselves with the hiragana table. When the testing period was finished the users completed a questionnaire for additional feedback. Recurring suggestions (such as placement of characters on the screen) led to improvements. The second group of usability testers were given the improved version of the courseware. Observation of their use of the learning object resulted in better sound files and improved graphics.

Even before usability testing had been carried out the object had been modified. Changes included adding a testing section and adapting the on-screen colour scheme to take account of possible colour blindness in users (a particular concern for men). A very basic consideration was the issue of colours on screen. Originally, the hiragana characters were black on a white screen. This was inspired by Japanese calligraphy which uses black ink on white paper. However, the contrast between these two colours was too stark: blue on white produces less glare on screen meaning that the object can be used for longer. Research cited by Hall and Hanna (2004, p. 3) showed the higher the contrast the better, with blue text and yellow background combinations being preferred by users (Figure 4).

The learning object also included a testing section, with 30y multiple choice items covering the whole hiragana table. Multiple choice testing encourages and motivates learners with partial knowledge over those who are simply guessing (Chang, Lin, & Lin, 2007). Learners do not take this set of questions 'against the clock'. Usability testing showed that competitive learners took the test before they could have successfully completed the table and they did not need the 'motivational effect' attributed to 'beat the clock' exercises

Figure 4. First screen from testing

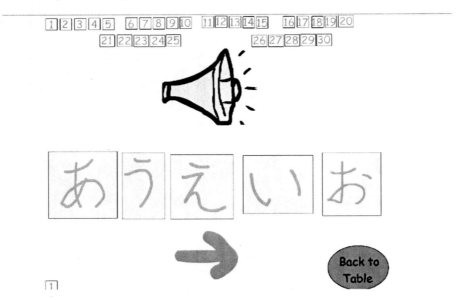

(Alessi & Trollip, 2001). The time-restrictive test was unnecessary and might demotivate some learner types due to the increased stress of working against the clock. Usability testing also suggested the addition of some English to navigation buttons and the reduction of the size of some graphics.

Pilot Study

A small-scale pilot study compared the speed of acquisition of learners using paper-based materials and the learning object. The control group and the experimental group both had three members. The control or Card Group studied the hiragana using the coloured cards over two two-hour sessions a week apart, while the Experimental Group used the object. The Card Group had two two-hour sessions learning hiragana using the coloured cards. The instructor introduced the colour combinations and the sounds associated with them as would be done in a zero-beginner class. The Experimental Group also had two two-hour sessions, using the object in the CALL lab. The Experimental Group were given no instruction, but interacted with the material in whatever way felt appropriate to them.

The Card Group participants were highly motivated and spoke to each other before the sessions began. However, the intensity of the activity meant that they needed frequent breaks; they decided not to learn to write the characters and felt nervous at the prospect of an informal test. Negative affective features impacted noticeably on the performance of this group. One participant was over-aware that she was not making as much progress as the others, and she appeared to become more and more stressed as the sessions went on. The other members of that group were also aware of her discomfort and spent a lot of time trying to encourage her. This participant's biggest problem was her lack of control of the amount of input she could get. Because she was embarrassed to ask the instructor to repeat as often as necessary for her needs, she ended up falling behind other participants and the whole group was affected. Here, the social dynamic as a problem in learning, even with a small and highly motivated group, became obvious.

By contrast, the Experimental Group sat at the computers in the lab and began using the object immediately. There was no social interaction among participants and no questions about how to use the object. What was very striking was that each participant used the learning object in a different way and began writing at a very early stage: one began writing characters in the air while another made charts in a notebook. They hardly noticed the two researchers in the room and worked productively without fatigue for two two-hour sessions. While it took the Card Group a half hour to become familiar with 20 hiragana characters, the Experimental Group had viewed the whole table during the first half-hour and had listened to the pronunciation of the characters as well as seeing them written. This study showed that the Experimental Group was twice as fast as the Card Group in familiarising themselves with the whole table of characters, and two of them had begun writing characters within the first five minutes. The Card Group, however, received all their input from the instructor at the same time and so they were not able to work at their own speed or decide how they would address the material. This added to the stress of the learners using paper-based materials.

The chart in Figure 5 was made from memory by one of the learners in the Experimental Group during the first 45 minutes using the learning object. What is notable about this is that he had the confidence to produce this after such little exposure to the material; that he was sufficiently motivated to write out the chart from memory and that there were no mistakes. In normal classes using paper-based materials it usually takes over six hours' contact time before learners will even attempt writing characters from memory. In general, the Experimental Group members were twice as fast at learning to read and write the hiragana as the Card Group.

The difference in the attitude of the two groups to the prospect of being tested was also

Figure 5. Half of chart made by experimental group learner within the first two hours

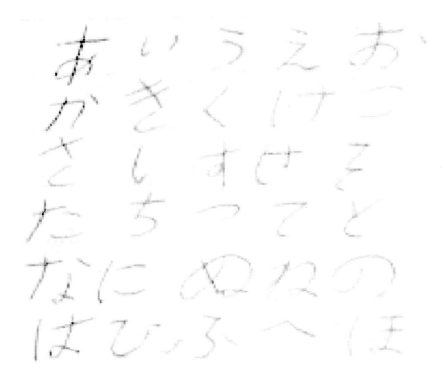

very marked. Both usability groups and the Experimental Group in the pilot study could hardly wait to get feedback by taking the test. Indeed, their anticipation of the testing was so great in the usability group that the button had to be removed to keep the Experimental Group in the pilot study from taking the test prematurely. This test was added as terminal evaluation, whereas some learners incorporated it into their acquisition of hiragana as a kind of formative evaluation. This shows how valuable it is to have the courage to hand over control to learners (Voller, 1997).

Use in Class

Learners used the software for the first time in class in September 2006. This was a multinational group (Irish, Spanish, Chinese and Latvian) of 25 zero-beginner students of Japanese. As with the usability and other groups who had tried out the object, 22 of the group began work immediately, each interacting with the object in a different but very productive manner. Only three students needed some direction, perhaps because they were older and less confident with the technology. A notable feature of the usability testing and classwork was that participants started to write without any prompting, some writing them in the air, some writing in a notebook. Some wrote in a chart format: others wrote the same character several times. The fact that learners were encouraged by the learning object to start practising writing spontaneously was an unexpected bonus (Figure 6).

The instructor's role in these sessions was primarily to observe and answer questions. There were very few questions, however; the lab was full of busy, completely engaged learners working enthusiastically with the object. There was a real feeling of autonomous learning taking place. Kupetz and Ziegenmeyer (2006) identify the following characteristics of educational technology promoting autonomy: it involves problem-solving activities; encourages active learning; is motivat-

Figure 6. Character being drawn

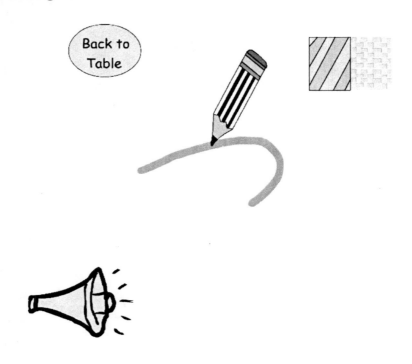

ing and relevant, is flexible, avoids embarrassment to students. They also mention that technology can involve a dialogue about learning. This is also a feature of the use of the learning object in Japanese classes at the University of Limerick; that students follow up sessions with the object by writing learner diaries.

Feedback from Learners

The instructor asked students to write learner diaries about their experiences with the object. The reaction was overwhelmingly positive. After the initial 30-minute session, one Irish student described the feeling of autonomous learning: 'The positive aspect of working with the CD was the fact that I could work on it at my own pace, and work on the parts of it that I wanted to' (Irish undergraduate, male).

Another student appreciated being able to take responsibility for his own learning and was enthusiastic about the testing element in the object:

I found this method of learning very effective as you work by yourself, at your own pace, and do not have to wait to ask a question. As clicking on a character will provide you with most of the information you need in learning them i.e. How to write? How to pronounce? It's like having your own personal tutor going through the hiragana with you ... I found the test excellent in familiarising yourself with the hiragana, as if you got one wrong you could go straight back and check which one was the correct answer. This is effective in that you will push yourself in making sure not to forget one you have gotten wrong already. I took the test multiple times. At first I didn't do too well but as I progressed I was recognising more and more hiragana, and towards the end I was flying through it. (Irish undergraduate, male)

Their speed of acquisition in one short session was surprising. With the cards, for learners to feel they could recognise most of the hiragana on the

table would have taken at least four hours' class time; many of this group felt confident that they could recognise most of the characters after 30 minutes. 'Now with hiragana I can recognise most of the symbols and can also write them. I have made some efforts at forming ... some words that I have already met in Japanese ... I find it fun and interesting to use and I'm excited at how quickly you can pick up the writing system using this method' (Irish undergraduate, female). This comment typifies the enthusiasm reported by the vast majority of the group. The three students who had had difficulty using the object in the lab tended to view it less favourably. One commented that she preferred more traditional methods: 'I can write more hiragana, but actually I preferred taking them out of a book than from the CD. I used the CD for pronunciations' (Irish undergraduate, female).

In summary, the object achieved the initial aim of enabling faster recognition of characters. Classes using the object in 2007 and 2008 achieved recognition of the characters in two weeks instead of the four weeks it had taken groups using paper-based materials. Analysis of learner diaries by the 2006 group of zero beginners using the learning object showed that 22 out of the 25 learners in that group achieved a high level of autonomous use as well as reporting positively on their experience. In particular, users reported a low level of stress as well as a higher level of motivation when compared to the use of paper-based materials.

REUSE OF DIGITAL LEARNING OBJECTS

In conclusion, the result of this extensive design, development, usability testing has been a shell which can be populated with new content without having to redesign navigation or basic graphics. Having this clean template allowed us to develop over a week (the first object took two months to develop from scratch) a version of the resource teaching the other phonetic Japanese syllabary, katakana. Many features of this new object show the benefit of extensive usability testing: the placement of graphics; sound quality; navigation and layout in the katakana object are all significantly improved, but the template for them already existed because of the previous design experience. The speed of development and the clearer design of the resulting object demonstrate the benefits of developing reusable digital learning objects. The speed of development of this new object was further accelerated because it could be developed with minimal interaction between the developer and the instructor since all the basic design decisions had already been made. While the optimal use of screen space was maintained in the new object's chart design, the design was cleaner because a typeset was used for characters on the chart. Each character was also of a uniform size

and shape, making the design neater and clearer. The original colour associations were maintained, but an invisible button made it easier for users to display the colours. The original sound files were reused, an improved recording having been done for the hiragana object. No further work on navigation or usability needed to be done; the structure was in place already and the placement of graphics and elements on screen had already been extensively tested. Based on this experience, once the structure, design and navigation have been put in place, content can be replaced, thus making optimal use of the time and resources needed to create these objects (Figure 7).

Instead of spending time using this object in class, we placed this on the university's learning management system, where it was easily accessible by learners. This also allowed us to

Figure 7. Katakana developed from Hiragana template

ア	イ	ウ	エ	オ
カ	キ	ク	ケ	コ
サ	シ	ス	セ	ソ
タ	チ	ツ	テ	ト
ナ	ニ	ヌ	ネ	ノ
ハ	ヒ	フ	ヘ	ホ
マ	ミ	ム	メ	モ
ヤ		ユ		ヨ
ラ	リ	ル	レ	ロ
ワ				ヲ
ン				

track learner usage. After three weeks and without special prompting from the instructor, the katakana resource had been accessed by half the class. Obviously, their successful use of the hiragana object encouraged learners to use the new object autonomously. Further development is needed in this object, in terms of assessment and more interactive learning features. A learning object teaching basic kanji characters based on this reusable template is planned. Because kanji characters are ideographic or logographic rather than phonetic, and because many of them are more complicated to write, this will add to the challenges in the design, development and usability processes in producing this new object. This type of object can also be used to teach other subjects: an object combining sound and animation with well-defined learning outcomes is being used in developing software to teach Gregg shorthand at the University of Limerick. Here, the same template and navigation structure is being reused. The Gregg shorthand system, similar to the Japanese hiragana and katakana systems, relies on phonetic sound and symbol association. The shorthand system, however, has hundreds of symbols which must be learned adding to the challenge of the development process. Collaborative development between a subject matter expert and an instructional designer results in a better object; if this is not possible, it is important to have well-defined learning outcomes, to conduct usability testing and to resist the lure of the added extras the authoring tool can deliver which distract from the purpose of the object.

REFERENCES

Alessi, S. M., & Trollip, S. R. (2001). *Multimedia for learning methods and development* (3rd ed.). Boston: Allyn and Bacon.

Caws, C., Friesen, N., & Beaudoin, M. (2006). A new learning object repository for language learning: Methods and possible outcomes. *Interdisciplinary Journal of Knowledge and Learning Objects, 2*, 111-124. Retrieved October 20, 2009, from http://ijklo.org/Volume2/v2p111-124Caws.pdf

Chang, S.-H., Lin, P.-C., & Lin, Z. C. (2007). Measures of partial knowledge and unexpected responses in multiple-choice tests. *Journal of Educational Technology & Society, 10*(4), 95–109.

Conger, S. Basu (2005). If there is no significant difference, why should we care? *The Journal of Educators Online, 2*(2). Retrieved October 20, 2009, from http://www.thejeo.com/Basu%20Conger%20Final.pdf

Cook, J., & Light, A. (2006). New patterns of power and participation? Designing ICT for informal and community learning. *E-Learning*. Special Issue of ICE2 Symposium, *3*(1), 51-61. Retrieved March 6, 2009, from http://www.wwwords.co.uk/elea/content/pdfs/3/issue3_1.asp

Gattegno, C. (1978). *Teaching foreign languages in schools: The silent way* (2nd ed.). New York: Educational Solutions.

Hall, R., & Hanna, P. (2004). The impact of web page text-background color combinations on readability, retention, aesthetics, and behavioral intention. *Behaviour & Information Technology, 23*(3), 183–195. doi:10.1080/01449290410001669932

Kruse, K. (2009). Introduction to instructional design and the ADDIE model. Retrieved April, 2009, from http://www.e-learningguru.com/articles/art2_1.htm

Kupetz, R., & Ziegenmeyer, B. (2006). Flexible learning activities: Fostering autonomy teaching training. *ReCALL, 18*(1), 63–82. doi:10.1017/S0958344006000516

Mohan, P., Greer, J., & McCalla, G. (2003). Instructional planning with learning objects. In P. Baumgartner, P.A. Cairns, M. Kohlhase, & E. Melis (Eds.), *Knowledge representation and automated reasoning for e-learning systems* (pp. 52-58). Retrieved November 12, 2009, from http://www.uni-koblenz.de/fb4/publikationen/gelbereihe/RR-16-2003.pdf

Nielsen, J. (2009). Usability 101: Introduction to usability. Retrieved April 4, 2009, from http://www.useit.com/alertbox/20030825.html

Oblinger, D. G., & Hawkins, B. L. (2006). The myth about no significant difference: Using technology produces no significant difference. *Educause Review, 41*(6), November/December. Retrieved April 10, 2009, from http://www.educause.edu/EDUCAUSE+Review/EDU-CAUSEReviewMagazineVolume41/TheMyth-aboutNoSignificantDiffe/158103

Sener, J. (2004). Escaping the comparison trap: Evaluating online learning on its own terms. *Innovate, 1*(2).

Taylor, J. (1998). Flexible delivery: The globalisation of lifelong learning. *Indian Journal of Open Learning, 7*(1) January, 55-65. Retrieved October 20, 2009, from http://www.usq.edu.au/users/taylorj/publications_presentations/1997india.doc

University of Illinois. (2007) Department of Ophthalmology and Visual Sciences. Retrieved April 10, 2009, from http://www.uic.edu/com/eye/LearningAboutVision/EyeFacts

Voller, P. (1997). Does the teacher have a role in autonomous language learning? In Benson, P., & Voller, P. (Eds.), *Autonomy and independence in language learning*. New York: Addison Wesley Longman.

Wiley, D. A. (2000). Connecting learning objects to instructional design theory: A definition, a metaphor, and a taxonomy. In D.A. Wiley (Ed.), *The instructional use of learning objects: Online version*, retrieved on April 29, 2008, from http://reusability.org/read/chapters/wiley.doc

Won, K., & Shih, T. K. (2004). On reusability and interoperability for distance learning. *Journal of Object Technology, 3*(8), 27-34. Retrieved April 10, 2009, from http://www.jot.fm/issues/issue_2004_09/column3

ADDITIONAL READING

Andrews, D. (2000). *Technical communication in the global community* (2nd ed.). New Jersey: Prentice Hall.

Boyle, T. (2003). Design principles for authoring dynamic, reusable learning objects. *Australian Journal of Educational Technology, 19*(1), 46-58. Retrieved October 20, 2009, from http://www.ascilite.org.au/conferences/auckland02/proceedings/papers/028.pdf

Brockman, J., & Rook, F. (1995). *Technical communication and ethics*. Arlington, VA: Society for Technical Communication.

Burnett, R. E. (2004). *Technical communication* (5th ed.). Fort Worth: Harcourt College Publishers.

Clark, R., & Mayer, R. (2003). *E-Learning and the science of instruction: Proven guidelines for consumers and designers of multimedia learning*. San Francisco: Jossey-Bass/Pfeiffer.

Hasegawa, N. (2005). Koukateki na hiragana jyugyou ni mukete *Nichigen Jisshuu Repoto*, Nagoya University. Retrieved July 17, 2008, from http://www.lang.nagoya-u.ac.jp/nichigen/menu5_folder/jisshu/2005/index.htm

Hatasa, K. (1983). Teaching Japanese syllabary with visual and verbal mnemonics. *CALICO Journal, 8*(3), 69–80.

Hoft, N. (1995). *International technical communication*. New York: Wiley.

IEEE Standards Committee. (2002). *IEEE Standard for Learning Object Metadata. IEEE Standard 1484.12.1*, New York: Institute of Electrical and Electronics Engineers. Retrieved October 10, 2007, from http://ieeexplore.ieee.org/iel5/8032/22180/01032843.pdf?arnumber=1032843

Jones, R. (2004). Designing adaptable learning resources with learning object patterns. *Journal of Digital Information, 6*(1). Retrieved October 20, 2009, from http://journals.tdl.org/jodi/article/viewArticle/60/62

Kamiyama, T. (1973). How to teach reading in the beginning 50 hours. *The Journal of the Association of Teachers of Japanese, 8*(2), 47–54. doi:10.2307/489198

McDowell, E. (1991). *Interviewing practices for technical writers*. Amityville, NY: Baywood.

Nielsen, J. (2000). *Designing web usability*. Indianapolis: New Riders.

O'Neill, P. G. (1967). *Japanese Kana workbook*. Tokyo, New York: Kodansha.

Oxford, R. L. (1999). Anxiety and the language learner: New insights . In Arnold, J. (Ed.), *Affect in language learning*. Cambridge: Cambridge University Press.

Quackenbush, H., Nakajyou, K., Nagatomo, K., & Tawada, I. (1989). Gojuppun hiragana dounyuhou - 'rensouhou' to 'irotsukikadohou' no hikaku *Nihongokyouiku 69*, 247-162.

Quackenbush, H., & Ohso, M. (1999). *Hiragana in 48 minutes*. Melbourne: Curriculum Corporation.

Ruddock, K. (2000). An argument for the use of authentic texts with beginners of Japanese as a foreign language. *CLCS Occasional Paper 58*. Dublin: Trinity College Dublin.

Shriver, K. (1997). *Dynamics in document design*. New York: Wiley and Sons.

Tavani, T. (2004). *Ethics and technology: Ethical issues in an age of information and communication technology*. New Jersey: Wiley.

Thompson, J. D., & Wakefield, J. F. (1996). *Picture this character: Using imagery to teach a Japanese syllabary*. Paper presented at the Annual Meeting of the Mid-South Educational Research Association, Alabama.

Warner, T. (1995). *Communication skills for information systems*. London: Pitman.

Weiss, E. (2005). *The elements of international English style*. New York: ME Sharpe.

ENDNOTE

[1] The suggestion to use colour combinations inspired by the Silent Way was by Prof. Naoko Aoki of Osaka University, to whom thanks are due.

Chapter 19
Web 2.0 to Pedagogy 2.0:
A Social–Constructivist Approach to Learning Enhanced by Technology

Judith A. Kuit
University of Sunderland, UK

Alan Fell
University of Sunderland, UK

ABSTRACT

Despite the extensive use of technology in teaching and supporting learning, teaching methods and approaches have for some academic staff remained largely unchanged. However, 21st century learners appear to have a different approach to learning and have different expectations regarding the use of technology in learning than their predecessors. For some academic staff this can be seen as a threatening scenario since they appear to believe that they have no role in future learning because it has been usurped by technology. Many suggest therefore, that the role of academic staff must change in the 21st century if they are to remain at the core of the learning process. The new learning paradigms of connectivism, navigationism, pedagogy 2.0 and heutagogy are described and discussed in the light of the role of academic staff. All of these paradigms have strong social constructivist learning theory underpinning their foundations and as such still have at their centre a fundamental role for academic staff. This is a role not in spite of the technology but rather one that is supported and enabled by the technology, particularly with respect to the Web 2.0 social networking tools.

INTRODUCTION

Despite the extensive current use of technology in teaching and supporting learning some have argued that teaching methods have remained largely unchanged in the last century, 'the school-master from 1909 would feel at home in the classroom in

DOI: 10.4018/978-1-61520-879-1.ch019

2009' (Elliott, 2009, p1). Some go even further by suggesting that 'lectures … have existed virtually unchanged for over 800 years' (Sheely, 2006, p. 770). If teaching has not changed then how about learning? Do 21st century learners, the so-called 'digital natives' (Prensky, 2001. p. 1) or 'Millenials' (Oblinger & Oblinger, 2003) learn differently from their predecessors? Prensky would argue that they do and that they are 'digitally wise' (Prensky,

2009, p. 1). Does this then suggest that the role of academic staff must change and that perhaps if learners are 'wise' then are academic staff necessary in the 21st century? This chapter will argue that academic staff are still vital instruments in terms of supporting learning, but that their new role in the 21st century is different from that of the 20th century.

The aim of this chapter is to posit that in order for learners to actively engage in effective learning enhanced by the use of technology then academic staff must change and adopt a new approach to teaching to enable this to happen, and it will do this by:

- considering the reasons why some academic staff do not engage, or engage very little with e-learning;
- considering the affordances to teaching and learning offered by Web 2.0 technologies;
- discussing paradigm shifts in teaching and learning which could occur with the use of Web 2.0 technologies.

BACKGROUND

In this early part of the 21st century there has been a rapid development of exciting new Web 2.0 tools which have the potential to be used in teaching and to develop a more active and deeper approach to learning. Despite this, there are still some academic staff who appear reluctant to engage in e-learning with their students, and research suggests that there are a number of reasons for this. Some of this research will be discussed below.

A Fear of Change

There appear to be many staff who fear the changes which e-learning brings either because it means exploring unknown territory or because they fear the consequences of the change. Research (Kuit & Fell, 2008; Margaryan & Littlejohn,

2008) has indicated that some academic staff feel threatened by the use of technology in teaching and perceive that they are usurped by the technology. As a consequence some feel that they either have a diminished role, or no longer have a role in supporting learners and learning. This is more apparent in those staff who have not grown up with technology. Kuit and Fell (2008) suggest that the term e-learning divides the views of some academic staff and that this division occurs around the hyphen. Some staff see only the 'e' that is the 'electronic', or technology part of the term but do not see the 'learning', part and as a consequence do not engage with e-learning. The reasons for this vary but Kuit and Fell (2008) suggest that it relates to fear of:

- a perceived, and often undisclosed, inability to use the technology;
- the time it will take to learn how to develop the necessary skills to use yet another piece of new technology;
- their teaching being 'exposed' to other staff and their lack of technical ability exposed to learners or to colleagues whom they often perceive as experts in e-learning;
- it threatening what they do in face-to-face sessions;
- their teaching being online so they will become under-employed or worse, unemployed.

In some instances this leads to some academic staff perceiving technology as a threat and therefore they do not engage with it. Consequently this becomes a problem for learners who 'observe their academic staff's lack of fluency with modern tools, and view them as "illiterate" in the very domain the kids know they will need for their future-technology' (Prensky, 2007, p. 40). These findings suggest that perhaps a more appropriate term to describe e-learning should be learning enhanced by technology because the learning should come first. This is a view now supported by the Higher Education Funding Council for England (HEFCE) who have revised their e-learning strategy by developing an approach of enhancing learning and teaching through the use of technology (HEFCE, 2009).

In contrast, there are some academic staff who commonly use e-learning in addition to their face-to-face teaching but find that it is difficult to make time in order to maintain both approaches effectively. This can be particularly problematic for their managers who can clearly allocate teaching duties for lectures and seminars on an hourly basis but who inevitably struggle with allocating equitable time for supporting online learning. There are other groups of academic staff known as the early adopters with clear IT skills who actively embrace every new technology because it is the latest tool or 'gadget'. This group use technology to support teaching because it is available but do not always ensure that it is used effectively and appropriately in the right context to enhance learning (Fell & Kuit, 2005). The first step in the critical design of learning enhanced by technology should therefore be to reflect on how the technology can be used in such a way as to ensure that effective learning takes place, rather than adopt a philosophy of 'I have a tool so how can I use it'. As Siemens (2006, p. 97) says 'the real value of a new tool is not the tool itself but what the tool enables'. However, too often the tool is imposed upon academic staff, not necessarily for pedagogical purposes, but because their institution has purchased a learning management system (LMS) such as a virtual learning environment (VLE) as a way of teaching increasingly large numbers of students both on-campus and off-campus.

Virtual Learning Environment

A VLE is a collection of integrated learning support tools which typically comes as a single, commercially available product such as Blackboard or else is available open source, for example Moodle. The VLE enables learning and the management of learning, online, for all students regardless of time and place, by providing a mechanism to deliver content and resources, student tracking and discussion fora. Their use in education at all levels is common and in many institutions the VLE sometimes becomes a strategic driver despite the reluctance by some academic staff to engage with it. Institutional insistence for staff to use it is in reality partly to justify the massive expenditure that an integrated VLE entails and this leads to senior managers insisting that 'we have a tool so you must use it'. Such a directive can be counter productive since it can often encourage staff to use the VLE in a very passive way since it is the easiest and quickest way to address the demand (Fell, 2004). For example, some academic staff simply deposit material such as lecture notes or powerpoint presentations on the VLE and then repeat the same lecture face to face with the learners. Staff often subsequently complain that learners are not attending lectures and wonder why this is happening. As has been argued, this is most often because these particular academic staff have translated their lecture notes to an on-line electronic document and have not actually transformed their teaching practice into online interactivity (Fetherston, 2001; Petre, Carswell, Price, & Thomas, 2000; Sheely, 2006). Consequently, their teaching 'modus operandi' has not evolved, despite the availability of the technology and the affordances offered by asynchronous text-based conferencing for active and reflective learning. Despite the excellent guidance provided by Salmon (2002) on e-moderating an online discussion, there is little incentive by academic staff to undertake this role as it is difficult to quantify in terms of work-loading. Similarly, students struggle to understand why they must communicate virtually with someone who in reality is sitting next to them (Fell, 2004). It is debatable as to whether this lack of appropriate and effective use of a VLE is the fault of the academic staff, the senior managers, the educational developers or perhaps the design of the VLE itself.

A VLE is often now perceived as a very cumbersome means of addressing the learning needs of the net generation. VLEs are seen to represent a way of controlling the learner's learning with little opportunity to develop or enhance it. Despite the recent additions of blogs and wikis to many existing VLEs they largely remain restricted to password-protected internal use, apparently in order to protect the copyright or intellectual property rights of the staff and/or the learners. However, current learners constantly use technology in their everyday life for example in the form of mobile phones or social networking sites such as Facebook and do not expect their access to be restricted. To these learners, a VLE uses a pre-21st century approach to teaching where the learner is the passive recipient of knowledge. The following quote from a frustrated member of academic staff, cited by Anderson (2007) supports this view.

I found out all my students were looking at the material in the VLE but going straight to Facebook to use the discussion tools and discuss the material and the lectures. I thought I might as well join them and ask them questions in their preferred space. (Anderson, 2007, p. 34)

McLoughlin and Lee (2008a) suggest that VLEs are models of a closed classroom and that they conform to the 'learner as an information consumer in their design' (p. 10) and as such they are becoming out of date. Sheely (2006) argues that VLEs are teacher-centric and more conducive to a traditional lecture hall whose purpose is to maximise the efficiency of teaching and not to enhance learning. It could be argued therefore that VLEs and other LMSs are redundant Web 1.0 technologies in the 21st century and that the affordances offered by the new Web 2.0 technologies will transform teaching because they have the potential and ability to transform learning (McLoughlin & Lee, 2008a; O'Reilly, 2005).

Web 1.0 and Web 2.0 Technologies

The tools which may be considered as belonging to Web 1.0 include: a learning platform such as a VLE; static learning materials published in electronic format for inclusion on an institution's VLE or some universally available website; domestic internet access via dial-up providing a rather limited bandwidth which tends to prevent, for example, the use of webcams and other dynamic interactive technology; email; hyperlinks to webpages selected by academic staff and deemed by her/him to be of interest and relevant to the chosen subject but not necessarily perceived by the learner as flexible learning (Hase & Kenyon, 2000).

It would not be unrealistic to suggest that while Web 1.0 affords greater freedom in terms of access to learning and where the learner is able to study, it does not support greater freedom in how the learner might study. That is to say Web 1.0 technology provides greater flexibility in terms of access regardless of time and place but it largely replicates in electronic format, the traditional classroom setting and the learning process continues to be steered and controlled by academic staff (Sheely, 2006). The level of interactivity afforded by Web 1.0 technologies is the principal indicator of the differences between Web 1.0 and Web 2.0.

To offer an enduring definition as to what constitutes Web 2.0 technologies is somewhat problematic since they are in a constant state of flux with new variations, facilities and tools emerging on an almost daily basis. Indeed very soon Web 2.0 technology will be replaced by Web 3.0 as access to increased bandwidth becomes more available. Despite this difficulty some indication does need to be provided here of what is Web 2.0 but with the caveat that this indication needs to be read in conjunction with the date of publication. The term Web 2.0 was originally coined by Dale Dougherty (though many argue it was Tim O'Reilly) and it essentially includes the use of all interactive technology which provides, and can support, various means of bilateral communication (O'Reilly, 2005). As the name suggests, Web 2.0 is regarded as the second generation of web technology which includes for example, blogs, podcasts, wikis and of course access to the internet via a broadband connection. However, Web 2.0 refers not simply to the technology itself but the manner in which it is applied and exploited. Web 2.0 has a much stronger focus upon interaction, communication and collaboration rather than, as was essentially the case with Web 1.0, the retrieval of static information. Although of course there remains with Web 2.0 a significant element of information retrieval this is much enhanced through access to a reliable broadband connection and to more effective search engines, principally Google.

Franklin and van Harmelen (2007) suggest that the most important applications of Web 2.0 tools for use in higher education are blogs, wikis, podcasts, social network sites and tagging. But Web 2.0 technologies are more than just a set of tools. Anderson (2004, p. 42) argues that Web 2.0 is a set of 'concepts, practices and attitudes' that define its scope. The two technological approaches of Web 1.0 and Web 2.0 reflect fundamental differences in the perception of knowledge with Web 1.0 representing the traditional view of knowledge as unbiased, evidence-based facts whilst Web 2.0 represents the 'collective agreement of a description that may combine with ... opinions, values and spiritual beliefs' (Dede, 2008, p. 80). Web 2.0 technologies rely on participation and a community of knowledge and practice where the wisdom of the crowd is more important than that of the individual. Therefore the more people who are networked together the greater the collective knowledge. Although the current tools which are described as Web 2.0 technologies will inevitably change and be replaced, the concept that individuals will interact and create new information and new networks will not (Siemens & Tittenberger, 2009).

It is clear from the discussion above and the differences outlined in Table 1 that Web 2.0 relies substantially upon the building of a community in which social networking is the crucial element. Through the building of an online community of learners the information retrieved and received from the web can be discussed, debated and internalised leading to a more informed understanding of the underlying principles through the process of social knowledge construction. While Web 2.0 affords the learner greater independence and autonomy when compared with more traditional approaches to learning, there remains the opportunity for academic staff to inform and guide the learning process. In a similar way to that used in asynchronous text-based conferencing academic staff can, with the prior agreement of the learners, observe the learners' discussions and exchanges and where appropriate intercede to guide or redirect the discussion (Fell, 2004; Fell & Kuit, 2005). Thus the role of academic staff is no longer to dictate what it is, or how, the learner learns but instead to guide, facilitate and, ideally, enhance both the learning and the process of learning. Conole and Creanor (2006) suggest that learners have high expectations of how they should learn, selecting technologies that best suit their needs and these are not necessarily what academic staff think that they should use. The use of Web 2.0 technologies and its successors in education will therefore affect how staff teach because it affects how learners learn.

HOW LEARNERS LEARN

There exists a variety of theories concerning the manner in which human beings learn and a very broad-brush taxonomy of these might include, among others, behaviourist learning theory, cognitive learning theory and social learning theory. It is beyond the scope of this book to describe them in detail but additional reading is provided in a list at the end of this chapter. Instead more emphasis

Table 1. Indicators of the Fundamental Differences between Web 1.0 and Web 2.0 Technologies (based upon O'Reilly, 2005)

Web 1.0 is about:	Web 2.0 is about:
Information consuming	Information prosuming (*through consuming and producing content in blogs/wikis/tagging etc.*)
Presenting knowledge	Constructing knowledge
Reading content	Creating new content (*through different combinations or applications*)
Individuals	Communities (*working collaboratively with others with similar interests or views*)
Home pages	Blogs (*posting comments and opinions online to which others can contribute*)
Portals	RSS (*Really Simple Syndication which pipes the latest information to the desktop*)
Wired	Wireless (*which permits mobility*)
Owning	Sharing (*with others online*)
Directories (taxonomy)	Tagging (*generating a folksonomy or personalised bookmarks which can be shared*)
Content Management Systems	Wikis (*which can be edited by anyone*)
Netscape	Google (*actively searching online*)

will be given to constructivist learning theory as this is particularly pertinent when considering the use of Web 2.0 technologies in teaching.

Constructivist Learning Theory

Whilst the definition of constructivism is controversial and complex (see Phillips, 1995 or Boghossian, 2006 in Additional Reading) for the purposes of this discussion the constructivist approach to learning is predicated upon the individual learner making sense of the new knowledge and materials which s/he encounters, that they have control over the learning process and that the process is learner centric. The thrust of constructivist learning theory is that the individual learner actively constructs personalised knowledge and that it is not simply knowledge received passively from others such as academic staff. There are, however, two strands of constructivist learning theory, cognitive and social. Cognitive constructivism, is where learners internalise or make sense of the content presented to them. Social constructivism occurs when learners construct meaning through the social interaction of discussion and combined exploration of content and concepts in order to

enhance and expand their knowledge and understanding. At the core of social constructivism lies the irrefutable need for communication and collaboration and in the 21st century world of learning enhanced by technology, and this can be provided by the adoption and exploitation of Web 2.0 social network technologies. The appropriate use of these technologies in this way will lead to a paradigm shift in teaching and learning.

Paradigm Shifts in Teaching and in Learning

Despite the argument that the process of teaching appears to have changed little over the decades or perhaps even centuries, there were a number of paradigm shifts in teaching and learning in the second half of the twentieth century. Brown (2005) suggests that these include:

- reproductive learning versus productive learning where the emphasis has shifted from memorising to application;
- behaviourism versus constructivism, i.e. moving from a change in the behaviour of the learner to a new construct of meaning by the learner;

315

- tutor-centred versus learner-centred, i.e. changing from the academic staff being the primary source of knowledge to the needs of the learner being central;
- teaching-centred versus learning-centred with educational activities now being focused upon the learning rather than the teaching;
- teaching versus learning facilitation, i.e. a move in the role of academic staff from being the only source of knowledge to role of facilitating the access, synthesis, interpretation and contextualisation of information into knowledge;
- content-based learning versus outcomes-based learning with a change in emphasis from what the learner knows to what the learner can actually do at the end of the learning process;
- content-based evaluation versus outcomes-based assessment which moves from the learner being able to demonstrate a change in content reproduction to being able to demonstrate mastery of learning outcomes.

Lave and Wenger's (1991) communities of practice theory is based on social constructivist principles and suggests that learners develop a 'community of practice' that develops shared resources, knowledge and experience. In a similar vein, Tangney, Fitzgibbon, Savage, Mehan, and Holmes (2001) propose a model of communal constructivism where learners actively create their own knowledge and contribute to the knowledge of the wider community. In both of these theories learners are clearly both consumers and producers of knowledge and the role of academic staff is to facilitate this by acting as a *'guide on the side'* (Stinson & Milter, 1996). It is clear that these theories could be applied to Web 2.0 technologies which they pre-date.

The application of Web 2.0 technologies in teaching and learning provides the opportunity for a further paradigm shift to develop new socio-constructivist theories of learning which underpin how learners engage with these tools to develop and create their own purpose-built knowledge (McKavanagh, Kanes, Bevan, Cunningham & Choy, 2002).

Connectivism

Siemens's theory of connectivism (2005) describes learning as a process of creating a network of personal knowledge and he argues that learning does not always take place inside a person. His theory is based on the premise that having the connection to information is more important than the information itself and the 'ability to learn what we need for tomorrow is more important than what we know today' (Siemens, 2005, p. 8). The theory of connectivism implies that we process, interpret and derive personal meaning from different information sources (Siemens, 2006) which any one individual is unable to synthesise alone. Instead it suggests that the individual off-loads this process to personal trusted networks of people and content to provide the knowledge for him or her. The individual develops this into personalised learning by a mash-up (or mix up) of external connections to social networks accessed via Web 2.0 technologies and the individual's personal interpretation through the neural networks of his or her brain (Siemens & Tittenberger, 2009).

Connectivism is predicated on the issue of dealing with information overload because anyone with an internet connection has the opportunity to access an unprecedented amount of rapidly changing information and knowledge.

While the world's codified knowledge base (i.e. all historical information in printed books and electronic files) doubled every 30 years in the earlier part of this [20th] century, it was doubling every seven years by the 1970s. Information library researchers say that by the year 2010, the world's codified knowledge will double every 11 hours. (Bontis, 2002, p. 22)

No one individual could possibly hold all of this knowledge let alone synthesise and evaluate it. Subsequently for academic staff it will become more difficult to continue to be the *sage on the stage* or even the *guide on the side* facilitating the learning process, and for learners it will become increasingly difficult to negotiate a way through the information without being overwhelmed by it. Oblinger (2008) suggests that educational institutions have an obligation to cultivate the skills of judgement, synthesis, research, practice and negotiation in their learners if they are to be capable of higher-order analysis and complex communication in using Web 2.0 technology. However, evidence from Windham (2005) indicates that many learners in higher education lack these increasingly important skills and are unable to navigate and select appropriate resources and information.

Navigationism

Brown (2005, p. 8) has partly addressed this concern in his novel learning paradigm, navigationism, where the role of academic staff has evolved beyond the metaphors of '*the sage on the stage*' and '*guide on the side*' to that of '*coach in touch*'. Brown posits that learning in the 21st century will be seen as

exploring, evaluating, manipulating, integrating and navigating. Successful learning takes place when learners solve contextual real life problems through active engagement in problem solving activities and extensive communication and collaboration. The aim of these activities is not to gain or create knowledge, but to solve problems. Knowledge is, of course, being created in the process, but knowledge creation is not the focus of the activities per se. (Brown, 2005, p. 8)

The theory of navigationism has evolved from social constructivist principles of knowledge creation to knowledge navigation and evaluation. If this paradigm shift were to be adopted then it would have profound affects on higher education. The role of the student would change from knowledge consumer to knowledge navigator whilst the role of academic staff would be to coach learners how to navigate through the ocean of knowledge and to mentor learners in the skills and competencies required to survive the journey through the immense network of information available to them. Similarly, instructional designers would need to concentrate on the design of coaching and navigating activities and navigation tools would need to be appropriately configured. Whilst universities would need to move from providing content for learners to providing a clearer 'focus on enabling learners to find, identify, manipulate and evaluate information and knowledge, to integrate this knowledge in their world of work and life, to solve problems and to communicate this knowledge to others' (Brown, 2005, p. 10).

However, McLoughlin and Lee (2008a, 2008b) would argue that learning is not simply using Web 2.0 technologies to facilitate networking and that the role of academic staff should support knowledge creation rather than simply coaching students in navigating. This is reflected in the fundamental differing structures of Web 1.0 and Web 2.0 technologies. Gillmor (2004) describes Web 2.0 as the read/write web because it facilitates participation and collaboration whilst Web 1.0 technology is read-only. The affordances of Web 2.0 lead to clear differences between the two in terms of the role of the learner and the role of the academic staff. Web 1.0 represents the presentation of knowledge which learners passively consume whilst Web 2.0 represents 'the active co-construction of resources by communities of contributors' (Dede, 2008, p. 80) where the learner is a part of the community as a creator of knowledge (Paavola & Hakkarainnen, 2005) but also as a consumer of knowledge. McLoughlin and Lee (2008a) develop this idea further and describe learners as '*prosumers*' and that in order to develop these skills in learners requires a substantial paradigm shift in teaching and a new pedagogy.

PEDAGOGY 2.0

Mcloughlin and Lee (2008a) propose that the metaphor of the network and that of knowledge creation requires a new pedagogy which they call Pedagogy 2.0.

Pedagogy 2.0 is a framework that aims to focus on desired learning outcomes in order to exploit more fully the affordances and potential for connectivity enabled by Web 2.0 and social software tools. It is envisioned as an overarching concept for an emerging cluster of practices that advocates learner choice and self-direction as well as engagement in flexible, relevant learning tasks and strategies. (McLoughlin & Lee, 2008a, p. 15)

They argue that the concept of Pedagogy 2.0 is fundamental in the critical design of learning activities enhanced by technology. This is more than instructional design alone but is a development of problem-based learning, connectivism and knowledge creation, all of which are based on social constructivist principles. Clearly the role of the academic staff is pivotal in this approach as the activity design, which enables this to happen, is their responsibility. McLoughlin and Lee (2008a) suggest a number of guidelines to inform this design which include:

- content which stimulates cognition and includes learner-generated resources;
- curriculum which is dynamic, negotiable, inter-disciplinary, blended and requiring learner input;
- communication which offers multiple opportunities for social interaction using multiple media types;

- learning processes which are contextualised, reflective, iterative and inquiry-based;
- resources which are media rich, global and inter-disciplinary;
- scaffolds provided by a network of academic staff as well as peers, experts and communities;
- learning tasks which are experiential and personal by allowing learners to create their own content and ideas.

These guidelines have been informed by the many exemplary practices available in the literature some of which are provided below.

Examples of Pedagogy 2.0

The following examples of Pedagogy 2.0 all demonstrate different ways in which students go beyond passively receiving knowledge to where they are actively contributing and disseminating their own knowledge and content. Many of these examples demonstrate that their adoption leads to higher-order thinking and meta-cognition (McLoughlin & Lee, 2008a). Further examples of these activities can be found in McLoughlin & Lee 2007, 2008a, 2008b and Siemens & Tittenberger, 2009.

Vod/Podcasts

Many academic staff have used podcasts in innovative ways to engage in a dialogue with students which go beyond the passive practice of simply recording a summary of a lecture. For example to engage in discussions about seminar material, students record their informal discussions and these are distributed to other students in the class (Miller, 2007, cited in McLoughlin & Lee, 2008a). Similarly Frydenberg (2008, cited in McLoughlin & Lee, 2008a) has encouraged students to produce vodcasts, i.e. their own novel video file, available online, on demand, of course content to teach to other students in their class. Podcasts are particularly valuable in developing skills in learning a foreign language and learning about a foreign culture and McCarty (2005, cited in McLoughlin & Lee, 2008a) has used this tool to persuade students to articulate podcast episodes in a foreign language about the foreign culture and history being studied.

Blogs

There are numerous examples of using web logs or blogs in creative ways but by no means all of them are necessarily examples of Pedagogy 2.0. However the example from McLoughlin, Brady, Lee and Russell (2007, cited in McLoughlin & Lee, 2008a) is an examplar of the application of Pedagogy 2.0. This particular application centred on students who were on a placement, or internship, as part of their course. They engaged in peer mentoring with geographically dispersed fellow placement students by sharing their work experiences and offering moral support and advice via a blog.

Wikis

Wikis (or what I know is) can be used for any form of collaborative writing or group work. For example, Sener (2007, cited in McLoughlin & Lee, 2008a) describes how a wiki-based encyclopaedia has been produced by students for their own joint use on a law and criminal justice course.

Social Bookmarking

Social bookmarking is a useful tool for sharing information, articles and resources from and between learners across a group. They can also be tagged so that bookmarks can be brought together to generate a folksonomy, i.e. a classification system created by the students themselves, for an assignment or group project for example.

These examples demonstrate how students are creating their own personal and collective knowledge through the medium of participating in a community of practice. Essentially, each example encompasses the three key elements of Pedagogy 2.0 which McLoughlin and Lee (2008a) describe as personalisation, participation and productivity, or the three Ps.

The Three Ps of Pedagogy 2.0

- **Personalisation:** Web 2.0 technologies allow individuals to access a wide range of resources, ideas and communities which they personally select as being appropriate to their own learning needs and preferences. This personalisation requires the learner to develop skills of self-regulation and autonomy.
- **Participation:** Learners participate in communities and global networks to share ideas, inquiry and problem-solving. Participation develops the skills of communication and collaborative working.
- **Productivity:** Pedagogy 2.0 requires learners to contribute to the social process of knowledge creation thereby generating new content. This generates the skills of creativity, innovation and of meta-cognition.

Although Pedagogy 2.0 is truly embedded in Web 2.0 technologies and is based on sound social constructivist principles it still does not address all the needs of learners in the 21st century. It may be more appropriate for younger students than for learners who are more mature in their approach to learning. For this type of learner, the learning paradigm of heutagogy may be more relevant.

Beyond Pedagogy 2.0 to Heutagogy

Learners in the 21st century are not just digitally wise they are also likely to have multiple career paths and as a consequence may need to be able to engage in lifelong learning so that they can become learners throughout their working life and beyond. In a world which is constantly evolving, where technology and information rapidly become obsolete and a job or career for life is no longer a likely prospect, learners need to be independent expert learners. As such they need the critical higher-order cognitive skills and maturity to be autonomous learners (McNickle, 2003) so that they can take advantage of future opportunities in their career. Although maturity can come with age this is not simply about andragogy as opposed to pedagogy. Learners in the 21st century need to be able to determine their own learning, taking into account intuition, experience and the ability to reflect on what has happened, and understanding how it challenges or supports existing values and assumptions; Hase and Kenyon (2000) call this heutagogy. It seems reasonable to suggest that heutagogy is an evolution of the personalisation aspect of Pedagogy 2.0.

In heutagogy a learner does not just identify his or her own learning needs but also reflects on novel experiences and evaluates how these may challenge or support existing assumptions and values, learning from them in the process. This is an approach based on the Humanistic theory of Rogers (1951) which Hase and Kenyon (2000) argue is ideally suited to develop capability in learners in higher education and to prepare them to use these abilities after graduation in their future career.

Despite heutagogy pre-dating Pedagogy 2.0 it can be seen as a natural progression of the Pedagogy 2.0 personalised prosumer approach to learning but developing it further so that learners are self-directed to continue to learn on their own. The idea of autonomous independent learning was used as a rationale for generating many self-study open learning courses which were usually paper-based and content-heavy. However, in reality the learner had no control over the content of what was taught and the requirement of what had to be learnt. The institutional provider still maintained control over the content which meant inevitably that it was totally inflexible. The affordances offered by Web 2.0 technologies and their successors do allow for inclusion of these elements of flexibility and autonomy and offer an opportunity for the paradigm shift from teacher-centric to learner-centric lifelong learning.

FUTURE RESEARCH DIRECTIONS

As with many paradigm shifts in teaching, Web 2.0 technologies have not been available long enough to determine whether or not they do actually impact on teaching and on learning in a positive way which is sustainable as well as measurable. Most research reported to date can only suggest that what happens in the short-term, in discrete cases may be transferable to the longer term.

The attitude of the teacher in these scenarios will also strongly influence how students approach the use of Web 2.0 tools. Indeed the work of Kvavik and Caruso (2005) suggests that the IT skills of academic staff influence how learners approach and utilise IT. Personal communication with students suggests that they work and study harder in order to please those academic staff who demonstrate an interest in them and their practice by developing creative and innovative ways of teaching. It is difficult to separate out the influence of a caring member of academic staff in any study of the effectiveness of teaching and of learning. It is also difficult to separate out the direct influence of face-to-face teaching on the effectiveness of teaching with Web 2.0 technologies. Unless the learners are the ultimate heutagogues who only learn independently, alone and online then it is very difficult to prove that it is the technology part of the usual blended learning experience which has had the most significant influence on learning and not the face-to-face element or the effective combination of face-to-face and online learning.

There is also very little evidence of how individual differences between learners with respect to age, gender, subject area, learning style, cultural background or digital literacy (Margaryan & Littlejohn, 2008; Mayes, 2004) can impact on learners' uses of Web 2.0 tools and technologies. The fear of change and lack of confidence in their own technical ability described earlier in relation to some academic staff is equally relevant to some students, particularly mature returners to education who may be unfamiliar with Web 2.0 technologies.

Until these studies are completed, if indeed that is possible, the claims made for these new pedagogies remain unsupported by evidence and this may have a profound and perhaps negative influence on those academic staff who are currently reluctant users of technology.

CONCLUSION

This chapter began by considering some of the reasons why some academic staff apparently do not engage with learning enhanced by technology. Some of these reasons relate to a fear of change and/or a fear of technology and it is understandable that even the early adopters of technology will not be able to keep up to date with the rapid developments and changes in Web 2.0 tools. But being fearful of the technology blinds some staff to the affordances to teaching and learning offered by Web 2.0 technologies. Although the role of the academic staff may appear to have changed with the introduction of Web 2.0 technologies, academic staff should not feel threatened by these new learning paradigms. They are all fundamentally based on familiar sound social constructivist principles and include Schön's reflective dialogue (1987) where learners challenge their assumptions rather than simply reacting to problems.

The introduction of Web 2.0 technologies for use in teaching appears at first sight to be challenging and innovative, however the pedagogies underpinning their effective use are fundamentally unchanged and constructivism is still as relevant in the 21st century as it was in the 20th. The role of the academic staff in this process is not redundant therefore, it has not fundamentally changed at all. It is still relevant and pertinent to cultivate the skills of judgement, synthesis, research, practice and negotiation in their learners so that they can become capable of higher-order analysis and complex communication (Oblinger, 2008). As Barnett (1999) states, in this age of 'supercomplexity ... students must be required to handle conflicting ideas and perspectives and uncertainties, through debate and structured workshops' (p. 160) and that this is the purpose of a university. The difference now is that the affordances of Web 2.0 technology enable this to happen more effectively and in a way which is more meaningful to the 21st century learner.

The implications of this for the learner are that with these new technologies, they can gain knowledge which is more personal, more productive and more participatory to them as individuals. In order to do this they will need to enhance their meta-cognitive development so that they are competent and capable in developing expertise in locating, evaluating, creating and sharing ideas. For these learners, unlike their colleagues confined to a lecture theatre, this is an active, independent and essentially a more demanding experience.

As Web 2.0 tools encourage learners to work more collaboratively, the same point may be made for university staff. Many of the skills of locating and navigating online resources have been the prerogative of library staff and whilst the value of these skills has not always been acknowledged by academic staff, the increasing use of Web 2.0 technologies should lead to an increasingly demanding role for library staff and for the library. Some (e.g. Anderson, 2007) have even suggested that perhaps libraries should lead in the introduction of such technologies in universities and should drive the necessary collaboration required between academic and non-academic staff if learning using Web 2.0 technologies is to be effective.

It should be recognised by universities that these Web 2.0 technological changes are not the sole drivers for pedagogical change in the 21st century. There are a host of factors including student expectations, lifelong learning, portfolio careers, economic turmoil and increasing globalisation which will drive out traditional teacher-centric models of teaching. Many universities may wish to hang on to their control of the content of what makes up their degrees (BECTA, 2008) and disregard the learner-centric autonomy of the pedagogy of Web 2.0 technologies. However, this is not sustainable and cannot continue if more and more prestigious international universities post their educational content online and make it freely available to all potential learners. If content is all that learners desire, there is no requirement to go to a university. These consumers are not learning but passively receiving and accruing content from others without constructing any meaning from it. Many of these learners do not have the ability or competence to be able to learn autonomously. Therefore the future role of the universities should be less reliant on content delivery than on teaching the learner the skills of critical evaluation and the ability to deal with uncertainty and to accredit them in the form of a degree. The challenge to universities will be to determine how to assess the individual's skills, knowledge and abilities that learners develop whilst working collaboratively with Web 2.0 tools. The issue therefore, is to be able to separate out and acknowledge the wisdom of the individual from the wisdom of the crowd.

REFERENCES

Anderson, P. (2007). *What is Web 2.0? Ideas, technologies and implications for education.* JISC Technology and Standards Watch. London, UK: JISC. Retrieved September 2, 2008, from http://jisc.ac.uk/media/documents/techwatch/tsw0701b.pdf

Anderson, T. (2004). Toward a theory of online learning . In Anderson, T., & Elloumi, F. (Eds.), *Theory and practice of online learning* (pp. 33–60). Athabasca, Alberta, Canada: Athabasca University.

Barnett, R. (1999). *Realizing the university in an age of supercomplexity.* Buckingham, UK: Society for Research into Higher Education and the Open University.

BECTA. (2008). *Web 2.0 technologies for learning at key stages 3 and 4.* Coventry, UK: British Educational Communications and Technology Agency. Retrieved September 2, 2008, from http://www.becta.org.uk

Bontis, N. (2002). The rising star of the Chief Knowledge Officer. *Ivey Business Journal,* March/April, 20-25.

Brown, T. H. (2005). Beyond constructivism: Exploring future learning paradigms. *Education Today, 2005* (2). Retrieved November 11, 2007, from http://www.bucks.edu/IDlab/Beyond_constructivism.pdf

Conole, G., & Creanor, L. (2006). In their own words: Exploring the learner's perspective on e-learning. London, UK. JISC. Retrieved September 7, 2008, from http://www.jisc.ac.uk/media/documents/programmes/elearningpedagogy/iowfinal.pdf

Dede, D. (2008). New horizons: A seismic shift in epistemology. *EDUCAUSE Review, 43*(3), 80–81.

Elliott, B. (2009). *E-pedagogy: Does e-learning require a new approach to teaching and learning?* Edinburgh: UK: Scottish Qualifications Authority. Retrieved March 13, 2009, from http://www.scribd.com/doc/932164/E-pedagogy

Fell, A. (2004, September). *Applications and advantages of synchronous and asynchronous text-based conferencing in support of online learners.* Paper presented at the Association of Learning Technology Conference 2004. Exeter, UK, University of Exeter.

Fell, A., & Kuit, J. A. (2005, November). *Developing the professional role of the e-tutor.* Paper presented at the Staff and Educational Developers Association Autumn Conference, Birmingham, UK.

Fetherston, T. (2001). Pedagogical challenges for the World Wide Web. *Association for the Advancement in Computing in Education Journal, 9*(1). Retrieved March 18, 2009, from http://www.editlib.org/index.cfm?fuseaction=Reader.TOC&sourceissue_id=164

Franklin, T., & van Harmelen, M. (2007). *Web 2.0 for learning and teaching in higher education.* London, UK: Observatory on Borderless Higher Education.

Gillmor, D. (2004). *We the media.* Retrieved August 2, 2006, from http://www.authorama.com/we-the-media-1.html

Hase, S., & Kenyon, C. (2000). *From andragogy to heutagogy.* Retrieved March 10, 2009, from http://www.ultibase.rmit.edu.au

HEFCE Higher Education Funding Council for England. (2009). *Enhancing learning and teaching through the use of technology. A revised approach to HEFCE's strategy for e-learning.* March 12, 2009. Retrieved March 31, 2009 from http://www.hefce.ac.uk/pubs/hefce/2009/09_12

Kuit, J. A., & Fell, A. (2008). The digital divide: is it the hyphen? In N. Whitton, & M. McPherson (Eds.), *Re-thinking the digital divide* (pp. 100-101). Research Proceedings of the 15th Association for Learning Technology Conference. Leeds, UK: University of Leeds.

Kvavik, R. V., & Caruso, J. B. (2005). *ECAR study of students and information technology, 2005: Convenience, connection, control and learning.* Boulder, CO: EDUCAUSE Center for Applied Research. Retrieved August 11, 2009, from http://net.educause.edu/ir/library/pdf/ers0506/rs/ers0506w.pdf

Lave, J., & Wenger, E. (1991). *Situated learning: Legitimate peripheral participation.* Cambridge, UK: Cambridge University Press.

Margaryan, M., & Littlejohn, A. (2008). *Are digital natives a myth or reality? Students' uses of technologies for learning.* Glasgow, UK: Glasgow Caledonian University, Caledonian Academy. Retrieved April 3, 2009, from http://www.academy.gcal.ac.uk/anoush/documents/DigitalNativesMythOrReality-MargaryanAndLitteljohn-draft-111208.pdf

Mayes, J. T. (2004). Stage 2: learner-centred pedagogy: Individual differences between learners. *JISC e-learning models desk study.* London, UK: JISC. Retrieved October 16, 2006, from http://www.jisc.ac.uk/uploaded_documents/Stage%202%20Learning%20Styles%20(Version%201).pdf

McKavanagh, C., Kanes, C., Bevan, F., Cunningham, A., & Choy, S. (2002). *Evaluation of web-based flexible learning,* Adelaide, Australia: NCVER. Retrieved April 21, 2006, from http://www.ncver.edu.au/research/proj/nr8007.pdf

McLoughlin, C., & Lee, M. (2007). Social software and participatory learning: Pedagogical choices with technology affordances in the Web 2.0 era. In *ICT: Providing choices for learners and learning. Proceedings ascilite Singapore 2007* (pp. 664-675). Sydney, Australia: CoCo, University of Sydney. Retrieved February 2, 2009, from http://www.ascilite.org.au/conferences/singapore07/procs/mcloughlin.pdf

McLoughlin, C., & Lee, M. (2008a). The three P's of pedagogy for the networked society: Personalization, participation and productivity. *International Journal of Teaching and Learning in Higher Education, 20*(1), 10–27.

McLoughlin, C., & Lee, M. (2008b). Future learning landscapes: Transforming pedagogy through social software. *Innovate, 4*(5). Retrieved February 2, 2009, from http://www.innovateonline.info/index.php?view=article&id=539.

McNickle, C. (2003). *The impact that ICT has on how we learn: pedagogy, andragogy or heutatgogy?* Paper presented at the 16th ODLAA Biennial Forum Conference Proceedings on Sustaining Quality learning Environments. Retrieved March 10, 2009, from http://www.odlaa.org/publications/2003Proceedings/pdfs/mcnickle.pdf

O'Reilly, T. (2005). *Web 2.0: Compact definition?* Retrieved March 18, 2009, from http://www.oreillynet.com/lpt/a/6228

Oblinger, D. (2008). Growing up with Google. What it means to education. In *Emerging Technologies for Learning,* Vol. 3. (pp.11-29). Coventry, UK: BECTA. Retrieved March 23, 2009, from http://publications.becta.org.uk/display.cfm?resID=35877&page=1835

Oblinger, D., & Oblinger, J. (2003). Introduction. In D. Oblinger, & J. Oblinger (Eds.), *Educating the net generation* (pp. 1.1-1.5). Washington, DC: Educause. Retrieved October 16, 2006, from http://www.educause.edu/content.asp?PAGE_ID=5989&bhcp=1

Paavola, S., & Hakkarainen, K. (2005). The knowledge creation metaphor: An emergent epistemological approach to learning. *Science and Education, 14*(6), 535–557. doi:10.1007/s11191-004-5157-0

Petre, M., Carswell, L., Price, B., & Thomas, P. (2000). Innovation in large-scale supported distance teaching: transforming for the internet not just translating . In Eisenstadt, M., & Vincent, T. (Eds.), *The knowledge web: Learning and collaborating on the net* (pp. 97–117). London, UK: Kogan Page.

Prensky, M. (2001). Digital natives, digital immigrants. *On the Horizon, 9*(5), 1-6. Retrieved October 16, 2006, from http://www.marcprensky.com/writing/Prensky%20-%20Digital%20Natives,%20Digital%20Immigrants%20-%20Part1.pdf

Prensky, M. (2007). How to teach with technology: Keeping both academic staff and learners comfortable in an era of exponential change. *Emerging technologies for learning* (Vol. 2, pp. 40-46). Coventry, UK: BECTA. Retrieved June 26, 2008, from http://partners.becta.org.uk/index.php?section=rh&rid=13768

Prensky, M. (2009). H. Sapiens digital: From digital immigrants and digital natives to digital wisdom. *Innovate* 5(3). Retrieved March 17, 2009, from http://www.innovateonline.info/index.php?view=article&id=705

Rogers, C. R. (1951). *Client centred therapy.* Boston, MA: Houghton Mifflin.

Salmon, G. (2002). *E-tivities. The key to teaching and learning online.* London, UK: Kogan Page.

Schön, D. A. (1987). *Educating the reflective practitioner.* San Francisco, CA: Jossey-Bass.

Sheely, S. (2006). Persistent technologies: Why can't we stop lecturing online? *Who's learning? Whose technology? Proceedings ascilite Sydney 2006* (pp.769-774). Sydney, Australia: University of Sydney. Retrieved March 16, 2009, from http://www.ascilite.org.au/conferences/sydney06/proceeding/pdf_papers/p167.pdf

Siemens, G. (2005). Connectivism: A learning theory for the digital age. *International Journal of Instructional Technology and Distance Learning, 2*(1). Retrieved March 16, 2006, from http://www.itdl.org/Journal/Jan_05/article01.htm

Siemens, G. (2006). *Knowing knowledge*. Manitoba, Canada: Lulu.

Siemens, G., & Tittenberger, P. (2009). *Handbook of emerging technologies for learning*. Manitoba, Canada: University of Manitoba. Retrieved March 20, 2009, from http://www.umanitoba.ca/learning-technologies/cetl/HETL.pdf

Stinson, J., & Milter, R. (1996). Problem-based learning in business education: Curriculum design and implementation issues . In Wilkerson, L. A., & Gijselaers, W. (Eds.), *Bringing problem-based learning to Higher Education: Theory and practice*. San Francisco, CA: Jossey-Bass.

Tangney, B., FitzGibbon, A., Savage, T., Mehan, S., & Holmes, B. (2001). Communal constructivism: Learners constructing learning *for* as well as *with* others. In C. Crawford et al. (Eds.), *Proceedings of Society for Information Technology and Academic Staff Education International Conference 2001* (pp. 3114-3119). Chesapeake, VA: Association for the Advancement of Computing in Education (AACE).

Windham, C. (2005). The learner's perspective . In Oblinger, D. G., & Oblinger, J. L. (Eds.), *Educating the net generation* (pp. 5.1–5.16). Washington, DC: Educause.

ADDITIONAL READING

Boghossian, P. A. (2006). *Fear of knowledge: Against relativism and constructivism*. New York: Oxford University Press.

Klamma, R., Cao, Y., & Spaniol, M. (2007, March). *Watching the blogosphere: Knowledge sharing in Web 2.0*. Paper presented at the International Conference on Weblogs and Social Media, Boulder, CO. Retrieved March 18, 2009, from http://www.icwsm.org/papers/2--Klamma-Cao-Spaniol.pdf

Phillips, D. C. (1995). The good, the bad and the ugly: The many faces of constructivism. *Educational Researcher, 24*(7), 5–12.

Piaget, J. (1972). *The psychology of the child*. New York: Basic Books.

von Gaserfeld, E. (1989). Constructivism in education . In Husen, T., & Postlethwaite, T. N. (Eds.), *The international encyclopaedia of education, Supplement 1* (pp. 162–163). Oxford, UK: Pergamon Press.

Vygotsky, L. S. (1978). *Mind in society*. Cambridge, MA: Harvard University Press.

Chapter 20
Sustainability through Staff Engagement:
Applying a Community of Practice Model to Web 2.0 Academic Development Programmes

Paul Gormley
National University of Ireland Galway, Ireland

Catherine Bruen
Trinity College Dublin, Ireland

Fiona Concannon
National University of Ireland Galway, Ireland

ABSTRACT

In many third-level institutions the innovative potential of technology has not been fully recognised or exploited at a strategic organisational level or embedded in mainstream educational work processes at a micro level. The sustainable integration of effective e-learning practices into higher education establishments remains a major challenge. This chapter discusses the challenges of designing staff development programmes which support the integration of e-learning into higher education by (1) leveraging the affordances presented by Web 2.0 technologies, coupled with (2) utilising a community of practice model to provide a sustainable peer-driven framework to share, support and embed technology-mediated teaching and learning practices. The chapter presents a practical example how a model of staff engagement was implemented within an Irish university, and concludes with suggestions on how others may benefit in considering a similar approach.

DOI: 10.4018/978-1-61520-879-1.ch020

INTRODUCTION

Technology has the potential to be used in a wide range of ways to support learning. Web 2.0 tools such as blogs and wikis are becoming increasingly commonplace in personal and workplace environments (O'Reilly, 2005), providing richer technological learning spaces for staff and students in higher education. The collaborative nature of Web 2.0 tools, and their appropriation into contexts where learning is more than just an isolated and individual activity, represents a promising new direction in facilitating effective learning. A key challenge for institutions is to provide innovative staff development supports to encourage faculty adoption and innovation with these e-learning technologies.

The concept of communities of practice has generated interest as an approach that might be effectively utilised to foster a more sustainable model of staff development (Blackwell & Blackmore, 2003; Chalmers & Keown, 2006; Donnelly, 2008). It represents an approach to staff development that recognises the importance of the community and extends beyond the traditional 'talking-head', trainer-led instructional design model to consider a more effective form of 'legitimate peripheral participation' (Lave & Wenger, 1991) to encourage the integration of technology into daily teaching practice. Within this academic realm, groups of people within disciplinary boundaries or subject domains share an interest in their teaching activities, and learn how to do it better through their interactions with one another in communities and professional networks. Academic staff development programmes in higher education ignore this at their peril as 'learning is ubiquitous in ongoing activity, though often unrecognised as such' (Lave, 1993, p. 5).

This chapter explores whether staff participation in a peer-supported, community-driven group can foster sustainable embedding of effective teaching practices mediated through Web 2.0 technologies in practice. Developing upon previous research on communities of practice undertaken within the Irish National Digital Learning Repository (NDLR) project, this chapter describes a 2008–2009 staff development initiative designed to work with existing communities at the National University of Ireland, Galway. By leveraging existing social structures, a staff development programme was designed and implemented by adapting the NDLR 3-Stage Community of Practice Model to support a network of staff with a shared interest of integrating Web 2.0 technology into the teaching and learning experience.

Initial evaluation results suggest that staff engagement can be effectively and sustainably supported through this community of practice (CoP) model. These findings represent a promising staff development approach towards sustainable, collaborative knowledge-sharing networks resulting in successful pedagogic experiences in embedding technology for the enhancement of teaching practice.

BACKGROUND

Academic Staff Development Approaches

Laurillard (2004) states that the difficulty of truly 'embedding' e-learning into everyday practice is undermined by poor leadership, lack of true innovation and lack of professional expertise. The organisation as a whole must enable and encourage the competence development of its individual members if it wants to strategically act in the field of e-learning-driven innovation. Staff development in higher education is typically supported at a distributed level at the college or faculty, and by central units such as Human Resource staff development and training service centres which have become increasingly prevalent in the last decade (often referred to as 'Centres for Teaching and Learning' or 'Educational Development Units' in Ireland and the UK) (Gosling, 2008).

These centres commonly work in an environment where universities aim to harness the opportunities that technological innovations offer, within a dynamic wider context that places increasing demands on staff developers and faculty. Segrave et al. (2005) have argued that a central challenge is to create and sustain quality e-learning environments of enduring value for teachers and learners which depend on innovative strategic academic professional development approaches (see also EDUCAUSE, 2009).

A literature analysis identifies key barriers to overcoming this challenge. For example, there is a perceived lack of buy-in and adoption of e-learning from academic staff. This is compounded by difficulties reported with staff development approaches in higher education that result in a lack of staff engagement. Many staff development approaches have targeted either the development of technologies or top-down policy aspirations, and not the human dimensions, scaling-up and embedding of innovation and the associated management of change (Tham & Werner, 2005). There is often a misalignment in staff development programme offerings with professional development programmes frequently 'disconnected from practice, fragmented and misaligned' (Schlager & Fusco, 2004, p. 205). Some programmes are perceived as being separated from teachers' daily work, contain inappropriate and irrelevant content, and are poorly focused (Sandholtz, 2002). Commentators have noted the difficulty posed for staff developers in 'trying to ensure that e-learning practices are driven by educational rather than technical, economic or administrative considerations' (Oliver & Dempster, 2003, p. 143). It is critical to ensure that pedagogy and improvement in teaching and learning practices are at the forefront of any e-learning continuing professional development (CPD) initiative, and assure staff that this motivation is central.

On an individual level, academic staff may lack the online experience of the Internet generation, and so not feel as confident in an online environment as they do in a traditional classroom setting. In this context the problem is a social rather than a pedagogic one, and lecturers may need to experience being an online student themselves in order to gain the necessary confidence to move to an online environment (Salmon, 2004).

A key concern of this chapter is the issue of CPD design. Most e-learning training and development provision is designed in the form of stand-alone workshops which are delivered in traditional face-to-face mode. This following section will consider some of the challenges inherent in the workshop training model, with particular reference to the development of pedagogic competencies.

The E-Learning Staff Development Workshop

Whilst professional development encompasses a range of activities, the staff development workshop is the most common form of training for educators (Guskey, 2000). This model of staff training aims to transfer the relevant tools and concepts within a formal two or three hour training session, with the expectation that staff can subsequently begin to consider how to integrate these into their own context. Three key shortcomings in applying this approach are considered here.

The first shortcoming is the assumption that e-learning mastery can be transmitted in an abstract setting, over a short duration, removed from the context of use. The complex activity of incorporating mediating technologies appropriately into mainstream teaching practice requires a shift from focusing on developing technical skills alone to considering the more complex endeavour of supporting practitioners to embed technology into their curriculum design. Research by Donnelly and O'Rourke (2007) warns against perpetuating academic staff misperceptions in considering an e-learning staff development programme as 'a course in ITCs rather than an effort to change or improve their teaching abilities' (p. 32). They report that approaching academic professional development in the use of web technologies in a one-off workshop has not been an immediately transformational experience.

Secondly, the one-off workshop approach to professional development raises the issue of sustainability. The sheer scale of resources required for a single support unit to communicate and engage with all academic staff is unsustainable within a large organisation, such as a university. With several thousand academic staff, and only a small number of learning technologists or educational developers, there is a shortage of resources necessary to collaborate and interact with the entire academic community. The development of expertise in e-learning practices of many working in higher education has been largely informal and ad hoc (Mansvelt, Suddaby, & O'Hara, 2008).

Thirdly, each subject-specific domain presents context-related pedagogic challenges. To overcome this difficulty, academics frequently turn to their own communities within their schools, subject area or research field (Becher & Trowler, 2001). In these, they establish their own practices, routines and conventions and frequently rely on each other to contextualise newly acquired knowledge in an informal and pervasive way.

Designing Sustainable CPD Programmes

It is clear that there is a need for academic teachers to develop or to improve ICT-related competences to cope with the technological challenges in their workplace (Johnson, 2003; Salmon, 2004). So how do we design staff development programmes that will facilitate staff buy-in and engagement in implementing Web 2.0 teaching and learning practices in their own contexts? And how can the peer-driven communities of practice provide sustainable supports and structures to embed innovative teaching and learning practices over the longer term?

Research in the field of professional development for teachers' learning presents useful pointers in applying constructivist principles to e-learning CPD design. Putnam and Borko (1997, p. 1224) identify four constructivist-based principles of professional development: (1) teachers should be treated as active learners who construct their own understandings; (2) teachers should be empowered and treated as professionals; (3) teacher education should be situated (Becher, 1989); and (4) teacher educators and professional developers should treat teachers as they expect their teachers to treat students (Putnam & Borko, 1997, p. 1224).

In terms of designing a continuing professional development model for academic staff in the area of e-learning, it is essential to regularly reassess the pedagogical methods employed, in order to ensure the best experience for the teacher (Donnelly & O'Rourke 2007). Therefore it is appropriate to revisit the traditional face-to-face workshop model approach to staff development with a view to incorporating community-based elements around this format.

Workshop models can be useful if structured in an appropriate manner. For example, workshops can explore and support a number of negotiated pedagogical aims, representing different teaching and learning contexts and a range of discipline areas, through a common technological approach. Well-designed workshops have the potential to offer valuable models of good practice in the use of technology to support student activities by giving lecturers a taste of e-learning from the students' perspective (Bennett, Priest, & Macpherson, 1999). Staff can develop through peer learning by discussing and sharing their concerns, needs and approaches as a group. Participants work from a valuable set of contextually relevant case studies that can provide exemplars for future runs of the programme and to engage the staff.

However, a considered approach to face-to-face workshop design that disseminates information to practitioners in this manner alone will not lead to understanding, engagement or impact (Conole & Oliver, 2002; Sharpe, 2004). Practitioners need to be supported in engaging with the concept or tool in order to understand its relationship to their own practice (de Freitas, Oliver, Mayes, & Mee, 2007) A strong model for staff development may be the combination of the workshop that introduces theoretical and research-based ideas and a programme of ongoing support during the year as teachers attempt to adapt their ideas and introduce them into the classrooms (Putham & Borko, 1997, p. 1260). This ongoing support may come from a community comprised of a number of stakeholders including professional developers and academic staff. Elton (2005) suggests that the most acceptable form of staff development and the one that probably has had the most success is that in which staff developers and academic teachers collaborate with the aim of improving the student experience.

At a strategic level staff developers must be cognisant that there are many possible ways to support e-learning: different combinations will be needed at different times, depending on the institutional context. For lecturers to be innovative, they need time for pedagogic analysis, development and exploration. Very little academic time is explicitly spent on such professional development (Dearing, 1997). To be effective, initiatives must be aligned with strategic encouragement so that staff are motivated to engage.

The approach at the individual level must seek to ensure that ownership of the content and pedagogy rests with the individual academic (and supports their own context-dependent academic environment). A wide variety of supportive mechanisms must underpin the continued developments of these change agents. If academic staff members gain a deeper and more comprehensive understanding for the impact of new technologies on their key work processes, they can use these new technologies to extend, re-work and innovate their research and teaching contexts (Graves, 2001).

On a community level, innovative staff-development approaches may include elements of formal training, measures for non-formal training embedded into immediate work environ-ment of academics, and support for communities of practice, peer groups and networks. The real work contexts and conditions, in which non- or informal learning processes take place, are highly relevant for the research on e-learning competency development. One key assumption for the design of adequate staff training measures is that self-organised learning, which takes place on or close to the job, is one important factor in ICT-related competence development (Kerres, Euler, Seufert, Hasanbegovic, & Voss, 2005). Therefore tapping into the existing informal social networks within the academic community is essential for sustainable academic development (Blackwell & Blackmore, 2003). The following section investigates the role of communities of practice in supporting and developing individual academic e-learning competencies to transform teaching practices into innovative teaching and learning activities.

The Role of Communities of Practice in Staff Development

Since the early work of Jean Lave and Etienne Wenger (1991), communities of practice have evolved as a theoretical approach to understanding how expertise and competency is developed. Hubert, Newhouse, and Vestal (2001) define communities of practice as

groups of people who come together to share and to learn from one another face-to-face and virtually. They are held together by a common interest in a body of knowledge and are driven by a desire and need to share problems, experiences, insights, templates, tools and best practices. Community members deepen their knowledge by interacting on an ongoing basis. (p. 2)

Community of practice theorists see their approach as addressing issues of engagement through continual negotiation and mutual responses that bind the group together to produce a shared repertoire of community knowledge and resources

(Wenger, cited in White, 2002, p. 2). There is an understanding that all have interesting and valid ideas that should be heard and where possible used by the community in working through issues.

Communities are fundamentally a self-organising collection of volunteers with a common goal or focus. Knowledge is shared within the community based on relationships with others, rather than direct transactions. Therefore a primary purpose is supporting knowledge flows between people.

At the simplest level they are a small group of people ... who've worked together over a period of time. ... They are peers in the execution of 'real work'. What holds them together is a common sense of purpose and a real need to know what each other know. (van Winkelen, 2003, p. 2)

In terms of staff development design, the community of practice offers a useful framework to extend the traditional face-to-face workshop model towards a sustainable approach to embed Web 2.0 teaching and learning practice. If the aim of the community is for academic staff to develop practices of employing technology, then the community must provide opportunities for them to participate in such practices. Hence, the technology becomes an important element in mediating communication.

This approach would aim to share stories across and within the academic communities, and use boundary objects – documents, concepts, and Web 2.0 tools – to broker connections across communities, opening new possibilities to encounter ideas and share practice beyond the traditional borders. Such an approach would acknowledge the social nature of learning and academic practice, and could in turn lead to the emergence, over time, of support and expertise through the community of practitioners embedding their use of learning technology.

Community of practice approaches applied to staff development are well documented. Chalmers and Keown (2006) report positive findings from employing a community of practice model, linked to a constructivist professional development framework for embedding e-learning practices in teaching and learning in New Zealand schools. The 'Elearning and Benchmarking and Pathfinder' project in the UK (Higher Education Academy, 2009), adopted a Collaboration Approach to the Management of E-Learning (CAMEL) method utilising a community of practice approach to explore and share effective e-learning good practice between partner institutions. This initiative led to the establishment of five special interest groups to disseminate innovative teaching and learning approaches to the wider community. These include the following: in the areas of e-learning design (CHEETAH team), quality assurance (PREEL 2 SIG), blended learning (CABLE Transfer group), podcasting (Digital Media SIG) and a capturing of the student learners' experiences (ELESIG). In each of these projects, Web 2.0 technologies were widely used as an integral part of the project process and outputs.

The Irish National Digital Learning Repository 3 Stage CoP Model

The National Digital Learning Repository (NDLR) is an Irish third-level sectoral initiative providing services and support to enable the sharing of digital learning content and teaching experience across Universities, Institutes of Technologies and associated Colleges funded by the Irish Higher Education Authority. The NDLR mission is 'to promote and support Higher Education sector staff in the collaboration, development and sharing of learning resources and associate teaching practices' (http://www.ndlr.ie). The NDLR provides (1) an online repository to support collaboration and sharing of teaching and learning resources within the Irish third-level education sector and (2) infrastructure to support subject or discipline based communities of practice in higher education.

The NDLR 3-Stage Community of Practice conceptual model was developed from working models (e.g. CAMEL model), case studies and research findings that were adapted and contextualised to the Irish higher education environment. The seven-principle framework of community development suggested by Wenger, McDermott, and Snyder (2002) informed the design of a flexible 'work-in-progress' model that aimed to provide a useful guide to generate momentum and sustain energy within the NDLR communities of practice. These guiding principles acknowledge that while communities of practice needed to be spontaneous and self-directed, guidelines and structures can be helpful in creating optimum conditions for communities to flourish. The three stages of the NDLR model are outlined in Table 1.

While respecting that each CoP has its own unique identity and needs, the NDLR 2008 Review explored some of the key features and principles that the fifteen active NDLR CoPs had in common during the four-year pilot stage of its project (2005–2008):

- Communities of practice take time to develop, typically a minimum of 18 months to establish the trust network although they made a surprising amount of progress in that time as social elements and face-to-face meetings can speed up the process.
- Participation needed to be of a voluntary nature and members of the community typically have shared goals and a shared passion, and often the community evolved from a member-driven need. The success

of the community of practice is dependent on commitment by all parties.
- Members had a strong feeling of identity with the community which could stimulate and inspire to give confidence to instigate changes in practice.
- Successful communities of practice investigated whether they were duplicating the activities and subject disciplines of existing communities, and. where those overlaps occurred, the communities were encouraged to collaborate together.

Research conducted in the areas of 'inter-organisational communities' further report that nurturing a 'culture of trust and openness' is needed to allow meaningful knowledge to be exchanged in successful communities of practice (Braun, 2002; van Winkelen, 2003). Building social capital (or the collective strength of the relationship within the group) requires an investment of time and effort. The noted benefits include access to information, greater influence and higher solidarity. To earn social capital, each party must have the opportunity, the motivation and the ability to contribute to the relationships (Adler & Kwon, 2002).

The following section details how the Learning Technologies team at the Centre for Excellence in Learning and Teaching at National University of Ireland (NUI) Galway applied key professional development and community of practice research findings to design and implement a new professional development programme to embed Web

Table 1. The NDLR 3-Stage Community of Practice Model

Stages	Activity
Stage 1 – Forming/Storming	In this early stage of the development of the community, the NDLR began to identify partners, build trust, identify common goals and experiences, begin to formalise informal relationships.
Stage 2 – Norming/Performing	In this second stage, the identity of the NDLR community began to form, with the sharing of resources, and good practice.
Stage 3 – Adjourning/Transforming	The NDLR is looking to the future, considering how to move forward and innovate, continue to build upon good practice (within each subject domain and nationally/internationally).

2.0 tools and activities in teaching and learning practices.

APPLYING THE COMMUNITY OF PRACTICE MODEL

Staff Development in E-learning Approaches at NUI Galway

At NUI Galway, staff development on the use of information and communication technology for on-campus and distance education is conducted through a central unit called the Centre for Excellence in Learning and Teaching (CELT). Established in 2002, the unit is involved in developing an institution-wide strategy for learning teaching and assessment, along with directly engaging with schools and colleges to explore opportunities for increasing student engagement. It also offers a Post-Graduate Certificate, Diploma and Masters-level programmes in Teaching and Learning in Higher Education, and supports Ph.D. students in the area of higher education policy and practice.

CELT also supports pedagogic innovations in the use of learning technologies. As is common in many higher education institutions, a key element of CELT's strategy has centred of the mainstreaming the use of the institutional Virtual Learning Environments (VLE) to enable technology-enhanced learning to inform teaching practice (Brown & Jenkins, 2003; OECD, 2005). The university hosts a VLE Blackboard platform for a population of approximately 15,000 students and 3,000 staff. As of April 2009, the NUI Galway VLE platform has 1,890 active modules, 1,478 instructor/leader users, and 12,174 active users. Over 48 face-to-face training sessions were delivered for university staff in 2008 to support staff in using this technology. This support is delivered within a changing institutional context in which the university aims to widen participation and access through the development of blended learning offerings. Requests for support from academic staff

are growing as the VLE becomes an increasingly mainstream technology on campus.

A 2008 CELT strategic review of support for staff in the use of learning technologies investigated approaches towards developing a more sustainable and diverse portfolio of staff development offerings both in content and delivery and an increased student-centric approach to VLE usage. This review incorporated a survey of the student perceptions and experiences in using the institution's VLE. The survey revealed a high satisfaction rate with the use of the institution's VLE to support teaching and learning (98% satisfied or strongly satisfied). However, the survey highlighted pedagogical concerns that the technology was being used primarily as a repository for lecturer resources, some use of discussion boards for collaboration activities and a general low level of active learning/active student engagement taking place. This finding is consistent with Irish and international research findings (Donnelly & O'Rourke, 2007; Jennings, 2005).

The review identified an opportunity to progress these approaches through the imminent integration of the Learning Objects Campus Pack building block to extend the functionality of the Blackboard platform through the provision of blogs, wikis and podcasting features. This opened up the potential to capitalise opportunities afforded by Web 2.0 technologies to engage staff and students through innovative teaching and learning activities, and in so doing advance the current VLE usage towards more student-centred, collaborative activities. Towards this end, the CELT Learning Technologies team designed and implemented a new staff development model utilising research findings from both staff development and community of practice domains with the aim of providing supports to assist the embedding of Web 2.0 tools and activities into teaching and learning practice at NUI Galway.

The first implementation instance of the model was the establishment of the 'NUIG Collaboration Special Interest Group (SIG)' to support participants of a new training workshop offering entitled 'Using Blackboard to Support Groupwork, Collaboration and Reflection'. The primary aim of the SIG was to support academic staff in considering how to develop and embed blog (group and individual) and wiki-based student activities in innovative and engaging ways. The secondary aim was to record and develop a number of local case studies at NUI Galway which would serve as exemplars of contextualised practice for local, national and international audiences.

Community of Practice Model Implementation

The NDLR 3-Stage community of practice approach was considered an appropriate tool to model the design of the new staff development programme in a community context. All members of the team had familiarity with the approach, having previously collaborated on the NDLR project at a number of levels (including as project board member, community of practice co-ordinator, institutional representative and from an end user perspective). The team aimed to leverage the experience of the NDLR project in fostering the development of communities of practice and felt that the fluid and evolutionary nature of the model would be suitably adaptable to the local contextualised needs of the NUI Galway teaching and learning environment. The adaption of the approach in each of the three stages is outlined here.

Stage 1. Forming/Storming: Early Stages of Development

As acknowledged by the literature, a community of practice takes time to develop to the level where the group becomes the point of reference for a member. Stage 1 of the model is a pilot phase for the emergent community of practices to identify a 'raison d'être', establish membership and demonstrate their active engagement. The trust element is

very important at this juncture and only develops fully over time through community activities.

The main activity in this first implementation instance of the model was to establish the special interest group. Stage 1 of the CELT staff development design model comprised three interrelated elements underpinned by Web 2.0 tools and activities: (1) the provision of an online SIG web space; (2) initiating a half-day face-to-face workshop series; and (3) coordinating post-workshop activities. These elements are described below.

Supporting the Forming Community with Web 2.0 Technology

In advance of the workshop roll-out, the Learning Technologies team created a folder set of Web 2.0 resources within a Blackboard module entitled 'The Teaching and Learning Forum' in which all NUI Galway staff members were enrolled. Within the folder there were three key elements: (1) a group blog; (2) a group wiki; and (3) a folder of workshop resources. A fourth element folder titled 'Case Studies: What Your Colleagues are Doing' was added to this space later on in the academic year to capture and share the NUIG academic experience with colleagues.

Participants gained access to the Web 2.0 group space, once they signed up to attend a face-to-face workshop. As each workshop was delivered, the number and diversity of participants on the online space increased, as did opportunities for peer support and collaboration within and between members from different academic disciplines. The individual elements of the Collaboration Special Interest Group (SIG) web space are described below, and in Figure 1.

(a) *SIG Blog:* This comprised of a collection of participant posts capturing their thoughts on how they might utilise blogs and/or wikis in their own teaching and learning contexts. These contributions are outputs from a work-

Figure 1. Collaboration Special Interest Group (SIG) Web 2.0 Space

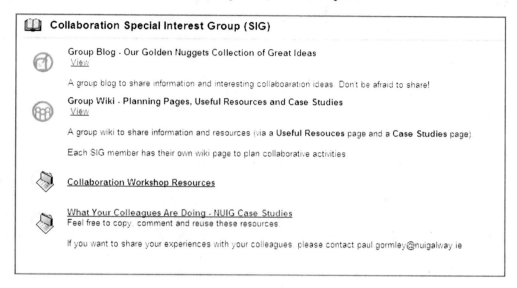

shop planning activity. The blog was referred to as 'Our Golden Nuggets Collection of Great Ideas'.

(b) *SIG Wiki:* The wiki consisted of a collection of useful resources, case studies and individual planning pages. The resources include planning sheets, YouTube videos, web links and research papers. Case studies were harvested from external sources initially, but are now being augmented and driven by local case studies. Participants add their own individual planning pages on the wiki to help develop their teaching and learning activities.

(c) *Group Folder – Workshop Resources:* A collection of MS PowerPoint presentations, planning sheets, videos, activities and sample files that are used in the face- to-face workshop session.

(d) *Group Folder – Case Studies*: *What Your Colleagues are Doing?*: The resources listed above were created prior to the workshop roll-out. This additional folder was added during the 2008–2009 academic year and is the key driver for knowledge sharing and transfer. The folder contains case studies

developed by NUI Galway staff embedding Web 2.0 technologies into their practice. Each case study contains a number of resources such as: wiki templates developed; learning tasks and student activities; evaluation tools such as student questionnaires or focus group questions; audio/video interviews with students; audio/video interviews with staff; lessons learned reflections.

The strategic aim of incorporating the Case Studies is to produce a critical mass of fifteen case studies from practitioners across the curriculum range. This feature of the online supporting space is envisaged as the catalyst for facilitating sustainable staff engagement with these technologies and to provide authentic voices to aid embedding e-learning into routine teaching and learning practices of staff.

(e) *Group Pages:* The group space lists all SIG participants, which enables colleagues to identify points of reference in their own subject domain, and/or colleagues who may be interested in collaborating on interdisciplinary projects.

Gráinne Conole has suggested that using new technologies requires a coordinated approach to design and that teaching practices and learning activities should be represented to better scaffold the sharing of good practice. She espouses the use of tools which seek to 'make explicit the pedagogical approaches and models that are implicit in practice' and 'might be used as an important prompt in this process' (Conole, 2008, p. 190). This mirrors the intention of the CELT Learning Technologies team to utilise collaborative Web 2.0 tools outlined above as a medium for communication amongst the community members. This served both as a community space to share information and resources, with the opportunity to practice and become proficient in understanding how Web 2.0 technologies offer particular affordances in facilitating knowledge sharing processes.

Staff Development Workshop Design

The highest profile community activity in Stage 1 was to offer a well-structured and targeted workshop that would begin to allow SIG members to meet face-to-face and become familiar with one another. The workshop format aimed to provide a common physical environment for academic staff to consider how to develop and embed blog (group and individual) and wiki-based student activities in innovative and engaging ways, and to support one another following the session.

The half-day face-to-face workshop 'Using Blackboard to Support Groupwork, Collaboration and Reflection' was designed for a maximum participation size of ten. A pre-requisite for workshop enrolment was that participants had previously attended a CELT 'Introduction to Blackboard' workshop and/or were comfortable with basic VLE activities, so that participants' contact time could focus on higher-order pedagogical issues.

The workshops were facilitated by a CELT Learning Technologist. Welcome comments set the context of the workshop by articulating that the aim of establishing the SIG was to provide

peer support for embedding Web 2.0 technologies into teaching and learning environments. Once the facilitator welcomed the participants to the NUIG Collaboration SIG group, participants logged into the SIG online resource area and were invited to use, contribute and communicate ideas and resources, either through the online resource area, or by contacting their peers listed in the group pages to investigate possible synergies. Staff were informed that the CELT Learning Technology team were keen to work with participants to develop local case studies over the coming months.

The workshop was structured around four main activities: (1) an introductory discussion of teaching and learning practice based around the opportunities and challenges afforded by Web 2.0 technologies; (2) hands-on technical activities in creating and using blogs and wikis; (3) showcasing Web 2.0 projects that peers are involved with; and (4) brainstorming and planning contextualised implementation of Web 2.0 activities into the participants' own teaching and learning environments.

Introductory group discussions provided a forum to help develop a shared understanding of pedagogical and technical issues associated with Web 2.0 tools by drawing on the experiences of the group where possible. A consistent theme emerged where the Web 2.0 pedagogical concepts were familiar to the group in an operational sense and that the terminology employed with Web 2.0 technologies provided the greatest concerns. Once the academics had explored the terminology and concepts collaboratively, they began to build up a greater confidence in their own understanding. Providing reflective space in the workshop allowed opportunities to contextualise the learning activities to participants' own environments as the group articulated their views on how learning can be designed effectively using technology enhancements.

The hands-on technical component provided an opportunity for the participants to get practical exposure to the Web 2.0 tools at their disposal.

Although the participants were required to have a working knowledge of the institutional VLE, a high proportion had not used Web 2.0 technologies before. This activity was designed to put participants at ease in order to see beyond the technology. A key output of the activity was to use the technology from a student perspective (e.g. add a post to the community blog and access some useful resources from the community wiki). The participants also created both a blog and a wiki in one of their active VLE courses. This provided an opportunity to implement the tool in participants' own teaching and learning context at a later stage.

The show-and-tell element of the workshop provided an opportunity for the participants to discover how Web 2.0 technologies were being implemented in a range of contexts by their peers. A powerful aspect of this workshop activity occurred when a member of the participating cohort demonstrated their own previous experience of using blogs and/or wikis. This provided opportunities for peer-driven question and answer discourse. When available, NUI Galway colleagues were invited into the workshops to demonstrate their use of these technologies, which added a degree of legitimacy to the experience.

The final brainstorming and planning activity provided an opportunity for the participants to apply their pedagogical and technical knowledge to implementing blogs and/or wikis into their own contexts. The academics downloaded planning sheets from the SIG wiki resource area and proceeded to identify a learning outcome which they wanted to address. Participants brainstormed in pairs to identify opportunities and constraints for successful implementation of the particular tool into their teaching and learning environments. There were two important outputs from this activity. Firstly, each participant was required to submit a three sentence summary (or 'Golden Nugget') idea post of what they would like to achieve with a particular tool into the community blog. Secondly, each participant was asked to create a personal planning page in the community

wiki resource area to progress their ideas outside of the contact time. This activity concluded with a one-minute round table verbal summary of participants' Golden Nuggets, along with a wider discussion based on these ideas.

Post-Workshop Activities

The workshop concluded with the facilitator outlining the CELT Learning Technologies team plan to provide development support in conjunction with the wishes of the SIG members. On a practical level, the facilitator articulated a range of forthcoming post-workshop opportunities and activities that were intended to support the members in implementing Web 2.0 activities into their teaching and learning contexts, namely: (1) staff were invited to work with the CELT Learning Technologies in developing Web 2.0 case studies; (2) participants were encouraged to network with group members; (3) members were invited to participate in future activities such as 'Show and Tell' informal sessions.

An important consideration in all professional development strategies is recognition of the importance of recording and evaluating the innovation experience. Participants intending to progress their intentions to incorporate Web 2.0 tools and activities into their teaching and learning contexts were encouraged to keep a reflective personal diary (a Web 2.0 tool) and to document both their own and the students' experience and, in doing so, to incorporate a light-weight systematic reflective process in their practice. Finally, the participants were encouraged to be mindful of potential research outputs from their case studies through non-disciplinary teaching and learning fora such as educational conferences.

Stage 2. Norming/Performing: The Maturing Community of Practice

At Stage 2 the community is beginning to mature as it grows in membership and depth of knowledge shared. It begins to define its role and its relationship to other communities. It needs to consider how it intends to proceed, self-organise and develop best practices to inform the group.

The main Stage 2 consideration of the CELT staff development design model was to identify how the community of practice could share and develop expertise in using Web 2.0 technologies for teaching in a sustainable fashion. The primary objective of this stage was to record a number of local case studies at NUI Galway which would serve as exemplars of contextualised practice for local, national and international audiences and to continue to build upon good practice.

Sharing Best Practices Amongst Members

The telling of stories and problem solving are essential elements of a community of practice to share news and information, build new knowledge and express an identity. A key Stage 2 activity of the SIG was to encourage the sharing of experiences, on the basis of the trust developed in Stage 1. The CELT Learning Technologies team facilitated sixteen workshops in the 2008–2009 academic year. SIG membership stands at 140 participants with members being drawn from across disciplines within the university. A wide variety of local case studies have been developed throughout NUI Galway utilising individual reflective blogs (e.g. with undergraduate Computer Science students and Software Development and postgraduate Education students), group blogs (e.g. with students based off-campus for a semester, including Modern Language students in Germany and Occupational Therapy students on work placement), individual wikis (e.g. 'Skills for Work Life' ePortfolio system for undergraduate Commerce students), and group wikis (e.g. with undergraduate Engineering and Marketing cohorts). Many academics have implemented Web 2.0 technologies who have not attended the CELT workshop. For example, staff in the School

of Commerce, Public Policy and Law have been particularly active in utilising group wikis for project management and problem-based case study activities. It is not clear whether the establishment of the collaboration SIG influenced non- member adoption of these technologies. However, it is reasonable to suggest that local experiences of implementing Web 2.0 technologies may have been discussed in local formal and informal networking contexts.

A number of scholarly research outputs have been realised with participants delivering conference papers and posters at the Blackboard World Europe 2009 conference. Five papers were been presented at the 2009 Irish Learning Technologies Users' Conference. At present, the CELT Learning Technologies team is capturing staff and student 2008–2009 experiences through video case study interviews. These case studies will be uploaded into the shared online space to reiterate the peer-driven dimension of the group, and provide local contact points for the community.

Stage 2 Special Interest Group Evaluation

CELT has recently surveyed the SIG members to gauge adoption trends in blogs/wikis and podcasting activities. Participant replies are ongoing, but a high-level analysis indicates a large take-up of blogs and wikis from the 2007–2008 to 2008–2009 academic cycle (when the functionality was deployed). When asked about intended use of collaboration tools in the 2009–2010 academic cycle, 63% indicated their plans to use group wikis, 57% reflective blog, 42% lecturer podcast, 35% group blog, 23% individual wiki, and 15% student-based podcasts. The trends suggest an increased embedding and mainstreaming of collaboration technologies amongst the SIG.

A number of staff have indicated that they would like to build on their initial successes to a wider student cohort (e.g. the student ePortfolio system in the School of Economics and Business has been extended to first- and third-year undergraduate Commerce students) or to an international context (e.g. the undergraduate Engineering module case study has extended their project to a German university cohort).

CELT is currently collating 2008–2009 staff experiences of their student-based collaboration activities. The SIG survey revealed that participants wished their colleagues to share (in order): (1) student engagement and motivation strategies; (2) marking, correcting and assessment strategies; and (3) the logistics of using wikis with larger groups

When asked how CELT could best support the academic community for 2009–2010, the SIG identified the following priorities:

- Uploading student and staff experience (e.g. case studies, videos, testimonies etc.);
- Conducting student research and evaluations (including student perceptions of learning technologies);
- Supporting academics to develop research-based practice; show and tell sessions (e.g. coffee mornings and informal gatherings);
- Working with academics to create case studies and conduct joint research activities.

Hence, it would seem that a coordinating role is still required from the SIG members, although this perceived value-added support of the team appears to have evolved along with the requirements of the SIG members, with the community collectively bearing the burden of support.

CELT surveyed and interviewed sample groupings of students and staff as an indication of engagement and sustainability. Staff interview responses to their experiences and the value of the SIG included:

'The students unprompted told me that they really liked it ... I really enjoyed it ... I think that they got more satisfaction out of it and that gave me a

lot more satisfaction out of it ... definitely I'd say the best thing that I could say is that I'll certainly be using it again and looking at ways in which I can bring it into other courses.' (Staff 1)

'In 14 years of teaching here in NUI Galway [I have never] actually witnessed students so engaged and so enthusiastic about a tool ... although the learning, the theories and the case studies were all similar, this just excited them like nothing else ... I think that there is a fear of technology for most people, including myself. I can definitely say that I can run with this now, on my own into the future. But I look forward to our next project and the next technologies that will engage our students in the learning process and to help them achieve the learning outcomes that we set them as academics.' (Staff 2)

Collaborating with a wide range of academics through the SIG has been an extremely positive and beneficial experience from a CELT perspective. The innovative nature of the of Web 2.0 technologies and the pedagogical fit have identified many reference point 'champions' to NUI Galway colleagues who may be interested in investigating learning technologies in their own teaching and learning contexts. Many academics have been enthusiastic in sharing their reflections for wider dissemination to the wider community.

Stage 3. Adjourning/ Transforming: The Established Community of Practice

Communities of practice at this stage of maturation typically displayed proof of a sustainable model. Established communities of practice progress through cycles of high and low activity. They often take active 'stewardship' of the knowledge and practices they share and consciously develop them (van Winkelen, 2003). These communities strive to maintain relevance, keeping the focus engaging, staying at the cutting edge. Research shows that the community may go through a transformation period where it evolves into another entity or merges with others communities.

It is hoped that the NUI Galway Collaboration SIG will move into Stage 3 of maturation. The NUI Galway Collaboration SIG has been established for ten months. The NDLR research reports that a community of practice takes a minimum of eighteen months to become established. A comprehensive qualitative and quantitative analysis of Stage 2 has provided positive indicators for the success of the community. There has been very high staff demand for attending the supporting workshops, as well as widespread reports of Web 2.0 implementation across the curriculum. A number of case-study-based research publications have been published by group members at national and international conferences. Anecdotal evidence indicates synergies between SIG staff. For example, staff have collaborated to provide guest speakers in each others' lectures as well as agreeing to employ common evaluation methods for capturing the student experience using group wikis for comparative analysis purposes.

Trend analysis indicates SIG members' intentions to incorporate a variety of Web 2.0 technologies in the upcoming academic year and provides useful pointers for how to best support the group in the next stage of the development model. However, wider economic human resource constraints have resulted in the reduction of the CELT Learning Technologies team by one full-time member. This will have practical implications for the development of the SIG in terms of the provision of face-to-face workshops (to increase the community membership and to widen the diversity and richness of community experiences), and in providing individual and community supports. The team must realign and prioritise available resources in light of these constraints. However, the redeployment of resources will provide a useful insight into sustainability of the SIG and its ability to progress to a truly

peer-driven community without the planned human resource support. Further research needs to be conducted to evaluate the development of the SIG into Stage 3 of the model, and to monitor the continuity and sustainability of Stage 2 activities in this new climate.

A Wider Application of the CELT Community of Practice Model

The authors suggest that this model and structure can be successfully adapted by third-level institutions in Ireland and overseas to meet local needs. To date, the NUI Galway staff development community of practice model has been successfully applied to a second Web 2.0 technology interest group focused on podcasting. This has been a relative seamless adaptation utilising the same community online space/half-day face-to-face workshop/post-workshop activities' structure.

The model has also been applied to the 2008–2009 collaboration strand of an Irish national e-learning project, 'Learning Technologies: From Pilot to Mainstream', between NUI Galway, Trinity College Dublin (TCD) and University College Cork (UCC). A key deliverable of the collaboration strand is to create and share information, practice and resources between the project partners. As part of this remit, NUI Galway Learning Technologies team developed a staff development podcasting workshop package in consultation with the project partners. The package consisted of a 'Train the Trainer' workshop, an academic staff development workshop and a set of reusable resources (trainer presentation materials, YouTube videos, participant work-pack activities, case studies and web links). All resources were stored in a shared wiki (PBWorks) site using the SIG space structure outlined above, and made available under the Creative Commons 2.0 Attribution, Non-Commercial and Share-Alike licence. Train-the-trainer and staff development podcasting workshops were facilitated by NUI Galway staff for their TCD counterparts in August 2008. The TCD Centre for Learning Technology officially launched their adapted podcasting workshop in April 2009 and have invited NUI Galway and UCC partners to participate in the local workshop rollout. TCD have uploaded all localised and original resources to the central wiki (PBWiki) site for comment and reuse. Further cross-institutional staff development workshops will be progressed in Autumn 2009. Thus, this initiative has provided many opportunities to work to help establish a Web 2.0 mediated framework for future information and resource exchange within a wider network.

CONCLUSION

This chapter explored whether staff participation in peer-supported community-driven groups fosters sustainable embedding of Web 2.0 technologies in teaching and learning. It highlighted how community of practice research and NDLR findings informed the development and implementation of community of practice driven Web 2.0 staff development programmes in the 2008–2009 academic year by the NUI Galway Learning Technologies team.

While initial evaluations suggest positive outcomes in terms of staff and student engagement using the community of practice model, more quantitative and qualitative research needs to be completed. The Collaboration SIG is moving towards the end of the Stage 2, where members of the community are sharing best practices and collaborating in a scholarly and collaborative fashion, sensitive to the constraints of their own contexts. The successful harvesting and sharing of participant experiences will be a key factor in the development and sustainability of the collective. Progression towards the next stage of the model will take place within an economically challenging environment which will test the robustness and sustainability of the local adaptation of the community of practice model to Web 2.0 academic

development programmes within the NUI Galway context and beyond.

FUTURE RESEARCH DIRECTIONS

The notion of communities of practice and the broader conceptualisation of learning as social and situated provides significant pointers for those involved in staff development. In this conclusion, we would like to highlight three of these.

Firstly, staff developers need to explore with practitioners how best to encourage membership and committed participation in communities of practice. Fostering strong communities of practice for continuing professional development in technology-enhanced education needs to be an important element of a staff developer's work, and is an important criterion for sustainable staff development with e-learning technologies

Secondly, there is no single solution for implementing a technology across situations or contexts. In each of the cases studies, the tools presented look very promising, but careful thought and consideration by the educator is required to leverage these emerging technologies into their own practice. Participation in a community that allows members to engage in joint activities, discussion, and build relationships that enable them to learn from one another will be essential to this change in practice. It also promotes scholarly reflection and peer review of the embedding of technology in a range of contexts amongst community members.

Thirdly, this chapter offers a glimpse of how Web 2.0 tools such as wikis can act as a useful mediating tool, as a sociable technology. This is particularly apparent when collecting a shared repertoire of resources, stories, and ways of addressing reoccurring problems. However, it is important to bear in mind that the technology merely serves to codify the explicit knowledge. That is not to say that it is not useful to document the experiences, but to acknowledge that it will rely on the community's tacit knowledge and social communication to be applied and shared.

Future directions in this approach will aim to broaden the community membership to others who share this interest, including the Irish Learning Technology Association (ILTA), the NDLR Technology-Enhanced Learning Community of Practice, and international research communities who share competence in this domain. Recent interest and participation from international partners may provide an exciting dimension along with greater opportunities for information and resource exchange and collaboration activities. This objective presents a challenge in retaining the trust and commitment of existing members, and sustaining interaction.

REFERENCES

Adler, P. S., & Kwon, S.-W. (2002). Social Capital: Prospects for a new concept. *Academy of Management Review, 27*(1), 17–40. doi:10.2307/4134367

Becher, T. (1989). *Academic tribes and territories: Intellectual inquiry and the cultures of disciplines. Milton Keynes*. UK: Society for Research into Higher Education and Open University Press.

Becher, T., & Trowler, P. (2001). *Academic tribes and territories: Intellectual enquiry and the cultures of disciplines* (2nd ed.). Bury St Edmunds, UK: Society for Research into Higher Education and Open University Press.

Bennett, S., Priest, A., & Macpherson, C. (1999). Learning about online learning: An approach to staff development for university teachers. *Australian Journal of Educational Technology, 15*(3), 207-221. Retrieved October 20, 2009, from http://www.ascilite.org.au/ajet/ajet15/bennett.html

Blackwell, R., & Blackmore, P. (2003). Rethinking strategic staff development . In Blackwell, R., & Blackmore, P. (Eds.), *Towards strategic staff development in Higher Education* (pp. 3–15). Maidenhead, UK: Society for Research into Higher Education and Open University Press.

Braun, P. (2002). Digital knowledge networks: Linking communities of practice with innovation. *The Journal of Business Strategy, 19*(1), 43–54.

Brown, T., & Jenkins, M. (2003). *VLE surveys: A longitudinal perspective between March 2001 and March 2003 for Higher Education in the United Kingdom*. Retrieved August, 2007, from http://www.ucisa.ac.uk/groups/tlig/vle/index_html

CAMEL. (Collaborative Approaches to the Management of E-Learning) model. Retrieved August, 2007, from http://www.jiscinfonet.ac.uk/camel/camel-model

Chalmers, L., & Keown, P. (2006). Communities of practice and professional development. *International Journal of Lifelong Education, 25*(2), 139–156. doi:10.1080/02601370500510793

Conole, G. (2008). Capturing practice: The role of mediating artefacts in learning design . In Lockyer, L., Bennett, S., Agostinho, S., & Harper, B. (Eds.), *Handbook of research on learning design and learning objects: Issues, applications and technologies* (pp. 187–207). Hersey, PA: IGI Global.

Conole, G., & Oliver, M. (2002). Embedding theory into learning technology practice with toolkits. *Journal of Interactive Media in Education, 2002*(8). Retrieved October 20, 2009, from http://www-jime.open.ac.uk/2002/8/conole-oliver-02–8.pdf

Dearing, R. (1997). The National Committee of Inquiry into Higher Education [Dearing report]. Retrieved October 20, 2009, from http://www.leeds.ac.uk/educol/ncihe de Freitas, S., Oliver, M., Mayes, T., & Mee, A. (2007). The practitioner perspective on the modelling of pedagogy and practice. *Journal of Computer Assisted Learning, 24*(1), 26-38.

Donnelly, R. (2008). Virtual problem-based learning communities of practice for teachers and teacher educators: An Irish higher education perspective . In Kimble, C., & Hildreth, P. (Eds.), *Communities of practice: Creating learning environments for educators* (*Vol. 2*). Charlotte, NC: Information Age Publishing.

Donnelly, R., & O'Rourke, K. (2007). What now? Evaluating e-learning CPD practice in Irish third-level education. *Journal of Further and Higher Education, 31*(1), 31–40. doi:10.1080/03098770601167864

EDUCAUSE. (2009). Top teaching and learning challenges for 2009. Retrieved August, 2007, from http://www.educause.edu/eli/challenges

Elton, L. (2005). Scholarship and the research and teaching nexus . In Barnett, R. (Ed.), *Reshaping the university* (pp. 108–118). Maidenhead, UK: Open University Press.

Gosling, D. (2008). *Educational development in the United Kingdom: Report to the Heads of Educational Development Group*. London, UK: Heads of Development Group.

Graves, W. H. (2001). Transforming traditional faculty roles . In Barone, C. A., & Hagner, P. R. (Eds.), *Technology-enhanced teaching and learning, Educause Leadership Strategies* (*Vol. 5*, pp. 35–44). New York: Wiley.

Guskey, T. R. (2000). *Evaluating professional development*. Thousand Oaks, CA: Corwin Press.

Hubert, C., Newhouse, B., & Vestal, W. (2001). *Building and sustaining communities of practice*. Houston, USA: APQC.

Jennings, D. (2005). Virtually effective: The measure of a learning environment. In G. O'Neill, S. Moore, & B. McMullin (Eds.), Emerging issues in the practice of university learning and teaching. Dublin: All Irish Society for Higher Education (AISHE).

Johnson, D. F. (2003). Toward a philosophy of online education . In Brown, D. G. (Ed.), *Developing faculty to use technology: Programs and strategies to enhance teaching* (pp. 9–12). Bolton: Anker Publishing.

Kerres, M., Euler, D., Seufert, S., Hasanbegovic, J., & Voss, B. (2005). *Lehrkompetenz für eLearning-Innovationen in der Hochschule (SCIL Report 6). St Gallen: Swiss Centre for Innovations in Learning*. SCIL.

Laurillard, D. (2004). The conversational framework . In Holliman, R., & Scanlon, E. (Eds.), *Mediating science learning through information and computing technology.* London: Routledge Falmer. doi:10.4324/9780203464007_chapter_1.2

Lave, J. (1993). The practice of learning . In Chaiklin, S., & Lave, J. (Eds.), *Understanding practice: Perspectives on activity and context* (pp. 3–32). Cambridge: Cambridge University Press. doi:10.1017/CBO9780511625510.002

Lave, J., & Wenger, E. (1991). *Situated learning: Legitimate peripheral participation*. Cambridge, UK: Cambridge University Press.

Mansvelt, J., Suddaby, G., & O'Hara, D. (2008). Learning how to e-teach? Staff perspectives on formal and informal professional development activity. Australian Society for Computers in Learning in Tertiary Education (ASCILITE) Conference, November 30 to December 3, 2008, Melbourne.

O'Reilly, T. (2005). *What is Web 2.0: Design patterns and business models for the next generation of software*. Retrieved October 20, 2009, from http://oreilly.com/web2/archive/what-is-web-20.html

OECD (2005). 'E-learning in Tertiary Education: Where do we stand?' *Education & Skills, 2005*(4), 1-293.

Oliver, M., & Dempster, J. A. (2003). Embedding e-learning practices . In Blackwell, R., & Blackmore, P. (Eds.), *Towards strategic staff development in higher education* (pp. 142–153). Berkshire, England: SRHE and Open University Press.

PBWorks (Formerly PBWiki). (2005-2009). Available http://www.pbwiki.com

Podcasting Resource Wiki, T. C. D. (2009). Retrieved from http://tcdpodcasting.pbworks.com/

Putnam, R. T., & Borko, H. (1997). Teacher learning: Implications of new views of cognition . In Biddle, B. J., Good, T. L., & Goodson, I. F. (Eds.), *International handbook of teachers and teaching* (*Vol. 2*, pp. 1223–1296). Dordrecht, The Netherlands: Kluwer.

Salmon, G. (2004). *E-moderating: The key to teaching and learning online* (2nd ed.). London: Taylor & Francis.

Sandholtz, J. H. (2002). Inservice training or professional development: Contrasting opportunities in a school/university partnership . *Teaching and Teacher Education, 18*(7), 815–830. doi:10.1016/S0742-051X(02)00045-8

Schlager, M. S., & Fusco, J. (2004). Teacher professional development, technology, and communities of practice: Are we putting the cart before the horse? In Barab, S., Kling, R., & Gray, J. (Eds.), *Designing virtual communities in the service of learning*. Cambridge: Cambridge University Press.

Segrave, S., Holt, D. M., & Farmer, J. (2005). The power of the 6[three] model for enhancing academic teachers' capacities for effective online teaching and learning: Benefits, initiatives and future directions. *Australasian Journal of Educational Technology, 21*(1), 118–135.

Sharpe, R. (2004). *A typology of effective interventions that support e-learning practice*. Bristol: JISC.

Tham, C. M., & Werner, J. M. (2005). Designing and evaluating e-learning in higher education: A review and recommendations. *Journal of Leadership & Organizational Studies, 11*(2), 15–25. doi:10.1177/107179190501100203

van Winkelen, C. (2003). *Inter-organizational communities of practice*. ESEEN Project. Retrieved August 2007, from http://www.elearningeuropa.info/directory/index.php?page=doc&doc_id=1483&doclng=6 and http://www.esen.eu.com

Wenger, E., McDermott, R., & Snyder, W. M. (2002). Cultivating communities of practice: A guide to managing knowledge. Harvard: Harvard Business School Press.

White, N. (2002). *Communities of practice: Learners connecting on-line*. Retrieved August, 2007, from http://flexiblelearning.net.au/nw2002/extras/commsofpractice.pdf

ADDITIONAL READING

Boisot, M. H. (1998). *Knowledge assets: Securing competitive advantage in the knowledge economy*. Oxford: Oxford University Press.

Brophy, C. (2007). *Exploring team roles in collaborative online games. Master of Science (Human-Computer Interaction with Ergonomics) in the Faculty of Life Sciences*. University College London.

Doolan, M. A. (2006). *Effective strategies for building a learning community online using a Wiki*. Proceedings 1st Annual Blended Learning Conference (pp. 51ff). Hertfordshire, UK: University of Hertfordshire.

Lave, J., & Wenger, E. (2002). Legitimate peripheral participation in communities of practice . In Lea, M. R., & Nicoll, K. (Eds.), *Distributed learning: Social and cultural approaches to practice* (pp. 56–63). London: RoutledgeFalmer.

Littlejohn, A. H. (2002). Improving continuing professional development in the use of ICT. *Journal of Computer Assisted Learning, 18*, 166–174. doi:10.1046/j.0266-4909.2001.00224.x

Maguire, T., & McAvinia, C. (2009) *Evaluating the National Digital Learning Repository Project: Evolving models for communities of practice.* EdTech2009: 20/20 Vision: Changing Learning Futures through Technology. National College of Ireland, May 21-22, 2009.

McKenzie, J., & Van Winkelen, C. (2003). *Understanding the knowledgeable organization: Nurturing knowledge competence.* London: Thomson Learning.

O'Keeffe, M., O'Regan, L., & Cashman, D. (2008). Supporting the development of communities of practice: Informal versus formal communities. ALT-C 2008: Rethinking the digital divide. University of Leeds, September, 9-11, 2008.

Oliver, R. (2002). Winning the toss and electing to bat: Maximising the opportunities of online learning. In C. Rust (Ed.), *Proceedings of the 9th improving student learning conference* (pp. 35-44). Oxford: OCSLD.

Owens, D., & Thompson, E. (2001). Fusing learning and knowledge at the St Paul Companies. *Knowledge Management Review, 4*(3), 24–29.

Palloff, R. M., & Pratt, K. (2005). *Collaborating online: Learning together in community.* San Francisco: Jossey-Bass.

Powazek, D. M. (2002). *Design for community. The art of connecting real people in virtual places.* Indianapolis, IN, USA: New Riders.

Preece, J. (2000). *Online communities: Designing usability, supporting sociability.* Chichester, UK: John Wiley & Sons.

Retallick, J., Cocklin, B., & Coombe, K. (1999). *Learning communities in education.* London, New York: Routledge.

Seely Brown, J., & Solomon Grey, S. (1995). The people are the company. *FastCompany Magazine, 1.*

Sharpe, R., & Oliver, M. (2007). Supporting practitioners' design for learning: Principles of effective resources and interventions. In Beetham, H., & Sharpe, R. (Eds.), *Rethinking pedagogy for a digital age. Designing and delivering e-learning* (pp. 117–128). London: Routledge.

Shaw, P. (1999). Purpose and process in effective learning communities . In Retallick, J., Cocklin, B., & Coombe, K. (Eds.), *Learning communities in education.* London, New York: Routledge.

van Winkelen, C., & Ramsell, P. (2002). *Building effective communities.* Henley Knowledge Management Forum Second Annual Conference. Henley Management College.

van Winkelen, C., & Ramsell, P. (2003). Aligning value is key to designing communities. *Knowledge Management Review, 5*(6), 20–23.

Chapter 21
Strategic Deployment of E-Learning

Pat Gannon-Leary
Bede Research & Consultancy, UK

James Carr
University of Edinburgh Business School, UK

ABSTRACT

Changes in higher education (HE) have continued in response to, or indeed in anticipation of, an increasingly competitive environment, technological advances and shifting demands of users. Introducing new technologies into a Higher Education Institute (HEI) requires management of complex change processes to deliver their full potential. Innovative ideas for technology and practice may be constrained, and compromised by people and cultural reactions thereby reducing their effectiveness and limiting their potential for improving teaching and learning. The management of change in organisational practices therefore involves attention to three aspects: processes, people, and culture. This chapter presents a longitudinal study of one HEI through the lens of two active participants in a number of e-learning initiatives, and discusses process, people and cultural change challenges. It proposes that new evaluation frameworks are required to establish success in the implementation of new and emergent delivery modes mediated through the use of ICTs, and provides one example, the Learning Technology Practice Framework. The use of such frameworks may help with engaging academics in thinking about how to embed e-learning successfully within courses, and at a broader level within the organisation. The changes in the roles of lecturers/tutors and learners is particularly important in light of the disorientation faced by both of these user groups as a result of changing organisational culture and work practices. Lecturers and students have to adapt to their new roles and be allowed the opportunity, time, rewards and training to allow them to adapt the technology to meet their needs in their different and particular contexts of use. Overall it is found that the adoption and diffusion of e-learning in higher education is likely to develop more slowly than imagined by some educational visionaries owing to the complex nature of technology implementation that is common across all sectors, be it industry or education.

DOI: 10.4018/978-1-61520-879-1.ch021

INTRODUCTION

The pursuit of technological transformation in higher education (HE) has become widespread internationally with the overarching pervasiveness of the Internet and the potential advantages this offers to higher education. In today's changing academic environment, leaders at Higher Education Institutions (HEIs) are confronted with increasing demands to transform their institutions, as stakeholders' expectations have risen and resources have diminished. HEIs compete intensely to attract students and to generate revenues as operating costs rise and they face greater scrutiny and accountability from outside agencies that impact on accreditation, funding and, in consequence, resources (Boyett, 1996; Newman, Couturier, & Scurry, 2004; Raelin, 1995). It may benefit HEIs to consider parallels in the corporate environment for, as Kotter (1995) suggests, examination of corporate change efforts is becoming increasingly relevant to even more organisations as environments become more and more competitive.

Across the HE sector, the rationale for e-learning and its benefits are largely accepted. The Higher Education Funding Council for England (HEFCE) strategy for e-learning (2009) demonstrates a commitment to supporting sustainable e-learning in HE institutions and is indicative of an acknowledgement that students learn in different ways and wish to have information presented in alternative formats and indicative also of a response to changing student needs including the desire for flexibility in study provision.

Changes in HE have continued in response to, or indeed in anticipation of, an increasingly competitive environment, technological advances and shifting demands of users. Introducing new technologies into a HEI requires management of complex change processes to deliver their full potential. Innovative ideas for technology and practice may be constrained, and compromised by people and cultural reactions (Calverley &

Dexter, 2007) thereby reducing their effectiveness and limiting their potential for improving teaching and learning. Change management in organisational practices therefore involves attention to three aspects: processes, people, and organisational culture (HEFCE, 2003). Pennington (2003) highlighted three corresponding themes that influence successful change management in higher education: the recognition of change as a complex social process, the identification of change agents with appropriate skills, and the creation of a cultural disposition towards change. Resistance to change can be managed through ensuring that information is disseminated, communication targeted and that opportunities for staff involvement are maximised.

People are central to the HE process and therefore, in technological transformation in HE, it is critical to address the concerns and perceptions of academic staff in the light of the need for changing their attitudes and maturation of their practices in effective use of information and communications technologies (ICTs) alongside the ICT maturation process (Calverley & Dexter, 2007; Evans & Franz, 1998; Taylor, Lopez, & Quadrelli, 1996). Increasing availability of ICTs is not enough in itself to improve poor processes. Staff need to be confident in the reliability and availability of e-learning developments and, concomitantly, in those supporting and delivering those developments. Staff at the 'coal face' who are engaged in delivering the learning, teaching and assessment may feel that control of ICTs is out of their hands and this can be a factor hindering take-up. There is a need to try to ensure commonality of approach and the availability of support and advice campus wide.

Staff structures must be in place to meet the new challenges of electronic learning, teaching and assessment. Lack of appropriate structures may result in stress associated with role conflict and ambiguity with staff feeling ill-prepared to face the challenges and alienated from new ways of working (Moses, 1997; Sarros, Gmelch, & Tanewski, 1997). Staff development may involve some questioning of the appropriateness of current learning, teaching and assessment mechanisms and whether their delivery may be enhanced using e-methods. Whilst change is responding to the possibilities of new technology and the needs of students, it needs also to retain a respect for the interests and strengths of staff.

BACKGROUND

In 1992 the UK Government granted several former polytechnic institutions university status. These post-'92 institutions have been termed 'new universities', 'modern universities', 'polytechnic universities' or 'plate glass universities', Beloff's (1968) term indicative of their distinctive architecture. The authors have borrowed Beloff's name for the post-'92 institution which forms the subject of this study.

At PlateGlass University which is the subject of this study, e-learning staff work alongside schools to facilitate e-learning developments which not only reflect disciplinary considerations, but also remain consistent with the university's overall strategy. Schools move at different speeds in e-learning activities and developments and natural champions emerge. Key supporting factors for the growth of e-learning identified by Browne, Jenkins, and Walker, (2006) include the development of such local champions (as described in Beastall & Walker's York model (2006) where champions are used to drive the involvement of departments and to disseminate their experience through awareness–raising events).

Aim of the Chapter

The aim of this chapter is to recount PlateGlass University's journey over the past 10 years in respect of e-learning implementation, as illustrated by a series of research projects designed to involve academic staff and enable them to have a feeling of ownership of the e-learning developments by canvassing their opinions and perspectives of the merits and demerits of various e-learning features. The research studies either directly relate to e-learning or have e-learning dimensions. Taken together they provide a picture of the e-learning journey taken by one institution viewed from a staff perspective. The chapter starts with early evaluations of aspects of e-learning and is followed by brief descriptions of a number of studies which have contributed to institutional knowledge of e-learning and aspects thereof. For value-added, whilst the institutional journey is sketched by someone from the research teams which conducted the projects, a management expert from outside the institution lends an evaluative perspective to the organisational change process.

This chapter addresses issues pertinent to academics who need guidance and advice when setting up e-learning courses; to ICT-literate academics; and to managers who are encouraging their staff to use e-learning platforms. It is anticipated that this chapter will give university managers greater insight into the issues academic staff are likely to encounter when designing e-learning material suitable for use to effectively enhance the learning experience of their students. Such issues need to be taken into account by university managers in general when encouraging staff to engage their students through the use of e-learning.

Methodology and Methods

The conceptual model for these studies drew on the intuitive Return on Investment (ROI) framework proposed by Collis and Moonen (2001). This framework addresses the concerns of many of the stakeholders involved in the universities e-learning developments. Typical questions asked by these stakeholders, including academics, are 'Is it working? Is it an improvement? Is it worth it?' These are not simply resource-driven questions about the 'bottom line' or evidence of resistance to change but may, for example, be an academic's attempt to resolve dilemmas of professional practice in a new context. The intuitive ROI model suggests that attempts to answer such questions should concentrate on changes occurring through the use of e-learning media such as BlackBoard (Bb), which are important and meaningful to those concerned. As Abrami (2006) points out, it is essential to balance the needs of all stakeholders, and the cost-benefit ratios of ICTs, in deciding not only what to use, but when and how to use.

Subsequent studies undertaken have focused on the inter-linked aspects of efficiency and effectiveness. With respect to efficiency, this involves consideration of time, effort and resources required for learning and teaching in this new context which claims 'ease of access' and 'flexibility'. With respect to effectiveness, the focus is on the quality of learning and teaching. Whilst adopting this framework, further studies have remained open to views of academic staff which may not fit in with the research teams' expectations. A series of brief accounts of the projects is presented to capture the flavour of some of these studies which have contributed to institutional knowledge of e-learning and the institutional journey.

Prior to each study, literature reviews were conducted and updates were sought from the schools within the institution to determine what divisions or programmes were using e-learning. From the information provided it was generally possible to identify key personnel and/or e-learning champions who would be appropriate interviewees and who would also be able to guide the team to other potential contacts.

Evaluation is central as it encourages reflective thinking. Whist some quantitative approaches were taken (e.g., in questionnaire survey work), the predominant approach taken was qualitative, using a modified grounded theory methodology. Firstly, this fitted with Glaser and Strauss's (1967) argument that theory (consisting of conceptual categories, their properties and relationships) should be derived from, and illustrated by, data. Secondly this fitted with the exploratory nature of the research and a desire to understand how academic staff 'define

the situation' (Thomas, in Marshall & Rossman 1989, p. 46). In line with the grounded theory approach, joint collection, coding and analysis of data was the underlying operation. The generation of theory, coupled with the notion of theory as process, required that these operations be completed together as far as possible. The research team worked through transcribed interviews and focus groups, comparing instances from the data in the hope that tentative categories and their properties could be identified. It was anticipated that emergent elements of the theory would be modified and developed by comparison with instances from subsequent fieldwork, and further categories and properties might emerge. Throughout the initial process the research team wrote analytic memos, which served to guide and record the emergent theory on the merits and demerits of e-learning from a staff and institutional perspective.

PART A. STAGES OF THE INSTITUTIONAL JOURNEY

Electronic Information Services

Early work undertaken in the late 1990s was based in a research institute at PlateGlass University and involved looking at use made of electronic information services (EIS) including the perspectives of library staff and academic staff. Initially research was conducted in the home institution but was widened out, thanks to external research funding, to examine the situation in other HEIs in the UK. This afforded an opportunity to make comparisons. The main objective of the study was to identify barriers and enablers to the use of EIS with a view to developing success criteria. In-depth fieldwork found that there was growing use of EIS such as bibliographic databases and websites in the curriculum but that practice varied both between institutions and between disciplines.

What emerged over the three-year period under study was a picture of academic staff struggling to keep on top of the information explosion (or at least on top of how to find information); trying to keep up with an ever-growing range of electronic resources (in the knowledge their students may approach them for help with these); and trying to keep up to date with developments in their discipline.

Even in the late 1990s some academic staff were still learning to use Word and Excel and had only just started using the web. This proved more of a challenge in the Humanities than in the Sciences and Social Sciences. Their own lack of IT and information handling skills was a sensitive issue for academic staff who were supposed to be preparing students for the world of work and, concomitantly, the technology out there. Not all academics proved familiar with services available or able to evaluate EIS for themselves and therefore it was more difficult for them to encourage the evaluative and critical skills of their students and to direct them to reliable and useful EIS, e.g. websites or electronic text centres.

Lessons learned from the EIS study highlighted the changing role of the academic. Their students were now coming into contact with support personnel, library staff, administrators and technicians, many of whom were also now involved in the delivery of learning. Sometimes ICT skills and information literacy skills were being taught by others, e.g. technical support staff and library staff. Sometimes such skills were taught as a separate entity, more rarely they were embedded into course design and delivery. The very transparency of the e-environment had the potential to make some academic staff feel insecure since technology could be associated with control.

In a recent study, Littlejohn et al. (2009) stress the fact that information management skills are an integral aspect of education. They advocate that library staff and teaching professionals work closely alongside each other in order that expertise in the management of EIS and resources can be combined with, and complemented by, expertise in e-learning.

External Evaluative Perspective

At a broader level, the advent of e-learning is seen by some commentators (e.g. Ford et al., 1996; Peters, 2000) to offer the chance for a revolution in the way teaching and learning is conducted in higher education. Benefits for the student may include enhanced learning experiences and increased access to learning opportunities, but moves to implement e-learning are perhaps driven more strongly by the external political environment (Mayes, 2001) and economic imperatives (Hase & Ellis, 2001). Mayes (1993, 1995) considers two main issues that are currently setting the agenda in the e-learning debate in the UK higher education sector. The first is the need to reduce the cost of education and training while simultaneously increasing provision to a growing customer base. The second is that quality must not only be maintained, but improved, and its relevance to industry increased. E-learning is emerging as a possible solution to current issues faced in higher education, but it has a 'long history of failed promises' (Mayes, 1995, p.1).

Commentators on e-learning in schools (e.g. Crook, 1994), which has an even longer history to draw upon, express surprise at such 'slow' progress. Universities are also being accused at being slow to adapt to technological change (Van Lieshout, Egyedi, & Bijker, 2001). One explanation for this slow innovation process may be a result of a concentration on supply-side (technology) rather than demand-side (learner needs) issues, as suggested by Laurillard (1994):

What students are most likely to need is not access to more information. Where understanding is difficult they need more guidance, practice and supervision. The technology does not easily offer that, however, and technology leads, not pedagogy, so it is rarely provided. (p. 1)

Thus technology–pedagogy imbalance may be a major factor in determining the success of e-learning learning technology implementation experiments by the higher education sector. However, more fundamentally the nature of technology and technology implementation indicates that the so-called 'slow' adaptation to technological change in education (Mayes, 1995; Van Lieshout et al., 2001) is actually a characteristic of major innovations, particularly those requiring significant organisational change (Freeman, 1997): technology implementation is a complex and uncertain socio-technical practice (Pollock & Cornford, 2003; Williams, 1996; Williams & Edge, 1996).

Virtual Learning Environments: Blackboard

Outside of the Internet and bibliographic databases, what other e-resources did students at that time use? It was becoming increasingly common for HEIs to adopt virtual learning environments (VLEs) and a subsequent internally funded study undertaken in 2002 evaluated the institution's adoption of the Blackboard (Bb) VLE with the objective of informing future developments in e-learning. It identified benefits, disadvantages and costs to relevant stakeholders by examining six case study courses that were using Bb as the main vehicle for e-learning. An additional objective was to illuminate the perspectives of academic staff involved.

As Conole, White and Oliver (2009) state, some universities had campus-wide initiatives in implementing VLEs; others adopted a more cautious approach letting practitioners decide the extent to which they wanted to use the VLE in their teaching. The latter approach was taken by PlateGlass University, where Bb implementation began in the academic year 2000/2001 and by 2002 Bb was used across a range of courses in all schools. Half the six case study courses in the university were campus-based. The others were flexible learning or distance learning (DL), either running in parallel with existing campus courses or being taken up by students who lived locally. This last point is impor-

tant because tutors were able to offer face-to-face tutorials to these 'distance' students.

Reasons for academic staff to be involved in early use of Bb included the University's push in this direction and the fact that the University's decision to adopt this particular VLE precluded use or experimentation with alternatives. Some academics chose to be a Bb 'pioneer' because they wanted to be at the forefront of university innovations; they were in search of something novel to engage the students' interest; they anticipated positive outcomes for students; they saw Bb as offering a means of making learning and teaching more effective and of handling materials more efficiently. Some saw it as a precursor to the possibility of introducing a distance learning course. One academic expressed a combination of the pioneering spirit coupled with the safety offered by Bb when they observed that:

'Going into the open Internet is like going out into the ocean whereas going onto Blackboard is like travelling up a river.'

As another academic commented, using the VLE was a 'relatively painless way' to make course materials available online. There was a general tendency for staff to feel, at this early stage, they had insufficient knowledge to know which functionalities of Bb were best to use for which purposes. In consequence, they were inclined to use the more basic offerings (i.e. as a repository for lecture notes and PowerPoint slides) until everyone was comfortable with these before attempting to use what were perceived as more sophisticated facilities. One academic expressed their feelings when they asked whether what you could not do with Bb was 'a downside of the system or more to do with your own limitations'. This academic went on to comment that they perceived Bb as a medium where much depended on how creative you were.

VLE systems are not intended to merely reproduce the classroom environment online but to use the technology to provide learners with new tools to facilitate their learning (Britain &

Liber, 1999). VLEs aim to accommodate a wider range of learning styles and goals to encourage collaborative and resource-based learning and to allow greater sharing and re-use of resources. One of the problems identified by Britain and Liber (1999) was how to determine whether a new technology could be embedded into the teaching and learning context of a given institution. Their report concluded that, among the factors slowing the uptake of VLEs in HEIs was the lack of a coherent framework within which to evaluate both the pedagogical benefits and the organisational changes required to effectively implement them. As Dearing's chapter on ICTs stressed, it is important to be 'led by educational imperative and not by technology' (1997, 13.2). Stress was placed by many academics on core values and the importance of maintaining these whilst seeing the technological revolution as an extension of learning and teaching rather than something that fundamentally changed things. As Oliver et al. (2009b) point out, VLE systems are chosen by management on the basis of institution-wide cost–benefit analysis, not through taking into account local learning and teaching practices. Foley and Ojeda (2008) discuss the complexity of the relationship between patterns of pedagogical beliefs and practices and the integration of ICTs in the HE classroom. There may be lack of alignment between lecturer beliefs, good practice and ICT usage, meaning that lecturing staff cannot consistently use ICTs in ways that support their core pedagogical beliefs.

For some staff the VLE was something they would take up and run with. For others, as one academic commented, 'it was like pulling teeth' in that it took enormous effort for them to reorientate their way of thinking about the process and they were likely to need much support. In the earlier study of EIS, personnel were described as 'beacons of good practice'. The equivalent in this study were Bb champions. These were creative and enthusiastic academics within the institution involved in the early stages, who could influence colleagues. Having such a person in a department could make everyone in that department Bb-aware. This enthusiasm might translate into cascading training to peers and the production of Bb templates for others to follow to cut down on individual effort.

As with the previous study, some academics experienced difficulties with perceived lack of skills in producing material for students in the format for Bb or for potential distance learners. Again, this proved to be not only an ICT skills issue but also an issue in that level of engagement of academics was more transparent with Bb. There was a sense of loss of control when someone else was posting their material onto Bb. One academic compared having material posted to Bb to being:

'Like submitting a journal article, you have got to polish the thing up before you put it out to the public domain. There's the fear it is not quite right.'

Oliver et al. (2009b) discuss experiences of disempowerment in relation to the curriculum and the ICTs that help manage and deliver it, fearing it will change their teaching practice and relationships with students. As Conole, White and Oliver (2009) point out, e-learning is a catalyst for change that cuts across institutional structures, impacting on – and making transparent – existing practices. Some PlateGlass academics were concerned over intellectual property rights (IPR) which made them reluctant to share material. Others perceived Bb as an imposition or a 'dumbing down' of learning and teaching. These reactions could result in problems for course leaders of getting commitment of a whole team – some of whom were enthusiastic and technically advanced whilst others had little interest and/or aptitude. This reliance on individuals' interests and willingness to take it up resulted in lack of uniformity in use of Bb.

Whilst a Bb champion was perceived as an asset, some academics expressed the feeling there needed to be more in the way of institutional policy.

'It is often left to people at our level to persuade colleagues to acquire the skills and use them. Perhaps it should be happening at a higher level with time set aside for all staff to, as a condition of contract, or at least a necessary part of training, learn how to use Bb.'

Therefore, amongst lessons learned, was a strong indication that the University and those involved in training programmes needed to promote Bb in order to get staff to use it to its full capacity.

E-Learning Audit

The objective of the internally funded e-learning audit of 2005 was to assess the current usage of e-learning across PlateGlass University schools and to determine what form such e-learning took, e.g. distance delivery, blended, on-campus, etc. The research team had information about what forms of e-learning were in existence in 2002, thanks to an earlier audit, so sent the information available to the school offices with a request that they update the information to reflect current practices.

By 2002 the term blended learning had emerged (Roberts, 2002) and when schools updated the PlateGlass research team on their e-learning programmes, this term appeared alongside distance learning, e-learning and flexible-learning. Definitions of these terms are imprecise, varying in the literature and in their use at different HEIs – and, indeed, at PlateGlass University, the usage varied slightly between schools with the terms 'blended' and 'flexible' being used interchangeably.

Those identified as e-learning champions on the basis of the school updates, claimed that their early adoption of new technologies was driven by their own interest and by what was happening in industry and the business world. Indeed, this became apparent in examining some of the offerings from these champions. In one instance, a portfolio of programmes was provided for a specific company via block release distance delivery with students studying independently in between block

release periods. In another instance, work-based e-learning modules had been developed with the workplace as the context of the learning. These focused on the professional/personal development needs of the learners and were negotiated by the employer and the learner. Therefore there was increasing awareness within the institution of the value of connections with industry and business and the capabilities of e-delivery to meet their needs. PlateGlass University was clearly developing along similar lines to other UK HEIs, as a HEFCE communication in 2004 stated:

recent consultation carried out by HEFCE with universities and colleges on developing an e-learning strategy reveals that they favour 'blended' approaches to e-learning – involving a mixture of IT, traditional, work-based and distance learning to meet the diverse needs of students – rather than concentrating on wholly e-based learning. (para 7)

Early evaluations had identified one of the main drivers for e-learning as a better experience for students on campus rather than combating distance but later studies revealed a drive to overcome geographical constraints. Schools were delivering and supporting learning to individuals all over the world via Bb. Supplementary material was being distributed via CD-ROM and/or hard copy study material. Some were using websites and web-based resources whilst on-line tutor support was available via Bb and e-mail.

Lessons learned centred on teaching and administrative processes geared up to students' physical presence. In terms of teaching, staff were wondering how they could offer an equivalent to some on-campus experiences such as guest speakers and fieldwork, to distance learners. They also felt that they were failing to obtain student feedback to the same degree as they were able to when they made face-to-face contact with them. In terms of administration there were interface issues between systems which failed to speak to each other involving enrolment, student records, invoicing and Bb, which involved several departments, e.g. Registry, Finance, IT services.

Issues of IPR and issues of control continued to be discussed as they had been with earlier studies. Those who ran course websites in parallel with their use of Bb claimed to have more sense of control and ownership with the former than with Bb. The concerns of those who raised IPR issues were typified by one academic who commented that: '*We give too much away within our modules. Nobody else gives as much detail electronically.*'

However alongside more local issues, there were some staff who saw participation in the varieties of e-learning as affording them a chance to be a world player in developing an e-learning community. Government agencies and professional associations were going down the road of e-learning platforms and blended learning and several academic staff saw distance learning as the future in what was now a global market.

Experiences of Developing Distance Learning Provision

The objective of this 2005 internally funded study was to determine critical success factors in developing a distance learning (DL) programme. This involved interviewing academic staff who had recently been involved in such a development. The PlateGlass research team wanted to find out how much support was forthcoming from e-learning staff, from IT staff and from school management. In addition the team wanted to determine the availability of staff development for those undertaking DL programme development. Whilst there were training sessions on offer and the e-learning team would also provide a customised training programme, the academic staff indicated that take-up for these was poor because of time constraints, indicative of a lack of school recognition of the requirements inherent in the development and of the resources needed, e.g. protected staff time. Once programmes were up and running, issues

similar to those reported in the e-learning audit arose, e.g. the fact that PlateGlass systems were geared to campus-based courses. For example, the systems such as that for student registration appeared to have difficulty recognising that a DL course could run across a calendar year rather than an academic year with students studying flexibly and at their own pace. Another issue harked back to the idea of 'champions' in that there were few academic staff with the expertise involved in the development. In consequence, these staff were having to do the 'lion's share' of the work. As one academic commented:

'*In the University we have academics who know a little about online learning. We have technicians who know a lot about ICTs. The shortfall is of people who know about learning and teaching online, who understand the needs and can translate them ...*'

Lessons learned from the study included the fact that academic staff involved in the developments were all 'at different points on the learning curve' and there was much reliance on the expertise of the e-learning and IT staff. There was a perceived lack of support from school management attributed to failure to appreciate the demands developing a DL programme imposed on staff and the time and effort expended in producing DL materials. There was consensus that if DL were to become something the Schools wished to encourage, they needed to recognise it required additional resources.

Asked about how the process could be improved, staff pointed out the importance of planning, of 'enculturing' those suspicious of online learning. Even those who had embarked on developing DL courses commented how it was '*A bit of a step into the dark.*' and that they were '*Unsure of what we were letting themselves in for.*' There was a sense that there was insufficient awareness of who had overall responsibility within

PlateGlass University and who was driving the move to DL: *'We have no battle plan: in fact we don't even know what war we are fighting!'*

External Evaluative Perspective

The concerns about lack of direction expressed by staff undertaking new e-learning initiatives as outlined above represent further examples of the high expectations often surrounding novel technologies coupled with complaints about the 'slow' pace of change that often follows their introduction are found to be common in industry as well as in the education setting. To unravel this 'mystery', there may be valuable lessons to be gained from research in the Social Shaping of Technology (SST) field. SST commentators argue that the diffusion of technology is not a linear process, but is a complex and uncertain process affected by an array of social, organisational, political and economic factors. SST research can thus offer important insights and points to the need for continued scepticism (Williams, 1996). For example, matching user requirements to new technical possibilities is likely to be a complex process and it is not clear whether the biggest contribution will come from building more societal knowledge into the design of new applications or from the design of generic offerings with final users learning how to adapt supplier offerings to their purposes (Williams, 1996).

If technology implementers are to begin to get to grips with the task at hand, an understanding of the nature of technology requires a broad and dynamic definition rather than a restricted narrow view. Technology implementation is also a difficult concept to define and is a highly complex and uncertain process, with a lack of simple recipes for success owing to the likelihood of different effects in different contexts of use. Implementation is seen to be the site for innovation as users 'struggle' to make technologies work in their particular organisational context. In the case of ICT implementation, SST commentators argue that the promotion of 'vapourware' by suppliers who have little knowledge of the end users' needs serves to add further difficulties to the chances of successful implementation outcomes (Williams, 1996).

PART B. STRATEGIC CONCERNS

Change Management and Transformation of Academic Practice Via E-Learning

There is much discussion in the change management literature about top-down and bottom-up approaches. Consensus is that neither approach is effective on its own but that there is a need to integrate the two (DeFreitas & Oliver, 2005; Fullan, 1994; Sarason, 1990; Trowler, Saunders, & Knight 2003). In addition to the bottom-up studies referred to above, PlateGlass University has also conducted some top-down studies. Risk assessments are crucial to success and these have been undertaken in order to inform policy at regular intervals to ensure that development of facets of e-learning, such as the virtual learning environment, remain in touch with institutional needs. Transformation of academic practice in the sharing and collaborative development of electronic learning, teaching and assessment raise issues such as access, copyright and IPR.

Risk Managing of a VLE: Strategic Implications for Learning Providers

Universities have changed from relatively stable institutions, insulated from the market, to rapidly changing institutions. The range of risks they now face is higher and their reputations have to be carefully monitored, protected and projected. (Leggett & Bunker, 2006, p. 275)

Mention was made above of the global market and of distance learning as the future. Another tactic for entering the global marketplace is by forging international connections with external partners (Craft, 2004). Increasingly, such partnerships involve arrangements whereby an HEI franchises all or part of the off-campus delivery of its taught courses and programmes to approved partners. In the UK this is normally referred to as 'collaborative provision' other terms include 'transnational education', 'off-shore teaching', or 'extra territorial provision'. This is a challenging enterprise, in terms of quality assurance, since the home university still carries full responsibility for control of the quality and standard of any certificate, diploma or degree delivered at a distance in its name.

The objective of this 2006 internally funded research was related to PlateGlass University's institutional strategic priorities and sought to identify areas of risk in relation to strategic change and growth. The university's key strategic vision involves being a world leader in the delivery of flexible and adaptable learning, globally. One of the most important dimensions of this is the use of the University's VLE, in relation to overseas and collaborative ventures and partnerships (OCVPs) and the research team investigated staff assessments of opportunities and risks inherent in using e-learning media.

By embarking on collaborative ventures, institutions choose to enter 'the zone of uncertainty' (Raban & Turner, 2003, para 81). This zone affords opportunities accompanied, inevitably, by risks. Opportunities include an enhanced profile for the university; financial benefits; an expanded student base; enhanced opportunities for student and staff mobility; development of new curricula; and the creation of a resource base in other locations which can be used strategically. The risks, as identified by the research team include administrative, procedural, contractual/legal, technical, financial, resourcing, teaching delivery and cultural. Therefore, matters to be considered revolved around streamlining of the systems to ensure academic quality, operational efficiencies, financial success and strategic relevance. Other matters of concern were areas of responsibility for administering the VLE infrastructure to ensure accessibility of learning materials, staff development (McSwiney & Parnell, 2003) and issues of equity.

Olsen (2005, p. 11) argues that a central international office needs to apply both a brake function and an accelerator function in collaborative education strategy. On the one hand the 'brake function' is to protect the university from financial and reputational risk, by applying good practice models to all proposed collaborative education initiatives. The 'accelerator function' comes into play by encouraging proposals for collaborative initiatives, in the target countries, ensuring that the proposals meet good practice benchmarks (ibid.). So, in effect, we have come full circle and Olsen highlights the need to take account of the risks as well as the opportunities arising from collaborative ventures.

Lessons learned included the fact that HEIs need to develop different business models for the exploitation of e-learning technology and e-learning content beyond the academic programme for which they were originally designed, in new geographical markets or in new markets outside HE. In so doing, HEIs are faced with an increased responsibility to mediate the transfer and exchange of information between copyright owners and users of that information and with a concomitant responsibility to ensure damage limitation through the adoption and reasonable implementation and dissemination of policies and procedures which safeguard copyright or IPR owners. On the other hand, there is a paradox that such policies and procedures may dictate a transmissive pedagogy which runs counter to the potential for the VLE to be used in a highly devolved way, capitalising on its embodiment of creativity, exploratory and self-directed learning.

Figure 1. Learning technology-practice framework

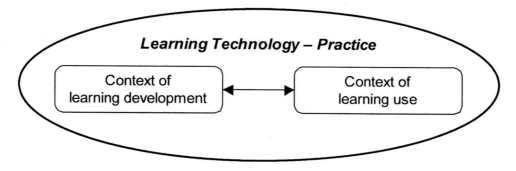

External Evaluative Perspective

Effective change management and the transformation of academic practice via e-learning requires a deep understanding of how to embed e-learning within courses and institutions and the avoidance of narrow technological determinist approaches:

In general, we see a neglect of the educational goals per se and accordingly a lack of attention to the potentially positive synergy between multimedia and innovative teaching. This lacuna can be traced down to the policies that intend to stimulate educational multimedia use, to the design of multimedia projects and to their results. A naïve technological determinist view is clear – if the technical infrastructure is in place, the rest will follow. (Van Lieshout et al., 2001, p. 316)

Carr (2005) proposes use of an e-learning implementation and evaluation framework called the Learning Technology Practice Framework, which is made up of two main elements, the *context of learning development* and the *context of learning use*. Its central premise is that alignment between these two contexts is necessary if successful implementation is to occur:

The *context of learning development* is the socio-technical milieu in which learning technology is developed, and includes issues such as: choice and design of media, defining learn-

ing objectives, identifying student' needs, and designing the learning activities. The *context of learning use* is the socio-technical milieu in which learning technology is used, and includes issues related to learning management, such as facilitator and learner preparation, changes in the role of facilitators and learners, integration with the course, pedagogic support, and logistics. Overarching issues in the framework concern the role of learning technology and the essential need for dialogue in the teaching-learning process. Thus in Figure 1 the central and most important issue is denoted as *learning technology-practice*, i.e. the working integration between the *context of learning development* and the *context of learning use* that is required for successful learning technology implementation to occur. However all too often e-learning use becomes alienated from development and the learning technology becomes packaged or artefactualised. This is illustrated in Figure 2 by the bold jagged lines representing the rupture between the *context of learning development* and the *context of learning use* that is commonplace in university's attempts to implement e-learning solutions:

HEIs do have a growing expertise in the development of e-learning educational solutions, but the demands become much more complex when trying to develop materials for learners from beyond the academic programme for which they were originally designed, or for learners in new

Figure 2. LTPF illustrating use alienated from development

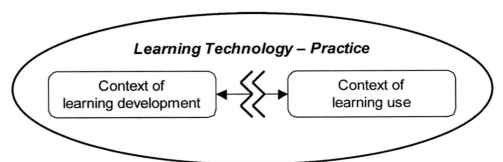

geographical markets or in new markets outside HE (e.g. the small business sector). When developing and implementing learning technology solutions for such learners, HE educators, learning technology developers and public funding bodies should recognise:

1. That e-learning implementation is a socio-technical practice;
2. The importance of informal learning to some types of learners, e.g. those working in small businesses (Carr and Gannon–Leary, 2007);
3. That the more the intended use of learning technology deviates from the developing institution's practice, the more attention must be paid to the *context of learning use*;
4. The value of involving end-users in the development stage to provide an understanding of the *context of learning use*;
5. The need for analytical frameworks (e.g. the Learning Technology Practice Framework) for studying learning technology in use to provide a feedback loop into the *context of learning development*.

PART C. CONCLUDING REMARKS

As illustrated in this chapter, the University has drawn on a broad range of institutional experiences to help to inform the strategy for the deployment of e-learning. It has taken a realistic approach to change management that has been informed both strategically and practically. This approach has been a consultative one which has sought feedback from staff and students on the planning, roll-out and implementation of e-learning technologies and pedagogies. The findings about drivers and barriers to an e-learning environment have been drawn together. Existing data about current practices and their impact have been analysed and new data gathered in order to identify staff and student needs and priorities.

E-learning developments involve managerial and change issues around human and resource factors. If a HEI is to ensure that e-learning transformations are as smooth as possible, strategic planning needs to be coupled with a methodical evaluation. There needs to be a clearly articulated vision of how learning teaching and assessment might not only develop but also how that learning, teaching and assessment might be evaluated.

For institution-wide e-Llearning, a better understanding of the educational components of change, provided by characterising and quantifying its elements, will help development of coordinated approaches to emerging operational areas such as handling staff and student expectations, experiences and learning. Developing and adapting techniques to measure and promote organisational change through encouraging evaluation of existing practice and embedding new practice can form the basis for continual improvement and quality enhancement across all areas of e-learning.

Monitoring and benchmarking are other approaches designed to measure change and combining change management techniques with benchmarking affords an approach to improving the embedding, longevity and practice of e-learning innovations (Calverley & Dexter, 2007).

PlateGlass University was one of a cohort of HEIs which participated in a Higher Education Academy (HEA) and Joint Information Systems Committee (JISC) initiative in 2008. This built upon work undertaken in a number of previous research projects, including those described in this chapter. It was hoped that the exercise could both celebrate achievements and identify areas for development. The summary of outcomes is divided into five categories, one of which focuses on staff experience, support and development, identifying and discussing strengths and areas for improvement. To complete the loop, the findings were fed back to management to influence future strategic planning.

Some of the areas to which the University will be looking in the future were highlighted. For example the need to ensure that decisions about developments respond effectively to pedagogic needs with more embedding and formalisation of liaison between those implementing e-learning developments and those using them at the 'chalk face'. Emphasis upon different emerging pedagogies relating to online learning could form a key strand in future staff development to ensure effective progression of new approaches to delivering programmes. The culture of good e-learning practice is not yet omnipresent and the work of e-learning champions needs to be more widely disseminated and applied.

LESSONS LEARNED

This chapter omits full reports on two other research studies undertaken at PlateGlass University, both of which canvassed staff and student opinions.

One study investigated interactive lectures using an audience response system whilst the other study looked at use of the Turnitin plagiarism detection software. Both studies served to illustrate how few staff were actually availing themselves of these developments. Both therefore highlighted one of the lessons learned from this body of research, i.e. that it is not enough to rely on champions or enthusiasts within schools without at least rewarding them in some way, e.g. dedicated time to disseminate their good practice. Conole, White and Oliver (2009) discuss organisational interventions in the achievement of organisational change by harnessing the potential of ICTs. They discuss the development of innovative approaches to learning and teaching; funds to enable practitioners to experiment with ICTs, evaluate and disseminate the results of their e-learning initiatives; the development of support materials and workshops on effective use of ICTs; and local events to disseminate activities across the institution.

PlateGlass University has taken on board some of these lessons learned. In terms of funding to enable practitioners to experiment with ICTs, in the summer of 2001 PlateGlass introduced a small grants scheme awarded to support innovation and dissemination of good practice in all forms of teaching, learning and assessment and learner support activity. Some 30–50 funding awards are made annually of between £1,000 and £3,000. In recognition of such funding, successful applicants are required to produce a report and a tangible output which can be disseminated and made publicly available.

In terms of support, early 2009 witnessed a merger of two PlateGlass teams – the VLE support team and the e-learning initiatives team – to provide a single point of contact for a service to help support staff in using technology, advising on issues such as curriculum design and development; materials design; production of online content; effective use of ICTs in teaching and assessment; copyright; approval procedures; and quality assurance of online programmes. Members of the newly merged team worked with individual and group members of staff on using ICTs to enhance the student learning experience in a number of ways, including house calls, drop in surgeries and collaboration on specific projects. They liaised with the academic staff development unit and learning and teaching advisors to offer a programme of staff development and dissemination activities across PlateGlass and worked closely with the library and IT services to maximise the success of any e-learning projects. As Bocz, Mihalyi and Kovacs (2009) indicate, the design and development of e-curricula and contents supporting e-learning require knowledge not only of the possibilities provided by ICTs, but also professional and pedagogical knowledge plus managerial skills and competencies such as cooperation, negotiation etc., and the merged team at PlateGlass achieves such synergy.

In terms of funding, the awards on offer at PlateGlass are not large. As Conole, Smith and White (2009) state, funding for e-learning has traditionally been short-term. Whilst the PlateGlass initiative affords practitioners an opportunity to experiment with the use of ICTs in learning and teaching, its short-term nature militates against long-term sustainability, sustainability or reflection on its impact. Fortunately the research team has been able to take a longitudinal perspective to aid understanding of how e-learning is being embedded at PlateGlass but clearly more funding would enable more reflective research to be undertaken. As Nicholas (2008) points out, unless a state of sustainable institutional embedding of e-learning is achieved, long-term e-learning activity may be limited to enthusiasts such as our identified 'beacons of good practice' or e-learning champions.

Also, in terms of funding, Conole, White and Oliver's (2009) suggestion that practitioners evaluate their own initiatives is problematic. Indeed, Oliver et al. (2009a) acknowledge that academics have rarely received training to perform such an evaluation, see no particular benefits and have

other priorities. Fortunately, in some instances, the research team has been able to conduct some evaluation of implementations, evidenced by this chapter, but awareness-raising of the process and significance of evaluation among practitioners is recommended.

Some present elements of evaluation (internal and external) are designed with conventional face-to-face delivery in mind and may be inappropriate to deal with new and emergent delivery modes mediated through the use of ICTs. The use of e-learning implementation and evaluation frameworks such as the Learning Technology Practice Framework (Carr, 2005) may help with engaging academics in thinking about how to embed e-learning successfully within courses, and at a broader level within the organisation. The changes in the roles of lecturers/tutors and learners is particularly important in light of the disorientation faced by both these user groups as a result of changing organisational culture and work practices (Campbell-Gibson, 2000). Lecturers and students have to adapt to their new roles and be allowed the opportunity, time, rewards and training to allow them to adapt the technology to meet their needs in their different and particular contexts of use. Peters' (2000, p. 11) recommendation for 'a bold wave of modernization such as never before' in the higher education sector may well be necessary in the current climate of educational change, but the adoption and diffusion of e-learning in higher education is likely to develop more slowly than imagined by some educational visionaries owing to the complex nature of technology implementation that is common across all sectors, be it industry or education. The first author of this chapter has practised what she preaches by enlisting the assistance of a second author with e-learning evaluation experience gained at other universities, thereby providing an external broad perspective to this account of PlateGlass University's e-learning journey over the past decade.

REFERENCES

Abrami, P. C. (2006). Review of e-learning in Canada: A rough sketch of the evidence, gaps and promising directions. *Canadian Journal of Learning and Technology, 32*(3), n.p. Retrieved June 22, 2009, from http://www.cjlt.ca/index.php/cjlt/article/viewArticle/27/25

Beastall, L., & Walker, R. (2006). Effecting institutional change through e-learning: An implementation model for VLE deployment at the University of York. *Journal of Organisational Transformation and Social Change, 3*(3), 285–299. doi:10.1386/jots.3.3.285_1

Beloff, M. (1968). *The Plateglass universities.* London: Secker & Warburg.

Bocz, T. K., Milhalyi, K., & Kovacs, K. (2009). A synthesis of competency requirements for electronic curriculum developers compiled within the framework of the ACVCD project. Paper given at *Innovation in Learning Communities: What did you invent for tomorrow?* Eden Annual Conference, Gdansk, Poland, 10-13 June.

Boyett, I. (1996). New leader, new culture, old university. *Leadership and Organization Development Journal, 17*(5), 24–30. doi:10.1108/01437739610127487

Britain, S., & Liber, O. (1999). *A framework for pedagogical evolution of virtual learning environments.* Report presented to the Joint Information Systems Committee's Technology Applications Programme (JTAP). Retrieved February 14, 2009, from http://www.leeds.ac.uk/educol/documents/00001237.htm

Browne, T., Jenkins, M., & Walker, R. (2006). A longitudinal perspective regarding the use of VLEs by Higher Education institutions in the UK. *Interactive Learning Environments, 14*(2), 177–192. doi:10.1080/10494820600852795

Calverley, G., & Dexter, H. (2007). Change management of organisational practices to promote successful e-learning. *Proceedings of the 2ⁿᵈ International Conference on E-learning* (ICEL) New York 28-29 June.

Campbell-Gibson, C. (2000). The ultimate disorienting dilemma: The online learning community . In Evans, T., & Nation, D. (Eds.), *Changing university teaching: Reflections on creating educational technologies* (pp. 133–146). London: Kogan Page.

Carr, J. (2005). The implementation of technology-based SME management development programmes. *Educational Technology & Society, 8*(3), 206-215. Retrieved October 22, 2009, from http://www.ifets.info/journals/8_3/18.pdf

Carr, J., & Gannon-Leary, P. (2007). Understanding the learning process in SMEs. *Education, Knowledge and Economy, 1*(2), Routledge. Retrieved October 22, 2009, from http://www.informaworld.com/smpp/title~content=g779588974~db=all

Collis, B., & Moonen, J. (2001). *Flexible learning in a digital world: Experiences and expectations.* London: Kogan Page.

Conole, G., Smith, J., & White, S. (2009). A critique of the impact of policy and funding. In G. Conole, & M. Oliver (Eds.), Contemporary perspectives in e-learning research: Themes, methods and impact on practice (pp. 38-54). Abingdon: Routledge.

Conole, G., White, S., & Oliver, M. (2009). The impact of e-learning on organisational roles and structures. In G. Conole, & M. Oliver (Eds.), Contemporary perspectives in e-learning research: Themes, methods and impact on practice (pp. 69-81). Abingdon: Routledge.

Craft, A. (2004). Assessment of quality risks in collaborative provision. *Quality in Higher Education, 10*(1), 25–29. doi:10.1080/1353832242000195897

Crook, C. (1994). *Computers and the collaborative experience of learning*. London: Routledge.

Dearing, R. (1997). Higher education in the learning society (National Committee of Inquiry into Higher Education) London: HMSO. Retrieved February 14, 2009, from https://bei.leeds.ac.uk/Partners/NCIHE/

DeFreitas, S., & Oliver, M. (2005). Does e-learning policy drive change in higher education? A case study relating models of organisational change to e-learning implementation. *Journal of Higher Education Policy and Management, 7*(1), 81–95. doi:10.1080/13600800500046255

Evans, F. J., & Franz, J. B. (1998). Managing change in the global university. In *Proceedings of the Towards the Global University: Strategies for the Third Millennium Conference*, Tours, April.

Foley, J., & Ojeda, C. (2008). Teacher beliefs, best practice, technology usage in the classroom: A problematic relationship. In K. McFerrin et al. (Eds.), *Proceedings of Society for Information Technology and Teacher Education International Conference* (pp. 4110-4117). Chesapeake, VA: AACE.

Ford, P., Goodyear, P., Heseltine, R., Lewis, R., Darby, J., & Graves, J. (1996). *Managing change in higher education: A learning environment architecture*. London: The Society for Research into Higher Education and Open University Press.

Freeman, C. (1997). *The economics of industrial innovation* (3rd ed.). London: Pinter.

Fullan, M. G. (1994.) Coordinating top-down and bottom-up strategies for educational reform. *Systematic Reform: Perspectives on Personalising Education,* September. Retrieved January 27, 2009, from http://www.ed.gov/pubs/EdReformStudies/SysReforms/fullan1.html

Glaser, B., & Strauss, A. (1967). *The discovery of grounded theory: Strategies for qualitative research*. Chicago: Aldine.

Hase, S., & Ellis, A. (2001). Problems with online learning are systemic, not technical . In Stephenson, J. (Ed.), *Teaching and learning online: Pedagogies for new technologies* (pp. 27–36). London: Kogan Page.

Higher Education Funding Council for England. (2003). *Effecting change in higher education. Report of the HEFCE Good Management Practice Project 2001*. Bristol: HEFCE.

Higher Education Funding Council for England. (2004). *Further briefing statement following the HEFCE Board Meeting on 25 February 2004*. Bristol: HEFCE. Retrieved February 12, 2009, from http://www.hefce.ac.uk/news/HEFCE/2004/euni/further.asp

Higher Education Funding Council for England. (2009). *Enhancing learning and teaching through the use of technology: A revised approach to HEFCE's strategy for e-learning*. Bristol: HEFCE. Retrieved June 16, 2009, from http://www.hefce.ac.uk/pubs/hefce/2009/09_12/

Kotter, J. P. (1995). Leading change: Why transformation efforts fail. *Harvard Business Review* March-April, 59-68. Retrieved January 27, 2009, from http://www.naph.org/NAPH/2008_Fellows/Leading_Change__Why_Transformations_Efforts_Fail_-_John_Kotter.pdf

Laurillard, D. (1994). Reinvent the steering wheel. *Association for Learning Technology Newsletter, 6*(1).

Leggett, M., & Bunker, A. (2006). Teaching portfolios and university culture. *Journal of Further and Higher Education, 30*(3), 269–282. doi:10.1080/03098770600802297

Littlejohn, A., Cook, J., Sclater, N., & Campbell, L. Davis, H., & Currier, S. (2009). Managing educational resources. In G. Conole, & M. Oliver (Eds.), Contemporary perspectives in e-learning research: Themes, methods and impact on practice (pp. 134-146). Abingdon: Routledge.

Marshall, C., & Rossman, G. B. (1989). *Designing qualitative research.* London: Newbury Park, Mayes, J.T. (1993). Distance learning and the new technology: A user-centred view. *Commissioned Report from the Centre for the Exploitation of Science and Technology, London*, Institute for Computer-Based Learning (ICBL), Heriot-Watt University, Retrieved July 28, 2000, from http://led.gcal.ac.uk/clti/staff/Tmpapers.html

Mayes, J. T. (1995). Learning technology and Groundhog Day. In W. Strang, V. Simpson and D. Slater (Eds.), Hypermedia at work: Practice and theory in higher education (pp. 21-37). Canterbury: University of Kent Press.

Mayes, T. (2001). Learning technology and learning relationships . In Stephenson, J. (Ed.), *Teaching and learning online: Pedagogies for new technologies* (pp. 16–26). London: Kogan Page.

McSwiney, C., & Parnell, S. (2003). Transnational expansion and the role of the university library: A study of academics and librarians in an Australian university. *New Review of Libraries and Lifelong Learning, 4*(1), 63–75. doi:10.1080/1468994042000240223

Moses, I. (1997). Redefining academic roles . In Sharpham, J., & Harman, G. (Eds.), *Australia's future universities* (pp. 176–202). Armidale, NSW: University of New South Wales Press.

Newman, F., Couturier, L., & Scurry, J. (2004). *The future of higher education: Rhetoric, reality, and the risks of the market.* San Francisco, CA: Jossey-Bass.

Nicholas, M. (2008). Institutional perspectives: The challenges of e-learning diffusion. *British Journal of Educational Technology, 39*(4), 598–609. doi:10.1111/j.1467-8535.2007.00761.x

Oliver, M., Harvey, J., Conole, G., & Jones, A. (2009a). Evaluation. In G. Conole, & M. Oliver (Eds.), Contemporary perspectives in e-learning research: Themes, methods and impact on practice (pp. 203-216). Abingdon: Routledge.

Oliver, M., Roberts, G., Beetham, H., Ingraham, B., & Dyke, M. (2009b) Knowledge, society and perspectives on learning technology. In G. Conole, & M. Oliver (Eds.), Contemporary perspectives in e-learning research: Themes, methods and impact on practice (pp. 21-37). Abingdon: Routledge.

Olsen, A. (2005).Transnational education programs: Strategy development. Seminar presentation, *Transnational Education: Strategy Considerations and Quality Issues*, Swinburne University of Technology, August 31.

Pennington, G. (2003). *Guidelines for promoting and facilitating change.* York: LTSN Generic Centre.

Peters, O. (2000). The transformation of the university into an institution of independent learning . In Evans, T., & Nation, D. (Eds.), *Changing university teaching: Reflections on creating educational technologies* (pp. 10–23). London: Kogan Page.

Pollock, N., & Cornford, J. (2003). *Putting the university online: Information, technology and organisational change.* Buckingham: Open University Press.

Raban, C., & Turner, E. (2003). *Academic risk: Quality risk management in higher education. Project Report for the Higher Education Funding Council for England.* Bristol: HEFCE.

Raelin, J. (1995). How to manage your local professor. *Academy of Management Journal, 12*, 207–212.

Roberts, G. (2002). *Technology assisted off campus programmes at Oxford Brookes University. Project Report (draft 5.2)*. Oxford: Oxford Brookes University.

Sarason, S. B. (1990). *The predictable failure of educational reform: Can we change course before it's too late?* San Francisco: Jossey Bass.

Sarros, J., Gmelch, W., & Tanewski, G. (1997). The role of the department head in Australian universities: Changes and challenges. *Higher Education Research & Development, 16*, 9–24. doi:10.1080/0729436970160102

Taylor, P., Lopez, L., & Quadrelli, C. (1996). *Flexibility, technology and academics' practices: Tantalising tales and muddy maps, evaluations and investigations programme*. Canberra: Department of Employment, Education, Training and Youth Affairs.

Trowler, P., Saunders, M., & Knight, P. (2003). *Change thinking, change practices: A guide to change for heads of department, subject centres and others who work middle-out*. York: LTSN Generic Centre.

Van Lieshout, M., Egyedi, T. M., & Bijker, W. E. (Eds.). (2001). Social learning technologies: The introduction of multimedia in education. Farnham: Ashgate.

Williams, R. (1996). The social shaping of information and communication technologies . In Kubicek, H., Dutton, W. H., & Williams, R. (Eds.), *The social shaping of information highways. European and American roads to the information society* (pp. 299–338). Frankfurt: Campus Verlag.

Williams, R., & Edge, D. (1996). The social shaping of technology . *Research Policy, 25*, 856–899. doi:10.1016/0048-7333(96)00885-2

ADDITIONAL READING

Bernath, U., Szucs, A., Tait, A., & Vidal, M. (2009). *Distance and e-learning in transition: Learning innovation, technology and social challenges.* London: ISTE/Wiley.

Bocz, T. K., Mihalyi, K., & Kovacs, K. (2009). *A synthesis of competency requirements for electronic curriculum developers compiled within the framework of the ACVCD project*. Innovation in Learning Communities: Eden Annual Conference, Gdansk, 10-13 June.

Bonal, X. (2003). The neoliberal educational agenda and the legitimation crisis: Old and new state strategies. *British Journal of Sociology of Education, 24*(2), 159–175. doi:10.1080/01425690301897

Donnelly, R., & McSweeney (2008). *Applied e-learning and e-teaching in higher education.* Hershey, PA: Idea Group Inc. (IGI).

Ertmer, P. A. (2005). Teacher pedagogical beliefs: The final frontier in our quest for technology integration? *Educational Technology Research and Development, 53*(4), 25–39. doi:10.1007/BF02504683

Grummell, B., Devine, D., & Lynch, K. (2009). The care-less manager: Gender, care and new managerialism in higher education. *Gender and Education, 21*(2), 191–208. doi:10.1080/09540250802392273

Jelfs, A., & Kelly, P. (2007). Evaluating electronic resources: Personal development planning resources at the Open University – A Case Study. *Assessment & Evaluation in Higher Education, 32*(5), 515–526. doi:10.1080/02602930601116755

Price, S., & Oliver, M. (2007). A framework for conceptualising the impact of technology on teaching and learning. *Educational Technology & Society, 10*(1), 16-27. Retrieved 22 June, 2009, from http://www.ifets.info/journals/10_1/3.pdf

Roberts, C. (2008). Implementing educational technology in higher education: A strategic approach. *Journal of Educators Online, 5*(1), n.p. Retrieved June 22, 2009, from http://www.thejeo.com/Archives/Volume5Number1/RobertsPaper.pdf

Sclater, N. (2009). *Embedding educational innovation.* Paper given at Innovation in learning communities. Eden Annual Conference, Gdansk, 10-13 June.

Shurville, S., Browne, T., & Whitaker, M. (2009). Accommodating the newfound strategic importance of educational technologists within higher education: A critical literature review. *Campus-Wide Information Systems, 26*(3), 201–231. doi:10.1108/10650740910967384

Compilation of References

A teacher's guide to the Common European Framework. New York: Pearson/Longman. Retrieved June 23, 2009, from http://www.pearsonlongman.com/ae/cef/cefguide.pdf

Abbey, B. (2000). *Instructional and cognitive impacts of web-based education.* Hershey, PA: Idea Group.

Abowd, G. D., & Mynatt, E. D. (2000). Charting past, present, and future research in ubiquitous computing. [TOCHI]. *ACM Transactions on Computer-Human Interaction, 7*(1), 29–58. doi:10.1145/344949.344988

Abrami, P. C. (2006). Review of e-learning in Canada: A rough sketch of the evidence, gaps and promising directions. *Canadian Journal of Learning and Technology, 32*(3), n.p. Retrieved June 22, 2009, from http://www.cjlt.ca/index.php/cjlt/article/viewArticle/27/25

Abrami, P. C., & Barrett, H. (2005). Directions for research and development on electronic portfolio. *Canadian Journal of Learning and Technology 31*(3), 1-15. Retrieved April 12, 2009, from http://www.cjlt.ca/index.php/cjlt/rt/printerFriendly/92/86

Abrandt Dahlgren, M., & Öberg, G. (2001). Questioning to learn and learning to question: Structure and function of problem-based learning scenarios in environmental science education. *Higher Education, 41*, 263–282. doi:10.1023/A:1004138810465

Adams, P. (1998). Teaching and learning with SimCity 2000. *The Journal of Geography, 97*(2), 47–55. doi:10.1080/00221349808978827

Adler, P. S., & Kwon, S.-W. (2002). Social Capital: Prospects for a new concept. *Academy of Management Review, 27*(1), 17–40. doi:10.2307/4134367

Afoullouss, H. (2009, June). *Integrating LOLIPOP ELP in a language course: A pilot project.* Paper presented at the symposium Learning to LOLIPOP: Learners and Teachers Reflect. Dublin City University, Dublin. Retrieved June 23, 2009, from http://www.lolipop-portfolio.eu/symposium/index.html

Agostinho, S., Harper, B., Oliver, R., Hedberg, J., & Wills, S. (2008). A Visual Learning Design Representation to facilitate dissemination and reuse of innovative pedagogical strategies in university teaching . In Botturi, L., & Stubbs, T. (Eds.), *Handbook of visual languages for instructional design: Theories and practices.* Hershey, PA: Information Science Reference.

Alessi, S. M., & Trollip, S. R. (2001). *Multimedia for learning methods and development* (3rd ed.). Boston: Allyn and Bacon.

Alexander, C. (1979). *The timeless way of building.* New York: Oxford University Press.

Allan, B., & Lewis, D. (2006). The impact of membership of a virtual learning community on individual learning careers and professional identity. *British Journal of Educational Technology, 37*(6), 841–852. doi:10.1111/j.1467-8535.2006.00661.x

Ambrose, L. (2001). *Learning online facilitation online.* Brisbane: Intellectual Property Unit, Southbank Institute of TAFE.

American Library Association. (1989). *Presidential Committee on Information Literacy: Final Report.* Retrieved March 23, 2009, from http://www.ala.org/ala/mgrps/divs/acrl/publications/whitepapers/presidential.cfm

Anderson, P. (2007). *What is Web 2.0? Ideas, technologies and implications for education.* JISC Technology and Standards Watch. London, UK: JISC. Retrieved September 2, 2008, from http://jisc.ac.uk/media/documents/techwatch/tsw0701b.pdf

Anderson, T. (2004). Toward a theory of online learning . In Anderson, T., & Elloumi, F. (Eds.), *Theory and practice of online learning* (pp. 33–60). Athabasca, Alberta, Canada: Athabasca University.

Anderson, T. (2009). Towards a theory of online learning. In T. Anderson, (Ed.), The theory and practice of online learning (2nd ed., pp. 45-74). Athabasca: Athabasca University Press.

Angeli, C., Valanides, N., & Bonk, C. (2003). Communication in a web-based conferencing system: The quality of computer-mediated interactions. *British Journal of Educational Technology*, *34*(1), 31–43. doi:10.1111/1467-8535.00302

Angelo, T. A., & Cross, K. P. (1993). *Classroom assessment techniques: A handbook for college teachers* (2nd ed.). San Francisco, CA: Jossey-Bass.

Antonelli, P. (1997). Curator's Essay. In *Achille Castiglioni: Design!* (A retrospective of the Italian architect and industrial designer), The Museum of Modern Art, New York. Retrieved July 27, 2009, from http://www.moma.org/exhibitions/1997/castiglioni/index.html

Apple Press Release. (2007). *Apple reinvents the phone with iPhone.* Retrieved April 15, 2009, from http://www.apple.com/pr/library/2007/01/09iphone.html

Apple Press Release. (2007). *Apple announces iTunes U on the iTunes store.* Retrieved April 15, 2009, from http://www.apple.com/pr/library/2007/05/30itunesu.html

Apple Press Release. (2009). *Apple reports third quarter results.* Retrieved August 26, 2009, from http://www.apple.com/pr/library/2009/07/21results.html

Apple, M. W. (1979). *Ideology and curriculum.* London: Routledge & Kegan Paul. doi:10.4324/9780203241219

Armstrong Moore, E. (2005). When iPod goes collegiate. *The Christian Science Monitor.* Retrieved April 15, 2009, from http://www.csmonitor.com/2005/0419/p11s01-legn.html

Armstrong, J., & Franklin, T. (2008). A review of current and developing international practice in the use of social networking (Web 2.0) in higher education. Retrieved December 29, 2008, from http://www.franklin-consulting.co.uk/LinkedDocuments/the%20use%20of%20social%20networking%20in%20HE.pdf

Army, U. S. (2009). America's army offical website. Retrieved May 7, 2009, from http://www.americasarmy.com

Association of American Colleges and Universities. (2007). *VALUE: Valid assessment of learning in undergraduate education.* Retrieved March 20, 2009, from http://www.aacu.org/value/index.cfm

Atkins, C. (2000). Lifelong learning – attitudes to practice in the rural context: A study using Bourdieu's perspective of habitus. *International Journal of Lifelong Learning*, *19*(3), 253–265.

Au, W. J. (2007, April 30). Surveying Second Life. *New World Notes.* Retrieved February 15, 2009, from http://nwn.blogs.com/nwn/2007/04/second_life_dem.html

Aviv, R., Erlich, Z., Ravid, G., & Geva, A. (2003). Network analysis of knowledge construction in asynchronous learning networks. *Journal of Asynchronous Learning Networks*, *7*(3), 1–23.

Bachman, L., & Palmer, A. (1996). *Language testing in practice.* Oxford: Oxford University Press.

Baker, M. (2007). iPhone may be freezing college network. Retrieved April 15, 2009, from http://www.msnbc.msn.com/id/19836992

Baker, R. K., Thornton, B., & Adams, M. (2008). An evaluation of the effectiveness of turnitin.com as a tool for reducing plagiarism in graduate student term papers [Electronic Version]. *College Teaching Methods & Styles Journal, 4*. Retrieved October 19, 2009 from http://www.cluteinstitute-onlinejournals.com/archives/abstract.cfm?ArticleID=2096

Barcan, R. (1996). The Body of the (Humanities) Academic, or, 'What is an Academic'. *Australian Humanities Review, 1*(3) September/November. Retrieved October 20, 2009, from http://www.australianhumanitiesreview.org/archive/Issue-Sept-1996/barcan.html

Bargh, J. A., McKenna, K. Y. A., & Fitzsimons, G. M. (2002). Can you see the real me? Activation and expression of the 'true self' on the Internet. *The Journal of Social Issues, 58*(1), 33–48. doi:10.1111/1540-4560.00247

Barnett, K., & Adkins, B. (2004). Engaging with the future: Older learners see the potential of computers for their lifestyle interests. Paper presented at *Social Change in the 21st Century Conference*. Queensland University of Technology: Centre for Social Change Research. Retrieved October 20, 2009, from http://eprints.qut.edu.au/643/1/barnett_adkins.pdf

Barnett, R. (1999). *Realizing the university in an age of supercomplexity*. Buckingham, UK: Society for Research into Higher Education and the Open University.

Baron, N. S. (2008). *Always on: Language in an online and mobile world*. Oxford: Oxford University Press.

Barrett, H. (2008, September 30). *Categories of ePortfolio tools*. Retrieved April 1, 2009, from http://electronicportfolios.org/categories.html

Barrett, H. (2009). *Balancing the two faces of ePortfolios*. Retrieved April 1, 2009, from http://electronicportfolios.org/balance

Barrett, T. (2005). Understanding problem-based learning. In T. Barrett, I. Mac Labhrainn, & H. Fallon (Eds.), Handbook of enquiry and problem-based learning. Irish case studies and international perspectives (pp. 13-25). Dublin: All Ireland Society for Higher Education (AISHE).

Bartoluci, S., Goodyear, P., & Retalis, S. (2004). E-LEN project: Working towards an e-learning design pattern language. *Learning Technology, 5*(4), 24–26. Retrieved July 27, 2009, from http://www.ieeetclt.org/issues/october2003/learn_tech_october2003.pdf

Bass, R. (1997). *Course portfolio page*. Retrieved March 19, 2009, from http://www9.georgetown.edu/faculty/bassr/portfolio.html

Bass, R., & Eynon, B. (2009, March 18). Electronic portfolios: A path to the future of learning. *Wired Campus*. Retrieved April 1, 2009, from http://chronicle.com/blogPost/Electronic-Portfolios-a-Pa/4582

Baumeister, R. F., & Leary, M. R. (1995). The need to belong: Desire for interpersonal attachments as a fundamental human motivation. *Psychological Bulletin, 117*, 497–529. doi:10.1037/0033-2909.117.3.497

Bayne, S. (2005). Deceit, desire and control: The identities of learners and teachers in cyberspace . In Land, R., & Bayne, S. (Eds.), *Education in cyberspace*. London: RoutledgeFalmer.

Bayne, S. (2008). Higher education as a visual practice: Seeing through the virtual learning environment. *Teaching in Higher Education, 13*(4), 395–410. doi:10.1080/13562510802169665

Beastall, L., & Walker, R. (2006). Effecting institutional change through e-learning: An implementation model for VLE deployment at the University of York. *Journal of Organisational Transformation and Social Change, 3*(3), 285–299. doi:10.1386/jots.3.3.285_1

Becher, T. (1989). *Academic tribes and territories: Intellectual inquiry and the cultures of disciplines. Milton Keynes*. UK: Society for Research into Higher Education and Open University Press.

Becher, T., & Trowler, P. (2001). *Academic tribes and territories: Intellectual enquiry and the cultures of disciplines* (2nd ed.). Bury St Edmunds, UK: Society for Research into Higher Education and Open University Press.

Beck, J., & Young, M. (2005). The assault on the professions and the restructuring of academic and professional identities: A Bernsteinian analysis. *British Journal of Sociology of Education, 26*(2), 183–197. doi:10.1080/0142569042000294165

BECTA. (2008). *Web 2.0 technologies for learning at key stages 3 and 4*. Coventry, UK: British Educational Communications and Technology Agency. Retrieved September 2, 2008, from http://www.becta.org.uk

Beetham, H. (2004). Review: Developing e-learning models for the JISC Practitioner Communities. *JISC*. Retrieved July 27, 2009, from http://www.elearning.ac.uk/resources/modelsreview

Beetham, H., & Sharpe, R. (2007). An introduction to rethinking pedagogy in the digital age . In Beetham, H., & Sharpe, R. (Eds.), *Rethinking pedagogy for a digital age: Designing and delivering e-learning* (pp. 1–10). London: Routledge.

Bell, D. (2008). The university in your pocket. In G. Salmon, & P. Edirisingha (Eds.), Podcasting for learning in universities (pp. 178-187). Open University Press: Society for Research into Higher Education.

Bell, J., & Motion, A. (2001). *The creative writing coursebook*. London: Macmillan.

Beloff, M. (1968). *The Plateglass universities*. London: Secker & Warburg.

Belz, J.A., & Kinginger, C. (2002). The cross-linguistic development of address form use in telecollaborative language learning: Two case studies. *The Canadian Modern Language Review/La revue canadienne des langue vivantes, 59*(2), 189-214.

Bennett, M. J. (1998). *Basic concepts of intercultural communication: Selected readings*. Yarmouth, MA: Intercultural Press.

Bennett, S., Priest, A., & Macpherson, C. (1999). Learning about online learning: An approach to staff development for university teachers. *Australian Journal of Educational Technology, 15*(3), 207-221. Retrieved October 20, 2009, from http://www.ascilite.org.au/ajet/ajet15/bennett.html

Benveniste, E. (1971). *Problems in general linguistics (trans. Mary Elizabeth Meek), 2 vols*. Coral Gables, FL: University of Miami.

Bereiter, C. (1995). A dispositional view of transfer . In McKeough, A., Lupart, J., & Marini, A. (Eds.), *Teaching for transfer: Fostering generalization in learning* (pp. 21–34). Mahwah, NJ: Lawrence Erlbaum.

Berge, Z. L. (1995). Facilitating computer conferencing: Recommendations from the field. *Educational Technology, 35*, 22–30.

Bergeron, B. P. (2006). *Developing serious games*. Hingham, MA: Charles River Media.

Bernath, U., Szucs, A., Tait, A., & Vidal, M. (Eds.). (2009). *Distance and e-learning in transition. Learning innovations, technology and social challenges*. Hoboken, NJ: Wiley-ISTE.

Berners-Lee, T. (2000). The web's brainchild [Interview]. Retrieved October 20, 2009, from http://www.unesco.org/webworld/points_of_views/berners-lee.shtml

Betz, J. (1996). Computer games: Increase learning in an interactive multidisciplinary environment. *Journal of Educational Technology Systems, 24*(2), 195–205.

Bhowmicka, A., Khasawnehb, M. T., Bowling, S. R., Gramopadhyea, A. K., & Melloya, B. J. (2007). Evaluation of alternate multimedia for web-based asynchronous learning. *International Journal of Industrial Ergonomics, 37*, 615–629. doi:10.1016/j.ergon.2007.04.004

Biggs, J. (2003). *Aligning teaching for constructing learning*. The Higher Education Academy. Retrieved October 20, 2009, from http://www.heacademy.ac.uk/assets/York/documents/resources/resourcedatabase/id477_aligning_teaching_for_constructing_learning.pdf

Biggs, J. (2006). *Teaching for quality learning at university: What the student does*. Maidenhead, UK: Open University Press.

Birch, D., & Burnett, B. (2009). Bringing academics on board: Encouraging institution-wide diffusion of e-learning environments. *Australasian Journal of Educational Technology, 25*(1), 117-134. Retrieved October 20, 2009, from http://www.ascilite.org.au/ajet/ajet25/birch.html

Blackboard Press Release. (2009). New Blackboard Learn(TM) for Apple(R) iPhone(TM) application lets users take learning on the go. Retrieved August 26, 2009, from http://www.blackboard.com/Company/Media-Center/Press-Releases.aspx?releaseid=1270202

Blackwell, R., & Blackmore, P. (2003). Rethinking strategic staff development . In Blackwell, R., & Blackmore, P. (Eds.), *Towards strategic staff development in Higher Education* (pp. 3–15). Maidenhead, UK: Society for Research into Higher Education and Open University Press.

Blair, K. L., & Takayoshi, P. (1997). Reflections in reading and evaluating electronic portfolios. In K.B. Yancey, & I. Weiser (Eds.), Situating portfolios: Four perspectives. Logan, UT: Utah State University Press. Cambridge, B., Kahn, S., Tompkins, D.P., & Yancey, K.B. (Eds.) (2001). Electronic portfolios: Emerging practices in student, faculty, and institutional learning. Sterling, VA: Stylus.

Bocz, T. K., Milhalyi, K., & Kovacs, K. (2009). A synthesis of competency requirements for electronic curriculum developers compiled within the framework of the ACVCD project. Paper given at *Innovation in Learning Communities: What did you invent for tomorrow?* Eden Annual Conference, Gdansk, Poland, 10-13 June.

Boghossian, P. (2006). *Fear of knowledge: Against relativism and constructivism*. Oxford: Oxford University Press.

Bologna Process. (2009). Official Bologna Process Website 2009-2010. Retrieved October 20, 2009, from http://www.ond.vlaanderen.be/hogeronderwijs/bologna/

Bolstad, R., & Gilbert, J. (2006). Creating digital age learners through school ICT projects: What can the Tech Angels project teach us? New Zealand Ccouncil for Educational Research. [Online] Retrieved November 3, 2009 from http://www.educationcounts.edcentre.govt.nz/__data/assets/pdf_file/0017/6614/ict-tech-angels.pdf

Bonnington, C. P., Oates, G., Parnell, S., Paterson, J., & Stratton, W. (2007). A report on the use of tablet technology and screen recording software in tertiary mathematics courses. In A. D'Arcy-Warmington, V. Martinez Luaces, G. Oates, & C. Varsavsky (Eds.), *Vision and change for a new century, Proceedings of Calafate Delta'07: 6th Southern Hemisphere Conference on Mathematics and Statistics Teaching and Learning* (pp. 19-32). Retrieved April 1, 2009, from http://www.bonnington.org/publications/TabletLectureRecording.pdf

Bontis, N. (2002). The rising star of the Chief Knowledge Officer. *Ivey Business Journal,* March/April, 20-25.

Boot, W., Kramer, A., Simons, D., Fabiani, M., & Gratton, G. (2008). The effects of video game playing on attention, memory, and executive control. *Acta Psychologica, 129*(3), 387–398.

Booth, A., & Nicholls, D. (2005). History teaching in Higher Education: Breaking down the barriers to progression and dialogue. Retrieved March 23, 2009, from http://www.history.ac.uk/education/conference/nichollsbooth.html

Botturi, L., & Stubbs, T. (Eds.). (2008). *Handbook of visual languages for instructional design: Theories and practices*. Hershey, PA: Information Science Reference.

Botturi, L., Derntl, M., Boot, E., & Figl, K. (2006). A classification framework for educational modeling languages in instructional design. In *Proceedings of the Sixth International Conference on Advanced Learning Technologies* (ICALT2006) (pp. 1216-1220). Los Alamitos, CA: IEEE.

Bourdieu, P. (1990). The logic of practice (R. Nice, trans.). Cambridge: Polity Press. (Originally published 1980 as Le Sens pratique. Paris: Les Editions de Minuit.)

Bourdieu, P. (1991). *Language and symbolic power.* Cambridge: Polity Press.

Bourdieu, P. (2000). Pascalian meditations (R. Nice, trans.). Cambridge: Polity Press. (Originally published 1997 as Meditations pascaliennes. Paris: Seuil.)

Bourdieu, P., & Wacquant, L. (1992). An invitation to reflexive sociology. (L. Wacquant, trans.). Cambridge: Polity Press. (Originally published 1992 as Responses: Pour une anthropologie reflexive. Paris: Seuil.)

Bowe, B., & Fitzmaurice, M. (2006). *Guide to writing learning outcomes.* Dublin: Dublin Institute of Technology.

Boyd, D. M. (2004, April). *Friendster and publicly articulated social networking.* Paper presented at the Conference on Human Factors in Computing Systems, Vienna, Austria.

Boyett, I. (1996). New leader, new culture, old university. *Leadership and Organization Development Journal, 17*(5), 24–30. doi:10.1108/01437739610127487

Boyle, T. (1997). *Design for multimedia learning.* Hemel Hempstead: Prentice Hall Europe.

Boyle, T. (2003). Design principles for authoring dynamic, reusable learning objects. *Australian Journal of Educational Technology, 19*(1), 46-58. Retrieved July 27, 2009, from http://www.ascilite.org.au/ajet/ajet19/boyle.html

Bradley, C., & Boyle, T. (2004). Students' use of learning objects. *Interactive Multimedia Electronic Journal of Computer-Enhanced Learning, 6*(2). Retrieved July 27, 2009, from http://imej.wfu.edu/articles/2004/2/01/index.asp

Bransford, J. D., & Schwartz, D. L. (1999). Rethinking transfer: A simple proposal with multiple implications. *Review of Research in Education, 24,* 61–100.

Bransford, J., Brown, A., & Cocking, R. (2003). *How people learn: Brain, mind, experience, and school.* Washington, DC: National Academy Press.

Braun, P. (2002). Digital knowledge networks: Linking communities of practice with innovation. *The Journal of Business Strategy, 19*(1), 43–54.

Brew, A. (2006). *Research and teaching: Beyond the divide.* Basingstoke: Palgrave Macmillan.

Brew, A. (2007). Research and teaching from the students' perspective. Retrieved March 23, 2009, from http://portal-live.solent.ac.uk/university/rtconference/2007/resources/angela_brew.pdf

Brighouse, T. (2005). 'Remote' leadership and cultural change . In Coleman, M., & Earley, P. (Eds.), *Leadership and management in education* (pp. 102–114). Oxford: Oxford University Press.

Brine, J. (2006, October). Lifelong learning and the knowledge economy: Those that know and those that do not – the discourse of the European Union. *British Journal of Educational Research, 32*(5), 649–665. .doi:10.1080/01411920600895676

Britain, S., & Liber, O. (1999). *A framework for pedagogical evolution of virtual learning environments.* Report presented to the Joint Information Systems Committee's Technology Applications Programme (JTAP). Retrieved February 14, 2009, from http://www.leeds.ac.uk/educol/documents/00001237.htm

British Market Research Bureau (BMRB). (2006). A quarter of all adult internet users will listen to a 'Podcast' in the next 6 months. *British Market Research Bureau.* Retrieved April 15, 2009, from http://www.bmrb.co.uk/news/article/a-quarter-of-all-adult-internet-users-will-listen-to-a-podcast-in-the-next-Burrows, P. (2009). App Store hits 500 million downloads. *BusinessWeek.* Retrieved April 15, 2009, from http://www.businessweek.com/technology/ByteOfTheApple/blog/archives/2009/01/the_app_store_s.html

Broad, M., Matthews, M., & McDonald, A. (2004). Accounting education through an online-supported virtual learning environment. *Active Learning in Higher Education, 5*(2), 135–151. doi:10.1177/1469787404043810

Brockbank, A., & McGill, I. (2007). *Facilitating reflective learning in higher education* (2nd ed.). London: Open University Press, McGraw Hill Education.

Brookfield, S. D. (2005). *The power of critical theory for adult learning and teaching.* Berkshire, England: Open University Press.

Brown, J. S., Collins, A., & Duguid, P. (1889). Situated cognition and the culture of learning . *Educational Researcher, 18*(1), 32–34.

Brown, T. H. (2005). Beyond constructivism: Exploring future learning paradigms. *Education Today, 2005* (2). Retrieved November 11, 2007, from http://www.bucks.edu/IDlab/Beyond_constructivism.pdf

Brown, T., & Jenkins, M. (2003). *VLE surveys: A longitudinal perspective between March 2001 and March 2003 for Higher Education in the United Kingdom.* Retrieved August, 2007, from http://www.ucisa.ac.uk/groups/tlig/vle/index_html

Browne, T., Jenkins, M., & Walker, R. (2006). A longitudinal perspective regarding the use of VLEs by Higher Education institutions in the UK. *Interactive Learning Environments, 14*(2), 177–192. doi:10.1080/10494820600852795

Bruce, B. C., & Levin, J. A. (1997). Educational technology: Media for inquiry, communication, construction and expression. *Journal of Educational Computing Research, 17*(1), 79–102.

Bruen, J., & Péchenart, J. (2007, May). *Vorsprung durch Technik: Developing an online version of the European Language Portfolio.* Paper presented at EDTech 2007: Eighth Annual Irish Technology Users' Conference, Dublin Institute of Technology, Dublin. Retrieved March 2, 2009, from http://www.ilta.net/edtech2008/index_edtech2008.html

Bruen, J., & Sherry, R. (2007). New perspectives in language learning: Transferable skills and the Language On-line Portfolio Project . In Conacher, J., & Kelly-Holmes, H. (Eds.), *New learning environments for language learning: Moving beyond the classroom* (pp. 111–122). Frankfurt am Main: Peter Lang.

Bruen, J., Péchenart, J., & Crosbie, V. (2007). Have portfolio, will travel: The intercultural dimension of the European Language Portfolio . In Pearson-Evans, A., & Leahy, A. (Eds.), *Intercultural spaces: Language, culture, identity* (pp. 115–125). New York: Peter Lang.

Budgett, S., Cumming, J., & Miller, C. (2007). *The role of Screencasting in statistics courses.* Paper presented at the International Statistical Institute conference, Lisbon.

Bush, M. (2008). Screencasting as a vehicle for learning & teaching. *Project application,* London: South Bank University. Retrieved April 1, 2009, from http://www.lsbu.ac.uk/lteu/documents/ltip0809/LTiPInd-0809MBush.pdf

Byram, M. (1997). *Teaching and assessing intercultural communicative competence.* Clevedon: Multilingual Matters Limited.

Byram, M., & Zarate, G. (1994). *Definitions, objectives and assessment of sociocultural competence.* Strasbourg: Council of Europe.

Byram, M., & Zarate, G. (1997). Defining and assessing intercultural communicative competence: Some principles and proposals for the European context. *Language Teaching, 29,* 239–243. doi:10.1017/S0261444800008557

Calverley, G., & Dexter, H. (2007). Change management of organisational practices to promote successful e-learning. *Proceedings of the 2nd International Conference on E-learning* (ICEL) New York 28-29 June.

CAMEL. (Collaborative Approaches to the Management of E-Learning) model. Retrieved August, 2007, from http://www.jiscinfonet.ac.uk/camel/camel-model

Campbell, D. (1988). Task complexity: A review and analysis. *Academy of Management Review, 13*(1), 40–52. doi:10.2307/258353

Campbell-Gibson, C. (2000). The ultimate disorienting dilemma: The online learning community . In Evans, T., & Nation, D. (Eds.), *Changing university teaching: Reflections on creating educational technologies* (pp. 133–146). London: Kogan Page.

Campos, M. (1998). Conditional reasoning: A key to assessing computer-based knowledge-building communication processes . *Journal of Universal Computer Science, 4*(4), 404–428.

Cann, A. J. (2007). Podcasting is dead. Long live video! *Bioscience Education ejournal*, 10. Retrieved April 1, 2009, from http://www.bioscience.heacademy.ac.uk/journal/vol10/beej-10-C1.pdf

Carbone, N. (2001). Turnitin.com, a pedagogic placebo for plagiarism [Electronic Version]. *Technical Notes*. Retrieved October 10, 2007 from http://bedfordstmartins.com/technotes/techtiparchive/ttip060501.htm

Carr, J. (2005). The implementation of technology-based SME management development programmes. *Educational Technology & Society, 8*(3), 206-215. Retrieved October 22, 2009, from http://www.ifets.info/journals/8_3/18.pdf

Carr, J., & Gannon-Leary, P. (2007). Understanding the learning process in SMEs. *Education, Knowledge and Economy, 1*(2), Routledge. Retrieved October 22, 2009, from http://www.informaworld.com/smpp/title~content=g779588974~db=all

Carraher, D., & Schliemann, A. (2002). The transfer dilemma. *Journal of the Learning Sciences, 11*(1), 1–24. doi:10.1207/S15327809JLS1101_1

Casey, J., & McAlpine, M. (2002). *Writing and using reusable educational materials: A beginners guide*. JISC Centre for Educational Technology Interoperability Standards. Retrieved July 27, 2009, from http://zope.cetis.ac.uk/groups/20010809144711/FR20020507112554

Casey, J., & Wilson, P. (2006). *A practical guide to providing flexible learning in Further and Higher Education*. Gloucester: Quality Assurance Agency for Higher Education. Retrieved July 27, 2009, from http://www.enhancementthemes.ac.uk/themes/FlexibleDelivery/publications.asp

Casey, J., Greller, W., & Brosnan, K. (2005). *Prospects for using learning objects and learning design as staff development tools in Higher Education*. Paper presented at Cognition and Exploratory Learning in Digital Age, CELDA 2005, December, 14–16 2005, Porto, Portugal. Retrieved October 20, 2009, from http://trustdr.ulster.ac.uk/outputs/casey_brosnan_greller_final.pdf

Casey, J., Proven, J., & Dripps, D. (2006). Modeling organisational frameworks for integrated e-learning: The experience of the TrustDR Project. In *Proceedings of the Sixth International Conference on Advanced Learning Technologies* (ICALT2006) (pp. 1216-1220). Los Alamitos, CA: IEEE.

Caws, C., Friesen, N., & Beaudoin, M. (2006). A new learning object repository for language learning: Methods and possible outcomes. *Interdisciplinary Journal of Knowledge and Learning Objects, 2*, 111-124. Retrieved October 20, 2009, from http://ijklo.org/Volume2/v2p111-124Caws.pdf

CEC Commission of the European Communities. (2006). *Communication from the Commission to the Council and the European Parliament: Delivering on the modernisation agenda for universities: education, research and innovation*. COM(2006) 208. Final. Brussels May 10, 2006. Retrieved October 20, 2009, from http://eur-lex.europa.eu/LexUriServ/LexUriServ.do?uri=COM:2006:0208:FIN:EN:PDF

CEDEFOP. (2009). *The shift to learning outcomes: Policies and practice in Europe*. CEDEFOP Reference Series: 72 Luxembourg: Office for Official Publications of the European Communities. Retrieved October 20, 2009, from http://www.cedefop.europa.eu/etv/Upload/Information_resources/Bookshop/525/3054_en.pdf

CETIS. (2009). *CETIS briefings on e-learning standards.* Retrieved July 27, 2009, from http://zope.cetis.ac.uk/static/briefings.html

Chaky, M., & Diekhoff, M. (2002). A comparison of traditional and internet cheaters. *Journal of College Student Development, 43*(6), 906–911.

Challis, M. (1999). AMEE medical education guide no. 11 (revised): Portfolio-based learning and assessment in medical education. *Medical Teacher, 21*(4), 370–386. doi:10.1080/01421599979310

Chalmers, L., & Keown, P. (2006). Communities of practice and professional development. *International Journal of Lifelong Education, 25*(2), 139–156. doi:10.1080/02601370500510793

Chamot, A., & O'Malley, J. (1994). *The CALLA handbook: Implementing the cognitive language learning approach.* Reading, MA: Addison Wesley.

Chang, S.-H., Lin, P.-C., & Lin, Z. C. (2007). Measures of partial knowledge and unexpected responses in multiple-choice tests. *Journal of Educational Technology & Society, 10*(4), 95–109.

Charp, S. (2002). Wireless vs. hard-wired network use in education. *T.H.E. Journal, 29*(8), 8–10.

Chen, H. L., & Mazlow, C. (2002). Electronic learning portfolios and student affairs. *Net Results.* Retrieved April 6, 2009, from http://www.naspa.org/netresults/PrinterFriendly.cfm?ID=825

Cheng, J. (2007) Duke solves iPhone network problem. *Ars Technica.* Retrieved April 15, 2009, from http://arstechnica.com/apple/news/2007/07/duke-solves-iphone-network-problem.ars

CHEPS. (2007). The extent and impact of higher education curricular reform across Europe. Final report of the Directorate-General for Education and Culture of the European Commission. Part 1. Comparative Analysis and Executive Summary. Enschede: Center for Higher Education Policy Studies (CHEPS) Retrieved October 20, 2009, from http://ec.europa.eu/education/pdf/doc244_en.pdf

Chester, A. (2004). *Presenting the self in cyberspace: Identity play online.* Unpublished doctoral dissertation, University of Melbourne.

Chester, A., & Bretherton, D. (2007). Impression management and identity online . In Joinson, A., McKenna, K., Postmes, T., & Reips, U. (Eds.), *The Oxford handbook of Internet psychology* (pp. 223–236). New York: Oxford University Press.

Choy, S. O., & Ng, K. C. (2007). Implementing wiki software for supplementing online learning. *Australasian Journal of Educational Technology, 23*(2), 209-226. Retrieved October 12, 2009, from http://www.ascilite.org.au/ajet/ajet23/choy.html

Churchill, T. (2005). E-reflections: A comparative exploration of the role of e-learning in training higher education lecturers. *Turkish Online Journal of Distance Education, 6*(3), 48–57.

Clark, D. R. (2004). *A brief history of instructional system design.* Retrieved July 27, 2009, from http://www.nwlink.com/~Donclark/history_isd/isdhistory.html   de Corte, E. (1990). Learning with new information technologies in schools: Perspectives from the psychology of learning and instruction, *Journal of Computer Assisted Learning, 6*(2), 69-87.

Clarke, A. (2001). *Designing computer-based learning materials.* Aldershot: Gower.

Cohen, A. (1998). *Strategies in learning and using a second language.* New York: Addison Wesley Longman.

Cole, D. J., Ryan, C. W., & Kick, F. (1995). *Portfolios across the curriculum and beyond.* California: Corwin Press.

Collis, B., & Moonen, J. (2001). *Flexible learning in a digital world: Experiences and expectations.* London: Kogan Page.

Common European Framework of Reference for Languages. (2001). *Learning, teaching, assessment.* Cambridge: Cambridge University Press.

Condie, R., & Livingston, K. (2007). Blending online learning with traditional approaches: Changing practices. *British Journal of Educational Technology, 38*(2), 337–348. doi:10.1111/j.1467-8535.2006.00630.x

Conger, S. Basu (2005). If there is no significant difference, why should we care? *The Journal of Educators Online, 2*(2). Retrieved October 20, 2009, from http://www.thejeo.com/Basu%20Conger%20Final.pdf

Connolly, M., Jones, C., & Jones, N. (2007). Managing collaboration across further and higher education: a cause in practice. *Journal of Further and Higher Education, 31*(2), 159–169. doi:10.1080/03098770701267630

Connolly, P. (2004). *Boys and schooling in the early years. Abingdon.* Oxon, UK: RoutledgeFalmer, Taylor and Francis Group.

Conole, G. (2008). Capturing practice: The role of mediating artefacts in learning design . In Lockyer, L., Bennett, S., Agostinho, S., & Harper, B. (Eds.), *Handbook of research on learning design and learning objects: Issues, applications and technologies* (pp. 187–207). Hersey, PA: IGI Global.

Conole, G. (2008). Stepping over the edge: The implications of new technologies for education. In M. Lee,& C. McLoughlin (Eds.), *Web 2.0-based e-learning: Applying social informatics for tertiary teaching.* [Online] Retrieved July 28, 2009, from http://www.online-conference.net/jisc/content2008/conole/Conole_in_lee_mcloughlin.doc

Conole, G., & Creanor, L. (2006). In their own words: Exploring the learner's perspective on e-learning. London, UK. JISC. Retrieved September 7, 2008, from http://www.jisc.ac.uk/media/documents/programmes/elearningpedagogy/iowfinal.pdf

Conole, G., & Oliver, M. (2002). Embedding theory into learning technology practice with toolkits. *Journal of Interactive Media in Education, 2002*(8). Retrieved October 20, 2009, from http://www-jime.open.ac.uk/2002/8/conole-oliver-02–8.pdf

Conole, G., & Oliver, M. (Eds.). (2007). Contemporary perspectives in e-learning research: Themes, methods and impact on practice. Abingdon: Routledge.

Conole, G., Smith, J., & White, S. (2009). A critique of the impact of policy and funding. In G. Conole, & M. Oliver (Eds.), Contemporary perspectives in e-learning research: Themes, methods and impact on practice (pp. 38-54). Abingdon: Routledge.

Conole, G., Thorpe, M., Weller, M., Wilson, P., Nixon, S., & Grace, P. (2007). *Capturing practice and scaffolding learning design.* Paper presented at the Eden Conference. Milton Keynes, The Open University. [Online] Retrieved July 28, 2009, from http://labspace.open.ac.uk/file.php/1/kmap/1176712833/references/eden_conole_et_al_learning%20design%20final.doc

Conole, G., White, S., & Oliver, M. (2009). The impact of e-learning on organisational roles and structures. In G. Conole, & M. Oliver (Eds.), Contemporary perspectives in e-learning research: Themes, methods and impact on practice (pp. 69-81). Abingdon: Routledge.

Cook, J., & Light, A. (2006). New patterns of power and participation? Designing ICT for informal and community learning. *E-Learning.* Special Issue of ICE2 Symposium, *3*(1), 51-61. Retrieved March 6, 2009, from http://www.wwwords.co.uk/elea/content/pdfs/3/issue3_1.asp

Cornford, I. (2005). Challenging current policies and policy makers' thinking on generic skills. *Journal of Vocational Education and Training, 57*(1), 25–45. doi:10.1080/13636820500200273

Costello, E. (2008). *Developing educational resources using Camtasia Studio.* National Digital Learning Repository Project (NDLR) workshop presentation. Retrieved March 20, 2008, from http://www.ndlr.ie/mshe

Cotteral, S. (1999). Key variables in language learning: What do learners believe about them? *System, 27,* 593–613. doi:10.1016/S0346-251X(99)00047-0

Cotterill, S. J., White, A., & Currant, B. (2007). Using Web 2.0 to support PDP. *PDP-UK, 12,* 7–8.

Council of Europe [Website] Retrieved October 15, 2008, from http://culture2.coe.int/portfolio

Crabtree, H. (2003). Improving student learning using an enquiry based approach. Retrieved March 23, 2009, from http://www.ece.salford.ac.uk/proceedings/theme2.php?id=2

Craft, A. (2000). *Continuing professional development: A practical guide for teachers and schools* (2nd ed.). New York: Routledge Falmer. doi:10.4324/9780203420041

Craft, A. (2004). Assessment of quality risks in collaborative provision. *Quality in Higher Education, 10*(1), 25–29. doi:10.1080/1353832242000195897

Cram, B. (1995). Self-assessment: from theory to practice. Developing a workshop guide for teachers. In G. Brindley (Ed.), *Language Assessment in Action*. Sydney: NCELTR. Dialang [Website] Retrieved March 24, 2009, from http://www.dialang.org

Crawford, C. M., & Gannon-Cook, R. (2002). *Faculty attitudes towards distance education: Enhancing the support and rewards system for innovative integration of technology within coursework*. Paper presented at 13th International Conference of the Society for Information Technology & Teacher Education. Nashville, TN. Retrieved March 4, 2007, from http://www.eric.ed.gov/ERICDocs/data/ericdocs2sql/content_storage_01/0000019b/80/1a/99/d5.pdf

Crook, C. (1994). *Computers and the collaborative experience of learning*. London: Routledge.

Csikszentmihalyi, M. (2002). *Flow: The classic work on how to achieve happiness* (Rev. ed.). London: Rider.

Cunningham, J. (1993). Habitus and misrecognition: An essay in response to Scahill. *Philosophy of Education*. University of Illinois Urbana-Champaign College of Education, Philosophy of Education Society 1996-2004. Retrieved September 8, 2007, from http://www.ed.uiuc.edu/EPS/PES-Yearbook/93_docs/CUNNINGH.HTM

Curry, P., Sherry, R., & Tunney, O. (2003). *What transferable skills do employers look for in third-level graduates?* Dublin: Transferable Skills Project.

Curtis, D., & Lawson, M. (2001). Exploring collaborative online learning. *Journal of Asynchronous Learning Networks, 5*(1), 21–34.

Curtis, P. (1997). Mudding: Social phenomena in text-based virtual reality . In Keisler, S. (Ed.), *Culture of the Internet* (pp. 121–142). Mahwah, NJ: Erlbaum.

Dahl, S. (2007). Turnitin. The student perspective on using plagiarism detection software . *Active Learning in Higher Education, 8*(2), 173–191. doi:10.1177/1469787407074110

Dalziel, F. (2007, June). *The European Language Portfolio: Its role and potential in university language teaching*. Paper presented at a Cercles Seminar, University College Dublin, Dublin. Retrieved February 24, 2007, from http://www.cercles.org/en/elp/seminar/presentations/Dalziel/ELP_Higher_Education.ppt

Davidson-Shivers, G. V. (2002). Instructional technology in higher education . In Reiser, R. A., & Dempsey, J. V. (Eds.), *Trends and issues in instructional design and technology* (pp. 256–268). New Jersey: Merrill Prentice Hall.

Davis, M. H., Ponnamperuma, G. G., & Ker, J. S. (2009). Student perceptions of a portfolio assessment process. *Medical Education, 43*(1), 89–98. doi:10.1111/j.1365-2923.2008.03250.x

Davis, R. H. (1979, March). A behavioral change model with implications for faculty development. *Higher Education, 8*(2), 123–140. .doi:10.1007/BF00138376

De Corte, E. (2003). Transfer as the productive use of acquired knowledge, skills, and motivations. *Current Directions in Psychological Science, 12*(4), 142–146. doi:10.1111/1467-8721.01250

De Wever, B., Schellens, T., Valcke, M., & Van Keer, H. (2006). Content analysis schemes to analyze transcriptions of online asynchronous discussion groups: A review. *Computers & Education, 46*(1), 6–28. doi:10.1016/j.compedu.2005.04.005

Dearing, R. (1997). Higher education in the learning society (National Committee of Inquiry into Higher Education) London: HMSO. Retrieved February 14, 2009, from https://bei.leeds.ac.uk/Partners/NCIHE/

Dede, C. (2008). New Horizons: A seismic shift in epistemology. *EDUCAUSE Review, 43*(3), 80-81. Retrieved October 12, 2009, from http://net.educause.edu/ir/library/pdf/ERM0837.pdf

DeFreitas, S., & Oliver, M. (2005). Does e-learning policy drive change in higher education? A case study relating models of organisational change to e-learning implementation. *Journal of Higher Education Policy and Management, 7*(1), 81–95. doi:10.1080/13600800500046255

Demiris, G. (2005). The diffusion of virtual communities in health care: Concepts and challenges. *Patient Education and Counseling, 62*, 178–188. doi:10.1016/j.pec.2005.10.003

Department of Education and Science. Ireland *Leaving Certificate English Syllabus*. Retrieved October 26, 2009, from http://www.education.ie/servlet/blobservlet/lc_english_sy.pdf?language=EN

Detterman, D. K. (1996). The case for the prosecution: Transfer as an epiphenomenon . In Detterman, D. K., & Sternberg, R. J. (Eds.), *Transfer on trial: Intelligence, cognition and instruction* (pp. 1–25). New York: Ablex.

Dewey, J. (1938). *Logic: The theory of inquiry*. New York: Holt.

Diez, M. (1994). *The portfolio: Sonnet, mirror, and map*. Paper presented at the conference on Linking Liberal Arts and Teacher Education: Encouraging Reflection through Portfolios, San Diego, CA.

DIT. (2009). Dublin Institute of Technology's Research Ethics Committee. Retrieved March 31, 2009, from http://www.dit.ie/researchandenterprise/research/researchsupportoffice/ethics/guidelines

Donnelly, R. (2008). Activity systems within blended problem-based learning in academic professional development. *International Journal of Applied Educational Studies, 3*(1), 38–59.

Donnelly, R., & Gardner, J. (2009). Content analysis of computer conferencing transcripts. *Journal of Interactive Learning Environments, 20*(4), 469–485.

Donnelly, R., & O'Rourke, K. (2007). What now? Evaluating e-learning CPD Practice in Irish Third-Level Education. *Journal of Further and Higher Education, 31*(1), 31–40. doi:10.1080/03098770601167864

Doolan, M. A. (2006). Effective strategies for building a learning community online using a Wiki. *Proceedings 1st Annual Blended Learning Conference* (pp. 51-55). Retrieved October 12, 2009, from https://uhra.herts.ac.uk/dspace/bitstream/2299/1721/1/901867.pdf

Dörnyei, Z. (2003). Attitudes, orientations and motivations in language learning: Advances in theory, research and applications. *Language Learning, 53*(1), 3–32. doi:10.1111/1467-9922.53222

Downes, S. (2003). *Design, standards and reusability*. Retrieved July 27, 2009, from http://www.downes.ca/post/54

Downes, S. (2005). *E-learning 2.0. eLearn Magazine*. October 16, 2005. Retrieved October 12, 2009, from http://www.elearnmag.org/subpage.cfm?section=articles&article=29–1

Draaijer, S., & van Boxel, P. (2006). *Summative peer assessment using 'Turnitin' and a large cohort of students: A case study*. Paper presented at the Computer-Assisted Assessment (CAA) Conference. Retrieved October 20, 2009, from http://hdl.handle.net/2134/4559

Dreyfus, H. L. (2009). *On the Internet* (2nd ed.). New York: Routledge.

Dubinsky, J. (2003). Creating new views on learning: ePortfolios. *Business Communication Quarterly*, *66*, 96–102. doi:10.1177/108056990306600410

Dumais, S. A. (2002, January). Cultural capital, gender, and school success: The role of habitus. [from http://socofedcomps.wikispaces.com/file/view/cult+capital+and+habitus+quant+article.pdf]. *Sociology of Education*, *75*(1), 44–68. Retrieved September 17, 2007. doi:10.2307/3090253

Eales, R. T. J. (2003). Supporting informal communities of practice within organizations . In Ackerman, M., Pipek, V., & Wulf, V. (Eds.), *Beyond knowledge management: Sharing expertise*. Cambridge, MA: MIT Press.

Edirisingha, P., Salmon, G., & Nie, M. (2008). Developing pedagogical podcasts. In G. Salmon, & P. Edirisingha (Eds.), Podcasting for learning in universities (pp. 153-168). Open University Press: Society for Research into Higher Education.

Education Technology Services. (2009). *e-Portfolios at Penn State*. Retrieved March 23, 2009, from http://portfolio.psu.edu

Educause (2006). 7 things you should know about ... Screencasting. *EDUCAUSE Learning Initiative Brief.* Retrieved April 1, 2009, from http://net.educause.edu/ir/library/pdf/ELI7003.pdf

EDUCAUSE. (2009). Top teaching and learning challenges for 2009. Retrieved August, 2007, from http://www.educause.edu/eli/challenges

Egenfeldt-Nielsen, S. (2005). *Beyond edutainment: Exploring the educational potential of computer games*. IT-University of Copenhagen.

Elbow, P. (1973). *Writing without teachers*. London: Oxford University Press.

Elbow, P. (1999). Inviting the mother tongue: beyond 'mistakes', 'bad English', and 'wrong language'. *Journal of Advanced Composition*, *19*(2), 359–388.

Elbow, P., & Belanoff, P. (1986). Portfolios as a substitute for proficiency examinations. *College Composition and Communication*, *37*(3), 336–340. doi:10.2307/358050

E-LEN Project. (2004). *Design expertise for e-learning centres: design patterns and how to produce them. E-LEN project workpackage deliverable*. Retrieved July 27, 2009, from http://www2.tisip.no/E-LEN/documents/ELEN-Deliverables/booklet-e-len_design_experience.pdf

Elgort, I., Smith, A. G., & Toland, J. (2008). Is wiki an effective platform for group course work? *Australasian Journal of Educational Technology*, *24*(2), 195–210.

Elliott, B. (2009). *E-pedagogy: Does e-learning require a new approach to teaching and learning?* Edinburgh: UK: Scottish Qualifications Authority. Retrieved March 13, 2009, from http://www.scribd.com/doc/932164/E-pedagogy

Elliott, L., San Antonio, T., Dalrymple, M., Schiflett, S., & Miller, J. (2004). Scaling scenarios: Development and application to c4isr sustained operations research . In Schiflett, S. G. (Ed.), *Scaled worlds: Development, validation, and applications* (pp. 119–133). Aldershot: Ashgate.

Ellsworth, J. B. (2000). *Surviving change: A survey of educational change models*. Syracuse: Eric Clearinghouse on Information & Technology.

Elsasser, G. N., Hoie, E. B., Destache, C. J., & Monaghan, M. S. (2009). Availability of Internet download lecture audio files on class attendance and examination performance. *International Journal of Instructional Technology and Distance Learning*, *6*(2), 19-24. Retrieved April 15, 2009, from http://www.itdl.org/Journal/Feb_09/article03.htm

Elton, G. R. (1967). *The practice of history*. London: Fontana.

Elton, L. (2005). Scholarship and the research and teaching nexus . In Barnett, R. (Ed.), *Reshaping the university* (pp. 108–118). Maidenhead, UK: Open University Press.

Ely, D. P. (1990). Conditions that facilitate the implementation of educational technology innovations. *Journal of Research on Computing in Education*, *23*(2), 298–305.

Ertmer, P. (2005). Teacher pedagogical beliefs: The final frontier in our quest for technology integration? *ETR&D, 53*(4), 25–39. doi:10.1007/BF02504683

Eshet, Y. (2004). Digital literacy: A conceptual framework for survival skills in the digital era. *Journal of Educational Multimedia and Hypermedia, 13*(1), 93–106.

European Commission. (2005). Towards a European qualifications framework for lifelong learning. Commission Staff Working Document. Brussels (SEC(2005)957). Retrieved October 20, 2009, from http://ec.europa.eu/education/policies/2010/doc/consultation_eqf_en.pdf

Evans, F. J., & Franz, J. B. (1998). Managing change in the global university. In *Proceedings of the Towards the Global University: Strategies for the Third Millennium Conference*, Tours, April.

Everett, R. (2006). *Addressing 'E': A pedagogic rationale for embedding e-learning in a large Further Education College*. Unpublished MA thesis, University of London: Institute of Education.

Everett, R. (2008). *Oaklands College Vision*. St Albans. [Online] Retrieved July 21, 2009, from http://info.rsc-eastern.ac.uk/file_security/get_file.aspx?id=1525

Fahlberg, T., Fahlberg-Stojanovska, L., & MacNeil, G. (2007). Whiteboard math movies. *Teaching Mathematics and Its Applications, 26*(1), 17–22. doi:10.1093/teamat/hrl012

Fairclough, N. (1993). *Critical discourse analysis: The critical study of language*. New York: Longman.

Felder, R. M., & Silverman, L. K. (1988). Learning and teaching styles in engineering education. *English Education, 78*(7), 674–681.

Fell, A. (2004, September). *Applications and advantages of synchronous and asynchronous text-based conferencing in support of online learners*. Paper presented at the Association of Learning Technology Conference 2004. Exeter, UK, University of Exeter.

Fell, A., & Kuit, J. A. (2005, November). *Developing the professional role of the e-tutor*. Paper presented at the Staff and Educational Developers Association Autumn Conference, Birmingham, UK.

Fetherston, T. (2001). Pedagogical challenges for the World Wide Web. *Association for the Advancement in Computing in Education Journal, 9*(1). Retrieved March 18, 2009, from http://www.editlib.org/index.cfm?fuseaction=Reader.TOC&sourceissue_id=164

Feurzeig, W., Munter, P., Swets, J., & Breen, M. (1964). Computer-aided teaching in medical diagnosis. *Journal of Medical Education, 39*(8), 645–754.

Fini, A. (2007). Editorial: Focus on e-learning 2.0. *Journal of e-Learning and Knowledge Society: The Italian e-Learning Association Journal, 3*(2).

Fink, L. D. (2003). *Creating significant learning experiences: An integrated approach to designing college courses*. San Francisco: Jossey-Bass.

Fisch, S., Kirkorian, H., & Anderson, D. (2005). Transfer of learning in informal education: The case of television . In Mestre, J. (Ed.), *Transfer of learning from a modern multidisciplinary perspective* (pp. 371–390). Greenwich: IAP.

Fitzpatrick, N. (2008). *Les Je(ux) de discours dans l'oeuvre de Brian Friel*. Lille: CNT.

Fitzpatrick, N., Hayes, N., & O'Rourke, K. C. (2009). Beyond constriction and control: Constructivism in online theory and practice . In Payne, C. (Ed.), *Information technology and constructivism in higher education: Progressive learning frameworks*. Hershey, PA: IGI Global.

Fleming, T. (2008). We are condemned to learn: Towards higher education as a learning society. *DIT-Level3, 6*(1). Retrieved October 20, 2009, from http://level3.dit.ie/html/issue6/fleming/fleming_1.html

Flottechmesch, K. (2000). Building effective interaction in distance education: A review of the literature. *Educational Technology, 40*(3), 46–51.

Flower, L., & Hayes, J. (1981). A cognitive process theory of writing. *College Composition and Communication, 32*(4), 365–387. doi:10.2307/356600

Foley, J., & Ojeda, C. (2008). Teacher beliefs, best practice, technology usage in the classroom: A problematic relationship. In K. McFerrin et al. (Eds.), *Proceedings of Society for Information Technology and Teacher Education International Conference* (pp. 4110-4117). Chesapeake, VA: AACE.

Ford, P., Goodyear, P., Heseltine, R., Lewis, R., Darby, J., & Graves, J. (1996). *Managing change in higher education: A learning environment architecture*. London: The Society for Research into Higher Education and Open University Press.

Foster, A. L. (2007, September 21). Professor Avatar: In the digital universe of Second Life, classroom instruction also takes on a new personality. *Chronicle of Higher Education*. Retrieved February 12, 2009, from http://chronicle.com/weekly/v54/i04/04a02401.htm

Foucault, M. (1966). *The order of things: An archaeology of the human sciences*. New York: Pantheon.

Fowler, S., Watson, C. E., & Zaldivar, M. (2009, January). *Institutionalizing the ePortfolio: Addressing assessment, pedagogy, and professional development issues for widespread adoption*. Paper presented at the annual meeting of the Educause Learning Initiative, Orlando, Florida.

Fox, S., & MacKeogh, K. (2003). Can e-learning promote higher-order learning without tutor overload? *Open Learning, 18*(June), 121–134. doi:10.1080/02680510307410

Fox, S., & Walsh, E. (2007). Task Oriented Online Learning (TOOL)—Social interaction in an online environment. In G. O'Neill, G. et al. (Eds.), *Case Studies of Good Practice in Assessment of Student Learning in Higher Education* Dublin: AISHE/HEA. Retrieved October 20, 2009, from http://www.aishe.org/readings/2007–1/No-06.html

Franciszkowicz, M. (2008). Video-based additional instruction. *Journal of the Research Center for Educational Technology, 4*(2), 5-14. Retrieved April 1, 2009, from http://www.rcetj.org/?type=art&id=90059& Gilbert, S. (2002). Low threshold applications. *Webpage*. Retrieved July 5, 2002, from http://www.tltgroup.org/resources/rltas.html

Franklin, T., & van Harmelen, M. (2007). *Web 2.0 for Content for learning and teaching in Higher Education*. Bristol: JISC. Retrieved October 12, 2009, from http://ie-repository.jisc.ac.uk/148/1/web2-content-learning-and-teaching.pdf

Frankola, K. (2001). Why online learners dropout. Retrieved August 30, 2005, from http://www.workforce.com/feature/00/07/29/

Frath, P. (2006). Le Portfolio européen des langues et le Cadre européen commun de référence: entre normalisation institutionnelle et responsabilité individuelle . In Sachot, M., & Schneider-Mizony, M. (Eds.), *Education et normativité*. Caen: Presses Universitaires de Caen.

Freeman, C. (1997). *The economics of industrial innovation* (3rd ed.). London: Pinter.

Friesen, N. (2004). Three objections to learning objects and e-learning standards . In McGreal, R. (Ed.), *Online education using learning objects* (pp. 59–70). London: Routledge.

Friesen, N., & Cressman, D. (2006). The political economy of technical e-learning standards. In A. Koolhang, & K. Harman (Eds.), *Learning objects: Theory, praxis, issues, and trends* (pp. 507-526). Warsaw: Informing Science Press. Retrieved July 27, 2009, from http://learningspaces.org/n/papers/standards_ant.doc

Fullan, M. (1999). *Change forces the sequel*. London, Philadelphia: Open University Press.

Fullan, M. (2001). *Leading in a culture of change*. San Francisco: Jossey-Bass.

Fullan, M. G. (1994.) Coordinating top-down and bottom-up strategies for educational reform. *Systematic Reform: Perspectives on Personalising Education,* September. Retrieved January 27, 2009, from http://www.ed.gov/pubs/EdReformStudies/SysReforms/fullan1.html

Gallagher, M. (2008). Improving institutional effectiveness: The relationship between assessing student learning outcomes and strategic planning in California Community Colleges. *Journal of Applied Research in the Community College, 15*(2), 101–108.

Gao, X. (2006). Has language learning strategy research come to an end? A response to Tseng et al. *Applied Linguistics, 28*(4), 615–620. doi:10.1093/applin/amm034

Garis, J. W. (2007). e-Portfolios: Concepts, designs, and integration with student affairs. *New Directions for Student Services, 119*(Fall), 3–15. doi:10.1002/ss.245

Garisson, D. R., Anderson, T., & Archer, W. (2000). Critical inquiry in a text-based environment: computer conferencing in higher education. *The Internet and Higher Education, 2*(2/3), 87–105.

Garrison, D. R. (1990). An analysis and evaluation of audio teleconferencing to facilitate education at a distance. *American Journal of Distance Education, 4*(3), 13–24. doi:10.1080/08923649009526713

Garrison, D. R. (2007). Online community of inquiry review: Social, cognitive, and teaching presence issues. *Journal of Asynchronous Learning Networks, 11*(1), 61–72.

Garrison, D. R., & Kanuka, H. (2004). Blended learning: Uncovering its transformative potential in higher education. *The Internet and Higher Education, 7,* 95–105. doi:10.1016/j.iheduc.2004.02.001

Garrison, D. R., Anderson, T., & Archer, W. (2001). Critical thinking, cognitive presence and computer conferencing in distance education. *American Journal of Distance Education, 15*(1), 7–23. doi:10.1080/08923640109527071

Gattegno, C. (1978). *Teaching foreign languages in schools: The silent way* (2nd ed.). New York: Educational Solutions.

Gayle, B. M. (2004). Transformations in a civil discourse public speaking class: Speakers' and listeners' attitude change. *Communication Education, 53*(2), 174–184. doi:10.1080/03634520410001682438

Gick, M., & Holyoak, K. (1980). Analogical problem solving. *Cognitive Psychology, 12*(3), 306–355. doi:10.1016/0010-0285(80)90013-4

Gilbert, J., Morton, S., & Rowley, J. (2007). e-Learning: The student experience. *British Journal of Educational Technology, 38*(4), 560–573. doi:10.1111/j.1467-8535.2007.00723.x

Giles, J. (2005). Internet encyclopaedias go head to head. *Nature, 438,* 900-901 (December 15).

Gillmor, D. (2004). *We the media.* Retrieved August 2, 2006, from http://www.authorama.com/we-the-media-1.html

Glaser, B., & Strauss, A. (1967). *The discovery of grounded theory: Strategies for qualitative research.* Chicago: Aldine.

Goddard, R., & Rudzki, R. (2005). Using an electronic text-matching tool (Turnitin) to detect plagiarism in a New Zealand university. *Journal of University Teaching & Learning Practice, 2.*

Goleman, D. (1994, October 11). Peak performance: Why records fall. *The New York Times.*

González, J. (2008). Promoting student autonomy through the use of the European Language Portfolio, *English Language Teaching (ELT) Journal, 10*(November), 1-10. Retrieved March 6, 2009, from http://eltj.oxfordjournals.org/cgi/reprint/ccn059v1.

Goodfellow, R. (2005). Virtuality and the shaping of Educational Communities. *Education Communication and Information, 5*(2), 113–129.

Goodman, A. (2003). *Now what? Developing our future: Understanding our place in the unfolding universe*. New York: Peter Lang Publishing.

Gosling, D. (2008). *Educational development in the United Kingdom: Report to the Heads of Educational Development Group*. London, UK: Heads of Development Group.

Gosling, S. D., Gaddis, S., & Vazire, S. (2007, March). *Personality impressions based on Facebook profiles*. Paper presented at the International Conference on Weblogs and Social Media, Boulder, Colorado.

Gourvès-Hayward, A., Kennedy, F., & Sudhershan, A. (2007, April). *The intercultural dimension in LOLIPOP. How interculturally competent are you?* Paper presented at the SIETAR EUROPA Annual Conference, East, West, North & South: Culture's Impact on Economy, Religion, Ecology, Politics. Sofia, Bulgaria.

Gourvès-Hayward, A., Péchenart, J., & Simpson, V. (2008, May). LOLIPOP, vers une plus grande autonomie dans l'apprentissage des langues. *Actes du 36ème Congres de l'UPLEGESS (Union des Professeurs de Langues des Grandes Ecoles)* (pp. 43-55). Paris, France.

Gourvès-Hayward, A., Simpson, V., & Morace, C. (2009, June). Using LOLIPOP for intercultural communication and management. Paper presented at the symposium *Learning to LOLIPOP: learners and teachers reflect*. Dublin City University, Dublin. Retrieved June 23, 2009, from http://www.lolipop-portfolio.eu/symposium/index.html

Grabe, M., & Christopherson, K. (2007). Optional student use of online lecture resources: Resource preferences, performance and lecture attendance. *Journal of Computer Assisted Learning, 24*(1), 1–10.

Grabinger, R. S., & Dunlap, J. C. (2000). Rich environments for active learning: A definition . In Squires, D., Conole, G., & Jacobs, G. (Eds.), *The changing face of learning technology* (pp. 8–38). Cardiff: University of Wales Press.

Graves, W. H. (2001). Transforming traditional faculty roles . In Barone, C. A., & Hagner, P. R. (Eds.), *Technology-enhanced teaching and learning, Educause Leadership Strategies* (*Vol. 5*, pp. 35–44). New York: Wiley.

Gray, B. (2004). Informal learning in an online community of practice. *Journal of Distance Education, 19*(1), 20–35.

Greeno, J., Smith, D., & Moore, J. (1996). Transfer of situated learning . In Detterman, D. K., & Sternberg, R. J. (Eds.), *Transfer on trial: Intelligence, cognition, and instruction* (pp. 99–167). New York: Ablex.

Grierson, H., Nicol, D., Littlejohn, A., & Wodehouse, A. (2004). Structuring and sharing information resources to support concept development and design learning. Paper presented at the *Network Learning Conference*, Exeter, UK (pp. 572-579), April 2004. Retrieved October 12, 2009, from http://www.networkedlearningconference.org.uk/past/nlc2004/proceedings/individual_papers/grierson_et_al.htm

Griffiths, D., & Blat, J. (2005). The role of teachers in editing and authoring units of learning using IMS Learning Design. *International Journal on Advanced Technology for Learning, Special Session on Designing Learning Activities: From Content-based to Context-based Learning Services, 2*(4). Retrieved July 27, 2009, from http://dspace.ou.nl/handle/1820/586

Group, N. D. P. (2008). The NPD Group: iPhone 3G leads U.S. consumer mobile phone purchases in the third quarter of 2008. Retrieved April 15, 2009, from http://www.npd.com/press/releases/press_081110.html

Grummell, B., Devine, D., & Lynch, K. (2009). The care-less manager: Gender, care and new managerialism in higher education. *Gender and Education, 21*(2), 191–208. doi:10.1080/09540250802392273

Guevarra Enriquez, J. (2009). Discontent with content analysis of online transcripts. *Association for Learning Technology Journal, 17*(2), 101–113.

Gunawardena, C., Lowe, C., & Anderson, T. (1997). Analysis of a global online debate and the development of an interaction analysis model for examining social construction of knowledge in computer conferencing. *Journal of Educational Computing Research, 17*(4), 397–431.

Gunter, H. M. (2000, December). Thinking Theory: The field of education management in England and Wales. *British Journal of Sociology of Education, 21*(4), 623-635. Retrieved December 6, 2006, from JSTOR database http://www.jstor.org/pss/1393386

Guskey, T. R. (2000). *Evaluating professional development*. Thousand Oaks, CA: Corwin Press.

Gustafson, K. L., & Branch, R. M. (2002). What is instructional design? In Reiser, R. A., & Dempsey, J. V. (Eds.), *Trends and issues in instructional design and technology* (pp. 16–25). New Jersey: Merrill Prentice Hall.

Hairston, M. (1982). The winds of change: Thomas Kuhn and the revolution in the teaching of writing. *College Composition and Communication, 33*(1), 76–88. doi:10.2307/357846

Hall, G. E. (1979). The concerns-based approach to facilitating change. *Educational Horizons, 57*(4), 202–208.

Hall, R. (2006). Battery farming or free ranging: Towards citizen participation in e-learning environments. *E-learning, 3*(4), 505–518. doi:10.2304/elea.2006.3.4.505

Hall, R., & Hanna, P. (2004). The impact of web page text-background color combinations on readability, retention, aesthetics, and behavioral intention. *Behaviour & Information Technology, 23*(3), 183–195. doi:10.1080/01449290410001669932

Halliday, M. A. K. (1978). *Language as social semiotic*. London: Arnold.

Halliday, M. A. K. (1985). *An introduction to functional grammar*. London: E. Arnold.

Ham, V., & Davey, R. (2005). Our first time: Two higher education tutors reflect on becoming a 'virtual teacher'. *Innovations in Education and Teaching International, 42*(3), 257–264. doi:10.1080/01587910500168017

Hammond, M., & Wiriyapinit, M. (2005). Learning through online discussion: A case of triangulation in research. *Australasian Journal of Educational Technology, 21*(3), 283–302.

Hammond, N. (2003). Learning technology in higher education in the UK: Trends, drivers and strategies. In M. van der Wende and M. van der Ven (Eds.), *The use of ICT in higher education: A mirror of Europe* (pp. 109–122). Utrecht: Lemma Publishers. Retrieved October 20, 2009, from http://www.psychology.heacademy.ac.uk/Publications/HammondMirror2003.pdf

Hancock, J. T., Thom-Santelli, J., & Ritchie, T. (2004). Deception and design: The impact of communication technologies on lying behaviour. In E. Dykstra-Erickson and M. Tscheligi (Eds.), *Conference on computer human interaction* (pp. 29-134). New York: ACM Press.

Hannah, S. B. (1995, December). The correlates of innovation: Lessons form best practice. *Public Productivity & Management Review, 19*(2), 216–228. doi:10.2307/3380499

Hargreaves, A., & Fullan, M. (2000). Mentoring in the new millennium. *Theory into Practice, 9*(1), 51–56.

Harris, J. (2008). eMentoring: The Future of online learner support. *Scientific Commons*. [Online] Retrieved April 10, 2009, from http://en.scientificcommons.org/40674734

Hartman, J., Moskal, P., & Dziuban, C. (2005). Preparing the academy of today for the learner of tomorrow. In D.G. Oblinger, & J.L. Oblinger (Eds.), *Educating the Net Generation*. Retrieved October 20, 2009, from http://www.educause.edu/Resources/EducatingtheNetGeneration/PreparingtheAcademyofTodayfort/6062.

Hase, S., & Ellis, A. (2001). Problems with online learning are systemic, not technical . In Stephenson, J. (Ed.), *Teaching and learning online: Pedagogies for new technologies* (pp. 27–36). London: Kogan Page.

Hase, S., & Kenyon, C. (2000). *From andragogy to heutagogy*. Retrieved March 10, 2009, from http://www.ultibase.rmit.edu.au

Haskell, R. E. (2001). *Transfer of learning: Cognition, instruction, and reasoning*. San Diego, CA: Academic Press.

Hawkey, K. (2003). Asynchronous text-based discussion: A case study with trainee teachers. *Education and Information Technologies*, *8*(2), 165–177. doi:10.1023/A:1024558414766

Hays, R. (2005). *The effectiveness of instructional games: A literature review and discussion*. Orlando, FL: Naval Air Warfare Center Training Systems Division.

HEFCE Higher Education Funding Council for England. (2009). *Enhancing learning and teaching through the use of technology. A revised approach to HEFCE's strategy for e-learning*. March12, 2009. Retrieved March 31, 2009 from http://www.hefce.ac.uk/pubs/hefce/2009/09_12

Hemmi, A., Bayne, S., & Land, R. (2009). The appropriation and repurposing of social technologies in higher education. *Computer Assisted Learning*, *25*(1), 19–30. doi:10.1111/j.1365-2729.2008.00306.x

Hendricks, V., & Maor, D. (2004). Quality of students' communicative strategies delivered through computer-mediated communications. *Journal of Interactive Learning Research*, *15*(1), 5–32.

Henri, F. (1992). Computer conferencing and content analysis . In Kaye, A. R. (Ed.), *Collaborative learning through computer conferencing: The Najaden Papers* (pp. 117–136). Berlin: Springer-Verlag.

Heppell, S. (2006). Play to learn, learn to play. Retrieved April 15, 2009, from http://www.heppell.net/weblog/stephen/otherwriting/2006/10/20/Playtolearnlearntoplay.html

Herring, S. C. (2004). Computer-mediated discourse analysis: An approach to researching online behavior. In S.A. Barab, R. Kling, & J.H. Gray (Eds.), *Designing for virtual communities in the service of learning* (pp. 338-376). New York: Cambridge University Press. Preprint. Retrieved April 26, 2009, from http://ella.slis.indiana.edu/~herring/cmda.pdf

Herring, S. C. (2004). Content analysis for new media: Rethinking the paradigm. In *New research for new media: Innovative research methodologies symposium working papers and readings* (pp. 47-66). Minneapolis, MN: University of Minnesota School of Journalism and Mass Communication. Retrieved April 26, 2009, from http://ella.slis.indiana.edu/~herring/newmedia.pdf

Herring, S. C. (2007). A faceted classification scheme for computer-mediated discourse. *Language@Internet*, 4, Article 1. Retrieved April 26, 2009, from http://www.languageatinternet.de/articles/2007/761

Higgins, E. T. (1987). Self-discrepancy: A theory relating self and affect. *Psychological Review*, *94*(3), 319–340. doi:10.1037/0033-295X.94.3.319

Higher Education Funding Council for England. (2003). *Effecting change in higher education. Report of the HEFCE Good Management Practice Project 2001*. Bristol: HEFCE.

Higher Education Funding Council for England. (2004). *Further briefing statement following the HEFCE Board Meeting on 25 February 2004*. Bristol: HEFCE. Retrieved February 12, 2009, from http://www.hefce.ac.uk/news/HEFCE/2004/euni/further.asp

Higher Education Funding Council for England. (2009). *Enhancing learning and teaching through the use of technology: A revised approach to HEFCE's strategy for e-learning*. Bristol: HEFCE. Retrieved June 16, 2009, from http://www.hefce.ac.uk/pubs/hefce/2009/09_12/

Hillman, D. C., Willis, D. J., & Gunawardena, C. N. (1994). Learner–interface interaction in distance education: An extension of contemporary models and strategies for practitioners. *American Journal of Distance Education*, *8*(2), 30–42. doi:10.1080/08923649409526853

Hiltz, S. R., Coppola, N., Rotter, N., & Turoff, M. (2000). Measuring the importance of collaborative learning for the effectiveness of ALN: A multi-measure, multi-method approach. *Journal of Asynchronous Learning Networks*, *4*(2), 103–125.

Hinman, L. M. (2002). The impact of the Internet on our moral lives in academia. *Ethics and Information Technology*, *4*(1), 31–35. doi:10.1023/A:1015231824812

Hokanson, B. (2008). The virtue of paper: Drawing as a means to innovation in instructional design . In Botturi, L., & Stubbs, T. (Eds.), *Handbook of visual languages for instructional design: Theories and practices*. Hershey, PA: Information Science Reference.

Holmes, B., Tangney, B., FitzGibbon, A., Savage, T., & Mehan, S. (2001). Communal constructivism: Students constructing learning for as well as with others. Retrieved December 5, 2006, from https://www.cs.tcd.ie/publications/tech-reports/reports.01/TCD-CS-2001–04.pdf

Holmes, T. (2008). Discourse structure analysis of chat communication. *Language@Internet*, 5. Retrieved October 26, 2009, from http://www.languageatinternet.de/articles/2008/1633

Hsiao, T., & Oxford, R. (2002). Comparing theories of language learning strategies: A confirmatory factor analysis. *Modern Language Journal*, *86*(iii), 368–383. doi:10.1111/1540-4781.00155

Hubert, C., Newhouse, B., & Vestal, W. (2001). *Building and sustaining communities of practice*. Houston, USA: APQC.

Hughes, G. (2007). Using blended learning to increase learner support and improve retention. *Teaching in Higher Education*, *12*(3), 349–363. doi:10.1080/13562510701278690

Hulme, M. K. (2004). Examining inter-space: A working paper exploring Bourdieu's concepts of 'habitus' and 'field' in relations to mobility related empirical research. Centre for the Study of Media, Technology and Culture. Retrieved November 4, 2009, from http://www.lancs.ac.uk/fass/centres/cemore/pastevents/altmobs/hulme.doc

Hutchings, B. (2006). Principles of enquiry-based learning. Retrieved March 23, 2009, from http://www.campus.manchester.ac.uk/ceebl/resources/papers/ceeblgr002.pdf

Illich, I. (1973). *Tools for conviviality*. London: Harper & Row.

IMS. (2009). *IMS Learning Design best practice and implementation guide*. Retrieved July 27, 2009, from http://www.imsglobal.org/learningdesign/ldv1p0/imsld_bestv1p0.html

Irgon, A., Zolnowski, J., Murray, K. J., & Gersho, M. (1990). Expert system development: A retrospective view of five systems. *IEEE Expert*, *5*(3), 25–40. doi:10.1109/64.54671

Issroff, K., & Scanlon, E. (2002). Educational technology: The influence of theory. *Journal of Interactive Media in Education*, 2002(6). Retrieved from www-jime.open.ac.uk/2002/6

Jackson, B., & Anagnostopoulou, K. (2001). Making the right connections: Improving quality in online learning . In Stephenson, J. (Ed.), *Teaching and learning online: Pedagogies for new technologies*. London: Kogan Page.

James, D., & Biesta, G. (Eds.). (2007). *Improving learning cultures in further education*. Oxon: Routledge.

James, R., Bexley, E., Devlin, M., & Marginson, S. (2007). Australian university student finances 2006: A summary of findings from a national survey of students in public universities. Canberra: Australian Vice-Chancellors' Committee.

Jelfs, A., & Colbourn, C. (2002). Do students' approaches to learning affect their perceptions of using computing and information technology? *Journal of Educational Media*, *27*(1-2), 41–53. doi:10.1080/0305498032000045449

Jenkins, R. (2002). *Pierre Bourdieu. Abingdon*. Oxon, UK: Routledge. (Original work published 1992)

Jennings, D. (2005). Virtually effective: The measure of a learning environment. In G. O'Neill, S. Moore, & B. McMullin (Eds.), Emerging issues in the practice of university learning and teaching. Dublin: All Irish Society for Higher Education (AISHE).

Johnson, D. F. (2003). Toward a philosophy of online education . In Brown, D. G. (Ed.), *Developing faculty to use technology: Programs and strategies to enhance teaching* (pp. 9–12). Bolton: Anker Publishing.

Johnson, D., & Post, D. (1996). Law and borders – The rise of law in cyberspace. *Stanford Law Review*, *48*(5), 1367–1402. doi:10.2307/1229390

Johnson, L. G. (1984). Faculty receptivity to an innovation: A study of attitudes toward external degree programs. *The Journal of Higher Education*, *55*(4), 481–499. doi:10.2307/1981444

Johnson, N. J., & Rose, L. M. (1997). *Portfolios: Clarifying, constructing, and enhancing*. Lancaster, PA: Technomic Publishing Company.

Johnson, R. S., Mims-Cox, J. S., & Doyle-Nichols, A. (2006). *Developing portfolios in education: A guide to reflection, inquiry, and assessment*. Thousand Oaks, CA: SAGE Publications.

Johnson, S. (2006). *Everything bad is good for you: How popular culture is making us smarter*. London: Penguin.

Joinson, A. (2003). *Understanding the psychology of Internet behaviour: Virtual worlds, real lives*. Basingstoke: Palgrave Macmillan.

Joint Information Systems Committee. (2009). *About us*. Retrieved March 24, 2009, from http://www.jisc.ac.uk/aboutus.aspx

Jonassen, D. H. (2003). *Learning to solve problems with technology: A constructivist perspective*. Upper Saddle River, NJ: Merrill.

Jonassen, D. H., & Reeves, T. C. (1996). Learning with technology: Using computers as cognitive tools . In Jonassen, D. H. (Ed.), *Handbook of research on educational communications and technology* (pp. 693–719). New York: Macmillan.

Jones, P. (2007). When a wiki is the way: Exploring the use of a wiki in a constructively aligned learning design. In R.J. Atkinson, C. McBeath, S.K.A. Soong, & C. Cheers (Eds.), *ICT: Providing choices for learners and learning*. Proceedings ascilite Singapore 2007. Centre for Educational Development, Nanyang Technological University, Singapore, 2-5 December. Retrieved October 12, 2009, from http://www.ascilite.org.au/conferences/singapore07/procs/

Jordan, A., Carlile, O., & Stack, A. (2008). *Approaches to learning*. Maidenhead: Open University Press.

Jung, T., Hyunsook, Y., & McClung, S. (2007). Motivations and self-presentation strategies on Korean-based 'cyworld' weblog format personal homepages. *Cyberpsychology & Behavior*, *10*(1), 24–31. doi:10.1089/cpb.2006.9996

Junglas, I. A., Johnson, N. A., Steel, D. J., Abraham, D. C., & MacLoughlin, P. (2007). Identity formation, learning styles and trust in virtual worlds. *The Data Base for Advances in Information Systems*, *38*(4), 90–96.

Kahn, P., & O'Rourke, K. (2004). Guide to curriculum design: Enquiry-based learning. Retrieved March 27, 2009, from http://www.campus.manchester.ac.uk/ceebl/resources/guides/kahn_2004.pdf

Kahn, P., & O'Rourke, K. (2005). Understanding enquiry-based learning. In T. Barrett, I. Mac Labhrainn, & H. Fallon (Eds.), Handbook of enquiry and problem-based learning: Irish case studies and international perspectives (pp. 1-12). Dublin: All Ireland Society for Higher Education (AISHE).

Kahn, S. (2001). Linking learning, improvement, and accountability: An introduction to electronic institutional portfolios . In Cambridge, B. (Ed.), *Electronic portfolios: Emerging practices in student, faculty, and institutional learning* (pp. 135–158). Sterling, VA: Stylus.

Kanter, B. (2008). Screencasting primer. *Webpage.* Retrieved April 1, 2009, from http://screencastingprimer. wikispaces.com/primer

Kanuka, H., & Kelland, K. (2008). Has e-learning delivered on its promises? Expert opinion on the impact of e-learning in higher education. *Canadian Journal of Higher Education, 38*(1), 45–65.

Kent, T. (2002). Supporting staff using WebCT at the University of Birmingham. *Proceedings of the European Conference on E-Learning* (pp. 157-168). Brunel University, Uxbridge, UK.

Kerres, M., & de Witt, C. (2003). A didactical framework for the design of blended learning arrangements. *Journal of Educational Media, 28*(203), 101–113. doi:10.1080/1358165032000165653

Kerres, M., Euler, D., Seufert, S., Hasanbegovic, J., & Voss, B. (2005). *Lehrkompetenz für eLearning-Innovationen in der Hochschule (SCIL Report 6). St Gallen: Swiss Centre for Innovations in Learning.* SCIL.

Kirkpatrick, D. L. (1959). Techniques for evaluating training programs . *Journal of American Society for Training and Development, 13*(11-12).

Kirschner, P. A., Hendricks, M., Paas, F., Wopereis, I., & Cordewener, B. (2004, October). Determinants for failure and success of innovation projects: The road to sustainable educational innovation. Paper given at *27th Association for Educational Communications and Technology.* Retrieved March 4, 2007, from http:// www.eric.ed.gov/ERICDocs/data/ericdocs2sql/content_ storage_01/0000019b/80/1b/a7/36.pdf

Kleck, C. A., Reese, C., Ziegerer-Behnken, D., & Sundar, S. (2007). *The company you keep and the image you project: Putting your best face forward in online social networks.* Paper presented at the annual meeting of the International Communication Association, San Francisco, California.

Kleiman, G. M. (2000). Myths and realities about technology in K-12 Schools . In Gordon, D. T. (Ed.), *The digital classroom. How technology is changing the way we teach and learn.* Cambridge, MA: The Harvard Education Letter.

Kleiman, G. M. (2004). Myths and realities about technology in k-12 schools: Five years later. *Contemporary Issues in Technology and Teacher Education, 4*(2). Retrieved October 20, 2009, from http://www.citejournal. org/vol4/iss2/seminal/article2.cfm

Knight, M. E., & Gallaro, D. (Eds.). (1994). *Portfolio assessment: Applications of portfolio analysis.* Lanham, MD: University Press of America.

Knight, W. E., Hakel, M. D., & Gromko, M. (2008). The relationship between electronic portfolio participation and student success. *Association for Institutional Research Professional File, 107*, 1–16.

Knoster, T., Villa, R., & Thousand, J. (2000). A framework for thinking about systems change . In Villa, R., & Thousand, J. (Eds.), *Restructuring for caring and effective education: Piecing the puzzle together* (pp. 93–128). Baltimore, MD: Paul H. Brookes Publishing Co.

Koory, M. A. (2003). Differences in learning outcomes for the online and f2f version of 'an introduction to Shakespeare'. *Journal of Asynchronous Learning Networks, 7*(2), 18–35.

Koper, R. (2003). Combining reusable learning resources and services with pedagogical purposeful units of learning . In Littlejohn, A. (Ed.), *Reusing on-line resources: A sustainable approach to e-learning.* London: Kogan Page.

Koper, R. (2005). An introduction to Learning Design . In Koper, R., & Tattersall, C. (Eds.), *Learning Design: A handbook on modelling and delivering networked education and training*. Berlin: Springer.

Koschmann, T. (Ed.). (2001). *CSCL: Theory and practice of an emerging paradigm* (pp. 1–23). Mahwah, NJ: Lawrence Erlbaum.

Kotter, J. P. (1995). Leading change: Why transformation efforts fail. *Harvard Business Review* March-April, 59-68. Retrieved January 27, 2009, from http://www.naph.org/NAPH/2008_Fellows/Leading_Change__Why_Transformations_Efforts_Fail_-_John_Kotter.pdf

Krause, K.-L. (2007). The Teaching-Research-Technology nexus: Implications for engaging the Net Generation. Retrieved March 30, 2009, from http://www.linkaffiliates.net.au/idea2007/files/IdeaConfKrauseFINAL.pdf

Kreijns, K., Kirschner, P. A., & Jochems, W. (2003). Identifying the pitfalls for social interaction in computer-supported collaborative learning environments: A review of the research. *Computers in Human Behavior*, *19*(3), 335–353. doi:10.1016/S0747-5632(02)00057-2

Kreitzberg, C., & Little, A. (2008). Usability in practice: Strategies for designing application navigation. *MSDN Magazine* (March). Retrieved June 23, 2009, from http://msdn.microsoft.com/en-us/magazine/dd458810.aspx

Kruse, K. (2009). Introduction to instructional design and the ADDIE model. Retrieved April, 2009, from http://www.e-learningguru.com/articles/art2_1.htm

Kuit, J. A., & Fell, A. (2008). The digital divide: is it the hyphen? In N. Whitton, & M. McPherson (Eds.), *Re-thinking the digital divide* (pp. 100-101). Research Proceedings of the 15th Association for Learning Technology Conference. Leeds, UK: University of Leeds.

Kupetz, R., & Ziegenmeyer, B. (2006). Flexible learning activities: Fostering autonomy teaching training. *ReCALL*, *18*(1), 63–82. doi:10.1017/S0958344006000516

Kvavik, R. V., & Caruso, J. B. (2005). *ECAR study of students and information technology, 2005: Convenience, connection, control and learning*. Boulder, CO: EDUCAUSE Center for Applied Research. Retrieved August 11, 2009, from http://net.educause.edu/ir/library/pdf/ers0506/rs/ers0506w.pdf

Lamb, B. (2004). Wide open spaces: Wikis ready or not. *Educause Review*, September/October, 36-48. Retrieved October 12, 2009, from http://net.educause.edu/ir/library/pdf/ERM0452.pdf

Land, R., & Bayne, S. (Eds.). (2005). Education in cyberspace. London and New York: RoutledgeFalmer.

Lang, S. (2000). A-level history: Changes and methodology. *History Today*, *50*(2), 16.

Language On-line Portfolio Project (LOLIPOP). Retrieved October 15, 2008, from http://lolipop-portfolio.eu

Laru, J., & Järvelä, S. (2008). Using Web 2.0 software and mobile devices for creating shared understanding among Virtual Learning Communities. Retrieved March 30, 2009, from http://ieeexplore.ieee.org/stamp/stamp.jsp?tp=&arnumber=4489827&isnumber=4489772

Laurillard, D. (1993). *Rethinking University Teaching: A framework for the effective use of educational technology*. London: Routledge.

Laurillard, D. (1994). Reinvent the steering wheel. *Association for Learning Technology Newsletter, 6*(1).

Laurillard, D. (2002). *Rethinking university teaching*. Abingdon: Routledge and Falmer.

Laurillard, D. (2004). The conversational framework . In Holliman, R., & Scanlon, E. (Eds.), *Mediating science learning through information and computing technology*. London: Routledge Falmer. doi:10.4324/9780203464007_chapter_1.2

Lave, J. (1993). The practice of learning . In Chaiklin, S., & Lave, J. (Eds.), *Understanding practice: Perspectives on activity and context* (pp. 3–32). Cambridge: Cambridge University Press. doi:10.1017/CBO9780511625510.002

Lave, J., & Wenger, E. (1991). *Situated learning: Legitimate peripheral participation*. Cambridge: Cambridge University Press.

Lavender, T. (2008). Homeless: It's no game – measuring the effectiveness of a persuasive videogame. In T. Conolly, & M. Stansfield (Eds.), *2nd European Conference on Games Based Learning* (pp. 261-266). Barcelona: Academic Publishing Limited.

Lea, M. (2001). Computer conferencing and assessment: New ways of writing in higher education. *Studies in Higher Education, 26*(2), 163–181. doi:10.1080/03075070120052099

Leary, M. R. (1995). *Self-presentation: Impression management and interpersonal behaviour*. Madison, WI: Brown and Benchmark.

Leberman, S., McDonald, L., & Doyle, S. (2006). *The transfer of learning: Participants' perspectives of adult education and training*. Aldershot: Gower.

Ledwith, A., & Risquez, A. (2008). Using anti-plagiarism software to promote academic honesty in the context of peer reviewed assignments. *Studies in Higher Education, 33*(4), 371–384. doi:10.1080/03075070802211562

Lee, A. T. (2005). *Flight simulation: Virtual environments in aviation*. Aldershot: Ashgate.

Lee, H. (2001, November). Teachers' perceptions of technology: Four categories of concerns. Paper given at *24th National Convention of the Association for Educational Communications and Technology: Vols. 1–2. Annual Proceedings of Selected Research and Development [and] Practice Papers* (pp. 239-244). Atlanta GA. Retrieved March 4, 2007, from http://www.eric.ed.gov/ERICDocs/data/ericdocs2sql/content_storage_01/0000019b/80/1a/85/fc.pdf

Lee, M. J. W., & Chan, A. (2007). Reducing the effects of isolation and promoting inclusivity for distance learners through podcasting, *Turkish Online Journal of Distance Education, 8*(1), 85-104. Retrieved October 26, 2009, from http://tojde.anadolu.edu.tr/tojde25/pdf/article_7.pdf

Lee, M. J. W., Pradhan, S., & Dalgarno, B. (2008). The effectiveness of screencasts and cognitive tools as scaffolding for novice object-oriented programmers. *Journal of Information Technology Education, 7*, 61–80.

Lee, S. (2005). Electronic spaces as an alternative to traditional classroom discussion and writing in secondary English classrooms. *Journal of Asynchronous Learning Networks, 9*(3), 25–46.

Legacy Games. (2009). *911 paramedic*. Retrieved May 7, 2009 from http://www.legacygames.com/download_games/861/911_paramedic

Legacy Games. (2009). *Pet pals: Animal doctor*. Retrieved May 7, 2009 from http://www.legacygames.com/download_games/154/pet_pals:_animal_doctor

Leggett, M., & Bunker, A. (2006). Teaching portfolios and university culture. *Journal of Further and Higher Education, 30*(3), 269–282. doi:10.1080/03098770600802297

Levy, P., & Petrulis, R. (2007). Towards transformation? First year students, inquiry-based learning and the research/teaching nexus. Retrieved March 30, 2009, from http://www.srhe.ac.uk/conference2007

Levy, S. (1984). *Hackers: Heroes of the computer revolution*. New York: Dell.

Light, V., Nesbitt, E., Light, P., & Burns, J. R. (2000). 'Let's you and me have a little discussion': Computer mediated communication in support of campus-based university courses. *Studies in Higher Education, 25*(1), 85–96. doi:10.1080/030750700116037

Little, D. (2005). *Learner autonomy: Drawing together the threads of self-assessment, goal-setting and reflection*. Graz: European Council for Modern Languages. Retrieved June 19, 2009, from http://www.ecml.at/mtp2/Elp_tt/Results/DM_layout/00_10/06/06%20Supplementary%20text.pdf

Little, D. (2008, August). David Little talks about the European Language Portfolio (ELP). *ELT News*. Retrieved February 24, 2009, from http://www.prosper.ro/EuroIntegrELP/materiale%20pentru%20site%20Euro-IntegrELP.../EN_ELT%

Little, D., & Perclová, R. (2001). *The European Language Portfolio: A guide for teachers and teacher trainers*. Strasbourg: Council of Europe. Retrieved March 2, 2009, from http://www.coe.int/T/DG4/Portfolio/documents/ELPguide_teacherstrainers.pdf

Little, D., & Simpson, B. (2003). *European Language Portfolio: The intercultural component and learning how to learn*. Strasbourg: Council of Europe.

Littlejohn, A. (2003). An incremental approach to staff development in the reuse of learning resources . In Littlejohn, A. (Ed.), *Reusing on-line resources: A sustainable approach to e-learning*. London: Kogan Page.

Littlejohn, A., Cook, J., Sclater, N., & Campbell, L. Davis, H., & Currier, S. (2009). Managing educational resources. In G. Conole, & M. Oliver (Eds.), Contemporary perspectives in e-learning research: Themes, methods and impact on practice (pp. 134-146). Abingdon: Routledge.

Lloyd, C. (1996). For realism and against the inadequacies of common sense: A response to Arthur Marwick. *Journal of Contemporary History, 31*, 192–207. doi:10.1177/002200949603100108

Löfström, E., & Nevgi, A. (2007). From strategic planning to meaningful learning: Diverse perspectives on the development of web-based teaching and learning in higher education. *British Journal of Educational Technology, 38*(2), 312–324. doi:10.1111/j.1467-8535.2006.00625.x

Lorenzi, F., MacKeogh, K., & Fox, S. (2004). Preparing students for learning in an online world: An evaluation of the Student Passport to eLearning (SPEL) model. *European Journal of Open Distance Learning (EURODL)* Jan–June 2004/1. Retrieved October 20, 2009, from http://www.eurodl.org/materials/contrib/2004/Lorenzi_MacKeogh_Fox.htm

Lorenzi, F., MacKeogh, K., & Fox, S. (2009). Preparing students for learning in an online world: The Student Passport to eLearning (SPeL) model . In Tait, A., Vidal, M., Bernath, U., & Szucs, A. (Eds.), *Distance and e-learning in transition? Learning innovation, technology and social challenges* (pp. 439–456). London: ISTE/Wiley.

Lucas, B. (2006). Bringing e-learning home: An experiment in embedding e-learning using e-learning departmental advocates. In L. Markauskaite, P. Goodyear, & P. Reimann (Eds.), *Proceedings of the 23rd Annual Conference of the Australasian Society for Computers in Learning in Tertiary Education: Who's Learning? Whose Technology?* (pp. 479–482). Sydney: Sydney University Press.

Lynch, K. (2006). Neo-liberalism and marketisation: The implications for higher education. *European Educational Research Journal, 5*(1), 1–14. doi:10.2304/eerj.2006.5.1.1

Lynch, M. M. (2002). *The online educator: A guide to creating the virtual classroom*. New York: RoutledgeFalmer. doi:10.4324/9780203458556

Macdonald, J., & Twining, P. (2002). Assessing activity-based learning for a networked course. *British Journal of Educational Technology, 33*(5), 603–618. doi:10.1111/1467-8535.00295

MacKeogh, K. (2006). Supervising undergraduate research using online and peer supervision. In M. Huba (Ed.) *7th International Virtual University Conference, Bratislava 14–15 December 2006* (pp. 19–24). Technical University Bratislava: Bratislava. Retrieved October 20, 2009, from http://doras.dcu.ie/82/

MacKeogh, K., & Fox, S. (2008). *An eLearning Strategy for DCU*. Dublin: DCU. Retrieved October 20, 2009, from http://www.dcu.ie/~foxs/elearning

MacKeogh, K., & Fox, S. (2009). Academic staff in traditional universities: Motivators and demotivators in the adoption of elearning . In Bernath, U., Szucs, A., Tait, A., & Vidal, M. (Eds.), *Distance and E-learning in Transition: Learning innovation, technology and social challenges* (pp. 217–233). London: ISTE/Wiley.

MacKeogh, K., & Lorenzi, F. (2007). Learning from the past and looking at the future. Closing the evaluation-revision-implementation cycle in an elearning module. *European Association of Distance Teaching Universities Annual Conference*, Lisbon, November 8–10, 2007. Retrieved October 20, 2009, from http://www.eadtu.nl/conference-2007/files/SAA2.pdf

Maguire, B., Mernagh, E., & Murray, J. (2007). Aligning learning outcomes descriptors in national and meta-frameworks of qualifications: Learning from Irish experience. *European Journal of Vocational Training, 42*(3), 70–83.

Mainemelis, C., Boyatzis, R. E., & Kolb, D. A. (2002). Learning styles and adaptive flexibility: Testing experiential learning theory. *Management Learning, 33*(5), 5–33. doi:10.1177/1350507602331001

Malley, A. (2009). Apple iPhone controls over 66% of all mobile web use. *AppleInsider*. Retrieved April 15, 2009, from http://www.appleinsider.com/articles/09/03/01/apple_iphone_controls_over_66_of_all_mobile_web_use.html

Mansvelt, J., Suddaby, G., & O'Hara, D. (2008). Learning how to e-teach? Staff perspectives on formal and informal professional development activity. Australian Society for Computers in Learning in Tertiary Education (ASCILITE) Conference, November 30 to December 3, 2008, Melbourne.

Margaryan, M., & Littlejohn, A. (2008). *Are digital natives a myth or reality? Students' uses of technologies for learning.* Glasgow, UK: Glasgow Caledonian University, Caledonian Academy. Retrieved April 3, 2009, from http://www.academy.gcal.ac.uk/anoush/documents/DigitalNativesMythOrReality-MargaryanAndLitteljohn-draft-111208.pdf

Marshall, C., & Rossman, G. B. (1989). *Designing qualitative research.* London: Newbury Park, Mayes, J.T. (1993). Distance learning and the new technology: A user-centred view. *Commissioned Report from the Centre for the Exploitation of Science and Technology, London,* Institute for Computer-Based Learning (ICBL), Heriot-Watt University, Retrieved July 28, 2000, from http://led.gcal.ac.uk/clti/staff/Tmpapers.html

Mason, R., & Rennie, F. (2006). *Elearning: The key concepts.* Oxon: Routledge.

Maton, K. (2008). Habitus . In Grenfell, M. (Ed.), *Pierre Bourdieu key concepts* (pp. 49–66). Stocksfield, UK: Acumen Publishing Ltd.

Mayes, J. T. (1995). Learning technology and Groundhog Day. In W. Strang, V. Simpson and D. Slater (Eds.), Hypermedia at work: Practice and theory in higher education (pp. 21-37). Canterbury: University of Kent Press.

Mayes, J. T. (2004). Stage 2: learner-centred pedagogy: Individual differences between learners. *JISC e-learning models desk study.* London, UK: JISC. Retrieved October 16, 2006, from http://www.jisc.ac.uk/uploaded_documents/Stage%202%20Learning%20Styles%20(Version%201).pdf

Mayes, T. (2001). Learning technology and learning relationships . In Stephenson, J. (Ed.), *Teaching and learning online: Pedagogies for new technologies* (pp. 16–26). London: Kogan Page.

Mays, J.T., & Morrison, D. (2008). You take the high road: National programmes for the development of elearning in higher education. *Reflecting Education,* 6-16.

McAndrew, P., Goodyear, P., & Dalziel, J. (2006). Patterns, designs and activities: unifying descriptions of learning structures. *International Journal of Learning Technology, 2*(2/3), 216–242. doi:10.1504/IJLT.2006.010632

McConnell, D. (2000). *Implementing computer supported cooperative learning* (2nd ed.). London: Kogan Page.

McConnell, D. (2006). *E-learning groups and communities.* Maidenhead: Society for Research into Higher Education & Open University Press.

McFerrin, K. M. (1999). Incidental learning in a higher education asynchronous online distance course. In J.D. Price, J.Willis, M. Jost, & S. Boger-Mehall (Eds.), SITE 99: Proceedings of the Society for Information Technology & Teacher Education International Conference (pp. 1418-1423). San Antonio TX, 28 Feb. to 4 Mar. (Charlotteville, VA: Association for the Advancement of Computers in Education (AACE)).

McGrath, O. (2002). *Building an instructional portal: Channeling the writing lab.* Paper presented at the 30th Annual ACM SIGUCCS Conference on User Services, New York.

McKavanagh, C., Kanes, C., Bevan, F., Cunningham, A., & Choy, S. (2002). *Evaluation of web-based flexible learning,* Adelaide, Australia: NCVER. Retrieved April 21, 2006, from http://www.ncver.edu.au/research/proj/nr8007.pdf

McKenna, K. Y. A., & Green, A. S. (2002). Virtual Group Dynamics. *Group Dynamics, 6*(1), 116–127. doi:10.1037/1089-2699.6.1.116

McKenna, K., & Seidman, G. (2005). You, me, and we: Interpersonal processes in electronic groups . In Amichai-Hamburger, Y. (Ed.), *The social net: Human behaviour in cyberspace* (pp. 191–217). Oxford: Oxford University Press.

McKinney, D., Dyck, J. L., & Luber, E. S. (2009). iTunes University and the classroom: Can podcasts replace Professors? *Computers & Education, 52*(3), 617–623. doi:10.1016/j.compedu.2008.11.004

McLoughlin, C. (2000). Creating partnerships for generative learning and systemic change: Redefining academic roles and relationships in support of learning. *The International Journal for Academic Development, 5*(2), 116–128. doi:10.1080/13601440050200725

McLoughlin, C., & Lee, M. (2007). Social software and participatory learning: Pedagogical choices with technology affordances in the Web 2.0 era. In *ICT: Providing choices for learners and learning. Proceedings ascilite Singapore 2007* (pp. 664-675). Sydney, Australia: CoCo, University of Sydney. Retrieved February 2, 2009, from http://www.ascilite.org.au/conferences/singapore07/procs/mcloughlin.pdf

McLoughlin, C., & Lee, M. (2008). The three P's of pedagogy for the networked society: Personalization, participation and productivity. *International Journal of Teaching and Learning in Higher Education, 20*(1), 10–27.

McLoughlin, C., & Lee, M. (2008). Future learning landscapes: Transforming pedagogy through social software. *Innovate, 4*(5). Retrieved February 2, 2009, from http://www.innovateonline.info/index.php?view=article&id=539.

McNair, L., Paretti, M., Knott, M., & Wolfe, M. L. (2006). *Using e-portfolio to define, teach, and assess ABET professional skills.* Paper presented at the annual meeting of the ASEE/IEEE Frontiers in Education.

McNickle, C. (2003). *The impact that ICT has on how we learn: pedagogy, andragogy or heutatgogy?* Paper presented at the 16th ODLAA Biennial Forum Conference Proceedings on Sustaining Quality learning Environments. Retrieved March 10, 2009, from http://www.odlaa.org/publications/2003Proceedings/pdfs/mcnickle.pdf

McSwiney, C., & Parnell, S. (2003). Transnational expansion and the role of the university library: A study of academics and librarians in an Australian university. *New Review of Libraries and Lifelong Learning, 4*(1), 63–75. doi:10.1080/1468994042000240223

Melling, M. E. (Ed.). (2006). *Supporting e-learning: A guide for library and information managers.* London: Facet Publishing.

Memory, D. M., Yoder, C. Y., Bolinger, K. B., & Warren-Wilson, J. (2004). Creating thinking and inquiry tasks that reflect the concerns and interests of adolescents. *Social Studies*, *95*(4), 147–154. doi:10.3200/TSSS.95.4.147-154

Meskill, C., & Sadykova, G. (2007). The presentation of self in everyday ether: A corpus analysis of student self-tellings in online graduate courses. *Journal of Asynchronous Learning Networks*, *11*(3), 123–138.

Mezirow, J. (1996). Adult education and empowerment for individual and community development . In Connolly, B., Fleming, T., McCormack, D., & Ryan, A. (Eds.), *Radical learning for liberation. Maynooth Adult and Community Education Occasional Series No. 1. Maynooth: MACE.*

Mileham, R. (2008). *Powering up: Are computer games changing our lives?* Chichester: Wiley/Dana Centre.

Millett, C. M., Payne, D. G., Dwyer, C. A., Stickler, L. M., & Alexiou, J. J. (2008). *A culture of evidence: An evidence centred approach to accountability for student learning outcomes.* Washington, DC: Educational Testing Services.

Mnookin, J. L. (1996). Virtual(ly) law: The emergence of law in LambdaMOO. *Journal of Computer-Mediated Communication, 2*(1). Retrieved April 12, 2009, from http://jcmc.indiana.edu/vol2/issue1/lambda.html

Mohan, P., Greer, J., & McCalla, G. (2003). Instructional planning with learning objects. In P. Baumgartner, P.A. Cairns, M. Kohlhase, & E. Melis (Eds.), *Knowledge representation and automated reasoning for e-learning systems* (pp. 52-58). Retrieved November 12, 2009, from http://www.uni-koblenz.de/fb4/publikationen/gelbereihe/RR-16-2003.pdf

Moon, J. (2002). *The module and programme development handbook: A practical guide to linking levels, outcomes and assessment criteria.* London: Routledge.

Moon, J. (2004, July). *Linking levels, learning outcomes and assessment criteria*. Paper presented at a conference Using Learning Outcomes, Edinburgh. Retrieved June 23, 2009, from http://www.bologna-bergen2005.no/EN/Bol_sem/Seminars/040701-02Edinburgh.HTM

Moore, M. (1989). Editorial: Three types of interaction. *American Journal of Distance Education*, *3*(2), 1–7. doi:10.1080/08923648909526659

Moore, M. G., & Anderson, W. G. (Eds.). (2003). *Handbook of distance education.* Mahwah, NJ: Lawrence Erlbaum Associates.

Morley, N. (n.d.). Making Wikipedia work for you ... Making use of Wikipedia to promote learning, not just warning students against it. Retrieved March 23, 2009, from http://www.heacademy.ac.uk/hca/resources/detail/assessment_making_wikipedia_work_for_you

Morrison, K. (2005, July). Structuration theory, habitus and complexity theory: Elective affinities or old wine in new bottles? *British Journal of Sociology of Education*, *26*(3), 311–326. .doi:10.1080/01425690500128809

Moses, I. (1997). Redefining academic roles . In Sharpham, J., & Harman, G. (Eds.), *Australia's future universities* (pp. 176–202). Armidale, NSW: University of New South Wales Press.

Mount, N., & Chambers, C. (2008). Podcasting and practicals. In G. Salmon, & P. Edirisingha (Eds.), Podcasting for learning in universities (pp. 43-56). Berkshire: Open University Press.

Murph, D. (2008). ACU dishing out iPhone/iPod touch to all incoming freshmen. *Endgadget*. Retrieved April 15, 2009, from http://www.engadget.com/2008/02/26/acu-dishing-out-iphone-ipod-touch-to-all-incoming-freshmen

Murphy, M., & Fleming, T. (2006). The application of the ideas of Habermas to adult learning . In Sutherland, P., & Crowther, J. (Eds.), *Lifelong learning: Concepts and contexts* (pp. 48–57). London: Routledge.

Murphy, S. (1997). Teachers and students: Reclaiming assessment via portfolios . In Yancey, K. B., & Weiser, I. (Eds.), *Situating portfolios: Four perspectives* (pp. 72–88). Logan, UT: Utah State University Press.

Murray, D. (1985). Composition as conversation: The computer as a medium of communication . In Odell, L., & Goswami, D. (Eds.), *Writing in non-academic settings* (pp. 203–227). New York: The Guilford Press.

Newman, F., Couturier, L., & Scurry, J. (2004). *The future of higher education: Rhetoric, reality, and the risks of the market*. San Francisco, CA: Jossey-Bass.

Ng'ambi, D. (2008). Podcasts for reflective learning. In G. Salmon, & P. Edirisingha (Eds.), Podcasting for learning in universities (pp. 132-145). Open University Press: Society for Research into Higher Education.

Nicholas, M. (2008). Institutional perspectives: The challenges of e-learning diffusion. *British Journal of Educational Technology*, *39*(4), 598–609. doi:10.1111/j.1467-8535.2007.00761.x

Nielsen, J. (2009). Usability 101: Introduction to usability. Retrieved April 4, 2009, from http://www.useit.com/alertbox/20030825.html

Nintendo. (2007). *Brain age*. Retrieved May 7, 2009 from http://www.brainage.com

Norman, D. (1999). *The design of everyday things*. Cambridge, MA: MIT Press.

NQAI. (2003). *National Framework of Qualifications. A framework for the development, recognition and award of qualifications in Ireland*. Dublin: National Qualifications Authority of Ireland.

Nusche, D. (2008). Assessment of learning outcomes in Higher Education: A comparative review of selected practices. OECD Working Papers No 15. Paris: OECD.

O'Donnell, E. (2008). *Can the use of e-learning improve the learning experience to better prepare students for work in industry?* Unpublished master's dissertation. Dublin City University.

O'Neill, K., Singh, G., & O'Donoghue, J. (2004). Implementing e-learning programmes for higher education: A review of the literature. *Journal of Information Technology Education*, *3*, 314–320.

O'Reilly, T. (2005). *Web 2.0: Compact definition?* Retrieved March 18, 2009, from http://www.oreillynet.com/lpt/a/6228

O'Reilly, T. (2005). *What is Web 2.0: Design patterns and business models for the next generation of software*. Retrieved October 20, 2009, from http://oreilly.com/web2/archive/what-is-web-20.html

Oaklands (2009). *Oaklands 2011–Vision to Reality*. St Albans. [Online] Retrieved July 21, 2009, from http://www.oaklands.ac.uk/about/strategy.aspx

Oblinger, D. (2008). Growing up with Google. What it means to education. In *Emerging Technologies for Learning*, Vol. 3. (pp.11-29). Coventry, UK: BECTA. Retrieved March 23, 2009, from http://publications.becta.org.uk/display.cfm?resID=35877&page=1835

Oblinger, D. G., & Hawkins, B. L. (2006). The myth about no significant difference: Using technology produces no significant difference. *Educause Review, 41*(6), November/December. Retrieved April 10, 2009, from http://www.educause.edu/EDUCAUSE+Review/EDUCAUSEReviewMagazineVolume41/TheMythaboutNoSignificantDiffe/158103

Oblinger, D., & Oblinger, J. (2003). Introduction. In D. Oblinger, & J. Oblinger (Eds.), *Educating the net generation* (pp. 1.1-1.5). Washington, DC: Educause. Retrieved October 16, 2006, from http://www.educause.edu/content.asp?PAGE_ID=5989&bhcp=1

OECD. (2005). *E-learning in tertiary education: Where do we stand?* Paris: Organisation for Economic Cooperation and Development.

OECD. (2007). Assessing Higher Education learning outcomes: Summary of a first meeting of experts. EDU (2007)8. Retrieved October 20, 2009, from http://www.oecd.org/dataoecd/15/5/39117243.pdf

OECD. (2007). Qualifications systems: Bridges to life-long learning. Paris: Organisation for Economic Co-operation and Development.

Oliver, M. (2002). What do learning technologists do? *Innovations in Education and Teaching International, 39*(4), 245–252. doi:10.1080/13558000210161089

Oliver, M., & Dempster, J. A. (2003). Embedding e-learning practices . In Blackwell, R., & Blackmore, P. (Eds.), *Towards strategic staff development in higher education* (pp. 142–153). Berkshire, England: SRHE and Open University Press.

Oliver, M., Conole, G., Cook, J., Ravenscroft, A., & Currier, S. (2002). Multiple perspectives and theoretical dialogue in learning technology. In *ASCILITE 2002 Proceedings*. Retrieved April 2, 2007, from http://www.ascilite.org.au/conferences/auckland02/proceedings/papers/075.pdf

Oliver, M., Harvey, J., Conole, G., & Jones, A. (2009a). Evaluation. In G. Conole, & M. Oliver (Eds.), Contemporary perspectives in e-learning research: Themes, methods and impact on practice (pp. 203-216). Abingdon: Routledge.

Oliver, M., Roberts, G., Beetham, H., Ingraham, B., & Dyke, M. (2009b) Knowledge, society and perspectives on learning technology. In G. Conole, & M. Oliver (Eds.), Contemporary perspectives in e-learning research: Themes, methods and impact on practice (pp. 21-37). Abingdon: Routledge.

Olsen, A. (2005).Transnational education programs: Strategy development. Seminar presentation, *Transnational Education: Strategy Considerations and Quality Issues*, Swinburne University of Technology, August 31.

Oud, J. (2009). Guidelines for effective online instruction using multimedia screencasts. *Reference Services Review, 37*(2), 164-177. Retrieved June 19, 2009, from http://www.ingentaconnect.com/content/mcb/240/2009/00000037/00000002/art00004

Overbaugh, R.C., & ShinYi, L. (2006). Student characteristics, sense of community, and cognitive achievement in web-based and lab-based learning environments. *Journal of Research on Technology in Education, 39*(2), 205–223.

Owston, R., Garrison, D., & Cook, K. (2006). Blended learning at Canadian universities: Issues and practices . In Bonk, C. J., & Graham, C. R. (Eds.), *The handbook of blended learning. Global perspectives, local designs* (pp. 338–350). San Francisco: Pfeiffer.

Oxford, R. (1990). *Language learning strategies*. New York: Newbury House.

Paavola, S., & Hakkarainen, K. (2005). The knowledge creation metaphor: An emergent epistemological approach to learning. *Science and Education, 14*(6), 535–557. doi:10.1007/s11191-004-5157-0

Pagnucci, G. S. (1998). Crossing borders and talking tech: Educational challenges. *Theory into Practice, 37*(1), 46-53. Retrieved March 4, 2007, from JSTOR database http://www.jstor.org/pss/1477512

Pajares, F., & Valiante, G. (2006). Self-efficacy beliefs and motivation in writing development . In MacArthur, C. A., & Graham, S. (Eds.), *Handbook of writing research*. New York: Guilford Press.

Palloff, R. M., & Pratt, K. (2005). *Collaborating online: Learning together in community*. San Francisco: Jossey-Bass.

Palmquist, M. (2003). A brief history of computer support for writing centers and writing-across-the-curriculum programs. *Computers and Composition, 20*(4), 395–413. doi:10.1016/j.compcom.2003.08.013

Park, H. (2005). Design and development of a mobile learning management system adaptive to learning style of students. Retrieved June 19, 2009, from http://ieeexplore.ieee.org/stamp/stamp.jsp?arnumber=01579236

Patrick, M. (2008). Fostering effective and appropriate use of online resources: (Or: How do we stop students copying their essays from Wikipedia?). *Discourse (Berkeley, Calif.), 8*(1), 99–111.

Paulson, F. L., Paulson, P. R., & Meyer, C. A. (1991). What makes a portfolio a portfolio? *Educational Leadership*, 60–63.

PBWiki (now PBWorks) (2009). [Homepage] http://pbworks.com

PBWorks (Formerly PBWiki). (2005-2009). Available http://www.pbwiki.com

Peach, B. E., Mukherjee, A., & Hornyak, M. (2007). Assessing critical thinking: A college's journey and lessons learned. *Journal of Education for Business, 82*(6), 313–320. doi:10.3200/JOEB.82.6.313-320

Pennington, G. (2003). *Guidelines for promoting and facilitating change*. York: LTSN Generic Centre.

Perl, S. (1977). The composing processes of unskilled college writers. *College Composition and Communication, 28*(8), 12–28.

Peters, O. (2000). The transformation of the university into an institution of independent learning . In Evans, T., & Nation, D. (Eds.), *Changing university teaching: Reflections on creating educational technologies* (pp. 10–23). London: Kogan Page.

Peterson, E. (2007). Incorporating screencasts in online teaching. *The International Review of Research in Open and Distance Learning, 8*(3). Retrieved April 1, 2009, from http://www.irrodl.org/index.php/irrodl/article/viewArticle/495/935

Peterson, S. (2006). Influence of gender on writing development . In MacArthur, C. A., & Graham, S. (Eds.), *Handbook of writing research*. New York: Guilford Press.

Petre, M., Carswell, L., Price, B., & Thomas, P. (2000). Innovation in large-scale supported distance teaching: transforming for the internet not just translating . In Eisenstadt, M., & Vincent, T. (Eds.), *The knowledge web: Learning and collaborating on the net* (pp. 97–117). London, UK: Kogan Page.

Picciano, D. (2002). *Educational leadership and planning for technology* (4th ed.). Columbus, OH: Prentice Hall.

Plowright, D., & Watkins, M. (2004). There are no problems to be solved, only inquiries to be made, in social work education. *Innovations in Education and Teaching International, 41*(2), 185–206. doi:10.1080/1470329042000208701

Podcasting Resource Wiki, T. C. D. (2009). Retrieved from http://tcdpodcasting.pbworks.com/

Pollock, N., & Cornford, J. (2000). Theory and practice of the virtual university. *ARIADNE, 24*. Retrieved July 27, 2009, from http://www.ariadne.ac.uk/issue24/virtual-universities/

Pollock, N., & Cornford, J. (2003). *Putting the university online: Information, technology and organisational change*. Buckingham: Open University Press.

Postle, G., Sturman, A., Reuschele, S., McDonald, J., Mangubhai, F., Vickery, B., & Cronk, P. (2003). *Online teaching and learning in Higher Education: A case study*. University of Southern Queensland. Retrieved July 27, 2009, from http://www.dest.gov.au/sectors/higher_education/publications_resources/profiles/online_teaching_and_learning_in_higher_education.htm

Powazek, D. M. (2002). *Design for community. The art of connecting real people in virtual places*. Indianapolis, IN: New Riders.

PowerPoint. (2009). Microsoft. Retrieved April 24, 2009, from http://office.microsoft.com/en-gb/powerpoint/default.aspx

Preece, J. (2000). *Online communities: Designing usability, supporting sociability*. Chichester, UK: John Wiley & Sons.

Prensky, M. (2001). *Digital game based learning*. New York: McGraw Hill.

Prensky, M. (2001). Digital natives, digital immigrants *On the Horizon, 9*(5). [Online] Retrieved October 20, 2009, from http://www.marcprensky.com/writing/Prensky%20-%20Digital%20Natives,%20Digital%20Immigrants%20-%20Part1.pdf

Prensky, M. (2005). *Complexity matters*. Retrieved October 20, 2009, from http://marcprensky.com/writing/Prensky-Complexity_Matters.pdf

Prensky, M. (2007). How to teach with technology: Keeping both academic staff and learners comfortable in an era of exponential change. *Emerging technologies for learning* (Vol. 2, pp. 40-46). Coventry, UK: BECTA. Retrieved June 26, 2008, from http://partners.becta.org.uk/index.php?section=rh&rid=13768

Prensky, M. (2009). H. Sapiens Digital: From digital immigrants and digital natives to digital wisdom. *Journal of Online Education. 5*(3). Retrieved April 15, 2009, from http://www.innovateonline.info/index.php?view=article&id=705

Putnam, R. T., & Borko, H. (1997). Teacher learning: Implications of new views of cognition . In Biddle, B. J., Good, T. L., & Goodson, I. F. (Eds.), *International handbook of teachers and teaching* (*Vol. 2*, pp. 1223–1296). Dordrecht, The Netherlands: Kluwer.

Raban, C., & Turner, E. (2003). *Academic risk: Quality risk management in higher education. Project Report for the Higher Education Funding Council for England.* Bristol: HEFCE.

Raelin, J. (1995). How to manage your local professor. *Academy of Management Journal, 12*, 207–212.

Rafaeli, S., Raban, D., & Kalman, Y. (2005). Social cognition online . In Amichai-Hamburger, Y. (Ed.), *The social net: Human behaviour in cyberspace*. New York: Oxford University Press.

Raman, M., Ryan, T., & Olfman, L. (2005). Designing knowledge management systems for teaching and learning with wiki technology. *Journal of Information Systems Education, 16*(3), 311.

Ramsden, P. (1988). *Improving learning: New perspectives*. London: Kogan Page.

Ramsden, P. (1992). *Learning to teach in higher education*. London: Routledge. doi:10.4324/9780203413937

Randel, J., Morris, B., Wetzel, C., & Whitehill, B. (1992). The effectiveness of games for educational purposes: A review of recent research. *Simulation & Gaming, 23*(3), 261–276. doi:10.1177/1046878192233001

Ravenscoft, A. (2000). Designing argumentation for conceptual development . *Computers & Education, 34*, 241–255. doi:10.1016/S0360-1315(99)00048-2

Reay, D. (1995). 'They employ cleaners to do that': Habitus in the primary classroom. *British Journal of Sociology of Education, 16*(3), 353–371. doi:10.1080/0142569950160305

Reay, D. (1998). 'Always knowing' and 'never being sure': Familial and institutional habituses and higher education choice. *Journal of Education Policy, 13*(4), 519–529. .doi:10.1080/0268093980130405

Reed, S., Ernst, G., & Banerji, R. (1974). The role of analogy in transfer between similar problem states. *Cognitive Psychology, 6*(3), 436–450. doi:10.1016/0010-0285(74)90020-6

Rees, M., & Emerson, L. (2009). The impact that Turnitin has had on text-based assessment practice. *International Journal for Educational Integrity, 5*(1), 20–29.

Reese, M., & Levy, R. (2009). Assessing the future: e-portfolio trends, uses, and options in higher education. *ECAR Bulletin, 4*. Retrieved October 20, 2009, from http://portfolio.project.mnscu.edu/vertical/Sites/%7B0D936A3C-B3B2-48B8-838C-F5A3B3E0AF6C%7D/uploads/%7B2231316D-EFA9-4A6D-B382-734A350E4510%7D.pdf

Reid, E. (1994). *Cultural formations in text-based virtual realities*. Unpublished master's thesis, University of Melbourne, Australia.

Reigeluth, C. (1999). What is Instructional-Design Theory and how is it changing? In Reigeluth, C. (Ed.), *Instructional-Design theories and models: A new paradigm of instructional theory* (*Vol. 2*). New Jersey: Lawrence Erlbaum Associates.

Resnyansky, L. (2002). Computer-mediated communication in higher education: Educators' agency in relation to technology. *Journal of Educational Enquiry, 3*(1), 35–58.

Rheingold, H. (1993). *The virtual community: Homesteading on the electronic frontier*. Reading, MA: Addison-Wesley.

Riedinger, B. (2006). Mining for meaning: Teaching students how to reflect . In Jafari, A., & Kaufman, C. (Eds.), *Handbook of research on ePortfolios* (pp. 90–101). Hershey, PA: Idea Group Reference.

Ring, G., & Foti, S. (2006). Using ePortfolios to facilitate professional development among pre-service teachers . In Jafari, A., & Kaufman, C. (Eds.), *Handbook of research on ePortfolios* (pp. 340–358). Hershey, PA: Idea Group Reference.

Roberts, G. (2002). *Technology assisted off campus programmes at Oxford Brookes University. Project Report (draft 5.2)*. Oxford: Oxford Brookes University.

Roberts, G., Aalderink, W., Cook, J., Feijen, M., Harvey, J., Lee, S., et al. (2005). *Reflective learning, future thinking: digital repositories, e-portfolios, informal learning and ubiquitous computing.* Paper presented at the ALT/SURF/ILTA1 Spring Conference Research Seminar, Trinity College, Dublin.

Robertson, J. W. (2003). Stepping out of the box: Rethinking the failure of ICT to transform schools. *Journal of Educational Change, 4*, 323–344. doi:10.1023/B:JEDU.0000006047.67433.c5

Rogers, C. R. (1951). *Client centred therapy*. Boston, MA: Houghton Mifflin.

Rogers, D. L. (2000). A paradigm shift: Technology integration for higher education in the new millennium. *Educational Technology Review, 13*, 19–27.

Rogers, E. (2003). *Diffusion of innovations* (5th ed.). New York: Free Press.

Rogers, E. M. (1963). What are innovators like? *Theory into Practice, 2*(5), 252–256. doi:10.1080/00405846309541872

Rogers, E. M. (1964). *Diffusion of innovations*. Glencoe: Free Press.

Rogers, E. M., & Beal, G. M. (1958). The importance of personal influence in the adoption of technological changes. *Social Forces, 36*(4), 329–335. doi:10.2307/2573971

Rogers, G. (2004). History, learning technology and student achievement: Making the difference? *The Institute of Learning and Teaching in Higher Education and SAGE Publications, 5*(2), 232–247.

Romano, S. (1999). On becoming a woman: Pedagogies of the self . In Hawisher, G. E., & Selfe, C. (Eds.), *Passions, pedagogies and the 21st century technologies* (pp. 249–267). Logan, UT: Utah State University Press.

Rosenberg, M. J. (2008). Taming the irrational expectations of high-tech learning. *T+D Training and Development.* Retrieved April 15, 2009, from http://www.marcrosenberg.com/images/ASTD_Technology_Euphoria_TD_0608.pdf

Rosser, J. Jr, Lynch, P., Cuddihy, L., Gentile, D., Klonsky, J., & Merrell, R. (2007). The impact of video games on training surgeons in the 21st century. *Archives of Surgery, 142*(2), 181–186. doi:10.1001/archsurg.142.2.181

Rowntree, D. (2002). *Preparing materials for open, distance and flexible learning*. Abingdon: Routledge Farmer.

Ruane, M., & Gauthier, V. (2006). Implementing the European Language Portfolio in an institution-wide language programme . In Gallagher, A., & O'Laoire, M. (Eds.), *Language education in Ireland: Current practice and future developments*. Dublin: Irish Association for Applied Linguistics.

Rubin, Z. (1975). Disclosing oneself to a stranger: Reciprocity and its limits. *Journal of Experimental Social Psychology, 11*, 233–260. doi:10.1016/S0022-1031(75)80025-4

Sacco, A. (2008). iPhone University: At ACU, students navigate college life via Apple iPhone. *CIO*. Retrieved March 7, 2009, from http://www.cio.com/article/452714/iPhone_University_At_ACU_Students_Navigate_College_Life_via_Apple_iPhone?page=1&taxonomyId=1436

Sakai (2009). Sakai 3 proposal: A proposal for a next-generation Sakai. Retrieved October 26, 2009, from http://confluence.sakaiproject.org/download/attachments/26444008/Sakai+3+Proposal+v08.pdf?version=1

Salmon, G. (2000). Computer mediated conferencing for management learning at the Open University. *Management Learning, 31*(4), 491–502. doi:10.1177/1350507600314005

Salmon, G. (2001). *E-moderating: The key to teaching and learning online*. London: Kogan Page.

Salmon, G. (2004). *E-moderating: The key to teaching and learning online* (2nd ed.). London: Taylor & Francis.

Salmon, G. (2006). *E-tivities: The key to active online learning*. Abingdon: Routledge Farmer.

Salmon, G., & Nie, M. (2008). Doubling the life of iPods. In G. Salmon, & P. Edirisingha (Eds.), Podcasting for learning in universities (pp. 1-11). Open University Press: Society for Research into Higher Education.

Sandholtz, J. H. (2002). Inservice training or professional development: Contrasting opportunities in a school/university partnership . *Teaching and Teacher Education, 18*(7), 815–830. doi:10.1016/S0742-051X(02)00045-8

Santa, T. (2008). *Dead letters: Error in composition 1873-2004*. Creskill, NJ: Hampton Press.

Sarason, S. B. (1990). *The predictable failure of educational reform: Can we change course before it's too late?* San Francisco: Jossey Bass.

Sarros, J., Gmelch, W., & Tanewski, G. (1997). The role of the department head in Australian universities: Changes and challenges. *Higher Education Research & Development, 16*, 9–24. doi:10.1080/0729436970160102

Savage, S. (2004). *Staff and student responses to a trial of Turnitin plagiarism detection software.* Paper presented at the Australian Universities Quality Forum 2004, Australia.

Savenye, W., Olina, Z., & Niemczyk, M. (2001). So you are going to be an online writing instructor: Issues in designing, developing, and delivering an online course. *Computers and Composition, 18*(4), 371–385. doi:10.1016/S8755-4615(01)00069-X

Sawchuk, S. (2009). Backers of '21st-century skills' take flak. *Education Week, 28*(23), 1–14.

Scanlon, P., & Neumann, D. R. (2002). Internet plagiarism among college students. *Journal of College Student Development, 43*(3), 374–385.

Schlager, M. S., & Fusco, J. (2004). Teacher professional development, technology, and communities of practice: Are we putting the cart before the horse? In Barab, S., Kling, R., & Gray, J. (Eds.), *Designing virtual communities in the service of learning*. Cambridge: Cambridge University Press.

Schneider, C. G. (2009). The proof is in the portfolio. *Liberal Education, 95*(1), 1–2.

Schön, D. A. (1987). *Educating the reflective practitioner*. San Francisco, CA: Jossey-Bass.

Scott Morton, M. S. (Ed.). (1991). *The Corporation of the 1990s: Information technology and organizational transformation*. Oxford: Oxford University Press.

Seely Brown, J., & Alder, R. P. (2008). Minds on fire: Open education, the long tail, and learning 2.0, *EDUCAUSE Review, 43*(1). Retrieved October 12, 2009, from http://net.educause.edu/ir/library/pdf/ERM0811.pdf

Segrave, S., Holt, D. M., & Farmer, J. (2005). The power of the 6three model for enhancing academic teachers' capacities for effective online teaching and learning: Benefits, initiatives and future directions. *Australasian Journal of Educational Technology, 21*(1), 118–135.

Seidensticker, B. (2006). *Future hype: The myths of technology change.* San Francisco: Berrett-Koehler Publishers.

Selwyn, N., Crook, C., Carr, D., Carmichael, P., Noss, R., & Laurillard, D. (2008). Education 2.0? Designing the web for teaching and learning: A Commentary by the Technology Enhanced Learning phase of the Teaching and Learning Research Programme. Retrieved December 29, 2008, from http://www.tlrp.org/tel/publications/files/2008/11/tel_comm_final.pdf

Sener, J. (2004). Escaping the comparison trap: Evaluating online learning on its own terms. *Innovate, 1*(2).

Sercu, L. (2002). Autonomous learning and the acquisition of intercultural communicative competence. *Language, Culture and Curriculum, 15*(1), 61–74. doi:10.1080/07908310208666633

Shaklee, B. D., Barbour, N. E., Ambrose, R., & Hansford, S. J. (1997). *Designing and using portfolios.* Boston, MA: Allyn and Bacon.

Shank, P. (2008). Web 2.0 and beyond: The changing needs of learners, new tools, and new ways to learn . In Carliner, S., & Shank, P. (Eds.), *The E-Learning Handbook: Past Promises, Present Challenges* (pp. 241–278). San Francisco: Pfeiffer.

SharpBrains. (2006). Cognitive training for basketball game-intelligence: Interview with Prof. Daniel. Gopher. Retrieved March 10, 2009, from http://www.sharpbrains.com/blog/2006/11/02/cognitivesimulations-for-basketball-game-intelligence-interview-with-prof-daniel-gopher/

Sharpe, R. (2004). *A typology of effective interventions that support e-learning practice.* Bristol: JISC.

Sharpe, R., Benfield, G., & Francis, R. (2006). Implementing a university e-learning strategy: Levers for change within academic schools. *ALT-J . Research in Learning Technology, 14*(2), 135–151.

Sharples, M. (1996). An account of writing as creative design . In Levy, C. M., & Ransdell, S. (Eds.), *The science of writing: Theories, methods, individual differences, and applications.* New Jersey: Erlbaum.

Sharples, M. (Ed.). (1993). *Computer supported collaborative writing.* London: Springer Verlag.

Sheely, S. (2006). Persistent technologies: Why can't we stop lecturing online? *Who's learning? Whose technology? Proceedings ascilite Sydney 2006* (pp.769-774). Sydney, Australia: University of Sydney. Retrieved March 16, 2009, from http://www.ascilite.org.au/conferences/sydney06/proceeding/pdf_papers/p167.pdf

Sheey, M., Marcus, G., Costa, F., & Taylor, R. (2006). Implementing e-learning across a faculty: Factors that encourage uptake. *Proceedings of the 23rd Annual Conference of the Australasian Society for Computers in Learning in Tertiary Education: Who's Learning? Whose Technology?* [Online] Retrieved July 21, 2009, from http://www.ascilite.org.au/conferences/sydney06/proceeding/pdf_papers/p120.pdf

Sheridan, J., Alany, R., & Brake, D.-J. (2005). Pharmacy students' views and experiences of Turnitin®—an online tool for detecting academic dishonesty. *Pharmacy Education, 5*(3/4), 241–250. doi:10.1080/15602210500288977

Shim, A., Crider, D., Kim, P., & Raffin, J. (2008). Can the use of video iPods promote cognitive residue in college health and wellness students? In G. Richards (Ed.), *Proceedings of World Conference on E-Learning in Corporate, Government, Healthcare, and Higher Education* 2008 (pp. 3197-3200). Chesapeake, VA: Association for the Advancement of Computing in Education (AACE).

Shirky, C. (2008). *Here comes everybody: The power of organizing without organizations.* New York: Penguin Press.

Siemens, G. (2005). Connectivism: A learning theory for the digital age. *International Journal of Instructional Technology and Distance Learning, 2*(1). Retrieved August 26, 2009, from http://www.itdl.org/Journal/Jan_05/article01.htm

Siemens, G. (2006). *Knowing knowledge.* Manitoba, Canada: Lulu.

Siemens, G., & Tittenberger, P. (2009). *Handbook of emerging technologies for learning.* Manitoba, Canada: University of Manitoba. Retrieved March 20, 2009, from http://www.umanitoba.ca/learning-technologies/cetl/HETL.pdf

Singley, M. K., & Anderson, J. R. (1989). *The transfer of cognitive skill.* Cambridge, MA: Harvard University Press.

Slevin, J. (2008). E-Learning and the transformation of social interaction in higher education. *Learning, Media and Technology, 33*(2), 115–126. doi:10.1080/17439880802097659

Sloep, P., Hummel, H., & Manderveld, J. (2004). Basic design procedures for e-learning courses . In Koper, R., & Tattersall, C. (Eds.), *Learning design: A handbook on modelling and delivering networked education and training* (pp. 139–160). Berlin: Springer.

Smith, G., Evans, J., Jastram, C., & Leader, W. G. (2008). *Enhancing plagiarism awareness and understanding among students through didactic review and TurnItIn.* Paper presented at the annual meeting of the American Association of Colleges of Pharmacy, July 19, 2008.

Snavely, L. (2004). Making problem-based learning work: Institutional challenges. *Portal-Libraries and the Academy, 4*(4), 521–531. doi:10.1353/pla.2004.0071

Society of College, National and University Libraries. (2003). *Information skills in higher education: A SCONUL position paper.* Retrieved April 2, 2009, from http://www.sconul.ac.uk/groups/information_literacy/papers/Seven_pillars.html

Squire, K. (2004). *Replaying history: Learning world history through playing Civilization III.* Dissertation, Instructional Systems Technology Department, Indiana University.

Stahl, G. (2003). *Communication and learning in online collaboration.* Paper presented at GROUP_03, Sannibel Island, Florida. Retrieved April 26, 2009, from http://www.cis.drexel.edu/faculty/gerry/publications/conferences/2003/group/group03.doc

Stanford Center for Innovations in Learning. (2002). *Folio thinking: Personal learning portfolios.* Retrieved March 23, 2009, from http://scil.stanford.edu/research/projects/folio.html

Stefani, L., Mason, R., & Pegler, C. (2007). *The educational potential of e-Portfolios: Supporting personal development and reflective learning.* London, UK: Routledge.

Steinkuehler, C. (2008). Massively multiplayer online games as an educational technology: An outline for research. *Educational Technology Magazine: The Magazine for Managers of Change in Education, 48*(1), 10–21.

Sterne, J. (2003). Bourdieu, technique and technology. [from http://sterneworks.org/BourdieuTechandTech.pdf]. *Cultural Studies, 17*(3/4), 367–389. Retrieved April 2, 2007.

Stinson, J., & Milter, R. (1996). Problem-based learning in business education: Curriculum design and implementation issues . In Wilkerson, L. A., & Gijselaers, W. (Eds.), *Bringing problem-based learning to Higher Education: Theory and practice.* San Francisco, CA: Jossey-Bass.

Stubbs, T., & Gibbons, S. (2008). Design drawing outside of ID . In Botturi, L., & Stubbs, T. (Eds.), *Handbook of visual languages for instructional design: Theories and practices.* Hershey, PA: Information Science Reference.

Sudhershan, A. (2009, June). *Savoir auto-évaluer: Exploring learners' experience of LOLIPOP self-assessment*. Paper presented at the symposium Learning to LOLIPOP: Learners and Teachers Reflect, Dublin City University, Dublin. Retrieved June 23, 2009, from http://www.lolipop-portfolio.eu/symposium/index.html

Súilleabháin, Ó. G. (2008). Player transfer: How learning transfer and serious games answer serious (and transferable) questions about one another. In T. Conolly & M. Stansfield (Eds.), *2nd European Conference on Games Based Learning* (pp. 349-357). Barcelona, Spain: Academic Publishing Limited.

Sujo de Montes, L., Oran, S. M., & Willis, E. M. (2002). Power, language, and identity: Voices from an online course. *Computers and Composition, 19*, 251–271. doi:10.1016/S8755-4615(02)00127-5

Sullivan, B. F., & Thomas, S. L. (2007). Documenting student learning outcomes through a research-intensive senior capstone experience: Bringing the data together to demonstrate progress. *North American Journal of Psychology, 9*(3), 321–329.

SumTotal Press Release. (2008). SumTotal introduces ToolBook 9.5 for faster learning content creation and access anytime, anywhere. Retrieved April 15, 2009, from http://www.sumtotalsystems.com/press/index.html/2008/09/09/1

Surry, D. W., Jackson, M. K., Porter, B. E., & Ensminger, D. C. (2006). An analysis of the relative importance of Ely's Eight Implementation Conditions. [Online] Retrieved March 4, 2007, from http://www.eric.ed.gov/ERICDocs/data/ericdocs2sql/content_storage_01/0000019b/80/1b/cf/1f.pdf

Sutherland-Smith, W., & Carr, D. (2005). Turnitin.com: Teachers' perspectives of anti-plagiarism software in raising issues of educational integrity. *Journal of University Teaching and Learning Practice, 3*(1b), 94–101.

Tangney, B., FitzGibbon, A., Savage, T., Mehan, S., & Holmes, B. (2001). Communal constructivism: Learners constructing learning *for* as well as *with* others. In C. Crawford et al. (Eds.), *Proceedings of Society for Information Technology and Academic Staff Education International Conference 2001* (pp. 3114-3119). Chesapeake, VA: Association for the Advancement of Computing in Education (AACE).

Taylor, I., Thomas, J., & Sage, H. (1999). Portfolios for learning and assessment: Laying the foundations for continuing professional development. *Social Work Education, 18*(2), 147–160. doi:10.1080/02615479911220151

Taylor, J. (1998). Flexible delivery: The globalisation of lifelong learning. *Indian Journal of Open Learning, 7*(1) January, 55-65. Retrieved October 20, 2009, from http://www.usq.edu.au/users/taylorj/publications_presentations/1997india.doc

Taylor, P., Lopez, L., & Quadrelli, C. (1996). *Flexibility, technology and academics' practices: Tantalising tales and muddy maps, evaluations and investigations programme*. Canberra: Department of Employment, Education, Training and Youth Affairs.

Taylor, S. (Ed.). (2001). *Ethnographic research: A reader*. London: Sage.

Tegrity Press Release. (2006). Kansas State University launches world's largest course podcasting initiative. Retrieved April 15, 2009, from http://www.tegrity.com/learn-more/press-releases/56-kansas-state-university-launches-worlds-largest-course-podcasting-initiative.html

Terborg, J., & Miller, H. (1978). Motivation, behavior, and performance: A closer examination of goal setting and monetary incentives. *The Journal of Applied Psychology, 63*(1), 29–39. doi:10.1037/0021-9010.63.1.29

Tham, C. M., & Werner, J. M. (2005). Designing and evaluating e-learning in higher education: A review and recommendations. *Journal of Leadership & Organizational Studies, 11*(2), 15–25. doi:10.1177/107179190501100203

Thelwall, M. (2008, January 15). MySpace, Facebook, Bebo: Social networking students. *ALT Newsletter*. Retrieved March 23, 2009, from http://newsletter.alt.ac.uk/e_article000993849.cfm von Glaserfeld, E. (1989). Cognition, construction of knowledge, and teaching. *Synthese, 80*, 121-140.

Thomas, M. J. W. (2002). Learning within incoherent structures: The space of online discussion forums. *Journal of Computer Assisted Learning, 18*, 351–366. doi:10.1046/j.0266-4909.2002.03800.x

Thomson, P. (2008). Field . In Grenfell, M. (Ed.), *Pierre Bourdieu key concepts* (pp. 67–84). Stocksfield, UK: Acumen Publishing Ltd.

Thorndike, E. L. (1906). *The principles of teaching based on psychology*. New York: A.G. Seiler. doi:10.1037/11487-000

Thorndike, E. L., & Woodworth, R. S. (1901). The influence of improvement in one mental function upon the efficiency of other functions. (I). *Psychological Review, 8*(3), 247–261. doi:10.1037/h0074898

Thorndike, E. L., & Woodworth, R. S. (1901). The influence of improvement in one mental function upon the efficiency of other functions. (II). The estimation of magnitudes. *Psychological Review, 8*(4), 384–395. doi:10.1037/h0071280

Thorndike, E., & Woodworth, R. S. (1901). The influence of improvement in one mental function upon the efficiency of other functions. (III). Functions involving attention, observation and discrimination. *Psychological Review, 8*(6), 553–564. doi:10.1037/h0071363

Thorne, S. L. (2006). Pedagogical and praxiological lessons from internet-mediated intercultural foreign language education research . In Belz, J. A., & Thorne, S. L. (Eds.), *Internet-mediated intercultural foreign language education* (pp. 2–30). Boston, MA: Heinle & Heinle.

Trayner, T. (2002). *Practical approaches to electronic engineering – an SFEU funded teaching intervention*. Falkirk: Falkirk College of Further and Higher Education. Retrieved July 27, 2009, from http://www.sfeu.ac.uk/projects/falkirk_intervention_1

Trees, A. R., & Jackson, M. H. (2007). The learning environment in clicker classrooms: Student processes of learning and involvement in large university-level courses using student response systems. *Learning, Media and Technology, 32*(1), 21–40. doi:10.1080/17439880601141179

Treleaven, L., & Cecez, K. (2001). Collaborative learning in a web-mediated environment: A study of communicative practices. *Studies in Continuing Education, 23*(2), 169–183. doi:10.1080/01580370120101948

Trifonova, A., & Ronchetti, M. (2004). A general architecture for M-Learning. *International Journal of Digital Contents, 2*(1), Special issue on 'Digital Learning-Teaching Environments and Contents'. In A. Méndez-Vilas, & J.A. Mesa González (Eds.), *Proceedings of the II International Conference on Multimedia and Information and Communication Technologies in Education (mICTE2003)*, Badajoz (Spain), December 3-6, 2003, pp. 31-36.

Trowler, P., Saunders, M., & Knight, P. (2003). *Change thinking, change practices: A guide to change for heads of department, subject centres and others who work middle-out*. York: LTSN Generic Centre.

Tseng, W., Dörnyei, Z., & Schmitt, N. (2006). A new approach to assessing strategic learning: The case of self-regulation in vocabulary acquisition. *Applied Linguistics, 27*(1), 78–102. doi:10.1093/applin/ami046

Turkle, S. (1994). Constructions and reconstructions of self in virtual reality: Playing in the MUDs. *Mind, Culture, and Activity, 1*(3), 158–167.

Turkle, S. (1995). *Life on the screen: Identity in the age of the Internet*. New York: Simon & Schuster.

Turner, J. (2007). Creating a work portfolio: Interview tips for engineers and computer scientists. *Graduating Engineers + Computer Careers*. Retrieved April 1, 2009, from http://www.graduatingengineer.com/articles/20071023/Creating-a-Work-Portfolio

Twigg, C. (2005*). Keynote summary: Improving learning and reducing costs – New models for on-line learning*. Paper presented at the ALT-C 2005 Conference, Manchester. Retrieved July 27, 2009, from http://www.alt.ac.uk/altc2005/keynotes.html#carol

Uhl, K., & Poulsen, L. (1970). How are laggards different? An empirical inquiry. *Journal of Marketing Research, 7*(1), 51-54. Retrieved March 4, 2007, from JSTOR database http://www.jstor.org/pss/3149506

UNFOLD Project. (2009). *Welcome to Unfold*. Retrieved July 27, 2009, from http://www.unfold-project.net

University of Illinois. (2007) Department of Ophthalmology and Visual Sciences. Retrieved April 10, 2009, from http://www.uic.edu/com/eye/LearningAboutVision/EyeFacts

van Joolingen, W. R., de Jong, T., & Dimitrakopoulou, A. (2007). Issues in computer-supported inquiry learning in science. *Journal of Computer Assisted Learning, 23*, 111–119. doi:10.1111/j.1365-2729.2006.00216.x

Van Lieshout, M., Egyedi, T. M., & Bijker, W. E. (Eds.). (2001). Social learning technologies: The introduction of multimedia in education. Farnham: Ashgate.

van Winkelen, C. (2003). *Inter-organizational communities of practice*. ESEEN Project. Retreived August 2007, from http://www.elearningeuropa.info/directory/index.php?page=doc&doc_id=1483&doclng=6 and http://www.esen.eu.com

Vandehey, M., Diekhoff, G., & LaBeff, E. (2007). College cheating: A twenty-year follow-up and the addition of an honor code. *Journal of College Student Development, 48*(4), 468–480. doi:10.1353/csd.2007.0043

VanDeventer, S., & White, J. (2002). Expert behavior in children's video game play. *Simulation & Gaming, 33*(1), 28–48. doi:10.1177/1046878102033001002

Veronikas, S. W., & Maushak, N. (2005). Effectiveness of audio on screen captures in software application instruction. [from http://www.proquest.com.eresources.shef.ac.uk]. *Journal of Educational Multimedia and Hypermedia, 14*(2), 199–205. Retrieved July 20, 2009.

Vogel, J. F., Vogel, D. S., Cannon-Bowers, J., Bowers, C. A., Muse, K., & Wright, M. (2006). Computer gaming and interactive simulations for learning: A meta-analysis. *Journal of Educational Computing Research, 34*(3), 229–243. doi:10.2190/FLHV-K4WA-WPVQ-H0YM

Voller, P. (1997). Does the teacher have a role in autonomous language learning? In Benson, P., & Voller, P. (Eds.), *Autonomy and independence in language learning*. New York: Addison Wesley Longman.

Vygotsky, L. S. (1978). *Mind in society: The development of higher psychological processes*. Cambridge, MA: Harvard University Press.

Wagner, E. D. (1994). In support of a functional definition of interaction. *American Journal of Distance Education, 8*(2), 6–29. doi:10.1080/08923649409526852

Wallace, M. (2002). Managing and developing online education: Issues of change and identity. *Journal of Workplace Learning, 14*(5), 198–208. doi:10.1108/13665620210433891

Wallace, P. (1999). *The psychology of the Internet*. Cambridge: Cambridge University Press.

Walters, D., Burhans, D., Kershner, H., & Alphonce, C. (2000). Early followers versus early adopters: The use of technology as a change lever leads to increased learning and decreased costs in a computer fluency course. Retrieved March 30, 2009, from http://connect.educause.edu/Library/Abstract/EarlyFollowersversusEarly/37714

Walther, J. B., van der Heide, B., Kim, S. Y., Westerman, D., & Tong, S. T. (2008). The role of friends' appearance and behaviour on evaluations of individuals on Facebook: Are we known by the company we keep? *Human Communication Research, 34*, 28–49.

Walvoord, B. E. (2004). *Assessment clear and simple.* San Francisco, CA: Jossey-Bass.

Ward, C., & Moser, C. (2008). E-portfolios as a hiring tool: Do employers really care? *EDUCAUSE Quarterly, 4*, 13–15.

Warren, W. J. (2007). Closing the distance between authentic history pedagogy and everyday classroom practice. *The History Teacher, 40*(2), 249–256. doi:10.2307/30036991

Warschauer, M. (1996). Computer assisted language learning: An introduction . In Fotos, S. (Ed.), *Multimedia language teaching* (pp. 3–20). Tokyo: Logos International.

Warschauer, M. (1998). Online learning in sociocultural context. *Anthropology & Education Quarterly, 29*(1), 68–88. doi:10.1525/aeq.1998.29.1.68

Warschauer, M., & Grimes, D. (2007). Audience, authorship, and artifact: The emergent semiotics of Web 2.0. *Annual Review of Applied Linguistics, 27*, 1–23. doi:10.1017/S0267190508070013

Warschauer, M., & Grimes, D. (2008). Audience, authorship and artifact: The emergent semiotics of Web2.0. [from http://www.gse.uci.edu/person/warschauer_m/docs/aaa.pdf]. *Annual Review of Applied Linguistics, 27*, 1–23. Retrieved October 26, 2009.

Webb, J., Schirato, T., & Danaher, G. (2002). *Understanding Bourdieu.* London: Sage Publications.

Weinberger, A., & Fischer, F. (2006). A framework to analyze argumentative knowledge construction in computer-supported collaborative learning. *Computers & Education, 46*, 71–95. doi:10.1016/j.compedu.2005.04.003

Weiss, E. (1995). 'Professional communication' and the 'odor of mendacity': The persistent suspicion that skilful writing is successful lying. *IEEE Transactions on Professional Communication, 38*(3), 169–175. doi:10.1109/47.406731

Weller, M. (2000). The use of narrative to provide a cohesive structure for a web based computing course. *Journal of Interactive Media in Education, 1.* Retrieved, April 26, 2009, from http://www-jime.open.ac.uk/00/1/

Wellman, B., & Haythornthwaite, C. (2002). *The Internet in everyday life.* Oxford: Blackwell. doi:10.1002/9780470774298

Wenden, A. (1998). Metacognitive knowledge and language learning. *Applied Linguistics, 19*, 515–537. doi:10.1093/applin/19.4.515

Wenden, A. (2002). Learner development in language learning. *Applied Linguistics, 23*, 32–55. doi:10.1093/applin/23.1.32

Wenger, E. (1998). *Communities of practice: Learning, meaning and identity.* Cambridge: Cambridge University Press.

Wenger, E., McDermott, R., & Snyder, W. M. (2002). *Cultivating Communities of Practice.* Boston, MA: Harvard Business School Press.

Wesch, M. (2007). Web2.0: The machine is us/using us [Video], Retrieved, April 26, 2009, from http://www.youtube.com/watch?v=6gmP4nk0EOE

White, M. (2005). Communities of practice: Sources of information. Retrieved on June 2, 2006, from http://www.intranetfocus.com

White, N. (2002). *Communities of practice: Learners connecting on-line.* Retrieved August, 2007, from http://flexiblelearning.net.au/nw2002/extras/commsofpractice.pdf

Whithaus, C., & Neff, J. M. (2006). Contact and interactivity: Social constructionist pedagogy in a video-based, management writing course. *Technical Communication Quarterly, 15*(4), 431–456. doi:10.1207/s15427625tcq1504_2

Wiley, D. A. (2000). Connecting learning objects to instructional design theory: A definition, a metaphor, and a taxonomy. In D.A. Wiley (Ed.), *The instructional use of learning objects: Online version*, retrieved on April 29, 2008, from http://reusability.org/read/chapters/wiley.doc

Williams, M. (2007). Avatar watching: participant observation in graphical online environments. *Qualitative Research, 7*(1), 5–24. doi:10.1177/1468794107071408

Williams, R. (1994). *The non-designer's design book: Design and typographic principles for the visual novice.* California: Pearson Education.

Williams, R. (1996). The social shaping of information and communication technologies . In Kubicek, H., Dutton, W. H., & Williams, R. (Eds.), *The social shaping of information highways. European and American roads to the information society* (pp. 299–338). Frankfurt: Campus Verlag.

Williams, R., & Edge, D. (1996). The social shaping of technology . *Research Policy, 25*, 856–899. doi:10.1016/0048-7333(96)00885-2

Wilson, B. G., & Christopher, L. (2008). Hype versus reality on campus: Why e-learning isn't likely to replace a professor any time soon . In Carline, S., & Shank, P. (Eds.), *The E-Learning Handbook: Past Promises, Present Challenges* (pp. 55–76). San Francisco: Pfeiffer, An Imprint of Wiley.

Wilson, G., & Stacey, E. (2004). Online interaction impacts on learning: Teaching the teachers to teach online. *Australasian Journal of Educational Technology, 20*(1), 33–48.

Windham, C. (2005). The learner's perspective . In Oblinger, D. G., & Oblinger, J. L. (Eds.), *Educating the net generation* (pp. 5.1–5.16). Washington, DC: Educause.

Wingate, U. (2006). Doing away with 'study skills'. *Teaching in Higher Education, 11*(4), 457–469. doi:10.1080/13562510600874268

Winterbottom, S. (2007). Virtual lecturing: Delivering lectures using screencasting and podcasting technology. *Planet, 8.* Retrieved April 1, 2009, from http://www.gees.ac.uk/planet/p18/sw.pdf

Witte, S. (2007). That's online writing, not boring school writing: writing with blogs and the Talkback project. *Journal of Adolescent & Adult Literacy, 51*(2), 92–96. doi:10.1598/JAAL.51.2.1

Won, K., & Shih, T. K. (2004). On reusability and interoperability for distance learning. *Journal of Object Technology, 3*(8), 27-34. Retrieved April 10, 2009, from http://www.jot.fm/issues/issue_2004_09/column3

Wright, V. (2006). *Promoting and evaluating the use of the European Language Portfolio.* United Kingdom Higher Education Academy: Subject Centre for Languages, Linguistics and Area Studies. Retrieved March 2, 2009, from http://www.llas.ac.uk/projects/2570

Wu, J. (2008). All about iPhone. *comScore Report.* Retrieved April 15, 2009, from http://www.comscore.com/press/release.asp?press=2545

Yancey, K. B. (1998). *Reflection in the writing classroom.* Logan, UT: Utah State University Press.

Yancey, K. B. (2001). Digitized student portfolios . In Cambridge, B. (Ed.), *Electronic portfolios: Emerging practices in student, faculty, and institutional learning* (pp. 15–30). Sterling, VA: Stylus.

Yates, S. J. (1996). Oral and written linguistic aspects of computer conferencing: A corpus-based study . In Herring, S. C. (Ed.), *Computer-mediated communication: Linguistic, social and cross-cultural perspectives.* Philadelphia: John Benjamins Publishing Co.

Young, J. R. (2009). Caught (unfortunately) on tape. *The Chronicle of Higher Education, 55*(28), A17. Retrieved April 1, 2009, from http://chronicle.com/free/v55/i28/28a01701.htm

Yun, K. (2005). Collaboration in the semantic grid: A basis for e-learning. *Applied Artificial Intelligence, 19*(9 & 10), 881–904.

Zhang, D. (2004). Virtual mentor and the LBA System: Towards building an interactive, personalized, and intelligent e-learning environment. *Journal of Computer Information Systems, 44*(3), 35–43.

Zhang, X., & Wang, Z. (2008). The design and implement of knowledge building classroom based on Web 2.0. In *Proceedings of the 7th international conference on Advances in Web Based Learning* (LNCS 5145, pp. 405-412). Berlin: Springer.

Zhen, Y., Garthwait, A., & Pratt, P. (2008). Factors affecting faculty members' decision to teach or not to teach online in Higher Education. *Online Journal of Distance Learning Administration, XI*(III). Retrieved April 15, 2009, from http://www.westga.edu/~distance/ojdla/fall113/zhen113.html

Zhengdong, G., Humphries, G., & Hamp-Lyons, L. (2004). Understanding successful and unsuccessful EFL students in Chinese universities . *Modern Language Journal, 88*(ii), 229–244. doi:10.1111/j.0026-7902.2004.00227.x

Zubizarreta, J. (2004). *The learning portfolio: Reflective practice for improving student learning.* San Francisco, CA: Anker Publishing Company.

About the Contributors

Dr **Roisin Donnelly** is Programme Chair for the MSc Applied eLearning in the Dublin Institute of Technology (DIT). Previously, she was a lecturer and research fellow in the University of Ulster and the University of New South Wales, Sydney. More recently, she has guest tutored on a range of international online courses, including the University of Queensland, Oxford Brookes University (UK), and the University of Tampere (Finland). She also tutors and supervises on postgraduate programmes in higher education for academic staff in DIT. She has a wide range of publications to date reflecting her teaching and research interests, including eLearning Pedagogy & Design, Supporting Virtual Communities, Blended Learning Models & Strategies, ePortfolios and Online Problem-based Learning. Her co-edited book on Applied eLearning and eTeaching is available through IGI Global Publishers: http://www.igi-global.com/reference/details.asp?id=7958

Dr **Jen Harvey** is currently the Head of the Learning, Teaching and Technology Centre (LTTC) of the Dublin Institute of Technology. She has been in this role from 2003, prior to this she was the DIT Head of Distance Education. Before moving to Dublin she worked as an Implementation Consultant for the LTDI a SHEFC funded project based in ICBL, Heriot Watt University, Edinburgh. Jen is involved in a number of local and national collaborative Strategic Innovation Projects relating to Work-based Learning, Learning Innovation and Education in Employment. Current research interests relate to the use of technology to support learning, student assessment strategies, practitioner based evaluations and Communities of Practice.

Kevin O'Rourke is currently Head of eLearning Support and Development at the Dublin Institute of Technology, Ireland. His professional career has spanned advertising, publishing and eLearning in Dublin, New York and London. Before joining DIT in May 2002, he worked in the UK as a senior producer for Fathom.com, the online learning consortium led by Columbia University. He holds a PhD in intellectual history from University College London and is author of *John Stuart Mill and Freedom of Expression: The Genesis of a Theory* (Routledge, 2001), as well as articles on education and eLearning.

* * *

Jennifer Bruen is a Lecturer in German in the School of Applied Language and Intercultural Studies, Dublin City University. Her research interests include language teaching and learning, in particular the teaching of German as a foreign language and the European Language Portfolio, language learning styles and strategies, the preparation of students for study abroad, and language planning and policy at EU level. In this capacity, she has acted as an advisor to the Irish branch of the Committee of the Regions.

Catherine Bruen is currently working as the manager for the National Digital Learning Repository Service. Before that she worked as An Senior Instructional Designer and eLearning Project Manager for the Centre for Learning Technology (CAPSL) at Trinity College. Her research interests include technology enhanced learning, open educational resources, adaptive hypermedia, personalised learning and simulations based learning. She has lectured part time for postgraduate programmes in computer Science and Education. She has collaborated with colleagues in Irish Higher Education sector on a number of publications in the area of technology enhanced learning, teacher training and staff development.

Dr **James Carr** is an experienced Innovation and Entrepreneurship teacher, researcher and consultant, with a particular focus on the implementation of ICT initiatives in various organisations and industry sectors. He holds a BSc Honours degree from the University of Aberdeen, an MBA from the University of Edinburgh Business School and a PhD from the University of Edinburgh School of Informatics. James is a London Irishman who usually resides in Edinburgh (Scotland), but at the moment he is employed as a Marie Curie Research Fellow in Barcelona (Catalonia) as part of a Digital Business Ecosystem knowledge transfer exchange project between MicroArt and the University of Edinburgh.

John Casey works as organiser of the Digitalinsite collective. Previously John has worked on a number of leading UK e-learning projects including: The UHI Millennium Institute. Jorum, UK national learning resources project. TrustDR a project to develop legal guidelines to support greater sharing of learning resources. The UK Higher Education Quality Assurance Agency for Higher Education Flexible Delivery Enhancement Project. John has a long-standing interest in cognitive psychology, the design of learning materials and learning activities. Through his involvement in the design of online and distance courses John has become increasingly interested in the cultural, economic and political aspects of e-learning and their implications for organisational and professional change in the public education system.

Yvonne Cleary is a Lecturer in Technical Communication at the University of Limerick. She teaches technical communication and e-learning modules on undergraduate and postgraduate programs. She is Course Director for the Graduate Certificate in Technical Writing by distance learning, and the Graduate Diploma / MA in Technical Communication. Her research interests include professional issues in technical communication, technical communication pedagogy, virtual teams, and international technical communication. She has published her work in international journals such as the *IEEE Transactions on Professional Communication* and the *International Journal on E-Learning*. She has also presented her research at international conferences in Ireland, Europe and the United States

Fiona Concannon is a Learning Technologist working in the Centre for Excellence in Learning and Teaching (CELT) at the National University of Ireland, Galway. Her interests lie in the area of Technology-Enhanced Learning, the Learning Sciences, HCI, Activity Theory and the student learning experience in Higher Education. Her educational development activities involve working with academic staff and raising institutional awareness of advances in technology, with its accompanying issues of pedagogic approach, design and usability.

Veronica Crosbie is a Lecturer in ESOL and Intercultural Communication in the School of Applied Language and Intercultural Studies, Dublin City University. Between 2004 and 2007 she coordinated a Socrates Lingua 2 funded project, the 'Language On-line Portfolio Project' (LOLIPOP), which consisted of a partnership of twelve institutions in eight countries in Europe working together to create an interactive digital version of the European Language Portfolio. She is currently studying for an EdD. with the University of Sheffield, UK, and is writing her thesis on capability and cosmopolitan identity in the Higher Education classroom.

Richard Everett is a specialist independent eLearning and new build consultant. His company *intelligentBuilders Limited* supports educational institutions in creating sound eLearning and new build strategies that can help deliver sound pedagogic aims. Richard has been published widely by organisations such as the The Guardian, Becta, LSIS, JISC, ALT, CIBSE, LSN, CEDA, IfL, BBC, Silicon. Com and more recently by the New Review of Information Networking.Richard previously held the position of Director of eLearning at Oaklands College in Hertfordshire and was a member of the Senior Management Team there. He led a ground-breaking and award winning eLearning team engaging with teachers and lecturers to encourage the use of technology for learning. Richard is proud to have been the inventor of the highly successful eMentors' concept (where students teach the teachers to use technology appropriately) which was awarded the Tony Burgess award by the Centre for Excellence in Leadership.

Alan Fell is a senior lecturer in the Department of Computing, Engineering & Technology at the University of Sunderland and currently is programme leader for the B.Eng Mechanical Engineering and the B.Eng Automotive Engineering degree programmes. His research interests include pedagogical aspects of networked and distance learning and use of e-technology to support online learners. His work in these areas informs his PhD supervisions and the development of two MSc programmes in the field of learning technology. The first is an MSc offered at the Arabian Gulf University in Bahrain where he was Visiting Professor of e-learning. The other, at Sunderland University, was the MSc Learning Technology, a programme supported almost exclusively online, for which he was the programme leader.

Noel Fitzpatrick graduated from UCD with a BA in English and Philosophy, and an MA in Philosophy. He then moved to France to continue his postgraduate research into contemporary French philosophy in particular the Phenomenological Hermeneutics of Paul Ricoeur. He then obtained an Mphil from the University of Paris VII in 'la linguistique d'énonciation' and Psycholinguistics. He received a fellowship from the university of Paris VII in 2003 and 2005. In 2005 he obtained his PhD with first class honours entitled ' I and the narrative self in the work of Brian Friel', this thesis developed new models of discourse analysis in pragmatic linguists and the philosophy of language. This thesis has been published as book in France. This book focused on the dialogic structure of the theatre and construction of the speaking subject in the work of Brian Friel. He has continued his research into the dialogic structure of meaning in computer mediated communication.

Seamus Fox has worked in online and distance education for almost twenty years. More recently, he has been academic coordinator of Oscail's BSc in Information Technology programme and has overseen its conversion into a fully online programme. His main research areas are online teaching and learning methods which promote higher order learning and educational policies which affect elearning. In 2008, he was a member of the HEA's Expert Panel on Open and Distance Learning and is currently involved in implementing elearning across the DCU campus.

Dr. **Pat Gannon-Leary** is a consultant and joint partner of Bede Research & Consultancy. Her many academic qualifications include a PhD in Communication Studies. Pat began her career as an information professional and worked in a number of academic libraries in the UK and the USA before moving to research. She is currently employed by Edinburgh University as a senior research fellow on the European CREANOVA project which aims to examine specific conditions and factors which are present in creative learning environments and promote innovation.. Prior to becoming a freelance researcher, Pat worked for two higher education institutions in the North of England and, during this period of her career, areas of research in which she was engaged included electronic information services, e-learning and multi-agency information sharing. Pat has published widely and presented at international conferences. Her unique name makes her publications record easy to track, just Google 'Gannon-Leary'!

Barbara Geraghty lectures in Japanese in the Department of Languages and Cultural Studies at the University of Limerick, and teaches on both undergraduate and postgraduate courses in Japanese Language and Culture as well as Comparative Literature. She is a member of the steering committee of the Post-Primary Languages Initiative. Her research interests are Self-directed learning, Computer Assisted Language Learning, Language and culture and Okinawan literature. Her teaching interests include affect and motivation in language learning and technology enhanced language learning. She has recently published on Language and Culture, Okinawan literature and Computer Assisted Language Learning.

Paul Gormley is an eLearning Developer and Trainer working in the Centre for Excellence in Learning and Teaching (CELT) at the National University of Ireland, Galway. His research interests include the application of knowledge management strategies to support the learning organisation, and the design of innovative community-driven staff development approaches in Higher Education. Paul's professional background includes teaching and leadership roles at second and third level institutions in the UK, Ireland and Australia as well as working as a member of the Asia-Pacific Cisco instructional design team for the current CNAP programme. Paul was the Coordinator of the National Digital Learning Repository (NDLR) Modern Languages Community of Practice and is the current Chair of the Irish Learning Technology Association (ILTA).

Dr. **Gráinne Kirwan** is the programme co-ordinator of the MSc in Cyberpsychology in Dun Laoghaire Institute of Art, Design and Technology, Ireland. She has seven years experience of lecturing and her primary areas of research are forensic psychology, virtual reality and cyberpsychology. Most recently she has completed research identifying potential juror's attitudes towards cybercriminals and their victims. She has been interviewed by several major publications about her expertise in the field of cyberpsychology, as well as providing interviews for both regional and national radio stations. She regularly presents work at international psychological conferences and reviews articles for *Cyberpsychology and Behaviour* and *Computers in Human Behaviour.*

Judith A. Kuit is the Head of Academic Development at the University of Sunderland and is responsible for the staff development of academic staff and those who support learning. She leads modules on the university's MA in Teaching and Learning in Higher Education and MSc in Learning Technology. Formerly, she was a Visiting Professor of e-learning support at the Arabian Gulf University in Bahrain. She has a particular interest in how learning can be supported by technology and how this influences teaching practice. The Higher Education Academy of the UK supported national e-learning benchmarking exercises and e-learning pathfinder projects during 2006/8 and Judith led both these projects in the university. She is a committee member of the UK's Quality Assurance and Enhancement of e-learning Special Interest Group.

Francesca Lorenzi joined DCU in 2000 as academic coordinator of distance education humanities programmes. In 2009 she took up a lecturing position in the School of Education, DCU. She gained a bachelor's degree in Philosophy from Bologna University, Italy; a master's degree in Applied Linguistics from Trinity College Dublin. Prior to joining DCU, she was an adult educator and secondary school teacher working in a variety of institutions in Italy and Ireland. She has researched learner autonomy and language learning and is currently focusing on teaching and learning as pedagogical dialogue, formative assessment, teaching for professional development and the establishment of learning communities via virtual learning environments. She is undertaking research for a doctorate in educational philosophy at NUI Maynooth.

Ann Marcus-Quinn currently teaches Technical Communication to Distance Learners in the Department of Languages and Cultural Studies at the University of Limerick. In addition, she works within the Centre for Teaching and Learning as a research officer with the National Digital Learning Repository (NDLR) project, where among other activities, she collaboratively develops reusable learning objects with faculty at the university. Her research interests include: distance learning, multimedia teaching, and ICT in the post-primary classroom. She has published on the use of Virtual Learning Environments in Distance Learning and also on Computer Assisted Language Learning.

Barbara Macfarlan has worked in Further Education Colleges for over ten years. She was a Language, Literacy and IT skills lecturer and managed a volunteer programme for supporting those learners in a large college in Melbourne, Australia. In recent years Barbara has been part of the eLearning and Technology Support (eLTS) team at Oaklands College. Barbara managed Oaklands College's eInnovations projects which gave teachers the opportunity to bid for college funds to trial and implement different pedagogical approaches utilising new and innovative technology. She has also been involved in projects exploring learning technologies for blended and online delivery and presented at regional and national conferences on the subject.

Dr **Kay Mac Keogh** has over twenty years experience of developing and coordinating distance and elearning programmes in Dublin City University. She has developed innovative pedagogical approaches designed to achieve a range of learning outcomes, including improving research skills and the quality of undergraduate dissertations. Her research, publications and conference presentations cover a wide range of higher education topics, including institutional, national and EU policies; student and tutor expectations and attitudes; and design and evaluation of pedagogical innovation. Her current research is on research competences and supervision, student evaluation and feedback methodologies, institutional elearning strategies, and student retention and performance.

Claire McAvinia is a Learning Technologist in the Centre for Teaching and Learning at NUI Maynooth in Ireland. Her research interests are in educational technology generally, specifically in computer-assisted language learning (CALL), new literacies, and the emerging 'cultures of use' of technology amongst students. She has written and published with colleagues in Ireland and the UK on a range of topics in CALL, e-learning, and educational development, and has taught in related areas at undergraduate and postgraduate levels.

Larry McNutt is currently Head of School of Informatics and Engineering at the Institute of Technology Blanchardstown. Prior to joining ITB, Larry was Senior Lecturer in the ITT Dublin and has lectured in Southern Cross University Australia, Letterkenny IT, DCU and Capella University. A Fellow of the Irish Computer Society, his research interests and publications include distance education, educational technology, instructional design and computer science education. He is currently involved in a number of collaborative research projects in the e-learning area funded by the Higher Education Authority – Strategic Innovation Fund. He is also completing his EdD studies at the National University of Ireland Maynooth where his work is exploring the habitus of educational technologists. Further details on this project are available on http://www.mosceal.com/ or http://mosceal.pbworks.com.

Eileen O' Donnell conferred with a B.Sc. in Information Technology from DCU in March 1997 and a Masters in Information Systems for Managers from DCU in November, 2008. Lecturing on the Post Graduate Diploma in Business Information Systems since 2006. Guest speaker at the Perspectives on Education Seminar Series in February 2009, the topic was: E-Learning and DIT's Strategic Plan. Currently collaborating on an article "Preparing graduates for employment – evaluating the role of e-learning" with Dr. Anne Morrissey, DCU, and Professor Wallace Ewart, formerly Pro-Vice-Chancellor and Provost (Belfast), University of Ulster. Also undertaking research on an evaluation of Adaptive e-learning by pursuing a PhD in the Knowledge and Data Engineering Group, Trinity College Dublin, Ireland.

Dr. **Eugene F.M. O'Loughlin** is a Lecturer in Computing at the National College of Ireland (NCI). He received his PhD in 1988 from the University of Dublin, Trinity College. He then worked as a Production Manager and later as Director of Global Services for over 13 years with the e-Learning company – SmartForce (now SkillSoft). Since 2002 he has been teaching in the School of Computing at NCI where the subjects he teaches include Project Management, Learning Technologies, and Business Systems Analysis at undergraduate and postgraduate levels. He is a keen enthusiast for using technology in the classroom. Dr. O'Loughlin is author of the recently published book *An Introduction to Business Systems Analysis*.

Gearóid Ó Súilleabháin is the Projects Manager for the DEIS Department of Education Development in the Cork Institute of Technology, a higher education institute where he also works as a lecturer at graduate and postgraduate level in modules relating to creativity, multimedia, educational psychology and technology-enhanced learning. He had been working in the educational technology space for over 12 years and has, over this time, published and presented widely on a range of related topics as well as personally managing over 25 national and European research and development projects. Gearóid's current research interests include the use of web2.0 technologies for learning, authentic/alternative web-based assessment, the implementation of educational technology in traditional higher education institutes and the use of simulations and games for learning. Gearóid holds two masters degrees, one in Library and Information Studies and a second in E-Learning (a modified version of this second thesis has been published as a monograph by the FernUniversität, The German Open University). At the time of writing he is working on his Phd in the area of learning transfer and computer games.

Juliette Péchenart is a Lecturer in French (Business) in the School of Applied Language and Intercultural Studies, Dublin City University. Her research interests include language teaching and learning, in particular French for Specific Purposes (Business, Tourism) and the European Language Portfolio (ELP), especially electronic ELP's. She was a member of the Foreign Language Pedagogy team of the 'Language On-line Portfolio project' (LOLIPOP).

Andrew Power is the Head of School of Creative Technologies at the Institute of Art, Design and Technology, Ireland. Prior to his academic career Andrew worked for sixteen years in industry, initially working for multinationals such as Digital Equipment Corporation and Intel, later for the Irish elearning company SmartForce. Andrew serves on the board of directors of Extern and Extern Ireland two cross boarder charities working directly with children, adults and communities affected by social exclusion throughout Ireland. Andrew is a Doctoral student at the Institute of Governance, Queens University Belfast, where the focus of his research is eGovernance, cyberlaw and online democracy.

Damien Raftery is a Lecturer in Mathematics and Information Technology at the School of Business and Humanities at the Institute of Technology Carlow. Since September 2008 he has been partially seconded to the Institute's Teaching and Learning Centre as eLearning Development Officer. He earned a BSc and an MSc in mathematical science from University College Dublin and an MA in management in education from Waterford Institute of Technology. Raftery is currently working on a Doctorate in Education (EdD) with the University of Sheffield and his research interests include quantitative literacy, learning and teaching in higher education, and elearning. He has been actively involved with the Irish Learning Technology Association and the National Digital Learning Repository.

Angélica Rísquez BA (psych), MBS. Angélica has been a researcher at the Centre for Teaching and Learning at the University of Limerick since 2003. She is committed to the use of innovative teacher and student support mechanisms at third level, and is directly involved on the implementation and support of the learning management system at UL as a technology enhanced learning facilitator. She also supports the use of plagiarism prevention software, and is involved in initiatives involving using technology to promote transferable skills (intercultural education, research skills, employability, etc.). She is currently finalising her PhD studies in the Spanish National Open University (UNED) in the area of peer electronic mentoring.

Martin J. Ryan is Teaching Fellow in Early Medieval History in the School of Arts, Histories, and Cultures at the University of Manchester. His principal research interests are Christianity and the Church in pre-Viking England and early medieval charters and diplomatic. He has published on the landed patrimony of the cathedral of Worcester and on the artistic and intellectual cultures of the Atlantic Archipelago. He is co-editor, with Alan Deyermond, of *Early Medieval Spain: A Symposium* (Proceedings of the Medieval Hispanic Research Seminar, forthcoming) and co-author, with Nick Higham, of *The Anglo-Saxon World* to be published by Yale University Press.

Dr. **Julie-Ann Sime** is acting Director of the Centre for Studies in Advanced Learning Technology, Educational Research Department, Lancaster University, UK, where she researches into the design of technology enhanced professional learning and teaches on a professional doctorate in e-Research & Technology Enhanced Learning. With a background in psychology, computer science and artificial intelligence, she adopts a multi-disciplinary approach to research into the design of interactive learning environments within professional development contexts in industry and higher education. She has been involved in research collaborations, for over 20 year, working with European industry and with higher education partners to look at complex training situations where 3D environments, games and simulations are used to support learning. Dr. Sime is interested in how educational theory is put into practice, and how designers and educators can be supported in their working practice in the use of new technologies. For further information see http://www.lancs.ac.uk/fass/edres/profiles/Julie-Ann-Sime/

Teggin Summers received her PhD from the University of Georgia in 2008, specializing in rhetoric and composition, theory, and humanities computing. Having taught writing, including online courses, over the past eight years, she has a breadth of experience with learning technologies and electronic portfolios, including the wide-scale adoption of ePortfolios across the University of Georgia's First-Year Composition program. Dr. Summers currently serves as the Assistant Director for ePortfolio Initiatives at Virginia Tech. In this role, she contributes to the development of ePortfolio-related curriculum for learning, assessment, and professional development, as well as faculty development and training. Her current research interests include the use the ePortfolios to facilitate learning and assessment in the 21st century.

Elaine Walsh is an eLearning Support Specialist for Oscail, the distance education provider in Dublin City University. She completed a Masters in e-Learning Design and Development in the University of Limerick in 2003. Initially involved in the conversion of the Bachelor of Science in Information Technology degree programme for online delivery, she has gained a wide range of experience in various aspects of distance education. Over the past five years, she has conducted research and presented at conferences on online assessment techniques, fostering higher order learning within an online environment and online real-world business simulation. Currently, she provides e-learning support for Oscail staff and students and temporary coordination of the Bachelor of Science in Information Technology degree.

Jamie Ward is presently the Systems Librarian in Dundalk Institute of Technology. He was also the systems librarian in Letterkenny Institute of Technology 2006-2007. He graduated with a Masters in Library and Information Studies from UCD in 2003 with a thesis entitled: Open Source Alternatives for Libraries. He has presented papers at the Online Information Conference, London 2005 on Open Source Software within libraries. He was a member of the Sub Committee LAI Working Group on Information Literacy whose report is soon to be published. He presented a paper to the IIUG conference on this LAI Sub Committee in 2007.

C. Edward Watson received his doctorate in Curriculum and Instruction in 2007 from Virginia Tech. As the Director of Professional Development and Strategic Initiatives within Learning Technologies at Virginia Tech, he directs the Faculty Development Institute and provides strategic vision for Online Course Systems as well as ePortfolio Initiatives. In addition to these activities, Dr. Watson also teaches courses on change agency, the diffusion of innovations, and educational psychology. His book, *Self-efficacy and Diffusion Theory: Implications for Faculty Development*, was published in 2008. Beyond faculty development, Dr. Watson's research interests include the scholarship of teaching and learning, interdisciplinary pedagogy, social learning theory, and learner motivation. Dr. Watson also serves on

Cengage Learning's advisory board and is an associate editor for the International Journal of Teaching and Learning in Higher Education. His team is also involved in an international ePortfolio research project (I/NCEPR).

Jamie Wood completed his undergraduate and postgraduate degrees at the University of Manchester in the Departments of History and Classics and Ancient History. His doctoral thesis examined the chronographic writings of the seventh century Spanish writer and bishop, Isidore of Seville. Jamie is now working as a Leverhulme Early Career Postdoctoral Fellow in the Department of Religions and Theology at the University of Manchester. He has individually and collaboratively published a number of articles on the history of late antique and early medieval Spain, including on the Byzantines in Spain, on Isidore's historical writings, on the afterlife in Visigothic Spain, and an English translation of Isidore's *Chronica Maiora*. From 2007 to 2009 he worked as a Learning Development and Research Associate at the Centre for Inquiry-based Learning in the Arts and Social Sciences at the University of Sheffield.

Marc Zaldivar is the director of ePortfolio Initiatives at Virginia Tech. He has a Ph.D. in Instructional Design and Technology from Virginia Tech (2008). Before becoming an instructional designer, he worked in the Department of English there, teaching composition and working in the university Writing Center. In the new position, his research focus is on the use of ePortfolios for assessment - both institutional and self-assessment - and on the use of ePortfolios for learning and professional development. He is currently working with a dozen other colleagues at Virginia Tech to research engagement and reflection practices that best facilitate student learning. In addition, his primary role is to assist in the adoption of ePortfolio pedagogy and technology across the university; currently, he is working with more than 30 different programs to develop ePortfolio strategies for students. He is a member of AECT, I/NCEPR, AAEEBL, and ePAC.

Index

Symbols

911 Paramedic (video game) 116

A

Abilene Christian University (ACU) 143, 144, 145, 154, 155
academic dishonesty 127, 128, 134
academic honesty 127, 128, 131, 132, 133, 134
academic libraries 227
academic staff 310, 311, 312, 313, 314, 315, 316, 317, 318, 320, 321, 322, 324, 328, 329, 330, 331, 333, 334, 336, 340
actual self 42, 43
agency 282
America's Army (video game) 116
analysis, design, development, implementation and evaluation (ADDIE) 218, 221, 224, 297, 307
anti-plagiarism software 127, 128, 131, 133, 134
Apple Inc. 141, 142, 143, 144, 145, 147, 148, 153, 154, 155
applications (Apps) 142, 153
asynchronous communications 56, 58, 61, 62, 64, 65, 66, 67, 69, 71
audio 213, 214, 217, 218, 219, 220, 221, 222, 223, 225
autonomy 280, 282, 289
avatars 40, 41, 42, 45

B

baby boomers 41
bandwidth 8, 9
behaviorism 144

Blackboard VLE 93, 97, 312, 349, 351, 352, 353, 354
blended learning 22, 36, 37, 38, 39, 40, 44, 45, 48, 49, 227, 228, 234, 240
blended learning programs 39, 45, 48, 49
blogging software 163, 167
blogs 93, 195, 196, 201, 202, 203, 206, 234, 235, 327, 333, 334, 336, 337, 338
Bologna Process 22, 23, 24, 35
Bourdieu, Pierre 72, 74, 80, 81, 82, 83, 84, 85, 86, 87, 88, 89, 90
Brain Training (video game series) 116
bricks and mortar 4

C

CABLE SIG 331
captions 217, 218, 220, 225
centres for teaching and learning 73, 84, 85, 86
change management 346
change management, cultural aspect 346, 347, 356, 359, 360, 361, 362
change management, people aspect 346, 347, 353, 354
change management, process aspect 346, 347, 348, 349, 350, 352, 353, 354, 355, 357, 360, 361
CHEETAH SIG 331
Civilization (video game series) 116, 124
cognitive load 218, 220
cognitivism 94, 144
Collaboration Approach to the Management of E-Learning (CAMEL) 331, 332, 342
collaborative design 294

Common European Framework of Reference
   for Languages (CEFR) 177, 178, 180,
   182, 186, 187, 188, 190, 191
communities 92, 93, 94, 95, 96, 106, 109, 110,
   111, 330, 331, 332, 339, 342, 344
communities of practice (CoP) 244, 246, 259,
   326, 327, 329, 330, 331, 332, 334, 339,
   341, 342, 343, 344, 345
community development 93, 95
community processes 94
computer-assisted language learning (CALL)
   294, 300, 302
computer games 113, 114, 116, 117, 118, 119,
   120, 121, 122, 123, 124, 125
computer labs 217
computer-mediated communication (CMC)
   55, 56, 57, 58, 59, 61, 62, 63, 64, 66, 71,
   269, 273
computer-mediated discourse analysis 55, 63
connectivism 144, 155, 310, 316, 318
constructive alignment 22, 24, 25, 32, 34
constructivism 55, 56, 57, 58, 59, 60, 66, 67,
   69, 94, 144, 283, 292, 310, 315, 316,
   317, 318, 319, 321, 329, 331
constructivism, cognitive 56, 59, 62, 65, 66,
   68, 69
constructivism, radical 56, 94
constructivism, social 55, 56, 57, 58, 59, 60,
   61, 63, 64, 65, 66, 68, 70, 71
continuing professional development (CPD)
   initiative 328, 329, 341, 343, 344
CoP, staff participation in 327, 341
course materials 295
creative learning environment 283
creativity 1, 2, 13
culture of change 247, 259

D

demogirl.com 216, 224
Department for Employment and Learning
   (DEL) 296
development process 294, 297, 298, 300, 307
digital generation 244
digital learning objects 294, 295, 296, 297, 306
Digital Media SIG 331
digital natives 78, 198, 244, 247, 310, 323, 324

digital projectors 215
digital wisdom 144, 155
Diigo.com social bookmarking 200, 201, 205,
   206
discussion boards 262, 263, 265, 266, 271, 272
distance educators 25
distance learning (DL) 351, 354, 355
DkIT project 227
dot.com generation 41
drop-out rate 4
Dublin City University 22, 25, 26
Dublin Institute of Technology 262, 265, 274
Dundalk Institute of Technology 227, 228, 230

E

early adopter 3
eChampion initiative 248
educational development units (EDU) 75
educational technologists 72, 74, 75, 76, 78,
   79, 80, 82, 83, 84, 85
e-ELPs 178
e-folio thinking 162, 163, 170
e-learning 1, 2, 3, 4, 5, 6, 10, 12, 14, 16, 17,
   18, 19, 20, 311, 312, 322, 323
e-learning and Technology Support (eLTS)
   248, 249, 250, 251, 252, 258
e-learning coordinators 73
e-learning implementation 348, 357, 358, 360,
   362
e-learning platforms 262, 263, 265, 267
e-learning programs 39
electronic information services (EIS) 349, 350,
   352
ELESIG special interest group 331
ELP, Biography 177, 178, 179, 180, 181, 185,
   187
ELP, Dossier 177, 178
ELP, Passport 177, 180, 181, 182, 184, 185,
   187, 188
e-mail 263, 265, 268
eMentoring system 244, 250, 252, 253, 260
eMentors scheme 244, 245, 248, 249, 250,
   251, 252, 253, 254, 257, 258, 259
engagement 228
engagement, collaborative model of 228

Enterprise in Higher Education (EHE) initiative 159
ePortfolio applications 157
e-portfolio capstone experiences 158
e-portfolio development 162
e-portfolio initiatives 159, 168, 169, 170, 171
e-portfolios 157, 158, 159, 162, 163, 164, 165, 166, 167, 168, 169, 170, 171, 172, 173, 174
european language portfolio (ELP) 176, 177, 178, 179, 180, 181, 182, 183, 184, 185, 186, 187, 188, 189, 190, 191, 192, 193
European Qualifications Framework 24
European Union 22, 23
Eve anti-plagarism software 127
experiential fidelity 114, 122
extended practice 113, 114

F

Facebook 42, 44, 50, 52, 164, 313
face-to-face communication 2, 3, 9, 10
field 72, 74, 76, 80, 81, 82, 83, 84, 85, 86, 88
fitness games 116
flexible learning 351
flexible learning environments 262
Flickr 164
folio thinking 157, 161, 162, 163, 173
folksonomies 229
foreign culture 177
foreign language 176, 177, 184, 188
further education (FE) 244, 245

G

game complexity 113, 114
Google page ranking algorithm 229

H

habitus 72, 74, 80, 82, 83, 84, 85, 86, 87, 88, 89
hand-held technologies 141, 142, 143, 144, 145, 147, 153
heutagogy 310, 319, 320, 323
Higher Education Funding Council for England (HEFCE) 296, 312, 323, 347, 353, 362, 363

higher education (HE) 1, 2, 3, 4, 5, 10, 13, 14, 15, 16, 20, 93, 94, 95, 96, 104, 107, 110, 346, 347, 352, 356, 358
higher education institutes (HEI) 346, 347, 349, 351, 352, 353, 356, 357, 358, 359
Hilfswissenschaften 196
hiragana 298, 299, 300, 301, 302, 303, 304, 305, 306, 307, 308, 309
History 195, 196, 197, 198, 208, 209, 210, 211
History seminar classes 195

I

iClassroom 141, 143, 144, 145, 147, 148, 149, 150, 151, 152, 153
ICT infrastructure 72
ideal self 42
identity 39, 41, 42, 47, 50, 51, 52
impression management 42, 43, 50, 51
IMS Learning Design 1, 2, 3, 5, 6, 11, 18, 19, 21
independent learning 199
information literacy 227, 228, 229, 230, 231, 232, 233, 234, 236, 237, 238, 239, 240, 241
information literacy programs 227
innovators 72, 74, 75, 76, 77, 78, 79, 80, 83, 86, 89
inquiry-based learning (IBL) 195, 196, 197, 198, 204, 205, 206, 207, 208, 211
Instructional Systems Design (ISD) 7, 8
interactive elements 218, 222
intercultural experiences 178
interlocution 55, 62, 63, 66, 71
interpersonal interactions 55
iPhone 141, 142, 143, 144, 145, 146, 147, 148, 150, 151, 152, 153, 154, 155, 156
iPod 141, 142, 143, 144, 145, 146, 147, 148, 150, 151, 152, 153, 154, 155, 156
iTouch 141, 142, 143, 144, 145, 146, 147, 148, 150, 151, 152, 153
iTunes App Store 142, 143, 154
iTunes U 142, 146, 148, 153

J

Japanese writing systems 294
Joint Information Systems Committee (JISC) (UK) 230, 296
Just In Time Learning (JITL) 12

K

kanji 298, 307
katakana 298, 306, 307

L

laggards 74, 90
language learning 176, 177, 178, 179, 181, 182, 184, 185, 187, 188, 189, 191, 192, 193, 194
language undergraduates 176
learner autonomy 177, 178, 179, 184, 186, 193
learner control 214
learning management systems (LMS) 262, 263, 265, 312
learning objectives 160
learning objects (LO) 1, 2, 3, 4, 7, 15, 17, 18, 20, 214, 218, 294, 295, 296, 297, 298, 299, 300, 301, 302, 303, 304, 305, 306, 307, 308, 309
learning outcomes paradigm 22, 23, 24, 25, 27, 29, 32, 33, 34, 35, 36, 37
learning preferences 270, 272
learning support mechanisms 228
learning technologies 245, 252, 256
learning technology practice framework 346, 357, 358, 360
learning transfer 113, 114, 115, 116, 117, 118, 119, 122, 125
lecturers 262, 263, 264, 265, 266, 267, 268, 269, 270, 272, 273, 274, 277
lectures 264, 267, 268, 269, 272, 273
legitimate peripheral participation (LPP) 246, 327
lifelong learning 115, 124, 159, 175
Linden Labs 41
linguistics 55, 57, 61, 62, 63, 66, 67
listening skills 178, 181

LOLIPOP ELP 176, 178, 179, 180, 181, 182, 183, 184, 185, 186, 187, 188, 189, 190, 191, 192, 193

M

managed learning environments (MLE) 229
Massachusetts Institute of Technology (MIT) 295
mathcasts 215, 216, 219, 224
media comparison studies (MCS) 296
metacognition 177
Millennials 41, 310
m-learning 141, 142, 151, 153
mobile learning 294
Moodle VLE 58, 93, 312
Multimedia Educational Resources for Learning and Online Teaching (Merlot) project 7
Murray, Dennis 56, 69
My Drop Box anti-plagarism software 127

N

National Digital Learning Repository (NDLR) (Ireland) 7, 229, 296, 327, 331, 332, 334, 340, 341, 342
National Framework of Qualifications (NFQ) (Ireland) 23
navigationism 310, 317
NCAT 4
Nintendo DS 116

O

Oaklands College 244, 245, 252, 259
OECD (Organisation for Economic Co-operation and Development) 22, 23, 37
online chat rooms 263
online communities 39, 41, 50, 52, 53
online identities 39, 40, 41, 44, 45, 47, 48, 49
online learning environments 266
online marking 128, 129
online pedagogical techniques 22, 25, 26, 29, 35
organisational culture 346, 347, 360
ought self 42

P

paper mills 127
pedagogies, inquiry-based 196, 197
pedagogy 2.0 310
peer and group online undergraduate research
        supervision (POURS) 26, 30, 31, 32, 33
peer review 128, 129, 135
Penn State University 163
personal support system 5
Pet Pals: Animal Doctor (video game) 116
plagiarism 127, 128, 129, 130, 131, 132, 133,
        134, 135, 136, 139
plagiarism prevention 128, 129, 132, 133
podcasting 93
podcasts 141, 142, 143, 144, 145, 146, 147,
        148, 149, 150, 151, 152, 154, 156, 266
political economy 3, 4, 18
portfolio for professional development 161
portfolio paradigm 160
portfolios 157, 158, 159, 160, 161, 162, 163,
        164, 165, 166, 167, 168, 169, 170, 171,
        172, 173, 174, 175
portfolios, non-electronic 162
PowerPoint 213, 214, 219, 225
PREEL 2 SIG 331
problem-based learning (PBL) 195, 196
professional games 116

Q

quality assurance 73, 74, 78, 81

R

reading skills 178, 181
reflection 158, 159, 160, 161, 162, 163, 164,
        165, 166, 167, 168, 172, 174, 175
résumés 166
return on investment (ROI) framework 348,
        349
reusable learning object (RLO) 213, 218, 225

S

Sakai VLE 280, 290, 291, 292, 293
SCORM (shareable content object reference
        model) 300

screencasts 213, 214, 215, 216, 217, 218, 219,
        220, 221, 222, 223, 224, 225, 226
Second Life 40, 41, 42, 45, 46, 50
self-assessment 159, 160, 161, 166
self-regulation 177, 193
serious games 113, 114, 119, 122, 123, 125
shareable content objects (SCO) 300
Silent Way pedagogy 298, 299, 309
SimCity (video game series) 116, 123
situated learning 246
social bookmarking 199
social bookmarking tools 195
social constructivism 56, 57, 58, 59, 60, 66, 94,
        310, 316, 317, 318, 319, 321
social interaction 55, 64
social networking 310, 313, 314
socio-constructivism 94
special interest groups (SIG) 331, 333, 334,
        335, 336, 337, 338, 339, 340, 341
spoken interaction skills 178, 180
spoken production skills 178, 185
staff development programs 326, 327, 329, 341
standard written English 282
strategic competence 177
student learning 195, 207, 208
Student Passport to e-Learning (SPeL) 26, 27,
        28, 29, 33, 36
students, on-campus 22, 23, 35
Sulis VLE 280, 281, 285, 287, 289, 290, 291

T

task oriented online learning (TOOL) 26, 29,
        30, 32, 33, 36
teachertrainingvideos.com 216, 224
technology, transformative capability of 73
Thorndike, Edward E. 113, 114, 120, 125, 126
transfer power 114, 122
transfer research 113
transformative learning 262, 263, 265, 266,
        268, 269
trolling 40
true self 42
Turnitin anti-plagarism software 127, 128, 129,
        130, 131, 132, 133, 134, 135, 136, 137,
        138, 139, 140

U

UK 244, 245, 260
University of Limerick 280, 281, 283
University of Sheffield 198
USA 22, 24, 25

V

videocasts 263, 265, 266, 267, 268, 270
video games 113, 114, 116, 117, 118, 119, 120,
    121, 122, 123, 124, 125
virtual environments 40, 42, 43, 45, 54
virtual learning 76, 86
virtual learning environments (VLE) 25, 26,
    58, 61, 62, 65, 92, 93, 94, 214, 215, 221,
    225, 227, 229, 237, 238, 239, 240, 262,
    274, 280, 281, 283, 285, 289, 290, 293,
    295, 300, 312, 313, 351, 352, 361
virtual worlds 58
vlogs (video based blogs) 167
vocational games 116
vodcasts 141, 142, 143, 144, 146, 147, 148,
    149, 150, 151, 152
voiceovers 218
Vygotsky, Lev 246, 260

W

WcopyFind anti-plagarism software 127
Web 1.0 313, 314, 315, 317
Web 2.0 77, 92, 93, 94, 104, 106, 111, 112,
    195, 196, 197, 198, 201, 202, 203, 204,
    205, 206, 207, 208, 209, 210, 310, 311,
    313, 314, 315, 316, 317, 318, 319, 320,
    321, 322, 323, 324, 325

Web 2.0 social networking tools 310
Web 2.0 teaching and learning practice 331
Web 2.0 technologies 195, 196, 197, 198, 202,
    203, 204, 205, 206, 207, 280
Web 2.0 tools 327, 331, 332, 333, 334, 336,
    337, 341
WebCT VLE 93
Wiki collaborative active spaces 92
Wikis 92, 93, 94, 95, 96, 97, 98, 99, 105, 107,
    108, 109, 110, 111, 263, 265, 271, 327,
    333, 334, 336, 337, 338, 339, 340, 341
Woodworth, Robert Sessions 113, 114, 125
working memory 218
World of Warcraft 42
writing across the curriculum (WAC) 283
writing centers 283
writing instruction 281
writing process 281, 282, 285, 287, 289, 290,
    291
writing self-efficacy beliefs 282
writing skills 178, 184, 185, 280, 281, 283,
    284, 285, 286, 288, 291
writing support 280, 281

Y

Yates' democratic theory 57
YouTube 164, 213, 216, 217, 221, 222, 224,
    225